THE INDEX OF PSYCHOANALYTIC WRITINGS

ALEXANDER GRINSTEIN, M.D.

Preface by Ernest Jones, M.D.

INTERNATIONAL UNIVERSITIES PRESS, INC.

New York, N. Y.

THE INDEX OF PSYCHOANALYTIC WRITINGS

VOLUME VII

GREENE—PETERS

47793—55833

INTERNATIONAL UNIVERSITIES PRESS, INC.

New York, N.Y.

Manufactured in the United States of America
by Hallmark Press, New York

CONTENTS

CONTENTS

LIST OF PRINCIPAL ABBREVIATIONS

ABBREVIATIONS OF NAMES OF PERIODICALS AND COLLECTED WORKS

Abbreviations of periodicals which appear in the Index, other than those listed below, were taken from the *World List of Scientific Periodicals, 1900-1950*, 3rd Edition, New York: Academic Press; London: Butterworth Publications, Ltd., 1952.

Act Np Arg	Acta Neuropsiquiátrica Argentina
Acta psycho-ther psy-chosom ortho-paedag	Acta Psychotherapeutica, Psychosomatica et Orthopaedagogica
Adv Psychiat	Cohen, M. B. (Ed) *Advances in Psychiatry* [43762]
AJP	American Journal of Psychology
Am Hbk Psychiat	Arieti, S. (Ed) *American Handbook of Psychiatry* [40687]
Am Im	American Imago
Am Psych	American Psychologist
AMA ANP	American Medical Association Archives of Neurology and Psychiatry
An Surv Psa	Frosch, J. (Ed) *The Annual Survey of Psychoanalysis* [46429, 46430, 46431]
Ann méd-psychol	Annales Médico-Psychologiques
Ann Rev Psychol	Farnsworth, P. R. (Ed) *Annual Review of Psychology* [45344]
Arch crim Psychodyn	Archives of Criminal Psychodynamics
Arch Crimin Neuropsiq, 2. ep.	Archivos de Criminologia, Neuro-Psiquiatria y Disciplinas Conexas, 2a epoca
Arch Neurol Psiquiat	Archivos de Neurologia y Psiquiatria, 2a epoca
Arch physical Med Re-habil	Archives of Physical Medicine and Rehabilitation
Art Psa	Phillips, W. (Ed) *Art and Psychoanalysis* [55903]
ASP	Journal of Abnormal and Social Psychology
Austral J Phil	Australian Journal of Philosophy
B Sexfschg	Beiträge zur Sexualforschung
Beh Sci	Behavioral Science

vii

BMC	Bulletin of the Menninger Clinic
Bol Hig Ment	Boletim de Higiene Mental
Brit J psychiatr soc Work	British Journal of Psychiatric Social Work
Brit med J	British Medical Journal
Bull Assoc Psa Belg	Bulletin de l'Association des Psychanalystes Belges
Bull Phila Ass Psa	Bulletin of the Philadelphia Association for Psychoanalysis
Case St Chd Dis	Gardner, G. E. (Ed) *Case Studies in Childhood Emotional Disabilities* [46947]
Case St Couns PT	Burton, A. (Ed) *Case Studies in Counseling and Psychotherapy* [43170]
Char Pers	Character and Personality
Chg Cpts Psa Med	Rado, S. & Daniels, G. E. (Eds) *Changing Concepts of Psychosomatic Medicine* [56441]
Child-Fam Dig	Child-Family Digest
Childhood Contemp Cult	Mead, M. & Wolfenstein, M. (Eds) *Childhood in Contemporary Cultures* [53665]
Clin Path	Journal of Clinical and Experimental Psychopathology
Clin Psych	Journal of Clinical Psychology
Clin Stud Cult Confl	Seward, G. H. (Ed) *Clinical Studies in Culture Conflict* [59297]
Clin Stud Pers	Burton, A. & Harris, R. E. (Eds) *Clinical Studies of Personality* [43171]
Coll P	Winnicott, D. W. *Collected Papers* [62561]
Couns PT Ment Retard	Stacey, C. L. & DeMartino, M. F. (Eds) *Counseling and Psychotherapy with the Mentally Retarded* [60128]
Curr App Psa	Hoch, P. H. & Zubin, J. (Eds) *Current Approaches to Psychoanalysis* [48856]
Direct Anal	Rosen, J. N. *Direct Analysis: Selected Papers* [57422]
Dr Af Beh	Loewenstein, R. M. (Ed) *Drives, Affects, Behavior* [52737]
Drms Pers Dyn	DeMartino, M. F. (Ed) *Dreams and Personality Dynamics* [44143]
Dynam Psychopath Child	Jessner, L. & Pavenstedt, E. (Eds) *Dynamic Psychopathology in Childhood* [49544]
Early Devel Mind	Glover, E. *On the Early Development of Mind* [47330]
Ego Psychol Dyn Casewk	Parad, H. J. (Ed) *Ego Psychology and Dynamic Casework* [55451]
EJP	Egyptian Journal of Psychology
Emot Dist Child	Gerard, M. W. *The Emotionally Disturbed Child* [47136]

Emot Prob Early Child	Caplan, G. (Ed) *Emotional Problems of Early Childhood* [43399]
Encéph	Encéphale (et Hygiène Mentale)
Existence	May, R.; Angel, E.; & Ellenberger, H. F. (Eds) *Existence: A New Dimension in Psychiatry and Psychology* [53546]
Expl Psa	Lindner, R. (Ed) *Explorations in Psychoanalysis* [52568]
Freud 20th Cent	Nelson, B. N. (Ed) *Freud and the 20th Century* [54959]
Group PT	Group Psychotherapy
Hndb N P	Frankl, V. E.; Gebsattel, V. E. von; Schultz, J. H. (Eds) *Handbuch der Neurosenlehre und Psychotherapie* [45952]
Homosex	Krich, A. M. (Ed) *The Homosexuals As Seen by Themselves and Thirty Authorities* [51023]
HPI	The Hogarth Press and the Institute of Psycho-Analysis
IJP	Indian Journal of Psychology
Ind med J	Indian Medical Journal
Ind med Rec	Indian Medical Record
Int J clin exp Hyp	International Journal of Clinical and Experimental Hypnosis
Int J grp PT	International Journal of Group Psychotherapy
Int J Sexol	International Journal of Sexology
Int J soc Psychiat	International Journal of Social Psychiatry
Int Psa Cong	International Psycho-Analytical Congress
Int Rec Med	International Record of Medicine
Intro Clin Psych 2	Pennington, L. A. & Berg, I. A. (Eds) *An Introduction to Clinical Psychology,* 2nd Ed. [55743]
IPC	Imago Publishing Company
IUP	International Universities Press
J	International Journal of Psycho-Analysis
JAbP	Journal of Abnormal Psychology
JAMA	Journal of the American Medical Association
J Am Psa Ass	Journal of the American Psychoanalytic Association
J anal Psych	Journal of Analytical Psychology
Jb Psychol Psychother	Jahrbuch für Psychologie und Psychotherapie
J Bras Psiquiat	Jornal Brasileiro de Psiquiatria
J chron Dis	Journal of Chronic Diseases
J clin exp Hyp	Journal of Clinical and Experimental Hypnosis
J genet Psych	Journal of Genetic Psychology
J Hillside Hosp	Journal of the Hillside Hospital
J Hist Ideas	Journal of the History of Ideas
J ind Psych	Journal of Individual Psychology
JMS	Journal of Mental Science
JNMD	Journal of Nervous and Mental Diseases
Jones	Jones, E. *The Life and Work of Sigmund Freud* [16560A]
J Pers	Journal of Personality

J proj Techn	Journal of Projective Techniques
J Psychol	Journal of Psychology
Judaism Psychiat	Noveck, S. (Ed) *Judaism and Psychiatry* [55117]
Lav Np	Lavoro Neuropsichiatrico
Lit & Psych	Literature and Psychology
M	British Journal of Medical Psychology
Menn Q	Menninger Quarterly
MH	Mental Hygiene
Mind-Body	Deutsch, F. (Ed) *On the Mysterious Leap from the Mind to the Body* [44198]
MMW	Münchner medizinische Wochenschrift
Mod Tr PSM	O'Neill, D. (Ed) *Modern Trends in Psychosomatic Medicine* [55248]
MPN	Monatsschrift für Psychiatrie und Neurologie
New Dir Psa	Klein, M.; Heimann, P.; Money-Kyrle, R. M. (Eds) *New Directions in Psycho-Analysis* [50581]
New Front Child Guid	Esman, A. H. (Ed) *New Frontiers in Child Guidance* [45133]
Nord Psyk Medl	Nordisk Psykiatrisk Medlemsblad
Note Psichiat, Pesaro	Note e Riviste di Psichiatria, Ospedale Psichiatrico Provinciale, Pesaro
NPAP	Psychoanalysis, Journal of the National Psychological Association for Psychoanalysis
NPPA J	National Probation and Parole Association Journal
NYSJM	New York State Journal of Medicine
Ops	American Journal of Orthopsychiatry
Out Psa 1955	Thompson, C.; Mazer, M.; Wittenberg, E. (Eds) *The Outline of Psychoanalysis* [61278]
P	American Journal of Psychiatry
Pers n s c	Kluckhohn, C.; Murray, H. A.; Schneider, D. M. (Eds) *Personality in Nature, Society, and Culture* [50655]
Pers Thy	David, H. P., & Bracken, H. von (Eds) *Perspectives in Personality Theory* [44062]
Pisani	"Il Pisani" Giornale di Patologia Nervose e Mentale
PPR	Psychoanalysis and the Psychoanalytic Review
Prak Psychiat	Praktische Psychiatrie
Prax Kinderpsychol	Praxis der Kinderpsychologie und Kinderpsychiatrie
Prax PT	Praxis der Psychotherapie
Pres Day Psychol	Roback, A. A. (Ed) *Present Day Psychology* [57214]
Pro Cl P	Brower, D. & Abt, L. E. (Eds) *Progress in Clinical Psychology* [42989]
Prob Hum Pleas Beh	Balint, M. *Problems of Human Pleasure and Behavior* [41072]
Proc RSM	Proceedings of the Royal Society of Medicine
Prog Neurol Psychiat	Spiegel, E. A. (Ed) *Progress in Neurology and Psychiatry* [59999]

Prog PT	Fromm-Reichmann, F. & Moreno, J. L. (Eds) *Progress in Psychotherapy*, Vol. 1 [11072A]. Masserman, J. H. & Moreno, J. L. (Eds) *Progress in Psychotherapy*, Vol. 2, 3, 4 [53471, 53472, 53473]
Ps	Psychiatry
Psa	American Journal of Psychoanalysis
Psa Psychiat Psychol	Knight, R. P. & Friedman, C. P. (Eds) *Psychoanalytic Psychiatry and Psychology* [50683]
Psa PT	Fromm-Reichmann, F. *Psychoanalysis and Psychotherapy* [46428]
Psa Sci Method Phil	Hook, S. (Ed) *Psychoanalysis, Scientific Method and Philosophy* [49087]
Psa Soc S	Muensterberger, W. & Axelrad, S. *Psychoanalysis and the Social Sciences*. NY: IUP
Psa Soc Wk	Heiman, M. (Ed) *Psychoanalysis and Social Work* [48618]
Psa St C	Eissler, R. S. et al. (Eds) *The Psychoanalytic Study of the Child*. NY: IUP
Psa St Soc	Muensterberger, W. & Axelrad, S. *The Psychoanalytic Study of Society* [54656]
Psa Vkb	Federn, P. & Meng, H. (Eds) *Das Psychoanalytische Volksbuch*. Bern: Huber
PSM	Psychosomatic Medicine
Psm Cpt Psa	Deutsch, F. (Ed) *The Psychosomatic Concept in Psychoanalysis* [44203)
Psychiat Bull GP	Psychiatric Bulletin for the Physician in General Practice
Psychiat Comm	Psychiatric Communications
Psychiat et Neurol jap	Psychiatria et Neurologia Japonica
Psychiat Q	Psychiatric Quarterly
Psychiat Res Rep	Psychiatric Research Reports
Psychiat World	Menninger, K. A. *A Psychiatrist's World: Selected Papers* [53987]
Psych Issues	Psychological Issues
Psychol Bull	Psychological Bulletin
Psychopathol	Reed, C. F.; Alexander, I. E.; Tomkins, S. S. (Eds) *Psychopathology: A Source Book* [56761]
Psychopathol Communic	Hoch, P. H. & Zubin, J. (Eds) *Psychopathology of Communication* [48880]
PT	American Journal of Psychotherapy
PUF	Presses Universitaires de France
Q	The Psychoanalytic Quarterly
R	The Psychoanalytic Review
Ra Pgc	Rassegna di Psicologie Generale e Clinica
Rd Psa Psychol	Levitt, M. (Ed) *Readings in Psychoanalytic Psychology* [52315]

Read Child   Martin, W. E. & Stendler, C. B. (Eds) *Readings in Child De-*
Devel   *velopment* [53333]
Read Psychol Strunk, O., Jr. (Ed) *Readings in the Psychology of Religion.*
Relig   Nashville, Tenn: Abingdon Pr 1959
Read Soc   Maccoby, E. E.; Newcomb, T. M.; Hartley, E. L. (Eds) *Read-*
Psychol   *ings in Social Psychology,* 3rd Ed. NY: Holt 1958
Res PT   Rubinstein, E. A. & Parloff, M. B. (Eds) *Research in Psycho-*
             therapy [58067]
Rev Bras   Revista Brasileira de Saúde Mental
Saúde ment
Rev gén belge Revue Générale Belge
Rev Neuro-   Revista de Neuro-Psiquiatria
psiquiat
Rev Neurol   Revista de Neurologia Psiquiatria e Higiene Mental
Psiquiat
Hig ment
Rev Psicoanál Revista de Psicoanálisis
Rev Psicol   Revista de Psicologia General y Aplicada, Madrid
gen apl,
Madrid
Rev Psicol   Revista de Psicologia Normal e Patológia
norm patol
Rev Psiquiat Revista de Psiquiatria y Psicologie Médica de Europa y América
Psicol   Latinas
Rev urug Psa Revista Uruguaya Psicoanálisis
RFPsa   Revue Française de Psychanalyse
Riv Pat nerv Rivista di Patologie Nervosa e Mentale
ment
Riv Psa   Rivista di Psicoanalisi
Rv Np inf   Revue Neuropsychiatrie Infantile et d'Hygiène Mentale d'Enfance
Sat Rev   The Saturday Review
Schiz Psa Off Rifkin, A. H. (Ed) *Schizophrenia in Psychoanalytic Office Prac-*
Pract   *tice* [57149]
Schiz Rev   Bellak, L. & Benedict, P. K. (Eds) *Schizophrenia: A Review of*
Syn   *the Syndrome* [41465]
Schweiz ANP Schweizer Archiv für Neurologie und Psychiatrie
Schweiz Z   Schweizerische Zeitschrift für Psychologie und ihre Anwen-
Psychol   dungen. [Revue Suisse de Psychologie Pure et Appliquée]
Sci Mon   Scientific Monthly
Sci Psa   Masserman, J. H. (Ed) *Science and Psychoanalysis* [53489]
SE   Strachey, J. (Ed) *Standard Edition of the Complete Psycho-*
             logical Works of Sigmund Freud [10707A]
Soc   American Journal of Sociology
Soc Casewk   Social Casework
Soc Probl   Social Problems
Soc Psych   Journal of Social Psychology
Soc S R   Social Service Review
Stud Pers   Brand, H. (Ed) *The Study of Personality. A Book of Readings*
             [42735]
Supp Vie Spir Supplément de la Vie Spirituelle

Tokyo J Psa	Tokyo Journal of Psychoanalysis
20 Yrs Psa	Alexander, F. & Ross, H. (Eds) *Twenty Years of Psychoanalysis* [40340]
Under Hum Motiv	Stacey, C. L. & DeMartino, M. F. (Eds) *Understanding Human Motivation* [60129]
Unif Theory Behav	Grinker, R. R. (Ed) *Toward a Unified Theory of Human Behavior* [47986]
WMW	Wiener medizinische Wochenschrift
YBPsa	Lorand, S. (Ed) *The Yearbook of Psychoanalysis.* NY:IUP
Z diag Psychol	Zeitschrift für diagnostische Psychologie und Persönlichkeitsforschung
Z Kinderpsychiat	Zeitschrift für Kinderpsychiatrie
Z PSM	Zeitschrift für psychosomatische Medizin
Z Psychol	Zeitschrift für Psychologie

ABBREVIATIONS USED FOR NAMES OF ABSTRACTORS, REVIEWERS, AND TRANSLATORS

AAB	Abraham A. Brill	JLan	Joseph Lander
ASt	Alix Strachey	JPG	Joseph P. Gutstadt
BL	Barbara Low	JR	John Rickman
CBr	Charles Brenner	JRiv	Joan Riviere
CJMH	C. J. M. Hubback	JS	James Strachey
CMB	Cecil M. Baines	KHG	Kenneth H. Gordon, Jr.
CR	Charles Rycroft	LCK	Lawrence C. Kolb
DB	Clement A. Douglas Bryan	LRa	Leo Rangell
DRu	David L. Rubinfine	MBr	Marjorie Brierley
EBMH	Ethilde B. M. Herford	MG	Martin Grotjahn
EBu	Edith Buxbaum	MGr	Milton Gray
ECM	E. Colburn Mayne	MK	Mark Kanzer
EFA	Edwin Frederick Alston	NR	Norman Reider
EG	Edward Glover	NRo	Nathaniel Ross
EJ	Ernest Jones	RCM	R. C. McWatters
EMW	Edward M. Weinshel	RdeS	Raymond de Saussure
ESt	Erwin Stengel	RDT	Robert D. Towne
GD	George Devereux	RJA	Renato J. Almansi
GPK	Geraldine Pederson-Krag	RRG	Ralph R. Greenson
GZ	Gregory Zilboorg	RTh	Ruth Thomas
HRB	H. Robert Blank	SG	Sigmund Gabe
HW	Herbert Weiner	STa	Sidney Tarachow
IFGD	I. F. Grant Duff	TFr	Thomas Freeman
JAA	Jacob A. Arlow	TGS	Tom G. Stauffer
JB	J. Bernays	VC	Victor Calef
JBi	Joseph Biernoff	Vega	Gabriel de la Vega
JFr	John Frosch	WH	Willi Hoffer
JKl	John Klauber		

THE INDEX OF
PSYCHOANALYTIC WRITINGS

VOLUME VII

GREENE, BERNARD L.

See Carlson, Helen B.

GREENE, GEORGE W., JR.

See Ross, George L.

GREENE, JANET S.

See Wolf, Alexander

GREENE, WILLIAM A., JR.

47793 Process in psychosomatic disorders. PSM 1956, 18:150-158
    Abs Fain RFPsa 1957, 21:301-302
47794 (& Miller, G.) Psychological factors and reticuloendothelial disease.
Observations on a group of children and adolescents with leukemia: an
interpretation of disease development in terms of the mother-child unit.
PSM 1958, 20:124-144
    Abs Afterman, J. Q 1959, 28:130-131
47795 (& Young, L. E.; Swisher, S. N.) Psychological factors and reticuloendothelial disease: observations on a group of women with lymphomas
and leukemias. PSM 1956, 18:284-303
    Abs R 1957, 44:486. Fain, M. RFPsa 1957, 21:620. Johnston, McL.
Q 1958, 27:134-135
47796 Psychological factors and reticuloendothelial disease: preliminary observations on a group of males with lymphomas and leukemias. PSM
1954, 16:220-230
    Abs Rev Psicoanál 1955, 12:324-325
47797 Role of a vicarious object in the adaptation to object loss. PSM 1958,
20:344-350
    Abs Prest, J. R. Q 1959, 28:425
47798 Role of a vicarious object in the adaptation to object loss: vicissitudes
in the role of the vicarious object. PSM 1959, 21:438-447
    Abs Powelson, H. Q 1960, 29:594

See Engel, George L.

GREENHILL, J. P.

47799 Traitement de la frigidité chez la femme. [Treatment of frigidity in
women.] Gynec Prat 1957, 8:139-149

GREENHILL, M.

See Berblinger, Klaus W.

GREENING, THOMAS C.

47800 Moral standards and defense against aggression. (Abs) Diss Abstr
1959, 19:3364-3365

See Allinsmith, Wesley

GREENSON, RALPH R.

47801 On boredom. J Am Psa Ass 1953, 1:7-21
Abs JFr An Surv Psa 1953, 4:219-222. Hoffer, W. J 1953, 34:274
47802 The classic psychoanalytic approach. Am Hbk Psychiat 2:1399-1416
47803 Empathy and its vicissitudes. (Read at 21st Int Psa Cong, Copenhagen, July 1959) J 1960, 41:418-424
47804 Forepleasure: its use for defensive purposes. J Am Psa Ass 1955, 3:244-254
Abs TFr J 1956, 37:209. Shentoub, S. A. RFPsa 1956, 20:568-569. Young, B. Q 1959, 28:560
47805 On moods and introjects. BMC 1954, 18:1-11
Abs JFr An Surv Psa 1954, 5:119-121. Rahman, L. Q 1955, 24:469
S-12440 The mother tongue and the mother.
Abs R 1953, 40:355
47806 Phobia, anxiety, and depression. J Am Psa Ass 1959, 7:663-674
47807 Problems of dosage, timing, and tact in interpretation. (Read at Boston Psa Soc & Inst, Nov 30, 1959)
Abs Swartz, J. Bull Phila Ass Psa 1960, 10:23-24
47808 Problems of identification. Introduction. J Am Psa Ass 1954, 2:197-199
Abs NRo An Surv Psa 1954, 5:60-61
47809 Psychiatric information for general practice. California Med 1958, 88:354-357
47810 On screen defenses, screen hunger and screen identity. J Am Psa Ass 1958, 6:242-262
Abs TFr J 1959, 40:361. Shentoub, S. A. RFPsa 1959, 23:147 TGS Q 1960, 29:428
47811 About the sound "mm . . ." (Read at Am Psa Ass, NY, Dec 4, 1953) Q 1954, 23:234-239
Abs JFr An Surv Psa 1954, 5:121-122. JKl J 1955, 36:423
47812 The struggle against identification. J Am Psa Ass 1954, 2:200-216
Abs HAW J Am Psa Ass 1953, 1:538-539. JFr An Surv Psa 1954, 5:174. NRo An Surv Psa 1954, 5:60; 61-62. TFr J 1955, 36:222-223. MGr Q 1956, 25:614-615
47813 Variations in classical psychoanalytic technique. (Read at 20th Int Psa Cong, Paris, 1957) J 1958, 29:200-201
Abs JLan Q 1959, 28:280-281

ABSTRACTS OF:
47814 Aronson, G. J. Delusion of pregnancy in a male homosexual with an abdominal cancer. Q 1953, 22:450-451
47815 Arnow, A. J. Verbal hallucinations: a restitutional symptom. Q 1953, 22:451
47816 Barnard, R. I. et al: The day hospital as an extension of psychiatric treatment. Q 1953, 22:127-128
47817 Benedek, T. Dynamics of the counter-transference. Q 1954, 23:617
47818 Bernfeld, S. & Bernfeld, S. C. Freud's first year in practice, 1886-1887. Q 1953, 22:127
47819 Bikales, V. W. et al: The effects of leadership upon morale in a group therapeutic setting. Q 1953, 22:452

47820 Blitzsten, N. L. & Fleming, J. What is a supervisory analysis? Q 1954, 23:467-468
47821 Bullard, D. M. Problems of clinical administration. Q 1953, 22:451-452
47822 Devereux, G. Psychiatry and anthropology: some research objectives. Q 1953, 22:451
47823 Ekstein, R. & Wright, D. The space child. Q 1953, 22:452-453
47824 Fingert, H. H. Comments on the psychoanalytic significance of the fee. Q 1953, 22:303-304
47825 Fleming, J. The role of supervision in psychiatric training. Q 1954, 23:468-469
47826 Gardiner, M. M. Meetings with the Wolf-Man. Q 1954, 23:303-304
47827 Gaw, E. A. et al: How common is schizophrenia? Q 1953, 22:612
47828 Holt, R. R. & Luborsky, L. Research on the selection of psychiatrists: a second interim report. Q 1953, 22:304-305
47829 Knight, E. H. Spelling disability as a symptom of emotional disorder. Q 1953, 22:303
47830 Knight, R. P. Borderline states. Q 1953, 22:611-612
47831 Knight, R. P. An evaluation of psychotherapeutic technique. Q 1953, 22:304
47832 Knight, R. P. Management and psychotherapy of the borderline schizo-phrenic patient. Q 1954, 23:468
47833 Menninger, K. What are the goals of psychiatric education? Q 1953, 22:450
47834 Menninger, K. Psychiatry and the practice of medicine. Q 1954, 23:469
47835 Munro, L. Clinical notes on internalization and identification. Q 1953, 22:600
47836 Paley, A. Hypnotherapy in the treatment of alcoholism. Q 1953, 22:127
47837 Pearlman, J. Psychodynamics in a case of severe hypochondriasis. Q 1953, 22:303
47838 Reider, N. A type of transference in institutions. Q 1954, 23:304
47839 Richfield, J. The role of philosophy in theoretical psychiatry. Q 1954 23:304
47840 Schmidl, F. Freud's sociological thinking. Q 1953, 22:126
47841 Schwarz, H. A case of character disorder. Q 1953, 22:127
47842 Solow, R. A. Chronic cyclic schizo-affective psychosis. Q 1953, 22:612
47843 Wiener, N. Problems of organization. Q 1954, 23:468
47844 Zulliger, H. Child psychotherapy without interpretation of unconscious content. Q 1954, 23:468

REVIEW OF:
47845 Jones, E. The Life and Work of Sigmund Freud. J 1954, 35:359-360

GREENWALD, HAROLD

47846 The Call Girl: A Social and Psychoanalytic Study. NY: Ballantine 1958, 245 p
47847 The call girl: a social and psychoanalytic study. NPAP 1958 6(1): 20-44
47848 (Ed) Great Cases in Psychoanalysis. NY: Ballantine 1959, 256 p
47849 Psychoanalytic profile of a factory. NPAP 1959, 5(4):27-37

47850 Sandra. From author's *The Call Girl: A Social and Psychoanalytic Study.* In Freeman, L. *Troubled Women,* World Publ Co 1959, 97-122

See Munzer, Jean

GREENWALD, LEONA M.
See Hulse, Wilfred C.

GREENWOOD, EDWARD D.

47851 The role of psychotherapy in residential treatment. Symposium 1954: The role of residential treatment for children. Ops 1955, 25:692-698
Abs Koenig RFPsa 1956, 20:583-584

See Robinson, J. Franklin

GREER, INA M.
See Lindemann, Erich

GREGG, ALAN

47852 The place of psychoanalysis in medicine. 20 Yrs Psa 28-49

See Lidz, Theodore

GREGORI, ELLEN

47853 Das Symbol im Märchen. [The symbol in the fairy tale.] Jb Psychol Psychother 1955, 3:88-94

GREGORY, CHRISTOPHER C. L.

47854 (& Kohsen, A.) Physical and Psychical Research: An Analysis of Belief. Reigate, Surrey: Omega Pr 1954, 213 p

GREGORY, HOOSAG K.

47855 The prisoner and his crimes: summary comments on a longer study of the mind of William Cowper. Lit & Psychol 1956, 6(2):53-59

GREGORY, JOSHUA CRAVEN

47856 Revelations and dreams. Contempor 1955, 187:177-182

GRENSTED, LAURENCE W.

47857 Foreword to Guntrip, H. J. S. *Mental Pain and the Cure of Souls*
47858 The Psychology of Religion. London: Oxford Univ Pr 1952, 175 p
Rv Rowley, J. T. J 1954, 35:80

GRESSOT, MICHEL

47859 (& Fierz, H. K.; Pulver, U.; Morf, A.; Reymond-Rivier, B.; Moser, U.; Blarer, A. von; Matalon, B.) Les critères de validité en psychanalyse. [Criteria in the validation of psychoanalysis. Symposium.] Schweiz Z Psychol 1959, 18:303-330

47860 Le désire d'être psychologue. [The desire to be a psychologist.]
Schweiz Z Psychol 1958, 17:127-133

47861 Les états de dépendance en psychothérapie. [States of dependence in
psychotherapy.] Schweiz ANP 1956, 77:30-39

47862 Les indications et la technique de la cure psychanalytique. [Indications
and technique of psychoanalytic therapy.] Rev méd Suisse rom 1953,
73:759-760

47863 Le mythe dogmatique du système moral des Manichéens. [The
dogmatic myth and the moral system of the Manicheans.] RFPsa 1953,
17:398-427

Abs RJA An Surv Psa 1953, 4:348-351

47864 Psychanalyse et analyse existentielle. [Psychoanalysis and "Daseinsanalyse".] Proc Int Cong Psychotherapy 1958, Barcelona

47865 Psychanalyse et connaissance. (Contribution à une épistemologie psychanalytique). [Psychoanalysis and knowledge (contribution to a psychoanalytic epistemology).] RFPsa 1956, 20:9-130

47866 Psychothérapie en clientèle privée. [Psychotherapy with private
patients.] Prak Psychiat 1953, 32:237-239

47867 Le transfert dans la médecine des sociétés primitives. [Transference
phenomena in the medicine of primitive cultures.] Evolut psychiat
1955, 251-270

Übertragungsphänomene in der Medizin der Primitiven. Psyche,
Heidel 1957, 10:714-732

47868 Le transfert en psychiatrie. [Transference and psychiatry.] Arch Suisses
Neurol Psychiatrie 1957, 79:409-411

47869 Valeur psychologique de la peine. [Psychological value of the penalty.]
Rev intern de Criminologie, Geneva 1958, 12:172-177

47870 Y a-t-il une éthique du psychanalyste? [Is there a psychoanalyst's
ethic?] Arch Suisses Neurol Psychiatrie 1958

GREWEL, FRITS

47871 The Frenum Praeputii and the defloration of the human male. Folia
Psychiatr Neerl 1958, 61:59-62

GREY, EARLE

47872 Shakespeare Festival, Toronto, Canada. Shakespeare Survey 1957,
10:111-114

GRIFFIN, WILLIAM J.

47873 The uses and abuses of psychoanalysis in the study of literature. Lit
& Psychol 1951, 1(5-6):9-18

GRIFFITH, EDWARD F.

47874 Die Bejahung der Sexualität in der Ehe. [Affirmation of sexuality in
marriage.] B Sexfschg 1958, (13):14-20

47875 Marriage and the Unconscious. London: Secker & Warburg 1957,
221 p

GRIFFITH, RICHARD MARION

47876 Typical dreams: a statistical study of personality correlates. (Abs) Diss
Abstr 1958, 18:1106

47877 (& Miyagi, O.; Tago, A.) Universality of typical dreams: Japanese vs.
Americans. Am Anthrop 1958, 60:1173-1179

GRIFFITHS, RUTH

47878 The Abilities of Babies. London: Univ London Pr 1954, 229 p
Rv EJA J 1955, 36:406; Rev Psicoanál 1959, 15:161

GRIMES, LOUISE IRELAND

See Powdermaker, Florence

GRIMSHAW, L.

47879 Anorexia nervosa: a contribution to its psychogenesis. M 1959, 32:44-49
Abs Riv Psa 1959, 5:87

GRIMSLEY, RONALD

47880 An aspect of Sartre and the unconscious. Philosophy Ja 1955, 33-44

GRINBERG, LEON

47881 Sobre algunos mecanismos esquizoides en relación con el juego de
ajedrez. [Concerning some schizoid mechanisms with chess playing.]
Rev Psicoanál 1955, 12:376-384

47882 Sobre algunos problemas de técnica psicoanalítica determinados por la
identificación y contraidentificación proyectivas. [On some technical
psychoanalytical problems determined by projective identification and
counter-identification.] Rev Psicoanál 1956, 13:507-511

47883 Aspectos mágicos en las ansiedades paranoides y depresivas. [Magical
aspects of paranoid and depressive anxieties.] Rev Psicoanál 1959, 16:
15-26

47884 Aspectos mágicos en la transferencia y en la contratransferencia. Sus
implicaciones técnicas. [Magic aspects of transference and countertransference. Its technical implications.] Rev Psicoanál 1959, 15:347-
368
Abs Vega Q 1959, 28:436

47885 Aspectos psicoanalíticos de una cefalea jaquecosa. [Psychoanalytic
aspects of a migraine type headache.] Rev Psicoanál 1954, 11:31-47
Abs JFr An Surv Psa 1954, 5:147-148. Vega Q 1956, 25:130-131

47886 (& Langer, M.; Rodrigué, E.) Bildung einer Gruppe. [Formation of a
group.] Psyche, Heidel 1959, 13:195-214

47887 Considerationes sobre un caso de jaqueca. [Considerations upon a case
of migraine.] Rev Psicoanál 1954, 11:169-177. In Garma, A. El Dolor
de Cabeza, Buenos Aires: Biblioteca de Psicoanálisis 1958
Abs JFr An Surv Psa 1954, 5:147. Vega Q 1956, 25:133

47888 Sobre la despersonalización en el curso de la neurosis transferencial.
[Depersonalization during transference neurosis.] Rev Psicoanál 1954,
11:314-347
Abs NRo An Surv Psa 1954, 5:345-346. Vega Q 1956, 25:297-298

47889   Motivaciones psicológicas de la superstición y el tabú; sus relaciones
        con la neurosis obsesiva y los mecanismos esquizoides. [Psychological
        motivations of superstition and taboo; their relations with obsessive
        neurosis and with schizoid mechanisms.] Act Np Arg 1958, 4:291-302
47890   La negación en el comer compulsivo y en la obesidad. [Denial in com-
        pulsive eating and in obesity.] Rev Psicoanál 1956, 13:160-169
47891   Palabras de apertura. [Opening remarks.] Rev Psicoanál 1959, 16:319-
        321
47892   Perturbaciones en la interpretación por la contraidentificación proyec-
        tiva. [Perturbations of interpretation caused by projective counter-
        identification.] Rev Psicoanál 1957, 14:23-28
S-12671 Psicoanálisis de una melancolia ansiosa: elaboracion tardia de un
        duelo.
            Abs JFr An Surv Psa 1952, 3:136-139. Vega Q 1954, 23:149
47893   (& Langer, M.; Rodrigué, E.) Psicoterapie del Grupo. Su Enfoque
        psicoanalítico. [Group Psychotherapy. Its Psychoanalytical Approach.]
        Buenos Aires: Ed. Paidos 1957, 242 p
            Psychoanalytische Gruppentherapie. Stuttgart: Ernst Klett 1960
47894   La psicoterapie del grupo y la Universidad. [Group psychotherapy and
        the University.] Psique en la Universidad 1958, 1(3):1-9
47895   Revisión de los conceptos sobre magia y omnipotencia. [Review of
        concepts on magic and omnipotence.] Rev Psicoanál 1957, 14:324-332
47896   La rivalidad y los sueños legendarios de José. [Rivalry and the legend-
        ary dreams of José.] Rev Psicoanál 1960, 17:27-45
47897   Si Yo Fuera Usted: Contribución al estudio de la identificación proyec-
        tiva. [If I Were You: Contribution to the study of the projective iden-
        tification.] Rev Psicoanál 1957, 14:355-367
            Abs Vega Q 1959, 28:135
S-12672 La situación traumática como etiología común del sueño y del síntoma
        agudo.
            Abs Brodsky, B. Q 1953, 22:461-462
47898   (& Grinberg, R.) Los sueños del dia lunes. [Dreams of moonlight.]
        Rev Psicoanál 1960, 17:449-455
47899   Vicisitudes de las relaciones entre analistas y sus motivaciones. [Changes
        in the relations between analysts and their motivations.] Rev Psicoanál
        1959, 16:368-380

        See Rodrigué, Emilio; Rolla, E. H.

        ABSTRACTS OF:
47900   Bergler, E. The problem of "magic gestures." Rev Psicoanál 1956,
        13:80
47901   Christensen, E. O. The magic cloak: a critical review. Rev Psicoanál
        1956, 13:195-196

        REVIEWS OF:
47902   Alexander, F. Psychogenic headache and migraine. Rev Psicoanál 1954,
        11:259
47903   Alexander, F. & Szasz, T. S. The psychosomatic approach in medicine.
        Rev Psicoanál 1954, 11:259
47904   Deutsch, H. Absence of grief. Rev Psicoanál 1954, 11:407

47905 Federn, P. Depersonalization. Rev Psicoanál 1954, 11:404

47906 Feigenbaum, D. Depersonalization as a defense mechanism. Rev Psicoanál 1954, 11:407-408

47907 French, T. M. The integration of behavior. Rev Psicoanál 1953, 10:238-239

47908 French, T. Physiology of behavior and choice of neurosis. Rev Psicoanál 1954, 11:241

47909 Gitelson, M. The emotional position of the analyst in the psychoanalytical situation. Rev Psicoanál 1953, 10:246-247

47910 Koolhaas, G. Psicoanálisis de una perturbacion visual. Rev Psicoanál 1953, 10:248-249

47911 Langer, M. Fantasias eternas a la luz del psicoanálisis. Rev Psicoanál 1957, 14:335-336

47912 Lowtzky, F. Mahatma Gandhi: a contribution to the psychoanalytic understanding of the causes of war and the means of preventing wars. Rev Psicoanál 1953, 10:245-246

47913 Oberndorf, C. P. The role of anxiety in depersonalization. Rev Psicoanál 1954, 11:403-404

47914 Róheim, G. Magic and schizophrenia. Rev Psicoanál 1956, 13:77

47915 Rosenfeld, H. Psychoanalysis of a schizophrenic state with depersonalization. Rev Psicoanál 1954, 11:408

47916 Seidenberg, R. Psychosexual headache. Rev Psicoanál 1954, 11:253

47917 Selinsky, H. Psychological study of the migrainous syndrome. Rev Psicoanál 1954, 11:239-240

47918 Tarachow, S. The analysis of a dream during a migraine attack. Rev Psicoanál 1954, 11:249

GRINBERG, REBECCA V. DE

47919 Caracteristicas de las relaciones de objeto en un claustrophobia. [Character of the object relationships in a phobic patient.] Rev Psicoanál 1959, 16:122-138

Abs Vega Q 1960, 29:446

47920 Evolución de la fantasía de enferedad a través de la construcción de casas. [Evolution of the fantasy of illness through house-building.] Rev Psicoanál 1958, 15:26-30

47921 Los significados de Mirar. [The significance of Mirar.] Rev Psicoanál 1960, 17:224-242

See Evelson, Elena; Grinberg, Léon

REVIEWS OF:

47922 Caplan, G. Emotional problems of early childhood. Rev Psicoanál 1958, 15:138

47923 Klein, M. The psychoanalytic play technique: its history and significance. Rev Psicoanál 1958, 15:138-139

47924 Ramirez, S. "El Mexicano"; psicologia de sus motivaciones. Rev Psicoanál 1960, 17:254-255

47925 Rosenfeld, E. Dream and vision. Some remarks on Freud's Egyptian bird dream. Rev Psicoanál 1956, 13:327-328

GRINEVICH, V.

47926 [On the pathography of S. Esenin.] (Russian) Klinischeskii arkhiv geneal'nosti i odarennosti 1927, 3(1):82-94

GRINKER, JULIUS

47927 Freud's psychotherapy. Illinois med J 1912, 22:185-195

GRINKER, ROY R.

47928 Alcoholism. Report of Committee. Inst Med Chicago 1959, 17 (10)

47929 Anxiety in "consciousness." In Abrahamson, H. A. *Problems of Consciousness, Transactions of the Fifth Conference,* NY: Josiah Macy, Jr. Foundation, 1955

47930 Anxiety as a significant variable for a unified theory of human behavior. AMA Arch gen Psychiat 1959, 1:537-546

47931 Breathing-holding time in anxiety states. Fed Proc 1946, 5(1)

47932 (& Robbins, F. P.) Brief therapy of a psychosomatic case. In Greenwald, H. *Great Cases in Psychoanalysis,* NY: Ballantine 1959, 219-226. From authors' *Psychosomatic Case Book*

47933 Closing comments. Sci Psa 1958, 1:174-175

47934 Closure. In author's *Mid-Century Psychiatry* 182-183

47935 Comment on Engel, G. L. & Reichsman, F. "Letter to the editor." J 1959, 40:61

47936 Comment on the psychodynamic position. In Kruse, H. D. *Integrating the Approaches to Mental Disease,* NY: Hoeber-Harper 1957, 145-146

47937 Contributor to Abrahamson, H. A. *Problems of Consciousness, Transactions of the Second Conference,* NY: Josiah Macy, Jr. Foundation 1951

47938 [Discussant on] Community resources for morale. In Galdston, I. *Panic and Morale,* NY: IUP 1958, 240-242

47939 Comparisons between systems of organization. Unif Theory Behav 135-141

47940 Contributor to Luski, *Interdisciplinary Team Research,* NY: Nat'l Training Laboratories 1958

47941 Discussion of Levine, M. "The impact of psychoanalysis on training in psychiatry." 20 Yrs Psa 75-83

47942 Discussion of Murphy, G. "Psychoanalysis as a unified theory of behavior." Sci Psa 1960, 3:176-177

47943 Discussion of symposium: "Neurohumoral factors in emotions." AMA ANP 1955, 73:138-140

47944 The effect of infantile disease on ego patterns. P 1953, 110:290-295 Abs NRo An Surv Psa 1953, 4:68-71. MK Q 1954, 23:303

47945 Every doctor a psychiatrist. Inst Med Chicago 1947, 15(16)

47946 [Contributor to panel discussion on] The family in psychotherapy. Sci Psa 1959, 2:204-206

47947 Foreword to Beck, S. J. *Rorschach Method, Vol. II,* NY: Grune & Stratton 1945

47948 Foreword to Piers, G. & Singer, M. B. *Shame and Guilt*

47949 Freud and medicine. Bull NY Acad Med 1956, 32:878-886. In Galdston, I. *Freud and Contemporary Culture*, NY: IUP 1957, 29-41

47950 Growth, inertia and shame: their therapeutic implications and dangers. J 1955, 36:242-253
    Abs Lebovici, S. RFPsa 1955, 19:639-640. JLan Q 1957, 26:278

S-12678 (& Gottschalk, L.) Headaches and muscular pains.
    Rv Liberman, D. Rev Psicoanál 1954, 11:257-258

47951 Hypothalamic functions in psychosomatic interrelations. PSM 1939, 1:19-47. In Alexander, F. & French, T. M. *Studies in Psychosomatic Medicine*, NY: Ronald Pr 1948, 46-84

47952 On identification. J 1957, 38:379-390
    Abs Auth Q 1958, 27:600

47953 Indications for specific psychiatric therapy. Bull Chicago Med Soc 1946, July

47954 The Institute for Psychosomatic and Psychiatric Research and Training, Michael Reese Hospital, Chicago. Mental Hosp 1956, 7:27

47955 The intrapersonal organization. Univ Theory Behav 3-15

47956 Introduction. In author's *Mid-Century Psychiatry* 3-7

47957 Introduction to Beck, S. J. *The Six Schizophrenias*

47958 (& Spiegel, J. P.) Men under stress. In Winch, R. F. & McGinnis, R. *Selected Studies in Marriage and the Family*, NY: Holt 1953, 562-569. From authors' *Men Under Stress* [12681]

47959 The mental health of our veterans. Northwestern Univ Reviewing Stand 1945, 6(3)

47960 (Ed) Mid-Century Psychiatry. Springfield, Ill: Charles C Thomas 1953, 183 p
    Rv Harris, H. I. Q 1954, 23:287

47961 [Discussant on] Morale: its nature and meaning. In Galdston, I. *Panic and Morale*, NY: IUP 1958, 80; 83

47962 A note on the derivation of speech patterns. Lancet 1946, 66:370

47963 Participant in symposium. In Kruse, H. D. *Integrating the Approaches to Mental Disease*, NY: Hoeber-Harper 1957, 160-383

47964 Peace of mind. Northwestern Univ Reviewing Stand, 1946, Oct.

47965 A philosophical appraisal of psychoanalysis. Sci Psa 1958, 1:126-142

47966 Preface to Lichtenberg, P. et al: *Motivation for Child Psychiatry Treatment*

47967 Problems of consciousness (a review, an analysis and a proposition). In Abrahamson, H. A. *Problems of Consciousness, Transactions of the Fourth Conference*, NY: Josiah Macy, Jr. Foundation 1954

47968 Psychiatric disorders in combat crews overseas and in returnees. Med Clinics N America 1945, May

47969 The psychiatric, medical and social aspects of war neurosis. Cincinnati J Med 1945, 26:241

47970 Psychiatric objectives of our time. Canad Med Ass J 1947, 56:153

47971 The psychiatrist's contribution to the concept of health and disease. Univ Chicago Round Table 688, 1951, June 3

47972 Psychosomatic approach to anxiety. P 1956, 113:443-447. J Amer Soc Psychosomatic Dentistry 1957, 4:13. In Crow, L. D. & Crow, A. *Read-*

ings in Abnormal Psychology, Ames, Iowa: Littlefield, Adams 1958, 168-175

Abs DRu Q 1959, 28:127

47973 (& Robbins, Fred P.) Psychosomatic Case Book. NY: Blakiston 1954, 346 p

Cliniques psychosomatiques. Paris: PUF 1959

Rv Johnson, A. M. Q 1955, 24:304-306

47974 Psychosomatic medicine. Mental Health Bull 1948, 26 (Mar-Apr)

47975 Psychosomatic processes: theory and experiment. In Beck, S. J. & Molish, H. B. *Reflexes to Intelligence,* Glencoe, Ill: Free Pr 1959, 249-262

47976 Psychosomatic Research. NY: W. W. Norton 1953, 208 p

Rv NR Q 1954, 23:130-131

47977 Rehabilitation of flyers with operational fatigue. Air Surgeon's Bull 1945, 2(1)

47978 (& Basowitz, H.; Korchin, S. J.) Response to a life stress: the experience of anxiety. Am Psych 1953, 8:318

47979 (& Spiegel, J. P.) The returning soldier—dissent. Hollywood Quart 1946, 1:321

47980 Sedation as a technique in psychotherapy. Bull NY Acad Med 1946, 22:185

47981 [Discussant on] The sociology of morale. In Galdston, I. *Panic and Morale,* NY: IUP 1958, 127-130; 150-151

47982 The soldier—by science, not by flags. Survey 1949, Aug

47983 Some current trends and hypotheses of psychosomatic research. Psm Cpt Psa 37-62

47984 Summary. Unif Theory Behav 365-375

47985 (& Korchin, S. J.; Basowitz, H.; Hamburg, D. A.; Sabshin, M.; Persky, H.; Chevalier, J. A.; Board, F. A.) A theoretical and experimental approach to the problems of anxiety. AMA ANP 1956, 76:420-431. Prog PT 1957, 2:44-60

47986 (& Hughes, H. McG.) Toward a Unified Theory of Human Behavior. NY: Basic Books 1956, xv + 375 p

47987 A transactional model for psychotherapy. Arch gen Psychiat 1959, 1:132-148

Abs KRu Q 1960, 29:438-439

47988 (& Sabshin, M.; Hamburg, D. A.; Board, F. A.; Basowitz, H.; Korchin, S. J.; Persky, H.; Chevalier, J. A.) The use of an anxiety-producing interview and its meaning to the subject. AMA ANP 1957, 77:406-419

47989 (& Braceland, F. J.; Meduna, L. J.) Use of drugs in the treatment of neurosis and in the office management of psychoses. Modern Med 1957, 25:190

47990 War neuroses. In *Encyclopedia Britannica Year Book 1946*

See Basowitz, Harold; Glickstein, Mitchell; Hamburg, David A.; Harrower, M. R.; Jeans, R. F.; Korchin, Sheldon J.; Persky, Harold; Sabshin, Melvin; Spiegel, John P.

GRINSTEIN, ALEXANDER

47991 The boy and the dike. J 1953, 34:265-270

Abs RJA An Surv Psa 1953, 4:347-348. Auth Q 1955, 24:152-153

47992 The convertible as a symbol in dreams. J Am Psa Ass 1954, 2:466-472
  Abs JFr An Surv Psa 1954, 5:222-223. TFr J 1955, 36:427-428.
  Aldendorff, H. Q 1957, 26:136
47993 The dramatic device: a play within a play. (Read at Am Psa Ass, Apr 1954) J Am Psa Ass 1956, 4:49-52
  Abs TFr J 1957, 38:133-134
47994 The Index of Psychoanalytic Writings, Five Volumes. (Preface: EJ) NY: IUP 1956-1960
47995 "Miracle in Milan": some psychoanalytic notes on a movie. Am Im 1953, 10:229-245
  Abs MK An Surv Psa 1953, 4:386-388
S-12699 A psychoanalytic study of Schwind's "The Dream of a Prisoner."
  Abs JFr An Surv Psa 1951, 2:260. MK An Surv Psa 1951, 2:475-476
47996 A specific defense met in psychoanalytic therapy: "Comes the knight in shining armor." (Read at Am Psa Ass, Atlantic City, N.J., May 1955) J Am Psa Ass 1957, 5:124-129
  Abs Shentoub, S. A. RFPsa 1957, 21:613. HW Q 1960, 29:279
S-12700 Stages in the development of control over fire.
  Abs STa An Surv Psa 1952, 3:461-462. MGr Q 1954, 23:140-141
47997 (& Sterba, E.) Understanding Your Family. NY: Random House 1957, v + 312 p
  Rv Abraham, H. C. J 1959, 40:346-347
47998 Vacations: a psychoanalytic study. J 1955, 36:177-186
  Abs JLan Q 1956, 25:614. Rv Usandivaras, R. Rev Psicoanál 1955, 12:431-432

GRODZICKI, W. D.

47999 Neue Wege in der Psychoanalyse? [New ways in psychoanalysis?] Psyche, Heidel 1956, 10:795-905
48000 The technical problem of "taking action" in analysis. (Read at 20th Int Psa Cong, Paris, 1957)
  Abs Auth J 1958, 39:291

GROEN, J.

48001 Behandeling van asthma bronchiale met de combinatie van ACTH en groeps (psycho) therapie. [Treatment of bronchial asthma with a combination of ACTH and group (psycho) therapy.] Nederl Tschr Geneesk 1954, 98:2212
48002 (& Groen-van Beverwijk, M.; Bastiaans, J.; Groen, A. S.; Vles, S. J.) De invloed van psychische factoren op het onstaan en het beloop van de long-tuberculose. [The influence of psychic factors on the genesis and course of pulmonary tuberculosis.] Amsterdam: Scheltema en Holkema 1952, 149 p
48003 (& Bastiaans, J.) Studies on ulcerative colitis: personality structure, emotional conflict situations and effects of psychotherapy. Mod Tr PSM 102-125

  See Bastiaans, J.

GROETHUYSEN, ULRICH C.

48004 (& Robinson, D. B.; Haylett, C. H.; Estes, H. R.; Johnson, A. M.)
Depth electrographic recording of a seizure during a structured interview: report of a case. PSM 1957, 19:353-362
    Abs Luchina Rev Psicoanál 1956, 14:427. Johnson, McC. Q 1958,
27:606

GROH, LESLIE S.

48005 A study of ego integration by means of an index of identification
derived from six TAT cards. J proj Techn 1956, 20:387-397

GRONSETH, ERIK

48006 Familien, Barnet og Samfunnet. [Families, Children and the Community.] Samtiden 1953, 62:591-602

GROOM, P. R. M.

See Buck, Alice E.

GROSCH, MARIA

48007 Über Hyperchondrie. [On hypochondria.] Z PSM 1958, 4:195-205

GROSS, ALFRED

S-12737 The secret.
    Abs JFr An Surv Psa 1951, 2:205-208

GROSS, GEORGE A.

See Luborsky, Lester B.

GROSS, LEONARD

48008 God and Freud. NY: David McKay 1959, vii + 215 p

GROSS, LLEWELLYN

48009 Society, maternal behavior and gastro-intestinal disorders. Psychiat Q
Suppl 1955, 29:23-37. Child-Fam Dig 1956, 14(2):9-23

GROSS, MARTIN L.

See Polatin, Philip

GROSS, ZOLTAN

See Masserman, Jules H.

GROSSBARD, HYMAN

See Goldsmith, Jerome M.

GROSSMAN, DAVID

48010 An experimental investigation of a psychotherapeutic technique. J
consult Psychol 1952, 16:325-331

GROSSMAN, EUGENE M.
See Guthrie, Thomas C.

GROSSMAN, NAOMI
48011 Participant in Clinical Conference: A problem of ego organization in a latency child. New Front Child Guid 173-209

GROSSMAN, SEARLES A.
48012 Psychological studies in planning and evaluating psychotherapy in a case of recurring depression. Case Reports Clin Psychol 1951, 2:16-28

GROTE, HERBIERTO DE
TRANSLATION OF:
Ross, Josephine H. [57559]

GROTJAHN, MARTIN
48013 The accident. Child-Fam Dig 1956, 14(2):29-36
48014 Analytic family therapy: a survey of trends in research and practice. Sci Psa 1959, 2:90-104
48015 Analytic psychotherapy with the elderly. R 1955, 42:419-427
     Psychothérapie analytique des gens agés. (Tr: Smirnoff, V.) Psychanalyse 1956, 2:243-255
     Abs JLan Q 1957, 26:285
48016 Beyond Laughter. NY: Blakiston Div, McGraw-Hill 1957, 285 p
     Abs J Am Psa Ass 1958, 6:168. Rv Ehrenzweig, A. J 1957, 38:364-365. GPK Q 1957, 26:541-542. Granoff, W. Psychanalyse 1958, 4:293-296
48017 On bullfighting and the future of tragedy. J 1959, 40:238-239
     Abs Weiss, J. Q 1960, 29:585. Rv Tabak Rev Psicoanál 1960, 17:262
48018 The defenses against creative anxiety in the life and work of James Barrie. Commentary to John Skinner's research of "The Boy Who Wouldn't Grow Up." Am Im 1957, 14:143-148
48019 Discussion of Kubie, L. S. "Some theoretical concepts underlying the relationship between individual and group psychotherapies." Int J grp PT 1958, 8:26-30
48020 History. An Surv Psa 1951, 2:1-19
S-12780 The inability to remember dreams and jokes.
     Abs JAA An Surv Psa 1951, 2:128-129
S-12783 Laughter in psychoanalysis.
     Rv Bensoussan, P. RFPsa 1954, 18:308
48021 A letter by Sigmund Freud with recollections of his adolescence. J Am Psa Ass 1956, 4:644-652
     Abs TFr J 1957, 38:433. JPW Q 1960, 29:137
48022 Neuere Fortschritte in der Entwicklung der psychotherapeutischen Technik. [Recent progress in the development of psychotherapeutic technique.] Psyche, Heidel 1953, 7:197-207
     Abs LCK An Surv Psa 1953, 4:503-504

48023 (& Treusch, J. V.) A new technique of psychosomatic consultations. Some illustrations of teamwork between an internist and a psychiatrist. A practical approach to psychosomatic medicine. R 1957, 44:176-192
    Abs J Lan Q 1958, 27:443

48024 Present trends in psychoanalytic training. 20 Yrs Psa 84-113

48025 Problems and techniques of supervision. Ps 1955, 18:9-16

S-12789 The process of maturation in group psychotherapy and in the group therapist.
    Abs R 1954, 41:69

48026 Psychoanalysis and the Family Neurosis. NY: W. W. Norton 1960, 320 p

48027 A psychoanalyst passes a small stone with big troubles. In Pinner, M. & Miller, B. F. *When Doctors Are Patients*, NY: W. W. Norton 1952, 89-95
    Der kleine Nierenstein eines Psychoanalytikers und seine grossen Beschwerden. In Pinner, M. & Miller, B. F. *Was Ärzte als Patienten erleben*, Stuttgart 1953, 111-119
    Um psicanalista elimina um pequeno calculo com grandes dificuldades. Rev bras Medicina 1953, 10:723

48028 The recognition of the Oedipus complex in Greek antiquity. Two quotations from Aristophanes. Samiksa 1955, Bose number, special issue: 28-34

48029 About the relation between psychoanalytic training and psychoanalytic therapy. (Read at 18th Int Psa Cong, London, July 1953) J 1954, 35:254-262
    Abs Auth J 1954, 35:285. JFr An Surv Psa 1954, 5:400-403. Lebovici, S. RFPsa 1954, 18:471. JLan Q 1955, 24:608-609

S-12804 About the representation of death in the art of antiquity and in the unconscious of modern men.
    Abs JAA An Surv Psa 1951, 2:153-154. JFr An Surv Psa 1951, 2:248-251. MK An Surv Psa 1951, 2:487

S-12805 The role of identification in psychiatric and psychoanalytic training.
    Abs R 1953, 40:78-79

48030 Sigmund Freud and the history of psychoanalysis from early times in Vienna to the contemporary scene in America. PSM 1954, 16:265-267

S-12809 Some analytic observations about the process of growing old.
    Abs GD An Surv Psa 1951, 2:537. NRo An Surv Psa 1951, 2:94-97

48031 Special aspects of countertransference in analytic group psychotherapy. Int J grp PT 1953, 3:407-416
    Abs LCK An Surv Psa 1953, 4:513-514. GPK Q 1955, 24:163

48032 Theorie und Praxis der Gruppenpsychotherapie. Ein bescheidener Versuch, einige Fragen und Bedenken von wohlwollenden Kritikern der Gruppenpsychotherapie zu beantworten. [Theory and practice of group psychotherapy. Answers to questions and complaints of critics.] (Tr: Vogel, H.) Z diagn Psychol 1957, 5:178-186

48033 Die Träume eines Kindes. Beobachtungen über eine Zeitspanne von 15 Jahren. [A child's dreams. Observations covering a period of 15 years.] Die Heilkunst 1956, 69:156-158

48034 Training the third ear: report on an attempt at teaching conjecture in psychotherapy. Expl Psa 221-229

48035 (& Ziferstein, I.) Working through, acting out, and psychodrama. Group PT 1954, 7:321-322

48036 Über die Zusammenarbeit von Psychotherapeut und Internist. [Collaboration of psychotherapist and internist.] Psyche, Heidel 1956, 10:530-550

See Jackson, James; Moreno, J. L.; Ziferstein, Isidore

ABSTRACTS OF:

48037 Bartemeier, L. Presidential address. J 1953, 34:75-76

48038 Bernfeld, S. Sigmund Freud, M.D., 1882-1885. An Surv Psa 1951, 2:5-7

48039 Bernfeld, S. C. Freud and archaeology. An Surv Psa 1951, 2:7-8

48040 Borkenau, F. Zwei Abhandlungen zur griechischen Mythologie. Q 1958, 27:455-456

48041 Brosin, H. W. Leo H. Bartemeier, M.D., President 1951-1952. J 1953, 34:75-76

48042 Burlingham, D. T. Precursors of some psychoanalytic ideas about children in the sixteenth and seventeenth centuries. An Surv Psa 1951, 2:17-19

48043 Buxbaum, E. Freud's dream interpretation in the light of his letters to Fliess. An Surv Psa 1951, 2:1-3

48044 Colby, K. M. On the disagreement between Freud and Adler. An Surv Psa 1951, 2:10-12

48045 Eissler, K. R. An unknown autobiographical letter by Freud and a short comment. An Surv Psa 1951, 2:4-5

48046 Freud, A. August Aichhorn, July 27, 1878-October 17, 1949: an obituary. An Surv Psa 1951, 2:12-14

48047 Margolin, S. G. Psychophysiological basis of medical practice. J 1954, 35:450

48048 Reich, A. The discussion of 1912 on masturbation and our present-day views. An Surv Psa 1951, 2:15-17

48049 Sterba, R. A case of brief psychotherapy by Sigmund Freud. An Surv Psa 1951, 2:8-10

48050 Weiss, E. Paul Federn: an obituary. An Surv Psa 1951, 2:14-15

48051 Weiss, E. Paul Federn's scientific contributions: in commemoration. An Surv Psa 1951, 2:14-15

REVIEWS OF:

48052 Allport, G. W. The Nature of Prejudice. Q 1954, 23:605

48053 Bergson, H. The World of Dreams. Q 1959, 28:418

48054 Brody, M. W. Observations on Direct Analysis. Q 1960, 29:251-252

48055 Bromberg, W. Man Above Humanity. Q 1956, 25:112

48056 Christie, R. & Jahoda, M. (Eds) Studies in the Scope and Method of "The Authoritarian Personality." Continuities in Social Research. Q 1954, 23:605-606

48057 Cohen, E. A. Human Behavior in the Concentration Camp. Q 1954, 23:458-459

48058 Eaton, J. W. & Weil, R. J. Culture and Mental Disorders. Q 1956, 25:109-110

48059   Eisenstein, V. W. (Ed) Neurotic Interaction in Marriage. Q 1957, 26:260-262
48060   Erikson, E. H. Young Man Luther. J 1959, 40:343-346
48061   Fabricant, N. (Ed) Why We Became Doctors. Q 1955, 24:457-458
48062   Feifel, H. (Ed) The Meaning of Death. Q 1960, 29:406-407
48063   Galdston, I. (Ed) Society and Medicine. Q 1956, 25:607-608
48064   Hasluck, M. The Unwritten Law in Albania. Q 1955, 24:457
48065   Heiman, M. (Ed) Psychoanalysis and Social Work. J 1953, 34:346-347
48066   Holt, R. R. et al: Personality Patterns of Psychiatrists. A Study of Methods for Selecting Residents. Q 1959, 28:405-407
48067   Hook, S. (Ed) Psychoanalysis, Scientific Method, and Philosophy. Q 1959, 28:536-537
48068   LaBarre, W. The Human Animal. Q 1955, 24:597-598
48069   MacDonald, J. M. Psychiatry and the Criminal. Q 1958, 27:435
48070   Mannheim, K. Essays on the Sociology of Culture. Q 1957, 26:132-133
48071   Marcuse, H. Eros and Civilization. Q 1956, 25:429-431
48072   Nuttin, J. Psychoanalysis and Personality. Q 1954, 23:450
48073   Phillips, W. (Ed) Art and Psychoanalysis. Q 1957, 26:544-545
48074   Podolsky, E. (Ed) The Neuroses and Their Treatment. Q 1958, 27:436
48075   Reik, T. Of Love and Lust. Q 1958, 27:113
48076   Schaffner, B. (Ed) Group Processes. Q 1959, 28:415-416
48077   Stokes, A. Greek Culture and the Ego. Q 1960, 29:404-406
48078   Tauber, E. S. & Green, M. R. Prelogical Experience. Q 1960, 29:126
48079   Vincent, C. E. (Ed) Readings in Marriage Counseling. Q 1957, 26:545-546

GROVES, MARION H.

See Boshes, Benjamin

GRUEN, ARNO

48080   Old age as a factor in motivation for therapy. Int J soc Psychiat 1957, 3:61-66

GRUENBERG, ERNEST M.

See Welsch, Exie E.

GRUENBERG, SIDONIE MATSNER

48081   (Ed) The Encyclopedia of Child Care and Guidance. NY: Doubleday 1954, 1016 p
48082   Foreword to Raymond, L. *Adoption and After*
48083   *The Lady from the Sea*, Psyche 1929, 9:84-92
48084   (& Arnstein, H.) Parent education in six White House Conferences. Child Stud 1959-60, 37:9-15
48085   Parents' Guide to Everyday Problems of Boys and Girls: Helping Your Child from Five to Twelve. NY: Random House 1957, xiv + 363 p

GRUENTHAL, MAX

48086   Aims and limitations of psychotherapy with schizophrenics and borderline cases in private practice. PT 1958, 12:465-472

48087 Testing of the limits in active psychotherapy. Acta psychother psychosom orthopaedag 1955, 3(Suppl):123-131

GRUGETT, ALVIN ELDRIDGE, JR.

48088 Sexual expression of identification conflicts. In Bender, L. *A Dynamic Psychopathology of Childhood,* Springfield, Ill: Charles C Thomas 1954, 130-171

See Bender, Lauretta; Gurevitz, Saul

REVIEW OF:
48089 Caplan, G. Emotional Problems of Early Childhood. NPAP 1955-56, 4(2):80

GRUHLE, HANS WALTER

48090 Verstehen und Einfühlen: gesammelte Schriften. [Understanding and Intuition: Collected Papers.] Berlin: Springer 1953, vi + 458 p
48091 Wernickes psychopathologische und klinische Lehren. [Wernicke's psychopathological and clinical theories.] Nervenarzt 1955, 26:505-507

GRUMMON, DONALD L.

48092 (& John, E. S.) Changes over client-centered therapy evaluated on psychoanalytically based Thematic Apperception Test Scales. In Rogers, C. R. & Dymond, R. *Psychotherapy and Personality,* Chicago: Univ Chicago Pr 1954, 121-144

GRÜNBAUM, ADOLF

48093 Remarks on Dr. Kubie's views [on psychoanalysis and scientific method]. Psa Sci Method Phil 225

GRUNBERGER, B.

48094 Conflit oral et hystérie. [Oral conflict and hysteria.] RFPsa 1953, 7:250-265
   Abs JFr An Surv Psa 1953, 4:183-184
48095 Considérations sur l'oralité et la relation d'objet orale. [Observations on orality and oral object relationship.] RFPsa 1959, 22:177-204
48096 Essai sur la situation analytique et le processus de guérison. [The analytic situation and the healing process.] RFPsa 1957, 21:373-458
48097 Esquisse d'une théorie psychodynamique du masochisme. RFPsa 1954, 18:193-214
   Psychodynamic theory of masochism. In Lorand, S. *Perversions: Psychodynamics and Therapy,* NY: Random House 1956, 183-208
   Abs JFr An Surv Psa 1954, 5:171-172. García Reinoso, D. Rev Psichoanál 1955, 12:541-542. Feldman, S. S. Q 1956, 25:128-129
48098 Etude sur la relation objectale anale. [Study of the anal object relation.] RFPsa 1960, 24:138-160; 166-168
48099 Interprétation pré-génitale. [Pregenital interpretation.] RFPsa 1953, 17:428-495
   Abs JFr An Surv Psa 1953, 4:183-184

48100 Participant in discussion of Luquet, C. J. "La place du mouvement masochique dans l'évolution de la femme." RFPsa 1959, 23:337-340

48101 Préliminaires à une étude topique du narcissisme. [Preliminaries to a topical study of narcissism.] RFPsa 1958, 22:269-295

Rv Zmud, F. & Fiasche, D. N. de Rev Psichoanál 1959, 16:194-195

48102 Über-Ich und Narzissmus in der analytischen Situation. [Superego and narcissism in the analytic situation.] Psyche, Heidel 1958, 12:270-290

GRUNES, MARK

REVIEW OF:

48103 French, T. M. The Integration of Behavior. Vol. III. The Reintegrative Process in a Psychoanalytic Treatment. PPR 1959, 46(4):120-122

GRÜNEWALD, ED

48104 Gewissensbildung und Symbolcharakter der Über-Ich-Projektionen. [Conscience formation and the symbolic character of superego projections.] Jb Psychol Psychother 1955, 3:80-87

48105 Kastrationsdrohung und Bettnässen. [Castration threat and bed-wetting.] Jb Psychol Psychother 1954, 2:364-367

GRÜTTER, EMIL

48106 Psychoanalytische Bemerkungen zur Jung'schen Heilmethode. [Psychoanalytic remarks on Jungian therapy.] Psyche, Heidel 1959, 13:536-553

GRYGIER, PATRICIA

48107 The personality of student nurses. Int J soc Psychiat 1956, 2:105-112

GRYGIER, TADEUSZ

48108 Homosexuality, neurosis and "normality"; a pilot study in psychological measurement. Brit J Delinq 1958, 9:59-61

48109 Oppression. NY: Grove Pr 1954, 362 p

GSCHWIND-GASS, RUTH

48110 (& Haffter, C.) Psychogene Ernährungsschwierigkeiten bei Säuglingen und Kleinkindern. [Psychogenic nourishment problems in babies and children.] Schweiz med Wschr 1957, 87:1124-1126

See Haffter, C.

GUARDINI, ROMANO

48111 Sigmund Freud und die Erkenntnis der menschlichen Wirklichkeit. [Sigmund Freud and the knowledge of human reality.] Jb Psychol Psychother 1958, 5:97-107

GUASTALLA, B. R.

48112 Concetti e sistemi di classificazione nel lavoro di casework. [Concepts and systems of classification in the field of casework.] Riv Psa 1959, 5:59-83

GUEHL, J. J.
See Vosburg, R. L.

GUENEAU
See Parrot, P.

GUERRA, C. VIANNA

48113   Regressão. [Regression.] Bol Inst Psicol Univ Brasil 1958, 8(7-8):35-43

GUEVARA OROPESA, MANUEL

48114   Consideraciones sobre el psicoanálisis; commentario. [Considerations on psychoanalysis; comments.] Gaceta méd Méx 1953, 83:305-307

GUEX, GERMAINE

48115   Conditions d'éveil du sens social. [Conditions for the awakening of a social sense.] Schweiz Z Psychol 1953, 12:143-152
48116   La névrose d'abandon. [The Neurosis of Abandonment.] Paris: PUF 1950, 140 p
        Spanish: 1959

GUGGENHEIM, PETER

48117   (& Cohen, L. B.) A case of schizophrenia in which manifestations of Parkinsonism appeared during the course of the psychosis and disappeared after lobotomy. PSM 1958, 20:151-160
        Abs Afterman, J. Q 1959, 28:131

GUI, WESTON A.

S-13154 Bottom's dream.
        Abs MK An Surv Psa 1952, 3:527-529

GUILLEMAIN, BERNARD

48118   Sade était masochiste. [Sade was masochistic.] Psyché, Paris 1953, 8:486-497

GUILYAROVSKY, V.

48119   The contemporary situation in Soviet psychotherapy. Prog PT 1958, 3:270-273

GUIORA, A. Z.

48120   The Zulliger 'Z' test. A diagnostic means in screening procedures. Acta med orient, Tel Aviv 1956, 15:250-261

GUIRAUD, PAUL

48121   La doctrine psychanalytique. [The psychoanalytic doctrine.] In author's Psychiatrie clinique, Paris: Le François 1956, 44-57
48122   Il problema della psicogenesi. (La querelle de la psychogenèse.) [The question of psychogenesis.] Note Psichiat, Pesaro 1956, 49:13-23
48123   Psychothérapie des névroses. Psychanalyse. [Psychotherapy of neuroses. Psychoanalysis.] In author's Psychiatrie clinique, Paris: Le François 1956, 264-267

48124 Rencontrés dans les profondeurs. [Encounters in the depths.] Evolut psychiat 1957, (2):181-205

See Dide, Maurice

GUIRDHAM, ARTHUR

48125 Christ and Freud: A Study of Religious Experience and Observance. (Pref: Durrell, L.) London: Allen & Unwin 1959, 193 p

GUITON, MICHELINE

48126 Les aspects psychologiques de la puériculture. [Psychological aspects of infant care.] Paris: Librairie Maloine 1951, 100 p
48127 Le bercement. Son rôle dans le développement du nourisson. Quelques hypothèses psychanalytiques. [Rocking. Its influence on infant development; some psychoanalytical hypotheses.] Sem Hop Paris (Annales de Pédiatrie) 1954, 30(64/4):2-7
48128 Les carences paternelles liées à la personnalité ou à l'activité professionnelle du chef de famille. [Paternal frustration connected with the personality or the professional activity of the father.] Extrait des entretiens de Bichat 1956, Médecine.
48129 Les suppositoires chez le petit enfant. Leur influence sur le développement psychologique de l'adolescent et de l'homme. [Suppositories in childhood. Their influence on the psychological development of adolescent and adult.] Extrait des Entretiens de Bichat 1957, 513-518

GUMBEL, ERICH

48130 [Freud: Open-eyed humanism.] (Hebrew) Molad 1956, 14:283-290
48131 Obituary: Dr. Gershon Barag. J 1958, 39:617-619
48132 Psychoanalysis in Israel: a historical sketch. Acta med orient, Tel-Aviv 1956, 15:206-208
48133 Sigmund Freud. Harefuah 1956, 50:215-219

GUMP, PAUL

48134 (& Sutton-Smith, B.) Activity setting and social interaction: a field study. Ops 1955, 25:755-760
         Abs DRu Q 1958, 27:137-138. Koenig, J. RFPsa 1956, 20:584-585

See Redl, Fritz

GUNDLACH, RALPH H.

48135 (& Riess, B. F.) A critique of the sampling, method and logic of Krugman's article on communism. Ps 1954, 17:207-209
48136 Research with projective techniques. J project Tech 1957, 21:350-354

GÜNTER, W.

48137 Psychotherapeutische Fragen des Kinderarztes. [Psychotherapeutic problems in pediatrics.] Therapiewoche 1952, 8-9:267-269

GUNTHER, HANNAH

See Margolin, Sydney G.

GUNTRIP, HENRY J. S.

48138 Centenary reflections on the work of Freud. Univ Leeds Med J 1956, 5:162-166
48139 Mental Pain and the Cure of Souls. (Foreword: Grensted, L. W.) London: Independent Pr 1956, 206 p. With title: Psychotherapy and Religion, NY: Harper 1957, 206 p
48140 Psychology for Ministers and Social Workers. London: Independent Pr 1949, 356 p; Chicago: Allenson 1953
° ° ° Psychotherapy and Religion. (Foreword: May, R.) See [48139]
48141 Psychotherapy and religion: the constructive use of inner conflict. Pastoral Psychol 1957, 8(74):31-40
48142 Recent developments in psychoanalytical theory. M 1956, 29:82-99
Abs EMW Q 1957, 26:442
S-13180A A study of Fairbairn's theory of schizoid reactions. Psychopathol 344-369
Abs KMC Q 1953, 22:461
48143 The therapeutic factor in psychotherapy. M 1953, 26:115-132
48144 You and Your Nerves. London: Allen & Unwin 1951, 195 p

GUPTA, N. N.

48145 Influence of Hindu culture and social customs on psychosomatic disease in India. PSM 1956, 18:506-510

GUREVITZ, SAUL

S-13181 Direct analytic therapy and symbolical fulfillment—reviewed as to their applicability in childhood schizophrenia.
Abs EBu & NRo An Surv Psa 1951, 2:304-305
48146 (& Helme, W. H.) Effects of electroconvulsive therapy on personality and intellectual functioning of the schizophrenic child. JNMD 1954, 120:213-226
48147 (& Bauer, I. L.) Group therapy with parents of schizophrenic children. Int J grp PT 1952, 2:344-357
48148 (& Grugett, A. E. Jr.) Letter to a mother of a schizophrenic child. Quart J Child Behav 1952, 4:281-288
48149 The parents of the schizophrenic child. NPAP 1954, 2(3):36-40
48150 Treatment of a schizophrenic child through activation of neurotic symptoms. Quart J Child Behav 1952, 4:139-155

See Bender, Lauretta

GURIN, MAIZIE GUSAKOFF

48151 Differences in the psychological characteristics of latency and adolescence: a test of relevant psychoanalytic propositions utilizing projective material. (Abs) Diss Abstr 1953, 13:433-434

GURVITZ, MILTON S.

48152 Personality dynamics in the vocational adjustment of psychiatric patients. Jewish soc Serv Quart 1954, 30:373-380

See Kavazanjian, Thomas

GUSRAE, RACHEL
See Becker, Benjamin J.

GUSSACK, HAROLD
See Basowitz, Harold

GUSSOW, ZACHARY

48153 *Pibloktoq* (hysteria) among the Polar Eskimo: an ethno-psychiatric study. Psa St Soc 1960, 1:218-236

GUSTAV, ALICE
REVIEW OF:
48154 Nichtenhauser, A. et al: Films in Psychiatry, Psychology and Mental Health. NPAP 1954, 2(4):68-71

GUSTAV, L.
See Wolf, Katherine M.

GUSTIN, JOHN C.

48155 Discussion of Meerloo's "On Ambivalence." NPAP 1953, 2(1):22-25
S-13185 Phantasy in frigidity.
        Abs JFr An Surv Psa 1952, 3:132-133
48156 The psychoanalyst-writer affair. PPR 1960, 47(1):106-115
48157 Psychology of the actor. NPAP 1955-56, 4(2):29-36
48158 Supervision in psychotherapy. PPR 1958, 45(3):63-72
48159 Theodor Reik. Expl Psa ix-xiii
48160 The well-tempered analyst. NPAP 1953, 1(4):2-6

GUT, WALTER

48161 "Übertragung" als Zeichen der Deutung des Menschen. ["Transference" as a sign of the individual's self-concept.] Acta psychother psychosom orthopaedag 1954, 2:210-228

GUTERMAN, NORBERT
TRANSLATION OF:
Binswanger, L. [42133]

GUTHEIL, EMIL A.

48162 Aktive Psychoanalyse (Stekel). [Active psychoanalysis (Stekel).] Hndbk N P 1959, 3:159-170
S-13189 Analyse eines Falles von Migräne.
        Rv Figueras, A. Rev Psicoanál 1954, 11:234

48163 Dreams as an aid in evaluating ego strength. PT 1958, 12:338-357
S-13205 The Handbook of Dream Analysis. NY: Grove Pr 1960, 710 p
48164 Music as adjunct to psychotherapy. PT 1954, 8:94-109
S-13216 The organic symptom in the dream (globus hystericus). Drms Pers Dyn 176-182
48165 Problem of therapy in obsessive-compulsive neurosis. PT 1959, 13:793-808
48166 Pseudoneurotic forms of depressive psychosis. PT 1955, 9:719-736
48167 The psychologic background of transsexualism and transvestism. PT 1954, 8:231-239
48168 Reactive depressions. Am Hbk Psychiat 1:345-352
48169 Recent developments in psychotherapy. Pres Day Psychol 645-678
48170 Sexual dysfunctions in men. Am Hbk Psychiat 1:708-726

See Lowy, S.; Lussheimer, Paul

GUTHRIE, THOMAS C.

48171 Oedipus myth in ancient Greece. Psychiat Q 1955, 29:543-554
S-13225AA (& Grossmann, E. M.) A study of the syndrome of denial. Abs LRa Q 1953, 22:458-459

See Beck, Aaron T.

GUTIERREZ AGRAMONTE, E. A.

48172 Neurosis cardiaca. [Cardiac neurosis.] Arch Neurol Psiquiat 1958, 8:3-7

GUTSTADT, JOSEPH P.

ABSTRACTS OF:
48173 Bay, J. C. Historical mindedness in medicine. Q 1960, 29:139
48174 Beech, H. R. An experimental investigation of sexual symbolism in anorexia nervosa employing a subliminal stimulation technique. Q 1960, 29:292
48175 Boorstein, S. Ego autonomy in psychiatric practice. Q 1960, 29:140
48176 Bridger, W. H. & Reiser, M. F. Psychophysiological studies of the neonate. Q 1960, 29:292
48177 Holzman, P. S. A note on Breuer's hypnoidal theory of neurosis. Q 1960, 29:140
48178 Lee, A. R. et al: Clinical symposium: Psychological and physiological aspects of marked obesity in a young adult female. Q 1960, 29:144-145
48179 Stunkard, A. Obesity and denial of hunger. Q 1960, 29:292

GUTTMACHER, MANFRED S.

48180 [Participant in discussion on] Psychiatric implications of surveys on sexual behavior. R 1956, 43:471-500
48181 (& Weihofen, H.) Psychiatry and the Law. NY: Norton 1952, viii + 476 p
       Rv Overholser, W. Q 1953, 22:586-587
48182 Why psychiatrists do not like to testify in court. BMC 1956, 20:300-307
       Abs Weiss, J. Q 1958, 27:294

GUTTMAN, SAMUEL A.

48183   Bisexuality in symbolism. Bull Phila Ass Psa 1952, 2:13. J Am Psa Ass 1955, 3:280-284
        Abs TFr J 1956, 37:209
48184   Certain aspects of ego theory. Bull Phila Ass Psa 1953, 3:3-7
48185   Child Psychiatry. (Monograph) Davis Cyclopedia of Medicine, Surgery & Specialties 1951, 11:479-594
48186   (Reporter) Criteria for analyzability. (Panel: Am Psa Ass, Phila, Apr 1959) J Am Psa Ass 1960, 8:141-151
48187   Dreams and affects. Bull Phila Ass Psa 1955, 5:45-53
        Abs Herman, M. Q 1958, 27:290
48188   A fantasy of a patient with ulcerative colitis. Bull Phila Ass Psa 1954, 4:19
48189   A note on anti-Semitism. Bull Phila Ass Psa 1952, 2:12
48190   A note on morning depression. J Am Psa Ass 1954, 2:479-483
        Abs JFr An Surv Psa 1954, 5:115-116. TFr J 1955, 36:428. MGr Q 1957, 26:137
48191   A note on the role of play in the life of a child. Davis Cyclopedia of Medicine, Service Vol. 1950
48192   (& Sears, F. M.; Dominguez, K. E.) Observations on an infant separated from his mother. Bull Phila Ass Psa 1952, 2:76
48193   The repetitive core in psychoanalysis. Bull Phila Ass Psa 1951, 1:3
48194   (& Sears, F. M.) Theoretical implications of anxiety observed in an infant. Bull Phila Ass Psa 1953, 3:40-41

See Biddle, Sydney G.

GUTTMANN, O.

48195   The psychobiological approach to the so-called stomach neuroses: on the basis of a case of "nervous vomiting." PT 1956, 10:263-272

GUY, WILLIAM B.

48196   (& Shoemaker, R. J.; McLaughlin, J. T.) Group psychotherapy in adult atopic eczema. AMA Arch Dermatol Syphilol 1954, 70:767-781
48197   (& Finn, M. H. P.) A review of autofellatio. A psychological study of two new cases. R 1954, 41:334-358
        Abs JLan Q 1956, 25:115

See McLaughlin, James T.; Shoemaker, R. J.

GUZE, HENRY

48198   Anesthesia and instrumentation trauma as revealed in hypnotherapy. J clin exp Hyp 1953, 1(2):71-74
48199   Basic psychological principles and hypnosis: an interpretation and analysis. In Kline, M. V. Hypnodynamic Psychology, NY: Julian Pr 1955, 207-243
48200   The involvement of the hypnotist in the hypnotic session. J clin exp Hyp 1956, 4:61-68

48201 Sexual factors in the physician-patient relationship. Int J Sexol 1952, 5:14-19

See Kline, Milton V.

GUZE, SAMUEL B.

See Saslow, George; Winokur, George

GUZZO, AUGUSTO

48202 Filosofia e analisi. [Philosophy and analysis.] Arch Filos 1952, 47-64

GWARTNEY, R. H.

48203 (& Auerback, A.; Nelken, S.; Goshen, C. E.) Panel discussion on psychiatric emergencies in general practice. JAMA 1959, 170(9):1022-1030

H

H., F.

48204 Ferenczi. Psychiat Q Suppl 1954, 28:10-14

HAAG, ERNEST VAN DEN

48205 Psychoanalysis and its discontents. Psa Sci Method Phil 104-116
  See Ross, Ralph

HAAK, NILS

48206 Comments on the analytical situation. J 1957, 38:183-195
  Abs JLan Q 1958, 27:440
48207 Hur nervositet påverkar hälsan. [How nervousness influences health.]
  In *Kvinnans egen läkarbok*, Stockholm: Natur och Kulturs 1956, 23 p
48208 Något om ungdomens sexualproblem från en praktiserande nervläkares
  synpunkt. [On the sexual problems of youth from the point of view
  of a physician in nervous diseases.] In *Ungdomssexualitet*, Stockholm:
  Albert Bonniers 1948, 33 p
48209 Psykoanalys. [Psychoanalysis.] In *Psykologiskpedagogisk uppslagsbok*,
  Stockholm: Natur och Kulturs 1956, 6 p

HAAS, LADISLAV

48210 [Doctors and psychoanalysis.] (Czech) Czechosl psa annual 1948
48211 [Frigidity and premenstrual syndrome.] (Czech) Summary in Russian
  and English. Československá psychiatrie 1957, 53:273-279

HAAS, STEPHANIE

48212 Psychiatric implications in gynecology and obstetrics. In Bellak, L.
  Psychology of Physical Illness, NY: Grune & Stratton 1952, 90-118

HAASE, H.-J.

48213 Die Erforschung der Ätiologie der Schizophrenien. [Investigations in
  the etiology of schizophrenia.] Med Klin 1958, 53:315-319

HABERLANDT, H.

48214 Archetypus und Psyche; Gedanken über ein neues Buch von C. G.
  Jung. [Archetype and psyche; comments on a new book by C. G.
  Jung.] Wien Arch Psychol Psychiat Neurol 1954, 4(3):161-166

HÄBERLIN, C.

48215 Ärztliche Seelenkunde. [Medical Psychology.] Leipzig 1928, vii + 181 p

48216 Lebensgeschehen und Krankheit. [Life Happenings and Illness.] Leipzig 1926, xii + 144 p

HACKER, FREDERICK J.

48217 On artistic production. Expl Psa 128-138

48218 Freud, Marx, and Kierkegaard. Freud 20th Cent 125-142

48219 The living image of Freud. BMC 1956, 20:103-111

48220 Scientific facts, religious values and the psychoanalytic experience. BMC 1955, 19:229-239

48221 Some thoughts on symbolism. (Read at 20th Int Psa Cong, Paris 1957) Abs J 1958, 39:291

48222 Symbole und Psychoanalyse. [Symbols and psychoanalysis.] Psyche, Heidel 1958, 11:641-671

HACKER, ROSE

48223 Telling the Teen-Agers. A Guide to Parents, Teachers and Youth Leaders. London: Deutsch 1957, 213 p

HADDEN, SAMUEL B.

48224 Countertransference in the group psychotherapist. Int J grp PT 1953, 3:417-423
        Abs LCK An Surv Psa 1953, 4:517-518. GPK Q 1955, 24:164

48225 Historic background of group psychotherapy. Int J grp PT 1955, 5:162-168

48226 Treatment of homosexuality by individual and group psychotherapy. P 1958, 114:810-815

See Peltz, William L.

HADFIELD, JAMES ARTHUR

48227 The cure of homosexuality. BMJ 1958, 5083:1323-1326

48228 Dreams and Nightmares. London, Baltimore: Penguin Books 1954, 235 p
        Rv Thornton, N. R 1955, 42:445

48229 Psychology and Morals: An Analysis of Character. NY: McBride 1958, 219 p

48230 The rationale of analysis in the treatment of the psychoneuroses. Med Pr 1953, 229:441-443

HADLEY, JOHN MILLARD

48231 Clinical and Counseling Psychology. NY: Knopf 1958, xxxiv + 682 p

HAEBERLE, ANN W.

48232 Quantification of observational data in various stages of research. Symposium 1958: Observational research with emotionally disturbed children: session II. Ops 1959, 29:583-589

HAFFTER, C.

48233 Zur Lage der Kinderpsychotherapie. [Concerning the present status of psychotherapy for children.] Pro Juventute 1958, 39:62-64

48234 (& Gschwind-Gass, R.) Das Verhalten der Eltern während der Psychotherapie mit dem Kind. [Behavior of parents during psychotherapy with the child.] Prax Kinderpsychol 1957, 6:249-253

See Gschwind-Gass, Ruth

HÄFNER, HEINZ

48235 A case of pseudo-neurotic schizophrenia. (Tr: Stierlin, H.) Case St Couns PT 282-308

48236 Zur Daseinsanalyse der Schwermut. [Existential analysis of depression.] Z Psychother med Psychol 1958, 8:223-235

48237 Das Gewissen in der Neurose. [Conscience in the neuroses.] Hndb NP 1959, 2:692-726

48238 (& Jordan, D.) Sobre la psicoterapia de las esquizofrenias. [Psychotherapy of the schizophrenias.] Folia clín internac Barcelona 1952, 2:498-502

48239 (& Freyberger, H.) Über psychogene Blindheit. [Psychogenic blindness.] Z Psychother med Psychol 1954, 4(5):224-235

48240 Zur Psychopathologie der halluzinatorischen Schizophrenie. [The psychopathology of hallucinatory schizophrenia.] ANP 1954, 192:241-258

48241 Schulderleben und Gewissen. Beitrag zu einer persönlichen Tiefenpsychologie. [Guilt Experience and Conscience. Contribution to an Individualized Depth Psychology.] Stuttgart: Klett 1956, 182 p

48242 Der Wert als psychotherapeutisches Problem. [Personal values as a psychotherapeutic problem.] Z Psychother med Psychol 1953, 3:252-261

48243 Wertanalyse der therapeutischen Begegnung. [Value analysis of the therapeutic encounter.] Acta psychother psychosom orthopaedag 1955, 3(Suppl.):132-139

See Winkler, Walter T.

HAGAN, HELEN R.

See Robinson, J. Franklin

HAGERTY, M.

See Fleck, Stephen

HAGGERTY, ARTHUR D.

See Kline, Milton V.

HAGOPIAN, JOHN V.

48244 Chaucer as psychologist in Troilus and Criseyde. Lit & Psych 1955, 5(1):5-11

48245 A psychological approach to Shelley's poetry. Am Im 1955, 12:25-45

HAGSPIHL, K.

48246 Analytische Psychotherapie eines jugendlichen Stotterers und Exhibitionisten. [Analytic psychotherapy with a young stutterer and exhibitionist.] Prax Kinderpsychol 1954, 3:6-11, 37-45

48247 Bemerkungen zu "Ärztliches Verhalten und Vorgehen bei psychisch bedingten funktionellen Störungen." [Remarks on "Medical attitude toward and management of psychogenic functional disturbances."] Z PSM 1957-58, 4:137-138

48248 Besitzproblem im auslösenden Konflikt bei Magen-darmerkrankungen. [The problem of possession in the conflict triggering gastric and intestinal illnesses.] (German) Z PSM 1954-55, 1:21

48249 [Psychoses from the psychosomatic viewpoint.] Z PSM 1954-55, 1:241-253

HAHN, F.

See Holzberg, Jules D.

HAHN, G.

48250 Aperçus sur l'infantilisme. [Outline of infantilism.] Suppl Vie Spir 1958, (46):336-354

HAHN, MILTON EDWIN

48251 (& MacLean, M. S.) Counseling Psychology (2nd ed) NY: McGraw-Hill 1955, 302 p

HAHN, PAULINE B.

48252 (& Peck, A. L.; Silver, M. L.) Two phases in the treatment of a hyper-active destructive boy. Case St Ch Dis 1956, 2:278-315

See Coolidge, John C.; Waldfogel, Samuel

HAIKER, E.

48253 Die früheste Kindheitserinnerung. [The earliest childhood memory.] Wien Archiv Psychol 1956, 19-27

HAINES, WILLIAM H.

See Perkins, Rollin M.

HAISCH, ERICH

48254 Fliegen als ein Befreiungerlebnis. Eine psychotherapeutische Studie. [Flying as a liberating experience. A psychotherapeutic study.] Acta psychother psychosom orthopaedag 1955, 3:251-258

48255 Über die psychoanalytische Deutung der Musik: ein Übersichtsbericht. [On the psychoanalytic interpretation of music: a review.] Psyche, Heidel 1953, 7:81-88

HAKEEM, MICHAEL

48256 A critique of the psychiatric approach. In Roucek, J. *Juvenile Delinquency*, NY: Philos Lib 1958, 79-112

HALDANE, F. P.

REVIEW OF:

48257 Rümke, H. C. Problems in the Field of Neurosis and Psychotherapy. J 1953, 34:336-337

HALEVY, MEYER

48258 (& Bernstein, M. W.; Melamed, L.; Aron, W.) Discussion regarding Sigmund Freud's ancestry. Yivo Annual of Jewish Social Sciences 1958-59, 12:297-300

HALEY, JAY

48259 Control in psychoanalytic psychotherapy. Prog PT 1959, 4:48-65

48260 Obiter dicta. The art of psychoanalysis. ETC. A review of general semantics, 1958, 15(3):190-200

48261 Paradoxes in play, fantasy, and psychotherapy. Psychiat Res Rep, Wash 1955, (2):52-58

See Jackson, Donald D.

HALL, BERNARD H.

48262 Editor of Menninger, K. A. *A Psychiatrist's World*

See Ekstein, Rudolf; Luborsky, Lester B.; Modlin, Herbert C.; Teitelbaum, Harry A.; Wallerstein, Robert S.

HALL, CALVIN SPRINGER

48263 A cognitive theory of dream symbols. J gen Psychol 1953, 48:169-186. In McClelland, D. C. *Studies in Motivation*, NY: App Cen Cr 1955, 30-43. Psychopathol 258-274

48264 A cognitive theory of dreams. J gen Psychol 1953, 49:273-282. Abridged: Drms Pers Dyn 123-134

48265 Current trends in research on dreams. Prog Cl P 1956, 2:239-257

48266 Diagnosing personality by the analysis of dreams. ASP 1947, 42:68-79. Abridged: Drms Pers Dyn 193-211. Stud Pers 250-263

48267 Freud's concept of anxiety. Pastoral Psychol 1955, 6(52):43-48

48268 The Meaning of Dreams. NY: Harper 1953, 244 p
    Rv Alexander, F. Q 1953, 22:438-440

48269 A Primer of Freudian Psychology. Cleveland: World Pub Co 1954, 137 p
    Abs J Am Psa Ass 1955, 3:158. Rv Abadi, M. Rev Psicoanál 1957, 14:419-420.

48270 (& Lindzey, G.) Psychoanalytic theory and its applications in the social sciences. In Lindzey, G. *Handbook of Social Psychology*, Cambridge, Mass: Addison-Wesley 1954, 1:143-180
    Abs GD An Surv Psa 1954, 5:423-425

48271 The significance of the dream of being attacked. J Person 1955, 24:168-180. Abridged: Drms Pers Dyn 110-123
    Abs Holzman, P. S. Q 1956, 25:455-456

48272 (& Lindzey, G.) Theories of Personality. NY: Wiley 1957, xi + 572 p

48273   What dreams tell us about man. Pastoral Psychol 1953, 3(30):34-38
48274   What people dream about. Scientific American 1951, 184:60-63. Drms
         Pers Dyn 55-63. In Daniel, R. S. *Contemporary Readings in General
         Psychology,* Boston: Houghton, Mifflin 1959, 204-208

         See Lindzey, Gardner

HALL, JENNY WAELDER

         See WAELDER-HALL, JENNY

HALL, JEROME

48276   Psychiatry and the criminal law. Yale Law J 1956, 65:761-785

HALL, MARY

         See Phillips, Ewing Lakin

HALL, TREVOR H.

         See Dingwall, Eric John

HALLE, MORRIS

         See Jakobson, Roman

HALLEN, O.

48277   Zur biographischen Genese des Phantomschmerzes. [The biographical
         genesis of phantom pains.] Z Psychother med Psychol 1956, 6:3-7

HALLER, W. V.

48278   Ein Fall von jugendlichem Fetischismus. [A case of juvenile fetishism.]
         Prax Kinderpsychol 1954, 3:257-260
48279   Das Problem der Poriomanie. [The problem of poriomania.] Nervenarzt
         1957, 28:385-389

HALLIDAY, JAMES L.

48280   Concept of a psychosomatic affection. The Lancet 1943, 145:692-696.
         In Weider, A. *Contributions toward Medical Psychology,* Vol. I, NY:
         Ronald Pr 1953, 173-186

HALLOWELL, ALFRED IRVING

48281   Aggression in Saulteaux society. Ps 1940, 3:395-407. Pers n s c, 260-
         275. In author's *Culture and Experience,* 277-290
48282   Culture and Experience. Phila: Univ Penn Pr; London: Oxford Univ
         Pr 1955, xvi + 434 p
48283   Fear and anxiety as cultural and individual variables in a primitive
         society. Soc Psych 1938, 9:25-47. In author's *Culture and Experience,*
         250-265. In Opler, M. K. *Culture and Mental Health,* NY: Macmillan
         1959, 41-62
48284   The Ojibwa self and its behavioral environment. In author's *Culture
         and Experience,* 172-182

48285 Personality structure and the evolution of man. Amer Anthrop 1950, 52. In author's *Culture and Experience*, 2-13

48286 Psychic stresses and culture patterns. P 1936, 92:1291-1310. In Opler, M. K. *Culture and Mental Health*, NY: Macmillan 1959, 21-39

48287 Psychological leads for ethnological field workers. In Haring, D. G. *Personal Character and Cultural Milieu*, NY: Syracuse Univ Pr 1948. Stud Pers, 265-308

48288 Psychology and anthropology. In Gillin, J. *For a Science of Social Man*, NY: Macmillan 1954, 160-226

48289 Psychosexual adjustment, personality, and the good life in a non-literate culture. In Hoch, P. W. & Zubin, J. *Psychosexual Development in Health and Disease*, NY: Grune & Stratton 1949. In author's *Culture and Experience*, 291-309

48290 The recapitulation theory and culture. In author's *Culture and Experience*, 14-31

48291 The self and its behavioral environment. In author's *Culture and Experience*, 75-110

48292 The social function of anxiety in a primitive society. Am Sociol Rev 1941, 7:869-881. In author's *Culture and Experience*, 266-276

48293 Some psychological characteristics of the Northeastern Indians. In Johnson, F. *Man in Northeastern North America* (Papers of the R. S. Peabody Found. for Archaeology) 1946, 3:195-225. In author's *Culture and Experience*, 125-150

48294 Values, acculturation, and mental health. Ops 1950, 20:732-743. In author's *Culture and Experience*, 358-366

HALLOWITZ, DAVID

48295 Residential treatment of chronic asthmatic children. Ops 1954, 24:576-587

48296 (& Stulberg, B.) The vicious cycle in parent-child relationship breakdown. Soc Casewk 1959, 40:268-275

HALLOWITZ, EMANUEL

48297 (& Rosenthal, L.; Henig, A.) The group psychotherapy literature—1954. Int J grp PT 1955, 5:299-321

48298 (& Rosenthal, L.; Leon, H.; Freeman, H.) The group psychotherapy literature—1955. Int J grp PT 1956, 6:197-215

HALL-SMITH, PATRICK

See Norton, Alan

HALMOS, PAUL

48299 Towards a Measure of Man: The Frontiers of Normal Adjustment. NY: Humanities Pr; London: Routledge & Kegan Paul 1957, 250 p

HALPERN, FLORENCE

ABSTRACT OF:

48300 Finn, M. H. P. & Brown, F. Training for clinical psychology. Q 1960, 29:421-423

HALPERN, HOWARD M.

48301 (& Lesser, L. N.) Empathy in infants, adults, and psychotherapists. PPR 1960, 47(3):32-42

HALPERN, L.

48302 [Freud as a neurologist.] (Hebrew) In author's [*Freud's Festival*] 9-12

48303 (et al) [Freud's Festival (to commemorate his centenary).] (Hebrew) Jerusalem: The Magnes Pr, Hebrew Univ 1957, 112 p

See Mazar, B.

HALPERT, ANITA

See Gabriel, Betty

HAM, GEORGE C.

48304 (Contributor to) Harrower, M. *Medical and Psychological Teamwork in the Care of the Chronically Ill.* Reports and disc of Conf March 28-31, 1954, Galveston, Texas. *American Lecture Series.* Springfield, Ill: C. C Thomas, 1955

48305 The development of concepts and methods. Psychiat Res Rep 1956, (3):67-73

48306 Discussion of Mirsky, I. A. "Psychoanalysis and the biological sciences." 20 Yrs Psa 177-181

48307 The management of the multiple complainer. In Liebman, S. *Management of Emotional Problems in Medical Practice,* Phila: Lippincott 1956, 93-109

48308 Psychosomatic investigation and management of gastrointestinal disorders. J med Soc NY 1952, 52:2250

48309 Psychosomatic Medicine. Britannica Book of Year 1957, Chicago: Encycl Brit 1957, 635-636. Britannica Book of Year 1960, 573-574

48310 (& Sandifer, M. G., Jr.) Psychosomatic medicine. Britannica Book of Year 1958, Chicago: Encycl Brit 1958, 569-570

S-697 (& Alexander, F.; Carmichael, H. T.) A psychosomatic theory of thyrotoxicosis.
Abs STa An Surv Psa 1951, 2:366-367. R 1953, 40:161-162

48311 Trends and issues in psychiatric programs. Member of Writing Committee, GAP Report No 31, 1955

48312 Who, what, when, why and where of health and illness. Abs of Psychiat for the Gen Practitioner 1959, 2(1)

See Benedek, Therese; Hargrove, Eugene A.

HAMBIDGE, GOVE, JR.

48313 On the ontogenesis of repression. R 1956, 43:195-203
Abs JLan Q 1957, 26:584

48314 Self-weaning and the growth of independence. Quart J child Behavior 1952, 4:196-208

48315   Structural play therapy. Symposium 1954: Therapeutic play techniques. Ops 1955, 25:601-607
          Abs Koenig, J. RFPsa 1956, 20:584-585
48316   (& Gottschalk, L. A.) Verbal behavior analysis—psychodynamic, structural and temporal correlates of specific variables. Psychopathol Communic 84-97

See Frank, Lawrence K.; Gottschalk, Louis A.

HAMBLING, JOHN

48317   Essential hypertension. Mod Tr PSM 184-206

HAMBURG, DAVID A.

48318   (& Sabshin, M. A.; Board, F. A.; Grinker, R. R.; Korchin, S. J.; Basowitz, H.; Heath, H.; Persky, H.) Classification and rating of emotional experiences: special reference to reliability of observation. AMA ANP 1958, 79:415-426

See Board, Francis; Eldred, Stanley H.; Fleming, Joan; Glickstein, Mitchell; Grinker, Roy R.; Korchin, Sheldon J.; Persky, Harold; Sabshin, Melvin S.

HAMBURGER, CHRISTIAN

48319   (& Sturup, G. K.; Dahl-Iversen, E.) Transvestism. Homosex 293-308

HAMBURGER, WALTER W.

48320   The occurrence and meaning of dreams of food and eating: I. Typical food and eating dreams of four patients in analysis. PSM 1958, 20:1-16
          Abs Afterman, J. Q 1959, 28:128-129
48321   Psychological aspects of obesity. Bull NY Acad Med 1957, 33:771-782

See Engel, George L.

HAMBURGER, WERNER

48322   A clinical observation on emotion and childbirth. Bull Phila Ass Psa 1957, 7:107-110
          Abs deSaugy RFPsa 1959, 23:158
48323   Legal guilt and the unconscious. Bull Phila Ass Psa 1957, 7:62-65
          Abs EFA Q 1958, 27:446

HAMILTON, DONALD M.

See Moss, Leonard M.

HAMILTON, GILBERT V.

48324   Changes in personality and psychosexual problems. In Cowdry, E. V. *Problems of Ageing.* 2nd ed. Baltimore: Williams & Wilkins 1942, 810-831
48325   Incest and homosexuality: the psychoanalytic approach. Homosex 214-226

HAMILTON, GORDON

S-13417A Theory and Practice of Social Casework.
Rv Bech, E. B. Q 1953, 22:590-593
48326 A theory of personality: Freud's contribution to social work. Ego Psychol Dyn Casewk 11-37

HAMILTON, M.

48327 Groupwork with children in a family agency. Brit J psychiat soc Wk 1959, 5:75-83

HAMILTON, VERNON J.

48328 Conflict avoidance in obsessionals and hysterics and the validity of the concept of dysthymia. JMS 1957, 103:666-676
48329 Perceptual and personality dynamics in responses to ambiguity. BJP 1957, 48:200-215

HAMLIN, ROY M.

48330 A compliant alcoholic. Clin Stud Pers 263-289

See Wolpin, M.

HAMLISH, ERNA

48331 (& Gaier, E. L.) Teacher-student personality similarity and grades. School Rev 1954, 62:265-273

HAMMER, ALFRED GORDON

48332 Contemporary theorising in abnormal psychology. Austral J Psychol 1958, 10:69-84

HAMMER, EMANUEL F.

48333 Areas of special advantages for projective drawings. In author's *The Clinical Application of Projective Drawings* 599-612
48334 The Clinical Application of Projective Drawings. Springfield, Ill: C. C Thomas 1958, 658 p
48335 Comparison of H-T-P's of rapists and pedophiles. J proj Tech 1954, 18:346-354
48336 A comparison of H-T-P's of rapists and pedophiles: II. The "dead" tree as an index of psychopathology. Clin Psych 1955, 11:67-69
48337 Doodles: an informal projective technique. In author's *The Clinical Application of Projective Drawings* 562-582
48338 An experimental study of symbolism on the Bender Gestalt. J proj Tech 1954, 18:335-345
48339 Frustration-aggression hypothesis extended to socio-racial areas: comparison of Negro and white children's H-T-P's. Psychiat Q 1953, 27: 597-607
48340 (& Piotrowski, Z. A.) Hostility as a factor in clinician's personality as it affects his interpretation of projective drawings (H-T-P). J proj Tech 1953, 17:210-216

48341 An investigation of sexual symbolism: a study of H-T-P's of eugenically sterilized subjects. J proj Tech 1953, 17:401-413

48342 Negro and white children's personality adjustment as revealed by a comparison of their drawings (H-T-P). Clin Psych 1953, 9:7-10

48343 Projection in the art studio. In author's *The Clinical Application of Projective Drawings*, 18-56

48344 Projection in the clinical setting. In author's *The Clinical Application of Projective Drawings*, 5-17

48345 The projective drawing battery. In author's *The Clinical Application of Projective Drawings*, 441-480

48346 The prognostic role of drawings in the projective battery. In author's *The Clinical Application of Projective Drawings*, 628-634

48347 A psychoanalytic hypothesis concerning sex offenders. J clin exp Psychopath 1957, 18:177-184

48348 (& Glueck, B. C., Jr.) Psychodynamic patterns in sex offenders: a four factor theory. Psychiat Q 1957, 31:325-345. In Hoch, P. & Zubin, J. *Psychiatry and the Law*, NY: Grune & Stratton 1955, 157-168

48349 Recent variations of the projective drawing techniques. In author's *The Clinical Application of Projective Drawings*

48350 Relationship between diagnosis of psychosexual pathology and the sex of the first drawn person. Clin Psych 1954, 10:168-170

48351 Retrospect and prospect. In author's *The Clinical Application of Projective Drawings*, 637-649

48352 The role of the H-T-P in the prognostic battery. Clin Psych 1953, 9:371-374

48353 Use of the Blacky pictures with a child whose oedipal desires are close to consciousness. Clin Psych 1951, 7:280-282

See Michal-Smith, Harold

HAMMERSCHLAG, HEINZ ERICH

48354 Möglichkeiten und Grenzen der Hypnose als psychosomatische Heilmethode. [The possibilities and limitations of hypnosis as psychosomatic therapy.] Die Heilkunst 1955, 68:44-46

48355 Schlusswort zur Diskussion über das Thema "Hypnose und Psychoanalyse." [Final remarks in the discussion on the subject of "Hypnosis and psychoanalysis."] Die Heilkunst 1957, 70:28-29

HAMOVITCH, M. B.

See Caplan, Gerald

HAMPSHIRE, ALICE

48356 The use of groups as motivation for analytic group psychotherapy. Int J grp PT 1954, 4:95-102

HAMPSON, JOAN G.

48357 (& Money, J.) Idiopathic sexual precocity in the female; report of three cases. PSM 1955, 17:16-35
        Abs EMW Q 1957, 26:142-143

See Money, John

HANDELMAN, M. S.

See Garner, Harry H.

HANFMANN, EUGENIA

48358 (& Dorris, R. J.; Levinson, D. J.) Authoritarian personality studied by a new variation of the sentence completion technique. ASP 1954, 49: 99-108

48359 Boris, a displaced person. Clin Stud Pers 642-667

48360 (& Beier, H.) Emotional attitudes of former Soviet citizens, as studied by the technique of projective questions. ASP 1956, 53:143-153

48361 (& Getzels, J. W.) Interpersonal attitudes of former Soviet citizens as studied by a semi-projective method. Psychol Monogr 1955, 69(4):1-37. In McGuigan, F. J. & Calvin, A. D. *Current Studies in Psychology*, NY: Appleton-Century-Crofts 1958, 193-211

48362 (& Beier, H.) The mental health of a group of Russian displaced persons. Ops 1958, 28:241-255

48363 (& Inkeles, A.; Beier, H.) Model personality and adjustment to the Soviet socio-political system. Hum Relat 1958, 11:3-22

48364 The non-projective aspects of the Rorschach experiment: III. The point of view of the research clinician. Soc Psych 1956, 44:199-202

48365 Social perception in Russian displaced persons and an American comparison group. Ps 1957, 20:131-149

48366 (& Getzels, J. W.) Studies of the sentence completion test. J proj Tech 1953, 17:280-294

48367 William Stern on "Projective techniques." J Person 1952, 21:1-21

HANKINS, JOHN E.

48368 Hamlet and Oedipus reconsidered. Shakespeare Newsletter 1956, 6(2): 11

HANKS, LUCIEN M., JR.

S-13434A The quest for individual autonomy in Burmese personality. Abs R 1953, 40:84-85

HANLON, NANCY

See Tisza, Veronica B.

HANNIBAL, OTTO

48369 Reifungskrisis und Appendektomie. [Puberty crisis and appendectomy.] Psyche, Heidel 1954, 8:234-240

HANN-KENDE, FANNY

S-13437 Az áttétel és viszontáttétel szerepéhez a pszichoanalizisben. On the role of transference and countertransference in psychoanalysis. In Devereux, G. *Psychoanalysis and the Occult*, NY: IUP 1953, 158-167

HANSBURG, HENRY G.

48370 Case of a bright child with oral disturbance and severe neurotic difficulties. Case Rep in Clin Psychol 1953, 3/2. Dept of Psychol King's County Hosp, Bkln 3, NY, 60-68
48371 A reformulation of the problem of reading disability. J child Psychiat 1956, 3:37-148

HANSELMANN, HEINRICH

48372 Einführung in die Heilpädagogik: praktischer Teil für Eltern, Lehrer, Anstaltserzieher, Jugendfürsorger, Richter und Ärzte. [Introduction to Ortho-Pedagogy: Practical Advice for Parents, Teachers, Principals, Youth Workers, Judges, and Doctors.] (5th ed) Zurich: Rotapfel-Verlag 1958, 612 p
48373 Psychologie und Säuglingsfürsorge. [Psychology and infant care.] Pro Juventute 1958, 39:468-471

HANSEN, E. BJERG

48374 Om indikationer for psykoanalytisk behandling. [Indications for psychoanalytic therapy.] Ugeskr laeger, Kbh 1956, 118:365-372
48375 Om kastrationskomplekset. [The castration-complex.] (Abs) Auth Nordisk Psykiatrisk Medlemsblad 1956, 10:261

HANSEN, FINN

48376 The conduct of psycho-therapy in West Germany and impressions of training in the psychosomatic section. Nord Psykol 1957, 9:142-144

HANSON, GORDON C.

48377 Educational psychology. Pres Day Psychol 297-319

HANSON, ROBERT C.

See Sorokin, Pitirim

HARABILL, C.

See Scheidlinger, Saul

HARADA, KAZUHIKO

48378 On the emotional reactions of psychoneuroses. Psychiatria et Neurologia Jap 1952, 54(4): 63
48379 On the group psychotherapy. Psychiatria et Neurologia Jap 1952, 54(4):154

HARARY, FRANK

See Cartwright, Dorwin

HARBOUR, P. B.

48380 The learning process in psychoanalytic therapy. I. General introduction. J Amer osteop Ass 1953, 53:181-188

48381 Psychoanalysis in a case of ecdysiasm. J Amer osteop Ass 1956, 56:210-212

48382 Tractable pain during psychoanalysis. J Amer osteop Ass 1954, 54: 197-200

HARDCASTLE, D. N.

REVIEWS OF:

48383 Baruch, D. & Miller, H. One Little Boy. J 1953, 34:167. Rev Psicoanál 1959, 15:159

48384 Eisler, R. Man into Wolf: An Anthropological Interpretation of Sadism, Masochism and Lycanthropy. J 1953, 34:170-171

48385 Jackson, L. A Test of Family Attitude. J 1953, 34:347. Rev Psicoanál 1959, 15:160

48386 Jaques, E. The Changing Culture of a Factory. J 1953, 34:340-341

48387 Jones, M. Social Psychiatry. J 1953, 34:340-341

48388 Maas, H. (Ed) Adventure in Mental Health. J 1953, 34:171

48389 Peters, F. The World Next Door. J 1953, 34:170

48390 Scott, J. F. & Lynton, R. P. Three Studies in Management. J 1953, 34:340-341

HARDENBERG, H. E. W.

REVIEWS OF:

48391 Bond, D. The Love and Fear of Flying. J 1953, 34:160-161

48392 Huxley, A. The Doors of Perception. J 1955, 36:357

48393 Walker, N. A Short History of Psychotherapy. J 1959, 40:351

HARDENBERG, JANET

48394 Editor of Winnicott, D. W. *The Child and the Outside World*

HARDER-MENZEL, RENATE

See Kretschmer, Wolfgang

HARDING, D. W.

48395 Social Psychology and Individual Values. London: Hutchinson's Univ Lib 1953, 184 p
Rv ESt J 1954, 35:372

HARDING, GÖSTA T.

48396 Freud och själsläkekonsten. [Freud and psychotherapy.] Hörde Ni (J Swed Broadcasting Corp) 1956, June, (6):464-472

48397 Gegenwärtiger Stand und Entwicklungstendenzen der Neurosenlehre und Psychotherapie. Nordeuropa: Schweden. [The present state and the tendencies of development of psychotherapy and the theory of neuroses. Northern Europe: Sweden.] Hnd N P 1957, 87-91

48398 Om hysteri hos barn. [About hysteria in children.] Medicinska föreningens tidskrift 1952, 30:82-91

48399 Psykoterapeutiska problem i Ibsens "Fruen fra havet." [Psychotherapeutic problems in Ibsen's "The Lady from the Sea."] Nordisk psykiatrist Medlemsblad 1958, Suppl. 1, 11:71-80

48400   Significado para la psicoterapie de algunos puntos de vista contenidos en las obras de Kierkegaard y de Ibsen. [Psychotherapeutic significance of several viewpoints in the works of Kierkegaard and Ibsen.] Rev Psiquiat Psicol 1959, 4:278-281

48401   Stand und Probleme der psychischen Hygiene in Schweden. [State and problems of mental hygiene in Sweden.] In Pfister-Ammende, M. *Geistige Hygiene—Forschung und Praxis.* Basel: Benno Schwabe 1955, 365-376

HARDING, JOHN

48402   (& Kutner, B.; Proshansky, H.; Chein, I.) Prejudice and ethnic relations. In Lindzey, G. *Handbook of Social Psychology,* Cambridge, Mass: Addison-Wesley Pub Co 1954, 1021-1061

HARDING, MARY ESTHER

48403   A dynamic approach to psychotherapy. J S C med Ass 1957, 53:387-388

48404   The psyche and the symbols of religion. In Wolff, W. *Psychiatry and Religion,* NY: MD Publications 1955, 3-7

HARDOY, GUILLERMO FERRARI

See FERRARI HARDOY, GUILLERMO

HARDRÉ, JACQUES

48405   Jean-Paul Sartre: literary critic. Stud Philol 1958, 55:98-106

HARE, A. PAUL

See Caplan, Gerald; Strodtbeck, F. L.

HARGROVE, EUGENE A.

48406   (& Ham, G. C.; Fleming, W. L.) Multidisciplinary teaching of human ecology in the first year of medicine. J med Educ 1957, 32:697-701

See Engle, Bernice

HARITZ, R.

48407   Die Geburt eines Kindes als auslösende Situation für das Auftreten neurotischer Symptome. Ein Beitrag zum Thema Geburt und Neurose. [The birth of a child as the precipitating situation of neurotic symptoms. A contribution to the subject of childbirth and neurosis.] Z PSM 1957-58, 4:81-91

HARKAVY, EDWARD E.

48408   The psychoanalysis of a gambler. (Read at NY Psa Soc, Mar 10, 1953; 18th Int Psa Cong, London, July 1953)
        Abs Auth J 1954, 35:285. Bromberg, N. Q 1954, 23:153-156

REVIEWS OF:
48409   Bellak, L. et al: Conceptual and Methodological Problems in Psychoanalysis. Q 1960, 29:400-401

48410 Fisher, S. & Cleveland, S. E. Body Image and Personality. Q 1959, 28:90-92

48411 Fromm-Reichmann, F. Psychoanalysis and Psychotherapy. Q 1960, 29:249-251

48412 Roback, A. A. Freudiana. Q 1957, 26:551-552

48413 Sakel, M. Schizophrenia. Q 1959, 28:87-88

48414 Steinfeld, J. I. A New Approach to Schizophrenia. Q 1957, 26: 258-260

HARLE, MARJORIE

See Dewald, Paul A.

REVIEWS OF:

48415 Fleming, C. M. Teaching: A Psychological Analysis. Q 1960, 29:419-421

48416 Inhelder, B. & Piaget, J. The Growth of Logical Thinking from Childhood to Adolescence. Q 1958, 27:589-591

48417 Schutz, W. C. FIRO. A Three-Dimensional Theory of Interpersonal Behavior. Q 1959, 28:274-275

HARLEY, MARJORIE

S-13476 Analysis of a severely disturbed three and a half year old boy. Abs EBu & NRo An Surv Psa 1951, 2:288-291

REVIEW OF:

48418 Tanner, J. M. & Inhelder, B. (Ed) Discussions on Child Development. Vol. III. A Consideration of the Biological, Psychological, and Cultural Approaches to the Understanding of Human Development and Behavior. Q 1959, 28:410-412

HARLOW, HARRY F.

48419 The nature of love. Am Psych 1958, 13:673-685

HARLOW, ROBERT G.

48420 Masculine inadequacy and compensatory development of physique. J Person 1951, 19:312-323

HARMS, ERNEST

48421 Essentials of Abnormal Child Psychology: A Survey Representing Twenty-Five Years' Work in the Field of Child Psychology. NY: Julian Pr 1953, 295 p

48422 The present status of knowledge of abnormal psychology of the child. Pres Day Psychol 687-710

48423 Simon-Andred Tissot (1728-1797): the Freudian before Freud. P 1956, 112:744

HARNACK, GUSTAV A. VON

48424 Bemerkungen zu der Arbeit von C. H. Mallet: Analyse des Grimm'schen Märchens "Der starke Hans." [Remarks on the article by C. H. Mallet: Analysis of Grimm's fairy tale "Strong John."] Prax Kinderpsychol 1953, 2:321

HARNIK, J.

S-13509 Pleasure in disguise, the need for decoration and the sense of beauty.
Rv Garma, A. Rev Psicoanál 1953, 10:126-127

HARPER, ROBERT ALLAN

48425 Neurotic interactions among counselors. J counsel Psychol 1958, 5:33-38

48426 Psychoanalysis and Psychotherapy; 36 Systems. Englewood Cliffs, N.J.: Prentice-Hall 1959, 182 p

HARRIES, MARGARET

S-13536 Sublimation in a group of four-year-old boys.
Abs NRo An Surv Psa 1952, 3:226-229. Auth J 1953, 34:280

HARRIMAN, PHILIP

48427 Abnormal psychology. Pres Day Psychol 355-374

HARRINGTON, MOLLY

48428 (& Hassan, J. W. M.) Depression in girls during latency. M 1958, 31:43-50
Abs Johnston, M. Q 1959, 28:134

HARRIS, ALBERT J.

See Liss, Edward

HARRIS, CATHERINE

48429 Sullivan's concept of scientific method as applied to psychiatry. Phil Sci 1954, 21:33-43

HARRIS, DALE B.

48430 (Ed) The Concept of Development: An Issue in the Study of Human Behavior. Minneapolis: Univ of Minnesota Pr 1957, x + 287 p

HARRIS, GEORGE S., JR.

See Jackson, Edith B.; Wessel, Morris A.

HARRIS, HAROLD J.

48431 (& Kemple, C.) Chronic brucellosis and psychoneurosis. PSM 1954, 16:414-425
Abs Fain RFPsa 1955, 19:492. EMW Q 1956, 25:449. Rv Garcia Reinoso, D. Rev Psicoanál 1955, 12:427-428

HARRIS, HERBERT I.

48432 (& Heald, F. P.) Psychotherapy of adolescents by pediatrician and psychiatrist at combined clinic and in-patient hospital level. In Balser, B. H. *Psychotherapy of the Adolescent*, NY: IUP 1957, 113-129

S-13548 Repression and the electroencephalogram.
Abs STa An Surv Psa 1952, 3:25-26. CR J 1953, 34:356

48433 Telephone anxiety. J Am Psa Ass 1957, 5:342-347
       Abs Shentoub RFPsa 1958, 22:127. HW Q 1960, 29:282
48434 (& Peters, C. M.) The treatment of psychosomatic disorders by the
       internist. Am Practit Dig Treatment 1954, 5:158-163

       See Gallagher, J. Roswell; Webster, T. G.

REVIEWS OF:
48435 Bett, W. R. The Infirmities of Genius. Q 1953, 22:594-595
48436 Grinker, R. R. (Ed) Mid-Century Psychiatry. Q 1954, 23:287
48437 Michaels, J. J. Disorders of Character. Q 1956, 25:106
48438 Reik, T. Myth and Guilt. Q 1957, 26:543-544
48439 Reik, T. The Secret Self. Q 1953, 22:595
48440 Sartre, J. P. Existential Psychoanalysis. Q 1955, 24:137
48441 Strauss, H. et al: Diagnostic Electroencephalography. Q 1953, 22:446-
       447
48442 Sutherland, J. D. Psychoanalysis and Contemporary Thought. Q 1960,
       29:116-117

HARRIS, HUNTER P.

48443 Some aspects of negativistic phenomena. Southern Med J 1952, 1:71

HARRIS, IRVING D.

48444 The analyst dream. (Read at Chicago Psa Soc, Jan 26, 1960)
       Abs Seitz, P. F. D. Bull Phila Ass Psa 1960, 10:59-60
S-13557 Characterological significance of the typical anxiety dreams.
       Abs NRo An Surv Psa 1951, 2:69-70. JFr An Surv Psa 1951, 2:259-
       260
48445 The dream of the object endangered. Ps 1957, 20:151-161
S-13559 Observations concerning typical anxiety dreams. Drms Pers Dyn 97-
       110
48446 On recognition of resemblance. Ps 1953, 16:355-364
48447 Typical anxiety dreams and object relations. J 1960, 41:604-611
48448 Unconscious factors common to parents and analysts. J 1960, 41:123-
       129

HARRIS, J. B.

48449 (& Hoff, H. E.; Wise, R. A.) Diaphragmatic flutter as a manifestation
       of hysteria. PSM 1954, 16:56-66
       Abs Weiss, J. Q 1955, 24:316. Rev Psicoanál 1955, 12:319

HARRIS, JACQUELINE B.

       See Levine, Abraham

HARRIS, L. M.

48450 Exploring the relationship between the teacher's attitudes and the
       overt behavior of the pupil; case study of an aggressive girl. Am J Ment
       Defic 1956, 60:536-544
48451 Reactions of adolescent, mentally deficient girls to a permissive at-
       mosphere in an academic schoolroom. Am J Ment Defic 1953, 57:434-
       446

HARRIS, LEBERT H.

See Tillman, William A.

HARRIS, MYRON W.

REVIEW OF:

48452   Phillipson, H. The Object Relations Technique (Book and Test Cards). Q 1957, 26:132

HARRIS, ROBERT E.

48453   Clinical methods: psychotherapy. Ann Rev Psychol 1956, 7:121-146

See Burton, Arthur; Kalis, Betty L.

HARRISON, EMMA

48454   Freud eulogized as parley opens. New York Times 1956, Apr 28
48455   Freud overruled on self analysis. New York Times 1956, Apr 24
48456   Physician urges no-fee analysis. New York Times 1956, Apr 29
48457   Psychiatry's tie to science noted. New York Times 1956, May 6

HARRISON, IRVING B.

48458   A clinical note on a dream followed by elation. J Am Psa Ass 1960, 8:270-280

HARRISON, SAUL I.

48459   Contribution to the symposium on Ambisexualism. Univ of Mich Med Bull 1959, April
48460   Direct supervision of the psychotherapist as a teaching method. In *Digest of Papers Presented at the 36th Annual Meeting,* Am Orthopsychiat Ass 1959, 48
48461   Modus operandi of psychoanalysis. Univ of Mich Med Bull 1957, 23: 456-457
48462   (& Fischer, H. K. et al) Observations from multiple therapy on the development of object relations. In *Scientific Papers.* Wash: Am Psychiat Ass 1957, 149-150

See Brody, Morris W.

HARROWER, MARY RACHEL (MOLLY)

48463   The application of clinical psychological tests to a fuller understanding of somatic disease. Texas Rep Biol Med 1953, 11:465-488
48464   Appraising Personality; The Use of Psychological Tests in the Practice of Medicine. NY: Norton 1952; London: Routledge & Kegan Paul 1953, 197 p
        Rv Sandler, J. J 1954, 35:372-373
48465   Clinical aspects of failures in the projective techniques. J proj Tech 1954, 18:294-302
48466   (& Kraus, J.) Experimental studies with the Szondi test. Szondi Newsletter 1953
48467   The first offender: a study of juvenile delinquents by the Szondi test. Szondi Newsletter 1958, June

48468 Group Rorschach. In Weider, A. *Contributions Toward Medical Psychology.* NY: Ronald Pr 1953, 620-624

48469 The measurement of psychological factors in marital maladjustment. Texas Rep Biol Med 1954, 12:72-85

48470 (Ed) Medical and Psychological Teamwork in the Care of the Chronically Ill. Texas Rep Biol Med 1954, 12:561-794. Springfield, Ill: Charles C Thomas 1955, xii + 232 p
Rv Little, M. J 1956, 37:488-489

48471 Mental Health and MS. NY: Nat Multiple Sclerosis Soc 1953

48472 The most unpleasant concept test: a graphic projective technique for diagnostic and therapeutic use. In Hammer, E. F. *The Clinical Application of Projective Drawings,* Springfield, Ill: Charles C Thomas 1958

48473 (& Kubie, L. S.) Neurotic depression in a child. In Burton, A. & Harris, R. E. *Case Histories in Clinical and Abnormal Psychology,* NY: Harper 1955. In Murphy, G. & Bachrach, A. J. *An Outline of Abnormal Psychology,* NY: Modern Lib 1954, 106-119

48474 A new pattern for mental health services in a children's court. Ops 1955, 25

48475 (& Peck, R. F.; Beck.) A New Pattern for Mental Health Services in a Children's Court. Springfield, Ill: C. C Thomas 1958

48476 Personality Change and Development as Measured by the Projective Techniques. NY: Grune & Stratton 1958

48477 Projective counseling—a psychotherapeutic technique. PT 1956, 10:74-86

48478 (& Herrmann, R.) Psychological Factors in the Care of Patients with Multiple Sclerosis. NY: Nat Mult Sclerosis Soc 1953

48479 Psychological factors in multiple sclerosis. Ann NY Acad Sci 1954, July

48480 A psychological testing program for entering students at the University of Texas School of Medicine, Galveston—a preliminary report. Texas Rep Biol Med 1955, 13:406-419

48481 Screening . . . for what? The relevant use of psychological tests in medical education. M 1957, 30

48482 (& Grinker, R. R.) The stress tolerance test. Preliminary experiments with a new projective technique utilizing both meaningful and meaningless stimuli. PSM 1946, 8:3-15

48483 Who comes to court? Ops 1955, 25

HART, HENRY HARPER

48484 Discussion of Cole, N. J. & Tabaroff, J. "The psychological problems of the congenitally blind child." Ops 1955, 25:627-643

48485 Fear of homosexuality in college students. In Wedge, B. M. *Psychosocial Problems of College Men,* New Haven: Yale Univ Pr 1958, 200-213

48486 The identification with the machine. Am Im 1953, 10:95-111
Abs GD An Surv Psa 1953, 4:325-328

S-13592 Masochism, passivity and radicalism.
Abs STa An Surv Psa 1952, 3:467

48487 Maternal narcissism and the Oedipus complex. (Read at 20th Int Psa Cong, Paris 1957) J 1958, 39:188-190
Abs J 1958, 39:291. JLan Q 1959, 28:280. Tabak Rev Psicoanál 1959, 16:189

48488 The meaning of circumstantiality. Samiksa 1953, 7:271-284
Abs JFr An Surv Psa 1953, 4:224-226. Levinson, G. J 1954, 35:448

48489 The meaning of passivity. Psychiat Q 1955, 29:595-611
Abs JBi Q 1956, 25:619

48490 (& Jenkins, R. L.; Axelrad, S.; Sperling, P. I.) Multiple factor analysis of traits of delinquent boys. J soc Psychol 1943, 17:191-201

48491 In memoriam: Clements Collard Fry, 1892-1955. Ops 1956, 26:188-189

48492 (& Axelrad, S.) The only-child delinquent contrasted with delinquents in large families. J crim Law Criminol 1941, 32:42-66

48493 A scarcely recognized factor in the Oedipus complex. Bull Phila Ass Psa 1956, 6:54-57

See Jenkins, Richard L.

ABSTRACT OF:
48494 Lacan, J. Some reflections on the ego. Q 1954, 23:608

HART, JOHN E.

48495 *The Red Badge of Courage* as myth and symbol. Univ of Kansas City Rev 1952-53, 19:249-256

HART DE RUYTER, THEODOOR

48496 Über die Bedeutung konstitutioneller Faktoren bei kindlichen Verhaltungsstörungen. [About the importance of constitutional factors in infantile behavior disturbances.] Folia Psychiat Neur Neurochir Neerlandia 1958, 61:63-73

48497 Bemerkungen zum Problem der Psychotherapie bei Ich-schwachen Jugendlichen. [Remarks on the problem of psychotherapy with ego-weak adolescents.] Z Kinderpsychiat 1958, 25:52-62

48498 De betekenis der psycho-analytische paedagogie voor de opvoeding van kinderen met aanpassingsstoornissen. [The value of psychoanalytical paedagogy in the education of children with adaptation disturbances.] T Buitengew Onderw Orthopadagogiek 1953, 33:173-178; 190-195; 1954, 34:38-43; 216-221

48499 Hyperesthetisch-emotionele zwaktoestanden bij kinderen. [Hyperesthetic-emotional anxiety states in children.] NTvG 1956, 100/II: 1546-1550

48500 Inleiding tot de kinderpsychologie; ontwikkelingsbeeld van het normale en het afwijkende kind. [Introduction to child psychology; the development of the normal and the retarded child.] Groningen 1952

48501 De ontwikkeling van de persoonlijkheid in de jeugd. [The development of personality in youth.] Ned Handboek der Psychiatrie 1958, 1:279-311

48502 Praeventieve Kinderspychiatrie. [Preventive child psychiatry.] Maandblad voor Kindergeneeskunde 1955, 23:58-65

48503 Psychiatrische aspecten van de zorg voor de jeugd in sociaal-labiel milieu. [Psychiatric aspects of youth care in socially-labelled surroundings.] 16th Conf of the Antonia Wilhelmina Fund, Uitg A W F 1956, 6-25

48504 A psycho-analytical approach to adolescence and juvenile neuroses. Folia Psychiat, Amst 1955, 58:408-421

48505 Therapeutische Gezinsverpleging. [Therapeutic family care.] De Koepel, Ned Maandblad v Kinderbescherming 1958 12(4):132-137. Tijdschr v Ziekenverpleging 1958, 12:350-354

HARTELIUS, H.

48506 Suicide in Sweden 1935-1950. A statistical analysis and psychodynamic interpretation. Acta Psychiat Neurol Scand 1957, 32:151-181

HARTLEY, RUTH EDITH

48507 (& Frank, L.; Goldenson, R.) Understanding Children's Play. London: Routledge & Kegan Paul 1952, xvi + 372 p
Rv Joseph, B. J 1953, 34:337. Rev Psicoanál 1959, 15:160

48508 (& Gondor, E. I.) The use of art in therapy. Prog Clin Psych 1956, 2:202-211

HARTMAN, A. ARTHUR

48509 Name styles in relation to personality. J general Psychol 1958, 59:289-294

48510 Personality factors in perceptual distortion. J general Psychol 1959, 61:181-188

HARTMAN, JAMES W. D.

48511 Midcentury psychosomatics. Pres Day Psychol 591-626

HARTMAN, LENORE D.

See Fromm, Erika

HARTMAN, MORTIMER A.

48512 Participant in Conference on d-lysergic acid diethylamide (LSD-25). In Abramson, H. A. *The Use of LSD in Psychotherapy; Transactions,* NY: Josiah Macy, Jr Found 1960, 7-240

48513 Psychoanalytic psychotherapy with LSD. In Abramson, H. A. *The Use of LSD in Psychotherapy; Transactions.* NY: Josiah Macy, Jr Found 1960, 7-24

HARTMANN, DORA

48514 Discussion of Freud, A. "Problems of technique in adult analysis." (Panel) Bull Phila Ass Psa 1954, 4:55

HARTMANN, HEINZ

48515 Comments on the scientific aspects of psychoanalysis. Psa St C 1958, 13:127-146
Abs RTh J 1960, 41:649-650

48516   Contributions to the metapsychology of schizophrenia. (Read at 18th
        Psa Cong, London, July 1953) Psa St C 1953, 8:177-198
            Abs JFr An Surv Psa 1953, 4:152-153. Auth J 1954, 35:285. RTh
        J 1955, 36:78
48517   The development of the ego concept in Freud's work. (Read at Brit
        Psa Soc, May 1956) J 1956, 37:425-438. Rd Psa Psychol 84-105
            Abs JLan Q 1957, 26:580-581. Lebovici RFPsa 1957, 21:615-616
48518   Discussion of Freud, A. "Child observation and prediction of develop-
        ment." Psa St C 1958, 13:120-122
48519   (& Kris, E.; Loewenstein, R. M.) The function of theory in psycho-
        analysis. Dr Af Beh 13-37
48520   To Herman Nunberg on his seventieth birthday. J 1954, 35:1
S-13658 Ich-Psychologie und Anpassungsproblem.
            Ego Psychology and the Problem of Adaptation. (Tr: Rapaport, D.)
        NY: IUP 1958, xi + 121 p
            Rv MBr J 1960, 41:566-568
S-13665 The mutual influences in the development of the ego and id.
            Die gegenseitigen Beeinflussungen von Ich und Es in der psycho-
        analytischen Theoriebildung. Psyche, Heidel 1955, 9(1):1-22
            Abs JAA An Surv Psa 1952, 3:32-36. WH J 1953, 34:276-277
48521   Notes on the reality principle. Psa St C 1956, 11:31-53
            Abs RTh J 1959, 40:72-73
48522   Notes on the theory of sublimation. Psa St C 1955, 10:9-29
            Bemerkungen zur Theorie der Sublimierung. Psyche, Heidel 1956,
        10:41-62. In Mitscherlich, A. Entfaltung der Psychoanalyse, Stuttgart:
        Klett 1956, 41-62
            Abs RTh J 1957, 38:292
48523   Obituary: Ernst Kris (1900-1957). Psa St C 1957, 12:9-15
48524   Problems of infantile neurosis. Psa St C 1954, 9:31-36; 50-51
            Abs RTh J 1956, 37:211-212
48525   Psychoanalysis and Moral Values. NY: IUP 1960, 121 p
48526   Psychoanalysis as a scientific theory. Psa Sci Method Phil 3-37
S-13681 (& Kris, E.; Loewenstein, R. M.) Some psychoanalytic comments
        on "Culture and Personality."
            Abs GD An Surv Psa 1951, 2:494-496
S-13685 Technical implications of ego psychology.
            Abs STa An Surv Psa 1951, 2:373-374. Cesio, F. R. Rev Psicoanál
        1956, 13:81

HARTMANN, KLAUS

48527   Über Wesenszüge der modernen amerikanischen Psychologie. [Char-
        acteristics of modern American psychology.] Nervenarzt 1957, 28:360-
        363

HARTOCH, ANNA

48528   The child's reaction to the Rorschach situation. In Murphy, L. B. Per-
        sonality in Young Children. Vol. I. Methods for The Study of Person-
        ality in Young Children, NY: Basic Books 1956, 153-180

HARTOGS, RENATUS
REVIEW OF:
48529   Reiwald, P. Society and Its Criminals. R 1954, 41:95-96

HARTWICH, ALEXANDER
48530   Geschichte einer Verdrängung oder Wie Oesterreich einen seiner grossen
        Söhne ehrte. [Story of a repression or how Austria honored one of her
        great sons.] Aufbau 1956, 22(30):11. Forum, Vienna 1956, June:205

HARTZ, JEROME
48531   Personality and stress in tuberculosis. In Sparer, P. J. *Personality,
        Stress, and Tuberculosis,* NY: IUP 1956, 190-207
48532   Psychological aspects of pulmonary tuberculosis. In Wittkower, E. D. &
        Cleghorn, R. A. *Recent Developments in Psychosomatic Medicine.*
        Phila: Lippincott 1954, 281

HARVEY, J. M.
48533   The causes of alcohol addiction. Univ Toronto Med J 1957, 34:175-
        178

HARVEY, WILLIAM A.
48534   (& Sherfey, M. J.) Vomiting in pregnancy: a psychiatric study. PSM
        1954, 16:1-9
        Abs Weiss, J. Q 1955, 24:316. Rev Psicoanál 1955, 12:314

        See Appel, Kenneth E.

HARWAY, NORMAN I.
        See Raush, Harold L.

HARWAY, VIVIAN
        See Reichsman, Franz

HASELKORN, F.
        See Bellak, Leopold

HASSAN, IHAB H.
48535   The victim: images of evil in recent American fiction. College English
        1959, 21:140-146

HASSAN, JANET W. M.
        See Harrington, Molly

HASSEL, LINDA
        See Conger, John J.

HASSLER, ROLF
48536   Cecile und Oskar Vogt. [Cecile and Oskar Vogt.] In Kolle, K. *Grosse
        Nervenärzte,* Stuttgart: Thieme 1959, 2:45-64

HASTINGS, DONALD

48537 Some psychiatric problems of mental deficiency. Am J Ment Defic 1948, 52:260-262. Couns PT Ment Retard 411-414

HASTINGS, MARGUERITE
See Eisenberg, Leon

HAU, THEODOR F.

48538 "Neuroticism" und Psychoanalyse. ["Neuroticism" and psychoanalysis.] Z PSM 1957-58, 4:261-268

48539 Zur psychodynamischen Einordnung der Promazinwirkung. [On the psychodynamic classification of the effect of promazine.] Z PSM 1958-59, 5

48540 Untersuchungen an Lehranalysierten auf sog. neurotische und Lügen-Tendenzen im MMQ. [MMQ study of so-called neuroticism and tendency toward lying in trained psychoanalysts.] Z PSM 1957-58, 4:115-117

48541 Vergleichende Untersuchungen an Schizophrenen und Neurotikern mit dem MMQ (Maudsley-Persönlichkeitsfragebogen). [Comparative examinations of schizophrenics and neurotics with the MMQ (Maudsley-personality-questionnaire).] Z exper angewandte Psychol 1957, 4

HAUCK, HERBERT
See Kaplan, Harold I.

HAUCK, PAUL A.
See Glatter, A. N.

HAUG, KARL

48542 Angst- und Schuldgefühle bei psychiatrischen Erkrankungen. [Guilt and anxiety in psychoses.] In Bitter, W. *Angst und Schuld*, Stuttgart: Ernst Klett 1959

HAUGE, INGVAR

48543 Freud, Marx eller Kristus: en linje I. W. H. Audens Diktning. [Freud, Marx or Christ; with reference to W. H. Auden's poetry.] Samtiden 1955, 64:335-345

HAUGEN, GERHARD B.

48544 (& Dixon, H. H.; Dickel, H. A.) A Therapy for Anxiety Tension Reactions. NY: Macmillan 1958, x + 110 p

HAUSER, ANDRÉE

48545 La doctrine d'Adler. [Adler's doctrine.] In *Problèmes de Psychanalyse*, Paris: Fayard 1957, 68-82

HAUSER, IRENE

48546 Das Kind und sein Spiel. [Child and play.] Heilpäd Werkbl 1953, 22:47-50

HAVEL, JOAN

See Freedman, Alfred M.; Frenkel-Brunswik, Else

HAVEMANN, ERNEST

48547   The Age of Psychology. NY: Simon & Schuster 1957, 115 p
        Abs J Am Psa Ass 1958, 6:172. Rv GPK Q 1958, 27:275-276

HAVENS, LESTON L.

See Semrad, Elvin V.

HAVERMANS, FRANCISCUS MARINUS

48548   (& Oosterbaan, W. M.) Sociale Psychiatrie voor Maatschappelijk
        Werkenden. [Social psychiatry for Social Workers.] Roermond: Romen
        1954, 394 p

HAVINGHURST, ROBERT J.

48549   Social and psychological needs of the aging. In Gorlow, L. & Katkovsky,
        W. *Readings in the Psychology of Adjustment*, NY: McGraw-Hill 1959,
        439-447

See Davis, Allison

HAVU, TOINI

TRANSLATION OF:
(& Mikkola, S.) Menninger, K. A. [22519]

HAWKINS, DAVID R.

See Baughman, E. Earl; Shands, Harley C.

HAWKINS, MARY O'NEIL

48550   Discussion of Freud, A. "Problems of technique in adult analysis."
        (Panel) Bull Phila Ass Psa 1954, 4:59-60

HAYAKAWA, S. I.

48551   Sexual fantasy and the 1957 car. ETC Rev gen Semant 1957, 14:163-
        168

HAYDEN, MARJORIE

See Brodey, Warren M.

HAYES, FRANCIS

48552   Gestures: a working bibliography. Southern Folklore Q 1957, 21:218-
        317

HAYFORD, HARRISON

48553   Melville's Freudian slip. Am Lit 1958-59, 30:366-368

HAYLETT, CLARICE H.

See Estes, Herbert R.; Groethuysen, Ulrich C.

HAYLEY, T. T. S.

48554   The Anatomy of Lango Religion and Groups. Cambridge, Engl: Cambridge Univ Pr 1947, 205 p

REVIEW OF:
48555   Carstairs, G. M. The Twice-Born. J 1958, 39:436-437

HAYMAN, ANNE

REVIEW OF:
48556   Hamlyn, D. W. The Psychology of Perception. J 1958, 39:429-430

HAYMAN, MAX

48557   Current attitudes to alcoholism of psychiatrists in Southern California. P 1956, 112:485-493
48558   (& Wilkins, P. A.) Polyneuropathy as a complication of disulfiram therapy of alcoholism. Quart J Stud Alcoh 1956, 17:601-607
48559   Traumatic elements in the analysis of a borderline case. J 1957, 38:9-21
            Abs JLan Q 1958, 27:127
48560   A unique day therapy center for psychiatric patients. MH 1957, 41:245-249
48561   What psychiatrists think about alcoholism. Calif Med 1955, 83:435-440

ABSTRACT OF:
48562   Rangell, L. Some rethinking on our psychoanalytic nosology. Bull Phila Ass Psa 1960, 10:158-160

HAYS, H. R.

48563   Satire and identification: an introduction to Ben Jonson. Kenyon Rev 1957, 19:267-283

HAYWARD, HELEN

See Krug, Othilda; Wise, Louis J.

HAYWARD, MALCOLM L.

48564   Diagnosis and prognosis. In Whitaker, C. A. *Psychotherapy of Chronic Schizophrenic Patients,* Boston: Little, Brown 1958, 3-30
48565   Direct analytic therapy. In *Cyclopedia of Medicine, Surgery and Specialties,* Phila: F. A. Davis Co. 1949, 393-400
48566   The emotional reactions of a schizophrenic patient to shock therapy. Psychiat Q 1951, 25:288-293
48567   Problems in the psychotherapy of schizophrenia. Penn Med J 1956, 59:470-474
48568   (& Taylor, J. E.) A schizophrenic patient describes the action of intensive psychotherapy. Psychiat Q 1956, 30:211-248
            Abs JBi Q 1957, 26:288

48569 (& Peters, J. J.; Taylor, J. E.) Some values of the use of multiple therapists in the treatment of the psychoses. Psychiat Q 1952, 26:244-249

See Taylor, James Edward

HEAD, DOROTHY
See Taylor, James Edward

HEALD, FELIX P.
See Harris, Herbert I.

HEALY, WILLIAM
48570 (& Bronner, A. F.) Orthopsychiatry: an overview. Ops 1955, 25:472-474

HEATH, DOUGLAS H.
48571 Individual anxiety thresholds and their effect on intellectual performance. ASP 1956, 52:403-408
48572 Projective tests as measures of defensive activity. J proj Tech 1958, 22:284-292

HEATH, HELEN A.
See Hamburg, David A.; Korchin, Sheldon J.; Persky, Harold

HEATH, ROBERT G.
48573 Biology and psychoanalysis. Sci Psa 1958, 1:143-144
48574 (& Leach, Byron E.) Multidisciplinary research in psychiatry. Chg Cpts Psa Med 201-224
48575 (& Leach, B. E.) Pharmacological and biological therapy in schizophrenia. Prog PT 1958, 3:219-231
48576 (Ed) Studies in Schizophrenia. A Multidisciplinary Approach to Mind-Brain Relationships. Cambridge, Mass: Harvard Univ Pr; London: Geoffrey Cumberlege 1954, xiv + 619 p
       Rv Corday, R. J. J 1955, 36:400
48577 The theoretical framework for a multidisciplinary approach to human behavior. In author's Studies in Schizophrenia, 9-55.

See Lidz, Theodore

HEAVER, L.
See Arnold, G. E.

HEBB, DONALD O.
48578 The mammal and his environment. P 1955, 111:826-831. Read Soc Psychol, 335-341.
       Abs Racamier, P. C. RFPsa 1956, 20:574-575. DRu Q 1958, 27:142

HEBERER, H.

48579 Psyche und Soma beim Weibe. [Psyche and body in woman.] Ann
Univ Sarrbrücken 1954, II(1):9-18

HECHLER, H.

48580 Die Lehre Pawlows im unüberwindlichen Gegensatz zur Psychoanalyse
und Psychosomatik. [The Pavlovian theory in insurmountable opposition to psychoanalysis and psychosomatics.] Z ärzt Fortbild 1954, 48:
730-738

HECHT, M. BERNARD

48581 Obesity in women: a psychiatric study. Psychiat Q 1955, 29:203-231
S-13842A Uncanniness, yearning and Franz Kafka's works.
Abs JAA An Surv Psa 1952, 3:85; MK An Surv Psa 1952, 3:537-539

HECKEL, ROBERT V.

48582 A factor analysis of Horney's concepts of moving toward, away from
and against others. Penn. State Univ. Abs Doct Diss 1955, 18:423-425

HECKHAUSEN, HEINRICH

See Kemmler, Lilly

HEDBERG, S. E.

See Hill, S. R.

HEFFERMAN, ANGELA

48583 A psychiatric study of fifty preschool children referred to hospital for
suspected deafness. Emot Prob Early Child, 269-292

HEGELER, STEN

48584 Hvordan, mor? [How, mummy?] Denmark: Branner & Koch 1948,
35 p
    Peter and Caroline. A Child Asks about Childbirth and Sex. (Draw-
ings by Nystad, Gerda; Foreword: Nixon, W. C. W.) London: Tavistock
Publ 1957, 29 p
    Rv CR J 1959, 40:354-355
48585 Peter og Marianne i skole. [Peter and Marianne at school.] Copenhagen: Branner & Koch 1953, 35 p

HEIDEGGER, M.

48586 Logos. [Logos.] (Tr. Lacan, J.) Psychanalyse 1953-55, 1:59-79

HEIDER, FRITZ

48587 Comments on Rapaport, D. "On the psychoanalytic theory of motivation." In Jones, M. R. Nebraska Symposium on Motivation, 1960, Lincoln, Neb: Univ of Nebraska Pr 1960, 253-257

48588 Comments on White, R. W. "Competence and the psychosexual stages of development." In Jones, M. R. *Nebraska, Symposium on Motivation, 1960,* Lincoln, Neb: Univ of Nebraska Pr 1960, 141-143

48589 The description of the psychological environment of Marcel Proust. Char Pers 1941, 9:295-314. Psych Issues 1959, 1(3):85-107

48590 Environmental determinants in psychological theories. Psych Issues 1959, 1(3):61-84

48591 The function of economical description in perception. Psych Issues 1959, 1(3):53-60

48592 Introductory remarks. Psych Issues 1959, 1(3):ix-xi

48593 Die Leistung des Wahrnehmungssystems. Z Psychol 1930, 114:371-394

The function of the perceptual system. Psych Issues 1959, 1(3):35-52

48594 On Lewin's methods and theory. Psych Issues 1959, 1(3):108-119

48595 On Perception and Event Structure, and the Psychological Environment. Psych Issues 1959, 1(3):1-123

48596 Thing and Medium. Psych Issues 1959, 1(3):1-34

German: Symposion 1926, 1:109-157

See Bruner, Jerome S.

HEIDER, GRACE MOORE

See Escalona, Sibylle

HEIDGERD, EVERETT

48597 Research in drawing techniques. In Hammer, E. F. *The Clinical Application of Projective Drawings,* Springfield, Ill: Charles C Thomas 1958, 482-507

HEIGL, F.

48598 Ein Fall von generalisiertem Tic. [A case of generalized tic.] Prax Kinderpsychol 1955, 4:202-205

48599 Die Handhabung der Gegenübertragung in der analytischen Psychotherapie. [The management of countertransference in analytic psychotherapy.] Z PSM 1958-59, 5:189-191

48600 Neurotische Arbeitsstörungen in der analytischen Psychotherapie. [Neurotic work disorders in analytic psychotherapy.] Z PSM 1954-55, 1:51-55; 135-140

48601 Die "rechthaberische Übertragung" im Vergleich mit Freud'schen Abwehrmechanismen. [The "self-righteous transference" compared with Freudian resistance mechanisms.] Z PSM 1958-59, 5:110-118

48602 Eine "Todeslinie" in der Hand. Bericht über die analytisch -psychotherapeutische Behandlung eines Patienten mit depressiver Charakterstruktur und Beziehungsidee. [A "death line" in the hand. Report on the analytic psychotherapy of a patient with depressive personality traits and delusions of reference.] Z PSM 1957-58, 4:254-261

48603 Vergleichende Betrachtung der prognostischen Faktoren bei Schultz-Hencke und Alexander. [Comparative study of the prognostic factors in the work of Schultz-Hencke and of Alexander.] Z PSM 1957-58, 4:108-144

See Gerson, W.

HEILBRUN, CAROLYN

48604   The character of Hamlet's mother. Shakespeare Quart 1957, 8:201-206

HEILBRUNN, GERT

48605   The basic fear. J Am Psa Ass 1955, 3:447-466
        Abs TFr J 1956, 37:210-211. Shentoub RFPsa 1956, 20:567. Young, B. Q 1959, 28:562
48606   Comments on a common form of acting out. Q 1958, 27:80-88
        Abs Sapochnik, L. Rev Psicoanál 1958, 15:305-306. JKl J 1959, 40:366
48607   Fusion of the Isakower phenomenon with the dream screen. Q 1953, 22:200-204. YBPsa 1954, 10:214-220
        Abs JFr An Surv Psa 1953, 4:249-250. Cesio, F. R. Rev Psicoanál 1954, 11:389. JKl J 1954, 35:441
48608   Juvenile delinquency—comments on etiology. Northwest Med 1956, 55:277-281
48609   Selection of patients for modern psychiatric pharmacotherapy in general practice. Northwest Med 1956, 55:1198-1205
48610   On weeping. (Read at Am Psa Ass, St. Louis, May 1954) Q 1955, 24:245-255
        Abs JKl J 1956, 37:203

REVIEWS OF:
48611   The Annual Survey of Psychoanalysis, vol. I. Q 1953, 22:267-268
48612   Loewenstein, R. M. (Ed) Drives, Affects, Behavior. Q 1954, 23:582
48613   Lorand, S. (Ed) The Yearbook of Psychoanalysis, Vol. VIII. Q 1954, 23:108-109

HEILIZER, FREDERICK H.

48614   (& Axelrad, H. S.; Cowen, E. L.) The correlates of manifest anxiety in paired associate learning. J Pers 1956, 24:463-474

HEILPERIN, L.

See HALPERN, L.

HEIM, ALICE W.

48615   The Appraisal of Intelligence. London: Methuen 1954, 171 p
        Rv Lindsay, S. F. J 1955, 36:418

HEIMAN, MARCEL

48616   Introduction. Psa Soc Wk x-xiv
48617   The problem of family diagnosis. In Eisenstein, V. W. *Neurotic Interaction in Marriage*, NY: Basic Books 1956, 221-234

48618 (Ed) Psychoanalysis and Social Work. NY: IUP 1953, 346 p
Abs JLan An Surv Psa 1953, 4:614-629. Rv Haldane, F. P. J 1953,
34:346-347. Lippman, Hyman S. Q 1954, 23:116-118

48619 Psychoanalytic evaluation of the problem of one-child sterility. Fertil &
Steril, NY 1955, 6:405-414

48620 Psychosocial influences in functional uterine bleeding. Obs & Gyn
1956, 7:3

48621 The relationship between man and dog. (Read at NY Psa Soc, June
10, 1952; Am Psa Ass, Dec 5, 1953) Q 1956, 25:568-585
Abs JKl J 1957, 38:435

48622 Reproduction: emotions and the hypothalamic-pituitary function. Fer-
tility & Sterility 1959, 10:162-173

48623 Rip Van Winkle: a psychoanalytic note on the story and its author.
Am Im 1959, 16:3-47

48624 On the role of animals. (Read at NY Psa Soc, June 10, 1952)
Abs Linn, L. Q 1953, 22:147-149

48625 The role of stress situations and psychological factors in functional
uterine bleeding. J Mt Sinai Hosp 1956, 23:775-781

48626 Separation from a love object as an etiological factor in functional
uterine bleeding. J Mt Sinai Hosp 1959, 26

HEIMANN, PAULA

48627 Bemerkungen zur Sublimierung. [Remarks on sublimation.] Psyche,
Heidel 1959, 13:397-414

48628 A combination of defence mechanisms in paranoid states. New Dir Psa
240-265

S-13874 A contribution to the problem of sublimation and its relation to processes of internalization.
Una contribución al problema de la sublimación y sus relaciones con
los procesos de internalización. Rev Psicoanál 1951, 8:550-568

S-13874A A contribution to the re-evaluation of the Oedipus complex—the early
stages. New Dir Psa 23-38
Abs JAA An Surv Psa 1952, 3:71-73. CBr Q 1953, 22:598-599.
Pichon-Rivière, A. A. Rev Psicoanál 1953, 10:384-385

S-13875 On counter-transference.
Abs R 1953, 40:361

S-13876 A discussion on archetypes and internal objects.
Rv Pichon-Rivière, A. A. de Rev Psicoanál 1953, 10:383-384

48629 Dynamics of transference interpretations. (Read at 19th Int Psa Cong,
Geneva, July 1955) J 1956, 37:303-310.
Zur Dynamik der Übertragungsinterpretationen. Psyche, Heidel
1957, 11:401-415
Abs Auth J 1956, 37:131. JLan Q 1957, 26:575

S-13878A Preliminary notes on some defense mechanisms in paranoid states.
Abs JFr An Surv Psa 1952, 3:143-144. Bychowski, G. Q 1953, 22:
605-606. Garma Rev Psicoanál 1953, 10:392.

48630 Problems of the training analysis. (Read at 18th Int Psa Cong, London,
July 1953) J 1954, 35:163-168

Abs Auth J 1954, 35:285-286. JFr An Surv Psa 1954, 5:412-413; 415. Lebovici, S. RFPsa 1954, 18:465-466. JLan Q 1955, 24:604. Rv Pichon-Rivière, A. A. Rev Psicoanál 1955, 12:430-431

See Klein, Melanie

REVIEW OF:
48631 Wolstein, B. Transference. J 1956, 37:491-493

HEIMLER, EUGENE

48632 Night of the Mist. (Tr from Hungarian: Ungar, A.) London: Bodley Head 1959, 191 p

HEIMPEL, ELIZABETH

48633 Märchen und Psychologie. [Fairy-tale and psychology.] Sammlung 1953, 8:278-293

HEIMS, LORA

See Kaufman, Irving

HEINE, RALPH W.

48634 A comparison of patients' reports on psychotherapeutic experience with psychoanalytic, non-directive and Adlerian therapists. PT 1953, 7:16-22
Abs Rev Psicoanál 1955, 12:140

HEINICKE, CHRISTOPH

48635 (& Whiting, B. B.) Bibliography on personality and social development of the child, and selected ethnographic sources on child training. Soc Sci Res Council Pamph 1953, (10), 130 p

HEISER, KARL F.

48636 Mental deficiency in the urban community. Ops 1957, 27:484-489
Abs Koenig RFPsa 1959, 23:167
48637 Organic and psychological factors in a mental defective. Clin Stud Pers, 431-454

HEISLER, IVAN C.

ABSTRACTS OF:
48638 Bruner, J. S. The cognitive consequences of early sensory deprivation. Q 1959, 28:570
48639 Deutsch, F. Correlations of verbal and nonverbal communication in interviews elicited by the associative anamnesis. Q 1959, 28:571
48640 Fisher, S. Extensions of theory concerning body image and body reactivity. Q 1959, 28:571
48641 Luby, E. D. et al: Stress and the precipitation of acute intermittent porphyria. Q 1959, 28:570
48642 Stuntz, E. C. The beard as an expression of bodily feelings in a schizophrenic. Q 1959, 28:570

HEISS, ROBERT

48643 Allgemeine Tiefenpsychologie: Methoden, Probleme und Ergebnisse. [General Depth Psychology: Methods, Problems, and Results.] Bern: Hans Huber; NY: Intercontinental Medical Book Corp 1956, 371 p

48644 Was ist Psychologie? Die heutige Situation der Psychologie. [What is psychology? The present state of psychology.] Psychotherapie 1956, 1:5-20

HELD, FRITZ

48645 Studie zur Psychologie der Meditation am Modell der indischen Lehren. [Study of the psychology of meditation on the model of Indian doctrines.] Z Psychother med Psychol 1955, 5:122-133

HELD, RENÉ R.

48646 Angoisse pré-operatoire. (Signification et psychothérapie). [Presurgical anxiety. (Meaning and psychotherapy).] Acta de l'Institut d'Anesthésiologie 1958, 7:5-31

48647 (& Chertok, L.) Anorexie mentale et potomanie. (Considérations psychosomatiques). [Mental anorexia and potomania. (Psychosomatic considerations).] Sem Hôp 1959, 35:1649-1652

48648 Le cercle vicieux psychosomatique dans la pathologie du cycle hormonal féminin. [The vicious psychosomatic circle in the pathology of the feminine hormonal cycle.] Évolut psychiat 1953, (3):415-441

48649 Sur la chlorpromazine et les médicaments neuroleptiques. Incidences psychothérapeutiques. [About chlorpromazine and neuroleptic medication. Psychotherapeutic repercussions.] Enceph (4):1000-1004

48650 Les critères de la fin du traitement psychanalytique. [Criteria for the termination of psychoanalytic treatment.] RFPsa 1955, 19:603-614

48651 Le dentiste et son patient. Quelques réflexions psychanalytiques. [The dentist and his patient. Some psychoanalytic remarks.] Rev franç d'Odonto-stomatologie 1958, 1-8

48652 Difficultés de l'analyse de certaines résistances intellectuelles. [About difficulties of the psychoanalysis of some intellectual resistances.] Bull d'Act Psa Belg 1957, (27)
        Greek: Athens 1958
        Abs Lebovici RFPsa 1957, 21:623

48653 Discussion of Berge, A. "L'équation personelle ou de l'art psychanalytique." RFPsa 1959, 23:468-469

48654 Fausse insomnie (étude psychanalytique et électroencéphalographique). [So-called insomnia. A psychoanalytic and electroencephalographic study.] Presse Med 1959, 67(4):141-143

48655 L'interrogatoire psychosomatique. [The psychosomatic interview.] In Volume des Entretiens de Bichat, Paris: L'Expansion scientifique française 1958

48656 Intervention aux journées de Bonneval sur la schizophrénie. [Participation in the Bonneval Symposium on Schizophrenia.] Évolut psychiat 1958, (2):484-496

48657 Intervention dans le colloque sur l'utilisation du matériel onirique en thérapeutique psychanalytique chez l'adulte. [Participation in a panel discussion on the use of dream material in the psychoanalytic therapeutics of the adult.] RFPsa 1959, 23:42-48

48658 Introduction à une étude clinique et psychopathologique de l'action des tranquillisants (avec référence particulière à l'hydroxyzine). [An introduction to a clinical and psychopathological survey of the effects of tranquilizers, with special reference to hydroxyzine.] Sem Hôp 1958, 34(9):1-3

48659 Névrose et grossesse. Quelques réflexions de clinique psychanalytique. [Neurosis and pregnancy. A few remarks on a psychoanalytic clinic.] In *Analgésie Psychologique en Obstétrique*, London, NY, Paris, Los Angeles: Pergamon Pr 1959, 89-93

48660 À propos des accidents d'automobile (quelques notes de clinique psychanalytique). [About automobile accidents. Some clinical psychoanalytic notes.] L'Ouest Médical 1959, 12(8):272-280

48661 À propos des dépressions. [About depressive states.] Discussion. Évolut psychiat 1955, (3):571-574

48662 Psychanalyse et médecine. In Nacht, S. *La Psychanalyse d'Aujourd'hui*, Paris: PUF 1956, 361-436
       Psychoanalysis and medicine. In Nacht, S. *Psychoanalysis of Today*, NY, London: Grune & Stratton 1959, 123-143

48663 Psychothérapie de l'impuissance sexuelle. [Psychotherapy of sexual impotence.] Évolut psychiat 1957, (3):489-554

48664 Religion, rationalisme et psychanalyse. [Religion, rationalism and psychoanalysis.] In *Les Cahiers Rationalistes*, Paris: Union Rationaliste 1959

S-13903 The therapeutic problem in psychosomatic medicine.
       Abs RdeS Q 1953, 22:311

       See Gilbert-Dreyfus; Nacht, Sacha; Schlumberger, Marc

HELLER, ABRAHAM

See Heller, Lora

HELLER, JUDITH BERNAYS

48665 Freud's mother and father. A memoir. Commentary 1956, 21:418-421

HELLER, LORA

48666 (& Heller, A.) Hamlet's parents: the dynamic formulation of a tragedy. Am Im 1960, 17:413-421

HELLER, PETER

48667 The creative unconscious and the spirit: a study of polarities in Hesse's image of the writer. Mod Lang Forum 1953, 38:28-40

48668 The masochistic rebel in recent German literature. J Aesthet 1953, 11:198-213

HELLERSBERG, ELIZABETH F.

48669 Child's growth in play therapy. PT 1955, 9:484-502

48670 Ego deficiency in school age. NPAP 1954, 2(3):21-35

48671 Unevenness of growth in its relation to vulnerability, anxiety, ego weakness, and the schizophrenic patterns. Ops 1957, 27:577-586

HELLIN, EMMY
REVIEW OF:
48672 Chapiro, M. La Révolution Originelle. PPR 1960, 47(2):107-111

HELLMAN, ILSE
48673 Psycho-analysis and the teacher. In Sutherland, J. M. *Psychoanalysis and Contemporary Thought,* London: HPI 1958, 58-76
48674 Research on adolescents in treatment. Proc RSM 1958, 51(11) Clinical Studies in Psycho-Analysis (Research project of the Hampstead Child Therapy Clinic) 5 p
48675 (& Friedmann, O.; Shepheard, E.) Simultaneous analysis of mother and child. Psa St C 1960, 15:369-377
48676 Some observations on mothers of children with intellectual inhibitions. Psa St C 1954, 9:258-273
          Abs NRo An Surv Psa 1954, 5:292-293. RTh J 1956, 37:215-216

See Bennett, Ivy

HELLMAN, LEON I.
See Brill, Norman Q.

HELLPACH, WILLY HUGO
48677 (& Rudder, B. de; Witte, W.) Klinische Psychologie. [Clinical Psychology.] Stuttgart: G. Thieme 1946, xiii + 224 p

HELME, WILLIAM H.
See Freedman, Alfred M.; Gurevitz, Saul

HELSDINGEN, R. J. VAN
48678 Beelden uit het onbewuste. [Images from the Unconscious.] Arnheim: Van Loghum Slaterus 1957, 131 p

HELSON, HARRY
48679 Psychiatric screening of flying personnel; perception and personality— a critique of recent experimental literature. USAF, Sch Aviat Med Proj Rep 1953, Proj No. 21-0202-0007 (Rep No. 1) v + 55 p

HELWEG, HJALMAR
48680 Soul Sorrow: The Psychiatrist Speaks to the Minister. (Tr: Grano, J.) NY: Pageant Pr 1955, 151 p
          Rv Murphy, W. F. Q 1956, 25:603-604

HENDERSON, DAVID KENNEDY
48681 (& Gillespie, R. D.; Batchelor, I. R. C.) A Text-book of Psychiatry for Students and Practitioners. London, NY: Oxford Univ Pr 1956, 746 p

HENDERSON, JOSEPH L.

48682 Analysis of transference in analytical psychology. PT 1955, 9:640-656
48683 Resolution of the transference in the light of C. G. Jung's psychology.
        Acta psychother psychosom orthopaedag 1954, 2:267-283
48684 Stages of psychological development exemplified in the poetical works
        of T. S. Eliot. J analyt Psychol 1956, 1:133-144; 1957, 2:33-49

HENDIN, HELEN

See Palmore, E.

HENDIN, HERBERT M.

48685 Psychoanalysis, modern art, and the modern world. Psychiat Q 1958,
        32:522-531
            Abs JBi Q 1959, 28:421-422
S-13960 Psychodynamic motivation factors in suicide. Encycl Aberr 513-516

See Lennard, Henry L.

HENDRICK, IVES

48686 Clinical psychology and medicine. The Commonwealth, Quart Bull
        Mass Dept of Pub Health 1935, 2(2)
48687 Concerning rejection. Child-Fam Dig 1949, 1(4):34-42
48688 Conscience and experience; a psychological point of view. Child Study
        1936, Jan:102
48688A Current problems of psychoanalytic technique. (Abs) Bull Am Psa
        Ass 1952, 7:229
48689 Discussion. Psm Cpt Psa 139-140
48690 Dream resistance and schizophrenia. J Am Psa Ass 1958, 6:672-690
            Abs TFr J 1959, 40:365. Shentoub RFPsa 1959, 23:439-440. TGS
            Q 1960, 29:433-434
S-13965 Early development of the ego: identification in infancy.
            Abs NRo An Surv Psa 1951, 2:74-76; JAA An Surv Psa 1951, 2:110-
            111
S-13972 Facts and Theories of Psychoanalysis. (3rd ed) NY: Knopf 1958, xxi
        + 385 + xvii p
48691 Homeostasis (re "physiologic infantilism"). In Dunbar, F. Synopsis of
        Psychosomatic Diagnosis and Treatment, St. Louis: C. V. Mosby 1948,
        55-56
48692 [Contributor to] The objective evaluation of psychotherapy. Round
        Table, 1948. Ops 1949, 19:467-470
48693 Presidential Address: Professional standards of the American Psycho-
        analytic Association. J Am Psa Ass 1955, 3:561-599
            Abs TFr J 1956, 37:510
S-13976 [Contribution to] Problems of Infancy and Childhood. Child-Fam
        Dig 1951, 5(6):18-23
48694 [Contributor to] The Psychiatrist, His Training and Development by
        John C. Whitehorn, Washington: American Psychiatric Assoc, 1953

48695 The structure of the total personality. In Linscott, R. N. & Stein, J. *Why You Do What You Do,* NY: Random House 1956, 10-16. From author's *Facts and Theories of Psychoanalysis* [13972]

48696 Summary of discussion. Transactions, National Conf on Mental Health, Wash, D. C., October 23, 1923

HENDRICKS, ROGER C.

REVIEWS OF:

48697 The Annual Survey of Psychoanalysis, Vol. V. Q 1960, 29:111-113

48698 Benedek, T. Psychosexual Functions in Women. Q 1953, 22:259-261

48699 Dunbar, F. Emotions and Bodily Changes. Q 1955, 24:584-585

48700 Lorand, S. (Ed) The Yearbook of Psychoanalysis, Vol. IX. Q 1955, 24:123-124

48701 Pederson-Krag, G. Personality Factors in Work and Employment. Q 1956, 25:601-602

48702 Schilder, P. Introduction to a Psychoanalytic Psychiatry. Q 1953, 22:95-96

48703 Schilder, P. Psychoanalysis, Man, and Society. Q 1953, 22:95-96

48704 Stallworthy, K. R. A Manual of Psychiatry. Q 1954, 23:457

HENDRICKSON, WILLARD J.

48705 (& Coffer, R. H.; Cross, T. N.) The initial interview. AMA ANP 1954, 71:24-30
      Abs Leavitt, M. Q 1956, 25:451

HENIG, ANTON J.

See Hallowitz, Emanuel

HENRIC, ÉTIENNETTE

See Ey, Henri

HENRY, GEORGE W.

48706 All the Sexes; A Study of Masculinity and Femininity. NY: Rinehart 1955, xxi + 599 p

HENRY, JULES

48707 An anthropological approach to cultural, idiosyncratic and universal factors in behavior. Prog PT 1958, 3:199-203

48708 Attitude organization in elementary school classrooms. Ops 1957, 27:117-133
      Abs Koenig RFPsa 1957, 21:873

48709 Cultural change and mental health. MH 1957, 41:323-326

S-14209 (& Henry, Z.) Doll play of Pilagá Indian children. Pers n s c 292-307

48710 Homeostasis in a special life situation. Unif Theory Behav 264-277

48711 The problem of spontaneity, initiative and creativity in suburban classrooms. Symposium 1958: The teacher's role in creativity. Ops 1959, 29:266-279

48712 (& Winokur, G.) Some aspects of the relationship between psychoanalysis and anthropology. Ops 1952, 22:644-648

48713   Types of institutional structure. In Greenblatt, M. et al: *The Patient and the Mental Hospital*, Glencoe, Ill: The Free Press 1957, 73-90

See Goodrich, Anne T.

HENRY, WILLIAM E.

48714   The Analysis of Fantasy. NY: Wiley; London: Chapman & Hall 1956, 305 p

48715   Problems of supervision and training in clinical psychology. Round table, 1952. 5. The language of fantasy—a problem in instruction and supervision. Ops 1953, 23:315-321

HENRY, ZUNIA

See Henry, Jules

HENSON, ISABELLE

See Talbot, Mira

HENTIG, HANS VON

48716   Die Kriminalität der lesbischen Frau. [Criminality of Lesbian women.] B Sexfschg 1958 (15): 83 p

HEPBURN, JAMES G.

48717   Disarming and uncanny visions: Freud's "The Uncanny" with regard to form and content in stories by Sherwood Anderson and D. H. Lawrence. Lit & Psych 1959, 9:9-12

HERBERG, WILL

48718   Freud, religion, and social reality. "The incomprehensible monster, man." Commentary 1957, 23:277-284

48719   Freud, the revisionists, and social reality. Freud 20th Cent 143-163

HERBERT, PHILIP S., JR.

48720   Creativity and mental illness. Psychiat Q 1959, 33:534-547
        Abs Engle, B. Q 1960, 29:436

HERBST, IRWIN

S-14051 Notes on the "Berit" in two dreams.
        Abs JFr An Surv Psa 1952, 3:187-189

HERLAND, LEO

48721   Gesicht und Charakter. [Face and Character.] 2nd ed. Zurich: Rascher 1956, 437 p

HERMA, HANS

48722   (& Kurth, G. M.) (Eds) Elements of Psychoanalysis. NY: World Publ 1957, xi + 333 p

HERMA, JOHN L.

See Ginsburg, Sol Wiener

REVIEWS OF:

48723 Glover, E. The Technique of Psycho-Analysis. NPAP 1955-56, 4(2):77-79

48724 Pederson-Krag, G. Personality Factors in Work and Employment. NPAP 1955, 4(1):78-79

HERMAN, MYRON

ABSTRACTS OF:

48725 Blanchard, P. A boy's effeminate behavior as a cover for aggression. Q 1958, 27:134

48726 Devereux, G. Denial of the anus in neurosis and culture. Q 1958, 27:133

48727 Galinsky, M. A clinical note on hostility. Q 1958, 27:131

48728 Gardiner, M. The lifeself and the death self. Q 1958, 27:132

48729 Gardiner, M. Make good the damage done—one motive of an exhibitionist. Q 1958, 27:132-133

48730 Guttman, S. A. Dreams and affects. Q 1958, 27:290-291

48731 Herskovitz, H. Childhood schizophrenia. Q 1958, 27:131

48732 Hunt, R. L. Aspects of a case of neurotic acting out. Q 1958, 27:290

48733 Johnson, D. E. A dream of fainting. Q 1958, 27:133

48734 Kaplan, A. J. Unconscious masturbation fantasies. Q 1958, 27:132

48735 Pearson, G. H. J. A brief survey of psychosis in children. Q 1958, 27:289-290

48736 Pearson, G. H. J. The fear of going berserk. Q 1958, 27:290

48737 Silverman, D. Analysis of a bug obsession. Q 1958, 27:130

48738 Spark, I. An instance of acting out in the analytic situation. Q 1958, 27:131

48739 Terzian, A. S. An early recognition of sex differences. Q 1958, 27:291

48740 Waelder, R. Notes on prejudice. Q 1958, 27:133-134

HERMANN, ALICE

48741 Emberré nevelés. [Education to humanship.] Budapest: Székesfövárosi Irodalmi és Müvészeti Intézet 1947, 203 p

HERMANN, IMRE

48742 Az Antiszemimizmus Lélektana. [Psychology of Antisemitism.] Budapest: Bibliotheca 1945, 110 p

48743 Augenleuchten, Schamgefühl und Exhibitionismus. [Ocular light reflection, feeling of shame, and exhibitionism.] Schweiz Z Psychol 1957, 16:50-53

48744 Bolyai János. Egy gondolat születésének története. [John Bolyai. The psychology of the birth of a thought.] Budapest: Anonymus 1945, 122 p

48745 Denken und Sprechen in ihrer gegenseitigen Abhängigkeit. [Thinking and speaking in their reciprocal dependency.] Acta Psychol 1955, 11:513-514

48746 On the dynamics of repression and ego subordination. M 1959, 32:210-212
    Abs RDT Q 1960, 29:445
48747 Az ember ósi ëztönei. [Primordial Instincts of Man.] Budapest: Pantheon 1943, 298 + xvi p
S-14079 The giant mother, the phallic mother, obscenity.
    Abs Perestrello, M. Rev Psicoanál 1956, 13:83
48748 Hibátlan Gondolkodsá, hibás gondolkodás. [Faultless thinking, faulty thinking.] In *Pszichológiai Tanulmányok*. Budapest: Akadémiai Kiadó 1958, 279-287
48749 Psychohygiene in der sexuellen Latenzperiode. [Psychohygiene of the latency period in sexuality.] In Pfister, M. *Die Psychohygiene*. Bern: Huber 1949, 1-9
48750 Das schöpferische und das schizoid-fehlerfreie Denken, erläutert an Johann Bolyais mathematischen Abhandlungen. [The productive and the schizoid-faultless thinking in John Bolyai's mathematical writings.] Psyche 1959, 12:706-718
48751 (& Fónagy, I.) Selbstregelung der Lautstärke. [Self-regulation of loudness.] Folia Phoniatrica 1958, 10:167-181

HERNER, T.

48752 Ein Fall von chronischer Schizophrenie. [A case of chronic schizophrenia.] Acta psychother psychosom orthopaedag 1957, 5:326-333

HERNFELD, FRED FARAU

See FARAU, ALFRED

HERR, MAURICE

48753 Psychanalyse de la politique française: après la chute de Mendès-France. [Psychoanalysis of French politics after the fall of Mendès-France.] Rev gén Belge 1955, 91:835-884

HERREN, RÜDIGER

48754 Zur Psychologie des abergläubischen Verbrechers. [The psychology of the superstitious criminal.] Psyche, Heidel 1954, 8:388-400

HERREROS, M. L.

48755 Factores psiquicos en la etiologia de la enfermedad de Basedow, sindromes afines y bocio simple (nota previa). [Psychic factors in the etiology of Basedow's disease, related syndromes, and simple goiter. (Preliminary note).] Semana Medica, Argentina 1953, 16:521-524
    Rv Amici di San Leo, G. Rev Psicoanál 1953, 10:385-386
48756 Tratamiento psicoanalitico de una neurosis obsesiva en una niña de trece años. [Psychoanalytic treatment of an obsessive neurosis in a thirteen-year-old girl.] Rev Clin Esp 1953, 50:307-309

HERRICK, JOAN

See Kaufman, Irving

HERRMANN, ROSALIND S.
See Caveny, Elmer L.; Day, Max; Harrower, Molly

HERSCHMANN, K.
TRANSLATION OF:
Ekstein, R. [7783]

HERSEY, FRANCIS
See Semrad, Elvin V.

HERSHER, LEONARD
48757 (& Moore, A. U.; Richmond, J. B.) Effect of post partum separation of mother and kid on maternal care in the domestic goat. Science 1958, 128(3335):1342-1343

HERSKO, MARVIN
See Winder, Alvin E.

HERSKOVITS, FRANCES
See Herskovits, Melville

HERSKOVITS, MELVILLE
48758 (& Herskovits, F.) Sibling rivalry, the Oedipus complex and myth. J Am Folklore 1958, 81:1-15

HERSKOVITZ, HERBERT H.
48759 (& Brenner, B. U.; Semple, R. A., III) Break through the Fog; painting and sculpture by an 18-year-old pre-psychotic girl with hypochondriacal and hysteric features. Santa Barbara, Calif.: Devereux Foundation 1955, 35 p
48760 Childhood schizophrenia. Bull Phila Ass Psa 1953, 3:70-74
     Abs Herman, M. Q 1958, 27:131
48761 (Chrm) (& Freedman, A. M.; Ekstein, R.; Sperling, M.; Fabian, A. A.; Gardner, G. E.; Kaplan, S.; Mahler, M. S.; Kanner, L.) Childhood schizophrenia. Round Table 1953. Ops 1954, 24:484-528
     Abs NRo An Surv Psa 1954, 5:275-277. MK Q 1955, 24:472
48762 Introductory remarks. Round table 1953: Childhood schizophrenia. Ops 1954, 24:484-486

See Hulse, Wilfred C.

HERTZ, D. G.
48762A (& Fellner, G. H.; Rosenbaum, M.) Psychosomatic approach to frontal lobe lesion. AMA ANP 1956, 75:78-82

HERTZMAN, MAX
48763 Psychology, literature, and the life situation. NPAP 1955, 3(2):46-57

HERZ, MARVIN
See Persky, Harold

HERZOG, EDGAR

48764 (& Herzog-Dürck, J.) Psychotherapie und menschliche Freiheit; das Lebenswerk Fritz Künkels. [Psychotherapy and man's freedom; the life work of Fritz Künkel.] Psyche, Heidel 1956, 10:404-414

HERZOG-DÜRCK, JOHANNA

48765 Der neurotische Widerstand gegen die Wandlung. [Neurotic resistance against change.] In Bitter, W. *Die Wandlung des Menschen in Seelsorge und Psychotherapie.* Göttingen: Verlag f med Psychol 1955

See Herzog, Edgar

HESNARD, ANGELO LOUIS MARIE

48766 Apport de la phénoménologie à la psychiatrie. [Contribution of phenomenology to psychiatry.] Paris: Masson 1959
48767 Comparaison de l'acquisition des conduites d'interdiction chez l'enfant et chez l'animal. [Acquisition of behavior control in children and in animals; a comparison.] Psychanalyse 1956, 2:311-313
S-14260 Évolution de la notion de surmoi dans la théorie de la psychanalyse. Abs JAA An Surv Psa 1951, 2:39-40. Edwards, F. H. J 1953, 34:282
S-14273 Manuel de Sexologie. 3rd ed. Paris: Payot 1959
48768 Moi et l'autre. [Myself and the other.] Psyché, Paris 1954, 9:481-496
48769 Morale sans Péché. [Morality Without Sin.] Paris PUF 1954
48770 Nature de la conscience. [The nature of consciousness.] Évolut psychiat 1959 (3):354-378
48771 L'Oeuvre de Freud et son Importance pour le Monde moderne. [Freud's Work and Its Importance for the Modern World.] (Pref: Merleau-Ponty, M.) Paris: Payot 1960, 395 p
48772 Psychanalyse de Lien interhumain. [Psychoanalysis of the Interhuman Bond.] Paris: PUF 1957, 231 p
Abs J Am Psa Ass 1960, 8:220; 595
48773 Psychanalyse et phénoménologie. [Psychoanalysis and phenomenology.] Psyché, Paris 1956, 11:193-202
48774 La psychologie, connaissance concrète de l'humain. [Psychology, a practical knowledge of the human.] Psyché, Paris 1953, 8:241-247
48775 Réflexions sur le "Wo Es war, soll Ich werden" de Freud. [Thoughts about "Wo Es war, soll Ich werden" by Freud.] Psychanalyse 1957, 3:317-324

HESS, VERENA

48776 Wandlungen eines paranoiden Menschen in der psychotherapeutischen Begegnung. [Changes of a paranoid person in the psychotherapeutic encounter.] Psyche, Heidel 1958, 12:131-158

HETZER, HILDEGARD

See Bühler, Charlotte; Wolf, Katherine M.

HEUSE, GEORGES A.

48777 Éléments de Psychologie Sociale Générale. [Elements of General Social Psychology.] Paris: J. Vrin 1954, xii + 110 p

HEUYER, GEORGES

48778 (& Lebovici, S.; Roumajon, Y.) A case of psychosis of affective etiology in a young child. Emot Prob Early Child 363-377

48779 (& Lebovici, S.; Bouvier) Epilepsie et obsessions. [Epilepsy and obsessions.] R Np inf 1954, 2:354-363

48780 L'équipment scientifique en neuro-psychiatrie infantile. [The scientific team in child psychiatry.] Z Kinderpsychiat 1958, 25:69-76

48781 Foreword to Stern, E. *Über Verhaltens- und Charakterstörungen bei Kindern und Jugendlichen*

48782 (& Lebovici, S.) Influence immédiatement décelable du film à partir de l'âge de 10 ans. [Immediately detectable influence of film from age of 10 years on.] Presse méd 1955, (50):1058-1060

48783 Psychiatrie et psychanalyse. [Psychiatry and psychoanalysis.] Bull Acad nat Méd 1953, 137(32/33):548-551

Psiquiatria y psicoanálisis. Rev Psicol gen apl, Madrid 1955, 10:123-128

48784 (& Lebovici, S.; Bertagna, L.) Recherches expérimentales filmologiques; compréhension et réactions des enfants débiles et caractériels. [Experimental studies of motion pictures; comprehension and reactions of feebleminded and character disturbed children.] R Np inf 1955, 3:1-4

48785 (& Lebovici, S.; Giabicani, A.) Le sens de la mort chez l'enfant. [The concept of death in children.] R Np inf 1955, 3:219-251

HEWER, VIVIAN

48786 (Ed) New Perspectives in Counseling. Univ of Minnesota Pr 1955, 60 p

HEWES, HENRY

48786A Freud and the theatre. Sat Rev 1956, May 5:10

HEWITT, C. C.

48787 Short-term analytic therapy. Psa 1952, 12:69-73

HEWITT, LESTER

See Jenkins, Richard L.

HEWLETT, IRMA

See Schneer, Henry I.

HEYER, GUSTAV RICHARD

48788 Vom Aufbau des Unbewussten. [The construction of the unconscious.] Jb Psychol Psychother 1953, 1:432-443

48789 Bildnereien aus dem Unbewussten. [Forming out of the unconscious.] In Speer, E. *Lindauer Psychotherapiewoche 1950*. Stuttgart: Hippokrates-Verlag 1951, 26-33. Hndb NP 1959, 4:278-289

48790 Carl Gustav Jung. In Kolle, K. *Grosse Nervenärzte*, Stuttgart: Thieme 1959, 153-174

48791 Komplexe psychologie (C. G. Jung). [The psychology of complexes. C. G. Jung).] Hndb N P 1959, 3:285-326

48792 Menschen in Not; Ärztebriefe aus einer psychotherapeutischen Praxis. [People in Trouble; Physician's Letters from a Psychotherapeutic Practice.] 3rd Rev Ed. Stuttgart: Hippokrates-Verlag 1957.

48793 (& Lelord, G.; Laroche, J.) Signification du transitivisme chez l'enfant à propos de deux observations. [The significance of transitivism in children. Two observations.] Rev Np inf 1958, 6:326-342

48794 Tiefenpsychologische Hintergründe der Entmannung. [Depth psychological backgrounds of emasculation.] Psychol Berater gesunde prakt Lebensgestalt 1952, 4:258-264

HEYER-GROTE, LUCY

48795 Freud und Jung: Ein Beitrag zur Geschichte der Tiefenpsychologie. [Freud and Jung: A contribution to the history of depth psychology.] Die Heilkunst 1956, 69:173-176

HEYMAN, MARGARET

See Appel, Kenneth E.

HEYMANN, GARY M.

48796 Some relationships among hostility, fantasy aggression, and aggressive behavior. Diss Abstr 1956, 16:793-794

HIATT, R. B.

See Flood, C.; Karush, Aaron

HIGGINS, JOHN W.

48797 Psychodynamics in the excessive drinking of alcohol. AMA ANP 1953, 69:713-726. In Podolsky, E. *Management of Addictions*, NY: Philos Lib 1955, 3-32
    Abs LRa Q 1955, 24:317-318

See Appel, Kenneth E.; Rosenbaum, Milton

HILER, EDWARD WESLEY

48798 An investigation of psychological factors associated with premature termination of psychotherapy. Diss Abstr 1954, 14:712-713

HILGARD, ERNEST R.

48799 Freud and experimental psychology. Beh Sci 1957, 2:74-79

48800 Freud's psychodynamics. In *Theories of Learning* (2nd ed), NY: Appleton-Century-Crofts 1956, 290-327

48801 Human motives and the concept of the self. Amer Psychologist 1949, 4:374-382. Under Hum Motiv 196-210. Stud Pers 347-361

48802 Unconscious Processes and Man's Rationality. Urbana, Ill: Univ Ill Pr 1958, 23 p

HILGARD, JOSEPHINE R.

48803 (& Newman, M. F.) Anniversaries in mental illness. Ps 1959, 22:113-121

Rv Euredjian Rev Psicoanál 1959, 16:272-273

48804 Anniversary reactions in parents precipitated by children. Ps 1953, 16:73-80

Abs JFr An Surv Psa 1953, 4:195-197

S-14376 Sibling rivalry and social heredity.

Abs CBr An Surv Psa 1951, 2:319-321. Rosengarten, L. Q 1953, 22:457

HILGEMAN, LOIS M.

See Loomis, Earl A., Jr.; Maier, Henry W.

HILL, DENIS

48805 Psychotherapy and the physical methods of treatment in psychiatry. JMS 1954, 100:360-374

HILL, GERALD

48806 The dynamic you-and-I relationship with a borderline personality. R 1956, 43:320-336

Abs JLan Q 1957, 26:586

REVIEWS OF:

48807 Fletcher, R. Instinct in Man. Q 1958, 27:433-435

48808 Hollingshead, A. B. & Redlich, F. C. Social Class and Mental Illness. Q 1959, 28:272-274

48809 McCary, J. L. (Ed) Psychology of Personality: Six Modern Approaches. Q 1959, 28:407-408

48810 Prince, M. The Dissociation of a Personality. Q 1958, 27:432-433

48811 Wedge, B. M. (Ed) Psychosocial Problems of College Men. Q 1959, 28:416-417

HILL, LEWIS B.

S-14382 Anticipation of arousing specific neurotic feelings in the psychoanalyst.

Abs STa An Surv Psa 1951, 2:397-399

48812 On being rather than doing in group psychotherapy. Int J grp PT 1958, 8:115-122

Abs GPK Q 1959, 28:431

48813 The drive for acquisition. Mental Hospitals 1958, March:3-5

S-14386 Infantile personalities.

Abs JFr An Surv Psa 1952, 3:159, 160. MK Q 1953, 22:448-449

48814 The nature of extramural schizophrenia. Schiz Psa Off Pract 3-9; 15-16

S-14387A Obituary: Ernest Elvin Hadley. J Am Psa Ass 1956, 4:382-384
S-14392A Psychotherapeutic Intervention in Schizophrenia. London: Cambridge Univ Pr; Chicago: Univ Chicago Pr 1955, vii + 216 p
    Abs Klein, H. S. J 1956, 37:489-490. TGS Q 1956, 25:424-426
48815 Psychotherapy of a schizophrenic. Psa 1957, 17:99-109
S-14397A (& Patton, J. D.) When physical therapy (shock) facilitates psychotherapy. P 1956, 113:60-65

REVIEWS OF:
S-14397B Arieti, S. Interpretation of Schizophrenia.. Q 1956, 25:98-99
S-14397c Brody, E. B. & Redlich, F. C. Psychotherapy with Schizophrenics: a Symposium. Q 1953, 22:430-434
S-14397D Bruch, H. Don't Be Afraid of Your Child. Q 1953, 22:440-441

HILL, S. R.

48816 (& Goetz, F. C.; Fox, H. M.; Murawski, B. J.; Krakauer, L. J.; Reifenstein, R. W.; Gray, S. J.; Reddy, W. J.; Hedberg, S. E.; St. Marc, J. R.; Thorn, G. W.) Studies on the adrenal cortical and psychological responses to stress in man. Arch Int Med 1956, 97:369

HILLARD, BEATRICE

48817 (& Ennis, J.) The role of child psychiatry in a program of education for childbirth. Workshop 1957: The collaboration of nursing and child psychiatry in a general hospital. Ops 1959, 29:89-93

See Blau, Abram

HILLSON, JOSEPH S.

See Worchel, Philip

HILTNER, SEWARD

48818 Freud for the pastor. Pastoral Psychol 1955, 5(50):41-57
48819 Freud, psychoanalysis and religion. Pastoral Psychol 1956, 7(68):9-21. In Doniger, S. Healing: Human and Divine, NY: Association Pr 1957, 71-100
48820 Healing. BMC 1958, 22:83-91
    Abs Weiss, J. Q 1959, 28:286
48821 The new concern of recent years. In Maves, P. B. The Church and Mental Health, NY, London: Scribner's 1953, 61-74
48822 Pastoral care and counseling. J Relig Thought 1956, 13:111-122
48823 Pastoral psychology and constructive theology. In Doniger, S. Religion and Human Behavior, NY: Association Pr 1954, 196-216
48824 Pastoral psychology and pastoral counseling. In Doniger, S. Religion and Human Behavior, NY: Association Pr 1954, 179-195
48825 Psychiatry and thoughts on God. BMC 1955, 19:217-226
48826 The psychological understanding of religion. Read Psychol Relig 74-104. Crozier Quart 1947, 24:3-36

HIMELHOCH, JEROME

48827   (& Fava, S. F.) Sexual Behavior in American Society. An Appraisal of
the First Two Kinsey Reports. NY: Norton 1955, 446 p
  Rv Canter, M. B. Psa 1955, 25:199. ESt J 1957, 38:368

HINCKLEY, MARY WHITE

48828   Discussion of Chrzanowski, G. "Treatment of asocial attitudes in ambulatory schizophrenic patients." Schiz Psa Off Pract 122-123

HINCKLEY, WILLIAM W.

48829   The Chestnut Lodge kiosk: observations on a psychiatric hospital's
work project. Part II. Int J grp PT 1957, 7:437-449
  Abs GPK Q 1959, 28:296

HINDLEY, COLIN B.

48830   Contributions of associative learning theories to an understanding of
child development. Symposium on the contribution of current theories
to an understanding of child development. M 1957, 30:230-269
  Abs EMW Q 1958, 27:620-621

HINKLE, BEATRICE

TRANSLATION OF:
Jung, C. G. [17468]

HINKLE, LAWRENCE E., JR.

48831   (& Christenson, W. N.; Kane, F. D.; Ostfeld, A.; Thetford, W. N.;
Wolff, H. G.) An investigation of the relation between life experience,
personality characteristics, and general susceptibility to illness. PSM
1958, 20:278-295
  Abs Simon, J. Q 1959, 28:292-293
48832   (et al) Studies in human ecology. Factors relevant to the occurrence
of bodily illness and disturbances in mood, thought, and behavior in
three homogeneous population groups. P 1957, 114:212-220
  Abs Dickes, R. Q 1959, 28:423

HINSIE, LELAND E.

48833   Anxiety. In Linscott, R. N. & Stein, J. *Why You Do What You Do,*
NY: Random House 1956, 88-104. From author's *Understandable
Psychiatry.* [14462]
48834   Introduction to Yost, O. R. *What You Should Know About Mental
Illness*
S-14448   (& Shatzky, J.) Psychiatric Dictionary, with Encyclopedic Treatment
of Modern Terms. 2nd ed with Suppl. NY: Oxford Univ Pr 1953,
vi + 781 p
  Abs R 1955, 42:106

HIRABAYASHI, NOBUTAKA

48835   [Psychological studies about a suicide in a TB sanatorium.] (Jap)
Nippon Iji Shinpo (Japanese Medical Journal) 1956, 1685

HIRE, A. WILLIAM

48836   An English bride in an Armenian-American family. Clin Stud Cult
Confl 531-560

HIRNING, L. CLOVIS

See Silverberg, William V.

HIRSCH, EDWIN W.

48837   Coital and non-coital sex technique as seen by a medical sexologist. In
Ellis, A. *Sex Life of the American Woman and the Kinsey Report*, NY:
Greenberg 1954, 161-174

HIRSCH, ERNEST A.

See Sargent, Helen D.

HIRSCH, J.

See Durkin, Helen E.

HIRSCH, J. M.

48838   Presente y future del psicoanálisis. [Present and future aspects of psychoanalysis.] Rev Policlín Cáracas 1951, 19(121):509-516

HIRSCH, M. W.

See Abramson, Harold A.

HIRSCH, SOLOMON

See Mendelson, Myer

HIRSCH, STANLEY I.

See Wynne, Lyman C.

HIRSCHBACH, FRANK DONALD

48839   The Arrow and the Lyre. A Study of the Role of Love in the Works
of Thomas Mann. The Hague, Netherlands: Martinus Nijhoff 1955,
195 p
Rv Kohut, H. Q 1957, 26:273-275

HIRSCHBERG, J. COTTER

48840   (& Mandelbaum, 'A.) Choice of interpretation in the treatment of
borderline and psychotic children. BMC 1957, 21:199-207
Abs Koenig RFPsa 1958, 22:127-128

48841   The education of emotionally disturbed children. 4. The role of education in the treatment of emotionally disturbed children through
planned ego development. Ops 1953, 23:684-690

48842   Parental anxieties accompanying sleep disorders in young children.
BMC 1957, 21:129-139
Abs Weiss, J. Q 1959, 28:108-109

48843   (& Bryant, K. N.) Problems in the differential diagnosis of childhood
schizophrenia. Proc Ass Res nerv Dis 1954, 34:454-461

HIRSCHFELD, M.
See Riese, Walther

HIRSH, ADA C.
48844 Possibilities of self-analysis. In Hartley, E. L. & Hartley, R. E. *Outside Readings in Psychology*, NY: Crowell 1957, 442-451

HITSCHMANN, EDWARD
S-14526 Experimentelle Wiederholung der infantilen Schlafsituation.
Abs Garma, A. Rev Psicoanál 1959, 15:163
S-14531 Franz Schubert's grief and love.
Abs R 1954, 41:367
S-14535 Freud's conception of love. YBPsa 1953, 9:23-36
Abs JAA An Surv Psa 1952, 3:66-68. MGr Q 1954, 23:141
S-37051 Gedankenübertragung während der Psychoanalyse. (Pub. anonymously)
Telepathy during psychoanalysis? In Devereux, G. *Psychoanalysis and the Occult*, NY: IUP 1953, 128-132
48845 Great Men; Psychoanalytic Studies. (Foreword: EJ. Ed: S. G. Margolin & H. Gunther). NY: IUP 1956, xiii + 278 p
Rv Wisdom, J. O. J 1958, 39:424-425. Kohut, H. J Am Psa Ass 1960, 8:567-586
S-14566 Zur Kritik des Hellsehens.
A critique of clairvoyance. In Devereux, G. *Psychoanalysis and the Occult*, NY: IUP 1953, 113-116
S-14566A Letter to Freud, May 6, 1916. Q 1956, 25:357-360
S-14601A Some psychoanalytic aspects of biography. (Read at 19th Int Psa Cong, Geneva, July 1955) J 1956, 37:265-269
Abs JLan Q 1957, 26:573
S-14606 Telepathie und Psychoanalyse.
Telepathy and psychoanalysis. In Devereux, G. *Psychoanalysis and the Occult*, NY: IUP 1953, 117-127

REVIEW OF:
S-14661A Baker, R. Sigmund Freud. Q 1953, 22:434-435

HITSON, H. M.
48846 (& Funkenstein, D. H.) Family patterns and paranoidal personality structure in Boston and Burma. Int J soc Psychiat 1959, 5:182-190

HJELHOLT, GUNNAR
48847 The neglected parent. Acta psychol 1958, 14:347-352. Nordisk Psykologi 1958, 10:347-352

HOBBS, NICHOLAS
48848 Client-centered psychotherapy. In McCary, J. L. *Six Approaches to Psychotherapy*, NY: Dryden Pr 1955, 11-60
48849 Science and ethical behavior. Am Psych 1959, 14:217-225

HOBMAN, D. L.

48850   Lou Andreas-Salomé. Hibbert J 1959-60, 58:149-156

HOBSON, R. F.

48851   An approach to group analysis. J Anal Psych 1959, 4:139-151

HOCH, PAUL H.

48852   Aim and limitations of psychotherapy. P 1955, 112:321-327. Prog PT 1956, 1:72-82

48853   (& Pool, L.; Ranschoff, J.; Cattell, J. P.; Pennes, H. H.) Case presentations of pseudo-neurotic schizophrenic patients treated with psychosurgery. JNMD 1954, 120:102-103

48854   (& Lewis, N. D. C.) Clinical psychiatry and psychotherapy. P 1957, 113:606-610; 1958, 114:599-602

48855   (& Lewis, N. D. C.) Clinical psychiatry including psychotherapy. P 1956, 112:522-526

48856   (& Zubin, J.) (Ed) Current Approaches to Psychoanalysis. NY: Grune & Stratton 1960, xiii + 207 p

48857   (& Zubin, J.) (Eds) Current Problems in Psychiatric Diagnosis. NY: Grune & Stratton 1953, vi + 291 p
         Rv Burnett, R. W. Q 1954, 23:286-287

48858   (& Zubin, J.) (Eds) Depression. NY: Grune & Stratton 1954, x + 277 p

48859   Discussion of Heath, R. G. & Leach, B. E. "Multidisciplinary research in psychiatry" and Rado, S. et al: "Schizotypal organization," Chg Cpts Psa Med 236-240

48860   Discussion of Rosen, J. N. "The treatment of schizophrenic psychosis by direct analytic therapy." Psychiat Q 1947, 21; Direct Anal 80-83

48861   Drug therapy. Am Hbk Psychiat 2; 1541-1551

48862   Drugs and psychotherapy. P 1959, 116:305-308

48863   The etiology and epidemiology of schizophrenia. Amer J Publ Hlth 1957, 47:1071-1076

48864   (& Zubin, J.) (Eds) Experimental Psychopathology. NY: Grune & Stratton 1957, x + 275 p

48865   Experimentally produced abnormal mental states. JNMD 1954, 119: 77-79

48866   Influence of Alfred Adler on psychoanalysis. Amer J Ind Psychol 1953, 10:54-58

48867   (& Zubin, J.) Foreword. Curr App Psa vii

48868   Masochism: clinical considerations. Sci Psa 1959, 2:42-43

48869   New aspects of treatment for mental illness. MH, NY 1957, 41:415-419

48870   Participant in: Conference on d-lysergic acid diethylamide (LSD-25). In Abramson, H. A. *The Use of LSD in Psychotherapy; Transactions.* NY: Josiah Macy, Jr. Found 1960, 7-240

48871   Pharmacologically induced psychoses. Am Hbk Psychiat 2:1697-1708

48872   Practical and theoretical applications of the new drug therapies in psychiatry. AMA ANP 1956, 75:325-328

48873   The problem of schizophrenia in the light of experimental psychopathology. In author's *Experimental Psychopathology* 205-217

48874 (& Zubin, J.) (Eds) Problems of Addiction and Habituation. NY, London: Grune & Stratton 1958, xii + 250 p

48875 Progress in psychiatric therapies. P 1955, 112:241-247

48876 (& Zubin, J.) (Eds) Psychiatry and the Law. NY: Grune & Stratton 1955, 232 p
   Rv Overholser, W. Q 1956, 25:594-596

48877 Psychoanalysis and psychiatric rationale. Sci Psa 1958, 1:159-161

48878 Psychoanalytic psychotherapy with LSD. In Abramson, H. A. *The Use of LSD in Psychotherapy; Transactions*. NY: Josiah Macy, Jr Found 1960, 7-24

48879 (& Zubin, J.) (Eds) Psychopathology of Childhood. NY: Grune & Stratton 1955, x + 303 p

48880 (& Zubin, J.) (Eds) Psychopathology of Communication. NY: Grune & Stratton 1958, xii + 305 p

48881 (& Pennes, H. H.; Cattell, J. P.) Psychoses produced by administration of drugs. Res Publ Ass nerv ment Dis 1953, 32:287-296. In Rinkel, M. & Denber, H. *Chemical Concepts of Psychosis*, NY: McDowell Oblensky 1958

48882 Psychoses-producing and psychoses-relieving drugs. Res Publ Ass Nerv Ment Dis 1958, 36:335-346

S-14835 Psychosomatic problems: methodology, research material and concepts.
   Abs JLan Q 1953, 22:301-302

48883 (& Pool, J. L.; Ranschoff, J.; Cattell, J. P.; Pennes, H. H.) The psychosurgical treatment of pseudoneurotic schizophrenia. P 1955, 111:653-658

48884 Remarks on LSD and mescaline. JNMD 1957, 125:442

48885 (& Cattell, J. P.; Pennes, H. H.) Report of the psychiatric discipline. In Mettler, F. A. *Psychosurgical Problems*, NY, Phila: Blakiston 1952, 279-307

48886 (& Lewis, N. D. C.) Review of psychiatric progress 1952: general clinical psychiatry, psychosomatic medicine, psychotherapy, and group therapy. P 1953, 109:503-505

48887 (& Lewis, N. D. C.) Review of psychiatric progress, 1953. Clinical psychiatry. P 1954, 110:503-507

48888 (& Lewis, N. D. C.) Review of psychiatric progress 1954: Clinical psychiatry. P 1955, 111:510-515

48889 Schools of psychiatry. In Wortis, J. *Basic Problems in Psychiatry*. NY: Grune & Stratton 1953, 126-145

48890 Some psychic manifestations in relation to brain function. Proc Rud Virchow med Soc, NY 1952, 11:108-114

48891 The use of tranquillizers in psychiatry. JMS 1958, 104:566-572

   See Cattell, James P.; Horwitz, William A.; Malitz, Sidney

HOCHHEIMER, WOLFGANG

48892 Abriss der Jung'schen Lehre als Beitrag zur Synthesen- und Amalgamdiskussion in der Psychotherapie. [Summary of the Jungian doctrine as contribution to the discussion of synthesis and amalgam in psychotherapy.] Psyche, Heidel 1952-53, 6:508-535

48893 Zur Analyse des therapeutischen Feldes. [Analyzing the psychotherapeutic field.] Psyche, Heidel 1954, 7:648-675

48894 Aufklärung und Gegenaufklärung in der Sexualanthropologie. [En-
lightenment and counter-enlightenment in sexual anthropology.] Psyche,
Heidel 1956-57, 10:763-784

48895 Zur Diskussion von Abgrenzungsfragen zwischen Psychotherapie und
ihren Nachbargebieten. [On questions of definition relating to psychotherapy and adjacent fields.] Psyche, Heidel 1955, 8:641-662

48896 Erziehung und Menschenbehandlung unter tiefenpsychologischem
Aspekt. [Education and handling of men in the view of depth psychology.] Studium Generale 1956, 9:154-162

48897 Zur Frage der Erfassung und Auswertung von Behandlungsgesprächen.
[On the question of compilation and evaluation of treatment interviews.] Psyche, Heidel 1954-55, 8(4):1-23

48898 Die Kinsey-Gerichte. [The Kinsey reports.] Psyche, Heidel 1954-55,
8(8):1-38

48899 Über Projektion. Einführung in die Thematik und Phänomenologie.
[Projection. An introduction into the theme and the phenomena.]
Psyche, Heidel 1955, 9:279-306

48900 Zur Psychologie von Goethes Wahlverwandtschaften. [On the psychology of Goethe's "Wahlverwandtschaften".] Psyche, Heidel 1953, 7:32-
54

48901 Psychologie und Psychoanalyse. [Psychology and psychoanalysis.] Der
Monat, Berlin 1956, 8:75-81

48902 Die Psychotherapie Carl Gustav Jungs. [The psychotherapy of Carl
Gustav Jung.] Psyche, Heidel 1957-58, 11:561-639

48903 Die Rolle des Unbewussten im zwischenmenschlichen Verhalten. [Roles
of the unconscious in interpersonal relations.] Psyche, Heidel 1953,
7:162-184

48904 Zur Tiefenpsychologie des pädagogischen Feldes. [On the depth psychology of the educational field.] Die Deutsche Schule, Berlin-Han-
nover-Darmstadt: Schroedel 1959, 51:101-119

HODGE, JAMES R.

48905 The passive-dependent versus the passive-aggressive personality. U S
Armed Forces med J 1955, 6:84-90

HODGES, DONALD CLARK

48906 The ethics of Freudian guilt. Arch crim Psychodyn 1957, 2:413-449

HODIN, J. P.

48907 The Dilemma of Being Modern. London: Routledge & Kegan Paul
1956, 271 p
Rv EJ J 1957, 38:126-127

48908 The future of surrealism. J Aesthet 1956, 14:475-484

HOEDEMAKER, EDWARD D.

48909 Preanalytic preparation for the therapeutic process in schizophrenia.
Ps 1958, 21:285-291

48910 Psycho-analytic technique and ego modifications. J 1960, 41:34-46
48911 The therapeutic process in the treatment of schizophrenia. J Am Psa Ass 1955, 3:89-109
    Abs TFr J 1956, 37:207. Shentoub RFPsa 1956, 20:566. Young, B. Q 1959, 28:557

HOEJER-PEDERSEN, WILLY
(See also Højer-Pedersen, Willy)

48912 An attempt at evaluating the contents of the concept of actual neurosis. Acta Ps et N Scandinavica 1956, 31:447-457
48913 Observations on duodenal ulcer patients admitted to a psychiatric department. Compared with the psychiatric findings in duodenal ulcer patients admitted to a medical department. Danish Med Bull 1959, 6:50-54
48914 Psykoanalytiske synspunkter inden for psykiatrien. [Psychoanalytic viewpoints inside psychiatry.] Mandesskrift for praktisk laegegerning og social medicin 1952, 240-252
48915 Om psykosomatisk medicin. [On psychosomatic medicine.] Ugeskrift for Laeger 1953, 115:1045-1053
48916 De psykosomatiske syndromers placering inden for psykiatrien. [The placing of the psychosomatic syndromes inside psychiatry.] Nordisk Psykiatrisk Medlemsblad 1958, 12(suppl 1):311-322

HOELEN, ED.

48917 Le cas dun fétichiste qui versait de l'encre sur les toilettes des jeunes femmes. [The case of a fetishist who poured ink on young women's dresses.] Psyché, Paris 1953, 8:1-11; 119-123

HOFF, H. C.
See Hoff, Hans

HOFF, H. E.
See Harris, Jacqueline B.

HOFF, HANS

48918 (& Ringel, E.) Anfänge der Psychopathie. [Origins of psychopathy.] Med Klin, Berl 1956, 51:423-425
48919 (& Hoff, H. C.) Ein Beitrag zu dem Symptomkomplex der weiblichen Frigidität. [On the symptomatology of female frigidity.] Wien Arch Psychol Psychiat Neurol 1954, 4(2):94-102
48920 Die Beziehung Sigmund Freuds zur Wiener Psychiatrischen Schule. [Sigmund Freud's relation to the Vienna psychiatric school.] Wien Zschr Nervenh 1956, 12:391-395
48921 The development of psychotherapy in Austria. Prog PT 1958, 3:262-266
48922 Foreword to Strotzka, H. *Sozial-psychiatrische Untersuchungen*

48923   (& Ringel, E.) L'influenza del nostro tempo sulle malattie psico-
        somatiche. [The influence of our time on psychosomatic diseases.] Med
        psicosom 1956, 1:189-194
48924   Über den klinischen Wert psychoanalytischer Erkenntnis. [On the
        clinical value of psychoanalytic knowledge.] Forum 1956, 3(29):174-
        176
48925   Zur Kritik des Begriffes der Managerkrankheit. [Criticism of the con-
        cept of managerial disease.] Acta psychother psychosom orthopaedag
        1955, 3:97-106
48926   Lehrbuch der Psychiatrie; Verhütung, Prognostik und Behandlung der
        geistigen und seelischen Erkrankung. [Principles of Psychiatry; Pre-
        vention, Prognosis and Treatment of Mental Illness.] Basel: Benno
        Schwabe 1956, xv + 922 p
           Rv ESt J 1958, 39:440. Viderman RFPsa 1958, 22:122
48927   Neurosen im Schiedsgerichtsverfahren. [Neuroses in judicial arbitra-
        tion.] WMW 1956, 106:516-522
48928   Die Prophylaxe der epileptischen Charakterveränderung. [Prophylaxis
        of epileptic character changes.] WMW 1953, 103:8-11
48929   Der psychiatrische Unterricht. [Instruction and training in psychiatry.]
        WMW 1955, 105:776-779
48930   (& Spiel, L.) Die psychische Einstellung des Behinderten. [The mental
        attitude of the handicapped.] WMW 1956, 106:1-13
48931   De psychische instelling van lichamelijk gebrekkigen. [The psycho-
        logical attitude of the physically handicapped.] Maandbl Geest Volks-
        gezondh 1956, 11:73-82
48932   (& Spiel, W.) Zur Psychosomatik im Kindesalter. [Psychosomatic in
        children.] Wien klin Wschr 1955, 67:756-759
48933   (& Ringel, E.) Die sogennante Soldatenbraut. Über eine besondere
        Form weiblicher Gefährdung in unserer Zeit. [The "soldier's girl." A
        special danger for women in our time.] Wien Arch Psychol Psychiat
        Neurol 1952, 2:140-154
48934   (& Ringel, E.) Stellungnahme "Zum Problem der Spezifizität der Per-
        sönlichkeitstypen und der Konflikte in der psycho-somatischen Medi-
        zin." [Discussion to "The problem of specificity of personality types
        and conflicts in psychosomatic medicine."] Z PSM 1957-58, 4:168-170
48935   (& Arnold, O. H.) Au sujet de la thérapie de la schizophrénie. [On the
        subject of the therapy of schizophrenia.] Enceph 1955, 44:1-25
48936   (& Ringel, E.) Zur Therapie psychosomatischer Erkrankungen. [Ther-
        apy of psychosomatic disorders.] Z PSM 1957-58, 4:10-14
           Rv Lustig, S. Rev Psicoanál 1958, 15:303-304. Zmud, F. & Fiasche,
        D. N. de. Rev Psicoanál 1959, 16:196-197
48937   Das veränderte Erscheinungsbild der Melancholie. [The changed pic-
        ture of melancholia.] Wien klin Wschr 1956, 68:730-734
48938   Zum 100. Geburtstag von Professor Sigmund Freud. [On the cen-
        tenary of Professor Sigmund Freud.] Wien klin Wschr 1956, 68(30)
48939   (& Berner, Ringel) Die Zeit und ihre Neurose. [The Time and Its
        Neuroses.] Vienna: (Schriftenreihe der Oesterr. UNESCO-Kommis-
        sion) 1956, 168 p

        See Arnold, O. H.

HOFFER, HEDWIG

48940 Obituary: Siegfried Bernfeld. 1892-1953. J 1955, 36:66-69

ABSTRACT OF:
48941 Sherwin, A. C. Reactions to music of autistic (schizophrenic) children. J 1954, 35:449-450

REVIEW OF:
48942 Sterba, E. & Sterba, R. Beethoven and His Nephew. J 1956, 37:507-508

HOFFER, WILLI

48943 Defensive process and defensive organization: their place in psychoanalytic technique. (Read at 18th Int Psa Cong, London, July 1953) J 1954, 35:194-198. Rd Psa Psychol 106-113
　　Abs Auth J 1954, 35:286. JLan Q 1955, 24:606. Lebovici RFPsa 1954, 18:468-469. NRo An Surv Psa 1954, 5:324-326
48944 Editorial. J 1955, 36:440
48945 Editorial: the Sigmund Freud centenary. J 1956, 37:1
48946 Letter: tribute to Ernest Jones. J 1958, 39:308-310
48947 Medicine since Freud. The Observer 1956, May 6
S-14921 The mutual influences in the development of ego and id: earliest stages.
　　Abs Auth J 1953, 34:277. JAA An Surv Psa 1952, 3:36-38

OBITUARIES:
48948 Dr. Douglas Noel Hardcastle 1892-1954. J 1955, 36:74
48949 Eduard Hitschmann. J 1958, 39:614-615
48950 Ernst Kris 1900-1957. J 1957, 38:359-362
48951 Clarence P. Oberndorf. J 1954, 35:375
48952 Oskar Pfister. J 1958, 39:616-617
48653 Psychoanalysis: Practical and Research Aspects. Baltimore: Williams & Wilkins 1955, 102 p
　　Rv Johnson, A. M. Q 1955, 24:573-574. ESt J 1956, 37:486-487. J Am Psa Ass 1957, 5:186
48954 To Sylvia May Payne on the occasion of her seventy-fifth birthday. J 1955, 36:369
S-14926 Three psychological criteria for the termination of treatment.
　　Abs R 1953, 40:369
48955 Transference and transference neurosis. (Read at 19th Int Psa Cong, Geneva, July 1955) J 1956, 37:377-379
　　Abs JLan Q 1957, 26:578

ABSTRACTS OF:
48956 Arlow, J. A. Masturbation and symptom formation. J 1953, 34:275
48957 Bonaparte, M. Masturbation and death or a compulsive confession of masturbation. J 1953, 34:280
48958 Eissler, K. R. The effect of the structure of the ego on psychoanalytic technique. J 1953, 34:276
48959 Fraiberg, S. A critical neurosis in a two-and-a-half-year-old girl. J 1953, 34:280

48960 Freud, A. The mutual influences in the development of the ego and id. Introduction to the discussion. J 1953, 34:277-278
48961 Gero, G. Defences in symptom formation. J 1953, 34:275
48962 Greenson, R. R. On boredom. J 1953, 34:274
48963 Hartmann, H. The mutual influences in the development of ego and id. J 1953, 34:276-277
48964 Jessner, L. et al: Emotional implications of tonsillectomy and adenoidectomy on children. J 1953, 34:280
48965 Kanzer, M. Past and present in the transference. J 1953, 34:276
48966 Klein, M. The mutual influences in the development of ego and id. Discussion. J 1953, 34:278
48967 Knight, R. P. The Journal of the American Psychoanalytic Association. J 1953, 34:274
48968 Kubie, L. S. The distortion of the symbolic process in neurosis and psychosis. J 1953, 34:275
48969 Lindemann, E. & Dawes, L. G. The use of psychoanalytic constructs in preventative psychiatry. J 1953, 34:282
48970 Meiss, M. L. The Oedipal problem of a fatherless child. J 1953, 34:280
48971 Nacht, S. The mutual influences in the development of the ego and id. Discussion. J 1953, 34:278
48972 Pearson, G. H. J. A survey of learning difficulties in children. J 1953, 34:281
48973 Reich, A. Narcissistic object choice in women. J 1953, 34:274-275
48974 Scott, W. C. M. The mutual influences in the development of ego and id. Discussion. J 1953, 34:278-279
48975 Sylvester, E. Discussion of techniques used to prepare young children for analysis. J 1953, 34:281
48976 Van der Waals, H. C. The mutual influences in the development of ego and id. Discussion. J 1953, 34:279

REVIEWS OF:
48977 Freud, S. Civilisation, War and Death. J 1955, 36:138-139
48978 Freud, S. A General Selection from the Works of Sigmund Freud. J 1955, 36:138
48979 Frosch, J. (Ed) The Annual Survey of Psychoanalysis, Vol. I. J 1953, 34:156-158
48980 Frosch, J. (Ed) The Annual Survey of Psychoanalysis, Vol. II, Vol. III. J 1956, 37:503-504
48981 Glover, E. The Technique of Psycho-Analysis. J 1956, 37:507

HOFFMAN, FRANCIS H.

48982 (& Brody, M. W.) The symptom, fear of death. R 1957, 44:433-438

HOFFMAN, FREDERICK J.

S-14950 Freudianism and the Literary Mind. 2nd ed. Baton Rouge: Louisiana State Univ Pr 1957, xi + 350 p. NY: Grove Pr 1959, xi + 350 p
48983 Psychoanalysis: influence on literature and art. In *Encyclopaedia Britannica*, Chicago, London, Toronto: Encyclopaedia Britannica Inc. 1954, 18:669-671

48984 Psychology and literature. Lit & Psychol 1956, 6:111-115
48985 Psychology and literature. Kenyon Rev 1957, 19:605-619

HOFFMAN, JAY L.

S-14951 A clinical appraisal of frontal lobotomy in the structure of Freud's thought.
Abs R 1954, 41:84

HOFFMAN, JULIUS

48986 Facial phantom phenomenon. JNMD 1955, 122:143-151
48987 Psychodynamic analysis of socio-economic determinants of personality formation in the Negro in the American culture. A compendium of psychiatric thought. Samiksa 1955, 9:129-137
48988 (& McDonald, M.) Use of artistic expression as an integral part of the psychotherapeutic process. PT 1955, 9:269-282

HOFFMAN, MARTIN L.

48989 Conformity as a defense mechanism and a form of resistance to genuine group influence. J Personality 1957, 25:412-424
48990 Some psychodynamic factors in compulsive conformity. ASP 1953, 48:383-394

See Weisskopf-Joelson, Edith A.

HOFFMAN, M. M.

See Dongier, M.

HOFFMANN, GERHARD

48991 Die Beziehungen zwischen Aktualneurosen, Psychoneurosen und Realitätsprinzip. [The connections between actual neuroses, psychoneuroses and reality principle.] Z PSM 1958-59, 5:24-27
48992 A hypothesis regarding the scope and limitations of psychotherapy. PT 1951, 5:339-361
48993 Transference and therapeutic goal. Acta psychotherap psychosom orthopaedag 1955 3(Suppl):139-145
Übertragung und therapeutisches Ziel. Psyche, Heidel 1956, 9:704-710

HOFFMANN, R.

See Schick, C. P.

HOFFMANN, WILHELM

48994 Epilogue to Schottlaender, F. *Das Ich und seine Welt*

HOFFMANN, WOLFHART

48995 Erarbeitung einer bipersonalen Ehe. [Setting up of bipersonality in matrimony.] Der Psychologe 1957, 9:98-103
48996 Der internationale Friede als psychologische Aufgabe. [International peace as a psychological task.] Der Psychologe 1959, 11:161-167

48997   Zum Problem der Ehereife. [On the problem of maturity for matri-
        mony.] Der Psychologe 1958, 10:175-181
48998   Probleme stationärer Heilpädagogik. [Problems of psychotherapeutical
        education in a home.] Der Psychologe 1958, 10:490-497
48999   Die Verteidigung des Friedens. [The defense of peace.] Der Psy-
        chologe 1958, 10:87-90

HOFLING, CHARLES K.

49000   (& Minnehan, R. W.) A case of an unusual impulse disorder. M 1956,
        29:150-161
            Abs EMW Q 1957, 26:443
49001   An interpretation of Shakespeare's Coriolanus. Am Im 1957, 14:407-
        435
49002   Notes on Raychaudhuri's "Jesus Christ and Sree Kisna." Am Im 1958,
        15:213-226

HOFSTÄTTER, PETER R.

49003   Die amerikanischen Töchterschulen der Psychoanalyse. [The Amer-
        ican finishing schools of psychoanalysis.] Hndb N P 1959, 3:507-530
49004   Psychotherapie und die Theorie der Lernvorgänge. [Psychotherapy
        and the theory of learning.] Psyche, Heidel 1953, 7:321-341
49005   Richtungen in der Psychologie? [Tendencies in psychology?] Psycho-
        therapie 1956, 1:187-197
49006   Die soziale Dynamik der psychotherapeutischen Situation. [The social
        dynamics of the psychotherapeutic situation.] Psyche, Heidel 1957,
        10:733-749

HOHMAN, LESLIE A.

49007   An atomistic biologic approach to human behavior. Curr App Psa 79-86

HOHMANN, GEORGE W.

49008   A stoic faces stress. Clin Stud Cult Confl 171-193

HÖHN, ELFRIEDE

49009   Theoretische Grundlagen der Inhaltsanalyse projektiver Tests. [Theory
        of content analysis of projective tests.] Psychol Forsch 1959, 26:13-74

        See Bühler, Charlotte

HØJER-PEDERSEN, WILLY
(See also Hoejer-Pedersen, Willy)

49010   On the significance of psychic factors in the development of peptic
        ulcer. Acta Ps et N Scandinavica 1958, suppl 119; vol 33. Copenhagen:
        Munksgard 1958, 232 p
            Rv Garma, A. J 1959, 40:68. Wilson, G. W. Q 1959, 28:93-96
49011   Symposium on disturbances of the digestive tract: IV. Neurotic states
        in duodenal ulcer patients. (Read at 21st Int Psa Cong, Copenhagen,
        July 1959) J 1960, 41:462-464

49012 Den traumatiske neuroses relation til psykosegruppen. [The relation between traumatic neuroses and psychoses.] Nord Psyk Medl 1957, 11:290-298

49013 Ulcussygdommen fra et psykosomatisk synspunkt. [The peptic ulcer from a psychosomatic point of view.] Manedsskrift for praktisk laegegerning og social medicin 1955, 291-304

HOKANSON, J. E.

See Gordon, Jesse E.

HOLDEN, MARJORIE

See Slavson, Samuel R.

HOLDEN, MELVIN

See Goodenough, Donald R.

HOLLAND, NORMAN N.

49014 Hobbling with Horatio. Hudson Rev 1959-60, 12:549-557

HOLLANDER, EDWARD E.

ABSTRACT OF:
49015 Lorand, S. Resistance. Q 1958, 27:462-464

HOLLENDER, MARC H.

49016 Ambulatory schizophrenia. J chronic Dis 1959, 9:249

49017 (& Boszormenyi-Nagy, I.) Hallucination as an ego experience. AMA ANP 1958, 80:93

49018 Is psychotherapy "real?" Amer Practitioner & Dig of Treatment 1958, 9:369

49019 (& Szasz, T. S.) Normality, neurosis and psychosis: some observations on the concepts of mental health and mental illness. JNMD 1957, 125: 599-607

49020 Observations on nasal symptoms: relationship of the anatomical structure of the nose to psychological symptoms. Psychiat Q 1956, 30:375

49021 Observations on the use of the placebo in medical practice. Amer Practitioner & Dig of Treatment 1958, 9:214

49022 The physician, the patient and cancer. Illinois Med J 1955, 107:20

49023 Psychiatry as part of a mixed internship. JAMA 1961, 175:489-490

49024 (& Brolley, M.) Psychological problems of patients with myasthenia gravis. JNMD 1955, 122:178

49025 The Psychology of Medical Practice. Phila: W B Saunders 1958

49026 (& Robbins, F. P.) The psychosomatic approach to medicine. In Tice-Sloan *Practice of Medicine*, Hagerstown, Md: W. F. Prior 1958

49027 Psychosomatic aspects of oral and pharyngeal diseases. In Hollender, A. R. *The Pharynx*, Chicago: Year Book Pub 1953

49028 The seeking of sympathy or pity. JNMD 1958, 126:579-584
    Abs Smolensky, G. Rev Psicoanál 1959, 16:94-95

See Szasz, Thomas S.

HOLLINGSHEAD, AUGUST B.

49029 (& Redlich, F. C.) Schizophrenia and social structure. P 1954, 110:
       695-701
          Abs MK Q 1954, 23:465
49030 (& Redlich, F. C.) Social Class and Mental Illness: A Community
       Study. NY: Wiley 1958, ix + 442 p
          Rv Hill, G. Q 1959, 28:272-274. Sherman, M. H. PPR 1960, 47(3):
       124-125
49031 (& Redlich, F. C.) Social mobility and mental illness. P 1955, 112:
       179-185
          Abs DRu Q 1958, 27:296-297
49032 (& Redlich, F. C.) Social stratification and psychiatric disorders. Am
       sociol Rev 1953, 18:163-169

       See Freedman, Lawrence Z.; Redlich, Fredrick C.

HOLLINGSWORTH, ALAN M.

49033 Freud, Conrad, and the future of an illusion. Lit & Psychol 1955, 5(4):
       78-83

HOLLIS, FLORENCE

49034 Personality diagnosis in casework. Ego Psychol Dyn Casewk 83-96
S-14983A Women in Marital Conflict: A Casework Study.
          Rv Zinkin, J. R 1953, 40:186-187

HOLLITSCHER, WALTER

49035 Introducción al Psicoanálisis. [Introduction to Psychoanalysis.] Buenos
       Aires: Ed Paidos 1956
          Rv Abadi, M. Rev Psicoanál 1957, 14:337

HOLLÓS, ISTVÁN (STEFAN)

S-15009 Wie sind die Geisteskranken zu verstehen und zu behandeln. Psa Vkb
       1957, 226-239

HOLMER, PAUL

49036 Child guidance clinics and community agencies. Bull Phila Ass Psa
       1953, 3:8-17

HÒLMES, ELIZABETH H.

       See Gardner, George E.; Kaufman, Irving

HOLMES, GORDON

       See Taylor, James

HOLMES, M. H.

49037 Mother and child; a case study of a four-year-old. Brit J psychiat soc
       Wk 1956, 3(3):25-28

HOLMES, MONICA BYCHOWSKI

49038 A cross-cultural study of the relationship between values and modal conscience. Psa St Soc 1960, 1:98-181

HOLMES, PAUL

49039 Towards a Measure of Man. The Frontiers of Normal Adjustment. London: Routledge & Kegan Paul
Rv Williams, A. H. J 1958, 39:435-436

HOLMES, THOMAS H.

49040 (& Ripley, H. S.) Experimental studies on anxiety reactions. P 1955, 111:921-929

S-15015A (& Wolff, H. G.) Life situation, emotions, and backache.
Abs NR Q 1953, 22:129. R 1953, 40:165

S-15015B (& Treuting, T.; Wolff, H. G.) Life situations, emotions, and nasal disease.
Abs R 1953, 40:165

See Stewart, Ann H.

HOLSTIJN, A. J. WESTERMAN
(See also Westerman-Holstijn, A. J.)

49041 Nieuwere opvattingen betreffende overdracht. [Recent concepts of transference.] NTvG 1955, 99:3826-3831
49042 The psychological development of Vincent van Gogh. JMS 1957, 103:1-17
Abs Lossy, F. T. Q 1958, 27:147

HOLSTROM, JOHN D.

See Perkins, Rollins M.

HOLT, ROBERT R.

49043 Gauging primary and secondary processes in Rorschach responses. J proj Tech 1956, 20:14-25
49044 Implications of some contemporary personality theories for Rorschach rationale. In Klopfer, B. et al: Developments in the Rorschach Technique. Vol. I. Technique and Theory, NY: World Book Co 1954, 501-560
49045 An inductive method of analyzing defense of self-esteem. BMC 1951, 15:6-15
49046 Personality growth in psychiatric residents. AMA ANP 1959, 81:203-215
49047 (& Luborsky, L.; Morrow, W. R.; Rapaport, D.; Escalona, S. K.) Personality Patterns of Psychiatrists. A Study of Methods for Selecting Residents. (Foreword: Knight, R. P.) NY: Basic Books 1958, Vol. I, 386 p; Vol. II, 400 p
Rv MG Q 1959, 28:405-407

S-21206A (& Luborsky, L.) Research in the selection of psychiatrists: a second interim report.
   Abs RRG Q 1953, 22:304-305
49048 (& Luborsky, L.) The selection of candidates for psychoanalytic training: on the use of interviews and psychological tests. J Am Psa Ass 1955, 3:666-681
   Abs TFr J 1956, 37:511. Shentoub RFPsa 1956, 20:568. Young, B. Q 1959, 28:565

See Goldberger, Leo; Klein, George S.; Klopfer, Bruno; Luborsky, Lester

ABSTRACT OF:
49049 Schafer, R. Psychoanalytic Interpretation in Rorschach Testing. An Surv Psa 1954, 5:530-539

HOLZBERG, JULES D.

49050 A carpenter with traumatic brain damage. Clin Stud Pers 407-427
49051 (& Hahn, F.) The picture-frustration technique as a measure of hostility and guilt reactions in adolescent psychopaths. Ops 1952, 22:776-797
49052 (& Bursten, B.; Santiccioli, A.) The reporting of aggression as an indication of aggressive tension. ASP 1955, 50:12-18

See Sohler, Dorothy Terry

HOLZKAMP, KLAUS

49053 Erziehungsberatung als sozialpsychischer Prozess. [Child guidance as a social-psychological process.] Prax Kinderpsychol 1958, 7:193-197

HOLZMAN, PHILIP S.

49054 (& Gardner, R. W.) Leveling and repression. ASP 1959, 59:151-155
   Abs Applebaum, S. A. Q 1960, 29:442
49055 (& Klein, G. S.) Motive and style in reality contact. BMC 1956, 20:181-191
   Abs Racamier RFPsa 1957, 21:123. Weiss, J. Q 1958, 27:293
49056 A note on Breuer's hypnoidal theory of neurosis. BMC 1959, 23:144-147
   Abs JPG Q 1960, 29:140
49057 (& Ekstein, R.) Repetition-functions of transitory regressive thinking. Q 1959, 28:228-235
   Abs Sapochnik Rev Psicoanál 1960, 17:265-266
49058 Repression and cognitive style. In Peatman, J. G. & Hartley, E. L. Festschrift for Gardner Murphy, NY: Harper 1960, 330-343

See Gardner, Riley; Klein, George S.

ABSTRACTS OF:
49059 Beach, F. A. The descent of instinct. Q 1957, 26:147
49060 Blum, G. S. & Miller, D. R. Exploring the psychoanalytic theory of "oral character." Q 1953, 22:310

49061   Fredericson, E. The effects of infantile experience upon adult behavior. Q 1953, 22:463
49062   Hall, C. S. The significance of the dream of being attacked. Q 1956, 25:455-456
49063   Levinson, D. J. Criminality from a sense of guilt. Q 1953, 22:311
49064   Litwinski, L. Toward the restatement of the concept of the self. Q 1953, 22:140-141
49065   Miller, D. R. & Stine, M. E. The prediction of social acceptance by means of psychoanalytic concepts. Q 1953, 22:309-310
49066   Pattie, F. & Cornett, S. Unpleasantness of early memories and maladjustment of children. Q 1953, 22:311
49067   Rapaport, D. The conceptual model of psychoanalysis. Q 1954, 23:620-621
49068   Rosenstock, E. M. Perceptual aspects of repression. Q 1953, 22:462
49069   Sarnoff, I. Identification with the aggressor: some personality correlates of anti-semitism among Jews. Q 1953, 22:310
49070   Schwartz, B. J. The measurement of castration anxiety and anxiety over loss of love. Q 1956, 25:456
49071   Weisskopf, E. A. Intellectual malfunctioning and personality. Q 1953, 22:463

REVIEW OF:
49072   Wechsler, D. The Measurement and Appraisal of Adult Intelligence. Q 1958, 27:592-594

HOME, H. J.
REVIEWS OF:
49073   Cole, W. G. Sex in Christianity and Psycho-Analysis. J 1957, 38:430
49074   Fordham, M. The Objective Psyche. J 1960, 41:84-85
49075   Geach, P. Mental Acts. J 1959, 40:356
49076   Jung, C. G. Flying Saucers. J 1960, 41:83-84
49077   O'Dea, T. F. The Mormons. J 1960, 41:84
49078   Some Considerations of Early Attempts in Cooperation between Religion and Psychiatry. Symposium No. 5. J 1959, 40:71
49079   Sprott, W. H. J. Human Groups. J 1960, 41:83
49080   Sutherland, J. D. (Ed) Psycho-Analysis and Contemporary Thought. J 1960, 41:81

HONIG, ALBERT M.
49081   The analytic treatment of schizophrenia. PPR 1958, 45(3):51-62
49082   Anxiety in schizophrenia: a contribution to direct analysis. PPR 1960, 47(3):77-90
49083   Negative transference in psychosis. PPR 1960, 47(4):105-114

HONIG, E. M.
49084   Psychosis and peptic ulcer. BMC 1955, 19:61-67
            Abs Racamier, P. C. RFPsa 1955, 19:631

HONIGMAN, J. J.
49085   Culture and Personality. NY: Harper 1954

HONZIK, MARJORIE

See MacFarlane, Jean W.

HOOK, SIDNEY

49086 Introduction. Psa Sci Method Phil xi-xiii
49087 (Ed) Psychoanalysis, Scientific Method, and Philosophy. A Symposium of the Second Annual New York University Institute of Philosophy, New York, March 28-29, 1958. NY: NYU Pr 1959, xiii + 370 p
   Abs J Am Psa Ass 1960, 8:595-596. Rv MG Q 1959, 28:536-537
49088 Science and methodology in psychoanalysis. Psa Sci Method Phil 212-224

HOOKER, EVELYN

49089 The adjustment of the male overt homosexual. J proj Tech 1957, 21: 18-31
49090 Male homosexuality in the Rorschach. J proj Tech 1958, 22:33-54
49091 A preliminary analysis of group behavior of homosexuals. J Psychol 1956, 42:217-225

HOOP, JOHANNES HERMANUS VAN DER

49092 Nieuwe richtingen in de zielkunde; het onbewuste en de persoon-lijkheid. [New directions in psychology; the unconscious and the personality.] (4th ed) Arnhem: Van Loghum Slaterus 1952, 240 p

HOOPER, H. ELSTON

49093 A Filipino in California copes with anxiety. Clin Stud Cult Confl 265-290

HOPKINS, PHILIP

49094 The general practitioner and the psychosomatic approach. Mod Tr PSM 1-28
49095 Psychotherapy in general practice. Lancet 1956, 271(6940):455-457

HOPKINS, PRYNCE

S-15144 A critical survey of the psychology of religion. Read Psychol Relig 46-61

HORA, THOMAS

49096 Beyond countertransference. PT 1956, 10:18-23
49097 Contribution to the phenomenology of the supervisory process. PT 1957, 11:769-773
49098 Ego oriented resistance analysis. R 1954, 41:263-266
   Abs JLan Q 1955, 24:614
49099 Existential communication and psychotherapy. NPAP 1957, 5(4):38-45
49100 Group psychotherapy in the rehabilitation process of the borderline patient. Int J grp PT 1957, 7:406-413
49101 Intrasystemic conflict: a metapsychological criterion of ego strength. PT 1954, 8:245-250
   Abs Rev Psicoanál 1955, 12:144-145

49102 Masochistic use of anxiety. PT 1953, 7:449-453
Abs JFr An Surv Psa 1953, 4:211-213. Rev Psicoanál 1955, 12:142
49103 Ontic perspectives in psychoanalysis. Psa 1959, 19:134-142
49104 Psychotherapy, existence and religion. PPR 1959, 46(2):91-98
49105 The structural analysis of transvestitism. R 1953, 40:268-274
Abs JFr An Surv Psa 1953, 4:235-236. JLan Q 1954, 23:462. Rev
Psicoanál 1954, 11:536

HORÁNYI, B.

49106 Über das Schweigen als Heilmittel. [On silence as a therapeutic agent.]
Z Psychother med Psychol 1959, 9:155-157

HORAS, PLÁCIDO ALBERTO

49107 Freud y el desarrollo de las teorías psicoanalíticas. [Freud and the
development of psychoanalytic theories.] San Luis, Argentina: Universidad Nacional de Cuyo, Facultad de Ciencias 1958, 48 p
49108 Orientación psicoanalítica de al educación. [Psychoanalytic orientation
of education.] Anales del Inst de Investigaciones Pedagóg, Univ de
Cuyo, San Luis, Arg 1957, 3:230-245

HORDERN, ANTHONY

S-15171A The response of the neurotic personality to abreaction.
Abs Colby, K. M. Q 1953, 22:465

HORKHEIMER, MAX

49109 Ansprache im Namen der philosophischen Fakultät der Universität
Frankfurt am Main. [Address on behalf of the Philosophical Faculty of
the University, Frankfurt am Main.] In Alexander, F. et al: *Freud in
der Gegenwart*, Frankfurt: Europäische Verlagsanstalt 1957, 31-35. In
*Reden gehalten in der Universität Frankfurt am Main anlässlich der
Wiederkehr des 100. Geburtstages von Sigmund Freud*, Frankfurt:
Klostermann 1956, 38-42
49110 (& Adorno, T.) Vorrede. [Foreword.] In Alexander, F. et al: *Freud
in der Gegenwart*. Frankfurt: Europäische Verlagsanstalt 1957, ix-xii

HORMIA, A.

49111 Ett fallav pseudologia phantastica. [A case of pseudologia phantastica.]
Nord Psykiat Medlemsbl 1957, 11:185-193

HORNEY, KAREN

49112 The basic conflict. In Gorlow, L. & Katkovsky, W. *Readings in the
Psychology of Adjustment*. NY: McGraw-Hill 1959, 311-316. From
author's *Our Inner Conflicts*, 34-37; 40-47
49113 (Moderator) Constructive forces in the therapeutic process: a round
table discussion. Psa 1953, 13:4-19
S-15184 Culture and neurosis. Under Hum Motiv 449-457
49114 The ever-tired editor. In Greenwald, H. *Great Cases in Psychoanalysis*, NY: Ballantine 1959, 187-200. From author's *Self-Analysis* [15229]

S-15207 The Neurotic Personality of Our Time.
        De Neurotische Persoonlijkheid van deze Tijd. Amsterdam 1951,
        243 p
S-15209 New Ways in Psychoanalysis.
        Neue Wege in der Psychoanalyse. (Tr: Neumann, H.) Stuttgart:
        G. Kilpper 1951, 319 p
49115   Occasional self-analysis. In Linscott, R. N. & Stein, J. *Why You Do What
        You Do*, NY: Random House, 1956, 274-289. From author's *Self-
        Analysis* [15229]
49116   The paucity of inner experiences. Psa 1952, 12:3-9
49117   The search for glory. Out Psa 1955, 369-385. In Moustakas, C. *The
        Self. Explorations in Personal Growth*, NY: Harper 1956, 220-231.
        From author's *Neurosis and Human Growth*
S-15229 Self Analysis.
        L'Auto-analyse. (Tr: Maroger) Paris: Stock 1953
        Rv David, C. RFPsa 1957, 21:607-609

        See Kelman, Harold

HORNSTRA, LEO

49118   Het Carmen-ballet van Roland Petit. [A psychoanalytic speculation
        about the Carmen-ballet of Roland Petit.] In *Kroniek van Kunst en
        Kultuur*, Amsterdam, Neth: 1954, 14(2)
49119   La fonction de la perception de l'aviateur. [The function of perception
        of the aviation pilot.] Schweiz Z Psychol 1955, 14:46-60
49120   Honderd jaar geleden werd Sigmund Freud in Moravië geboren. [A
        hundred years ago Sigmund Freud was born in Moravia.] Haarlems
        Dagblad, Haarlem, Neth 1956, April 7
49121   De mens in de organisatie van de arbeid. [Man in the Organization of
        Labor; a Psychoanalytic Approach of Industrial Psychology.] Amster-
        dam, Neth: Noordholl Uitg Mij 1951-52, 160 p
49122   Neurotische verhoudingen in de arbeidsfeer. [Neurotic relations in in-
        dustrial life.] In *De Betekenis der neurosen voor het arbeidsproces.
        [The Importance of the Neuroses in Industry.] The Hague, Neth:
        Dutch Soc Industrial Psychol 1953
49123   Psychologie van de belastingbetaler. [Psychology of the Taxpayer.]
        Leiden, Neth: Ned Uitg Mij 1953, 61 p
49124   Over de vermoeidheit. Een experimenteel onderzoek en enige beschou-
        wingen. [On fatigue. An experimental investigation and some theoreti-
        cal remarks.] Mens en Onderneming, Leiden 1955, 9(2-&3)

        See Sterren, H. A. van der

HOROWITZ, MILTON H.
See Furer, Manuel

HOROWITZ, WILLIAM S.
REVIEW OF:
49125   Brazier, M. A. B. (Ed) The Central Nervous System and Behavior.
        Q 1959, 28:545-547

HORST, M. VAN DER

TRANSLATION OF:
Josselyn, I. M. [49645]

HORST-OOSTERHUIS, C. J. VAN DER

49126 Het therapeutisch contact in de psychotherapie. [Transference in psychotherapy.] Ned Tijdschr Psychol 1955, 10(2):81-88
49127 Thérapie figurative. [Art therapy.] Evolut psychiat 1959, (4):585-593
49128 "Der Unbekannte:" Eine zentrale magische Figur ["The unknown one:"
A central magic figure.] Z Psychother med Psychol 1959, 9:1-8

HORTON, DONALD

49129 The functions of alcohol in primitive societies. Quart J Stud Alcohol
1943, 4:292-303. Pers n s c 680-690

HORTON, M. M.

See Senn, Milton J. E.

HORTON, WILLIAM D.

REVIEW OF:
49130 Reports and Symposiums, Vol. III. 1956-1959. Q 1960, 29:417

HORWITZ, WILLIAM A.

49131 Insulin shock therapy. Am Hdk Psychiat 2:1485-1498
49132 (& Polatin, P.; Kolb, L.; Hoch, P. H.) A study of cases of schizophrenia treated by "direct analysis." P 1958, 114:780-783
Abs Loeb, L. Q 1959, 28:424

HOSE, W.

49133 [Psychic factors in induratio penis plastica.] (German) Z PSM 1955-56,
2:20
49134 (& Cremerius, J.; Elhardt, S.; Kilian, H.) [Results of psychosomatic
research on diabetes.] (German) Psyche, Heidel 1955, 9:815

See Cremerius, Johannes

HÖSLI, L.

49135 Jugendträume als Künder eines aussergewöhnlichen Schicksals. [Child-
hood dreams as harbingers of an extraordinary destiny.] Schweiz ANP
1953, 72:77-133

HOSPERS, JOHN

49136 Free-will and psychoanalysis. In Sellars, W. S. & Hospers, J. *Readings
in Ethical Theory*, NY: Appleton-Century-Crofts 1952, 560-575
49137 Philosophy and psychoanalysis. Psa Sci Method Phil 336-357

HOTCHKISS, G.

See Lidz, Theodore

HOTKINS, ALBERT
See Scherer, Marvin

HOTT, LOUIS R.
See Sheiner, Sarah B.

HOUSTON, MARIETTA
See Allen, David W.; Bowman, Karl M.

HOVEY, RICHARD B.
49138 Psychiatrist and saint in *The Cocktail Party*. Lit Psychol 1959, 9:51-55

HOVLAND, CARL I.
49139 (& Janis, I. L.) (Ed) Personality and Persuasibility. New Haven: Yale Univ Pr 1959, 333 p

See Janis, Irving L.

HOWARD, THOMAS WILLIAM
49140 Diagnostic, physiological and Rorschach indices of anxiety. Amer Psychologist 1954, 9:396-397

HOWE, LOUISA P.
49141 Some sociological aspects of identification. Psa Soc S 1955, 4:61-79

HOWE, REVEL L.
See Farber, Leslie H.

HOYER, THOMAS V.
49142 Pseudologia fantastica. A consideration of "the Lie" and a case presentation. Psychiat Q 1959, 33:203-220

HSU, FRANCIS L. K.
49142A An anthropologist's view of the future of personality studies. Psychiat Res Rep 1955, 2:155-168
49143 (Ed) Aspects of Culture and Personality. NY: Abelard-Schuman 1954, xiii + 305 p
49144 Religion, Science and Human Crises. London: Routledge & Kegan Paul 1952, x + 142 p
       Rv MBr J 1953, 34:338

HUBER, G.
49145 Das Wahnproblem (1939-1954). [The problem of delusion (1939-1954).] Fortschr Neurol 1955, 23:6-56

HUCKEL, HELEN
49146 More than bread: six cases of compulsive eating. NPAP 1955, 4(1):53-63

49147 One day I'll live in the castle! Cinderella as a case history. Am Im 1957, 14:303-314
49148 The tragic guilt of Prometheus. Am Im 1955, 12:325-335
49149 Vicarious creativity. NPAP 1953, 2(2):44-55

HUEBSCHMANN, H.

49150 [On the pathogenesis of tuberculosis.] (German) Psyche, Heidel 1950, 3:741
49151 [The psyche and tuberculosis.] (German) Dtsch med Wschr 1951, 76:605
49152 [The Psyche and Tuberculosis.] (German) Stuttgart: Enke 1952
49153 [Social factors in disease.] (German) Beitr Klin Tuberk 1954, 3:555
49154 Von der Übertragung bei der psychischen Behandlung Tbc-Kranker. [On transference in the psychic treatment of tuberculotics.] Acta psychother psychosom orthopaedag 1955, 3(Suppl):145-149

HUFFMAN, P. E.

See Levinson, Daniel J.

HÜGEL, KÄTHE

TRANSLATIONS OF:
Balint, M. [41508]. Erikson, E. H. [8060]

HUGENHOLTZ, P. T.

49155 Enkele opmerkingen betreffende het bewustzijn. III. Over de luciditeit van het bewustzijn. [Notes on consciousness. III. The lucidity of consciousness.] Ned Tijdschr Psychol 1955, 10:485-498

HUGGLER, M.

49156 Die Überwindung der Lebensangst im Werk von Edvard Munch. [The overcoming of existential anxiety in the paintings of Edvard Munch.] Confin Psychiat, Basel 1958, 1:3-16

HUGHES, H. STUART

49157 Consciousness and Society: The Reorientation of European Social Thought. NY: Knopf 1958, xi + 433 p

HUGHES, HELEN MACGILL

See Grinker, Roy R.

HUGHES, R. E.

49158 Browning's "Childe Roland" and the broken taboo. Lit & Psychol 1959, 9(2):18-19

HULBECK, CHARLES R.

49159 Completeness-incompleteness: the human situation. Psa 1956, 16:54-62
49160 Psychoanalytical thoughts on creativity. Psa 1953, 13:84-86

HULDENFELD, KARL VON

See Caruso, Igor A.

HULETT, JAMES EDWARD, JR.

49161 Introduction to "Interdisciplinary relations in social psychology." In author's *Problems in Social Psychology*, 1-6
49162 (& Stagner, R.) (Ed) Problems in Social Psychology, an Interdisciplinary Inquiry. Urbana, Ill: Univ of Ill Pr 1952, viii + 271 p

HULL, JAMES

49163 Psychoanalytical problems in the writings of Aldous Huxley. Lib of Swiss Psychoanalytic Soc, Zurich 1955, May
49164 Remarks on counter-transference in the treatment of a chronic schizophrenic. Rosen Symposium, Cong Rep of 2nd Int Cong Psychiat, Zurich 1957, Sept, 4

HULL, R. F. C.

TRANSLATIONS OF:
Jung, C. G. [49678, 49685]. Neumann, E. [54990]

HULSE, WILFRED C.

49165 (& Durkin, H.; Glatzer, H. T.; Kadis, A. L.; Wolf, A.) Acting out in group psychotherapy. PT 1958, 12:87-105
49166 (& Lowinger, L.) Acute anxiety states and their treatment. Amer Practit Dig Treatment 1950, 1:926-932; 1024-1030
49167 The American adolescent girl in a changing world. (An experience in group counseling.) In *Growing Up in a Changing World*. London: World Federation for Mental Health 1958
49168 Behavior disorders in childhood—a challenging problem in general practice and public health. NYSJM 1959, 59:231-236
49169 (& Lowinger, L.) The child of school age. Amer Practit Dig Treatment 1950, 1:595-598
49170 The child-psychiatrist's function in foster home care. Foster Parents' News, Dept of Welfare, NYC 1957, 2(4 & 5)
49171 Childhood conflict expressed through family drawings. J proj Tech 1952, 16:65-79
49172 (& Davis, W. S.; Michal-Smith, H.) Children under stress in a pediatric clinic. Acta Paediatrica, Stockholm 1957, 46:32-42
49173 The child's reaction to parental "failure." Child Care Institute, Federation of Protestant Welfare Agencies, NY 1955
49174 Contributor to Brill, Norman Q. & Beebe, Gilbert W. *A Follow-Up Study of War Neuroses*, VA Medical Monograph, Govt Printing Off 1956
49175 Contributor to: *Psychiatric Consultation in the Family Service Agency*. NY: Family Serv Assoc of Amer 1956
49176 Contributor to Volmat, R. *L'Art psychopathologique*. Paris: PUF 1956, 109-115

49177 Dementia infantilis. JNMD 1954, 119:471-477

49178 Denial and infantilization: two pitfalls in the upbringing of blind children. New Outlook Blind 1958, 52:257-260

49179 Discussion: The struggle for ego boundaries in a psychotic child. PT 1956, 10:600-602

49180 Discussion: Guilt and the dynamics of psychological disorders. *Proceedings of the International Conference On Medical Psychotherapy, London, Vol. III.* NY: Columbia Univ Pr 1948, 52

49181 Discussion on the treatment of a schizophrenic adolescent. Jewish Soc Serv Q 1953, 30:278-281

49182 (& Carpentieri, J.; Bender, L.; Spencer, H.; Glickman, E.; Wechsler, D.; Herskovitz, H.; Young, R. J.; Rinehart, A. M.; Lourie, R. S.; Schmideberg, M.; Robinson, J. F.; Sontag, L. W.) Discussions. Round Table 5: Basic emotional factors in delinquency. In Karpman, B. *Symposia in Child and Juvenile Delinquency,* Wash: Psychodynamics Series 1959, 253-303

49183 Dynamics and techniques of group psychotherapy in private practice. Int J grp PT 1954, 4:65-73

49184 Emergency psychotherapy in general practice: The doctor and the patient: General psychotherapeutic considerations. Amer Practit 1948, 3(2):77-81

49185 The emotionally disturbed child. In Michal-Smith, H. *Pediatric Problems in Clinical Practice,* NY: Grune & Stratton 1954, 31-50

49186 The emotionally disturbed child draws his family. Quart J child Behav 1951, 3:152-174

49187 Freuds Geburtstagstisch mit Büchern. [Books on Freud's birthday table.] Aufbau 1956, 22(21):16

49188 Group approaches in the treatment of marital problems. III. Group psychotherapy. In Eisenstein, V. W. *Neurotic Interaction in Marriage,* NY: Basic Books 1956, 303-310

49189 Group psychotherapy and the First International Congress of Psychiatry. Grp PT 1950, 3:250-252

49190 Group psychotherapy at the Fourth International Congress on Mental Health, Mexico City, Dec. 1951—a communication. Int. J grp PT 1952, 2:270-272

49191 Group psychotherapy during and after the war. Proc Rudolf Virchow Med Soc 1947, 6:106-116

49192 Group psychotherapy in private practice. In Slavson, S. R. *The Fields of Group Psychotherapy.* NY: IUP 1956

49193 Group psychotherapy with soldiers and veterans. Military Surgeon 1948, 103(2):116-121

49194 Group therapy. In Wolff, W. *Contemporary Psychotherapists Examine Themselves.* Springfield, Ill: C. C Thomas 1956, 120-130

49195 (& Lowinger, L.) Hysteria and epilepsy. Amer Practit 1949, 4:135-141

49196 The impact of the environment on masturbation in children. In *Verhandlungen der deutschen Gesellschaft für Kinderheilkunde in Dresden, 1931,* Berlin: F C W Vogel 1932, 420

49197 International aspects of group psychotherapy. Int J grp PT 1951, 1:172-177

49198 On juvenile delinquency. In Karpman, B. *Symposia on Child and Juvenile Delinquency,* Wash: Psychodynamics Monograph Series 1959, 253-255

49199 Kurt Goldstein—80 years. Aufbau 1958, Oct 31

49200 Leben und Leiden des Doktor Freud. [The life and sorrows of Dr. Freud.] Aufbau 1954, 20(5):15-16

49201 The management of sexual conflicts in general practice. JAMA 1952, 150:846-849

49202 (& Lowinger, L.) Mother and child. Amer Practit Dig Treatment 1950, 1:139-141

49203 (& Lowinger, L.) The newborn infant. Amer Practit Dig Treatment 1950, 1:141-145

49204 Obituary, Ernest Jones. Aufbau 1958, Feb 21

49205 Observations on child development in a sightless world. In *Current Principles and Practices in Service to Young Blind Children,* NY: Guild for the Jewish Blind 1954

49206 (& Vergara, M. D.; Whitfield, R. E.) "On-the-spot" psychotherapy in a children's institution. Psychiat Q Suppl 1954, 28:121-130

49207 The physician and juvenile delinquency. NY Medicine, Editorial, Feb 20, 1958

49208 (& Murphy, J. J.; Simmons, A.; Vergara, M. D.) Preliminary report on the psychiatrically focused program of a temporary shelter for dependent and neglected children. J child Psychiat 1952, 2:285-301

49209 (& Lowinger, L.) The pre-school child. Amer Practit Dig Treatment 1950, 1:592-595

49210 Psychiatric aspects of the upbringing of severely handicapped children. Int Rev Pediatrics, Basel 1959, July

49211 Psychohygiene und Gruppentherapie. [Mental hygiene and group therapy.] In Federn, P. & Meng, H. *Die Psychohygiene,* Bern: Hans Huber 1949, 48-60

49212 (& Lowinger, L.) The psychologic treatment of children. Amer Practit Dig Treatment 1950, 1:588-591

49213 (& Lowinger, L.) The psychological management of the pre- and postoperative patient. Amer Practit Dig Treatment 1956, 7(6)

49214 Psychotherapy with ambulatory schizophrenic patients in mixed analytic groups. AMA ANP 1958, 79:681-687

49215 Psychotherapy with parent and child in behavior disorders of childhood. Sauvegarde de l'Enfance 1951, 181

49216 (& Lowinger, L.) The psychotic patient. Amer Practit Dig Treatment 1950, 1:706-716

49217 (& Greenwald, L. M.; Anchel, M.) Rehabilitation of a brain injured child with severe visual handicap. J Jewish Communal Serv 1958, 35:202-209

49218 Remarks on child psychiatry. Proc First Internat Cong Psychiat, Paris, 1950

49219 Remarks on group psychotherapy. Compt rend des Séances du Premier Congrès mondial de Psychiatrie, Vol. V. Paris: Hermann & Co 1950

49220 Report on various experiences in group psychotherapy. Jewish Soc Serv Quart 1948, 25(2). In *Group Therapy Brochure No. 28,* NY: Amer Grp Ther Assoc 1949, 203-224

49221 The role of group psychotherapy in preventive psychiatry. MH 1951, 36:531-547. In Proceedings of the Fourth International Congress of Mental Health, La Prensa medica mexicana, 193-204

49222 The role of the psychiatrist in child guidance. Medical News 1949, November

49223 (& Goldfield, R.) The role of the psychiatrist in child guidance. Amer OSE Rev 1951, 8(1):29-33

49224 (& Goldfield, R.) Die Rolle des Psychiaters in der Eltern- und Kinderberatungsstelle. [The role of the psychiatrist in the parent and child guidance center.] Gesundheit und Wohlfahrt (Revue suisse d'Hygiène) 1950, 30:557-563

49225 (& Reens, R. G.) Self-reporting in group therapy. R 1953, 40:117-124
   Abs Rev Psicoanál 1954, 11:535-536

49226 Das Sexualleben des Mannes. [The sexual life of man.] Schweiz ANP 1949, 64:507-512

49227 Sigmund Freud und der kleine Hans. (Eine Betrachtung über die Anfänge der psychoanalytischen kinderpsychiatrie). [Sigmund Freud and Little Hans. (Reflections on the beginnings of psychoanalytic child psychiatry.)] Die Heilkunst 1956, 69:154-156

49228 Sigmund Freud: Zum Ende der Centenar Feier. [At the end of the Sigmund Freud Centennial celebration.] Aufbau 1958, 24(4):15-16

49229 Sigmund Freud und die Gesellschaft im 20. Jahrhundert. [Sigmund Freud and 20th century society.] Aufbau 1956, 22(21):17-18

49230 The social meaning of current methods in group psychotherapy. Grp PT 1950, 3:59-66

49231 (& Slobody, L. B.) The socially and emotionally deprived child in institutional care. In *Management of the Handicapped Child*, NY: Grune & Stratton 1957

49232 Symbolic painting in psychotherapy. PT 1949, 3:559-584

49233 Symptomwahl der Kriegsneurosen. [Choice of symptom in the war neuroses.] MPN 1950, 119:286-306

49234 The therapeutic management of group tension. Ops 1950, 20:834-838

49235 Training for group psychotherapy in the U.S.A. and abroad. Int J grp PT 1958, 8:257-264

49236 Transference, catharsis, insight and reality testing during concomitant individual and group psychotherapy. Int J grp PT 1955, 5:45-53
   Abs GPK Q 1956, 25:453

49237 (& Lulow, W. V.; Rindsberg, B. K.; Epstein, N. B.) Transference reactions in a group of female patients to male and female co-leaders. Int J grp PT 1956, 6:430-435

49238 (& Lowinger, L.) Understanding the alcoholic. GP 1951, 3:35-40

See Blau, Abram; Davis, William S.; Stein, Aaron

HUME, PORTIA BELL

49239 Mental health: a discussion of various program approaches used in California and the basic assumptions involved. Calif Med 1957, 86:309-313

49240 A note on psychiatric developments in the San Francisco Bay area. P 1958, 114:926-930

49241   Proposed program for community mental health services. Brochure, State of Calif, Dept of Mental Hygiene 1954

49242   Report on Community Mental Health Services and Outpatient Clinics. *Second Partial Report, Senate Interim Committee on the Treatment of Mental Illness.* Community Mental Health Centers, Senate of the State of Calif 1956, 75-89

49243   The Short-Doyle Act for community mental health services: an informational brochure for the development of local mental health programs. State of Calif, Dept of Mental Hygiene 1957

49244   The Short-Doyle Act: its implications and implementation. Bull Los Angeles County Med Assoc 1958, 88(2):54-57

HUMPHREY, ROBERT

49245   Stream of Consciousness in the Modern Novel. Berkeley: Univ of Calif Pr 1954, vii + 127 p

HUMPHREYS, E. J.

49246   Widening psychiatric horizons in the field of mental retardation. In Crow, L. D. & Crow, A. *Readings in Abnormal Psychology,* Ames, Iowa: Littlefield, Adams 1958, 322-332

HUMPHREYS, LLOYD G.

See Sanford, Nevitt

HUNGERFORD, EDWARD A.

49247   Mrs. Woolf, Freud, and J. D. Beresford. Lit. & Psych 1955, 5(3):49-51

HUNGERLAND, HELMUT

49248   The aesthetic response reconsidered. J. Aesthet 1957, 16:32-43

49249   Selective current bibliography for aesthetics and related fields, January 1, 1954–December 31, 1954. J Aesthet 1955, 13:550-564

HUNT, FLORA M.

49250   Initial treatment of a client with anxiety hysteria: a case presentation. Smith Coll Stud soc Wk 1957, 27(3). Ego Psychol Dyn Casewk 174-182

49251   The neurotic client. Smith Coll Stud soc Wk 1957, 27:203-210

HUNT, JOSEPH McV.

49252   (Chm) Group discussion on Methods for Assessment of Change (b). Res PT 221-234

49253   (& Ewing, T. N.; LaForge, R.; Gilbert, W. M.) An integrated approach to research on therapeutic counseling with samples of results. J Couns Psychol 1959, 6:46-54

HUNT, ROBERT L.

49254   Aspects of a case of neurotic acting out. Bull Phila Ass Psa 1955, 5:33-42

        Abs Herman, M. Q 1958, 27:290

HUNT, SAMUEL P.
ABSTRACTS OF:
49255 De Monchy, R. Oral components of the castration complex. Q 1954, 23:144-145
49256 Rycroft, C. Some observations on a case of vertigo. Q 1955, 24:150-151

HUNT, WILLIAM ALVIN
49257 The Clinical Psychologist. Springfield, Ill: Thomas 1956, 206 p

See Caveny, Elmer L.

HUNT, WINSLOW
49258 On bullfighting. Am Im 1955, 12:343-353

HUNTER, DUGMORE
49259 An approach to psychotherapeutic work with children and parents. Proc 11th Inter-Clinic conf, Nat Ass for Mental Health, London, 1955
49260 Object-relation changes in the analysis of a fetishist. J 1954, 35:302-312
        Abs JFr An Surv Psa 1954, 5:200-201. Lebovici RFPsa 1955, 19:636. JLan Q 1956, 25:113-114
49261 Training in child psychotherapy. (Proc 4th Int Cong of Child Psychiatry, Lisbon 1958). A Criança portuguesa 1958, 17:185-196

HUNTER, R. C. A.
See Taylor, F. Kräupl

HUNTER, RICHARD A.
49262 (& Macalpine, I.; Payne, L. M.) The county register of houses for the reception of lunatics, 1798-1812. JMS 1956, 102:856-863
49263 (& Macalpine, I.) Follow-up study of a case treated in 1910 by "the Freud psychoanalytic method." M 1953, 26:64-67
        Abs SG An Surv Psa 1953, 4:18-20. Norman, H. F. Q 1954, 23:619

See Greenberg, P.; Macalpine, Ida

HUNTTING, I.
See Semrad, Elvin V.

HURKAN, JOHN
49264 To the end of thought. Cambridge Rev 1955, (4):232-280

HURLOCK, ELIZABETH B.
49265 Developmental Psychology. NY, Toronto, London: McGraw-Hill 1953, ix + 556 p
        Rv MBr J 1954, 35:373

HURVICH, MARVIN S.
See Beck, Aaron T.

HURWITZ, S.
See Jacobsohn, H.

HUSSONG, WALLACE B.
49266 Neurotic suffering in iatrogenic illness. Bull Camden County Med Soc 1955, 28(3)

HUSTON, PAUL E.
See Cohen, Bertram D.; Lowinger, Paul

HUTIN, SERGE
49267 Note sur C.-G. Jung et l'astrologie. [Note on C. G. Jung and astrology.] La Tour Saint-Jacques 1956, (4):124-125

HUTSCHNECKER, ARNOLD A.
49268 Love and Hate in Human Nature. NY: Thomas Y. Crowell 1955, x + 278 p
49269 The Will to Live. London: Victor Gollancz 1952, 278 p. New Rev Ed, Englewood Cliffs, N. J.: Prentice-Hall 1958, 292 p
       Rv Taylor, J. M. J 1953, 34:166

HUTT, MAX L.
49270 Actuarial and clinical approaches to psychodiagnosis. Psychol Rep 1956, 2:413-419
49271 (& Gibby, R. G.) The Child: Development and Adjustment. Boston: Allyn & Bacon 1959, xiii + 401 p
49272 (& Gibby, R. G.) Patterns of Abnormal Behavior. Boston: Allyn & Bacon 1957, 452 p
49273 Problems of supervision and training in clinical psychology. Round table, 1952. 7. Discussion. Ops 1953, 23:328-331
49274 Toward an understanding of projective testing. J proj Tech 1954, 18:197-201

HUTTEN, ERNEST H.
49275 On explanation in psychology and in physics. Brit J. Phil Sci 1956, 7:73-85
49276 The methodology of psychoanalysis. Brit J Phil Sci 1955, 6:78-88

HUTTON, LAURA
49277 The unmarried. In Neville-Rolfe, S. *Sex in Social Life.* NY: Norton 1950. In Krich, A.M. *Women.* NY: Dell 1953, 189-219

HUXLEY, ALDOUS
49278 The history of tension. Ann NY Acad Sci 1957, 67:675-684

HYDE, ROBERT W.
See Goldberg, Naomi

HYLAND, H. H.

49279 Disturbances of sleep and their treatment. Med Clin N Amer 1952, Toronto No.:539-555

HYMAN, HERBERT H.

49280 (& Sheatsley, P. B.) "The authoritarian personality"—a methodological critique. In Christie, R. & Jahoda, M. *Studies in the Scope and Method of "The Authoritarian Personality."* Glencoe, Ill: Free Pr 1954, 50-122

HYMAN, STANLEY EDGAR

49281 Freud and Boas: secular rabbis? Vienna Gaon; Tsaddik of Morningside Heights. Commentary 1954, 17:264-267
49282 Freud and the climate of tragedy. Partisan Rev 1956, 23:198-214. With title: Psychoanalysis and the climate of tragedy. Freud 20th Cent 167-185
S-15429A Maude Bodkin and psychological criticism. Art Psa 473-501
* * * Psychoanalysis and the climate of tragedy. See [49282]
49283 Some trends in the novel. College English 1958, 20:1-9
49284 The whole round world. New Mexico Q 1959, 29:277-291

HYPPOLITE, J.

49285 Commentaires sur des textes de Freud. Commentaire parlé sur la "Verneinung" de Freud. [Commentaries to texts by Freud. Spoken commentary to Freud's "Verneinung."] Psychanalyse 1953-55, 1:29-39
49286 Phénoménologie de Hegel et psychanalyse. [Hegel's phenomenology and psychoanalysis.] Psychanalyse 1957, 3:17-32

HYROOP, MURIEL HALL

S-15430 The factor of omnipotence in the development of paranoid reactions. Abs JFr An Surv Psa 1951, 2:190-191
49287 The significance of helplessness. PT 1953, 7:672-679
        Abs Rev Psicoanál 1955, 12:143

I

IBÉRICO, MARINO
See Delgado, Honorio

IDELSON, DAVID
49288 [Youth in Danger.] (Hebrew) Merhavia: Sifriyat Poalim 1956, 160 p

IFLUND, BORIS
49289 Selective recall of meaningful material as related to psychoanalytic formulation in certain psychiatric syndromes. Ph D thesis, U Calif 1953

IGERSHEIMER, WALTER W.
49290 Analytically oriented group psychotherapy for patients with psychosomatic illness. Part I. The selection of patients and the forming of groups. Part II. Int J grp PT 1959, 9:71-92; 225-238

See Freedman, Daniel X; Redlich, Frederick C.

IGERT, M.
49291 Introduction à la psychopathologie marocaine. [Introduction to the psychopathology of the Moroccan population.] Maroc méd 1955, 34:1309-1331
49292 Présence de Freud. [Presence of Freud.] Maroc méd 1958, 37(392) 21-31

IKEDA, KAZUYOSHI
49293 Obsessive symptom of neuroses. In *Progress of Psychiatry*, Tokyo: Med & Dental Publ 1957
49294 Psychopathological study on anxiety. Ann Rep of Educ Faculty, Kyushu Univ, Japan 1958, (5)
49295 Psychopathology of neuroses. J clin exper Med 1959, 36(4)
49296 Psychosomatic medicine observed from the viewpoint of psychiatry. Fukuoka Acta Med 1954, 45(9)
49297 Psychotherapy for Children. Tokyo: Keio Publ 1959
49298 Some considerations about neuroses. Kyushu Neuropsychiat 1955, 4(3-4)
49299 Study on neuroses. J clin exper Med 1953, 30(11)
49300 Study on neurotic children. Jap Med J 1958, (1766)
49301 Therapy of neuroses. Report 15th annual meet Jap Med Assoc 1959

IKEDA, YOSHIKO

49302 Hospitalism. Seishin Shintai Igaku Koza. [Psychosomatic Medicine, Vol. 3. Disease and Mind.] Tokyo: Nippon Kyobunsha Co 1957, 301-317

49303 [Play therapy.] (Japanese) J clin Pediatry 1954, 9(7)

49304 [Psychiatric study on benzedrine addiction among children.] (Japanese) J mental Health 1953, 1

49305 [Psychiatric study on institutionalized infants. A. Physical and mental development. B. Social maturity and speech. C. Initial reaction and chronic reaction. D. Experimental psychological study.] (Japanese) J mental Health 1955, 3:42-99

49306 [Psychoanalysis and Education.] (Japanese) Tokyo: Shinkokaku Publ Co 1955, 238 p

49307 [Psychotherapy of a child with phobia.] (Japanese) J mental Health 1957, 5:1-44

49308 [Study on hospitalism.] (Japanese) J mental Health 1954, 2:30-59

See Imura, Tsunero

IKIN, ALICE GRAHAM

49309 New Concepts of Healing: Medical, Psychological, and Religious. (Amer Intro: Oates, W. E.) Rev Amer Ed. NY: Association Pr 1956, 262 p

ILAN, ELI

49310 [Analysis of a conflict in family education and its influence.] (Hebrew) Ofakim 1953, 7:242-250

49311 [The concept of "transference" of Freud and his pupils.] (Hebrew) Ofakim 1956, 10:156-159

ILG, FRANCES LILLIAN

49312 (& Ames, L. B.) Child Behavior. London: Hamilton 1955, 364 p

ILIFFE, ALAN

49313 Lessons of the conference for teachers of psychology. Sociol Rev Monograph 1958, 1:109-117

ILLING, HANS A.

49314 Einige Probleme der Gruppenpsychotherapie in Strafanstalten. [Some problems of group therapy in penal institutions.] Z Diagnost Psychol 1957, 5:288-294

49315 Einige Probleme der psychoanalytischen Gruppentherapie. [Some problems of psychoanalytic group psychotherapy.] Psyche, Heidel 1959, 13:215-228

49316 Freud and Wagner-Jauregg. A contribution to Freudiana. Am Im 1958, 15:267-273

49317 Eine historische Perspektive zur Gruppenpsychotherapie. [A history of group psychotherapy.] Z PSM 1956, 2:131-147

49318 Jung's theory of the group as a tool in therapy. Int J grp PT 1957, 7:392-397

49318A Psychoanalytische Gruppenpsychotherapie. [Psychoanalytic group psychotherapy.] Psa Vkb 1959
49319 Der psychoanalytische Lebensraum in Social Work. [The place of psychoanalysis in social work.] Die Heilkunst 1956, 69:164-169
49320 Transference role of the visitor in group psychotherapy. Int. J grp PT 1955, 5:204-212
49321 The "visitor" and his role of transference in a group therapy. J crim Law Crimin 1954, 44:753-758

See Bach, George R.

IMBERCIADORI, E.

49322 L'aggressività nelle psicosi. [Aggressiveness in psychoses.] Neopsichiatria 1956, 22:21-62
49323 Indagini preliminari sul sentimento di colpevolezza (metodo Snoeck-Cargnello) nei malati di mente. [Preliminary investigations on the guilt feeling in mental patients (method Snoeck-Cargnello).] Neopsichiatria 1958, 24:189-212
49324 (& Manganaro, D.) Del suicidio; rassegna sintetico-critica. [Suicide; a synthetic and critical review.] Riv Pat nerv ment 1955, 76:141-180

IMHOF, BEAT

49325 Bettnässer in der Erziehungsberatung. [Enuretics in child guidance.] Heilpädag Werkbl 1956, 25:122-127

IMPALLARIA, CONSTANCE

49326 The contribution of social group work. Round Table, 1954: The hospitalized child. Ops 1955, 25:306-312

See Jensen, Reynold A.

IMPASTATO, DAVID J.

49327 (& Berg, S.; Pacella, B. L.) Electroshock therapy: focal spread technic. A new form of treatment of psychiatric illness. Conf neurol 1953, 13:266-271

See Pacella, Bernard L.

IMURA, SYOZO

49328 [Some aspects of the neuroses of marriageable females.] (Japanese) Jap J Psa 1959, 6(1):27-31

IMURA, TSUNERO

49329 (& Ikeda, Y.) [Psychotherapy.] (Japanese) Modern Psychology. Tokyo: Nakayama Publ Co 1954

INGHAM, HARRINGTON V.

49330 (& Love, L. R.) The Process of Psychotherapy. NY: McGraw-Hill 1954, ix + 270 p

INHELDER, BÄRBEL

49331 Die affektive und kognitive Entwicklung des Kindes. [The affective and cognitive development of the child.] Schweiz Z Psychol 1956, 15:251-268

49332 (& Piaget, J.) De la Logique de l'Enfant à la Logique de l'Adolescent. Paris: PUF 1955, 314 p
The Growth of Logical Thinking from Childhood to Adolescence. NY: Basic Books 1958, 356 p
Rv Harle, M. Q 1958, 27:589-591. Kaplan, D. PPR 1960, 47(2):125-127

49333 Participant in symposium. In Tanner, J. M. & Inhelder, B. *Discussions on Child Development*, Vol. III. NY: IUP 1958, 223 p

See Piaget, Jean; Tanner, J. M.

INKELES, ALEX

49334 (& Levinson, D. J.) National character: the study of modal personality and sociocultural systems. In Lindzey, G. *Handbook of Social Psychology*, Cambridge, Mass: Addison-Wesley Publ Co 1954, 977-1020

49335 Psychoanalysis and sociology. Psa Sci Method Phil 117-129

See Hanfmann, Eugenia

INMAN, WILLIAM S.

49336 Clinical thought-reading. J 1958, 39:386-396
Abs HW Q 1960, 29:129

S-19452 Emotion and eye symptoms. Mod Tr PSM 224-241

49337 Emotional factors in eye disease. Trans Ophthal Soc 1955, 75:685-689

49338 Nine-monthly scleritis in a childless woman. M 1955, 28:177-182
Abs EMW Q 1956, 25:625

49339 Time and G.B.S. Concerning the death of George Bernard Shaw. The Portsmouth Reader 1951, 14(2):17

INSTITUT FÜR PSYCHOTHERAPIE UND TIEFENPSYCHOLOGIE

49340 Im Kampf mit der Neurose. [Fighting Neurosis.] Stuttgart: Ernst Klett 1957, 224 p

INWOOD, EUGENE R.

49341 Leadership and the incidence of trench foot. U S Armed Forces Med J 1952, 3:1795-1800

49342 The problem of the hostile relative. U S Armed Forces Med J 1953, 4:1734-1747. Child-Fam Dig 1954, 10(3):53-67

49343 A procedure for the systematic analysis of psychotherapeutic interviews. Ps 1954, 17:337-345

49344 Psychiatric casualties evacuated from Korea. U S Armed Forces Med J 1952, 3:991-1001

49345 The role of the leader in the prevention of disease. Army Stress Symposium, March 1953, 261-267

49346 Therapeutic interviewing of hostile relatives. P 1952, 109:455-459

See Eldred, Stanley H.

IRONS, LUCIA

49347 Discussion (of symposium on learning problems). Ops 1959, 29:333-336

IRVINE, E. E.

49348 The ordeal of motherhood. Brit J psychiat soc Wk 1953, (7):3-6
49349 Research into problem families: theoretical questions arising from Dr. Blacker's investigations. Brit J psychiat soc Wk 1954 (9):24-33
49350 Transference and reality in the casework relationship. Brit J psychiat soc Wk 1956, 3(4):15-24
49351 The use of small group discussions in the teaching of human relations and mental health. Brit J psychiat soc Wk 1959, 5:26-30

IRWIN, ORVIS C.

See Brodbeck, Arthur J.

ISAACS, NATHAN

S-15476 Methodology and research in psycho-pathology.
Abs NRo An Surv Psa 1951, 2:48-49

ISAACS, SUSAN

S-15486 The Children We Teach
Rv Pichon-Rivière, A. A. de. Rev Psicoanál 1953, 10:503-504; 1958, 15:143-144
S-15494 The educational value of the nursery school.
Rv Pichon-Rivière, A. A. de. Rev Psicoanál 1958, 15:111
S-15497 Fatherless children.
Rv Morera, M. E. Rev Psicoanál 1958, 15:118
S-15504 Intellectual Growth in Young Children.
Rv Morera, M. E. Rev Psicoanál 1958, 15:107-108
S-15507 The mental hygiene of the preschool child.
Rv Morera, M. E. Rev Psicoanál 1958, 15:116
S-15513 The Nursery Years.
Rv Pichon-Rivière, A. A. de. Rev Psicoanál 1958, 15:111-113
S-15518 Property and possessiveness.
Rv Morera, M. E. Rev Psicoanál 1953, 10:524
49352 Rebellious and defiant children. In author's *Childhood and After*, 23
Rv Pichon-Rivière, E. Rev Psicoanál 1953, 10:522-523
S-15523 Recent advances in the psychology of young children.
Rv Morera, M. E. Rev Psicoanál 1958, 15:117-118
S-15526 Social Development in Young Children.
Rv Morera, M. E. Rev Psicoanál 1958, 15:108
S-15529 A special mechanism in a schizoid boy.
Rv Morera, M. E. Rev Psicoanál 1953, 10:523-524
S-15530 Temper tantrums in early childhood and their relation to internal objects.
Rv Pichon-Rivière, E. Rev Psicoanál 1954, 11:409; 1958, 15:118-119

S-15532 Troubles of Children and Parents.
>Parents et Enfants, Leurs Difficultés Quotidiennes. Paris: PUF 1953
Rv Pichon-Rivière, A. A. de. Rev Psicoanál 1953, 10:502-503; 1958, 15:131-132

ISAKOWER, OTTO

49353 Spoken words in dreams: a preliminary communication. (Read at Amer Psa Ass, NY, Dec 1948) Q 1954, 23:1-6
Abs JFr An Surv Psa 1954, 5:216-217. JKl J 1955, 36:421

ISCOE, IRA

49354 Some problems of mental hygiene research with children. MH, NY 1953, 37:441-444

ISHAM, A. CHAPMAN

49355 The ego and identification. PT 1955, 9:18-26
49356 The ego, consciousness, motor processes, and thought. R 1955, 42:61-71
Abs JLan Q 1956, 25:444-445
49357 Ego movement and identification. R 1956, 43:1-17
Abs Auth Q 1957, 26:435
49358 Emotion, instinct, and pain-pleasure. R 1954, 41:99-113
Abs JLan Q 1955, 24:466
49359 Imitation and identification. R 1956, 43:397-410
Abs JLan Q 1958, 27:128
49360 William James and the ego problem. PT 1953, 7:217-224

ISRAEL, HYMAN A.

See Kubie, Lawrence S.

IVANCICH, P.

49361 Aspectos del significado del canto a través de una sesión psicoanalítica. [Aspects of the meaning of singing during a psychoanalytical interview.] Rev Psicoanál 1954, 11:463-467
Abs NRo An Surv Psa 1954, 5:293

IVERSEN, TORBEN

See Bruch, Hilde

IVERSON, MARVIN A.

49362 (& Reuter, M. E.) Ego involvement as an experimental variable. Psychol Rep 1956, 2:147-181

IVEY, EVELYN P.

49363 Recent advances in the psychiatric diagnosis and treatment of phobias. PT 1959, 13:35-49

IVIMEY, MURIEL

S-15606 How does analysis help? In Linscott, R. N. & Stein, J. Why You Do What You Do, NY: Random House, 1956, 290-305

IZNER, SANFORD M.

49364 On the appearance of primal scene content in dreams. J Am Psa Ass
1959, 7:317-328
      Abs Shentoub RFPsa 1959, 23:533. McLaughlin, J. T. Q 1960,
29:593-594. Rv Morera, M. E. Rev Psicoanál 1959, 16:270-271
49365 (& Warshaw, L.; Leiser, R.; Sterne, S. B.) The clinical significance and
theory of sodium amytal Rorschach testing. J proj Techn 1954, 18:248-
251
49366 (& Goldman, J.; Leiser, R.) Hysterical amnesia treated by hypnosis
(psychiatric and psychological aspects). Dis nerv Syst 1953, 14:313-
315

J

JACKEL, MERL M.

ABSTRACTS OF:

49367 Brody, S. On the self-rocking of infants. Q 1959, 28:443-445
49368 Bychowski, G. The release of internal images. Q 1957, 26:148-150
49369 Durkin, H. E. Clinical management of masochism. Q 1958, 27:606
49370 Falstein, E. I. et al: Anorexia nervosa in the male child. Q 1958, 27:605
49371 Furer, M. et al: Internalized objects in children. Q 1958, 27:606
49372 Jacobson, E. Depersonalization. Q 1958, 27:626-628
49373 Levy, D. M. Capacity and motivation. Q 1958, 27:605
49374 Rexford, E. N. & Van Amerongen, S. T. The influence of unsolved maternal oral conflicts upon impulsive acting out in young children. Q 1958, 27:605-606
49375 Spiegel, L. A. Self, self-feeling, and perception. Q 1959, 28:445-447

JACKSON, DONALD DE AVILA

49376 The changing role of psychiatry in multi-disciplinary research. Program Guide, Psychiatry and Neurology Service, Office of the Chief Medical Director, Veterans Administration, Washington 25, D. C., June 1, 1955
49377 Countertransference and psychotherapy. Prog PT 1956, 1:234-238
49378 A critique of the literature on the genetics of schizophrenia. In author's *The Etiology of Schizophrenia*, 37-87
49379 An episode of sleepwalking. J Am Psa Ass 1954, 2:503-508
      Abs JFr An Surv Psa 1954, 5:126-127. TFr J 1955, 36:428. Shentoub RFPsa 1955, 19:501. MGr Q 1957, 26:137
49380 (Ed) The Etiology of Schizophrenia. NY: Basic Books 1960, 456 p
49381 Family interaction, family homeostasis and some implications for conjoint family psychotherapy. Sci Psa 1959, 2:112-141
49382 [Contribution to panel review on] The family in psychotherapy. Sci Psa 1959, 2:211-212
49383 Family and sexuality. In Whitaker, C. A. *Psychotherapy of Chronic Schizophrenic Patients*, Boston: Little, Brown 1958, 110-143
49384 Guilt and the control of pleasure in schizoid personalities. M 1958, 31:124-130
      Abs Weiss, J. Q 1959, 28:433-434
49385 The managing of acting out in a borderline personality. Case St Couns PT 168-189

49386 A note on the importance of trauma in the genesis of schizophrenia. Ps 1957, 20:181-184
49387 Office treatment of ambulatory schizophrenics. Calif Med 1954, 81:263-267
49389 A psychiatrist answers his critics. Med Econ 1955, August
49390 (& Block, J.; Block, J.; Patterson, V.) Psychiatrists' conceptions of the schizophrenogenic parent. AMA ANP 1958, 79:448-459
49391 The psychosomatic factors in ulcerative colitis. PSM 1946, 8:278-280
49392 Psychotherapy for schizophrenia. Scient Amer 1953, 188 (Jan):58
49393 Some factors influencing the Oedipus complex. (Read at San Francisco Psa Soc, Jan 11, 1954; Amer Psa Ass May 1, 1954) Q 1954, 23:566-581
       Abs JFr An Surv Psa 1954, 5:161-164. JKl J 1955, 36:426. Rev. Psicoanál 1955, 12:312
49394 Suicide. Sci Amer 1954, 191(5):88-96
49395 Suicide and the physician. The Prescribed 1955, March
49396 Theories of suicide. In Schneidman, E. S. & Farberow, N. L. *Clues to Suicide,* NY, London, Toronto: Blakiston Div, McGraw-Hill 1957, 11-21
49397 The therapeutic uses of hypnosis. Stanford med Bull 1944, 2(Nov):193
49398 The therapist's personality in the therapy of schizophrenics. AMA ANP 1955, 74:292-299
49399 (& Bateson, G.; Haley, J.; Weakland, J. H.) Towards a theory of schizophrenia. Behav Sci 1956, 1(3)

REVIEW OF:
49400 Perry, J. W. The Self in Psychotic Process. Q 1955, 24:138-140

JACKSON, EDGAR NEWMAN

49401 Understanding Grief: Its Roots, Dynamics, and Treatment. NY: Abingdon Pr 1957, 255 p

JACKSON, EDITH B.

49402 Child development patterns in the United States and childbirth patterns in the United States. In Soddy, K. *Mental Health and Infant Development,* Vol. I. London: Routledge & Kegan Paul 1955
49403 The development of rooming-in at Yale. Yale J Biol & Med 1953, 25(June)
S-15623 (& Klatskin, E. H.; Wilkin, L. C.) Early child development in relation to degree of flexibility of maternal attitude.
       Abs NRo An Surv Psa 1952, 3:210-214. RTh J 1953, 34:282
S-15624 (& Trainham, G.) (Ed) Family Centered Maternity and Infant Care. Rv Briehl, M. H. Q 1954, 23:122-126
49404 New trends in maternity care. Am J Nursing 1955, 55(5)
49405 (& Wilkin, L. C.; Auerbach, H.) Statistical report on incidence and duration of breast feeding in relation to personal-social and hospital maternity factors. Pediatrics 1956, 17:700-715

See Barnes, George R.; Freedman, Lawrence Z.; Klatskin, Ethylyn H.; Wessel, Morris A.

JACKSON, JAMES

49406 (& Grotjahn, M.) The concurrent psychotherapy of a latent schizophrenic and his wife. Ps 1959, 22:153-160
Rv Euredjian Rev Psicoanál 1959, 16:274

49407 (& Grotjahn, M.) The efficacy of group therapy in a case of marriage neurosis. Int J grp PT 1959, 9:420-428
Abs GPK Q 1960, 29:598

49408 (& Grotjahn, M.) The re-enactment of the marriage neurosis in group psychotherapy. JNMD 1958, 127:503-510

49409 (& Grotjahn, M.) The treatment of oral defenses by combined individual and group psychotherapy. Int J grp PT 1958, 8:373-382

See Grotjahn, Martin

JACKSON, JOAN K.

See Ripley, Herbert S.

JACKSON, JOHN HUGHLINGS

49410 Selected Writings. (Ed: Taylor, J.; Holmes, G.; Walshe, F. M. R.) Vol. I: On Epilepsy and Epileptiform Convulsions. Vol. II: Evolution and Dissolution of the Nervous System, Speech, Various Papers, Addresses and Lectures. NY: Basic Books 1958
Rv Woodhead, B. J 1960, 41:82-83

JACKSON, LYDIA

49411 Aggression and Its Interpretation. London: Methuen 1954, 237 p
Rv Philips, F. J 1955, 36:362

49412 "Non-speaking children." M 1950, 23:87-100

49413 Non-speaking children: seven years later. M 1958, 31:92-103

49414 A Test of Family Attitudes. London: Methuen 1952, 37 p
Rv Hardcastle, D. N. J 1953, 34:347; Rev Psicoanál 1959, 15:160

JACKSON, M.

See Plaut, Alfred B. J.

JACOB, W.

49415 Erfahrungen mit der Narkoanalyse als diagnostische und therapeutische Methode. [Experiences with narcoanalysis as diagnostic and therapeutic method.] Psychiat Neurol med Psychol, Leipzig 1953, 5:355-358

JACOBI, JOLANDE

49416 A case of writer's cramp. Case St Couns PT 111-140

49417 Complex, Archetype, Symbol in the Psychology of C. G. Jung. NY: Pantheon Books 1959, xii + 236 p

49418 Editor of Psychological Reflections. An Anthology of the Writings of C. G. Jung.

49419 Freud und Jung. [Freud and Jung.] Neue Zürcher Zeitung 1956, May 6

49420 Versuch einer Abgrenzung der wichtigsten Konzeptionen C. G. Jungs
       von denen S. Freuds. [An attempted differentiation of the most im-
       portant ideas of C. G. Jung from those of S. Freud.] Psyche, Heidel
       1955, 9:261-278

JACOBS, ALFRED

49421 Responses of normals and mental hospital patients to freudian sexual
       symbols. J consult Psychol 1954, 18:454

JACOBS, J. J. M.

REVIEWS OF:
49422 Bosselman, B. C. The Troubled Mind. J 1955, 36:361
49423 Caplan, G. (Ed) Emotional Problems of Early Childhood. J 1957,
       38:366-367
49424 Cohen, A. K. Delinquent Boys. J 1956, 37:491; Rev Psicoanál 1958,
       15:162

JACOBS, JAMES S. L.

49425 Cancer: host-resistance and host-acquiescence. In Gengerelli, J. A. &
       Kirkner, F. J. *The Psychological Variables in Human Cancer*, Berkeley
       & Los Angeles: Univ of Calif Pr 1954, 128-135

JACOBS, MELVILLE

49426 The Content and Style of an Oral Literature. Clackamas Chinook
       Myths and Tales. Chicago: Univ of Chicago Pr 1959, viii + 285 p

JACOBS, R.

49427 Tiefenpsychologische Aspekte von Märchenmotiven. Diskussionsbe-
       merkungen zu diesem Thema. [Depth psychologic aspects of fairy tale
       themes. Discussional remarks on the subject.] Prax Kinderpsychol 1956,
       5:313-314

JACOBSEN, CARLYLE

See Whitehorn, John C.

JACOBSOHN, H.

S-15656A (& Franz, M. L. von; Hurwitz, S.) Zeitlose Dokumente der Seele.
       Rv Zinkin, J. R 1954, 41:388-389

JACOBSON, EDITH

49428 The affects and their pleasure-unpleasure qualities in relation to the
       psychic discharge processes. Dr Af Beh 38-66
49429 Contribution to the metapsychology of cyclothymic depression. In
       Greenacre, P. *Affective Disorders*, NY: IUP 1953, 49-83
49430 Contribution to the metapsychology of psychotic identifications. J Am
       Psa Ass 1954, 2:239-262
       Abs HAW J Am Psa Ass 1953, 1:543-547. JFr An Surv Psa 1954,
       5:97. NRo An Surv Psa 1954, 5:60; 64-67. Rev Psicoanál 1954, 11:532-
       533. TFr J 1955, 36:223. Galin, I. Q 1956, 25:616-617

49431 Denial and repression. J Am Psa Ass 1957, 5:61-92
    Abs Shentoub RFPsa 1957, 21:614. J 1958, 39:66. HW Q 1960, 29:278-279
49432 Depersonalization. J Am Psa Ass 1959, 7:581-610
    Abs Q 1958, 27:626-628
49433 The "Exceptions." An elaboration of Freud's character study. Psa St C 1959, 14:135-154
49434 Federn's contributions to ego psychology and psychoses. J Am Psa Ass 1954, 2:519-525
    Federns Beitrag zur Ichpsychologie und den Psychosen. Psyche Heidel
49435 Interaction between psychotic partners. I. Manic-depressive partners. In Eisenstein, V. W. *Neurotic Interaction in Marriage*, NY: Basic Books 1956, 125-134
49436 Normal and pathological moods: their nature and functions. Psa St C 1957, 12:73-113
    Abs RTh J 1959, 40:368
49437 Problems of infantile neurosis. A discussion. Psa St C 1954, 9:49-50
49438 On psychotic identifications. (Read at NY Psa Soc, June 9, 1953; at 18th Int Psa Cong, London, July 1953) J 1954, 35:102-108
    Über psychotische Identifikationen. Psyche, Heidel 1954, 8:272-283
    Abs Auth J 1954, 35:286. JFr An Surv Psa 1954, 5:97. Lebovici, S. RFPsa 1954, 18:459-460. NRo An Surv Psa 1954, 5:67-68. Wangh, M. Q 1954, 23:160-163, JLan Q 1955, 24:601
49439 The self and the object world, vicissitudes of their infantile cathexes and their influence on ideational and affective development. Psa St C 1954, 9:75-127
    Abs NRo An Surv Psa 1954, 5:68-77; 260. RTh J 1956, 37:212-213
49440 Sullivan's interpersonal theory of psychiatry. J Am Psa Ass 1955, 3:149-156
49441 Transference problems in the psychoanalytic treatment of severely depressive patients. J Am Psa Ass 1954, 2:595-606
    Abs NRo An Surv Psa 1954, 5:307; 344-345. TFr J 1955, 36:429. Shorr, J. Q 1958, 27:280-281

REVIEW OF:
49442 Cloward, R. A. et al: Theoretical Studies in Social Organization of the Prison. Q 1960, 29:577-579

JACOBSON, S.

See Redl, Fritz

JACOBS VAN MERLEN, T.

49443 De la psychothérapie des parents. [On the psychotherapy of parents.] Bull Assoc Psa Belg n.d. No. 21
    Abs Lebovici RFPsa 1955, 19:495

JAEGER, JACOB O. S.

49444 Mechanisms in depression. PT 1955, 9:441-451

JAEGER, MARTHA

49445 Reflection on the work of Jung and Rank. J Psychother relig Proc 1955, 2:47-57

JAFFE, B.

See Weiss, Edward

JAFFE, DANIEL S.

49446 Analysis of a repetitive dream with painful content. Bull Phila Ass Psa 1957, 7:50-55
49447 Colon surgery: some psychological implications for the patient. Am J Proctol 1955, 6:453-459
49448 Countertransference: its influence on a patient's capacity for awareness. J clin exp Psychopath 1954, 15:323-327
49449 Psychosomatic mechanisms in constipation and diarrhea. Am J Proctol 1957, 8:223-228

JAFFE, JOSEPH

49450 (& Slote, W. H.) Interpersonal factors in denial of illness. AMA ANP 1958, 80:653-656
49451 (& Kahn, R. L.) Psychotherapeutic techniques with electroshock patients. J Hillside Hosp 1958, 7:17-25

JAFFE, RUTH

49452 [The catatonic spasm of the lip.] (Hebrew) Harefuah 1956, 50:225-226
49453 [Gestation psychoses.] (Hebrew) Harefuah 1951, 40(6):81-82

JÄGER, OTTO

49454 Gegen das Lampenfieber. [Counteracting stagefright.] Der Psychologe 1953, 5:101-105

JAGGI, J. W.

TRANSLATION OF:
Laforgue, R. [51254]

JAHODA, GUSTAV

49455 Sex differences in preferences for shapes: a cross-cultural replication. BJP 1956, 47:126-132

JAHODA, HEDWIG

See Goldfarb, William

JAHODA, MARIE

49456 Conformity and independence. Hum Relat 1959, 12:99-120
49457 Current Concepts of Positive Mental Health. NY: Basic Books 1958, xxi + 136 p
        Abs Lowenfeld, Y. Q 1960, 29:122-124. ESt J 1960, 41:568

49458   Introduction. In Christie, R. & Jahoda, M. *Studies in the Scope and Method of "The Authoritarian Personality,"* Glencoe, Ill: Free Pr 1954, 11-23

49459   The meaning of "psychological." Proc nat Conf soc Wk 1953, 197-204

49460   (& Cook, S. W.) Security measures and freedom of thought. Yale Law J 1952, March

See Ackerman, Nathan W.; Christie, Richard; Cooper, Eunice

JAKOBSON, ROMAN

49461   (& Halle, M.) Fundamentals of Language. The Hague: Mouton & Co., 1956, 87 p
Rv Glauber, I. P. Q 1957, 26:548-551

JAMES, MARTIN

49462   Premature ego development. Some observations on disturbances in the first three months of life. (Read at 21st Int Psa Cong, Copenhagen, July 1959) J 1960, 41:288-294

REVIEWS OF:
49463   Freud, S. On Dreams. J 1954, 35:360-361
49464   Freud, S. Totem and Taboo. J 1954, 35:360-361

JAMESON, JEAN
See Ovesey, Lionel

JAMPOLSKY, PIERRE

49465   L'étude systematique du rôle des premières expériences sociales dans la psychogenèse de la personnalité. [A systematic study concerning the role of the first social experiences in the psychogenesis of the personality.] Rv Np inf 1959

49466   Psychologie et psychiatrie. [Psychology and psychiatry.] R Np inf 1959, (9-10)

JANCKE, H.

49467   Vom Sinn und Unsinn des Psychisch-Unbewussten. [Sense and non-sense of the psychical unconscious.] MPN 1953, 125:494-514

49468   Über die Verwendbarkeit von Träumen in der Psychotherapie (mit einem Exkurs über die Biogenese des Träumens, des Bewusstseins und des sog. Unbewussten). [The utilizability of dreams in psychotherapy (with a digression on the biogenesis of dreaming, consciousness and the so-called unconscious).] MPN 1952, 124:304-327

JANIS, IRVING LESTER

49469   Anxiety indices related to susceptibility to persuasion. ASP 1955, 51:663-667

49470   Attitude change and the resolution of motivational conflicts. Proc 15th Int Cong of Psychol, 1957. Acta Psychol, Hague, 388-389

49471   (& Field, P. B.) A behavioral assessment of persuasibility: consistency of individual differences. In Hovland, C. I. & Janis, I. L. *Personality and Persuasibility*, New Haven, Conn: Yale Univ Pr 1959, 29-54

49472 (& Hovland, C. I.; Kelley, H. H.) Communication and Persuasion: Psychological Studies of Opinion Change. New Haven, Conn: Yale Univ Pr 1953, 306 p

49473 Decisional conflict: a theoretical analysis. J Confl Resolution 1959, 3:6-27

49474 (& Williams, R.; Fisher, B.) Educational desegregation as a context for basic social science research. Amer Sociol Rev 1956, 577-583

49475 (& Astrachan, M.) The effects of electro-convulsive treatments on memory efficiency. ASP 1951, 46:501-511

49476 (& Feshbach, S.) Effects of fear-arousing communications. ASP 1953, 48:78-92. In Katz, D. et al: *Public Opinion and Propaganda*, NY: Dryden Pr 1954, 320-336

49477 Emotional inoculation: theory and research on effects of preparatory communications. Psa Soc S 1958, 5:119-154

49478 (& Milholland, W.) The influence of threat appeals on selective learning of the content of a persuasive communication. J Psychol 1954, 37:75-80

49479 Meaning and the study of symbolic behavior. Ps 1943, 6:425-439

49480 Memory loss following electric convulsive treatments. J Personal 1948, 17:29-32

49481 Motivational effects of different sequential arrangements of conflicting arguments: A theoretical analysis. In Hovland, C. I. *The Order of Presentation in Persuasion*, New Haven: Yale Univ Pr 1957, 170-186

49482 Motivational factors in the resolution of decisional conflicts. In Jones, M. R. *Nebraska Symposium on Motivation: 1959*, Lincoln, Neb: Univ of Nebraska Pr 1959, 198-231

49483 Personality correlates of susceptibility to persuasion. J Personal 1954, 22:504-518

49484 (& Feshbach, S.) Personality differences associated with responsiveness to fear-arousing communications. J Personality 1954, 23:154-166. In Crow, L. D. & Crow, A. *Readings in Educational Psychology*, Ames, Iowa: Littlefield, Adams 1956, 254-264

49485 (& Rife, D.) Persuasibility and emotional disorder. In Hovland, C. I. & Janis, I. L. *Personality and Persuasibility*, New Haven, Conn: Yale Univ Pr 1959, 121-137

49486 (& Chapman, D. W.; Gillin, J. P.; Spiegel, J.) The Problem of Panic. Civil Defense Technical Bulletin T.B.-19.2. (Prepared for the Committee on Disaster Studies of the National Research Council & National Academy of Sciences). Wash: U.S. Govt Print Off 1955

49487 Problems of theory in the analysis of stress behavior. J soc Issues 1954, 10(3):12-25

49488 Proposals for field research on the psychological impact of peacetime disasters. RAND Corp 1949

49489 The psychoanalytic interview as an observational method. In Lindzey, G. *Assessment of Human Motives*, NY: Rinehart 1958, 149-181

49490 Psychologic effects of electric convulsive treatments. I. Post-treatment amnesias. II. Changes in word association reactions. III. Changes in effective disturbances. JNMD 1950, 111:359-382; 383-397; 469-489

49491 Psychological aspects of vulnerability to atomic bomb attacks. RAND Corp 1949

49492 Psychological effects of atomic disasters. Industrial College of the Armed Forces, Wash, D. C. Pub No L54-134, 1954

49493 Psychological effects of the atomic attacks on Japan. RAND Corp 1950

49494 The psychological impact of air attacks: a survey and analysis of observation on civilian reactions during World War II. RAND Corp, Crisis and Disaster Study, 1949

49495 Psychological problems of A-bomb defense. Bull Atomic Scientists 1950, 6:256-262

49496 Psychological Stress: Psychoanalytic and Behavioral Studies of Surgical Patients. NY: John Wiley 1958, xiv + 439 p
       Rv Linn, L. Q 1959, 28:271

49497 (& Field, P. B.) Sex differences and personality factors related to persuasibility. In Hovland, C. I. & Janis, I. L. *Personality and Persuasibility*, New Haven, Conn: Yale Univ Pr 1959, 55-68

49498 (& Janis, M. G.) A supplementary test based on free associations to Rorschach responses. Rorschach Res Exch 1946, 10:1-19

See Hovland, Carl I.; Spiegel, John P.

JANIS, M. G.

See Janis, Irving Lester

JANOWICZ, RUTH

See Coleman, Jules V.

JANOWITZ, MORRIS

See Bettelheim, Bruno

JANSE DE JONGE, ADRIAAN L.

49499 (& Marsman, W.) Dualiteitsverschijnselen. [Duality phenomenon.] Ned Tijdschr Psychol 1956, 11:10-53

49500 De werkelijkheidsbeleving. [The experience of reality.] Ned Tijdschr Psychol 1956, 11:375-380

JANZ, D.

49501 [Rage and the onset of a convulsion.] (German) Psyche, Heidel 1949, 2:97

JANZARIK, W.

49502 Zur Differentialtypologie der Wahnphänomene. [The differential typology of delusional phenomena.] Nervenarzt 1959, 30:153-159

JAQUES, ELLIOTT

49503 The Changing Culture of a Factory. London: Tavistock Publ 1951, xvii + 341 p
       Rv Hardcastle, N. J 1953, 34:340-341

49504 The clinical use of the Thematic Apperception Test with soldiers. ASP 1945, 40:363-375. In McClelland, D. C. *Studies in Motivation*, NY: App Cen Cr 1955, 71-82

49505 Disturbances in the capacity to work. (Read at 21st Int Psa Cong, Copenhagen, July 1959) J 1960, 41:357-367

49506 On the dynamics of social structure: a contribution to the psychoanalytical study of social phenomena. Hum Relat 1953, 6:3-24

49507 Fatigue and lowered morale caused by inadequate executive planning. Roy Soc of Health J 1958, 78(5)

49508 Measurement of Responsibility. A Study of Work, Payment, and Individual Capacity. London: Tavistock Publ 1956, xiii + 143 p
      Rv Menzies, I. E. P. J 1957, 38:287-288

49509 Psycho-analysis and the current economic crisis. In Sutherland, J. M. *Psycho-analysis and Contemporary Thought*, London: HPI 1958, 125-144

49510 Psycho-pathology in industrial life. Ment Hlth, Lond 1959, 18, Summer:50-55

49511 Psychopathology in industry. Twentieth Century 1956, April

49512 Social systems as a defense against persecutory and depressive anxiety. New Dir Psa 478-498

49513 Standard earning progression curves: a technique for examining individual progress in work. Hum Relat 1958, 11(2)

REVIEWS OF:
49514 Mead, M. & Metraux, R. (Eds) The Study of Culture at a Distance. J 1955, 36:416-417
49515 Radin, P. The Trickster. J 1957, 38:429-430
49516 Roheim, G. The Gates of the Dream. J 1954, 35:362

JARAST, ELÍAS

49517 La receptividad incondicional prenatal transferida a la figura del analista. [Prenatal unconditional receptivity transferred to the analyst's figure.] Rev Psicoanál 1958, 15:80-85
      Abs Vega Q 1959, 28:435-436

49518 (& Rascovsky, A.) Vivencias prenatales en la transferencia. [Prenatal existence in transference.] Rev Psicoanál 1956, 13:512-516
      Abs Auth Rev Psicoanál 1958, 15:200

See Rascovsky, Arnaldo

JARAST, SARA G. DE

49519 El duelo en relación con el aprendizaje. [Mourning in relation to learning.] Rev Psicoanál 1958, 15:31-35
      Abs Vega Q 1959, 28:435-436

REVIEW OF:
49520 Pearson, G. H. J. Emotional Problems of Living. Rev Psicoanál 1958, 15:145

JARVIK, MURRAY E.

See Abramson, Harold A.; Lennard, Henry L.

JARVIS, VIVIAN

49521 Clinical observations on the visual problem in reading disability. Psa St C 1958, 13:451-470
Abs Resta Riv Psa 1959, 5:193-194. RTh J 1960, 41:654

JARVIS, WILBUR

49522 "When I grow big and you grow little." Q 1958, 27:397-399
Abs JKl 1960, 41:166

JASPERS, KARL

S-15742 Zur Kritik der Psychoanalyse.
Contributo alla critica della psicanalisi. [Criticism of psychoanalysis.] Arch Filos 1952, 37-46

JAUR, JEANNE MARIE

49523 Étude expérimentale sur le test de Zulliger. [Experimental study of the Zulliger Test.] Arch Psicol Neurol Psichiat 1953, 14:159-166

JAVITS, J. K.

See Kelman, Harold

JEANS, R. F.

49523A (& Toman, J. E. P.; Grinker, R. R.) Anxiety and other factors modifying electroshock seizure latency in man. Am J Physiol 1954, 179:647-648

JEKELS, LUDWIG

S-15770 Fehlleistungen im täglichen Leben. Psa Vkb 1957, 123-145
49524 On the psychology of comedy. Tulane Drama Rev 1958, 2:55-61
S-15788 Selected Papers.
Rv Shor, J. NPAP 1953, 1(4):77-80. Thorner, H. A. J 1954, 35:361-362. Weigert, E. Q 1954, 23:96-97. R 1954, 41:294

JENKIN, NOEL

49525 Affective processes in perception. Psychol Bull 1957, 54:100-127
49526 The resolution of perceptual ambiguity: a technique for personality diagnosis. Bull Marit Psychol Assn 1955, 4:21-31
49527 Some relationships between projective test behavior and perception. Clin Psych 1955, 11:278-281
49528 Two types of perceptual experience. Clin Psych 1956, 12:44-49

JENKINS, RICHARD L.

49529 Breaking Patterns of Defeat. Phila: J. B. Lippincott 1953, 266 p
49530 Motivation and frustration in delinquency. Ops 1957, 27:528-537
Abs Koenig RFPsa 1959, 23:167-168
49531 (& Hart, H. H.; Sperling, P. I.; Axelrad, S.) Prediction of parole success. J crim Law Crimin 1942, 33:38-46

49532 (& Hewitt, L.) Types of personality structure encountered in child guidance clinics. Ops 1944, 14:84-94. In Glueck, S. *The Problem of Delinquency*, Boston: Houghton Mifflin 1959, 101-108

See Hart, Henry Harper

JENSEN, ARTHUR ROBERT

49533 Aggression in fantasy and overt behavior. Diss Abstr 1956, 16:794

See Symonds, Percival M.

JENSEN, REYNOLD A.

49534 (Chm) (& Bremner, E. A.; Kessler, J. W.; Barnes, M. J.; Impallaria, C.; Rolnick, A. R.) The hospitalized child. Round table, 1954. Ops 1955, 25:293-318
   Abs DRu Q 1956, 25:448

See Warson, Samuel R.

JENSEN, VIGGO W.

49535 Evaluating the suicide impulse in the university setting. Lancet 1955, 75:441-444

49536 (& Petty, T. A.) The fantasy of being rescued in suicide. Q 1958, 27:327-339
   Abs Auth J 1960, 41:165. Dreyfus RFPsa 1959, 23:434-435. Rv Sapochnik Rev Psicoanál 1959, 16:276

JEROME, J.

49537 Psychologie aristotélicienne et psychologie contemporaine de la volonté. [Aristotelian psychology and the contemporary psychology of the will.] Suppl Vie Spir 1953, (27):446-468

JERSILD, ARTHUR THOMAS

49538 Child Psychology. 4th Ed. NY: Prentice-Hall 1954, 676 p
   Rv HRB Q 1955, 24:302-303

49539 Emotional development. In Carmichael, L. *Manual of Child Psychology*, 2nd Ed, NY: Wiley; London: Chapman 1954, 833-867

49540 The Psychology of Adolescence. NY, London: Macmillan 1957, 438 p

49541 When Teachers Face Themselves. NY: Teachers Coll. Columbia Univ 1955, 169 p

JESSNER, LUCIE

49542 (& Kaplan, S.) "Discipline" as a problem in psychotherapy with children. Nerv Child 1952, 9:147-155

49543 Discussion. Psm Cpt Psa 161-164

49544 (& Pavenstedt, E.) (Eds) Dynamic Psychopathology in Childhood. NY, London: Grune & Stratton 1959, xi + 315 p

49545 (& Lamont, J.; Long, R.; Rollins, N.; Whipple, B.; Prentice, N.) Emotional impact of nearness and separation for the asthmatic child and his mother. Psa St C 1955, 10:353-380
   Abs RTh J 1957, 38:297-298

S-16423 (& Blom, G. E.; Waldfogel, S.) Emotional implications of tonsillectomy and adenoidectomy on children.
Abs NRo An Surv Psa 1952, 3:222-226. WH J 1953, 34:280

49546 (& Sandifer, M. G., Jr.) Der gegenwärtige Stand der psychosomatischen Medizin in den Vereinigten Staaten; ein Überblick. [Review of psychosomatic medicine in the U. S. A.] Psychiatria et Neurologia 1958, 136: 260-308

49547 Some observations on children hospitalized during latency. Dynam Psychopath Child 257-268

JÉSUS-MARIE, P. BRUNO DE

49548 Psychologie des profondeurs ou psychologie des hauteurs? [Psychology of the depths or psychology of the heights?] Jb Psychol Psychother 1955, 3:258-262

JOËL, W. D.

49549 A glimpse at the group psychotherapy literature. Int J grp PT 1957, 7:191-195

49550 Transference reactions of chronic regressed schizophrenic patients in group psychotherapy. Acta psychotherap psychosom orthopaedag 1955, 3(Suppl):150-156

JOFFE, W. G.

REVIEW OF:
49551 Zilboorg, G. The Psychology of the Criminal Act and Punishment. J 1955, 36:410-411

JOHANSSON, ALLAN

49552 Psychotherapeutische Behandlung eines Falles von Schizophrenie. [Psychotherapeutic treatment of a case of schizophrenia.] Psyche, Heidel 1956, 10:568-587

JOHN, EVE S.

See Grummon, Donald L.

JOHNSON, ADELAIDE M.

49553 The adolescent and his problems. Am J occup Ther 1957, 11(4, Part II):255-261

S-16440 A case of migraine.
Rv Garma Rev Psicoanál 1954, 11:248-249

49554 Collaborative psychotherapy: team setting. Psa Soc Wk 79-108

49555 Discussion. Workshop 1955: School phobia. Ops 1957, 27:307-309
Abs KHG Q 1959, 28:566

49556 The emotionally disturbed child. Univ Mich Med Bull 1956, 22:98-109

49557 (& Szurek, S. A.) Etiology of antisocial behavior in delinquents and psychopaths. JAMA 1954, 154:814-817. Focus 1955, 34:44-49. With title: Parental sanction of delinquency, Child-Fam Dig 1955, 13(4):72-81

49558 Factors in the etiology of fixations and symptom choice. (Read at Chicago Psa Soc, Oct 28, 1952) Q 1953, 22:475-496
    Abs JFr An Surv Psa 1953, 4:138-140. NRo An Surv Psa 1953, 4:109-110. Rev Psicoanál 1954, 11:390-391. JKl J 1955, 36:219

S-16443 (& Szurek, S. A.) The genesis of antisocial acting out in children and adults.
    Abs JFr An Surv Psa 1952, 3:181-184. CR J 1953, 34:355

49559 Individual antisocial behavior. Amer J Dis Child 1955, 89:472-475

49560 Juvenile delinquency. Am Hbk Psychiat 1:840-856

49561 (& Giffin, M. E.; Watson, E. J.; Beckett, P. G. S.) Observations on ego functions in schizophrenia. Ps 1956, 19:143-148

49562 (& Burke, E. C.) Parental permissiveness and fostering in child rearing and their relationship to juvenile delinquency. Proc Staff Meet Mayo Clin 1955, 30:557-565

49563 Psychoanalytic therapy. 20 Yrs Psa 242-257

S-16446 (Reporter) Psychotherapy in medical and surgical hospitals.
    Abs JAA An Surv Psa 1952, 3:347-354

49564 (& Robinson, D. B.) The sexual deviant (sexual psychopath). Causes, treatment and prevention. JAMA 1957, 164:1559-1565. Child-Fam Dig 1957, 16(5):3-20

49565 (& Giffin, M. E.) Some applications of psychoanalytic insights to the socialization of children. Ops 1957, 27:462-474
    Abs KHG Q 1959, 28:567

S-16449 Some etiological aspects of repression, guilt and hostility.
    Abs JAA An Surv Psa 1951, 2:37-39; 114. NRo An Surv Psa 1951, 2:85. CR J 1953, 34:271

See Barry, Maurice J.; Beckett, Peter G. S.; Estes, Hubert R.; Giffin, Mary E.; Groethuysen, Ulrich C.; Kohlsaat, Barbara; Kolb, Lawrence C.; Litin, Edward M.; Ross, Helen; Szurek, Stanislaus; Watson, E. Jane; Williams, George E.

REVIEWS OF:

49566 Abraham, J. & Varon, E. Maternal Dependency and Schizophrenia. Q 1955, 24:300-302

49567 Cohen, A. K. Delinquent Boys. Q 1957, 26:267-268

49568 Grinker, R. R. & Robbins, F. P. Psychosomatic Case Book. Q 1955, 24:304-306

49569 Hoffer, W. Psychoanalysis: Practical and Research Aspects. Q 1955, 24:573-574

49570 Lorand, S. (Ed) The Yearbook of Psychoanalysis, Volume X. Q 1956, 25:263-265

JOHNSON, ALVIN

49571 Love of friends. In Montagu, M. F. A. *The Meaning of Love*, NY: Julian Pr 1953, 195-207

JOHNSON, CHARLES S.

49572 The influence of social science on psychiatry. In Grinker, R. R. *Mid-Century Psychiatry*, Springfield, Ill: C. C Thomas 1953, 144-156

JOHNSON, DEAN

49573 The understanding and use of the self in counseling. BMC 1953, 17: 29-35. In Vincent, C. E. *Readings in Marriage Counseling*, NY: Crowell 1957, 191-197

JOHNSON, DON E.

49574 A depressive retirement syndrome. Geriatrics 1958, 13:314-319
49575 A dream of fainting. Bull Phila Ass Psa 1954-55, 4:32-34
        Abs Herman, M. Q 1958, 27:133
49576 The neurotic character of a gentleman. Bull Phila Ass Psa 1957, 7:66-74
        Abs EFA Q 1958, 27:446-447

ABSTRACT OF:
49577 Waelder, R. The nature of brainwashing. Bull Phila Ass Psa 1960, 10:160-161

JOHNSON, HIRAM

49578 Psychoanalysis: some critical comments. P 1956, 113:36-40
        Abs DRu Q 1959, 28:123-124

JOHNSON, LAVERNE C.

49579 Body cathexis as a factor in somatic complaints. J consult Psychol 1956, 20:145-149

JOHNSON, M.

See Fineberg, Henry H.

JOHNSON, NAN L.

See Warkentin, John

JOHNSON, PAUL EMANUEL

49580 Jesus as psychologist. In Doniger, S. *Religion and Human Behavior*, NY: Association Pr 1954, 47-57
49581 Personality and Religion. NY: Abingdon Pr 1957, 297 p
49582 Psychology of Religion. Nashville, Tenn: Abingdon Pr 1959, 304 p

JOHNSON, R.

See Cohen, S.

JOHNSON, RUTH F.

See Sarvis, Mary A.

JOHNSON, VIRGINIA

49583 Child Psychology. Columbia, Mo: Lucas Bros 1953, 162 p

JOHNSTON, M. H. S.

See Phillips, E. Lakin

JOHNSTON, McCLAIN
ABSTRACTS OF:
49584 Albino, R. C. & Thompson, V. J. The effects of sudden weaning on Zulu children. Q 1957, 26:590-591
49585 Board, F. et al: Psychological stress and endocrine functions. Q 1958, 27:135-136
49586 Bowlby, J. et al: The effects of mother-child separation: a follow-up study. Q 1957, 26:591
49587 Dongier, M. et al: Psychophysiological studies in thyroid function. Q 1958, 27:135
49588 Engel, G. L. Studies of ulcerative colitis, IV. Significance of headaches. Q 1958, 27:136
49589 Fisher, S. & Cleveland, S. E. Relationship of body image to site of cancer. Q 1958, 27:135
49590 Freeman, T. Aspects of perception in psychoanalysis and experimental psychology. Q 1959, 28:132-133
49591 Greenberg, P. et al: Sir Kenelm Digby on *folie à deux*. Q 1957, 26:591-592
49592 Greene, W. A., Jr. et al: Psychological factors and reticuloendothelial disease, II. Q 1958, 27:134-135
49593 Groethuysen, U. C. et al: Depth electrographic recording of a seizure during a structured interview. Q 1958, 27:606
49594 Harrington, M. & Hassan, J. W. M. Depression in girls during latency. Q 1959, 28:134
49595 Knapp, P. H. & Nemetz, S. J. Personality variations in bronchial asthma. Q 1958, 27:608
49596 Knapp, P. H. & Nemetz, S. J. Sources of tension in bronchial asthma. Q 1958, 27:608
49597 Lyle, J. G. & Gilchrist, A. A. Problems of T.A.T. interpretation and the diagnosis of delinquent trends. Q 1959, 28:134
49598 Main, T. F. Perception and ego function. Q 1959, 28:132
49599 Menzer, D. et al: Patterns of emotional recovery from hysterectomy. Q 1958, 27:606-607
49600 Meyer, B. C. & Weinroth, L. A. Observations on psychological aspects of anorexia nervosa. Q 1958, 27:607
49601 Renneker, R. E. Countertransference reactions to cancer. Q 1958, 27:607-608
49602 Rubinstein, L. H. Psychotherapeutic aspects of male homosexuality. Q 1959, 28:133
49603 Sandler, J. et al: Patterns of anxiety: the correlates of social anxieties. Q 1959, 28:133
49604 Sandler, J. Psychosomatic pathology. Q 1959, 28:133

JONAS, H.
See Kelman, Harold

JONES, ARTHUR
49605 An infantile fear of Lincoln. NPAP 1953, 2(2):71-75
49606 Sexual symbolism and the variables of sex and personality integration. ASP 1956, 53:187-190

JONES, C. E.

49607   Homosexuality as a neurosis. Arch crim Psychodyn 1957, 2:949-953

JONES, D. S.

See Sarbin, Theodore R.

JONES, ERNEST

49608   The achievement of Sigmund Freud. The Listener 1956, May 10:589

S-16479A The achievements of Sigmund Freud. Current of the World 1956, Dec

S-16480A Address on the occasion of the unveiling of a plaque at the Salpêtrière in honour of Sigmund Freud. J 1957, 38:301

49609   Allocution. [Remarks (on Freud at the Salpêtrière).] In *1856-1956: Centenaire de la Naissance de Sigmund Freud,* Paris: PUF 1957, 9-10

S-16485A An anniversary greeting. ASP 1956, 52:290

S-16500B The birth and death of Moses. (Read at 20th Int Psa Cong, Paris, July-Aug 1957) J 1958, 29:1-4
        Abs JLan Q 1959, 28:106. Racamier RFPsa 1959, 23:153

S-16507 The concept of a normal mind. In Halmos, P. & Iliffe, A. *Readings in General Psychology,* NY: Philos Lib; London: Routledge & Paul 1959, 167-184

S-16512A The dawn of conscience. The Observer 1955, February

S-16513 The death of Hamlet's father. Art Psa 146-150

S-16523A The early history of psychoanalysis. JMS 1954, 100:198-210
        Abs WH J 1955, 36:224. Norman, H. F. Q 1955, 24:319-320

49610   Excerpt from the letter dated 26. 3. 54 to the President, Indian Psychoanalytical Society. Samiksa 1955 Bose Number, Special issue: 1.

S-16529A Les fiançailles de Freud. [Freud's engagement.] La Table Ronde 1956, Dec (108):11

49611   Foreword to Hitschmann, E. *Great Men: Psychoanalytic Studies*

S-16532A Free Associations: Memoirs of a Psychoanalyst. NY: Basic Books 1959, 264 p
        Abs J Am Psa Ass 1960, 8:589. Rv NR Q 1960, 29:243-244

S-16534A Freud and his achievements. BMJ 1956, (4974):997-1000

S-16534B Freud's early travels. (Read at 18th Int Psa Cong, London, July 27, 1953) J 1954, 35:81-84
        Abs Auth J 1954, 35:286. SG An Surv Psa 1954, 5:5-6. JLan Q 1955, 24:600

S-16539 The genesis of the superego. Out Psa 1955, 39-47

S-16542 Der Gottmensch-Komplex. Psyche, Heidel 1958, 12:1-17

S-16549A The inception of "Totem and Taboo." (Read at 19th Int Psa Cong, Geneva, July 1955) J 1956, 37:34-35
        Abs JLan Q 1957, 26:433

S-16560A The Life and Work of Sigmund Freud. Vol. 1. The Formative Years and the Great Discoveries, 1856-1900. NY: Basic Books, London: Hogarth Pr 1953, xiv + 428 p. Vol. 2. Years of Maturity, 1901-1919. NY: Basic Books, London: Hogarth Pr 1955, xiii + 512 p. Vol. 3. The Last Phase, 1919-1939. NY: Basic Books, London: Hogarth Pr 1957, xvi + 537 p

Extrait du livre d'Ernest Jones: La vie et l'oeuvre de Sigmund Freud. [An extract from Jones' "Life and Work of Sigmund Freud."] RFPsa 1956, 20:316-331

Vida y Obra de Sigmund Freud. Buenos Aires: Ed Nova 1959

Abs SG An Surv Psa 1953, 4:3-9. J Am Psa Ass 1956, 4:190.

Rv MBr J 1954, 35:359; J 1956, 37: 478-480; J 1958, 39:422-424. Cesio, F. Rev Psicoanál 1960, 17:116. RRG J 1954, 35:359-360. Levi, J. NPAP 1958, 6(1):74-77. Lowenfeld, H. J Am Psa Ass 1956, 4:682-691. Okonogi, K. Jap J Psa 1956, 3(9-10). Piotrowski, Z. A. R 1956, 43:121-123. Reik, T. NPAP 1955, 4(1):68-74. Rubins, J. L. Psa 1955, 15:83. Sulzberger, C. F. NPAP 1953, 2(2):77-80. GZ Q 1954, 23:250-259; Q 1956, 25:260-261; Q 1958, 27:253-262. Zinkin, J. R 1954, 41:299-401

S-16568A A modern Iphigenia. Tribune 1955, Nov

S-16574A Nature of genius. Sci Mon, NY 1957, 84: 75-83. BMJ 1956, 56 (Aug 4)

De la nature du génie. RFPsa 1957, 21:64-82.

La naturaleza del genio. Rev Psicol gen apl, Madrid 1957, 12:13-35

Rv Morra Riv Psa 1957, 3:224-225

S-16574B The nature of morality. The Observer 1955

S-16575A On the Nightmare. NY: Grove Pr 1959, 374 p

S-16583A Obituary J. C. Flugel. J 1956, 37:193-194

S-16597A Pain. J 1957, 38:255

S-16604AC Preface to Grinstein, A. *The Index of Psychoanalytic Writings*

S-16604AD Preface. New Dir Psa v

S-16604AE Preface to Lesser, S. O. *Fiction and the Unconscious*. Boston: Beacon Pr 1957

49612 Preface. Dr Af Beh 9

49613 Preface to Nacht, S. (Ed.) *La Psychanalyse d'Aujourd'hui*. Paris: PUF 1956, vii-viii

Preface. In *Psychoanalysis of Today*. NY, London: Grune & Stratton 1959, vii

49614 Psychoanalyse und religion. [Psychoanalysis and religion.] Psa Vkb 1957, 397-406

S-16668A Sandor Ferenczi's last years. [Letter to the editor: reply to M. Balint] J 1958, 39:68

S-16670A Sigmund Freud; Four Centenary Addresses. NY: Basic Books 1956, 150 p

Rv Lowenfeld, H. J Am Psa Ass 1956, 4:682-691. MBr J 1957, 38: 282-283. Niederland, W. G. Q 1957, 26:118-119

S-16596A Our attitude toward greatness. J Am Psa Ass 1956, 4:626-643

Abs TFr J 1957, 38:433

REVIEWS OF:

49614A De Forest, I. The Leaven of Love. J 1956, 37:488

S-16833A Doolittle, H. Tribute to Freud. J 1957, 38:126

S-16846A Collected Papers of Otto Fenichel. Brit med J 1955, Aug 13

S-16864A Freud, S. Interpretation of Dreams. (Ed: JS) Brit med J 1955, Nov 12. Rev Psicoanál 1959, 16:58-71

S-16872A Gemelli, A. Psycho-Analysis Today. J 1957, 38:127

S-16873A Glover, E. The Technique of Psychoanalysis. Brit med J 1955, May 21
S-16898A Hodin, J. P. The Dilemma of Being Modern. J 1957, 38:126-127
S-16932A Lee, R. S. Psychology and Worship. J 1955, 36:407-408
S-16976A Philp, H. L. Freud and Religious Belief. J 1957, 38:125-126
S-17023A Székely-Kovács, O. & Berény, R. Caricatures of 88 Pioneers in Psychoanalysis. J 1956, 37:470-481

JONES, H. GWYNNE

49615 Neurosis and experimental psychology. JMS 1958, 104:55-62

JONES, HAROLD E.

49616 (& Kaplan, O. J.) Psychological aspects of mental disorders in later life. In Kaplan, O. J. *Mental Disorders in Later Life*, Stanford: Stanford Univ Pr; London: Oxford Univ Pr 1945, 69-115; 2nd ed, 1956, 98-156

JONES, KATHERINE

49617 King Mark disguised as himself. Am Im 1959, 16:115-125

REVIEWS OF:
49618 Bottome, P. Alfred Adler, Apostle of Freedom. J 1959, 40:66-67
49619 Reik, T. The Creation of Woman. J 1960, 41:646
49620 Robb, J. Working Class Anti-Semite. J 1960, 41:570

JONES, LUCY

49621 Traitement d'une hystérie d'angoisse. [Treatment of a case of anxiety hysteria.] RFPsa 1954, 18:215-243

JONES, MERVYN

49622 Ernest Jones: Funeral Address. J 1958, 39:307

JONES, RICHARD M.

49623 An Application of Psychoanalysis to Education. (Introd: Kubie, L. S.) Springfield, Ill: C. C Thomas; Toronto: Ryerson Pr 1960, xi + 124 p
49624 The differential effects of negated word associations on ability to recall "Traumatic" and "Non-Traumatic" stimulus words. J proj Tech 1958, 22(1)
49625 Dr. Freud coaching at third. The Reporter 1955, Apr 21
49626 A model of transitional thought: organization. Am Im 1958, 15:3-39
49627 The negation TAT; a projective method for eliciting repressed thought content. J proj Tech 1956, 20:297-303

REVIEW OF:
49628 Marcuse, H. Eros and Civilization; a Philosophical Inquiry into Freud. Am Im 1958, 15:175-180

JONG, U. J. DE
See Bruyn, G. W.

JORDAN, JO H.

See Bogen-Tietz, Esther

JORSWIECK, EDUARD

49629 Analyse eines 12 jährigen, intelligenzgeschädigten Kindes. Ein kasuistischer Beitrag zur psychoanalytischen Technik bei Schwachsinn. [Analysis of a 12-year-old child with damaged intelligence. A case contribution to psychoanalytic technique in feeblemindedness.] Prax Kinderpsychol 1958, 7:251-254

JOSEPH, BETTY

49630 An aspect of the repetition compulsion. J 1959, 40:213-222
Abs Weiss, J. Q 1960, 29:584. Rv Tabak Rev Psicoanál 1960, 17:260-261
49631 Some characteristics of the psychopathic personality. (Read at 21st Int Psa Cong, Copenhagen, July 1959) J 1960, 41:526-531

REVIEW OF:
49632 Hartley, R. et al: Understanding Children's Play. J 1953, 34:337

JOSEPH, EDWARD D.

49633 Cremation, fire, and oral aggression. Q 1960, 29:98-104
49634 (& Balser, B.; Brown, F.; Brown, M.; Phillips, D.) Mental health workshop in a public school system. P 1955, 112:199-205
49635 (& Winkelstein, C.; Brown, F.) Some psychiatric observations of ulcerative colitis with report of a case. JNMD 1958, 127:51-57
49636 An unusual fantasy in a twin with an inquiry into the nature of fantasy. Q 1959, 28:189-206
Abs Dreyfus RFPsa 1960, 24:207-208. Rv Sapochnik Rev Psicoanál 1960, 17:263-264

JOSEPH, HARRY

49637 (& Zern, G.) The Emotional Problems of Childhood. NY: Crown Publ 1954, ix + 310 p
Rv EJA J 1955, 36:404. Leonard, M. R. Q 1955, 24:592-593. Rev Psicoanál 1958, 15:161
49638 Freudian psychoanalytic progress. Prog Clin Psych 1958, 3:107-124

ABSTRACT OF:
49639 Silbermann, I. A contribution to the problem of pregenital character disorder. Q 1955, 24:327-328

JOSSELYN, IRENE M.

S-17239 The Adolescent and His World.
Rv Spiegel, L. A. Q 1953, 22:441-442
49640 (& Simon, A. J.; Eells, E.) Anxiety in children convalescing from rheumatic fever. Ops 1955, 25:109-119
49641 Cultural forces, motherliness and fatherliness. Ops 1956, 26:264-271
Abs Koenig RFPsa 1957, 21:305

49642 The ego in adolescence. Ops 1954, 24:223-237
  Abs NRo An Surv Psa 1954, 5:266-269. MK Q 1955, 24:315
49643 Emotional Problems of Illness. Chicago: Science Research Associates 1953, 48 p
49644 The family as a psychological unit. Soc Casewk 1953, 34:336-343. Proc nat Conf soc Wk 1953, 183-197
49645 The Happy Child: A Psychoanalytic Guide to Emotional and Social Growth. NY: Random House 1955, 410 p
  Het gelukkige kind. (Tr: Horst, M. van der) Leiden: I. Stafleu 1958, 384 p
S-17246 (Reporter) Panel on child analysis.
  Abs EBu & NRo An Surv Psa 1951, 2:293-297
49646 A psychiatrist looks at adoption. In Schapiro, M. *A Study of Adoption Practice*, Vol. II, NY: Child Welfare League of America 1955, 9-20
49647 The psychoanalytic psychology of the adolescent. Rd Psa Psychol 70-83
49648 Psychological aspects of adolescence. Symposium 1955: Our young citizens: promise and problem. Ops 1956, 26:478-485
  Abs Koenig RFPsa 1957, 21:122
49649 Psychology of fatherliness. Smith Coll Stud soc Wk 1956, 26(2):1-13
49650 Psychotherapy of adolescents at the level of private practice. In Balser, B. H. *Psychotherapy of the Adolescent*, NY: IUP 1957, 13-38
49651 A type of predelinquent behavior. Ops 1958, 28:606-612
  Abs Van Dam, H. Q 1960, 29:143

  See Mohr, George J.

JOST, F.

49652 (& Weilgart, W.; Sin, W.) Zum Traumerleben im präpsychotischen Stadium. [The experience of dreaming in the pre-psychotic stage.] Wien Arch Psychol Psychiat Neurol 1955, 5:101-115

  See Geertz, U.; Weilgart, W.

JOURARD, SIDNEY M.

49653 (& Secord, P. F.) Body-cathexis and personality. BJP 1955, 46:130-138
49654 Ego strength and the recall of tasks. ASP 1954, 45:51-58
49655 Personal Adjustment: An Approach through the Study of the Healthy Personality. NY: Macmillan 1958, 462 p

  See Secord, Paul F.

JOUVE, PIERRE-JEAN

49656 Le Don Juan de Mozart. [Mozart's *Don Giovanni*.] Univ of Fribourg Pr 1942

JOYCE, JAMES M.

  See Koren, Louis

JUCOVY, M. E.

ABSTRACT OF:
49657 Winnicott, D. W. Transitional objects and transitional phenomena. Q 1954, 23:611-612

JUDAS, ILSE

49658 (& Falstein, E. I.; Mendelsohn, R. S.) The role of the psychiatrist in a well-baby clinic. Ops 1957, 27:621-629
       Abs Koenig RFPsa 1959, 23:168

See Falstein, Eugene I.; Goldstein, Irving M.

JUDSON, ABE J.

49659 (& Wernert, C.) Need affiliation, orality, and the perception of aggression. Psychiat Q Suppl 1958, 32:76-81

JUEL-NIELSEN, N.

49660 (& Linnemann, E.) Neurosestudier af tvillinger. [Studies of neurosis in twins.] Nord Psykiat Medlemsbl 1958, 12 (suppl 1):139-156

See Bruch, Hilde

JUNDT, PIERRE

TRANSLATION OF:
Daim, W. [43991]

JUNG, CARL GUSTAV

49661 Analysis of two homosexual dreams. Homosex 286-293
49662 The anxious young woman and the retired business man. In Greenwald, H. *Great Cases in Psychoanalysis*, NY: Ballantine 1959, 155-174. From author's *Two Essays on Analytical Psychology* [17459]
49663 The Archetypes and the Collective Unconscious. Collected Works, Vol IX, Pt 1. NY: Pantheon 1959, xi + 462 p
49664 Basic Writings. (Ed: Staub de Laszlo, V.) NY: Modern Library 1959, xxiii + 552 p
49665 Development of Personality. Collected Works, Vol XVII (Bollingen Series XX). NY: Pantheon 1954, viii + 235 p
       Rv Piotrowski, Z. A. R 1956, 43:252-253
49666 The development of personality. In Moustakas, C. E. *The Self: Explorations in Personal Growth*, NY: Harper 1956, 147-159. From author's *The Development of Personality*
49667 Dream analysis in its practical application. Out Psa 1955, 159-182. From author's *Modern Man in Search of a Soul*
49668 Flying Saucers. London: Routledge & Kegan Paul n.d., 184 p.
       Rv Home, H. J. J 1960, 41:83-84
49669 Foreword to Fordham, M. S. M. *New Developments in Analytical Psychology*
S-17347A Foreword to Neumann, E. *The Origins and History of Consciousness*
49670 Foreword to Schmaltz, G. *Komplexe Psychologie und körperliches Symptom*
49671 La Guérison Psychologique. (Pref: Cahen, R.) Geneva: Georg 1953
49672 Introduction to Perry, J. W. *The Self in Psychotic Process: Its Symbolization in Schizophrenia*

49673 Morte e rinascita. [Death and resurrection.] In Zolla, E. *La Psico-analisi*, Milan: Garzanti 1960, 76-79

S-17386 (& Pauli, W.) Naturerklärung und Psyche
 The Interpretation of Nature and the Psyche. NY: Pantheon Books 1955, vii + 247 p
 Rv Waller, H. R 1954, 41:389-390

49674 L'opposition entre Freud et Jung. [Opposition between Freud and Jung.] Concours médical 1954, 76:1771-1776

49675 Pathologic mind: the vast unexplored. In Beck, S. J. & Molish, H. B. *Reflexes to Intelligence*, Glencoe, Ill: Free Pr 1959, 90-100. From author's "On the psychogenesis of schizophrenia." [17410]

49676 The Practice of Psychotherapy: Essays on the Psychology of the Transference and Other Subjects. NY: Pantheon Books 1954, xi + 377 p

49677 Le Problème du Transfert chez Jung. [The transference problem according to Jung.] Paris: Libraire de l'Université 1953
 Rv Shentoub RFPsa 1956, 20:549-552

49678 Psyche and Symbol; A Selection from the Writings of C. G. Jung. (Ed: S. de Laszlo, V.) (Tr: Baynes, C. & Hull, F. C. R.) Garden City, NY: Doubleday 1958, 363 p

49679 Psychological Reflections. An Anthology of the Writings of C. G. Jung. (Selected, ed: Jacobi, Jolande) London: Routledge & Kegan Paul 1953, xxvii + 342 p
 Abs J Am Psa Ass 1955, 3:548. Rv Fairbairn, W. R. D. J 1955, 36:362

S-17416 Psychologie und Alchemie. 2nd Rev Ed. Zurich: Rascher 1952, 708 p
 Psychology and Alchemy. Collected Works, Vol. XII. NY: Pantheon Books 1953, xxiii + 563 p

49680 Psychothérapie pratique. Fondaments généraux. [Practical psychotherapy. General concepts.] Encéph 1952, 41:407-430

49681 Psychotherapists or the clergy. Pastoral Psychol 1956, 7(63):27-44

49682 On the relation of analytical psychology to poetic art. In Vivas, E. & Krieger, M. *The Problems of Aesthetics*, NY: Holt, Rinehart & Winston 1960, 162-179. From author's *Contributions to Analytical Psychology*, 225-249

49683 Il simbolo della croce. [The symbol of the cross.] In Zolla, E. *La Psicoanalisi*, Milan: Garzanti 1960, 79-92

49684 The source of religious experience. Read Psychol Relig 122-123. From author's *The Undiscovered Self*

S-17459 Two Essays on Analytical Psychology. (Tr: Hull, R. F. C.) NY: Pantheon Books 1953, ix + 329 p. NY: Meridian Books 1956, 347 p

49685 The Undiscovered Self. (Tr from German: Hull, R. F. C.) Boston: Little, Brown 1958, 113 p

S-17463 Versuch einer Darstellung der psychoanalytischen Theorie. 2nd ed. Zurich: Rascher Verlag 1955, 195 p

49686 A visionary rumour. J analyt Psychol 1959, 4:5-19

S-17468 Wandlungen und Symbole der Libido
 Psychology of the Unconscious; A Study of the Transformations and Symbolisms of the Libido; A Contribution to the History of the Evolution of Thought. (Tr & intro: Hinkle, B. M.) NY: Dodd, Mead 1957, lv + 566 p

49687 Welt der Psyche; eine Auswahl zur Einführung [The World of the
       Psyche.] Zurich: Rascher 1954, 165 p
49688 Von den Wurzeln des Bewusstseins. Studien über den Archetypus.
       [From the roots of consciousness. Studies on the archetype.] Zurich:
       Rascher 1954, x + 681 p

JUNG INSTITUT, ZÜRICH

49689 Studien zur analytischen Psychologie C. G. Jungs. [Studies on the
       Analytical Psychology of C. G. Jung.] 2 vols. Zürich: Rascher 1955

K

KAAM, A. L. VAN

49690 Phenomenal analysis: exemplified by a study of the experience of "really feeling understood." J ind Psych 1959, 15:66-72

KADIS, ASYA L.

49691 The alternate meeting in group psychotherapy. PT 1956, 10:275-291
49692 La busqueda de la figura paterna en psicoterapia y educación. [The search for the father figure in psychotherapy and education.] Criminalia, Mexico 1956, 22:318-322
49693 Early childhood recollections as aids in group psychotherapy. J ind Psych 1957, 13:182-187
49694 Early childhood recollections—an integrative technique of personality test data. Am J ind Psych 1953, 10:31-42
49695 Group psychotherapy. Prog Cl P 1958, 3
49696 The latency phase. Prog Cl P 1953, 1:361-368
49697 Re-experiencing the family constellation in group psychotherapy. Am J ind Psych 1956, 12:63-68
49698 The role of co-ordinated group meetings in group psychotherapy. Acta psychother psychosom orthopaed 1959, 7(Suppl):175

See Hulse, Wilfred C.; Lazarsfeld, Sophie; Wolf, Alexander

KAFKA, JOHN S.

49699 A method for studying the organization of the time experience. P 1957, 114:546-553
   Abs Dickes, R. Q 1959, 28:424

KAGAN, JEROME

49700 The child's perception of the parent. ASP 1956, 53:257-258
49701 The concept of identification. Psych Rev 1958, 65:296-305
49702 (& Mussen, P. H.) Dependency themes on the TAT and group conformity. J consult Psych 1956, 32:20-29
49703 The measurement of overt aggression from fantasy. ASP 1956, 52:390-393
49704 (& Sontag, L. W.; Baker, C. T.; Nelson, V. F.) Personality and IQ change. ASP 1958, 56:261-266

49705 Psychological study of a school phobia in one of a pair of identical twins. J proj Tech 1956, 20:78-87

49706 Socialization of aggression and perception of parents in fantasy. Child Developm 1958, 29:311-320

49707 The stability of TAT fantasy and stimulus ambiguity. J consult Psych 1959, 23:266-271

49708 (& Moss, H. A.) Stability and validity of achievement fantasy. ASP 1959, 58:357-364

See Moss, H. A.; Mussen, Paul Henry

KAGAN, NORMAN

See Goldsmith, Jerome M.

KAHANA, RALPH J.

49709 (& Weiland, I. H.; Snyder, B.; Rosenbaum, M.) The value of early memories in psychotherapy. Psychiat Q 1953, 27:73-82
       Abs Rev Psicoanál 1955, 12:135

KAHANE, MURRAY

49710 An experimental investigation of a conditioning treatment and a preliminary study of psychoanalytic theory of the etiology of nocturnal enuresis. Unpubl doctoral Thesis. Los Angeles: available from Grad Libr of Univ of Calif

KAHLER, ERICH

49711 The nature of the symbol. In May, R. Symbolism in Religion and Literature, NY: G. Braziller 1960, 50-73

KAHN, EUGEN

49712 Über Angst. [Anxiety.] MPN 1953, 125:519-525

49713 An appraisal of existential analysis. Psychiat Q 1957, 31:203-227; 417-444

49714 A marginal note on interpretation. P 1955, 112:393-395

See Redlich, Fredrick C.

KAHN, J. B., JR.

See Gottschalk, Louisa

KAHN, JACOB P.

49715 Treatment of a withdrawn girl. Ops 1953, 23:629-643. In Murphy, G. & Bachrach, A. J. An Outline of Abnormal Psychology, NY: Modern Library 1954, 79-105.

KAHN, MARVIN W.

49716 The effect of severe defeat at various age levels on the aggressive behavior of mice. J genetic Psych 1951, 74:117-130

49717 Infantile experience and mature aggressive behavior of mice: some maternal influences. J genetic Psych 1954, 84:65-75

KAHN, ROBERT LOUIS

49718 (& Fink, M.; Weinstein, E. A.) The Amytal Test in mental illness. J Hillside Hosp 1955, 4:3-13

49719 (& Fink, M.) Changes in language during electroshock therapy. In Hoch, P. & Zubin, J. *Psychopathology of Communication*, NY: Grune & Stratton 1958, 126-139

49720 (& Graubert, D.; Fink, M.) Delusional reduplication of parts of the body after insulin coma therapy. J Hillside Hosp 1955, 4:134-147

49721 (& Cannell, C. F.) The Dynamics of Interviewing; Theory, Technique, and Cases. NY: Wiley; London: Chapman & Hall 1957, 368 p

49722 (& Pollack, M.; Fink, M.) Social factors in the selection of therapy in a voluntary mental hospital. J Hillside Hosp 1957, 6:216-228

49723 (& Pollack, M.) Sociopsychological factors affecting therapist-patient relationships. (Read at Acad of Psa, Phila, April 1959) Sci Psa 1960, 3:155-168

See Goldfarb, Alvin I.; Jaffe, Joseph; Linn, Louis; Tarachow, Sidney; Weinstein, Edwin A.

KAHN, SAMUEL

49724 Psychoanalysis for Thirty Years. Vol V. Ossining, N. Y.: Dynamic Psych Soc Pr 1957, 417-674

KAHN, SHIRLEY

49725 (& Prestwood, A. R.) Group therapy of parents as an adjunct to the treatment of schizophrenic patients. Ps 1954, 17:177

KAHN, THEODORE C.

49726 Personality projection on culturally structured symbols. J proj Tech 1955, 19:431-442

49727 (& Giffen, M. B.) Psychological Techniques in Diagnosis and Evaluation. London: Pergamon Pr 1959, 200 p

KAHR, MADLYN

See Kahr, Sidney

KAHR, SIDNEY

TRANSLATION OF:
(& Kahr, M.) Nunberg, H. [24392]

KAIRYS, DAVID

49728 Conscience and guilt: a psychiatric view. Judaism Psychiat, 13-23

See Kaufman, M. Ralph

REVIEW OF:
49729 Marcondes, D. A Medicina e a Psicologia. Q 1953, 22:442-443

KAISER, HELLMUTH

49730 The problem of responsibility in psychotherapy. Ps 1955, 18:205-211. Adv Psychiat 234-246

Le problème de la responsabilité en psychothérapie. (Tr: Smirnoff, V.) Psychanalyse 1956, 2:257-268
Abs Usandivaras Rev Psicoanál 1956, 13:325

KAKETA, KATSUMI

49731 Psychoanalysis in Japan. Psychologia 1957, 1:247-252

KALDECK, RUDOLPH

49732 Group psychotherapy with mentally defective adolescents and adults. Int J grp PT 1958, 8:185-192
Abs GPK Q 1959, 28:432

KALFF, D.

49733 The significance of the hare in Reynard the fox. J analyt Psych 1957, 3:183-193

KALINOWSKY, LOTHAR B.

49734 Die neueren Entwicklungen in der amerikanischen Psychiatrie einschliesslich der Psychochirurgie [Newer developments in American psychiatry including psychosurgery.] Dtsche med Wschr 1955, 80:671-675
49735 Problems of psychotherapy and transference in shock treatments and psychosurgery. PSM 1956, 18:399-403
49736 Transference problems in connection with shock treatments and psychosurgery. JNMD 1955, 121:181-182

KALIS, BETTY L.

49737 (& Bennett, L. F.) The assessment of communication: 5. The relation of clinical improvement to measured changes in communicative behavior. J consult Psych 1957, 21:10
49738 The assessment of communication. IV: Role differentiation in a psychiatric patient. Am Psych 1956, 11:476
49739 (& Harris, R. E.; Sokolow, M.; Carpenter, L. G.) Response to psychological stress in patients with essential hypertension. Am Heart J 53:572
49740 (& Harris, R. E.; Bennett, L. F.; Sokolow, M.) Psychosomatic predisposition and ego identity. Am Psych 1956, 11:366
49741 Some relationships between size perception and ego adequacy. J Personality 1957, 25:439

KALLEJIAN, VERNE J.

See Klemes, Marvin A.

KALLEN, HORACE M.

49742 The love of mankind. In Montagu, A. *The Meaning of Love*, NY: Julian Pr 1953, 211-230
49743 Psychoanalysis. In Seligman, E. R. A. & Johnson, A. *Encyclopaedia of the Social Sciences*, NY: Macmillan 1934, 12:580-588

KALLICH, MARTIN

49744 Psychoanalysis, sexuality, and Lytton Strachey's theory of biography. Am Im 1958, 15:331-370

KALLMANN, FRANZ J.

49745 Heredity in Health and Mental Disorder. Principles of Psychiatric Genetics in the Light of Comparative Twin Studies. NY: W. W. Norton 1953, 315 p

Rv Leonard, M. R. Q 1954, 23:436-441. Zinkin, J. R 1954, 41:401-402. TFr J 1955, 36:140-141

KALLSTEDT, FRANCES E.

See Bühler, Charlotte

KALMANSON, DENISE

49746 Psychanalyse d'une névrose obsessionnelle chez un enfant de 11 ans. [Psychoanalysis of an obsession-neurosis in an 11-year-old boy.] RFPsa 1957, 21:683-706

See Lebovici, Serge

KALZ, F.

See Fortin, John H.

KAMAL, FAZL

49747 Repression. Proc 6th Pakistan Sci Conf, Karachi 1954, Pt 3:269

KAMAL, S.

49748 [Emotional troubles of our children.] (Urdu) Urdu Psych 1955, 6(7):75-80

KAMM, BERNARD A.

S-17607 Depressive, aggressive and paranoid reactions.
Abs CBr An Surv Psa 1951, 2:316-317

49749 The problem of a "scientific evaluation" of psychoanalysis. Samiksa 1959, 13:24-28

49750 Reality: past and present. Samiksa 1953, 7:1-12
Abs NRo An Surv Psa 1953, 4:121-125. Levinson, G. J 1954, 35:447

KAMMAN, GORDON RICHARD

49751 Harmful effects of interpretative psychotherapy in certain involutional depressions. Minn Med 1956, 39:451-453, 458

KAMMER, G.

49752 Zwei kurze Mitteilungen aus der Traumarbeit. [Two brief reports of dream work.] Psychotherapie 1957, 2:150-152

KAMMERER, T.

49753 Rôle conscient et inconscient de certaines médications dans l'esprit du médecin. [Conscious and unconscious role of certain drugs in the physician's mind.] Strasbourg Méd 1957, 8:741-743

KAMP, L. N.

49754   Transference and counter-transference in nondirective psychotherapy. Acta psychother psychosom orthopaedag 1955, 3 (Suppl.), 156-161

KANE, F.

49755   Clothing worn by an outpatient. A case study. Psychiat Comm 1959, 2:71-74

49756   Clothing worn by out-patients to interviews. Psychiat Comm 1958, 1:58-62

KANE, R.

49757   Case report of a six-year-old psychotic girl. Psychiat Comm 1958, 1:121-128

KANIZSA, GAETANO

49758   Frustrazione ed aggressività: un contributo sperimentale. [Frustration and aggressiveness: an experimental study.] Riv Psa 1955, 1(2):21-34

KANNER, LEO

49759   Child Psychiatry. (Pref: Whitehorn, J. C.; Meyer, A.; Park, E. A.) (3rd Ed.) Springfield, Ill: Thomas; Oxford: Blackwell 1957, 777 p

49760   General concept of schizophrenia at different ages. Proc Ass Res nerv Dis 1954, 34:451-453

49761   (& Eisenberg, L.) Notes on the follow-up studies of autistic children. Proc Am Psychopath Ass 1954 (1955):227-239; discussion, 285-289

49762   Parents' feelings about retarded children. Am J Ment Defic 1953, 53:375-383. Couns PT Ment Retard, 381-390

49763   A psychiatric study of Ibsen's Peer Gynt. ASP 1925, 19:Jan

49764   Psychodynamics of child delinquency. Further contributions. Round Table, 1953. Ops 1955, 25:238-254

49765   Review of psychiatric progress 1952: Child psychiatry. Mental deficiency. P 1953, 109:511-514

49766   The role of the school in the treatment of rejected children. Child-Fam Dig 1953, 8(3):64-80

49767   Types of delinquents. In Karpman, B. *Symposia on Child and Juvenile Delinquency,* Wash: Psychodynamics Series 1959, 217-224

See Eisenberg, Leon; Gardner, George E.; Herskovitz, Herbert H.; Karpman, Ben

KANT, OTTO

S-17640 Technique of dream analysis. Drms Pers Dyn 182-193

KANTER, A.

49768   Narkoanalyse i psykoterapien. [Narcoanalysis in psychotherapies.] Nord Psyk Medl 1953, 7:15-20

KANTER, S. K.

See Wool, M. L.

KANTER, STANLEY S.

See Watson, Peter D.

KANTER, VICTOR B.

See Sandler, Joseph J.

REVIEWS OF:

49769 Bonaparte, M. Chronos, Eros, Thanatos. J 1954, 35:68-69
49770 Phillipson, H. The Object Relations Technique. J 1957, 38:430-431

KANZER, MARK

49771 (Reporter) Acting out and its relation to impulse disorders. (Panel: Am Psa Ass, Chicago, Apr 1956) J Am Psa Ass 1957, 5:136-145
49772 Acting out, sublimation and reality testing. J Am Psa Ass 1957, 5:663-684
   Abs Shentoub RFPsa 1958, 22:396. KHG Q 1960, 29:288-289
49773 Anality in inspiration and insight. Bull Phila Ass Psa 1955, 5:114-115
49774 Applied psychoanalysis: art and aesthetics. An Surv Psa 1951, 2:438-493; 1952, 3:511-546
49775 Applied psychoanalysis: literature, arts and aesthetics. An Surv Psa 1953, 4:355-389; 1954, 5:457-468
49776 Autobiographical aspects of the writer's imagery. J 1959, 40:52-58
   Abs JBi Q 1960, 29:275-276. Rv Tabak Rev Psicoanál 1959, 16:270
S-17647 The central theme in Shakespeare's works.
   Abs An Surv Psa 1951, 2:471-472
49777 The communicative function of the dream. J 1955, 36:260-266
   Abs JLan Q 1957, 26:279
49778 Contemporary psychoanalytic views of aesthetics. J Am Psa Ass 1957, 5:514-524
49779 (& Eidelberg, L.) Discussion of "The Metapsychology of Pleasure." I. The structural description of pleasure. (Read at 21st Int Psa Cong, Copenhagen, July 1959) J 1960, 41:368-371
49780 A field-theory perspective of psychoanalysis. J Am Psa Ass 1954, 2:526-534
49781 "The Figure in the Carpet." Am Im 1960, 17:339-348
49782 Gogol—a study on wit and paranoia. J Am Psa Ass 1955, 3:110-125
   Abs TFr J 1956, 37:207. Young, B. Q 1959, 28:558
49783 Image formation during free association. Q 1958, 27:465-484
   Abs Dreyfus RFPsa 1959, 23:533
S-17650 Manic-depressive psychoses with paranoid trends.
   Abs JFr An Surv Psa 1952, 3:141-143. Auth Q 1953, 22:597-598
49784 The mental hygiene workshop program in Westchester County. J Hillside Hosp 1956, 5:312-319
49785 The metapsychology of the hypnotic dream. J 1953, 34:228-231
   Abs JFr An Surv Psa 1953, 4:243-244. Auth Q 1955, 24:149-150
49786 Observations on blank dreams with orgasms. (Read at Amer Psa Ass, Dec 1953.) Q 1954, 23:511-520
   Abs JFr An Surv Psa 1954, 5:220-222. Dreyfus RFPsa 1955, 19:506. JKl J 1955, 36:425. Rev Psicoanál 1955, 12:310
49787 Past and present in the transference. (Read at NY Psa Soc, Mar 11, 1952) J Am Psa Ass 1953, 1:144-154
   Abs JLan An Surv Psa 1953, 4:425-426. Sillman, L. R. Q 1953, 22:145-146. WH J 1953, 34:276

49788   The reality-testing of the scientist. R 1955, 42:412-418
            Abs JLan Q 1957, 26:284
49789   The recollection of the forgotten dream. J Hillside Hosp 1959, 8:74-85
            Abs Osher, S. Q 1959, 28:569
S-17657 The self-analytic literature of Robert Louis Stevenson.
            Abs An Surv Psa 1951, 2:457
S-17658A The transference neurosis of the Rat Man.
            Abs NRo An Surv Psa 1952, 3:400-401. CR J 1953, 34:353-354
S-17659 The vision of Father Zossima from *The Brothers Karamazov.*
            Abs Auth An Surv Psa 1951, 2:461-462
49790   Wit and paranoia. (Read at NY Psa Soc, Feb 9, 1954)
            Abs DRu Q 1954, 23:482-485
49791   Writers and the early loss of parents. J Hillside Hosp 1953, 2:148-151

        See Frank, Richard L.

ABSTRACTS OF:
49792   Adams, L. A new look at Freud's dream "the breakfast ship." Q 1954,
        23:464
49793   Allport, G. W. The trend in motivational theory. Q 1953, 22:453
49794   Bahia, A. B. Content and defense in artistic creation. An Surv Psa
        1952, 3:514-516
49795   Baranger, W. Depresión, introyección y creación literaria en Marcel
        Proust. An Surv Psa 1952, 3:519-520
49796   Baranger, W. Tentativa de aproximación al psicoanalisis de las ideolo-
        gias filosoficas. An Surv Psa 1954, 5:417-473
49797   Barnes, M. J. The working-through process in dealing with anxiety
        around adoption. Q 1954, 23:305
49798   Barrett, W. G. Mark Twain's osteopathic cure. An Surv Psa 1953,
        4:364-365
49799   Bender, L. & Keeler, W. R. The body image of schizophrenic children
        following electroshock therapy. Q 1953, 22:128-129
49800   Beres, D. A dream, a vision, and a poem: a psychoanalytic study of
        "The Rime of the Ancient Mariner." An Surv Psa 1951, 2:447-449
49801   Bergler, E. Literary critics who can spell but not read. An Surv Psa
        1951, 2:491
49802   Bergler, E. A note on Herman Melville. An Surv Psa 1954, 5:465-466
49803   Bergler, E. Proust and the "torture-theory" of love. An Surv Psa 1953,
        4:367
49804   Bergler, E. True feelings and "tear jerkers" in literary work. An Surv
        Psa 1953, 4:369-370
49805   Bergler, E. Writers and ulcers. An Surv Psa 1953, 4:367
49806   Berman, S. Psychotherapeutic techniques with adolescents. Q 1955,
        24:315
49807   Bettelheim, B. Mental health and current mores. Q 1953, 22:128
49808   Blau, Abram: The diagnosis and therapy of health. Q 1954, 23:464
49809   Bolgar, H. Consistency of affect and symbolic expression. Q 1955,
        24:472
49810   Brenner, A. B. The fantasies of W. S. Gilbert. An Surv Psa 1952,
        3:534-536

49811 Brosin, H. W. Psychoanalytic training for psychiatric residents and others. The associated psychiatric faculties of the Chicago experiment. Q 1953, 22:303

49812 Bychowski, G. From catharsis to work of art: the making of an artist. An Surv Psa 1951, 2:439-440

49813 Bychowski, G. The metapsychology of artistic creation. An Surv Psa 1951, 2:440-442

49814 Bychowski, G. Walt Whitman: a study in sublimation. An Surv Psa 1951, 2:453-457

49815 Desmonde, W. H. Jack and the beanstalk. An Surv Psa 1951, 2:447

49816 Dewald, P. & Harle, M. Utilization of the psychiatric case worker as a consultant during the psychoanalytically oriented therapy of a patient. Q 1954, 23:470

49817 Dracoulides, N. N. Profil psychanalytique de Charles Baudelaire. An Surv Psa 1953, 4:363-364

49818 Dracoulides, N. N. Repercussions de sevrate précoce sur les tableaux d'un peintre moderne. An Surv Psa 1953, 4:368

49819 Edel, L. Hugh Walpole and Henry James: The fantasy of the "killer and the slain." An Surv Psa 1951, 2:457-461

49820 Eissler, K. R. On Hamlet. An Surv Psa 1953, 4:357-358

49821 Engelman, A. A case of transexion upon viewing a painting. An Surv Psa 1952, 3:543

49822 Esman, A. H. Jazz—a study in cultural conflict. An Surv Psa 1951, 2:482-483

49823 Esman, A. H. Mozart: a study of genius. An Surv Psa 1951, 2:483-484

49824 Evans, W. N. Two kinds of romantic love. An Surv Psa 1953, 4:367-368

49825 Feldman, A. B. The confessions of William Shakespeare. An Surv Psa 1953, 4:359-361

49826 Feldman, A. B. Othello's obsessions. An Surv Psa 1952, 3:529-531

49827 Freud, S. Postscript to my paper on the Moses of Michelangelo. An Surv Psa 1951, 2:473

49828 Friedman, J. & Gassel, S. Orestes: a psychoanalytic approach to dramatic criticism. An Surv Psa 1951, 2:488-490

49829 Friedman, J. J. Psychology of the audience in relation to the architecture of the theater. An Surv Psa 1953, 4:376-377

49830 Friend, M. R. et al: Observations on the development of transvestitism in boys. Q 1955, 24:472

49831 Gale, R. L. Freudian imagery in James's fiction. An Surv Psa 1954, 5:464

49832 Garma, A. Algunos significados de la ornamentación y la genesis del arte plástico. An Surv Psa 1953, 4:374-376

49833 Garma, A. The Indo-American winged or feathered serpent, the step coil and the Greek meander. An Surv Psa 1954, 5:467-468

49834 Gerard, M. W. & Dukette, R. Techniques for preventing separation trauma in child placement. Q 1955, 24:314

49835 Geyer, H. C. The mystique of light. An Surv Psa 1953, 4:380-382

49836 Giwjorra, M. Über die psychotherapeutische Aktivierung gestaltischer Fähigkeiten als Ausdrucksweg für unbewusste Erlebnisinhalte. An Surv Psa 1954, 5:466

49837 Glauber, H. The impact of the shift in the psychological constellation of the family on the treatment of a stuttering boy. Q 1954, 23:469-470

49838 Gombrich, E. H. Psychoanalysis and the history of art. An Surv Psa 1954, 5:462-463, 466

49839 Gonzalez, A. Aportación clinica al estudio psicoanalitico de la musica. An Surv Psa 1954, 5:460-461

49840 Goodrich, A. T. et al: Laughter in psychiatric staff conferences: a sociopsychiatric analysis. Q 1955, 24:315

49841 Goshen, C. E. The original case material of psychoanalysis. Q 1953, 22:125

49842 Grinker, R. R. The effect of infantile disease on ego patterns. Q 1954, 23:303

49843 Grinstein, A. "Miracle of Milan." Some psychoanalytic notes on a movie. An Surv Psa 1953, 4:386-388

49844 Grinstein, A. A psychoanalytic study of Schwind's "The Dream of a Prisoner." An Surv Psa 1951, 2:475-476

49845 Grotjahn, M. About the representation of death in the art of antiquity and in the unconscious of modern men. An Surv Psa 1951, 2:487

49846 Gui, W. Bottom's dream. An Surv Psa 1952, 3:527-529

49847 Hecht, M. B. Uncanniness, yearning and Franz Kafka's works. An Surv Psa 1952, 3:537-539

49848 Herskovitz, H. H. et al: Childhood Schizophrenia. Round Table 1953, Q 1955, 24:472

49849 Hill, L. B. Infantile personalities. Q 1953, 22:448-449

49850 Hollingshead, A. B. & Redlich, F. C. Schizophrenia and social structure. Q 1954, 23:465

49851 Josselyn, I. The ego in adolescence. Q 1955, 24:315

49852 Kligerman, C. The character of Jean Jacques Rousseau. An Surv Psa 1951, 2:464-465

49853 Kohut, H. The psychological significance of musical activity. An Surv Psa 1951, 2:480-481

49854 Krapf, E. E. El judío de Shakespeare—una contribución a la psicologica del antisemitismo. An Surv Psa 1951, 2:465-469

49855 Levi, J. Hawthorne's *The Scarlet Letter*. An Surv Psa 1953, 4:361-363

49856 Linn, L. Psychological implication of the "activating system." Q 1954, 23:303

49857 Lowenberg, R. D. From Immanuel Kant's self-analysis. An Surv Psa 1953, 4:365-366

49858 Macalpine, I. & Hunter, R. Rossini: piano pieces for the primal scene. An Surv Psa 1952, 3:526-527

49859 Manheim, L. F. The personal history of David Copperfield. An Surv Psa 1952, 3:522-524

49860 Margolis, N. M. A theory on the psychology of jazz. An Surv Psa 1954, 5:468

49861 Meerloo, J. The monument as a delusional token. An Surv Psa 1954, 5:466-467

49862 Meerloo, J. A. M. Three artists: an essay on creative urge and artistic perturbation. An Surv Psa 1953, 4:368-369

49863 Menninger, K. A. Recording the findings of the psychological examination ("mental status"). Q 1953, 22:124

49864 Michaels, J. J. Delinquency and control. Q 1955, 24:315

49865 Milner, M. Aspects of symbolism in comprehension of the notself. An Surv Psa 1952, 3:515-516

49866 Mosse, E. P. Psychological mechanisms in art production. An Surv Psa 1951, 2:152-153

49867 Noble, D. et al: Psychiatric disturbances following amputation. Q 1954, 23:464

49868 Oberndorf, C. P. Function in psychiatry. Q 1954, 23:303

49869 Odenwald, R. P. Advisability of undertaking psychotherapy against the will of the patient. Q 1953, 22:125

49870 Pauncz, A. The Lear complex in world literature. An Surv Psa 1954, 5:461-462

49871 Pauncz, A. Psychopathology of Shakespeare's King Lear. An Surv Psa 1952, 3:531-532

49872 Pederson-Krag, G. The genesis of a sonnet. An Surv Psa 1951, 2:449-451

49873 Pederson-Krag, G. "Oh poesy! For thee I hold my pen." An Surv Psa 1951, 2:451-452

49874 Petty, T. A. The tragedy of Humpty Dumpty. An Surv Psa 1953, 4:382-383

49875 Plank, E. N. & Plank, R. Emotional components in arithmetical learning as seen through autobiographies. An Surv Psa 1954, 5:470-471

49876 Plank, E. N. Memories of early childhood in autobiographies. An Surv Psa 1953, 4:356-357

49877 Proctor-Gregg, N. Variation on a theme. An Surv Psa 1953, 4:358-359

49878 Racker, E. Las relaciones de la musica con el inconsciente. An Surv Psa 1954, 5:459-460

49879 Racker, H. Contribution to psychoanalysis of music. An Surv Psa 1951, 2:481-482

49880 Rado, S. Dynamics and classification of disordered behavior. Q 1954, 23:463-464

49881 Read, H. Psychoanalysis and the problem of aesthetic value. An Surv Psa 1951, 2:443-446

49882 Reid, J. R. & Finesinger, J. E. The role of definitions in psychiatry. Q 1953, 22:448

49883 Reid, J. R. & Finesinger, J. B. The role of insight in psychotherapy. Q 1953, 22:124-125

49884 Reik, T. "Jessica, my child!" An Surv Psa 1951, 2:469-470

49885 Resnik, S. Actividad musical y reparación. An Surv Psa 1954, 5:461

49886 Riviere, J. The inner world in Ibsen's Master Builder. An Surv Psa 1952, 3:516-519

49887 Riviere, J. The unconscious phantasy of an inner world reflected in examples from English literature. An Surv Psa 1952, 3:516

49888 Róheim, G. Fairy tale and dream. An Surv Psa 1953, 4:383-384

49889 Róheim, G. Hansel and Gretel. An Surv Psa 1953, 4:385-386

49890 Róheim, G. The wolf and the seven kids. An Surv Psa 1953, 4:384-385

49891 Rosenfeld, E. M. The pan-headed Moses—a parallel. An Surv Psa 1951, 2:473-475

49892 Rosenthal, M. J. Relationships between form and feeling in the art of Picasso. An Surv Psa 1951, 2:476-478

49893 Safier, B. A psychological orientation to dance and pantomime. An Surv Psa 1953, 4:372-374

49894 Scharfstein, B. A. & Ostow, M. The unconscious sources of Spinoza's philosophy. An Surv Psa 1952, 3:539-540

49895 Schmideberg, M. The psychoanalysis of delinquents. Q 1953, 22:453

49896 Schneck, J. M. Countertransference in Freud's rejection of hypnosis. Q 1955, 24:313

49897 Schnier, J. Psychoanalysis of the artist. An Surv Psa 1954, 5:457-459

49898 Schnier, J. The symbolic bird in medieval and renaissance art. An Surv Psa 1952, 3:540-542

49899 Segal, H. A psycho-analytic approach to aesthetics. An Surv Psa 1952, 3:511-514

49900 Segy, T. Initiation ceremony and African sculpture. An Surv Psa 1953, 4:377-379

49901 Servadio, E. Il mangiatore di sogni. An Surv Psa 1952, 3:544

49902 Servadio, E. An unknown statuette of Moses. An Surv Psa 1951, 2:473

49903 Simenauer, E. "Pregnancy envy" in Rainer Maria Rilke. An Surv Psa 1954, 5:464

49904 Spira, M. Tentativas de reparación y creación literaria. An Surv Psa 1954, 5:459

49905 Steinberg, S. & Weiss, J. The art of Edward Munch and its function in his mental life. An Surv Psa 1954, 5:464-465

49906 Sterba, E. The role of the child analyst as a consultant. Q 1953, 22:128

49907 Sterba, E. The schoolboy suicide in André Gide's novel *The Counterfeiters*. An Surv Psa 1951, 2:490-491

49908 Sterba, R. & Sterba, E. Beethoven and his nephew. An Surv Psa 1952, 3:524-526; 1954, 5:465

49909 Sterren, H. A. van der: The *King Oedipus* of Sophocles. An Surv Psa 1952, 3:532-534

49910 Stone, L. On the principal obscene word in the English language: an inquiry with an hypothesis regarding its origin and persistence. An Surv Psa 1954, 5:469-470

49911 Tarachow, S. Circuses and clowns. An Surv Psa 1951, 2:487-488

49912 Wahl, C. W. Some antecedent factors in the family history of 392 schizophrenics. Q 1954, 23:464

49913 Watkins, J. G. Concerning Freud's paper on "The Moses of Michelangelo." An Surv Psa 1951, 2:473

49914 Webster, P. D. A critical examination of Franz Kafka's *The Castle*. An Surv Psa 1951, 2:460-464

49915 Weinstein, E. A. & Malitz, S. Changes in symbolic expression with amytal sodium. Q 1955, 24:468

49916 Weiss, J. Cézanne's technique and scoptophilia. An Surv Psa 1953, 4:379-380

49917 Westerman-Holstijn, A. J. The psychological development of Vincent van Gogh. An Surv Psa 1951, 2:478-480

49918 White, J. S. Georg Buechner or the suffering through the father. An Surv Psa 1952, 3:521-522

49919 Whitehorn, J. C. The meaning of medical education in our society. Q 1953, 22:302

49920 Wormhoudt, A. Cold pastoral. An Surv Psa 1951, 2:452-453

49921 Wormhoudt, A. Ivanhoe and the teacher. An Surv Psa 1953, 4:370-372

REVIEWS OF:

49922 Ehrenzweig, A. The Psychoanalysis of Artistic Vision and Hearing. J Am Psa Ass 1957, 5:514-524

49923 Ginzberg, Eli et al: The Ineffective Soldier. Lessons for Management and the Nation. Q 1959, 28:408-410

49924 Kris, E. Psychoanalytic Explorations in Art. J Am Psa Ass 1957, 5:514-524

49925 Lewis, N. D. C. & Engle, B. (Eds) Wartime Psychiatry. Q 1955, 24:445-447

49926 Schneider, D. E. The Psychoanalyst and the Artist. J Am Psa Ass 1957, 5:514-524

49927 Sievers, W. D. Freud on Broadway. Q 1956, 25:100-101

KAPLAN, ABRAHAM

49928 American ethics and public policy. In Morrison, E. *The American Style.* NY: Harper 1958

49929 Freud and modern philosophy. Freud 20th Cent 209-229

49930 Obscenity as an aesthetic category. In Hook, S. *American Philosophers at Work,* NY: Criterion Books 1956, 397-417

49931 The philosophical point of view. Psychiat Res Rep 1956, 6:199-211

See Lasswell, Harold D.

KAPLAN, ABRAHAM IRVING

49932 Hypochondriasis: some psychodynamic aspects. Psychotherapy 1956, 1:351-358

KAPLAN, ALBERT J.

49933 A clinical note on identification. Bull Phila Ass Psa 1952, 2:74-75

49934 Homosexuality in the father as a cause for promiscuity in daughter. Bull Phila Ass Psa 1952, 2:71-74

49935 A note on masturbation without conscious fantasy. Bull Phila Ass Psa 1958, 8:66-67

49936 An oral transference resistance. Bull Phila Ass Psa 1960, 10:137-147

49937 Unconscious masturbation fantasies—a case report. Bull Phila Ass Psa 1954, 4:1-16

Abs JFr An Surv Psa 1954, 5:214-215. Herman, M. Q 1958, 27:132

KAPLAN, ALEX H.

49938 (& Abrams, M.) Ejaculatory impotence. J Urol 1958, 79:964-968

49939 Love, hate and mental health. J Am Ass Univ Women 1955, 48:195-198

49940 Psychiatric syndromes and the practice of social work. J soc Casework 1956, 37:107-112

49941 Psychological aspects of the practice of dentistry. J Am Dental Ass 1958, 57:835-843

KAPLAN, ARTHUR

49942   (& Wolf, L.) The role of the family in relation to the institutionalized
mental patient. In Crow, L. D. & Crow, A. *Readings in Abnormal
Psychology,* Ames, Iowa: Littlefield, Adams 1958, 175-180

KAPLAN, BERT

49943   (& Plaut, T. F. A.) Personality in a Communal Society. An Analysis of
the Mental Health of the Hutterites. Lawrence, Kansas: University of
Kansas Publications 1956, 116 p
Rv Posinsky, S. H. Q 1957, 26:564-565
49944   (Ed) Primary Records in Culture and Personality. Vol. II. Madison,
Wisc: Microcard Foundation 1957, 209 microcards

KAPLAN, DONALD

REVIEWS OF:
49945   Atkinson, J. W. (Ed) Motives in Fantasy, Action and Society. PPR
1959, 46:127-128
49946   Feigl, H. et al (Ed) Minnesota Studies in the Philosophy of Science.
Vol. II. Concepts, Theories, and the Mind-Body Problem. PPR 1958,
45(1-2):150-154
49947   Freud, S. On Creativity and the Unconscious. PPR 1959, 46(1):122-124
49948   Inhelder, B. & Piaget, J. The Growth of Logical Thinking from Childhood to Adolescence. PPR 1960, 47(2):125-127
49949   Masserman, J. H. & Moreno, J. L. (Ed) Progress in Psychotherapy.
Vol II. Anxiety and Therapy. PPR 1958, 45(1-2):147-150
49950   Nelson, B. (Ed) Freud and the 20th Century. PPR 1959, 46(1):122-
124
49951   Szasz, T. S. Pain and Pleasure. NPAP 1957, 5(4):82-88

KAPLAN, ELIZABETH A. BREMNER

49952   The role of a birth injury in a patient's character development and his
neurosis. Bull Phila Ass Psa 1959, 9:1-18
Abs EFA Q 1960, 29:138

ABSTRACT OF:
49953   Peller, L. Language and symbols. Their use in childhood. Bull Phila
Ass Psa 1960, 10:108-110

KAPLAN, HAROLD I.

49954   Analysis and discussion of cases. In Williams, R. H. (Ed) *Institute for
Vocational Rehabilitation Counselors—Columbia University, Jan. 25-29,
1954.* Washington: U.S. Dept Health, Education & Welfare, 1954
49955   Combined psycho-medical therapy of psychosomatic disorders. Dis
nerv Syst 1957, 18:176-182
49956   (& Kaplan, H. S.) Current trends in psychosomatic medicine. In Dorf-
man, W. *Transactions of Academy of Psychosomatic Medicine, Fifth
Annual Meeting,* Oct 9, 1958. NY: Academy of Psychosomatic Medicine, 1958

49957 (& Kaplan, H. S.) Emotional problems and vocational adjustment. Psychiat Q Suppl 1956, 30(part 1):34-60

49958 (& Kaplan, H. S.) An historical survey of psychosomatic medicine. JNMD 1956, 124:546-568

49959 (& Kaplan, H. S.) The psychosomatic approach in medicine. Ann Intern Med 1957, 46:1063-1078

49960 (& Kaplan, H. S.) A psychosomatic concept. PT 1957, 11:16-38

49961 (& Kaplan, H. S.) The psychosomatic concept of obesity. JNMD 1957, 125:181-201

49962 The psychosomatic concept of peptic ulcer. JNMD 1956, 123:93-111

49963 (& Sager, C. J.) Psychosomatic detection. Conn State Med J 1956, 20:533-538

49964 (& Kaplan, H. S.; Leder, H.) Psychosomatic management of obesity. NYSJM 1957, 57:2815

49965 The schizophrenic reaction with psychopathic features: clinical characteristics and response to therapy. A comprehensive study of seven cases. AMA ANP 1952, 68:258-265

49966 (& Reisch, M.) Universal alopecia: a psychosomatic appraisal. NYSJM 1952, 52:1144-1146

49967 (& Hauck, H.; Kleinman, M. L.) An unusual response to the thematic apperception test. P 1952, 108:918-920

KAPLAN, HELEN SINGER

49968 (& Kaplan, H. I.) Current theoretical concepts in psychosomatic medicine. P 1959, 115:1091

See Kaplan, Harold I.

KAPLAN, LILLIAN K.

49969 Foster home placement. Psa Soc Wk 153-168

49970 (& Turitz, L. L.) Treatment of severely emotionally traumatized young children in a foster home setting. Ops 1957, 27:271-285
Abs Koenig RFPsa 1958, 22:257-258. KHG Q 1959, 28:566

KAPLAN, LILLIAN P.

See Rosow, H. Michael

KAPLAN, LOUIS

49971 "Keeper of the harem." Bull Phila Ass Psa 1955, 5:107-109

KAPLAN, MAURICE

49972 (& Ryan, J. F.; Nathan, E.; Bairos, M.) The control of acting out in the psychotherapy of delinquents. P 1957, 113:1108

KAPLAN, OSCAR J.

49973 (Ed) Mental Disorders in Later Life. 2nd Ed. Stanford, Calif: Stanford Univ Pr; London: Oxford Univ Pr, 1956, ix + 508 p

See Jones, Harold E.

KAPLAN, SAMUEL

49974 Childhood schizophrenia. Ops 1954, 24:521-523
49975 A child's reaction to adenoidectomy. In Miles, H. W. et al: *Case Histories in Psychosomatic Medicine*, NY: W. W. Norton 1952
49976 Enuresis. In Miles, H. W. et al: *Case Histories in Psychosomatic Medicine*, NY: W. W. Norton 1952
49977 Feeblemindedness or pseudo-retardation. In Miles, H. W. et al: *Case Histories in Psychosomatic Medicine*, NY: W. W. Norton 1952
49978 (Reporter) The latency period. (Panel: Am Psa Ass, NY, Dec 1956) J Am Psa Ass 1957, 5:525-538

See Gardner, George E.; Herskovitz, Herbert H.; Jessner, Lucie; Putnam, Marian C.; Rank, Beata

KAPLAN, STANLEY M.

49979 (& Gottschalk, L. A.; Fleming, D. E.) Modifications of oropharyngeal bacteria with changes in the psychodynamic state. AMA ANP 1957, 78:656-664
49980 (& Gottschalk, L. A.) Modifications of the oropharyngeal bacteria with changes in the psychodynamic state. PSM 1958, 20:314-320
       Abs Luchina Rev Psicoanál 1958, 15:426. Simon, J. Q 1959, 28:293
49981 Psychological aspects of cardiac disease. PSM 1956, 18:221-233
       Abs EMW Q 1957, 26:589
49982 (& Rosenbaum, M.) Thyrotoxicosis; psychosomatic conference of the Cincinnati General Hospital. PSM 1954, 16:148-155
       Abs Rev Psicoanál 1955, 12:322

See Gottschalk, Louis A.; Rosenbaum, Milton

KAPOTAS, CHARLES NICHOLAS

49983 An investigation of the psychoanalytic theory of psychosexual genesis of paranoid schizophrenia. Diss Abstr 1956, 16:385-386

KAPP, FREDERIC T.

49984 Adoption. Cincinnati J Med 1948, 29:703-705
49985 Intractable pain syndromes. In Weiss, E. & English, O. S. *Psychosomatic Medicine*, (3rd Ed) Phila: W. B. Saunders Co 1957, 528-529
49986 (& Ross, W. D.) New drugs for patients with emotional disorders. JAMA 1955, 157:665
49987 The peptic ulcer problem. Cincinnati J Med 1948, 29:224-225
49988 The psychiatrist and the general practitioner. Southwestern Ohio Soc Gen Prac News 1954, 5:2
49989 Psychosomatic aspects of Graves' syndrome. Proceedings Am Feder Clinical Research 1944, 1:7

See Blagg, David V.; Gottschalk, Louis A.

KARASIC, JEROME

49990 Some notes on a fantasy of female castration. Bull Phila Ass Psa 1960, 10:18-20

KARDINER, ABRAM

49991 Adaptational theory: the cross cultural point of view. Chg Cpts Psa Med 59-68

49992 Cultural factors in prophylaxis. Symposium 1956: Orthopsychiatry and prevention. Ops 1957, 27:231-238

49993 Discussion of Murphy, G. "Psychoanalysis as a unified theory of be-behavior." Sci Psa 1960, 3:169-172

49994 Discussion of Whiting, J. W. M. "Totem and taboo—a re-evaluation." Sci Psa 1960, 3:173-174

49995 Explorations in Negro personality. In Opler, M. K. *Culture and Mental Health,* NY: Macmillan 1959, 413-423

49996 Foreword to Wolberg, L. R. *Hypnoanalysis*

49997 Freud: the man I knew, the scientist, and his influence. Freud 20th Cent 46-58

S-17789 (& Ovesey, L.) The Mark of Oppression: A Psychological Study of the American Negro.
Rv Axelrad, S. Q 1954, 23:111-114

49998 (& Karush, A.; Ovesey. L.) A methodological study of Freudian theory. JNMD 1959, 129:11-19; 133-143; 207-221; 341-356
Abs Gelman, R. L. Q 1960, 29:599-601

49999 New horizons and responsibilities of psychoanalysis. Psa 1958, 18:115-126

50000 Psychoanalysis and anthropology. Sci Psa 1958, 1:152-158

50001 The relation of culture to mental disorder. In Hoch, P. H. & Zubin, J. *Current Problems in Psychiatric Diagnosis,* NY: Grune & Stratton 1953, 157-179

50002 Sex and Morality. NY: Bobbs-Merrill Co, Inc 1954, 266 p
Rv Ansell, C. NPAP 1955, 3(3):77-79. Murphy, W. F. Q 1955, 24: 581-584

50003 Social and cultural implications of psychoanalysis. Psa Sci Method Phil 81-103

50004 Traumatic neuroses of war. Am Hbk Psychiat 1:245-257

50005 Values in Alorese society. In McClelland, D. C. *Studies in Motivation,* NY: App Cen Cr 1955, 278-286. From author's *Psychological Frontiers of Society,* 234-238; 251-258

See DuBois, Cora Alice; Welsch, Exie E.

KARDOS, ELIZABETH

50006 (& Peto, Andrew) Contributions to the theory of play. M 1956, 29: 100-112
Abs EMW Q 1957, 26:442

KARLEN, SAUL H.

See Rado, Sandor

KARON, BERTRAM P.

50007 (& Rosberg, Jack) The homosexual urges in schizophrenia. PPR 1958, 45(4):50-56

50008   Some clinical notes on the significance of the number four. Psychiat
Q 1958, 32:281-288

See Rosberg, Jack

KARPE, MARIETTA

50009   (& Karpe, R.) The meaning of Barrie's Mary Rose. J 1957, 38:408-411
50010   The origins of Peter Pan. R 1956, 43:104-110
Abs JLan Q 1957, 26:437

See Karpe, Richard

KARPE, RICHARD

50011   Behavior research in collective settlements in Israel. Ops 1958, 28:547-548
Abs Koenig RFPsa 1959, 23:431-432. Van Dam, H. Q 1960, 29:143
50012   (& Ohtsuki, K.; Karpe, M.) [Discussion on Barrie.] (Japanese) Tokyo
J Psa 1958, 16:46, 52
50013   Freud's reaction to his father's death. Bull Phila Ass Psa 1956, 6:25-29
50014   My trip to Israel. Conn State Med J 1955, 19:841; 19:981-982; 1956,
20:39-40
Hebrew: Ofakim 1958
S-17831A (& Schap, I.) Nostopathy—a study of pathogenic homecoming.
Abs NRo An Surv Psa 1952, 3:296-297

See Karpe, Marietta; Mahl, George F.; Morse, Philip W.

KARPF, FAY B.

50015   Comments on case material. In Standal, S. W. & Corsini, P. J. *Critical
Incidents in Psychotherapy.* Englewood, N.J.: Prentice-Hall 1959, 48-50, 111-113, 121-123, 209-211, 250-252, 292-293
50016   The Psychology and Psychotherapy of Otto Rank; an Historical and
Comparative Introduction. NY: Philos Library 1953, ix + 129 p
Rv Wride, F. J 1953, 34:348
50017   Rankian will or dynamic relationship therapy. Prog PT 1957, 2:132-139

KARPMAN, BENJAMIN

S-17841A The Alcoholic Woman.
Rv Kelley, D. M. R 1953, 40:187-189
50018   A case of fulminating pyromania. JNMD 1954, 119:205-232
50019   Contrasting psychodynamics in two types of psychopathic behavior. A
case of symptomatic psychopathy. Arch crim Psychodyn 1959, 3:69-152; 349-420
50020   Criminal psychodynamics: a platform. Arch crim Psychodyn 1955,
1:2-100
50021   Criminal psychodynamics—a platform (a summary). J crim Law
Crimin 1956, 47(1)
50022   Dream life in a case of hebephrenia. Psychiat Q 1953, 27:262-316
Abs JBi Q 1954, 23:465-466

50023 Dream life in a case of pyromania. R 1955, 42:44-60
50024 Dream life in a case of uxoricide. Arch crim Psychodyn 1957, 2:597-675; 866-925
50025 The emotional and dream life of a criminal paretic: toward the psychodynamics of organic conditions. Arch crim Psychodyn 1955, 1:656-711
50026 The Hangover: A Critical Study in the Psychodynamics of Alcoholism. Springfield, Ill: Charles C Thomas 1957, xxiii + 531 p
    Rv Pfeffer, A. Z. Q 1958, 27:119-120
50027 On history, histories, and psychotherapy. Arch crim Psychodyn 1957, 2:154-159
50028 Iniquities and inconsistencies existing in criminal law and psychiatric testimony. Arch crim Psychodyn 1955, 1:397-444
S-17869 Lying. Encycl Aberr 288-300
50029 A paranoiac murder. Arch crim Psychodyn 1955, 1:908-939
50030 Predatory crimes. Proceedings of 2nd Intern Congress on Criminology 1952-1955, 3:369-373
S-17891 A psychoanalytic study of a case of murder.
    Abs JFr An Surv Psa 1951, 2:228-230
S-17892 A psychoanalytic study of a fraternal twin.
    Abs CBr An Surv Psa 1951, 2:321-322
50031 Psychodynamics in a fraternal twinship relation. R 1953, 40:243-267
50032 (& Chess, S.; Lurie, L. A.; Schmideberg, M.; Sontag L. W.) Psychodynamics of child delinquency. Round Table, 1952, Ops 1953, 23:1-69
50033 (& Kanner, L.; Robinson, J. F.; Sontag, L. W.; Schmideberg, M.; Peck, H. B.) Psychodynamics of child delinquency: further contributions. Round Table, 1953. Ops 1955, 25:238-282
    Abs DRu Q 1956, 25:447-448
50034 [Summarization. Round Table 1953] Psychodynamics of child delinquency. Further contributions. Ops 1955, 25:273-282
50035 [Summing up. Round Table, 1952] Psychodynamics of child delinquency. Ops 1953, 23:43-69
50036 [Round Table 4] Psychodynamics of childhood delinquency. Summing-up. In author's Symposia on Child and Juvenile Delinquency, 188-216
50037 Psychogenic (hysterical) dysphagia: report of a case. Op 1953, 23:472-500
50038 [Round Table 1] The psychopathic delinquent child. Summary and concluding remarks. In author's Symposia on Child and Juvenile Delinquency, 41-47
50039 [Round Table 2] Psychopathic Behavior. Summary and concluding remarks. In author's Symposia on Child and Juvenile Delinquency, 81-91
50040 Psychosis as a defense against yielding to perversive (paraphiliac) sexual crimes. J crim Law Crimin 1953, 44:22-29
50041 Psychosomatic neurosis as expression of a barrier against indulgence in craved but prohibited sexual drives. J crim Law Crimin 1954, 44:746-752
50042 On reducing tensions and bridging gaps between psychiatry and the law. J crim Law Crimin 1957, 48:164-174

50043   The Sexual Offender and His Offences. NY: Julian Pr 1954, xiii + 744 p
        Rv Berkeley, R. P. NPAP 1954, 2(4):71-74
50044   A survey of contributions of American psychoanalysis to criminology.
        Proc of 2nd Intern Congress on Crimin 1952-1955, 3:37-97
50045   (Ed) Symposia on Child and Juvenile Delinquency. Wash, D.C.:
        Psychodynamics Series 1959, 364 p
        Rv Alby, N. RFPsa 1960, 24:333-334
50046   Synthesis. In author's *Symposia on Child and Juvenile Delinquency,*
        304-364
50047   Uxoricide and infanticide in a setting of oedipal jealousy. Arch crim
        Psychodyn 1957, 2:107-141; 339-401

        See Palmer, James O.; Sontag, Lester W.

        TRANSLATION OF:
        Lippmann, W. O. [20786]

KARPMAN, S. B.

50048   Four levels of emotional involvement in psychotherapy. Georgetown
        Med Bull 1960, 14:150-154

KARSON, MARC

50049   The psychology of trade union membership. MH 1957, 41:87-93
        Abs JLan Q 1958, 27:299

KARSON, SAMUEL

        See Stern, F.

KARTUS, IRVING

50050   (& Schlesinger, H. J.) The psychiatric hospital physician and his
        patient. In Greenblatt, M. et al: *The Patient and the Mental Hospital,*
        Glencoe, Ill: Free Pr 1957, 286-299

KARUSH, AARON

50051   People who seek help: a diagnostic survey. Chg Cpts Psa Med 69-84
50052   (& Hiatt, R. B.; Daniels, G. E.) Psychophysiological correlations in
        ulcerative colitis. PSM 1955, 17:36-56
        Abs Fain, M. RFPsa 1955, 19:631-632. Garcia Reinoso, D. Rev
        Psicoanál 1956, 13:193-194. EMW Q 1957, 26:143. R 1957, 44:480
50053   (& Daniels, G.) Ulcerative colitis; the psychoanalysis of two cases.
        PSM 1953, 15:140-167
        Colitis Ulcerosa; Psychoanalyse zweier Fälle. Psyche, Heidel 1953,
        7:401-452
        Abs LCK An Surv Psa 1953, 4:496-497. VC Q 1954, 23:470

        See Flood, C. A.; Kardiner, Abram

KASPER, AUGUST M.

50054   The doctor and death. In Feifel, H. *The Meaning of Death,* NY;
        Toronto, London: McGraw-Hill 1959, 259-270

KASSOFF, ARTHUR I.

50055 Advantages of multiple therapists in a group of severely acting-out adolescent boys. Int J grp PT 1958, 8:70-75
Abs GPK Q 1959, 28:431

KATAN, ANNY

50056 Distortions of the phallic phase. (Read at 18th Int Psa Cong, London, July 1953) Psa St C 1960, 15:208-214
Abs Auth J 1954, 35:286
50057 The nursery school as a diagnostic help to the child guidance clinic. Psa St C 1959, 14:250-264
S-17982 Die Rolle der "Verschiebung" bei der Strassenangst.
Abs JAA An Surv Psa 1951, 2:122. JFr An Surv Psa 1951, 2:194-196. Rv Bensoussan, P. RFPsa 1954, 18:309

KATAN, MAURITS

50058 [Participant in] Clinical symposium on schizophrenia. J Hillside Hosp 1956, 5:111-118
50059 Comments on "ego distortion." J 1959, 40:297-303
Abs Weiss, J. Q 1960, 29:586
50060 Contribution to the panel on ego-distortion ("as-if" and "pseudo as-if"). (Read at 20th Int Psa Cong, Paris 1957) J 1958, 29:265-270
Abs JLan Q 1959, 28:283
50061 Discussion of Freud, A. "Problems of technique in adult analysis." Bull Phila Ass Psa 1954, 4:57-58
50062 Discussion of Pressman, M. D. "An unusual technical problem in the analysis of an agoraphobia." Bull Phila Ass Psa 1958, 8:38-48
50063 Discussion of Sloane, P. "Resistance as a narcissistic defense." Bull Phila Ass Psa 1957, 7:24-28, 35-36
50064 Dream and psychosis: their relationship to hallucinatory processes. (Read at 21st Int Psa Cong, Copenhagen, July 1959) J 1960, 41:341-351
50065 Freud's article on Schreber. (Read at Phila Ass Psa, November 1958)
Abs Silverman, D. Bull Phila Ass Psa 1959, 9:112-113
S-17985 Further remarks about Schreber's hallucinations.
Abs JFr An Surv Psa 1952, 3:149-150. Auth Q 1954, 23:141-142
50066 De Gronbeginselen van de Waanvorming. [Basic principle of delusion formation.] Thesis for Doctor of Medicine. Holland: Univ of Leiden 1946
50067 The importance of the nonpsychotic part of the personality in schizophrenia. (Read at 18th Int Psa Cong, London, July 1953) J 1954, 35:119-128. Rd Psa Psychol 162-180
Abs Auth J 1954, 35:286. JFr An Surv Psa 1954, 5:102-104. JLan Q 1955, 24:602. Rv Lebovici, S. RFPsa 1954, 18:461
50068 Introduction to discussion of Freud's article on Schreber. Bull Phila Ass Psa 1959, 9:102-103
50069 Mania and the pleasure principle: primary and secondary symptoms. In Greenacre, P. *Affective Disorders*, NY: IUP 1953, 140-209

S-17989 Schreber's hallucinations about the "little men."
>   Abs R 1953, 40:355-356
50070 Schreber's hereafter. Its building-up (Aufbau) and its downfall. Psa
>   St C 1959, 14:314-382
50071 Schreber's prepsychotic phase. J 1953, 34:43-51. YBPsa 1954, 10:47-63
>   Abs SG An Surv Psa 1953, 4:17-18. Auth Q 1954, 23:610. Rv
>   Bensoussan, P. RFPsa 1956, 20:557
50072 (Chairman) Seminar on a schizophrenic patient. (Phila Ass Psa, Novem-
>   ber, 1958)
>   Abs Silverman, D. Bull Phila Ass Psa 1959, 9:48-50
50073 Some remarks on observation of symbolization in a 15½ month old
>   boy. Bull Phila Ass Psa 1956, 6:94-95
S-17990 Structural aspects of a case of schizophrenia.
>   Aspects structuraux d'un cas de schizophrénie. Psychanalyse 1958,
>   4:179-225
50074 Those wrecked by success, bisexual conflicts, and ego defense. (Read
>   at NY Psa Soc, Nov 30, 1954)
>   Abs Waldhorn, H. F. Q 1955, 24:477-478

KATCHER, ALLAN

50075 (& Levin, M.) Children's conception of body size. Child Develpm
>   1955, 26:103-110

KATCHER, NAOMI

50076 The Freud centenary celebration of the American Psychoanalytic Asso-
>   ciation. Samiksa 1955, 9:255-256

KATO, M.

50077 Report on psychotherapy in Japan. Int J soc Psychiat 1959, 5:56-60

KATZ, BARNEY

50078 (& Lehner, G. F. J.) Mental Hygiene in Modern Living. NY: Ronald
>   Pr 1953, 544 p
50079 (& Thorpe, L. P.) Understanding People in Distress; Emotional and
>   Mental Disorders, Their Cause, Care and Cure. NY: Ronald Pr 1955,
>   357 p

KATZ, DANIEL

See Sarnoff, Irving

KATZ, DAVID

50080 Fünf Jahrzehnte im Dienst der psychologischen Forschung; auto-
>   biographische Aufzeichnungen und Bibliographie. [Five decades in
>   the service of psychological research; autobiographical notes and bibli-
>   ography.] Psychol Beitr 1954, 1:470-491

KATZ, JOSEPH

50081 Balzac and Wolfe: a study of self-destructive overproductivity. NPAP
>   1957, 5(2):3-20

50082 A new figure drawing technique for diagnosis and evaluation. PPR 1960, 47(2):103-105

See Taterka, John H.

KATZ, MELVIN MYRON

50083 Psychodynamics of peptic ulcer pathogenesis in hospitalized schizophrenic patients. PSM 1954, 16:47-55
  Abs Weiss, J. Q 1955, 24:316, Rev Psicoanál 1955, 12:317-318

KATZENELBOGEN, SOLOMON

50084 Analyzing Psychotherapy. NY: Philosophical Library 1958, 126 p
50085 Participant in: Conference on d-lysergic acid diethylamide (LSD-25). In Abramson, H. A. *The Use of LSD in Psychotherapy; Transactions,* NY: Josiah Macy Jr Found 1960, 7-240
50086 Psychoanalytic psychotherapy with LSD. In Abramson, H. A. *The Use of LSD in Psychotherapy; Transactions,* NY: Josiah Macy Jr Found 1960, 7-24

KATZENSTEIN, ALFRED

50087 Psychotherapie in Amerika und ihre theoretischen Grundlagen. [Psychotherapy in America and its theoretic basis.] Psychiat Neurol med Psychol, Leipzig 1955, 7:18-32

KAUFER, GEORGE

See Nyswander, Marie

KAUFMAN, CHARLOTTE A.

50088 (& Kaufman, H.) Some problems of treatment arising from the Federal Loyalty and Security Program. Workshop, 1955. Ops 1955, 25:813-825
  Abs DRu Q 1958, 27:140

KAUFMAN, HERBERT

See Kaufman, Charlotte A.

KAUFMAN, IRVING

50089 (& Heims, L.) The body image of the juvenile delinquent. Ops 1958, 28:146-159
  Abs Koenig RFPsa 1959, 23:172
50090 (& Rosenblum, E.; Heims, L.; Willer, L.) Childhood schizophrenia—treatment of children and parents. Ops 1957, 27:683-690
  Abs KHG Q 1960, 29:141
50091 The contribution of protective services. Child Welfare 1957, February
50092 Discussion of Kahn, J. P. Treatment of a withdrawn girl. In Murphy, G. & Bachrach, A. J. *An Outline of Abnormal Psychology,* NY: Modern Library 1954, 101-104
50093 (& Peck, A. L.; Tagiuri, C. K.) The family constellation and overt incestuous relations between father and daughter. Ops 1954, 24:266-277

50094   (& Frank, T.; Heims, L.; Herrick, J.; Willer, L.) Four types of defense
        in mothers and fathers of schizophrenic children. Workshop 1958:
        Parents of schizophrenic children. Ops 1959, 29:460-472
50095   (& Makkay, E. S.; Zilbach, J.) The impact of adolescence on girls with
        delinquent character formation. Ops 1959, 29:130-143
            Abs Koenig RFPsa 1959, 23:535
50096   (& Holmes, E. H.) Intensive treatment of a predelinquent boy with a
        learning disability. Case St Chd Dis 1953, 1:265-299
50097   Relationship between therapy of children and superego development.
        J Am Psa Ass 1960, 8:130-140
50098   The role of the psychiatric consultant. Ops 1956, 26:223-233
            Abs Koenig RFPsa 1957, 21:304-305
50099   Some consideration of the "borderline" personality structure and the
        psychodynamics of the therapeutic structure. Smith Coll Stud soc Wk
        1956, 26(3):7-17
50100   Superego development and pathology in childhood. (Panel, Am Psa
        Ass, NY, Dec 1957) J Am Psa Ass 1958, 6:540-551
50101   Therapeutic considerations of the borderline personality structure.
        Smith Coll Stud Soc Wk 1956, 26(3). Ego Psychol Dyn Casewk, 99-110
50102   Three basic sources for pre-delinquent character. Nerv Child 1955,
        11:12-15
50103   (& Makkay, E. A.) Treatment of the adolescent delinquent. Case St
        Chd Dis 1956, 2:316-352
* * *   Typical ego deviations of social agency clients. See [50101]

        See Simcox, Beatrice R.

KAUFMAN, I. CHARLES

50104   Some ethological studies of social relationships and conflict situations.
        J Am Psa Ass 1960, 8:671-685
50105   Symposium on "Psychoanalysis and ethology." III. Some theoretical
        implications from animal behavior studies for the psychoanalytic con-
        cepts of instinct, energy, and drive. (Read at 21st Int Psa Cong,
        Copenhagen, July 1959) J 1960, 41:318-326

        See Bandler, Bernard

KAUFMAN, LAWRENCE

50106   Contributor to Standal, S. W. & Corsini, R. J. *Critical Incidents in
        Psychotherapy*, Englewood Cliffs, NJ: Prentice-Hall 1959

KAUFMAN, M. RALPH

50107   Discussion of Bralove, R. S. & Milrod, D. "Clinical conference: a case
        of geriatric neurosis." J Hillside Hosp 1954, 3:240-245
50108   (& Franzblau, A.; Kairys, D.) The emotional impact of ward rounds.
        J Mt Sinai Hosp 1956, 23:782-803
50109   Graduate education for general practice from the viewpoint of psychi-
        atry. JAMA 1957, 163:1600-1601
50110   Preface. Psa Soc Wk ix

50111 The problem of psychiatric symptom formation. J Michigan State Med Soc 1958, 57:71-76

50112 Problems of therapy. Psm Cpt Psa Med 96-138

50113 (& Bernstein, S.) A psychiatric evaluation of the problem patients: study of a thousand cases from a consultation service. JAMA 1957, 163:108-111

50114 (& Lehrman, S.; Franzblau, A.; Tabbat, S.; Weinroth, L.; Friedman, S.) Psychiatric findings in admissions to a medical service in a general hospital. J Mt Sinai Hosp 1959, 26:160-170

50115 A psychiatric unit in a general hospital. J Mt Sinai Hosp 1957, 24:572-579

50116 Psychoanalysis in mid-century. In Grinker, R. R. *Mid-Century Psychiatry,* Springfield, Ill: Charles C Thomas 1953, 122-132

50117 Psychotherapies in a general hospital. J Michigan State Med Soc 1958, 57:252-256

50118 Psychotherapy in general practice: indications and limitations. Med Clin N America 1958, 42:733-739

50119 The role of the psychiatrist in a general hospital. Psychiat Q 1953, 27:367-381

See Abramson, Harold A.; Levine, A.; Stein, Aaron

KAUFMAN, S. HARVARD

50120 (& Ripley, H. S.) New approach to undergraduate teaching of psychiatric problems of children. J med Educ 1953, 28:21-25

KAUFMAN, SAMUEL S.

50121 Adolescence and conceptual thinking. Psychotherapy 1956, 1:120-140

50122 Adolescence and schizophrenia. Psychotherapy 1956, 1:321-350

50123 Counter-transference. Psychotherapy 1956, 1:209-220

50124 Cultural influences in adolescence. Psychotherapy 1956, 1:257-262

50125 Discussion on selection of patients for a psychiatric day hospital. Proc 1958 Day Hosp Conf, Am Psychiat Ass 1958, 68-71

50126 [Contribution to Round Table on:] Doctor-patient: the psychotherapeutic relationship. Psychotherapy 1955, 1:76-88

50127 Further notes on the psychiatric day hospital. Psychotherapy 1956, 1:376-380

50128 Notes on the day hospital. Psychotherapy 1956, 1:287-288

50129 The program of an integrated psychotherapeutic center. Psychotherapy 1955, 1:89-96

50130 The psychopathic personality. Psychotherapy 1956, 1:265-271

KAUFMANN, WALTER

50131 Existentialism and death. In Feifel, H. *The Meaning of Death,* NY, Toronto, London: McGraw-Hill 1959, 39-63

50132 Sigmund Freud. In Ferm, V. *Encyclopedia of Morals,* NY: Philos Lib 1956, 171-178

50133 Some emotional uses of money. Acta psychother psychosom orthopaedag 1956, 4:20-41

50134 Some psychosomatic aspects of food allergy. PSM 1954, 16:10-40
          Abs Rev Psicoanál 1955, 12:314-316
50135 Transference in the psychotherapy of patients with food allergies.
          Acta psychother psychosom orthopaedag, 1955, 3 (Suppl), 162-169

KAVAN, EVA
See Whitman, Roy M.

KAVAZANJIAN, THOMAS
50136 (& Gurvitz, M. S.) The W% on the Rorschach as a measure of orality.
          J Hillside Hosp 1953, 2:213-218

KAY, ELEANOR
See Sohler, Dorothy Terry

KAY, PAUL
ABSTRACT OF:
50137 Sperling, M. Pavor nocturnus. Q 1958, 27:155-156

KAYE, ABRAHAM
See Swartz, Jacob

KAYE, HARVEY E.
50138 Convulsions complicating ataractic therapy, their incidence and theo-
          retic implications. NYSJM 1957, 57:2967-2972
50139 Drop-out from outpatient psychiatric treatment, personality and situa-
          tional determinants. AMA ANP 1958, 80:657-666

KAYSER, FRIEDRICH
See Baltrusch, Hans-Joachim F.

KAYTON, ELOISE C.
50140 Development of sexual identity in a little girl. PPR 1960, 47(1):116

KAYWIN, LOUIS
50141 On the concept of the self. J Hillside Hosp 1959, 8:86-93
50142 Emotional factors in urticaria. PSM 1947, 9:131-136
50143 An epigenetic approach to the psychoanalytic theory of instincts and
          affects. J Am Psa Ass 1960, 8:613-658
50144 Notes on the concept of self-representation. J Am Psa Ass 1957, 5:293-
          301
          Abs Shentoub RFPsa 1958, 22:126. HW Q 1960, 29:281

KAZAN, AVRAAM T.
50145 (& Ostrow, E. K.; Cumings, R.; Kline, M. V.) Teaching mental
          hygiene; a problem in resistances. Psychiat Q Suppl 1953, 27:1-27

KAZIN, ALFRED

50146   The Freudian revolution analyzed. NY Times Magazine 1956, May 6.
Freud 20th Cent 13-21

50147   Portrait of hero [Sigmund Freud]. Partisan Rev 1956, 23:188-214

50148   Psychoanalysis and contemporary literary culture. PPR 1958, 46 (1-2):
41-51

KECSKEMETI, P.

50149   Editor of Mannheim, K. *Essays on Sociology and Social Psychology*

KEEHN, J. D.

See Mowrer, O. Hobart

KEELER, W. RAYMOND

50150   Autistic patterns and defective communication in blind children with
retrolental fibroplasia. Psychopathol Communic, 64-83

See Bender, Lauretta

KEES, WELDON

See Ruesch, Jurgen

KEHRER, FERDINAND ADALBERT

50151   Kritisches und Katamnestisches zum Schizophrenieproblem. [Critical
and catamnestic aspects of the schizophrenia problem.] Schweiz med
Wschr 1953, 83 (38 Suppl):1508-1512

50152   Die Psychoneurotic der zweiten Lebenshälfte und ihre Behandlung.
[Psychoneuroses in later life and their treatment.] Hndb NP 1959,
2:384-427

KEILSON, HANS

50153   De gevoelsmatige ontwikkeling van de puber in verband met de sexuele
opvoeding. [The emotional development of the adolescent in relation
with the sexual pedagogy.] Lecture cyclus 1957. Publishers Instit "De
Koepel," Rotterdam, 22-41

50154   De noodzakelijkheid voogdijkinderen voortelichen omtrent hun afkomst
en voorgeschiedenis. [The necessity to inform foster children about
their origin and past history.] De Koepel nederl maandbld v gestichts-
paedag en gezinsverpleging 1955, 9:326-332

50155   Psychologische aspecten van sexuele moeilijkheden bij kinderen. [Psy-
chological aspects of sexual difficulties of children.] Maandbld geest
volksgez 1954, 9:262-272

50156   Sexuele voorlichting als trauma. [Sexual information as trauma.]
Maandbld geest volksgez 1953, 8:355-364

KEISER, SYLVAN

S-18069 Body ego during orgasm. YBPsa 1953, 9:146-157
Abs JFr An Surv Psa 1952, 3:130-132. CR J 1953, 34:353

50157 Disturbances in abstract thinking and body-image formation. J Am Psa Ass 1958, 6:628-652
Abs TFr J 1959, 40:365. Shentoub RFPsa 1959, 23:438-439. TGS Q 1960, 29:433
50158 Female sexuality. J Am Psa Ass 1956, 4:563-574
50159 A manifest Oedipus complex in an adolescent girl. Psa St C 1953, 8:99-107
Abs NRo An Surv Psa 1953, 4:291-293. RTh J 1955, 36:76. Chaio, J. Rev Psicoanál 1958, 15:190
50160 Orality displaced to the urethra. J Am Psa Ass 1954, 2:263-279
Abs JFr An Surv Psa 1954, 5:113-114. Rev Psicoanál 1954, 11:533. TFr J 1955, 36:223-224. Shorr, J. Q 1956, 25:617
50161 The technique of supervised analysis. (Panel: Am Psa Ass, NY, Dec 1955) J Am Psa Ass 1956, 4:539-549

ABSTRACTS OF:
50162 Benedek, T. F. Psychosexual Functions in Women: Studies in Psychosomatic Medicine. An Surv Psa 1952, 3:547-556
50163 Bonaparte, M. Female Sexuality. An Surv Psa 1953, 4:541-548

KELLAM, SHEPPARD G.

See Finesinger, Jacob E.

KELLER, A.

50164 Aus der Frühzeit der psychoanalytischen Bewegung. [Early times in the psychoanalytic movement.] Schweiz Z Psychol 1956, 15:122-125

KELLER, M.

See Ganzaraín, Ramón; Redlich, Fredrick C.

KELLER, TINA

50165 Der Mann und die Weiblichkeit. [The male and femininity.] Psychol Berater gesunde prakt. Lebensgestalt. 1952, 4:279-282

KELLEY, DOUGLAS M.

50166 Foreword to Kupper, W. H. *Dictionary of Psychiatry and Psychology.*

REVIEWS OF:
50167 Abramson, H. A. (Ed) Problems of Consciousness. R 1954, 41:290-291
50168 Alford, L. B. Cerebral Localisation. R 1953, 40:374-375
50169 Bett, W. R. The Infirmities of Genius. R 1954, 41:383
50170 Bond, D. D. The Love and Fear of Flying. R 1954, 41:383-385
50171 Chesser, E. Cruelty to Children. R 1954, 41:385-387
50172 Dax, E. C. Experimental Studies in Psychiatric Art. R 1955, 42:212-213
50173 Devereux, G. (Ed) Psychoanalysis and the Occult. R 1954, 41:398-399
50174 Eisler, R. Man into Wolf. R 1954, 41:386-387

50175   Gottlober, A. B. Understanding Stuttering. R 1954, 41:378-380
50176   Griffith, E. F. A Sex Guide to Happy Marriage. R 1954, 41:294
50177   Karpman, B. The Alcoholic Woman. R 1953, 40:187-189
50178   Kris, E. Psychoanalytic Explorations in Art. R 1954, 41:391-392
50179   Pollak, O. Social Science and Psychotherapy for Children. R 1954, 41:393-394
50180   Reik, T. The Unknown Murderer. R 1953, 40:189-190
50181   Watson, R. I. The Clinical Method in Psychology. R 1954, 41:380-381
50182   Widening Horizons in Medical Education, a Study of the Teaching of Social and Environmental Factors in Medicine, 1945-1946, R 1953, 40:90-91
50183   Wolff, C. The Hand in Psychological Diagnosis. R 1954, 41:396-397

KELLEY, HAROLD H.

See Janis, Irving L.

KELLEY, KENNETH

50184   (& Daniels, G. E.; Poe, J.; Easser, R.; Monroe, R.) Psychological correlations with secondary amenorrhea. PSM 1954, 16:129-147
        Abs Rev Psicoanál 1955, 12:321

KELLY, E. LOWELL

See Shakow, David

KELMAN, HAROLD

50185   (& Kelman, N.; Javits, J. K.; Lemkau, P. V.; Lussheimer, P.; Freeman, N.) Addresses delivered at official opening of the Karen Horney Clinic at Hotel Plaza 1955, May 6. Psa 1955, 15:169-170
50186   The Analytic Process—A Manual. Privately printed, 1948, 86 p
50187   Attitudes toward sex. NYSJM 1945, 45:625-628
50188   Communing and relating. Part I. Past and current perspectives. Psa 1958, 18:77-98
50189   Communing and relating. Part 2. The mind structure of East and West. Psa 1958, 18:158-170
50190   Communing and relating. Part 3. Examples: general and clinical. Part 4. Communing as therapy. Psa 1959, 19:73-105
50191   Communing and relating. Part 5. Separateness and togetherness. Psa 1959, 19:188-215
50192   The concept "unconscious." Psa 1952, 12:101-103
50193   (& Horney, K.; Ackerly, S.; Allen, F. H.; Freeman, N.; Fromm-Reichmann, F.; Weiss, F. A.) Constructive forces in the therapeutic process. Psa 1953, 13:4-19
50194   Diagnosing and prognosing in psychoanalysis. Psa 1955, 15:49-70
50195   The diagnosis and treatment of head injuries. Hospital News, U.S. Public Health Service, 1939, 6(9):21-23
50196   Discussion of Eros and Thanatos: a critique and evaluation of Freud's death wish by Iago Galdston. Psa 1955, 15:132-134
50197   Eastern influences on psychoanalytic thinking. Psychologia: An Intern J of Psychol in the Orient 1959, 2(2)

50198 [Fear of anxiety—brief discussion.] (Japanese) (Tr: Ohtsuki, K.)
       Tokyo J Psa 1958, 16(7):44-48
50199 (& Diethelm, O.; Kilpatrick, E.; Ackerman, N. W.; Weiss, F. A.;
       Dreikurs, R.) Goals in therapy: a round table discussion. Psa 1956,
       16:3-23
50200 (et al) Group analysis. Some problems and promises. A symposium.
       Psa 1952, 12:78-81
50201 The holistic approach (Horney). Am Hbk Psychiat 2:1433-1452
50202 Holistic psychoanalysis. Samiksa 1958, 12:77-112
           Japanese: (Tr. Ohtsuki, K.) Tokyo J Psa 1958, 16(6):37
           Thai: (Tr: Ratanakorn, P.) J Thailand Psychiatric Ass 1959, 4(2):91-
       110
50203 (& Weiss, F. A.; Tillich, P.; Horney, K.) Human nature can change.
       (Symposium). Psa 1952, 12:62-63
50204 How to Choose a Psychoanalyst. Pamphlet, 4 p Aux Council, Ass Ad-
       vance Psa 1946
50205 (& Weiss, F. A.; Pankow, G.; Jonas, H.) Kurt Goldstein's influence on
       psychoanalytic thought. Psa 1959, 19:149-156
50206 Life history as therapy. Part 1. Evaluation of literature. Psa 1955, 15:
       144-162
50207 Life history as therapy: part 2. On being aware. Psa 1956, 16:68-78
50208 Life history as therapy: part 3. The symbolizing process. Psa 1956,
       16:145-173
50209 Masculinity and femininity. Pamphlet, 4 p Aux Council, Ass Advance
       Psa 1946
50210 Masochism and self-realization. Sci Psa 1959, 2:21-30
50211 A modern conception of essential hypertension. Hospital News, U.S.
       Public Health Service, 1940, 7(1):1-17
50212 The neuropsychiatric aspects of back injuries. Hospital News, U.S.
       Public Health Service, 1939, 6(4):22-32
50213 Observations in catatonia with mixtures of carbon dioxide and oxygen.
       Psychiat Q 1932, 6:513-522
50214 Prognosis in therapy. Samiksa 1958, 12:29-48. Med College J (Agra,
       India) 1959, 19(2):128-140
           Japanese: (Tr. Kondo, A.) Osaka J Mental Hygiene 1958, Sept,
       Dec; Tokyo J Psa 1959, April:20-31
50215 Psychoanalysis and science: a preliminary study. Psa 1953, 13:38-58
           Spanish: Rev Psicol gen apl, Madrid 1955, 10:195
50216 Psychoanalytic thought and Eastern wisdom. (Read at Acad of Psa,
       NY, Dec 7, 1958) Sci Psa 1960, 3:124-132
50217 The psychology of the returning veteran. Pamphlet, 4 p Aux Council,
       Ass Advance Psa, October 4, 1944
50218 (& Field, H.) Psychosomatic relationships in pruriginous lesions. JNMD
       1938, 88:627-643
50219 Psychotherapy in the Far East. Prog PT 1959, 4:296-305
50220 Rational and irrational authority. Psa 1952, 12:50-61
50221 The role of sex in the life of man. Pamphlet, 4 p Aux Council, Ass
       Advance Psa, December 15, 1942
50222 The theoretical approaches: round table discussion. Curr App Psa 63-
       74

50223 Tribute. [to Karen Horney] Psa 1954, 14:9-10
50224 A unitary theory of anxiety. Psa 1957, 17:127-160
        Japanese: (Tr: Ohtsuki, K.) Tokyo J Psa 1958, 16(9):1-9
50225 The use of the analytic couch. Psa 1954, 14:65-82
        Über den Gebrauch der Couch in der Analyse. (Tr: Stierlin) Psyche 1955, 9:783-792
50226 What are your doubts about analysis? In Horney, K. et al: *Are You Considering Psychoanalysis,* NY: W. W. Norton & Co 1946, 93-133
50227 Who should your analyst be? In Horney, K. et al: *Are You Considering Psychoanalysis,* NY: W. W. Norton & Co 1946, 135-157

See Lussheimer, Paul; Martin, Alexander R.

KELMAN, HERBERT C.

50228 (& Parloff, M. B.; Frank, J. D.) Comfort, effectiveness, and self-awareness as criteria of improvement in psychotherapy. P 1954, 111:343-351
50229 Compliance, identification, and internalization: three processes of attitude change. J Conflict Resolution 1958, 2:51-60
50230 (& Lerner, H. H.) Group therapy, group work and adult education: the need for clarification. J soc Issues 1952, 8(2):3-10
50231 (& Parloff, M. B.) Interrelations among three criteria of improvement in group therapy. ASP 1957, 54:281-288
50232 (& Alexander, F.; Stein, M. I.) Some psychological correlates of six somatic disturbances. (Abstract) Am Psychol 1958, 13:321
50233 Two phases of behavior change. J soc Issues 1952, 8(2):81-88

See Lerner, Henry H.; Parloff, Morris B.

KELMAN, NORMAN

50234 Clinical aspects of externalized living. Psa 1952, 12:15-23
50235 Goals of analytic therapy—a personal viewpoint. Psa 1954, 14:105-114
50236 (& Nathanson, J.; Taylor, H.; Martin, A. R.) Human values in a mechanized age: a symposium. Psa 1953, 13:72-80
50237 Obituary: Karen Horney, M.D. 1885-1952. R 1953, 40:191-193. Psa 1954, 14:5-7
50238 Psychoanalysis and morality. Amer Scholar 1955, 24:158-170
50239 Therapy of the resigned patient. Psa 1953, 13:90-91
50240 What is psychotherapy: The viewpoint of the Karen Horney group. Ann Psychother, Monogr 1959, (1):37-43

See Kelman, Harold

KELNAR, J.

50241 (& Sutherland, J. D.) Some current developments in psychotherapy in Great Britain. Prog PT 1956, 1:277-283

KELSEY, DENYS E. R.

50242 Phantasies of birth and prenatal experiences recovered from patients undergoing hypnoanalysis. JMS 1953, 99:216-223

KELTY, EDWARD J.

See Busse, Ewald William

KEMMLER, LILLY

50243 Ein Fall von pavor nocturnus. Diagnose und Therapie. [A case of pavor nocturnus. Diagnosis and therapy.] Prax Kinderpsychol 1957, 6:296-300

50244 (& Heckhausen, H.) Entstehungsbedingungen der kindlichen Selbständigkeit. Der Einfluss der mütterlichen Selbständigkeitserziehung auf die seelischsoziale Schulreife der Söhne. [Conditions of origin of independence in childhood. Influence of independence training by mothers on the social maturity of their sons at school age.] Z exper angew Psychol 1957, 4:603-622

50245 (& Hechhausen, H.) Mütteransichten über Erziehungsfragen. [Opinions of mothers on upbringing of children.] Psychol Rundschau 1959, 10:83-93

50246 Untersuchungen über den frühkindlichen Trotz. [Research on temper tantrums in early childhood.] Psychol Forschung 1957, 25:279-338

KEMP, A.

50247 Considerations on mental disorders in some diseases of the eye. Folia Psychiat Neerl 1958, 61:94-102

KEMPER, K. A.

50248 Angstsymptome, Erziehungs—und Schulschwierigkeiten bei einem 9 jährigen Jungen. (Verlauf einer analytischen Psychotherapie.) [Anxiety symptoms and difficulties with training and school in a boy of 9 years. Course of an analytic psychotherapy.] Prax Kinderpsychol 1953, 1:141-149

50249 Kurztherapie eines Falles von chronifiziertem Asthma bronchiale. [Brief therapy in a case of chronic bronchial asthma.] Prax Kinderpsychol 1954, 3:125-129; 167-173

50250 Psychosomatische Reaktion aufgrund praegenitaler Mechanismen bei akuter Sexualproblematik. Ausschnitt aus einer fortgeschrittenen Analyse. [Psychosomatic reaction based upon pregenital mechanisms with acute sex problems. Excerpts from an advanced stage in analysis.] Z PSM 1955-56, 2:47-51

50251 Widerspiegelung einer Kinderkurztherapie in der Scenodarstellung. [Reflection of a brief child analysis in a sceno-performance.] Prax Kinderpsychol 1955, 4:85-90

KEMPER, WERNER WALTER

50252 Die "Abstinenzregel" in der Psychoanalyse. [The "rule of abstinence" in psychoanalysis.] Psyche, Heidel 1955, 8:636-640

50253 Analyse des heutigen psychoanalytischen Ausbildungsganges. [Analysis of present day psychoanalytic training.] Psyche, Heidel 1959, 13:122-149

50254 Analyse zweier eindrucksvoller Wahrträume. [Analysis of two striking prophetic dreams.] Psyche, Heidel 1954, 8:450-467
   Abs JFr An Surv Psa 1954, 5:229-232

50255 Ärztliches Verhalten und Vorgehen bei psychisch bedingten funktionellen Störungen. [Medical attitude toward and management of psychogenic functional disturbances.] Z PSM 1957-58, 4:60-65; 137-138; 292-294

50256 Die Ausbildung zum Psychoanalytiker. [The training of a psychoanalyst.] Hndbk N P 1957, 1:1486-1497

50257 Die besonderen Probleme einer psychischen Hygiene in Brasilien. [The special problems of mental hygiene in Brazil.] In Pfister-Meng: Geistige Hygiene, Forschung und Praxis, Basel: Benno Schwabe 1955, 289-310

50258 Como fazer-se psicoanalista. [How to become a psychoanalyst.] Rev brasil med 1955, 12:829-832

50259 Erfahrungsbericht über eine didaktische Gruppen-Analyse mit psychoanalytischen Ausbildungskandidaten. [Report on an experiment in didactic group-analysis made with psychoanalytical training candidates.] In Grinberg, L. et al: El grupo psicológico: sus aplicaciones a la terapia, a la ensenanza y a la investigación, Buenos Aires: Edit Nova 1959

50260 Erwägungen zur psycho-somatischen Medizin. [Thoughts on psychosomatic medicine.] Z PSM 1954-55, 1:38-44; 123-130

50261 Zum ersten Latein-Amerikanischen Kongress für Gruppentherapie. [On the occasion of the 1st Latin-American Congress for group-psychotherapy.] Psyche, Heidel 1958, 11:716-720

50262 Frühkindliche Erlebniswelt, Neurose und Psychose. [Early childhood experiences behind neurosis and psychosis.] Psyche, Heidel 1953, 6:641-667
   Abs NRo An Surv Psa 1953, 4:66, 267-269

50263 Die Gegenübertragung, grundsätzliches und praktisches. [Countertransference. Its principles and practical importance.] Psyche, Heidel 1954, 7:593-626

50264 Zum Geleit (der Zeitschrift für Psycho-somatische Medizin). [Introduction (to the "Zeitschrift für Psycho-somatische Medizin).] Z PSM 1954-55, 1:1-2

50265 Grundregeln für die psychotherapeutische Praxis. [Fundamental rules for the psychotherapeutical clinic.] Hndbk N P 1957, 1:2467-2524

50266 Zur heutigen Gruppen-Psychotherapie. [Group psychotherapy today.] Psyche, Heidel 1958, 11:707-715

50267 De hipnose a medicina psicosomatica. [From hypnosis to psychosomatic medicine.] Brasil-Médico 1958, 72(1):35-40

50268 The manifold possibilities of therapeutic evaluation of dreams. (Read at 20th Int Psa Cong, Paris 1957) J 1958, 29:125-128
   Abs J 1958, 29:291. JLan Q 1959, 28:278. Usandivaras & Tabak Rev Psicoanál 1959, 16:89-90

50269 "Organwahl" und psychosomatische Medizin. ["Organ choice" and psychosomatic medicine.] Z Psychother med Psychol 1954, 4:101-113

50270 Zur Pathogenese der Enuresis. [Contribution to the pathogenesis of enuresis.] Ärztl Wschr 1953, 8:575-578; 597-602

50271 Persönlichkeitsstruktur, Confliktart, Organwahl und psycho-somatische Medizin. [Personality structure, conflict type, organ choice and psycho-somatic medicine.] Z PSM 1957-58, 4:186-192

50272 Zur Praxis der therapeutischen Traumdeutung. [The practice of therapeutic dream interpretation.] Z Psychother med Psychol 1956, 6:233-244

50273 Preface to Grinberg, L. et al: *Psychoanalytische Gruppenpsychotherapie in Theorie und Praxis.*

50274 Sóbre a prescricão de analgésicos. [About the prescription of analgesics.] Rev Brasil Med 1958, 15:1

50275 Problemas das anormalidades no desenvolvimento psíquico. [Problems of deviations in mental development.] Rev Brasil Estúdos pedagóg 1950, 14(40):58-75

50276 Über das Prospektive im Traum. [The prospective aspects of the dream.] Psyche, Heidel 1956, 9:561-583

50277 A psicanálise como fator cultural. [Psychoanalysis as a cultural factor.] Cultura, Publ by Brazil Ministr of Educ 1951, 1(4):23-27

50278 Psicanálise—retrospecto e porvir. [Psychoanalysis—retrospect and preview.] Rev Bras Saúde ment 1956, 2(2):11-17

50279 Psychoanalyse. Gegenwärtiger Stand und Entwicklungstendenzen in Südamerika. [Psychoanalysis; its actual position and tendencies for development in South-America.] Hndbk N P 1957, 1:226-232

50280 Psychoanalyse und Gruppen-Psychotherapie. [Psychoanalysis and group psychotherapy.] Z Psychother med Psychol 1959, 9:125-133

50281 Psychoanalytische Gruppenpsychotherapie. 1. Lateinamerikanischer Kongress für Gruppen-Psychotherapie (24. -28. 9. 1957, Buenos Aires, Argentinien). [Psychoanalytic group psychotherapy. 1. Latin-American Congress for Group Psychotherapy (September 24-28, 1957, Buenos Aires, Argentina).] Z PSM 1957-58, 4:221-223

50282 Roer unhas. [Nail biting.] Rev Brasil Med 1957, 14(2)

50283 Ser canhote é defeito? [Is it a defect to be left-handed?] Rev Bras Medicina 1951, 8(11):813

50284 Subjektstufen-und kategoriale Interpretation des Traumes. [Subject-level interpretation and categorial interpretation of dreams.] Psyche, Heidel 1957, 11:64-76

50285 Der Traum und seine Bedeutung. [The Dream and Its Significance.] Hamburg: Rowohlt-Taschenbuch 1955, 220 p
       Dutch: 1959
       O sonho, este desconhecido. Lisbõa: Livros do Brasil 1957, 245 p
       Rv Bychowski, G. Q 1957, 26:123. Friedmann, O. A. J 1957, 38:127.
       Garma, A. Rev Psicoanál 1957, 14:336

50286 Die Übertragung im Lichte der Gegenübertragung. [Transference in the light of counter-transference.] Acta psychotherap psychosom orthopaedag 1955, 3 (Suppl), 169-176

KEMPF, EDWARD J.

S-18182A Abraham Lincoln's organic and emotional neurosis. Abs LRa Q 1953, 22:306

50287 Biodynamics of everyday life. Trans NY Acad Sci 1959, Series 2, 21: 216-323

50288 The conflicting conditioned, self-determining attitude—basic mechanism of neuroses. In Gantt, H. W. *Physiological Bases of Psychiatry*, Springfield, Ill: Thomas 1958

50289 Neuroses as conditioned, conflicting, holistic, attitudinal, acquisitive-avoidant reactions. Ann NY Acad Sci 1953, 56:307-329

KEMPLE, CAMILLA

See Harris, Harold J.

KEMPSTER, STEPHEN W.

See Schacht, Mervyn

KENDALL, P.

See Wolf, Katherine M.

KENDLER, HOWARD H.

50290 An observation by an experimental psychologist. Psa Sci Method Phil 268

KENJI, SHINOZAKI

50291 [Psychoanalysis of a depressive hysteria with special reference to its symptomatic chromatopsia.] (Japanese) Hiroshima J med Sci 1953, 2(1-2): 175-179

KENNEDY, GAIL

50292 Psychoanalysis: protoscience and metapsychology. Psa Sci Method Phil 269-281

KENNEDY, J. S.

50293 Is modern ethology objective? Brit J Anim Behav 1954, 2:12-19

KENNEDY, JANET A.

S-18206 Problems posed in the analysis of Negro patients.
       Abs NRo An Surv Psa 1952, 3:436-440

KENNEY, WILLIAM

50294 Dr. Johnson and the psychiatrists. Am Im 1960, 17:75-82

KENWORTHY, MARION E.

50295 Foreword to Menninger, K. A. *A Psychiatrist's World*

KEPECS, JOSEPH G.

50296 Ambiguity and repression. AMA ANP 1958, 80:502-512

S-18226A (& Rabin, A.; Robin, M.) Atopic dermatitis.
       Abs R 1953, 40:160-161

50297 (& Robin, M.) Life situations, emotions and atopic dermatitis. In: *Life Stress and Bodily Disease*. Vol. 219, Proc Ass Res nerv Dis (1949), 1010-1015, 1950

50298 Observations on screens and barriers in the mind. (Read at Chicago Psa Soc, Nov 25, 1952) Q 1954, 23:62-77
    Abs NRo An Surv Psa 1954, 5:83, 364-366. Dreyfus RFPsa 1955, 19:496. JKl J 1955, 36:422. Rev Psicoanál 1955, 12:307
50299 The oral triad applied to psychosomatic disorders. Q 1957, 26:461-475
    Abs Auth J 1958, 39:452. Dreyfus RFPsa 1958, 22:743
50300 Psychiatric disorders in Puerto Rican troops. War Med 1945, 8:244-249
S-18227A (& Robin, M.; Brunner, M. J.) Relationship between certain emotional states and exudation into the skin.
    Abs R 1953, 40:161
50301 (& Robin, M.; Munro, C.) Responses to sensory stimulation in certain psychosomatic disorders. PSM 1958, 20:351-365
    Abs Prest, J. R. Q 1959, 28:425-426
50302 Some patterns of somatic displacement. PSM 1953, 15:425-432
    Abs Rev Psicoanál 1954, 11:551-552
50303 (& Robin, M.) Studies on itching. 1. Contributions toward an understanding of the physiology of masochism. PSM 1955, 17:87-95
    Abs Fain RFPsa 1955, 19:632. Garcia Reinoso, D. Rev Psicoanál 1956, 13:194. EMW Q 1957, 26:143-144
50304 (& Robin, M.) Studies in itching. 2. Some psychological implications of the interrelationships between the cutaneous pain and touch systems. AMA ANP 1956, 76:325-340
50305 (& Robin, M.; Munro, C.) Tickle. The organization of a patterned response. (Read at Chicago Psa Soc, Nov 29, 1959.)
    Abs Seitz, P. F. D. Bull Phila Ass Psa 1960, 10:24-25
S-18228 A waking screen analogous to the dream screen.
    Abs JFr An Surv Psa 1952, 3:129-130. CR J 1953, 34:353. Perestrello, M. Rev Psicoanál 1956, 13:80-81

    See Rabin, Albert; Robin, Milton

KEPPLER, LENE

50306 Editor of Schottlaender, F. *Das Ich und seine Welt.*

KERDMAN, LOUIS

50307 (& Peek, J. E.) Modes of communication in the psychotherapeutic process. PT 1957, 11:599-617
    Rv Usandivaras Rev Psicoanál 1957, 14:421

KERENYI, A. B.

50308 (& Koranyi, E. K.; Sarwer-Foner, G. J.) The use of intravenous methylphenidate (Ritalin) in psychiatric interviewing. Canad Med Ass J 1959, 80:963-967

KERENYI, KARL

50309 Zum Porträt des Oedipus. [On the portrait of Oedipus.] Neue Zürcher Zeitung 1956, May 6

KÉRI, HEDVIG

50310 Ancient games and popular games. Psychological essay. Am Im 1958, 15:41-89

KERLINGER, FRED N.

50311 Behavior and personality in Japan: a critique of three studies of Japanese personality. Soc Forces 1953, 31:250-258

KERMAN, EDWARD F.

50312 Psychodiagnosis and psychodynamics from an object-relations frame of reference. Psychiat Q 1958, 32:708-757
       Abs Engle, B. Q 1960, 29:144

KERNBERG, O.

50313 Estudio de orientación psicoanalitica del contenido del test de Rorschach en la homosexualidad masculina. [Psychoanalytical study of the contents of the Rorschach test in male homosexuality.] Rev psiquiat, Santiago 1956-57, 21-22:45-57

KERNER, OLIVER J. B.

50314 Stress, fantasy and schizophrenia: a study of the adaptive processes. Genetic Psychol Monog 1956, 53:189-281

KERR, MADELINE

50315 The People of Ship Street. London: Routledge & Kegan, Paul; NY: Humanities Pr 1958, 215 + vii p
50316 Personality and Conflict in Jamaica. Liverpool Univ Pr 1952, 221 p
       Rv Rey, T. H. J 1953, 34:345

KERSTEN, U.

50317 Der Wortsplitterversuch nach Müller-Hegemann im Rahmen der Assoziationsexperimente und seine Anwendung in der psychologischen und psychiatrischen Diagnostik. [The Müller-Hegemann word-fragment test in the domain of association experiments and its use in psychological and psychiatric diagnosis.] Psychiat Neur med Psychol 1956, 8:56-59

KERT, M. J.

See Marmor, Judd

KERVRAN, R.

See Marty, Pierre

KESSLER, JANE W.

50318 The interrelationship between clinical psychology and pediatrics. Round Table, 1954: The hospitalized child. Ops 1955, 25:297-300

See Jensen, Reynold A.

KESSLER, MORRIS M.

50319 Acute and subacute mobilization of defenses following a sudden leg amputation. Bull Phila Ass Psa 1959, 9:87-95

50320 The double manner by which an appendage organ like the penis presents itself sensorially to the ego and its importance in the production of castration anxiety. J Hillside Hosp 1956, 5:368-374
Abs Afterman, J. Q 1958, 27:610

KESSLER-SZILAGYI, I.

See Maslow, Abraham H.

KESTEMBERG, E.

50321 Problèmes diagnostiques et cliniques posés par les névroses de caractère. [Diagnostic and clinical problems presented by character neuroses.] RFPsa 1953, 17:496-517
Abs JFr An Surv Psa 1953, 4:204-205

50322 Quelques considérations à propos de la fin du traitement des malades à structure psychotique. [Considerations in terminating the treatment on patients of psychotic structure.] RFPsa 1958, 22:297-341
Rv Zmud, F. & Fiasche, D. N. de. Rev Psicoanál 1959, 16:194

See Diatkine, R.; Lebovici, Serge

KESTEN, JACOB

50323 Learning for spite. NPAP 1955, 4(1):63-67

KESTENBERG, JUDITH S.
(See also Silberpfennig, Ida)

50324 On the development of maternal feelings in early childhood. Observations and reflexions. Psa St C 1956, 11:257-291
Abs Faergeman, P. Q 1957, 26:295-296. RTh J 1959, 40:75

50325 The history of an "autistic" child: clinical data and interpretation. J Child Psychiat 1954, 3:5-52

50326 Notes on ego development. J 1953, 34:111-122
Abs NRo An Surv Psa 1953, 4:66-68. Auth Q 1954, 23:613-614. Rv Renard, W. RFPsa 1953, 17:581

50327 Vicissitudes of female sexuality. J Am Psa Ass 1956, 4:453-476
Abs TFr J 1957, 38:299. JPW Q 1960, 29:136

ABSTRACTS OF:

50328 Fontana, A. E. Colite ulcéreuse, présentation d'un cas. RFPsa 1959, 23:443-444

50329 Perez Morales, F. Un cas de névrose d'examen. RFPsa 1959, 23:442-443

REVIEWS OF:

50330 Garma, A. Quelques significations de l'ornamentation et la genèse de l'art plastique. RFPsa 1954, 18:308

50331 Garma, E. La masturbation défendue et le développement psychologique. RFPsa 1953, 17:584-585

50332   Gonzales, J. L. Asthme, abandon et traumatisme de naissance. RFPsa
        1954, 18:311
50333   Robinson, J. F. et al: Psychiatric Inpatient Treatment for Children.
        Q 1959, 28:97-98
50334   Winnicott, D. W. Mother and Child. Q 1958, 27:268-269

KEW, CLIFTON E.

50335   (& Kew, C. J.) Group psychotherapy in a church setting. Pastoral
        Psychol 1951, 1(10)
50336   (& Kew, C. J.) I have a little shadow. In author's *You Can Be Healed*,
        Prentice-Hall, 1954. Child-Fam Dig 1955, 12(1):53-63
50337   (& Kew, C. J.) Principles and values of group psychotherapy under
        church auspices. Pastoral Psychol 1955, 6(53):37-48
50338   (& Kew, C. J.) You Can Be Healed. NY: Prentice-Hall 1953, 186 p

KEW, CLINTON J.

See Kew, Clifton E.

KHAN, M. MASUD R.

50339   Clinical aspects of the schizoid personality: affects and technique.
        (Read at 21st Int Psa Cong, Copenhagen, July 1959) J 1960, 41:430-
        437
50340   Regression and integration in the analytic setting. A clinical essay on
        the transference and counter-transference of these phenomena. J 1960,
        41:130-146

See Winnicott, Donald Woods

REVIEWS OF:
50341   Bettelheim, B. Symbolic Wounds: Puberty Rites and the Envious Male.
        J 1955, 36:416
50342   Field, J. On Not Being Able to Paint. J 1953, 34:333-336
50343   Naumberg, M. Schizophrenic Art: Its Meaning in Psychotherapy. J
        1953, 34:164
50344   Pickford, R. W. The Analysis of an Obsessional. J 1955, 36:414

KIDORF, I. W.

See Magnussen, M. G.

KIELHOLZ, ARTHUR

50345   Analytische Beiträge zur Kirchengeschichte des Urchristentums. [Ana-
        lytical contributions to the history of the ancient Christian church.]
        Der Psychologe 1955, 7(11 & 12)
50346   Archäologie und Psychopathologie. [Archaeology and psychopathol-
        ogy.] Schweiz ANP 1956, 77:40-47
50347   Zur Behandlung und Verhütung von Depressionen bei Pensionierten.
        [On the treatment and prevention of depressions in pensioners.]
        Schweiz med Wschr 1953, 83:1117
50348   Von der Besserung nicht verbrecherischer Geisteskranken. [About the
        improvement of less than criminally insane patients.] Der Psychologe
        1952, 4(11)

50349 Biographie Adolf Weibel. [Biography of Adolf Weibel.] Lexikon, 840
50350 Biographie Konrad Frey. [Biography of Konrad Frey.] Lexikon, 234
50351 Einige Gedanken zur helfenden Sondererziehung. [Some thoughts on corrective special education.] Schweizer Lehrerzeitg. 1956, 35:919
50352 Freud und der Alkoholismus. [Freud and alcoholism.] Die Heilkunst 1956, 69:170-173
50353 Zur Geschichte der Psychiatrie im Aargau. [On the history of psychiatry in the Aargau.] Schweiz ANP 1956, 78:396-397
50353A Hans Zulliger. Schweiz Z Psychol 1953, 12:4-5
50354 Heilanstalt und Dichtung. [Sanatorium and fiction.] Prak Psychiat 1955, 34:173-174
50355 Von Heilgöttern und von Zahnärzten. [About healing gods and dentists.] Schweizer Mtschr Zahnheilkunde 1953, (5):452
50356 Von der Heilung durch Suggestion und Hypnose. [Therapy through suggestion and hypnosis.] Der Psychologe 1954, 6 (7 & 8)
50357 Von einem interessanten Amerikaner. [About an interesting American.] Prak Psychiat 1952, 31:229-233
50358 Von einem interessanten Engländer. [About an interesting Englishman.] Prak Psychiat 1954, 33:182-187
50359 Von einem interessanten Schweizer. [About an interesting Swiss.] Prak Psychiat 1956, 35:222-226
50360 Jakob Boehme und Baruch Spinoza als Vorläufer der Psychologie. [Jakob Boehme and Baruch Spinoza as forerunners of psychology.] Gesundheit u Wohlfahrt 1955, 35(6)
50361 Vom Kairos. Zum Problem der Kurpfuscherei. [On the problem of quackery.] Schweiz med Wschr 1956, 86:982
50362 Kinderbücher, ihre Dichter und das Unbewusste. [Children's books, their poets, and the unconscious.] Gesundheit und Wohlfahrt 1953, 6:(277)
50363 Zu einer kleinen Geschichte der psychoanalytischen Bewegung in der Schweiz. [Contribution to a short history of the psychoanalytic movement in Switzerland.] In *Festschrift zum 70. Geburtstag von Dr. Hans Christoffel*, Frankfurt a Main: Verlag Schau 1958
50364 Von der Krankheit, nicht krank sein zu können. [About the sickness, not to be able to be sick.] Praeventivmedizin 1957, 2:47
50365 Oskar Pfister. Schweiz Z Psychol 1953, 12:2-4
50367 Probleme der psychischen Hygiene in Anstalten. [Problems of mental hygiene in institutions.] Fachblatt Schweizer Anstaltswesen 1954, 25:242
50368 Von der Psychoanalyse seit Freud. [About psychoanalysis since Freud.] Der Psychologe 1956, 8(5/6)
50369 Psychohygiene im Werk von Prof. Heinrich Meng. [Psychohygiene in the work of Prof. Heinrich Meng.] Der Psychologe 1957, 9(8-9)
50370 Psychohygienische und psychotherapeutische Beiträge zu den Erscheinungen der modernen Völkerwanderung. [Psychohygienic and psychotherapeutic contributions to the phenomena of the modern migration of peoples.] Praeventivmedizin 1957, 2(3)
50371 Vom Rauchen und Trinken. [About smoking and drinking.] Gesundheit u Wohlfahrt 1955, 35(11)

50372 Sigmund Freud und das Problem des Krieges. [Sigmund Freud and the problem of war.] Junge Schweiz 1954, 11/12

50373 Von der Verbrechens-Verhütung in Anstalten. [About the prevention of crimes in institutions.] Gesundheit u Wohlfahrt 1954, 34:283. Prak Psychiat 1955, 34:2-9; 27-33.

50374 Zur Verhütung von Alterspsychosen. [Concerning the prevention of old-age psychoses.] Gesundheit u Wohlfahrt 1954, (8):365

50375 Von der Verhütung seelischer Störungen. [On the prevention of mental disturbances.] Jahresberichte des Hilfsvereins für Geisteskranke des Kantons Schaffhausen, 1951

KIELL, NORMAN

50377 The Adolescent Through Fiction: A Psychological Approach. NY: IUP 1959, 345 p
Abs J Am Psa Ass 1960, 8:599-600

KIESLINGER, GERTRUD M.
(See also Kurth, Gertrud M.)

50378 Der irdische Aufenthalt und die Erscheinungsform der Toten im europäischen Volksglauben. [The earthly abode and the form of appearance of the dead in European folk belief.] Arch Anthrop 1934, 23(2):79-149

KIEV, ARI

50379 Primitive therapy: a cross-cultural study of the relationship between child training and therapeutic practices related to illness. Psa St Soc 1960, 1:185-217

KIHN, BERTHOLD

50380 Über E. T. A. Hoffmann. [About E. T. A. Hoffmann.] In Speer, E. Lindauer Psychotherapiewoche, 1950, Stuttgart: Hippokrates-Verlag 1951, 110-121

50381 Die Kontaktpsychologie nach Ernst Speer. [Contact psychology according to Ernst Speer.] Hndb N P 1959, 3:413-424

50382 Über die Misserfolge in der Psychotherapie durch die Persönlichkeit des Arztes. [On the failure of psychotherapy due to the physician's personality.] In Speer, E. Die Vorträge der 5. Lindauer Psychotherapiewoche 1954, Stuttgart: Georg Thieme 1955, 136-142

50383 Psychotherapie des Massenmenschen. [Psychotherapy of collective man.] In Speer, E. Die Vorträge der 4. Lindauer Psychotherapiewoche 1953, Stuttgart: George Thieme 1954, 85-89

KILIAN, HANS

50384 Psychoanalyse und Anthropologie. [Psychoanalysis and anthropology.] In Riemann, F. Lebendige Psychoanalyse, Munich: Verlag C. H. Beck, 1956, 60-78

See Hose, W.

KILPATRICK, ELIZABETH

50385 Discussion of Robbins, B. "Schizophrenic consciousness and practice."
Schiz Psa Off Pract 22-25
50386 Training analysis. Psa 1953, 13:20-24
50387 Tribute to Karen Horney. Psa 1954, 14:8

See Kelman, Harold; Lussheimer, Paul; Van Bark, Bella S.

KIMBELL, ISHAM, JR.
See Redlich, Fredrick C.

KIND, H.
See Benedetti, Gaetano

KING, GERALD F.
See Rabin, Albert I.

KING, H. E.
See Lewis, Nolan D. C.

KING, STANLEY H.

50388 Psychosocial factors associated with rheumatoid arthritis. J chronic Dis
1955, 2:287-302. In Jaco, E. G. *Patients, Physicians and Illness*,
Glencoe, Ill: Free Pr 1958, 61-74

See Funkenstein, Daniel H.; Scheidlinger, Saul

KINGET, G. MARIAN

50389 The drawing completion test. In Hammer, E. F. *The Clinical Application of Projective Drawings*, Springfield, Ill: Thomas 1958, 344-364

KINNAIRD, JOHN

50390 The paradox of an American "identity." Partisan Review 1958, 25:380-
405

KINNEMANN, E. J.

50391 Prognosen ved psykoterapi. [Prognosis in psychotherapy.] Nord Med
1952, 47:727-730

KINNEY, MARGARET M.
See Bry, Ilse

KINSEY, A. C.

50392 [Participant in discussion on] Psychiatric implications of surveys on
sexual behavior. R 1956, 43:471-500

KIRBY, KATHRYN

50393 (& Priestman, S.) Value of a daughter (schizophrenic) and mother
therapy group. Int J grp PT 1957, 7:281-288
Abs Pivnick, H. Q 1959, 28:295

KIRCHHOFF, HANS W.
See Reindell, H.

KIRK, A'LELIA J.
See Warson, Samuel R.

KIRK, MARGARET
See Bernstein, Lotte

KIRKNER, FRANK J.
See Gengerelli, Joseph A.

KIRKPATRICK, MILTON E.

50394 Discussion. Round Table 1957: Segregation-integration: some psychological realities. Ops 1958, 28:31-33

KIRSCH, J.

50395 The enigma of Moby Dick. J analyt Psychol 1958, 3:131-148

KIRSCHBAUM, RUTH H.
See Prugh, Dane G.

KISKER, KARL PETER

50396 Zur Frage der Sinngesetzlichkeit. [The law of existential significance.] Schweiz ANP 1955, 76:5-22

KISSEN, DAVID M.

50397 Some psychological aspects of pulmonary tuberculosis. Int J soc Psychiat 1958, 3:252-259
Rv Salzi, J. RFPsa 1959, 23:294-295

KISSIN, BENJAMIN

50398 (& Gottesfeld, H.; Dickes, R.) Inhibition and tachistoscopic thresholds for sexually charged words. J Psychol 1957, 43:333-339

KITAMI, YOSHIO

50399 [Children's dreams and desires—analysis of dreams.] (Japanese) Child Study (ed & publ by Soc for Child Study in Tokyo Univ of Education) 1958, 12(2):45-50
50400 [The history of the progress of psychoanalysis in pre-war Japan.] (Japanese) Jap J Psa 1956, 3(9-10):2-6
50401 [School education and psychoanalysis.] (Japanese) Jap J Psa 1956, 3(4):1-11
50402 [Studies on typical dreams.] (Japanese) Jap J Psa 1957, 4(5, 6):1-12; 1958, 5(1):4-9; 1959, 6(1):1-7
50403 [Zen and psychoanalysis.] (Japanese) Bull of Soc for Psa Research, Tokyo 1952, 1(3):1-7

KITAMURA, SEIRO

50404 [A study of the fundamental ego.] (Japanese) Jap J Psychol 1953, 24:89-95

KITAYAMA, RIVU

50405 Der Romanschreiber Seseke Natume als Neurotiker. [The novelist Seseke Natume as a neurotic.] Tokio Z Psa 1938, 6:Sept

KITCHENER, HOWARD L.

See Dittmann, Allen T.

KIVISTO, P.

See Pasto, Tarmo A.

KLACKENBERG, GUNNAR

50406 Studies in maternal deprivation in infants' homes. Acta paediatr, Stockh 1956, 45:1-12

KLAF, FRANKLIN S.

50407 Napoleon and the Grand Army of 1812: a study of group psychology. PPR 1960, 47(3):67-76
50408 (& Brown, W.) Necrophilia: brief review and case report. Psychiat Q 1958, 32:645-652
    Abs Engle, B. Q 1960, 29:143
50409 "Night Song"—Nietzsche's poetic insight into the psychotic process. PPR 1959, 46(4):80-84

KLAPMAN, JACOB W.

50410 Group psychotherapy in relation to correctional psychiatry. J soc Ther 1957, 3:211-224
50411 Group psychotherapy in reverse. Dis nerv Syst 1952, 13:81-85
50412 Group Psychotherapy: Theory and Practice. (2nd ed) NY: Grune & Stratton 1959, x + 301 p
50413 Psychoanalytic or didactic group psychotherapy? Psychiat Q 1954, 28:279-286
    Rv Lamana, I. L. de. Rev Psicoanál 1955, 12:429

KLATSKIN, ETHELYN H.

50414 (& Jackson, E. B.; Wilkin, L. C.) The influence of degree of flexibility in maternal child care practices on early childhood behavior. Ops 1956, 26:79-93. Psychopathol 25-40
    Abs Koenig RFPsa 1957, 21:302-303. DRu Q 1959, 28:111
50415 (& Jackson, E. B.) Methodology of the Yale rooming-in project on parent-child relationship. Ops 1955, 25:81-108; 393-397

See Jackson, Edith B.

KLAUBER, JOHN

50416 Obituary: Dr. John Sheals Pratt. J 1956, 37:474-475

ABSTRACTS OF:

50417 Aarons, Z. A. Effect of the birth of a sister on a boy in his fourth year. J 1955, 36:218

50418 Aarons, Z. A. Notes on a case of *maladie des tics*. J 1960, 41:79

50419 Alexander, F. A contribution to the theory of play. J 1960, 41:79

50420 Alexander, F. Two forms of regression and their therapeutic implications. J 1957, 38:131-132

50421 Altman, L. L. The waiting syndrome. J 1958, 39:453

50422 Arlow, J. A. Notes on oral symbolism. J 1956, 37:202

50423 Azima, H. & Wittkower, E. D. Anaclitic therapy employing drugs: a case of spider phobia with Isakower phenomenon. J 1958, 39:450

50424 Bacon, C. L. Psycho-analytic observations on cardiac pain. J 1955, 36:421

50425 Bacon, C. L. The role of aggression in the asthmatic attack. J 1957, 38:132

50426 Barker, W. J. The stereotyped Western story. J 1956, 37:203

50427 Barrett, W. G. Mark Twain's osteopathic cure. J 1955, 36:220

50428 Barrett, W. G. On the naming of Tom Sawyer. J 1956, 37:204

50429 Bellak, L. & Smith, M. B. An experimental exploration of the psychoanalytic process. J 1957, 38:133

50430 Berliner, B. The role of object relations in moral masochism. J 1959, 40:365-366

50431 Bernabeu, E. P. Science fiction. J 1958, 39:453

50432 Bernabeu, E. P. Underlying ego mechanisms in delinquency. J 1960, 41:165-166

50433 Bernstein, I. The role of narcissism in moral masochism. J 1958, 39:451

50434 Bisi, R. H. Dermatosis in a case of postpartum psychosis. J 1957, 38:132-133

50435 Blank, H. R. Depression, hypomania and depersonalisation. J 1955, 36:421

50436 Blank, H. R. Psychoanalysis and blindness. J 1958, 39:448

50437 Blau, A. A unitary hypothesis of emotion. 1. Anxiety, emotions of displeasure and affective disorders. J 1956, 37:202

50438 Brady, M. W. The unconscious significance of the corner of a building. J 1954, 35:440

50439 Brody, M. W. Clinical manifestations of ambivalence. J 1957, 38:434

50440 Bunker, H. A. A dream of an inhibited writer. J 1955, 36:219

50441 Bunker, H. A. "Tantalus": a pre-Oedipal figure of myth. J 1954, 35:440

50442 Bychowski, G. The ego and the introjects. J 1957, 38:130

50443 Bychowski, G. General aspects and implications of introjection. J 1957, 38:434-435

50444 Bychowski, G. The structure of homosexual acting out. J 1955, 36:422

50445 Carroll, E. J. Acting out and ego development. J 1955, 36:425

50446 Cohn, F. S. Time and the ego. J 1958, 39:450

50447 Deutsch, F. A footnote to Freud's "Fragment of an Analysis of a Case of Hysteria." J 1958, 39:449-450

50448 Deutsch, H. The impostor. Contribution to ego psychology of a type of psychopath. J 1956, 37:204-205

50449 Devereux, G. Penelope's character. J 1958, 39:451

50450 Eisenbud, J. Behavioral correspondences to normally unpredictable future events. J 1955, 36:423; 424

50451 Eisenbud, J. Time and the Oedipus. J 1957, 38:133

50452 Evans, W. N. Evasive speech as a form of resistance. J 1955, 36:220

50453 Evans, W. N. Two kinds of romantic love. J 1954, 35:440

50454 Factor, M. A woman's psychological reaction to attempted rape. J 1955, 36:423

50455 Faergeman, P. M. Fantasies of menstruation in men. J 1956, 37:202

50456 Feldman, S. S. Blanket interpretations. J 1960, 41:79

50457 Feldman, S. S. Motives of "minor offences" in two dreams. J 1955, 36:423

50458 Fliess, R. The déjà raconté: a transference-delusion concerning the castration complex. J 1957, 38:132

50459 Fliess, R. The hypnotic evasion: a clinical observation. J 1955, 36:219

50460 Fox, H. M. Narcissistic defences during pregnancy. J 1960, 41:165

50461 Friedman, J. J. Psychology of the audience in relation to the architecture of the theater. J 1955, 36:220

50462 Garma, A. Vicissitudes of the dream screen and the Isakower phenomenon. J 1956, 37:204

50463 Giovacchini, P. L. Some affective meanings of dizziness. J 1960, 41:79

50464 Glauber, I. P. A deterrent in the study and practice of medicine. J 1955, 36:218-219

50465 Grauer, D. Homosexuality and the paranoid psychoses as related to the concept of narcissism. J 1956, 37:205

50466 Greenacre, P. The impostor. J 1960, 41:165

50467 Greenacre, P. "It's my own invention": a special screen memory of Mr. Lewis Carroll, its form and history. J 1956, 36:203

50468 Greenacre, P. The mutual adventures of Jonathan Swift and Lemuel Gulliver. J 1956, 37:202

50469 Greenson, R. R. About the sound "mm . . ." J 1955, 36:423

50470 Heilbrunn, G. Comments on a common form of acting out. J 1959, 40:366

50471 Heilbrunn, G. Fusion of the Isakower phenomenon with the dream screen. J 1954, 35:441

50472 Heilbrunn, G. On weeping. J 1956, 37:203

50473 Heiman, M. The relationship between man and dog. J 1957, 38:435

50474 Isakower, O. Spoken words in dreams. A preliminary communication. J 1955, 36:421

50475 Jackson, D. D. Some factors influencing the Oedipus complex. J 1955, 36:426

50476 Jarvis, W. When I grow big you grow little. J 1960, 41:166

50477 Johnson, A. M. Factors in the etiology of fixations and symptom choice. J 1955, 36:219

50478 Kanzer, M. Observations on blank dreams with orgasms. J 1955, 36:425

50479 Kepecs, J. G. Observations on screens and barriers in the mind. J 1955, 36:422

50480 Knapp, P. H. Sensory impressions in dreams. J 1957, 38:132
50481 Kolb, L. C. & Johnson, A. M. Aetiology and therapy of overt homosexuality. J 1956, 37:205
50482 Krapf, E. E. The choice of language in polyglot psychoanalysis. J 1956, 37:204
50483 Krapf, E. E. Transference and motility. J 1958, 39:453
50484 Kubie, L. S. The fundamental nature of the distinction between normality and neurosis. J 1955, 36:423
50485 Kubie, L. S. Research into the process of supervision in psychoanalysis. J 1960, 41:79
50486 Kubie, L. S. Some implications for psychoanalysis of modern concepts of the organisation of the brain. J 1954, 35:439-440
50487 Lacombe, P. A special mechanism of pathological weeping. J 1960, 41:79
50488 Laughlin, H. P. King David's anger. J 1955, 36:422
50489 Levine, J. & Redlich, F. C. Failure to understand humour. J 1956, 37:205-206
50490 Lewin, B. D. Dream psychology and the analytic situation. J 1956, 37:202-203
50491 Lewin, B. D. Reconsideration of the dream screen. J 1954, 35:440-441
50492 Lewin, B. D. Sleep, narcissistic neurosis, and the analytic situation. J 1955, 36:424-425
50493 Linn, L. The discriminating function of the ego. J 1955, 36:421-422
50494 Litin, E. M. et al: Parental influence in unusual sexual behavior in children. J 1957, 38:130
50495 Macalpine, I. & Hunter, R. A. The Schreber case. A contribution to the schizophrenia, hypochondria and psychosomatic symptom-formation. J 1955, 36:218
50496 Martin, P. Note on inhibition of scientific productivity. J 1957, 38:133
50497 Menaker, E. Masochism—a defense reaction of the ego. J 1954, 35:441-442
50498 Murphy, William F. A note on the significance of names. J 1958, 39:449
50499 Naftalin, M. Footnote to the genesis of Moses. J 1960, 41:166
50500 Needles, W. A note on orgastic loss of consciousness. J 1955, 36:219
50501 Niederland, W. G. River symbolism. J 1957, 38:434; 1958, 39:449
50502 Novey, S. The meaning of the concept of representation of objects. J 1959, 40:366
50503 Ostow, M. The illusory reduplication of body parts in cerebral disease. J 1959, 40:366-367
50504 Ostow, M. A psychoanalytic contribution to the study of brain function. Part II: The temporal lobes. III: synthesis. J 1956, 37:204
50505 Pederson-Krag, G. The use of metaphor in analytic thinking. J 1957, 38:131
50506 Posinsky, S. H. Instincts, culture, and science. J 1959, 40:365
50507 Racker, H. The meanings and uses of countertransference. J 1958, 39:450-451
50508 Racker, H. Notes on the theory of transference. J 1955, 36:422
50509 Rappaport, E. A. The management of an erotized transference. J 1957, 38:434

50510 Reichard, S. A reexamination of *Studies in Hysteria*. J 1957, 38:131
50511 Richfield, J. An analysis of the concept of insight. J 1955, 36:424
50512 Róheim, G. The individual, the group and mankind. J 1957, 38:130
50513 Róheim, G. The wolf and the seven kids. J 1954, 35:442
50514 Romm, M. E. The unconscious need to be an only child. J 1956, 37:203-204
50515 Rothenberg, S. & Brenner, A. B. The number 13 as a castration fantasy. J 1956, 37:205
50516 Saul, L. J. et al: On earliest memories. J 1957, 38:132
50517 Saul, L. J. The ego in a dream. J 1954, 35:442
50518 Saul, L. J. An etymological note on love and wish. J 1955, 36:219
50519 Saul L. J. The psychoanalytic diagnostic interview. J 1958, 39:449
50520 Sheppard, E. & Saul, L. J. An approach to a systematic study of ego function. J 1960, 41:79
50521 Siegman, A. J. Emotionality—a hysterical character defence. J 1955, 36:424
50522 Siegman, A. J. The psychological economy of *déjà raconté*. J 1957, 38:131
50523 Silverberg, W. V. Acting out versus insight. A problem in psychoanalytic technique. J 1956, 37:205
50524 Slap, J. The genesis of Moses. J 1960, 41:166
50525 Solomon, J. C. Fugue in a four-year-old. J 1959, 40:367
50526 Sperling, M. Etiology and treatment of sleep disturbances in children. J 1956, 37:204
50527 Sperling, M. Food allergies and conversion hysteria. J 1955, 36:219-220
50528 Sperling, O. E. A psychoanalytic study of social-mindedness. J 1956, 37:203
50529 Sperling, O. E. Psychodynamics of group perversions. J 1957, 38:130
50530 Starr, P. H. Psychoses in children: their origin and structure. J 1955, 36:426
50531 Stein, M. H. The marriage bond. J 1957, 38:132
50532 Stein, M. H. Premonition as a defence. J 1954, 35:440
50533 Steinberg, S. & Weiss, J. The art of Edvard Munch and its function in his mental life. J 1955, 36:424
50534 Sterba, R. Clinical and therapeutic aspects of character resistance. J 1954, 35:438-439
50535 Stern, M. M. Trauma, projective technique, and analytic profile. J 1954, 35:442
50536 Szasz, T. S. A contribution to the psychology of bodily feelings. J 1958, 39:448-449
50537 Szasz, T. S. Psychoanalysis as method and as theory. J 1959, 40:366
50538 Szurek, S. A. Teaching and learning of psychoanalytic psychiatry in medical school. J 1958, 39:451-452
50539 Weiss, J. Cézanne's technique and scoptophilia. J 1955, 36:219
50540 Weissman, P. Ego and super-ego in obsessional character and neurosis. J 1955, 36:425-426
50541 Weissman, P. Some aspects of sexual activity in a fetishist. J 1958, 39:452-453

50542 Wolf Man: Letters pertaining to Freud's "History of an infantile neurosis." J 1958, 39:452

50543 Zwerling, I. The favorite joke in diagnostic and therapeutic interviewing. J 1956, 37:202

REVIEWS OF:

50544 Halmos, P. Solitude and Privacy: A Study of Social Isolation, Its Causes and Therapy. J 1953, 34:339-340

50545 Meerloo, J. A. M. Conversation and Communication: A Psychological Inquiry. J 1953, 34:161-163

50546 Ruesch, J. & Bateson, G. Communication: The Social Matrix of Psychiatry. J 1953, 34:161-163

50547 Schneider, D. E. The Psycho-Analyst and the Artist. J 1955, 36:411

50548 Toulmin, S. The Philosophy of Science. J 1953, 34:345-346

KLAUBER, L. D.

See Meerloo, Joost A. M.

KLEIMAN, CHARLES

See Tarachow, Sidney

KLEIN, BETTY

50549 Participant in Clinical Conference: A problem of ego organization in a latency child. New Front Child Guide, 173-209

See Friend, Maurice R.

KLEIN, DAVID BALLIN

50550 The experimental production of dreams during hypnosis. Univ Texas Bull 1930, no. 3009:5-71. Abridged: Drms Pers Dyn 237-260

50551 Mental Hygiene; A Survey of Personality Disorders and Mental Health. NY: Henry Holt 1956, xviii + 654 p.

KLEIN, DONALD C.

50552 (& Ross, A.) Kindergarten entry: a study of role transition. In Krugman, M. *Orthopsychiatry and the School*, NY: Am Orthopsychiatric Ass 1958, 60-69

KLEIN, EMANUEL

50553 The psychoanalytic concept of the ego and its functions. Psa Soc Wk 22-52

ABSTRACT OF:

50554 Kris, E. Psychoanalytic Explorations in Art. An Surv Psa 1952, 3:586-605

KLEIN, GEORGE S.

50555 (& Spence, D. P.; Holt, R. R.; Gourevitch, S.) Cognition without awareness: subliminal influences upon conscious thought. ASP 1958, 57:255-266

Abs Applebaum, S. A. Q 1960, 29:296

50556 Cognitive control and motivation. In Lindzey, G. Assessment of Human Motives, NY: Rinehart 1958, 87-118

50557   Consciousness in psychoanalytic theory: some implications for current
        research in perception. J Am Psa Ass 1959, 7:5-34
            Abs Shentoub RFPsa 1959, 23:529. McLaughlin, J. T. Q 1960,
        29:588. TFr J 1960, 41:78. Rv Morera Rev Psicoanál 1959, 16:189
50558   The Menninger Foundation research on perception and personality,
        1947-1952: review. BMC 1953, 17:93-99. Menn Q 1954, 8:11-15
50559   Need and regulation. In Jones, M. R. *Nebraska Symposium on Motiva-
        tion: 1954,* Lincoln, Neb: Univ of Neb Pr 1954, 224-274
50560   A note to the reader [on Fritz Heider]. Psych Issues 1959, 1(3):v-vii
50561   Perception, motives and personality: a clinical perspective. In McCary,
        J. L. *Psychology of Personality,* NY: Logos Pr 1956, 122-199
50562   (& Holzman, P. S.; Laskin, D.) The perception project: progress re-
        port for 1953-1954. BMC 1954, 18:260-266
            Abs Rahman, L. Q 1956, 25:118
50563   (& Holt, Robert R.) Problems and issues in current studies of sub-
        liminal activation. In Peatman, J. G. & Hartley, E. L. *Festschrift for
        Gardner Murphy.* NY: Harper 1960, 75-93
50564   On subliminal activation. JNMD 1959, 128:293-301
50565   (& Smith, G. J. W.; Spence, D. P.) Subliminal effects of verbal stimuli.
        ASP 1959, 59:167-176

        See Bruner, Jerome S.; Gardner, Riley; Holzman, Philip S.; Smith,
        Gudmund J. W.

KLEIN, H. SYDNEY

50566   Analytic therapy. Mod Tr PSM 333-346
50567   Contribution to symposium on group therapy. M 1952, 25:223

        REVIEWS OF:
50568   Hill, L. B. Psychotherapeutic Intervention in Schizophrenia. J 1956,
        37:489-490
50569   Róheim, G. Magic and Schizophrenia. J 1958, 38:367-368
50570   Schilder, P. Medical Psychology. J 1955, 36:357-358
50571   Stokes, A. Michelangelo. J 1958, 39:429

KLEIN, HENRIETTE R.

50572   The Columbia Psychoanalytic Clinic: a development in psychoanalytic
        training. Chg Cpts Psa Med 4-14
50573   (& Potter, H.) On nursing behavior. Ps 1957, 20:39-46
50574   Pregnancy and childbirth. Prog PT 1957, 2:98-102
50575   A study of changes occurring in patients during and after psycho-
        analytic treatment. Curr App Psa 151-175
50576   Study of one hundred unselected patients attending gastrointestinal
        clinic. P 1948, 104:433-439

        See Potter, Howard W.

KLEIN, MELANIE

* * *   The child who couldn't sleep. See [18493].
S-18466 A contribution to the psychogenesis of manic-depressive states.
            Rv Badaracco Garcia. RFPsa 1955, 19:479-488

S-18467 A contribution to the theory of anxiety and guilt.
  Rv Garma Rev Psicoanál 1953, 10:518
S-18468 A contribution to the theory of intellectual inhibition.
  Rv Garma Rev Psicoanál 1953, 10:519-520
S-18470 Criminal tendencies in normal children.
  Le tendenze criminali nei bambini normali. (Tr: Savaral, A.) Riv
  Psa 1957, 3:3-18
  Rv Pichon-Rivière, A. A. Rev Psicoanál 1953, 10:521-522
S-18471 On criminality.
  Rv Pichon-Rivière, A. A. de. Rev Psicoanál 1953, 10:521
S-18472 On the criteria for the termination of a psycho-analysis.
  Abs R 1953, 40:359-360; 370
50577 On the development of mental functioning. (Read at 20th Int Psa
  Cong, Paris 1957) J 1958, 29:84-90
  Abs JLan Q 1959, 28:276. Usandivaras & Tabak Rev Psicoanál 1959,
  16:87
S-18473 The early development of conscience in the child.
  Sviluppo precoce della coscienza nel bambino. (Tr: Saraval, A.) Riv
  Psa 1956, 2:163-172
  Rv Garma Rev Psicoanál 1958, 15:124-125
50578 Envy and Gratitude. A Study of Unconscious Sources. London:
  Tavistock Pub Ltd; NY: Basic Books 1957, 101 p
  Rv Zetzel, E. R. Q 1958, 27:409-412. Rosenfeld, H. J 1959, 40:64-
  66
S-18480 Early stages of the Oedipus conflict.
  Stadi precoci del conflitto edipico. (Tr: Saraval, A.) Riv Psa 1956,
  2:3-15
50579 On identification. New Dir Psa 309-345
S-18483 The importance of symbol-formation in the development of the ego.
  L'importance de la formation du symbole dans le développement du
  moi. (Tr: Spira, M.) Psychanalyse 1956, 2:269-287
S-18484 Infantile anxiety situations reflected in a work of art and in the creative
  impulse.
  Rv Goode, E. Rev Psicoanál 1958, 15:123-124
50580 (& Riviere, J.) Love, Hate and Reparation. London: HPI 1953, 119 p
  Rv Lindsay, S. F. J 1955, 36:138
S-18488 The mutual influences in the development of the ego and id: discus-
  sion.
  Abs JAA An Surv Psa 1952, 3:42-43. WH J 1953, 34:278
50581 (& Heimann, P.; Money-Kyrle, R. E.) (Eds) New Directions in Psy-
  choanalysis. The Significance of Infant Conflict in the Pattern of Adult
  Behavior. NY: Basic Books 1955, 534 p; London: Tavistock Publ 1955,
  xiii + 534 p
  Rv Beres, D. Q 1957, 26:406-411. Lorand, S. J 1957, 38:283-285.
  Thorner, H. A. Rev Psicoanál 1957, 14:410-417
S-18491 Notes on some schizoid mechanisms.
  Notas sobre algunos mecanismos esquizoides. Rev Psicoanál 1948,
  6:82-113
S-18493 An obsessional neurosis in a six-year-old girl. With title: The child who

couldn't sleep. In Greenwald, H. *Great Cases in Psychoanalysis*, NY: Ballantine 1959, 63-91

S-18494 The Oedipus complex in the light of early anxieties.
El complejo de edipo a la luz de las ansiedades tempranas. Rev Psicoanál 1953, 10:439-496

S-18495 The origins of transference. YBPsa 1953, 9:37-46
Abs NRo An Surv Psa 1952, 3:405-406. Bernstein, I. Q 1954, 23: 142-143

S-18497 Die Psychoanalyse des Kindes.
The psychoanalysis of children. (Tr: Strachey, A.) NY: Grove Pr 1960, 399 p
La psychanalyse des enfants. (Tr: Boulanger, J. B.) Paris: PUF 1959, 320 p
Rv Goode, E. Rev Psicoanál 1958, 15:120. Pichon-Rivière, A. A. de Rev Psicoanál 1958, 15:109-111

S-18498 Die psychologischen Grundlagen der Frühanalyse.
Rv Garma, A. Rev Psicoanál 1958, 15:121

50582 The psycho-analytic play technique: its history and significance. Ops 1955, 25:223-237. New Dir Psa 3-22
Die psychoanalytische Spieltechnik: ihre Geschichte und Bedeutung. Psyche, Heidel 1959, 12:687-705
Abs DRu Q 1956, 25:447. Rv Grinberg, R. Rev Psicoanál 1958, 15:138-139

S-18499 The Psychotherapy of the Psychoses.
Rv Garma, A. Rev Psicoanál 1953, 10:520-521

50583 Rebellious and defiant children. In author's *Childhood and After*.
Rv Pichon-Rivière Rev Psicoanál 1958, 15:119

S-18502 Die Rollenbildung im Kinderspiel.
Rv Garma, A. Rev Psicoanál 1954, 11:406-407; 1958, 15:120-121

S-18506 Some theoretical conclusions regarding the emotional life of the infant.
Rv Chaio, J. Rev Psicoanál 1958, 15:132-133

50584 A study of envy and gratitude. (Read at 19th Int Psa Cong, Geneva, July 1955)
Neid und Dankbarkeit. Psyche, Heidel 1957, 11:241-255
Abs Auth J 1956, 37:131-132

S-18507 Symposium in child analysis.
Rv Pichon-Rivière, A. A. Rev Psicoanál 1958, 15:121-123

50585 Symposium on "Depressive Illness": V. A note on depression in the schizophrenic. (Read at 21st Int Psa Cong, Copenhagen, July 1959)
J 1960, 41:509-511

S-18514 Weaning.
Rv Resta Riv Psa 1958, 4:71-72

KLEIN, SIDNEY

50586 Obituary: Philip R. Lehrman, 1895-1958. Bull Am Psa Ass 14(1):380-382

KLEIN, VIOLA

50587 The feminine character. Out Psa 1955, 386-408. From author's *The Feminine Character*

KLEIN-LIPSHUTZ, EVA

50588 Comparison of dreams in individual and group psychotherapy. Int J grp PT 1953, 3:143-149
    Abs GPK Q 1955, 24:160

KLEINBERGER, ELIZABETH

50589 (& Barker, S.) The collaborative role of the child psychiatrist in the pediatric service. Workshop 1957: The collaboration of nursing and child psychiatry in a general hospital. Ops 1959, 29:83-85

See Barker, Sylvia; Blau, Abram

KLEINER, ROBERT J.

See Tuckman, Jacob

KLEINMAN, MILTON L.

See Kaplan, Harold I.

KLEINSCHMIDT, HANS JOACHIM

50590 The death of Elpenor. On a distinct type of self-destructive reaction in a rejected youth. J Hillside Hosp 1956, 5:320-327
    Abs Afterman, J. Q 1958, 27:609
50591 (& Waxenberg, S. E.; Cuker, R.) Psychophysiology and psychiatric management of thyrotoxicosis: a two year follow-up study. J Mt Sinai Hosp 1956, 23:131-153
50592 Psychotherapy with borderline schizophrenics; a review of current literature dealing with technique. Acta med orient 1955, 14(5):123-128

ABSTRACT OF:
50593 Spehlmann, R. Sigmund Freuds neurologische Schriften: Eine Untersuchung zur Vorgeschichte der Psychoanalyse. An Surv Psa 1953, 4:693-706

KLEINSORGE, H.

See Klumbies, G.

KLEITMAN, NATHAN

50594 Patterns of dreaming. Sci Amer 1960, 203:82-88

KLEMES, MARVIN A.

50595 (& Kallegian, V. J.) The group psychotherapist in industry: a preventive approach. Int J grp PT 1955, 5:91-98
    Abs GPK Q 1956, 25:454

KLEMPERER, EDITH

50596 Changes of the body image in hypnoanalysis. J clin exp Hyp 1954, 2:157-162

50597   Social anxiety, early sexual and aggressive theories as revealed through hypnoanalysis. R 1957, 44:81-87
50598   The spontaneous self-portrait in hypnoanalysis. J clin exp Hyp 1955, 3:28-33

KLEPZIG, H.

See Reindell, H.

KLIGERMAN, CHARLES

S-18529 The character of Jean Jacques Rousseau.
        Abs MK An Surv Psa 1951, 2:464-465
50599   A psychoanalytic study of the confessions of St. Augustine. (Read at Amer Psa Ass, NY, Dec 1956) J Am Psa Ass 1957, 5:469-484
        Abs Shentoub RFPsa 1958, 22:254-255. KHG Q 1960, 29:284-285
50600   The psychology of Herman Melville. R 1953, 40:125-143

ABSTRACT OF:
50601   Ehrenzweig, A. The Psychoanalysis of Artistic Vision and Hearing. An Surv Psa 1953, 4:578-590

REVIEW OF:
50602   Galdston, I. (Ed) Medicine in a Changing Society. Q 1957, 26:568-569

KLIJNHOUT, A. E.

50603   Régression ou évolution? (La sexualité humaine et animale.) [Regression or evolution? (The sexuality of humans and animals.)] Criança Port 1953, 11:245-264

KLINE, MILTON V.

50604   The application of hypnosis to non-directive psychotherapy. Clin Psych 1951, 7:283-287
50605   Childhood fears in relation to hypnotic age regression: a case report. J genet Psychol 1953, 82:137-142
50606   Delimited hypnotherapy: the acceptance of resistance in the treatment of a long standing neurodermatitis with a sensory-imagery technique. J clin exp Hyp 1953, 1(4):18-22
50607   The dynamics of hypnotically induced anti-social behavior. J Psych 1958, 45:239-245
50608   Editorial. J clin exp Hyp 1955, 3(1)
50609   Freud and hypnosis: a critical evaluation. Brit J med Hypnot 1953, 4(3):2-11
50610   Freud and hypnosis: II. Further observations on resistance and acceptance. J clin exp Hyp 1955, 3:124-129
50611   Freud and Hypnosis: The Interaction of Psychodynamics and Hypnosis. NY: Julian Pr 1958, xii + 207 p
50612   (Ed) Hypnodynamic Psychology. An Intergrative Approach to the Behavior Sciences. NY: Julian Pr 1955, 367 p
50613   Hypnosis and age progression: a case report. J genetic Psychol 1951, 78:195-205

50614 Hypnotherapy. Pres Day Psychol 797-834

50615 Hypnotic age regression and intelligence. J genetic Psych 1950, 77:129-132

50616 An hypnotic experimental approach to the genesis of occupational interests and choice. II. The thematic apperception test: a case report. J genetic Psychol 1953, 38:79-82

50617 (& Haggerty, A. D.) An hypnotic experimental approach to the genesis of occupational interests and choice: III. Hypnotic age regression and the thematic apperception test—a clinical case study in occupational identification. J clin exp Hyp 1953, 1(3):18-31

50618 Hypnotic retrogression: a neuropsychological theory of age regression and progression. J clin exp Hypn 1953, 1(1):21-28

50619 Living out "future" experience under hypnosis. Science 1954, 120 (3130):1076-1077

50620 The meaning of hypnotic behavior. In author's *A Scientific Report of "The Search for Bridey Murphy."* NY: Julian Pr 1956, 151-187

50621 A measure of mental masculinity and femininity in relation to hypnotic age progression. J genetic Psych 1951, 78:207-215

50622 A note on primate-like behavior induced through hypnosis; a case report. J genetic Psych 1952, 81:125-131

50623 An outline of the nature of some sexual reactions to the induction of hypnosis. Psychiat Q Supp 1952, 26(2):230-238

50624 Psoriasis and hypnotherapy: a case report. J clin exp Hypn 1954, 2:318-322

50625 Stimulus transformation and learning theory in the production and treatment of an acute attack of benign paroxysmal peritonitis. J clin exp Hyp 1954, 2:93-98

50626 Symptom control by direct suggestion including control of pain. In Dorcus, R. M. *Hypnosis and Its Therapeutic Applications,* NY: McGraw-Hill 1956

50627 Theoretical and conceptual aspects of psychotherapy. In author's *Hypnodynamic Psychology,* 77-203

50628 Toward a theoretical understanding of the nature of resistance to the induction of hypnosis and depth hypnosis. J clin exp Hypn 1953, 1(2):32-41

50629 (& Guze, H.) The use of a drawing technique in the investigation of hypnotic age regression and progression. Brit J med Hypn 1951, winter

50630 (& Shapiro, A.) The use of hypnosis in evaluating the physiological and psychological components in the functional impairments of the patient with multiple sclerosis. J clin exp Hypn 1956, 4(2):69-78

See Kazan, Avraam T.; Schneck, Jerome M.; Ventur, P.

KLINE, NATHAN S.

50631 (Ed) Approaches to the Study of Human Personality: Papers Presented at a Regional Research Conference Held under the Joint Auspices of the American Psychiatric Association and the Department of Psychiatry of the Graduate School of the National University of Mexico. Washington, D.C.: American Psychiatric Ass 1956, 176 p

50632   (& Barsa, J. A.; Bruckman, N. S.; Saunders, J. C.) The use of pro-
clorperazine (compazine) in a variety of psychiatric conditions. Psychiat Res Rep 1958, (9):5

See Ostow, Mortimer

KLINEBERG, OTTO

50633   The father's role. Best Articles and Stories 1958, 2(2):48-51
50634   Social Psychology. NY: Holt 1954, 578 p

KLOOS, G.

50635   [The psychopathology of tubercular patients.] (German) Dtsch med
Wschr 1949, 264

KLOPFER, BRUNO

50636   (& Ainsworth, M. D.; Klopfer, W. G.; Holt, R. R.) Developments in
the Rorschach Technique. Vol. 1: Technique and Theory. Yonkers,
NY: World Book Co 1954, 726 p. Vol 2: Fields of Application, 1956,
828 p.
Rv Kurth, G. M. Q 1955, 24:595-597; 1958, 27:276-278. Brown, F.
J Am Psa Ass 1957, 5:164-182

50637   (& Spiegelman, M.) Differential diagnosis. In author's *Developments in
the Rorschach Technique*, 2:282-317

50638   Discussion of Blumberg, E. M. "Results of psychological testing of
cancer patients." In Gengerelli, J. A. & Kirkner, F. J. *The Psychological
Variables in Human Cancer*, Berkeley, Los Angeles: Univ Calif Pr
1954, 62-65

50639   Discussion of Ellis, F. W. & Blumberg, E. M. "Comparative case summaries with psychological profiles in representative rapidly and slowly
progressive neoplastic diseases." In Gengerelli, J. A. & Kirkner, F. J.
The Psychological Variables in Human Cancer, Berkeley, Los Angeles:
Univ Calif Pr 1954, 93-94

50640   Jungian modification of Freudian ego psychology. In author's *Developments in the Rorschach Technique*, 1:565-575

50641   (& Crumpton, E.; Grayson, H. M.) Manual for rating scales for ego
functioning applicable to diagnostic testing. Distributed by UCLA
Students' Store, Feb 1958

50642   (& Spiegelman, M.) Methodological research problems. In author's
Developments in the Rorschach Technique, 2:267-280

50643   Projective techniques, ego psychology and analytic psychology. In
Contribution to Analytic Psychology, Vol 1: Zurich: Rascher 1955

50644   Psychological variables in human cancer. J proj Tech 1957, 21:331-
340

50645   (& Crumpton, E.; Grayson, H. M.) Rating scales for ego functioning
applicable to diagnostic testing. J. proj Tech 1958, 22:70-81

50646   (& Spiegelman, M.) Rorschach reactions and child therapy. In author's
Developments in the Rorschach Technique, 2:45-87

50647   (& Parker, J. W.; Franz, M. L. von) Sexual aggression and the need for
tenderness. Case St Couns PT, 190-217

KLOPFER, WALTER G.

See Bellak, Leopold; Klopfer, Bruno

KLOSINSKI, WERNER

50648 Die Handschrift vor und nach der analytischen Psychotherapie; Nachweis der Charakterwandlung. [Handwriting before and after analytic psychotherapy; proof of the change in character.] In Bitter, W. *Die Wandlung des Menschen in Seelsorge und Psychotherapie*, Göttingen: Verlag f med Psychol 1956

KLOSKA, G.

50649 Zur Bedeutung der Übertragung. [Significance of transference.] Hippokrates, Stuttg 1956, 27:38-39

KLOTH, EDWARD

ABSTRACT OF:
50650 Mittelmann, B. Motor patterns in infants, gestures, and genital behavior with a note on fetishism. Q 1956, 25:306-307

KLOTZ, MAURICE

See Masserman, Jules H.

KLUCKHOHN, CLYDE

50651 Culture and behavior. In Lindzey, G. *Handbook of Social Psychology*, Cambridge, Mass: Addison-Wesley Pub Co 1954, 921-976
50652 The educational process. In Goldschmidt, W. *Exploring the Ways of Mankind*, NY: Holt, Rinehart & Winston 1960, 179-187
50653 Ethical relativity: sic et non. J Philos 1955, 52:663-667
50654 The impact of Freud on anthropology. Bull NY Acad Med 1956, 32:903-907. In Galdston, I. *Freud and Contemporary Culture*, NY: IUP 1957, 66-72
50655 (& Murray, H. A.; Schneider, D. M.) (Ed) *Personality in Nature, Society, and Culture*. (2nd Ed, Rev & Enl) NY: Knopf 1956, xi + 701 p
50656 (& Murray, H. A.) Personality formation: the determinants. Pers n s c, 53-67
50657 Recurrent themes in myths and mythmaking. Daedalus (Proc Am Acad Arts & Sci) 1959, 88:268-279
S-18543 (& Morgan, W.) Some notes on Navaho dreams.
Abs JAA An Surv Psa 1951, 2:31-32. GD An Sur Psa 1951, 2:507. JFr An Surv Psa 1951, 2:244

See Kroeber, Alfred L.; Murray, Henry A.

REVIEWS OF:
50658 Róheim, G. Hungarian and Vogul Mythology. Q 1956, 25:99-100
50659 Steiner, F. Taboo. Q 1959, 28:540-541

KLUCKHOHN, RICHARD

See Whiting, John W. M.

KLUMBIES, G.

50660 (& Kleinsorge, H.) Kritische Untersuchungen zu einer Theorie der unbewussten Vorstellungen (zu den Bemerkungen von Dr. Karl Schmitz über Hypnose und Psychoanalyse). [Critical investigations leading to a theory of unconscious fantasies; apropos the remarks of Dr. Karl Schmitz on hypnosis and psychoanalysis.] Die Heilkunst 1956, 69:423-427

KLÜWER, KARL

50661 Zum neuen Verständnis der psychischen Entwicklung des Kindes durch Freud. [On the new understanding of the psychological development of the child through Freud.] In Riemann, F. *Lebendige Psychoanalyse*, Munich: Verlag C H Beck 1956, 79-97

See Schmeer, G.

KLÜWER, ROLF

50662 Psychoanalyse und religiöser Glaube. [Psychoanalysis and religious belief.] In Riemann, F. *Lebendige Psychoanalyse*, Munich: Verlag C H Beck 1956, 98-113

KLYCKHOHN, FLORENCE

See Spiegel, John P.

KNAPP, BARTON W.

REVIEW OF:
50663 Notcutt, B. The Psychology of Personality. R 1955, 42:308

KNAPP, PETER HOBART

50664 Conscious and unconscious affects: a preliminary approach to concepts and methods of study. Psychiat Res Rep 1957, 8:55-74
50665 Discussion [on the mysterious leap from the mind to the body.] Mind-Body 250-252
50666 The ear, listening and hearing. J Am Psa Ass 1953, 1:672-689. YBPsa 1954, 10:177-192
    Abs NRo An Surv Psa 1953, 4:111-113. Shentoub RFPsa 1954, 18:306. TFr J 1954, 35:446-447. MGr Q 1955, 24:611
50667 [Discussant] Is the term "mysterious leap" warranted? Mind-Body 18-19
50668 (& Nemetz, S. J.; Gilbert, R. R.; Lowell, F. C.; Michelson, A. L.) Personality variations in bronchial asthma. A study of forty patients: notes on the relationship to psychosis and the problem of measuring maturity. PSM 1957, 19:443-465
    Abs Johnson, McC. Q 1958, 27:608
50669 Sensory impressions in dreams. Q 1956, 25:325-347
    Abs JK1 J 1957, 38:132
50670 (& Nemetz, S. J.) Sources of tension in bronchial asthma. PSM 1957, 19:466-485
    Abs Johnson, McC. Q 1958, 27:608

50671 (& Levin, S.; McCarter, R. H.; Wermer, H.; Zetzel, E.) Suitability for psychoanalysis: a review of one hundred supervised analytic cases. Q 1960, 29:459-477

REVIEW OF:

50672 Ehrenwald, J. New Dimensions of Deep Analysis. Q 1956, 25:110-111

KNAPP, P. W.

See Dorsey, John M.

KNEHR, EDELTRAUT

50673 Ein schwer zu liebendes Kind. [A child difficult to love.] Prax Kinderpsychol 1955, 4:90-95

KNIGHT, EDWARD H.

S-18553A Spelling disability as a symptom of emotional disorder.
    Abs RRG Q 1953, 22:303

See Watkins, Charles

KNIGHT, JOHN

S-18554 The Story of My Psychoanalysis.
    Rv Garma Rev Psicoanál 1953, 10:116

KNIGHT, ROBERT P.

50674 Borderline states. Dr Af Beh 203-215. BMC 1953, 17:1-12. Psa Psychiat Psychol 1954, 1:97-109
    Abs JFr An Surv Psa 1953, 4:144-146. RRG Q 1953, 22:611-612

S-18558 A critique of the present status of the psychotherapies. Psa Psychiat Psychol 1954, 1:52-64. Bull NY Acad Med 1949, 25:100-114. J Med, Cincinnati 1949, 30:482-489

S-18559 Determinism, "freedom," and psychotherapy. Psa Psychiat Psychol 1954, 1:365-381

50675 Discussion of Ritvo, S. & Solnit, A. J. "Influences of early mother-child interaction on identification processes." Psa St C 1958, 13:90-91

S-18561 An evaluation of psychotherapeutic techniques. Psa Psychiat Psychol 1954, 1:65-76
    Abs NRo An Surv Psa 1952, 3:302-303. RRG Q 1953, 22:304

50676 (& Lewin, B. D.; Loewenstein, R. M.) Foreword. An Surv Psa 1951, 2:xi

50677 Foreword to Holt, Robert P. et al: *Personality Patterns of Psychiatrists.*

50678 The Journal of the American Psychoanalytic Association. J Am Psa Ass 1953, 1:5-6
    Abs WH J 1953, 34:274

50679 Management and psychotherapy of the borderline schizophrenic patient. BMC 1953, 17:139-150. Psa Psychiat Psychol 1954, 1:110-122
    Abs LCK An Surv Psa 1953, 4:470-473. RRG Q 1954, 23:468

50680 Obituary: Alfred Gross, 1893-1957. Q 1959, 28:250

50681 The present status of organised psychoanalysis in the United States. J Am Psa Ass 1953, 1:197-221. Psa Psychiat Psychol 1954, 1:7-26
    Abs JFr An Surv Psa 1953, 4:457-460. TFr J 1954, 35:442-443. MGr Q 1955, 24:156
S-18570 Psychiatric issues in the Kinsey Report on males. Psa Psychiat Psychol 1954, 1:311-320
50682 Psychiatry today. Oberlin Alumni Magazine, 1958, March
55683 (& Friedman, C. R.) (Eds) Psychoanalytic Psychiatry and Psychology: Clinical and Theoretical Papers. NY: IUP 1954, 391 p
    Abs Furer, M. J Am Psa Ass 1955, 3:161-162. Rv Barrett, W. G. Q 1955, 24:574-576. TFr J 1956, 37:486
50684 Seventeen ways to help or spoil a child. Science Illustrated 1947, 40
50685 Some remarks on psychotherapy. Dig Neurol Psychiat 1954, 22:150

    See Brenman, Margaret

KNOBEL, MAURICIO
See Dalma, Giovanni (Juan)

KNOBLOCH, F.
50686 [Contributions to the interpretation of dream mechanisms by the Pavlovian theory of conditioned reflexes.] Czechosl psa annual 1948

KNOBLOCH, HILDA
See Pasamanick, Benjamin

KNOEPFEL, H. K.
50687 (& Redlich, F. C.) Psychiatrische Ausbildung in USA. [Psychiatric training in the United States.] Psyche, Heidel 1953, 7:67-78

    See Redlich, Fredrick C.

KNOFF, WILLIAM F.
See Szasz, Thomas S.

KNOPF, OLGA
S-18610 Preliminary report on personality studies in 30 migraine patients. Rv Baranger, W. Rev Psicoanál 1954, 11:235-236

KNOWLTON, PETER
50688 Some principles of psychotherapy with atypical children. Ops 1954, 24:789-796
50689 (& Burg, M.) Treatment of a borderline psychotic five-year-old girl. Emot Prob Early Child. 451-488

KNOX, CRAWFORD
50690 The Idiom of Contemporary Thought. London: Chapman & Hall 1956, x + 206 p
    Rv Williams, A. H. J 1959, 40:355-356

KÖBERLE, D. ADOLF

50691 Das Schuldproblem in theologischer und tiefenpsychologischer Sicht. [The problem of guilt in the light of theology and of psychoanalysis.] In Bitter, W. *Psychotherapie und Seelsorge.* Stuttgart 1954

50692 Der Seelsorger lernt vom Psychotherapeuten. [The pastor learns from the psychotherapist.] Die Heilkunst 1958, 71:343-345

50693 Vatergott, Väterlichkeit und Vaterkomplex im christlichen Glauben. [Fathergod, fatherliness and father-complex in the Christian religion.] In Bitter, W. *Das Vaterproblem in Psychotherapie, Religion und Gesellschaft.* Stuttgart: Hippokrates 1955

KOBLENTZ, A. E.

See Tissenbaum, Morris J.

KOCH, A.

50694 Omnipotencia y sublimación. [Omnipotence and sublimation.] Rev Psicoanál 1956, 13:456-460

KOCH, HELEN L.

50695 Some emotional attitudes of the young child in relation to characteristics of his sibling. Child Develop 1956, 27:393-426

KOCH, SIGMUND

50696 Comments on Miller, D. R. & Swanson, G. E. "The study of conflict." In Jones, M. R. *Nebraska Symposium on Motivation:1956,* Lincoln, Neb: Univ of Neb Pr 1956, 175-179

KOCKEL, ELSA

50697 Freudsche und Jungsche Anschauungen in der Kasuistik. [Freudian and Jungian views in casuistry.] Psyche, Heidel 1953, 7:286-302
         Abs LRa An Surv Psa 1953, 4:49-51

KOCOUREK, KURT

50698 (& Niebauer, E.; Polak, P.) Ergebnisse der klinischen Anwendung der Logotherapie. [Results of the clinical application of Logotherapy.] Hndb NP 1959, 3:737-764

KOEGLER, RONALD R.

50699 In defense of the pun. Am Im 1959, 16:231-235

KOENIG

ABSTRACTS OF:
50700 Abramovitz, A. B. Methods and techniques of consultation. RFPsa 1959, 23:172

50701 Ackerman, N. Disturbances of mothering and criteria for treatment. RFPsa 1957, 21:304

50702 Alpert, A. A special therapeutic technique for certain developmental disorders in prelatency children. RFPsa 1958, 22:257

50703   Alpert, A. The treatment of emotionally disturbed children in a thera-
        peutic nursery. RFPsa 1956, 20:585-586

50704   Apteker, H. H. & Wertz, F. J. Clinique d'hygiene mentale dans le
        cadre d'une "agence sociale." RFPsa 1959, 23:432-433

50705   Baranger, M. Le fantasme de la maladie et le développement de
        l'insight dans l'analyse de l'enfant. RFPsa 1958, 22:255

50706   Behrens, M. L. & Goldfarb, W. Types of interaction in the families of
        schizophrenic children in residential treatment. RFPsa 1959, 23:173

50707   Bellak, L. et al: Rehabilitation of the mentally ill through controlled
        transitional employment. RFPsa 1957, 21:305

50708   Bender, L. & Grugett A.: A study of certain epidemiological factors in
        a group of children with childhood schizophrenia. RFPsa 1957, 21:303

50709   Blau, A. et al: The collaboration of nursing and child psychiatry in a
        general hospital. RFPsa 1959, 23:535

50710   Brody, N. M. & Hayden, M. Intra-team reactions: their relation to the
        conflicts of the family in treatment. RFPsa 1958, 22:258

50711   Brody, S. Signs of disturbance in the first year of life. RFPsa 1959,
        23:173-174

50712   Bromberg, N. Maternal influences in the development of moral masoch-
        ism. RFPsa 1956, 20:585

50713   Brown, B. S. & Nyswander, M. The treatment of masochistic adults.
        RFPsa 1957, 21:306

50714   Caplan, G. The role of deviant maturation in the pathogenesis of
        anxiety. RFPsa 1957, 21:303

50715   Clausen, J. A. & Kohn, M. L. Parental authority, behavior and schizo-
        phrenia. RFPsa 1957, 21:305-306

50716   Cook, R. Guides to the therapy of the alcoholic. RFPsa 1956, 20:586

50717   Eidelberg, E. A comparative pathology of the neuroses. RFPsa 1956,
        20:563-564

50718   Eisenberg, L. The fathers of autistic children. RFPsa 1959, 23:169

50719   Eisenberg, L. et al: Diagnostic services for maladjusted foster children.
        RFPsa 1959, 23:433

50720   Falstein, E. I. et al: Fantasies in children prior to herniorrhaphy.
        RFPsa 1959, 23:169-170

50721   Fried, E. Ego-strengthening aspects of hostility. RFPsa 1957, 21:303-
        304

50722   Furer, M. et al: Internalized objects in children. RFPsa 1957, 21:872

50723   Gardner, G. E. Present-day society and the adolescent. RFPsa 1959,
        23:167

50724   Gordon, G. & Siegel, L. The evolution of a program of individal psycho-
        therapy for children with aggressive acting-out disorders. RFPsa 1957,
        21:872

50725   Hallowitz, D. et al: The treatment process with both parents together.
        RFPsa 1959, 23:168

50726   Heiser, K. F. Mental deficiency in the urban community. RFPsa 1959,
        23:167

50727   Henry, J. Attitude organization in elementary school classrooms. RFPsa
        1957, 21:873

50728   Hertzman, M. Human relations in the classroom. RFPsa 1957, 21:122

50729   Hirschberg, J. C. & Mandelbaum, A. Choice of interpretation in the treatment of borderline and psychotic children. RFPsa 1958, 22:127-128

50730   Inglis, D. & Marsh, E. J. Usage des hôpitaux psychiatriques pour enfants. RFPsa 1959, 23:433

50731   Jenkins, R. L. Motivation and frustration in delinquency. RFPsa 1959, 23:167-168

50732   Josselyn, I. Cultural forces, motherliness and fatherliness. RFPsa 1957, 21:305

50733   Judas, I. et al: The role of the psychiatrist in a well-baby clinic. RFPsa 1959, 23:168

50734   Kaplan, L. K. & Turitz, L. L. Treatment of severely emotionally traumatized young children in a foster home setting. RFPsa 1958, 22:257-258

50735   Kaufman, I. et al: The impact of adolescence on girls with delinquent character formation. RFPsa 1959, 23:535

50736   Kaufman, I. & Heims, L. The body image of the juvenile delinquent. RFPsa 1959, 23:172

50737   Klatskin, E. H. et al: The influence of degree of flexibility in maternal child care practices on early child behavior. RFPsa 1957, 21:302-303

50738   Koret, S. & Rubin, E. Z. Utilization of projective tests as a prediction of casework movement. RFPsa 1958, 22:259

50739   Lagache, D. Le problème de transfert. RFPsa 1958, 22:256-257

50740   Lindzey, G. & Tejessy, C. TAT and aggression. RFPsa 1957, 21:122

50741   Lourie, R. S. Basic science and the failure of orthopsychiatry. RFPsa 1959, 23:431

50742   Mitchell, H. E. & Mudd, E. H. Anxieties associated with the conduct of research in a clinical setting. RFPsa 1958, 22:258

50743   Molish, H. B. & Beck, S. J. Further explorations of the "6 schizophrenias": type S-3. RFPsa 1959, 23:431

50744   Murphy, L. B. Psychoanalysis and child development. RFPsa 1958, 22:127

50745   Panel: The evaluation of rehabilitation in the individual. RFPsa 1956, 21:871-872

50746   Panel: Social group work in psychiatric residential settings. RFPsa 1957, 21:621-622

50747   Peck, H. B. Delinquency, a laboratory for public health psychiatry. RFPsa 1959, 23:172

50748   Peltz, W. et al: Group experiences with medical students as a method of teaching psychiatry. RFPsa 1957, 21:873

50749   Pereira Anavitarte, J. Notes sur l'activité ludique de l'adulte. RFPsa 1958, 22:256

50750   Pichon-Rivière, A. de: L'arrêt de l'acquisition du langage chez un enfant de six ans. RFPsa 1958, 22:256

50751   Piotrowski, Z. A. et al: Psychoanalytic concepts and principles discernible in projective personality tests. RFPsa 1959, 23:170-171

50752   Plank, E. N. et al: A general hospital child care program to counteract hospitalism. RFPsa 1959, 23:535

50753   Proctor, J. T. Hysteria in childhood. RFPsa 1959, 23:174

50754 Rexford, E. & Van Amerongen, S. T. The influence of unsolved maternal oral conflicts upon impulsive acting-out in young children. RFPsa 1957, 21:872

50755 Rexford, E. N. The life space interview. RFPsa 1959, 23:534-535

50756 Roy, F. Van: L'enfant infirme. Rev Psicoanál 1957, 14:563

50757 Segall, A. Report of a constipated child with fecal withholding. RFPsa 1959, 23:170

50758 Seidenfeld, R. Psychological implications of breathing difficulties in poliomyelitis. RFPsa 1956, 20:585

50759 Siegel, L. A catalyst in the growing pains of a residential treatment unit. RFPsa 1958, 22:259

50760 Sperry, B. et al: Renunciation and denial in learning difficulties. RFPsa 1959, 23:171-172

50761 Spotnitz, H. et al: Ego-reinforcement in the schizophrenic child. RFPsa 1957, 21:303

50762 Symposium: Behavior research in collective settlements in Israel. RFPsa 1959, 23:431-432

50763 Symposium: Childhood schizophrenia. RFPsa 1957, 21:122

50764 Symposium: Our young citizens: promise and problem. RFPsa 1957, 21:122

50765 Symposium on role of residential treatment for children, 1954. RFPsa 1956, 20:583-584

50766 Symposium on therapeutic play techniques, 1954. RFPsa 1956, 20:584-585

50767 Tathbun, C. et al: The restitutive process in children following radical separation from family and culture. RFPsa 1959, 23:174

50768 Waldfogel, S. et al: The development, meaning and management of school phobia. RFPsa 1959, 23:169

50769 Watson, E. J. & Johnson, A. M. The emotional significance of acquired physical disfigurement in children. RFPsa 1959, 23:172

50770 Workshop: Changing concepts in the care of the aged. RFPsa 1959, 23:173

50771 Workshop: Psychiatric consultation in residential treatment. RFPsa 1959, 23:173

50772 Workshop: School phobias. RFPsa 1958, 22:258

50773 Workshop: Traitement des toxicomanies. RFPsa 1959, 23:433

50774 Workshop. The use of the consultant. RFPsa 1958, 21:304-305

REVIEW OF:

50775 Braatoy, T. Fundamentals of Psychoanalytic Technique: A Fresh Appraisal of the Methods of Psychotherapy. RFPsa 1956, 20:562-563

KOENIG, RICHARD
See Whitman, Roy M.

KOENIGS, C.

50776 Psychische Faktoren bei Endokrinopathien. [Psychic factors in endocrine disorders.] Z PSM 1957, 3:157-172

KOESTLER, ARTHUR

50777 A guide to political neuroses. Encounter 1953, 1(2):25-32

KOFF, ROBERT H.

50778 A definition of identification. A review of the literature. (Read at Chicago Psa Soc, March 22, 1960)

Abs Seitz, P. F. D. Bull Phila Ass Psa 1960, 10:103-104

50779 The therapeutic man Friday. (Read at Am Psa Ass, Chicago, May 1956) J Am Psa Ass 1957, 5:424-431

Abs KHG Q 1960, 29:283

KOGA, MARY

See Boshes, Benjamin

KOGAN, NATHAN

50780 Authoritarianism and repression. ASP 1956, 53:34-37

KOGAN, YA

50781 [Identification and its role in artistic creativity.] (Russian) In [*Problems in the Theory and Practice of Psychoanalysis.*] Odessa: 1926, 78 p

50782 [Tattooing of Criminals.] (Russian) Odessa: 1928, 64 p

KOGERER, H.

50783 Psychotherapie und psychische Hygiene. [Psychotherapy and mental hygiene.] Wien Beitr Hyg 1955, 4:53-82

KOHL, RICHARD N.

50784 (& Flach, F. F.) Intensive dynamic psychotherapy of depressions. JNMD 1954, 120:90-91

KOHLSAAT, BARBARA

50785 (& Johnson, A. M.) Some suggestions for practice in infant adoptions. Soc Casewk 1954, 35:91-99

KOHN, LYNETTE GAYLE

See Siegel, Alberta E.

KOHN, MARTIN

See Esman, Aaron H.

KOHSEN, ANITA

See Gregory, Christopher Clive Langton

KOHUT, HEINZ

50786 Beyond the bounds of the basic rule. Some recent contributions to applied psychoanalysis. J Am Psa Ass 1960, 8:567-586

50787 (Reporter) Clinical and theoretical aspects of resistance. (Panel: Amer Psa Ass, NY, Dec 1956) J Amer Psa Ass 1957, 5:548-555
50788 *Death in Venice* by Thomas Mann: a story about the disintegration of artistic sublimation. Q 1957, 26:206-228
       Abs Auth J 1958, 39:450
50789 Introspection, empathy, and psychoanalysis. An examination of the relationship between mode of observation and theory. J Am Psa Ass 1959, 7:459-483
50790 Observations on the psychological function of music. (Read at Am Psa Ass, Chicago, May 1956) J Am Psa Ass 1957, 5:389-407
       Abs Shentoub RFPsa 1958, 22:253. KHG Q 1960, 29:282-283
50791 Psychoanalysis and introspection. (Read at 20th Int Psa Cong, Paris, July 1957)
       Abs J 1958, 39:292
S-18672 The psychological significance of musical activity.
       Abs MK An Surv Psa 1951, 2:480-481
50792 (Reporter) The psychology of imagination. (Panel: Am Psa Ass, Phila, Apr 1959) J Am Psa Ass 1960, 8:159-166
50793 Some psychological effects of music and their relation to music therapy. Music Therapy 1955, 5:17-20

ABSTRACT OF:
50794 (& Michel, A.) Michel, A. Psychanalyse de la Musique. An Surv Psa 1951, 2:662-675

REVIEWS OF:
50795 Greenacre, P. Swift and Carroll. J Am Psa Ass 1960, 8:576-586
50796 Hirschbach, F. D. The Arrow and the Lyre: A Study of the Role of Love in the Works of Thomas Mann. Q 1957, 26:273-275
50797 Hitschmann, E. Great Men: Psychoanalytic Studies. J Am Psa Ass 1960, 8:567-586
50798 Macalpine, I. & Hunter, R. A. (Eds) Daniel Paul Schreber, Memoirs of My Nervous Illness. J Am Psa Ass 1960, 8:567-586
50799 Michel, A. Psychanalyse de la musique. Q 1952, 21:109-111
50800 Reik, T. The Haunting Melody. Q 1955, 24:134-137
50801 Sterba, E. & Sterba, R. Beethoven and His Nephew. Q 1955, 24:453-455. J Am Psa Ass 1960, 8:567-586

KOLANSKY, HAROLD

50802 Castration anxiety following recovery from the rash of measles during the oedipal period. Bull Phila Ass Psa 1957, 7:110-113
       Abs de Saugy RFPsa 1959, 23:158-159
50803 A clinical note on the unconscious equation, machine = penis. Bull Phila Ass Psa 1957, 7:136-139
       Abs EFA Q 1958, 27:604. de Saugy RFPsa 1959, 23:159
50804 Obsessional thinking and conversion reaction in a case of psychogenic fever. Bull Phila Ass Psa 1957, 7:74-76
50805 Treatment of a three-year-old girl's severe infantile neurosis: stammering and insect phobia. Psa St C 1960, 15:261-285. Abridged: Bull Phila Ass Psa 1960, 10:113-129

KOLB, LAWRENCE C.

50806 Anxiety and anxiety reactions. J chron Dis 1959, 9:199

50807 Discussion of Zilboorg, G. "The conceptual vicissitudes of the idea of schizophrenia." Schiz Psa Off Pract 38-39

50808 Disturbances of the body-image. Am Hbk Psychiat 1:749-769

50809 (& Johnson, A. M.) Etiology and therapy of overt homosexuality. (Read at Am Psa Ass, NY, Dec 4, 1953) Q 1955, 24:506-515
    Abs Dreyfus RFPsa 1956, 20:572. JKl J 1956, 37:205

50810 (& Montgomery, J.) An explanation for transference cure: its occurrence in psychoanalysis and psychotherapy. P 1958, 115:414-421. Prog PT 1959, 4:66-75
    Abs Loeb, L. Q 1960, 29:289

50811 The mental hospitalization of the aged: is it being overdone? P 1956, 112:627-636

50812 Pain as a biosocial phenomenon. Dig Neurol Psychiat 1955, 23:207. Conn State med J 1956, 20:116

50813 Pain as a psychiatric problem. The Journal-Lancet, Minneapolis 1952, 72(2):50

50814 The Painful Phantom: Psychology, Physiology, and Treatment. Springfield, Ill: Charles C Thomas 1954, ix + 50 p

50815 Psychiatric experiences with painful phantom limb. AMA ANP 1955, 73:457-458. JNMD 1955, 121:89-90

50816 The psychiatric viewpoint in training residents. JAMA 1956, 161:21-24

50817 Psychiatry. Annual Review of Medicine 1956, 7:109-122

50818 Psychoanalytic studies in psychiatry. An Surv Psa 1953, 4:469-525

50819 Psychotherapeutic evolution and its implications. Psychiat Q 1956, 30:579-597
    Abs JBi Q 1957, 26:438-439

50820 Treatment of the acute painful phantom limb. Proc Staff Meet May Clinic 1952, 27:110-118

See Horwitz, William A.; Noyes, Arthur P.; Smith, Lauren H.

ABSTRACTS OF:

50821 Ackerman, N. W. (Reporter) Panel: Problems of hypertension. An Surv Psa 1953, 4:486-489

50822 Bergler, E. Writers and ulcers. An Surv Psa 1953, 4:495

50823 Cushing, M. M. The psychoanalytic treatment of a man suffering with ulcerative colitis. An Surv Psa 1953, 4:497-498

50824 Eissler, K. R. Notes upon the emotionality of a schizophrenic patient and its relation to problems of technique. An Surv Psa 1953, 4:473-474

50825 Flescher, J. The "primary constellation" in the structure and treatment of psychoses. An Surv Psa 1953, 4:474-475

50826 Foulkes, S. H. Some similarities and differences between psychoanalytic principles and group-analytic principles. An Surv Psa 1953, 4:505-506

50827 Frank, G. H. The literature on counter-transference. An Surv Psa 1953, 4:510-513

50828 Garma, A. The internalized mother as harmful food in peptic ulcer patients. An Surv Psa 1953, 4:493-495

50829 Golden, M. M. Some mechanisms of analytic group psychotherapy. An Surv Psa 1953, 4:506-508

50830 González, J. L. Asma, abandono y trauma del nacimiento. An Surv Psa 1953, 4:498-499

50831 Grotjahn, M. Neuere Fortschritte in der Entwicklung der psychotherapeutischen Technik. An Surv Psa 1953, 4:503-505

50832 Grotjahn, M. Special aspects of countertransference in analytic group psychotherapy. An Surv Psa 1953, 4:513-514

50833 Hadden, S. B. Countertransference in the group psychotherapist. An Surv Psa 1953, 4:517-518

50834 Karush, A. & Daniels, G. Ulcerative colitis: the psychoanalysis of two cases. An Surv Psa 1953, 4:496-497

50835 Knight, R. P. Management and psychotherapy of the borderline schizophrenic patient. An Surv Psa 1953, 4:470-473

50836 Kotkov, B. Analytically oriented group psychotherapy of psychoneurotic adults. An Surv Psa 1953, 4:508-510

50837 Kubie, L. S. The central representation of the symbolic process in psychosomatic disorders. An Surv Psa 1953, 4:483-486

50838 Langer, M. & Ochandorena, R. P. El espasmo de las trompas como origen de esterilidad; sus causas, mechanismo y tratameniento. An Surv Psa 1953, 4:499

50839 Lebovici, S. A propos de la psychanalyse de groupe. An Surv Psa 1953, 4:510

50840 Linn, L. Psychological implication of the "activating system." An Surv Psa 1953, 4:481-483

50841 Loeser, L. H. & Bry, T. The position of the group therapist in transference and countertransference: an experimental study. An Surv Psa 1953, 4:519-521

50842 Mahl, G. F. & Karpe, R. Emotions and hydrochloric acid secretion during psychoanalytic hours. An Surv Psa 1953, 4:489-491

50843 Reider, N. A type of transference to institutions. An Surv Psa 1953, 4:479-480

50844 Rosenthal, L. Countertransference in activity group therapy. An Surv Psa 1953, 4:522-524

50845 Ruffler, G. Grundsätzliches zur psychoanalytischen Behandlung körperlich Kranker. An Surv Psa 1953, 4:500-503

50846 Saul, L. J. Brief therapy of a case of torticollis. An Surv Psa 1953, 4:475-476

50847 Saul, L. J. Psychosomatic aspects of peptic ulcer. An Surv Psa 1953, 4:491-493

50848 Schindler, W. Countertransference in "family pattern group psychotherapy." An Surv Psa 1953, 4:521-522

50849 Slavson, S. R. Sources of countertransference and group-induced anxiety. An Surv Psa 1953, 4:515-517

50850 Sperling, M. Food allergies and conversion hysteria. An Surv Psa 1953, 4:499

50851 Tarachow, S. & Fink, M. Absence of a parent as a specific factor determining choice of neurosis: preliminary study. An Surv Psa 1953, 4:469-470

50852   Wayne, G. J. Modified psychoanalytic therapy in senescence. An Surv
        Psa 1953, 4:476-479

KOLLE, KURT

50853   (Ed) Grosse Nervenärzte. [Great Neurologists.] Stuttgart: Georg
        Thieme, 1956.
50854   Hans Berger. In author's *Grosse Nervenärzte* 1956, 1:1-16
50855   Introduction. In author's *Grosse Nervenärzte* 1:v-vii
50856   Karl Jaspers. In author's *Grosse Nervenärzte* 1956, 1:145-152
50857   Kraepelin und Freud: Beitrag zur Neueren Geschichte der Psychiatrie.
        [Kraepelin and Freud: Contribution to the Newer History of Psy-
        chiatry.] Stuttgart: Georg Thieme 1957, 88 p
50858   Psychotherapie; Vorlesungen zur Einführung in das Wesen und die
        Probleme der seelischen Krankenbehandlung. [Psychotherapy; Intro-
        ductory Lectures to the Nature and Problems of the Psychologic
        Treatment of Illness.] Basel, Switz: S Karger 1953, viii + 112 p.
50859   Sigmund Freud zum 100. Geburtstag; 1856-1939. [On the 100th
        anniversary of birth of Sigmund Freud; 1856-1939.] Dtsche med
        Wschr 1956, 81:1045-1047

KOLODNEY, ETTA

50860   The lessening of dependency needs through casework therapy. Ops
        1954, 24:98-110
50861   Participant in Clinical Conference: A problem of ego organization in a
        latency child. New Front Child Guid 173-209

KONDO, AKIHISA

50862   Intuition in Zen Buddhism. Psa 1952, 12:10-14
50863   Morita therapy: a Japanese therapy for neurosis. Psa 1953, 13:31-37

TRANSLATION OF:
Kelman, H. [50214]

KONOPKA, GISELA

50864   Discussion: Group therapy in the treatment of adolescent delinquents.
        Proc Nat Ass of Training Schools and Juvenile Agencies, May 1958,
        Chicago, Ill, 54:168-171
50865   The generic and the specific in group work practice in the psychiatric
        setting. Soc Work 1956, 1:72-80
50866   Group Work in the Institution: A Modern Challenge. NY: Assoc Pr
        1954, 304 p
            Psicologia Del Grupo. NY: Whiteside Inc & W. Morrow & Co 1957,
        345 p
50867   Resistance and hostility in group members. The Group 1953, 16:3-10
50868   The role of the group in residential treatment. Symposium, 1954; The
        role of residential treatment for children. Ops 1955, 25:679-684
            Abs Koenig RFPsa 1956, 20:583-584
50869   The role of the group worker in the psychiatric setting. Ops 1952,
        22:176-185

50870   The social group work method: its use in the correctional field. Federal
         Probation 1956, 20:25-30
50871   Social group work in relation to treatment. Proc 1955 Social Work
         Progress Institute 1955, April 6. Univ of Mich, Ann Arbor, 16-30
50872   Social group workers and mental health. Pamphlet; NY: Nat Ass Soc
         Workers 1959
50873   Therapeutic Group Work with Children. Minn Pr 1949
             Gruppenarbeit mit 11-17 jährigen Jungen in einem amerikanischen
         Auffangheim. München-Düsseldorf: Wilhelm Steinebach 1954, 84 p
50874   The troubled child. Minn J of Educ 1954, 35:33

KONUMA, MASUHO

50875   [On the case-studies about neuroses in my clinic.] (Japanese) Noshin-
         kei Ryoiki 1953, No. 2-3:127-138
50876   [On psychoanalysis for the psychogenesis of a case with depressive
         syndrome.] (Japanese) Hiroshima Igaku: Suppl. Ed 1952, 5(10):18-20
50877   [On the psychomechanisms of the persons described in the master-
         piece "Sasameyuki" by the famous novelist Jyunichiro Tanizaki.]
         (Japanese) Hiroshima Igaku, Suppl Ed 1952, 5:407-411

KOOLHAAS, GILBERTO

50878   El origen psicótico de la neurosis. [The psychotic origin of neurosis.]
         Rev Urug Psa Montevideo 1958, 2(4)
50879   Priapismo. Sobre las fantasías inconscientes de la erección. [Priapism.
         About the unconscious fantasies expressed by erection.] Rev Urug
         Psa Montevideo 1956, 1(1)
50880   Psicoanálisis de una perturbación visual. [The psychoanalysis of a
         visual disturbance.] Rev de Psiquiatría del Uruguay 1952, Aug
             Rv Grinberg, L. Rev Psicoanál 1953, 10:248-249
50881   (& Baranger, W.) Un sueño típico: el ascensor. [A typical dream: the
         elevator.] Rev Psicoanál 1956, 13:403-408
50882   El tiempo de la disociación, de la represión, de la reparación. [Time
         structure of dissociation, repression and reparation.] Rev Urug Psa
         Montevideo 1957, 2(1-2)

KOPPEL, SYLVIA

TRANSLATION OF:
(& Angel, E.) Gebsattel, V. E. von [11480]

KORANYI, E. K.

See Kerenyi, A. B.

KORCHIN, SHELDON J.

50883   (& Levine, S.) Anxiety and verbal learning. ASP 1957, 54:234-240
50884   (& Singer, J. L.; Ballard, R. G.) The effect of frustration on the re-
         production of visually-perceived forms. Personality 1951, 1:54-66
50885   (& Basowitz, H.; Grinker, R. R.; Hamburg, D. A.; Persky, H.; Sab-
         shin, M.; Heath, H.; Board, F. A.) Experience of perceptual distor-
         tion as a source of anxiety. AMA ANP 1958, 80:98-113

50886 (& Basowitz, H.) The judgment of ambiguous stimuli as an index of cognitive functioning in aging. J Personality 1956, 25:81-95

50887 (& Basowitz, H.) Perceptual adequacy in a life stress. J Psychol 1954, 38:495-502

50888 (& Basowitz, H.; Chevalier, J.; Grinker, R. R.; Hamburg, D. A.; Sabshin, M.; Persky, H.) Visual discrimination and the decision process in anxiety. AMA ANP 1957, 78:425-438

See Basowitz, Harold; Glickstein, Mitchell; Grinker, Roy R.; Hamburg, David A.; Persky, Harold; Sabshin, Melvin S.

KOREN, LOUIS

50889 (& Joyce, J. M.) The treatment implications of payment of fees in a clinic setting. Ops 1953, 23:350-357

KORET, SYDNEY

50890 (& Rubin, E. Z.) Utilization of projective tests as a prediction of casework movement. Ops 1957, 27:365-374
   Abs Koenig RFPsa 1958, 22:259

KORGER, MATTHIAS E.

50891 (& Polak, P.) Der geistesgeschichtliche Ort der Existenzanalyse. [The place of existentialist analysis in intellectual history.] Hndb N P 1959, 3:632-662

KORIN, HYMAN

50892 (& Fink, M.; Kwalwasser, S.) Relation of changes in memory and learning to improvement in electroshock. Confinia Neurologica 1956, 16:88-96

See Tarachow, Sidney

KORKES, LENORE
See Lewis, Nolan D. C.

REVIEWS OF:
50893 Bordin, E. S. Psychological Counseling. R 1955, 42:444-445
50894 Braatoy, T. Fundamentals of Psychoanalytic Technique. R 1957, 44:115-116
50895 Rado, S. & Daniels, G. E. (Eds) Changing Concepts of Psychoanalytic Medicine. R 1957, 44:114-115

KORMAN, ROBERT
See Lichtenberg, Philip

KORNBERG, LEONARD
See Scherer, Marvin

KORNER, ANNELIESE F.

50896 Limitations of projective techniques: apparent and real. J proj Tech 1956, 20:42-47

See Reider, Norman

KORNER, IJA N.

See Branch, C. H. Hardin

KORNETSKY, CONAN

See Abramson, Harold A.; Levine, Abraham

KORTLAND, A.

50897 Aspects and prospects of the concept of instinct. (Vicissitudes of the hierarchy theory). Arch Neerland de Zool 1955, 11:155-284. Leyden: E J Brill 1955

KOSAWA, HEISAKU

50898 [For understanding psychoanalysis.] (Japanese) Tokyo: Publ Dept of Hiyoshi Psychiatric Hosp 1958, 315 p

TRANSLATIONS OF:
Freud, S. [10547, 10696]. (& Okonogi, K.) Reich, W. [26812]

KOSSEFF, JEROME WILLIAM

50899 A study of changes in body image during psychotherapy. Ann Arbor: University Microfilms, 1952

KOTELIANSKY

See Woolf, Virginia

KOTHARI, N. J.

50900 Psychoanalytical views of epilepsy. Samīksā 1954, 8:58-60
    Abs JFr An Surv Psa 1954, 5:161

KOTINSKY, RUTH

50901 (& Witmer, Helen L.) (Eds) Community Programs for Mental Health. Theory Practice, Evaluation. Cambridge, Mass: Harvard Univ Pr for the Commonwealth Fund 1955, 362 p
    Rv Bech, E. B. Q 1956, 25:608-610

See Witmer, Helen L.

KOTKOV, BENJAMIN

50902 Analytically oriented group psychotherapy of psychoneurotic adults. R 1953, 40:333-350
    Abs LCK An Surv Psa 1953, 4:508-510
50903 Common forms of resistance in group psychotherapy. R 1957, 44:88-96
    Abs JLan Q 1958, 27:289

50904   Goals of short-term group psychotherapy. JNMD 1956, 123:546-552
50905   The group as a training device for a girls' training school staff. Int J grp PT 1954, 4:193
50906   Group psychotherapy with wayward girls. Dis nerv Syst 1953, 14:308
50907   Psychoanalytic application to levels of group psychotherapy with adults. Dis nerv Syst 1958, 19:379-385
50908   Unresolved sexual fantasies in group therapy. R 1957, 44:313-322

KOUPERNIK, CYRILLE

50909   Le développement du nourrisson: normes, techniques et hypothèses de travail. [The development of the infant: norms, techniques, and working hypotheses.] Evolut psychiat 1956, (3):613-630
        Abs Lebovici RFPsa 1957, 21:299

        See Berge, André

KOURETAS, D.

S-18786A [Abnormal Characters in the Ancient Drama.]
        Rv Lyketsos, G. Q 1953, 22:110-112
50910   [The centenary of birth of S. Freud and psychoanalysis.] (Greek) Radamanthys (Greece) 1956, December
50911   [Elements of psychoanalysis.] (Greek) A supplement to the Greek translation of Cecil, L. R. *Internal Pathology*, Vol. IV. Athens: Karavias Pr 1959
50912   De Freud à Hippocrate. RFPsa 1958, 22:733-736
        From Freud to Hippocrates. (Tr: Destounis, N.) Psychiat Comm 1959, 2:34-35
        Rv de Fiasche Rev Psicoanál 1959, 16:281
50913   [Freud and literature.] (Greek) Nea Hestia (Athens), 1956:June 1
50914   [Freud's personality formation on the basis of his personal childhood experiences and their influence upon the genesis of psychoanalysis.] (Greek) Arch med sci (Athens) 1956, July
50915   Introductory remarks to the Greek translation of Sigmund Freud's *Die Traumdeutung*. Athens, 1957
50916   ["Know Thyself" as an emblem of psychoanalysis.] (Greek) Helliniki Iatriki 1956, May
50917   [The meaning of fate in Euripides' "Medea" from a psychological standpoint.] (Greek) Akrokorinthos (Athens) 1955-56
50918   Motivation of Medea's infanticide. 55th Cong of French Neurol and Psychiat Soc (Lyon), 273-279
50919   (& Tsoukantos, G.) [Melampus's treatment by psychocatharsis of the "childlessness" of Iphicles.] (Greek) Helliniki Iatriki 1955, 24:1025-1029
        Abs Zavitzianos, G. Q 1957, 26:147
50920   La névrose sexuelle des Danaides. [The sexual neurosis of the Danaïdes.] Proc 54th Cong of the French Neurol and Psychiat Soc (Bordeaux), 398-399. RFPsa 1957, 21:597-602
        Abs Roman, R. E. Q 1958, 27:149
50921   [The problem of alcoholism in the light of psychoanalysis.] (Greek) Kinoniki Pronia (Athens) 1959, No 12

50922 [Psychic health in everyday life.] (Greek) Kinoniki Pronia (Athens), 1958, July: No 10

50923 [Psychoanalysis in Greece.] (Greek) Kathimerini, Greece, 1956, May 8

50924 [Psychoanalysis and the problem of psychic heredity.] (Greek) Kinoniki Pronia (Athens), 1957, January:No 4

50925 [Psychoanalytic interpretation of the Danaïdes myth.] (Greek) Neon Athineon (Greece) 1955, 255

50926 [Psychoanalytic remarks upon the criminality in Greece.] (Greek) Peloponesian Hestia (Athens), 1955, No 3-4

50927 [The psychoanalytic symbolism of the Danaïdes myth.] (Greek) Academic Medicine (Greece), 1957:December

50928 [Psychoanalytic views on the ancient Greek drama.] (Greek) Helliniki Iatriki (Greece), 1956:Jan

50929 [Some fundamental principles of psychoanalysis.] (Greek) Helios (Athens), 1953:July 4

50930 [On some motives of resistance to psychoanalysis.] (Greek) Radamanthys (Athens), 1957:Jan

50931 [Some remarks on psychogenic impotence.] (Greek) Helliniki Iatriki (Greece) 1959, No 5

TRANSLATION OF:
Devereux, G. [44256]

KOUSSY, ABDEL AZIZ

50932 Editor of Menninger, W. C. *Understanding Yourself* (Arabic)

KOVACS, ARTHUR L.

50933 Some antecedents of denial in fantasy as a defense against anger. Diss Abstr 1959, 19:3366-3367

KOVITZ, BENJAMIN

See Agoston, Tibor; Bateman, J. F.

KOVSHAROVA, G.

50934 [Psychoanalytic polyclinic in Berlin.] (Russian) Vrachebnoe delo 1923, No 3-5:109-110

KOWAL, SAMUEL J.

50935 Emotions as a cause of cancer. 18th and 19th century contributions. R 1955, 42:217-227
       Abs JLan Q 1957, 26:139

KRAELING, DORIS

See Miller, Neal E.

KRAEMER, WILHELM GUENTHER PAUL

50936 The dangers of unrecognized counter-transference. J analyt Psychol 1958, 3:29-41

50937 The difficult child. Davidson Clinic 1952

50938 The family clinic. London: Guild of Pastoral Psychology 1947
50939 Group therapy at the Davidson Clinic, Edinburgh, Scotland. Int J grp
       PT 1951, 1:281-284
50940 The happy child. Davidson Clinic, Edinburgh 1947
50941 The neurotic alternative. London: Guild of Pastoral Psychology 1958
50942 A study in group neurosis. Davidson Clinic Bull, Edinburgh 1948
50943 Success and failure in analysis. Brit Psychol Soc Bull, London 1957
50944 Transference and countertransference. M 1957, 30:63-74
           Abs Allen, D. W. Q 1958, 27:300-301

KRAFT, T. B.

50945 (& Burg, P. J. A. Van der) Über einen Fall von Folie à deux. [A case
       of "folie à deux."] Folia psychiat 1954, 57:35-52

KRAGH, ULF

50946 The actual-genetic model of perception-personality. Lund, Sweden:
       C W K Gleerup; Copenhagen, Denmark: Ejnar Munksgaard 1955,
       394 p
           Rv Faergeman, P. M. Q 1956, 25:597-601

KRAKAUER, L. J.
See Hill, S. R.

KRAMER, EDITH

50947 Art Therapy in a Children's Community. Springfield, Ill: Thomas 1958,
       xvii + 238 p
           Rv Peller, L. Q 1960, 29:125-126

KRAMER, MARIA K.

50948 On the continuation of the analytic process after psychoanalysis. (A
       self-observation). J 1959, 40:17-25
           Abs JBi Q 1960, 29:274. Rv Tabak Rev Psicoanál 1959, 16:269-270

KRAMER, PAUL

50949 On discovering one's identity. A case report. Psa St C 1955, 10:47-74
           Abs RTh J 1957, 38:293
50950 Early capacity for orgastic discharge and character formation. Psa St
       C 1954, 9:128-141
           Abs JFr An Surv Psa 1954, 5:164-167. RTh J 1956, 37:213
50951 Note on one of the preoedipal roots of the superego. J Am Psa Ass
       1958, 6:38-46
           Shentoub RFPsa 1959, 23:142. TGS Q 1960, 29:424

KRÄMER, RICHARD

50952 Psychotherapie bei endogenen Depressionen. [Psychotherapy in en-
       dogenous depressions.] Hndb N P 1959, 4:418-420
50953 Psychotherapie bei Psychosen. [Psychotherapy in psychoses.] Hndb
       N P 1959, 4:367-382

KRANEFELDT, WOLFGANG M.

50954 Therapeutische Psychologie: Ihr Weg durch die Psychoanalyse. [Therapeutic Psychology: Its Path through Psychoanalysis.] (3rd ed) Berlin: Walter De Gruyter 1956, 152 p

KRANSDORFF, M.
See Ventur, P.

KRANZ, HEINRICH

50955 Die schizoide Fehlhaltung. [Schizoid disturbances.] Hndb N P 1959, 2:263-315

See Fischer, Gert Heinz

KRAPF, E. EDUARDO

50956 Accidentes y operaciones como expresión de tendencias autodestructivas. [Accidents and operations as expressions of self-destructive tendencies.] Rev Psiquiat Crim 1944, 9:145-150

50957 Acerca de los problemas morales relacionados con la lobotomia prefrontal. [Moral problems related to pre-frontal lobotomy.] Rev Asoc méd argent 1951, 65:712-715

50958 On ageing. Proc RSM 1953 46:957-963

S-18813A Angustia, Tensión, Relajación, 2nd edition, 1959
Rv Langer, M. Rev Psicoanál 1953, 10:384. Vega Q 1954, 23:601-602

50959 Die Bedeutung der Psychoanalyse für unser Bild vom Menschen. [The influence of psychoanalysis on our concept of man.] Wien Zschr Nervenh 1956, 12:381-386

50960 The choice of language in polyglot psychoanalysis. Q 1955, 24:343-357
Über die Sprachwahl in der Psychoanalyse von Polyglotten. Psyche, Heidel 1955, 9:401-413
Abs Dreyfus RFPsa 1956, 20:571. JKl J 1956, 37:204

50961 Cultural influences on group formation. Prog PT 1958, 3:259-261

S-18816 Sur la dépersonnalisation.
Abs JFr An Surv Psa 1951, 2:198-199

50962 The education of the international sense and mental health in children. Int Child Welf Rev 1955, 9:146-153
L'éducation du sens international et la santé mentale de l'enfant. Rev int Enfant 1955, 19:133-140

50963 Entwicklungslinien der psychoanalytischen Technik. [Lines of development of psychoanalytic technique.] In Alexander, F. et al: *Freud in der Gegenwart*. Frankfurt: Europäische Verlagsanstalt 1957, 151-172

50964 Freud in der Gegenwart. [Freud today.] Frankfurter Beiträge zur Soziologie 1957, 6:173-184

50965 Homosexualidad. Hechos y teorías. [Homosexuality. Facts and theories.] Iatria (Buenos Aires) 1952, 23:172-179

S-18820 El judío de Shakespeare—una contribución a la psicologia del antisemitisme.
Abs MK An Surv Psa 1951, 2:465-469. GD An Surv Psa 1951, 2:515

50966 Über Kälte-und Wärmeerlebnisse in der Übertragung. Psyche, Heidel 1956, 10:216-221
Cold and warmth in the transference experience. (Read at 19th Int Psa Cong, Geneva, July 1955) J 1956, 37:389-391
Abs JLan Q 1957, 26:579

50967 Lichtenberg and Freud. Acta psychother psychosom orthopaedagog 1953-54, 1:241-255

50968 El medio siglo de la medicine psicosomático. [A half-century of psychosomatic medicine.] Cursos y Conf (Buenos Aires) 1953, 29:367-377

50969 Obituary: Abraham A. Brill. Rev Psicoanál 1948, 5:1076-1077

50970 Obituary: Smith Ely Jelliffe. Rev Psicoanál 1946, 4:158-160

50971 Obituary: Charles Odier. Rev Psicoanál 1955, 12:337

50972 On the pathogenesis of epileptic and hysterical seizures. Bull Wld Hlth Org 1957, 16:749-762

50973 Sur les phénomènes moteurs dans le transfert. [Motor phenomena in transference.] Acta psychother psychosom orthopaedag 1955, 3:231-241

50974 Physiogenèse et psychogenèse des états convulsifs. [Physiogenesis and psychogenesis of the convulsive state.] Evolut psychiat 1953, 4:607-622

50975 Prólogo. [Prologue.] In Oliverira, W. J. de: El matricidio en la Fantasía, Buenos Aires: Editorial Nova 1957, 13-15

50976 A propos des aphasies chez les polyglottes. [Concerning aphasias in polyglots.] Enceph 1957, 46:623-629

50977 Psicología médica y medicina psicosomática. [Medical psychology and psychosomatic medicine.] Rev Psicol gen apl 1955, 10:791-800. Pren méd argent 1956, 149-152

50977A Psicología de la sexualidad. [Psychology of sexuality.] In Problemas de la Higiene Sexual, Buenos Aires: Editorial Criterio 1954, 25-32
Psychologie de la sexualité. Concours méd 1959, 81

50978 Psychoanalyse und Religion. [Psychoanalysis and Religion.] In Alexander, F. et al: Freud in der Gegenwart, Frankfurt: Europäische Verlagsanstalt 1957, 173-184

50979 Psychoanalysis and the self understanding of man. Acta psychother psychosom orthopaedag 1958, 6:239-253

50980 Die Sexualerziehung. [Sex education.] In Meng, H. Psychohygienische Vorlesungen, Basel: Schwab & Co 1958, 104-116

50981 Shylock and Antonio. A psychoanalytic study of Shakespeare and antisemitism. R 1955, 42:113-130

50982 El significado del psicoanálisis para nuestra imágen del hombre. [The significance of psychoanalysis for our image of man.] Nosotros, Buenos Aires 1956, No. 242

50983 Die soziale Therapie der Schizophrenie. [The social therapy of schizophrenia.] Psyche, Heidel 1958, 12:408-414. Prak Psychiat 1959, 38:102-108
La thérapeutique social de la schizophrénie. Hyg ment 1958, 47:236-244

50984 Über das Sprachverhalten Hirngeschädigter Polyglotter. [Linguistic behavior of polyglots with brain injuries.] Wien Z Nervenheilk 1955, 12:121-133

50985 Tâches et possibilités du médecin de famille dans le domaine l'hygiène mentale. [Tasks and opportunities of the family physician in the field of mental hygiene.] Schweiz ANP 1956, 77:47-56

50986 Transference and motility. Q 1957, 26:519-526

REVIEWS OF:

50987 Wittkower, E. & Wittkower, R. Emotional factors in skin diseases. Rev Psicoanál 1955, 12:425; 1957, 14:337-338

50988 Wolstein, B. Transference: its meaning and function in psychoanalytic treatment. Rev Psicoanál 1955, 12:424; 1957, 14:338

KRAUS, ANTHONY R.

50989 Shifts in the levels of operating defenses induced by blurring of inkblot slides. Clin Psych 1956, 12:337-341

KRAUS, JANE

See Harrower, Molly

KREBS, G.

50990 Analytische Psychotherapie eines Zwangsneurotikers. [Analytic psychotherapy of an obsessive-compulsive neurotic.] Z PSM 1958-59, 5:36-43

KRECH, DAVID

50991 (& Crutchfield, R. S.) Elements of Psychology. NY: Alfred A. Knopf, Inc 1958, 694 p
       Rv Posinsky, S. H. Q 1958, 27:426-427

KREITLER, HANS

50992 Klinische Psychologie und Laienanalyse. [Clinical psychology and lay analysis.] Psyche, Heidel 1958, 12:124-130

50993 Die psychodynamische und klinische Bedeutung eines Mechanismus des schizophrenen Denkens. [The psychodynamic and clinical significance of a mechanism of schizophrenic thinking.] Schweiz Z Psychol Anwend 1958, 17:22-77

KREMER, MALVINA W.

50994 Consciousness in childhood. Psychotherapy 1956, 1:251

50995 Transference and countertransference. Schiz Psa Off Pract 66-68

KRENT, JUSTIN

ABSTRACT OF:

50996 Bond, D. The Love and Fear of Flying. An Surv Psa 1952, 3:556-564

KRETSCHMER, ERNST

50997 The image of man in psychotherapy. Psa 1954, 14:40-47

50998 Psychologie und Psychotherapie der Paranoiker. [Psychology and psychotherapy of paranoics.] In Speer, E. *Lindauer Psychotherapiewoche 1950*, Stuttgart: Hippokrates-Verlag 1951, 122-125

50999 Übertragung und Widerstand. [Transference and resistance.] Z Psychother med Psychol 1956, 6:1-3

KRETSCHMER, WOLFGANG, JR.

51000 (& Harder-Menzel, R.) Über archaische Erlebnisweisen bei Schizophrenen. [Concerning archaic experience modes in schizophrenia.] Z Psychother med Psychol 1954, 4:55-64

51001 Die Atem-Sprechschule im Rahmen kombinierter Psychotherapie. [Breathing-speech training within the frame of combined psychotherapy.] Z Psychotherap med Psychol 1953, 3:158-166

51002 Die Bedeutung der Mythologie für den modernen Menschen. [The importance of mythology for modern man.] Jahrbuch "Psychologie," Zurich: Rascher 1955

51003 Indikation und Methodik der Psychotherapie (ohne Psychoanalyse). [Indication and methodology of psychotherapy (without psychoanalysis).] In *Psychiatrie der Gegenwart I.* Heidelberg: Springer 1959

51004 Konstitution und Neurose. [Constitution and neurosis.] Hnbk N P 1957

51005 Meditation in der Psychologie und Psychiatrie der Gegenwart. [Meditation in contemporary psychology and psychiatry.] Zschr Religions-u Geistesgeschichte 1958, 10

51006 Die mythisch-archaische Welt des Schizophrenen als Krankheits-und Heilungsweg. [The mythical-archaic world of the schizophrenic as a course of illness and cure.] Z Psychotherap med Psychol 1957, 7:204-213

51007 Die Neurose als Reifungsproblem. (Konstitutionelle Grundlagen der Neurosenentwicklung). [Neurosis as a problem of maturation. Constitutional foundations for the development of neuroses.] Stuttgart: Thieme 1952

La neurosis como problema de maduración. Madrid: Alhambra 1953

51008 Die protreptischen Verfahren. [The protreptical processes.] Hnbk N P 1957

51009 La psicoterapia en los tiempos modernos. [Modern methods of psychotherapy.] Rev psicol gen apl 1953, 8:641-656

51010 Psychologische Weisheit der Bibel (Urbilder des Seins und Werdens im biblischen Schöpfungsbericht). [Psychological wisdom of the Bible. Prototypes of existence and genesis in the Biblical report of the creation.] Munich: Lehnen 1956

51011 Psychotherapie der Geisteskranken. [Psychotherapy of the mentally ill.] Universitas 1958, 13

51012 Psychotherapie und Seelsorge. [Psychotherapy and ministry.] Jb Psychol Psychotherap 1954, 2:175-183

51013 Selbsterkenntnis und Willensbildung im ärztlichen Raume. (Beiträge zu einer synthetischen Psychotherapie). [Self-knowledge and formation of the will in the medical realm. Contributions to a synthetical psychotherapy.] Stuttgart: Thieme 1958

51014 Sigmund Freud. Neuralmedizin 1956, 4

51015 Synthetische Psychotherapie. [Synthetical psychotherapy.] In *Handbuch der klinischen Psychologie. II.* Zurich: Rascher 1957

51016 Die Übertragung bei Verwendung psychotherapeutischer Hilfsmethoden. [Transference in the use of subsidiary methods in psychotherapy.] Acta psychotherap psychosom orthopaedag 1955, 3(Suppl), 177-180

KREVELEN, A. VAN

51017   Reflexiones sobre el complejo de inferioridad de los españoles. (Anotaciones al libro del profesor doctor Juan José López Ibor.) [The inferiority complex of the Spaniards. (Comments on the book by Professor Juan José López Ibor, M.D.)] Act Luso-Esp Neurol Psiquiat 1954, 13:222-225

KREVELEN, D. ARN VAN

51018   Die Anwendung des Pigem-Tests in der kinderpsychiatrischen Diagnostik. [Use of Pigem's test for diagnostic purposes in child psychiatry.] Z Kinderpsychiat 1953, 20:2-12
51019   Betteln im Kindersalter. [Begging in childhood.] Z Kinderpsychiat 1957, 24:33-42
51020   Hysterie bij kinderen, voorheen en thans. [Hysteria in children, previously and to-day.] NYvG 1955, 99:1890-1894
51021   Probleme der Übertragung in der Psychotherapie des Kindes. [Problems of transference in child psychotherapy.] Acta psychotherap psychosom orthopaedag 1955, 3(Suppl):181-188

KRICH, ARON M.

51022   Beyond psychology. In Baran, P. A. et al: *Marxism and Psychoanalysis,* NY: Monthly Review Pr 1960, 20-25
51023   (Ed) The Homosexuals: As Seen by Themselves and 30 Authorities. NY: Citadel Pr 1954, xi + 346 p
        Rv Frankel, E. NPAP 1955, 3(3):70
51024   Parent, child and expert. NPAP 1955, 3(3):25-35
51025   Preface. Homosex vii-xi

See Berg, Charles; Mudd, Emily Hartshorne

KRICHHAUFF, G.

51026   Der Asthmatiker und seine Innenwelt. [The asthmatic and his world within.] Z PSM 1955-56, 2:118-126
51027   [Remarks on genetic and neurotic-structural factors in endogenous eczemas.] (German) Z PSM 1955-56, 2:184

KRIEGER, MARGERY H.

51028   (& Worchel, P.) A quantitative study of the psychoanalytic hypotheses of identification. Perceptual and Motor Skills 1959

KRIEGER, MURRAY

See Vivas, Eliseo

KRIEGMAN, GEORGE

51029   (& Wright, H. B.) Brief psychotherapy with enuretics in the Army. P 1947, 104:254-258
51030   Group security and individual difference. Virginia J Educ 1956, 49(8)

KRIES, ILSE VON

51031 Zur Differentialdiagnose der Angstneurose und Angsthysterie. Ein Beitrag zur Entwicklungsgeschichte der psychoanalytischen Theorie. [The differential diagnosis between anxiety neurosis and anxiety hysteria. The history of the development of the psychoanalytical theory.] Psyche, Heidel 1957, 11:28-63

KRINSKY, L. W.

See Rolo, Andre

KRIPPENDORF, I.

51032 Rainer Maria Rilke, Psyche und Werk. I. Die Persönlichkeit und ihre Wandlungen. II. Die Dichtungen als Spiegel der Persönlichkeit. [R. M. Rilke, his psychology and works. I. The personality and its changes. II. Poetry as a mirror of the personality.] Z Psychother, Stuttgart 1952, 2:61-76; 2:110-122

KRIS, ERNST

51033 Bibliography. Psa St C 1958, 13:562-573
51034 The contribution and limitations of psychoanalysis. Art Psa 271-291. From author's *Psychoanalytic Explorations in Art.*
S-18905 The development of ego psychology.
    Abs JAA An Surv Psa 1951, 2:99-102. Levinson, G. J 1953, 34:282
S-18905A Discussion of Kubie, L. S. "Some implications for psychoanalysis of modern concepts of the organization of the brain." Q 1953, 22:64-67
S-18907 Ego psychology and interpretation in psychoanalytic therapy. Out Psa 1955, 77-93
    Abs STa An Surv Psa 1951, 2:371-372
51035 Freud in the history of science. The Listener 1956, May 17:631. J Philos 1957, 54:153-154
S-18912A To Helene Deutsch on her seventieth birthday. J 1955, 36:209
S-18923A Neutralization and sublimation. Observations on young children. Psa St C 1955, 10:30-46
    Abs RTh J 1957, 38:292-293
S-18923B New contributions to the study of Freud's *The Interpretation of Dreams.* A critical essay. J Am Psa Ass 1954, 2:180-191
S-18927 Opening remarks on psychoanalytic child psychology
    Abs EBu & NRo An Surv Psa 1951, 2:263-265
S-18928A The personal myth: a problem in psychoanalytic technique. J Am Psa Ass 1956, 4:653-681
    Abs TFr J 1957, 38:433-434. JPW Q 1960, 29:137-138
S-18931A (Chairman) Symposium: Problems of infantile neurosis. Psa St C 1954, 9:16-71
    Abs NRo An Surv Psa 1954, 5:241-248
S-18933A Psychoanalysis and the study of creative imagination. Bull NY Acad Med 1953, 29:334-351
S-18934 Psychoanalytic Explorations in Art. London: Allen & Unwin 1953
    Abs Klein, E. An Surv Psa 1952, 3:586-605. Rv Lee, H. B. Q 1953, 22:280-284. DR J 1954, 35:362-364. Kelley, D. M. R 1954, 41:391-392. MK J Am Psa Ass 1957, 5:514-524

S-18937B The recovery of childhood memories in psychoanalysis. Psa St C
1956, 11:54-88
Abs RTh J 1959, 40:73
S-18941 The significance of Freud's earliest discoveries.
Abs R 1953, 40:362-363
S-18942 Some comments and observations on early autoerotic activities.
Abs NRo An Surv Psa 1951, 2:77-79. JAA An Surv Psa 1951, 2:106
S-18943AA On some vicissitudes of insight in psychoanalysis. J 1956, 37:445-
455
Abs Donadeo, J. Q 1957, 26:445-447. JLan Q 1957, 26:581. Lebo-
vici RFPsa 1957, 21:616-617

See Coleman, Rose; Hartmann, Heinz

REVIEW OF:
S-18960A Naumberg, M. Schizophrenic Art: Its Meaning in Psychotherapy.
Q 1953, 22:98-101

KRIS, MARIANNE

51036   Discussion of Freud, A. "Problems of technique in adult analysis"
(Panel). Bull Phila Ass Psa 1954, 4:63-64, 65
51037   The use of prediction in longitudinal study. Psa St C 1957, 12:175-189
Abs RTh J 1959, 40:370

See Kubie, Lawrence S.

KRISCHE, PAUL

51038   Marx und Freud. [Marx and Freud.] In: *Neue Wege in der Weltan-
schauung und Ethik der Freidenker,* Leipzig-Plagwitz: Verlagsanstalt
für proletarische Freidenker 1924, 55 p

KROEBER, ALFRED L.

S-18977A (& Kluckhohn, C. et al) Culture: A Critical Review of Concepts and
Definitions.
Rv Muensterberger, W. Q 1954, 23:604

KROEF, C. V. D.

51039   (& Stokvis, B.) Eheschwierigkeiten bei psychosomatisch Kranken.
[Marital difficulties in psychosomatic patients.] Der Psychologe 1958,
10(4-5)

KROGER, WILLIAM S.

51040   Hypnotherapy in obstetrics and gynecology. J clin exp Hyp 1953,
1(2):61-70
51041   Hysterectomy: psychosomatic factors of the preoperative and postoperative aspects and management. West J Surg 1957, 65:317-323
51042   (& Freed, S. C.) Psychosomatic factors in functional amenorrhoea.
Brit J med Hypnot 1953, 5(2):5-14

See Bergler, Edmund

KROHN, HARRY
See Goldsmith, Jerome M.

KROJANKER, R.

51043 Congreso de psicoanalisis; resumenes parciales de los congresos nacionales psicoanaliticos y psiquiatricos reunidos en Mayo de 1957 en la ciudad de Chicago. [Congress of psychoanalysis; partial summaries of the national psychoanalytic and psychiatric congresses held in May 1957 in the city of Chicago.] Arch Crimin Neuropsiq 2 ep 1957, 5:376-393

51044 La musica en la psicologia clinica. [Music in clinical psychology.] Arch Crimin Neuropsiq 2 ep 1958, 6:25-105

51045 El surital sodico por goteo endovenoso en el narcoanalisis. [Intravenous surital sodium in narcoanalysis.] Arch Crimin Neuropsiq 2 ep 1955, 3:255-275

See Endara, Julio

TRANSLATION OF:
Piotrowski, Z. [56010]

KRONFELD, G.

51046 A psicanálise como contribuição para a personalização progressiva. [Psychoanalysis as a contributing factor toward progressive personalization.] Rev Psicol norm patol 1957 3:526-540

KRONHAUSEN, EBERHARD W.

51047 (& Kronhausen, P. C.) Family milieu therapy: the non-institutional treatment of severe emotional disturbances. NPAP 1957, 5(3):45-62

51048 (& Kronhausen, P. C.) The psychology of sexual relations. Helicon Records, New Rochelle, NY, 1958

51049 Sex and modern youth. Candida 1959, 1(3)

51050 (& Kronhausen, P. C.) The therapeutic family—the family's role in emotional disturbance and rehabilitation. Marriage Fam Living 1959, 21:29-35

KRONHAUSEN, PHYLLIS C.
See Kronhausen, Eberhard W.

KRONOLD, EDWARD

51051 Discussion of Freud, A. "Problems of technique in adult analysis." (Panel) Bull Phila Ass Psa 1954, 4:64

KROUT, MAURICE H.

51052 Measuring personality in developmental terms: the personal preference scale. Genetic Psychol Monogr 1954, 50:289-335

51053 A new procedure for the study of anxiety patterns in human subjects. Proc Int Psychol Cong, Brussels 1957

51054 (Ed) Psychology, Psychiatry, and the Public Interest. Minneapolis, Minn: Univ of Minn Pr 1956, xv + 217 p

KROWN, SYLVIA

See Alpert, Augusta

KRUG, OTHILDA

51055 The application of principles of child psychotherapy in residential treatment. P 1952, 108:695-700
51056 Child guidance home, 1958. Cincinnati J Med 1958, 39:568-574
51057 (& Stuart, Barbara L.) Collaborative treatment of mother and boy with fecal retention, soiling and a school phobia. Case St Chd Dis 1953, 2:2-28
51058 Discussion of case symposium: Holmes, E. H. & Lord, J. P. "Artie, a victim of an inconsistent parental relationship." Ops 1952, 22:41-45
51059 The dynamic use of the ego functions in casework practice. Soc Casewk 1955, 443-450
51060 The education of emotionally disturbed children. 5. A concept of education in the residential treatment of emotionally disturbed children. Ops 1953, 23:691-696
51061 (& Beck, H. L.) A guide to better discipline. Science Research Associates, Chicago 1954. In Menninger, W. C. *How to Help Your Children,* Sterling Publ 1959, 381-416
51062 (& Hayward, H.; Crumpacker, B.) Intensive residential treatment of a nine-year-old girl with an aggressive behavior disorder, petit mal epilepsy and enuresis. Ops 1952, 22:405-427. Case St Chd Dis 1953, 1:155-177
51063 Maladjustment in the adolescent. Ohio's Health 1952, 4(4):6-11
51064 Problems of inpatient psychiatric treatment for children. Proc 3rd Annual Psychiatric Inst, New Jersey Psychiatric Inst, Princeton, N.J. 1955

See Wise, Louis J.

KRÜGER, ELFRIEDE

51065 Erfahrungen aus der Jugendfürsorge über die Bedeutung der Familie für die Entwicklung des Kindes. [Experiences in child guidance work on the significance of the family for the development of the child.] Prax Kinderpsychol 1953, 2(5-6):133-138

KRUGER, MURIEL S.

51066 A psychoanalytic study of a normal child. South African J Sci 1933, 30:675-681

KRUGMAN, HERBERT E.

51067 Rejoinder to Gundlach and Riess. Ps 1954, 17:209-210
51068 The role of hostility in the appeal of communism in the United States. Ps 1953, 16:253-261

KRUSE, F.

51069 Grundsätzliche Unterschiede in der Übertragung männlicher und weiblicher Patienten. [Fundamental differences in the transference of male and female patients.] Acta psychother psychosom orthopaedag 1955, 3(Suppl):188-196

KRUSE, H. D.

51070 (Ed) Alcoholism as a Medical Problem. NY: Hoeber-Harper 1956, 102 p

51071 (Ed) Integrating the Approaches to Mental Disease. NY: Hoeber-Harper 1957, xvi + 393 p

KUBIE, LAWRENCE K.

51072 (& Glaser, G.) Affectivity and psychosurgery. In Mettler, F. A. & Overholser, W. "Evaluation of change in patients after psychosurgery; proceedings of the second research conference on psychosurgery." Wash: Nat Inst of Health, Public Health Service, Federal Security Agency 1953 (Pub Hlth Serv Publ No 156) 65-74

51073 (et al) Applied art: "An educational luxury?"; a symposium. Vassar Alumnae Magazine 1950, 35:Feb(No 3)20-24

51074 Are we educating for maturity? NEA Journal 1959, 48:58-63

51075 Authority and freedom: some insights from psychoanalysis. J relig Thought 1951-52, 9:40-47. In Bryson, L. et al: *Freedom and Authority in Our Time,* NY: Harper 1953, 385-391

51076 To break the hold of the past; the seminar on psychiatry and psychology as a tool for lawyers. Bar Bull, NY County Lawyers Ass 1959, 16:139-144

51077 The central representation of the symbolic process in psychosomatic disorders. PSM 1953, 15:1-7. In Wittkower, E. D. & Gleghorn, R. A. *Recent Developments in Psychosomatic Medicine,* London: I Pitman & Sons 1954, 126-133

      Abs LCK An Surv Psa 1953, 4:483-486. VC Q 1954, 23:306-307

51078 The challenge of the partial cure. J chron Dis 1959, 9:292-297. J Rehabilit 1959, 25(2):6-8

51079 Chronic illness and hidden neurotic difficulties. Texas Reports Biol Med 1954, 12:608-610. In Harrower, M. *Medical and Psychological Teamwork in the Care of the Chronically Ill,* Springfield: Thomas 1955, 41-43

51080 Competitive sports and the awkward child. Child Study 1954, 31:10-15

51081 The complex scientific challenge in chronic illness. In Harrower, M. *Medical and Psychological Teamwork in the Care of the Chronically Ill,* Springfield: Thomas 1955, 175-177

51082 The concept of normality and neurosis. Psa Soc Wk 3-14. From author's *Practical and Theoretical Aspects of Psychoanalysis; The neurotic potential, the neurotic process and the neurotic state.*

51083 Dedication to Dr. Ernest Jones. Bull Am Psa Ass 1939-40, 3(June)

51084 Dedication to the memory of Sigmund Freud. Bull Am Psa Ass 1938-39, 2(June)

51085 Discussion of Bellak, L. "The unconscious." Ann NY Acad Sci 1959, 76:1089-1090; 1092

51086 Discussion of Frank, J. "Group psychotherapy with chronic hospitalized schizophrenics." In Brody, E. & Redlich, F. *Psychotherapy with Schizophrenics,* NY: IUP 1952, 238-240

51087 Discussion of Kasanin, J. "Defense reactions in anxiety states of central origin." Q 1942, 11:500-501

51088   Discussion of Szasz, T. S. "A critical analysis of some aspects of the libido theory: the concepts of libidinal zones, aims, and modes of gratification." Ann NY Acad Sci 1959, 76:994-995; 996; 1002-1003; 1004

51089   Diskussionsbeitrag von Lawrence S. Kubie. [Kubie's contribution to the discussion of Margolin's lecture.] Psyche, Heidel 1952, 6:460-464

51090   The distortion of the symbolic process in neurosis and psychosis. J Am Psa Ass 1953, 1:59-86
        Abs WH J 1953, 34:275. NRo An Surv Psa 1953, 4:60-63. Rev Psicoanál 1954, 11:529-530

51091   Dr. Kinsey and the medical profession. PSM 1955, 17:172-184
        Abs EMW Q 1957, 26:144

51092   To the Editors of the International Journal of Group Psychotherapy. Int J grp PT 1958, 8:359-362

51093   Education and the process of maturation. From *Today's Children Are Tomorrow's World*, Associates of Bank Street Coll of Education, 5th Annual Conf Feb 1957, NY: 7-18

51094   The financial problems of the academic life: two possible solutions. Harvard Alumni Bull 1955, 58:21-22, 28-29

51095   The forgotten man of education. Harvard Alumni Bull 1954, 56:349-353. The Standard, Pub of Am Ethical Union, 1956, (Mar-Apr): 40-44

51096   A fortieth reunion in 2156—a salute from Harvard 1916. Harvard Alumni Bull 1956, 59:2,4. Reprinted in part with title: Hidden brain power, Sat Rev 1956, (Oct 13) 26

51097   Freud and human freedom. Sat Rev 1956, 39:9-10, 36-37

51098   Freud's legacy to human freedom. Proc Rudolf Virchow Med Soc 1956, 15:34-48. Perspectives in Biol and Med 1957, 1:105-118. Neurology, M Indian Med Profession, Bombay, India 1958, 6:33-37

51099   The fundamental nature of the distinction between normality and neurosis. (Expanded version of paper read before NY Psa Soc Dec 5, 1952) Q 1954, 23:167-204
        Abs HRB Q 1953, 22:620-621. JFr An Surv Psa 1954, 5:88-90. NRo An Surv Psa 1954, 5:31-32. Dreyfus RFPsa 1955, 19:497. JKl J 1955, 36:423

51100   The impact of behavioral medicine on pre-professional education for the future medical student. Conf on Pre-Professional Educ for Med, Oct 18, 19 1956. State Univ of NY, Downstate Med Cent, Coll of Med, 24-37

51101   Influence of symbolic processes on the role of instincts in human behavior. PSM 1956, 18:189-208
        Abs EMW Q 1957, 26:588-589

51102   An institute for basic research in psychiatry. BMC 1956, 20:281-287
        Abs Racamier RFPsa 1959, 23:155

51103   Introduction to Jones, R. M. *An Application of Psychoanalysis to Education.*

51104   The investigation of the pharmacology of psychological processes: some methodologic considerations from the point of view of clinical psychoanalysis. In Pennes, H. H. *Psychopharmacology.* NY: Hoeber-Harper 1958, 302-315

51105 Is preventive psychiatry possible? Daedalus (Proc Am Acad Arts & Sci) 1959, 88:646-668

51106 Letter to the Editor [concerning statistics of psychoanalytic practice.] Bull Am Psa Ass 1948, 4:41-43

51107 Limitations of aptitude tests; reply to Humphreys, L. G. "The importance of aptitude tests in the selection of Air Force personnel." Amer Scientist 1955, 43:105-108

51108 Minutes of the meetings of the American Psychoanalytic Association. JAMA 1939, 112:1986-1987

51109 Minutes, Special Committee on the Relationship of the American Psychoanalytic Association to the International Psycho-Analytical Association. Bull Am Psa Ass 1939-40, 3:28-53

51110 Need for a new subdiscipline in the medical profession. AMA ANP 1957, 78:283-293

51111 Neurotic Distortion of the Creative Process. Lawrence, Kansas: Univ Kansas Pr 1958, 151 p
    Abs J Am Psa Ass 1960, 8:219; 592. Rv Beres, D. Q 1959, 28:85-86. CR J 1960, 41:81-82. Schwerner, A. PPR 1960, 47(2): 106-107

S-19121 The neurotic potential, the neurotic process and the neurotic state.
    Abs JAA An Surv Psa 1951, 2:22-23

51112 The neurotic process as the focus of physiological and psychoanalytic research. JMS 1958, 104:518-536. Psychiat et Neurol jap 1959, 61:291-309
    Abs Allen, D. W. Q 1959, 28:574

51113 The normal and the neurotic. From author's Practical and Theoretical Aspects of Psychoanalysis. In Linscott, R. N. & Stein, J. Why You Do What You Do, NY: Random House 1956, 3-10

51114 Obituary: Dr. William Herman, 1891-1935. Q 1935, 4:345-346

51115 Obituary: Clarence P. Oberndorf, 1882-1954. J Am Psa Ass 1954, 2:546-551

51116 Obituary: Herbert A. Wiggers, 1907-1953. Q 1953, 22:321-323

51117 Participant in symposium. In Kruse, H. D. Integrating the Approaches to Mental Disease, NY: Hoeber-Harper 1957, 160-383

51118 Pavlov, Freud and Soviet psychiatry. Monthly Rev 1958, 9:259-362. Behav Sci 1959, 4:29-34

S-19130 A pilot study of psychoanalytic practice in the United States.
    Abs R 1954, 41:76-77

51119 The place of emotions in the feedback concept. In von Foerster, H. Transactions of the Ninth Conference on Cybernetics, NY: Josiah Macy Jr Foundation 1952, 48-72

S-19132 Practical and Theoretical Aspects of Psychoanalysis.
    Psychoanalyse ohne Geheimnis. Rowohlt deutsche Enzyklopädie (No 11) Hamburg, Germany: Rowohlt Taschenbuch Verlag GmbH, 1956, 173 p

51120 Preface to Hart, M. Lady in the Dark, NY: Random House 1941, 182 p

51121 (& Cobb, C. B. P.; Kris, M.; Levine, M. I.; Putnam, M. C.) Preventive use of psychotherapy in childhood; transcription of a panel meeting on therapeutics. Bull NY Acad Med 1956, 32:33-56

51122 The problem of maturity in psychiatric research. J med Educ 1953, 28(10):11-27

51123 The problem of specificity in the psychosomatic process. Psm Cpt Psa 63-81. In Wittkower, E. D. & Cleghorn, R. A. *Recent Developments in Psychosomatic Medicine.* Phila: Lippincott 1954, 29-40. Modern Medicine 1955, 23:158-164

51124 The pros and cons of a new profession: a doctorate in medical psychology. Texas Reports on Biology and Medicine 1954, 12:692-737. In Harrower, M. *Medical and Psychological Teamwork in the Care of the Chronically Ill.* Springfield: C. C Thomas 1955, 125-170
       Abs J 1956, 37:512-513. Gosselin, R. Q 1956, 25:299-300

S-19140 Psychiatric implications of the Kinsey Report. In Himelhoch, J. & Fava, S. F.: *Sexual Behavior in American Society; An Appraisal of the First Two Kinsey Reports.* NY: W. W. Norton 1955, 270-293

51125 Psychiatric and psychoanalytic considerations of the problem of consciousness. *Brain Mechanisms and Consciousness,* Oxford, Eng: Blackwell Scientific Publ 1954, 444-469

51126 Psychiatry in relation to authority and freedom. In Bryson, L. et al: *Freedom and Authority in Our Time,* NY: Harper 1953, 385-391

51127 Psychoanalysis as a basic science. 20 Yrs Psa 120-145

51128 Psychoanalysis and marriage: practical and theoretical issues. In Eisenstein, V. W. *Neurotic Interaction in Marriage,* NY: Basic Books 1956, 10-43

51129 Psychoanalysis and psychopharmacology. Psychiat Res Rep 1958, 9:61-67

51130 Psychoanalysis and scientific method. Psa Sci Method Phil 57-77

51131 The psychodynamic position on etiology. In Kruse, H. D. *Integrating the Approaches to Mental Disease,* NY: Hoeber-Harper 1957, 14-33

51132 A reply to a reply. Bull Am Psa Ass 1951, 7:146-147

51133 (Chairman) Report of study group on training and teaching. In Harrower, M. *Medical and Psychological Teamwork in the Care of the Chronically Ill,* Springfield: Thomas 1955, 108-124

51134 Research into the process of supervision in psychoanalysis. Q 1958, 27:226-236
       Abs Rev Psicoanál 1958, 15:430. JKl J 1960, 41:79

51135 Research possibilities in psychoanalysis. Acta psychol 1955, 11:123

51136 The Riggs Story: The Development of the Austen Riggs Center for the Study and Treatment of the Neuroses. NY: P. B. Hoeber 1960, 182 p

51137 (& Israel, H. A.) "Say you're sorry." Psa St C 1955, 10:289-299
       Abs RTh J 1957, 38:297

51138 The seeds of a new spirit—a salute to Sidonie Matsner Gruenberg on her 75th birthday. Child Study 1956, 33:3,4

51139 Social forces and the neurotic process. In Leighton, A. H. et al: *Explorations in Social Psychiatry,* NY: Basic Books 1957, 77-104. JNMD 1959, 128:65-80

51140 Some implications for psychoanalysis of modern concepts of the organization of the brain. (Read at Amer Psa Ass, NY, Dec 9, 1951) Q 1953, 22:21-52; 67-68
       Abs NRo An Surv Psa 1953, 4:53-60. JKl J 1954, 35:439-440

51141 Some theoretical concepts underlying the relationship between individual and group psychotherapies. Int J grp PT 1958, 8:3-43
    Abs GPK Q 1959, 28:430
51142 Some unsolved problems of psychoanalytic psychotherapy. Prog PT 1956, 1:87-102
51143 Some unsolved problems of the scientific career. Am Scientist 1953, 41:596-613; 1954, 42:104-112
51144 Symbolic distortion in neurosis and psychosis, some psychophysiological considerations. *Transactions of American Neurological Associations,* Richmond, Va: William Bird Pr 1951, 42-43
51145 Theory of psychoanalytic therapy. A few rarely asked and never answered questions about psychoanalytic therapy, emotions, and insight. (Read at NY Psa Soc, Apr 15, 1952)
    Abs Sillman, L. R. Q 1953, 22:466-467
51146 The use of psychoanalysis as a research tool. Psychiat Res Rep 1956, (6):112-136
51147 What is normal. Look Magazine 1955, (May 3):51-59

See Harrower, Molly; Manrique, M.

REVIEWS OF:
51148 Brian, W. R. The Contribution of Medicine to Our Idea of the Mind. Q 1953, 22:435-436
51149 Brian, W. R. Mind, Perception, and Science. Q 1953, 22:435-436
51150 Jones, M. The Therapeutic Community. Q 1954, 23:443-445
51151 Whitehorn, J. C. et al (Eds): The Psychiatrist—His Training and Development. Q 1955, 24:128-130
51152 Whitehorn, J. C. et al (Eds): Psychiatry and Medical Education. Q 1953, 22:436-438

KUBO, SHUNICHI

51153 Researches and studies on incest in Japan. Hiroshima J med Sci 1959, 8:99-159

KUCERA, OTAKAR

S-19191 The mechanisms of regression in the poetry of Baudelaire and his followers.
    Abs R 1953, 40:362
51154 [The origin of the "damned poet" Ducasse-Lautréamont.] (Czech) Czechosl psa annual 1948
51155 [On sublimation.] (Czech) Czechosl psa annual 1947
51156 On teething. J Am Psa Ass 1959, 7:284-291
    Abs J 1958, 39:292. Shentoub RFPsa 1959, 23:532. McLaughlin, J. T. Q 1960, 29:592. Rv Morera, M. E. Rev Psicoanál 1959, 16:271-272

KUDARAUSKAS, E. N.
See Fox, Henry M.

KUENEN, D. J.
See Schiller, Claire H.

KUETHE, JAMES L.

See Eriksen, Charles W.; Strickland, John F.

KUHLEN, RAYMOND G.

51157 Psychological trends and problems in later maturity. Intro Clin Psych 2, 448-479

KUHLENBECK, H.

51158 Further remarks on brain and consciousness: the brain-paradox and the meanings of consciousness. Confin Neurol, Basel 1959, 19:462-484

KUHN, ROLAND

51159 The attempted murder of a prostitute. (Tr: Angel, E.) MPN 1948, 116:66-151. Existence, 365-425
51160 Daseinsanalytische Studie über die Bedeutung von Grenzen im Wahn. [Existential analytical study of the significance of limits in the delusion.] MPN 1952, 124:354-382
51161 [On the existential analysis of anorexia nervosa.] (German) Nervenarzt 1951, 55:11
51162 Griesingers Auffassung der psychischen Krankheiten und seine Bedeutung für die weitere Entwicklung der Psychiatrie. [Griesinger's conception of psychical diseases, and his significance for the further development of psychiatry.] Psychiat Neurol, Basel 1957, suppl 100:41-67
51163 Der Mensch in der Zwiesprache des Kranken mit seinem Arzt und das Problem der Übertragung. [Man in the rapport of the patient with his physician and the problem of transference.] MPN 1955, 129:189-206

KÜHNEL, G.

51164 Tiefenpsychologische Erkenntnisse über depressive Symptomenbilder. [Depth psychologic findings of depressive syndromes.] Z PSM 1956-57, 3:249-256
51165 Die Übertragung in der Gruppenanalyse. [Transference in group analysis.] Acta psychother psychosom orthopaedag 1955, 3(Suppl):196-200

KUIPER, P. C.

51166 Aanpassing als centraal begrip in de moderne psychiatrie. [Adjustment as central concept in modern psychiatry.] NTvG 1956, 100:1896-1899
51167 Anthropologische en fenomenologische gezichtspunten. [Anthropological and phenomenological points of view.] In *Handboek der Psychiatrie*, Arnhem: V Loghum Slaterus 1958, 49-72
51168 De biologische fundering der psychopathologie. [The biological basis of psychopathology.] Groningen: J B Wolters 1958, 20 p
51169 De freqentie der neurotische stoornissen en de betekenis van de affectafweer. [The frequency of neurotic disturbances and the significance of repression of affects.] NTvG 1955, 99:3918-3924
51170 (& Mik, G.) Gedragstoornissen door conflictsituatie ten gevolge van masturbatie. [Behaviour disturbances resulting from a conflict due to masturbation.] NTvG 1954, 98-III (28):1932-1941

51171 Kan men ouders aansprakelijk stellen voor het ontstaan van neurotische aanpassingsstoornissen bij hun kinderen? [Are the parents responsible for the neurosis of their children?] NTvG 1957, 102:2449-2451

51172 Onechtheid een neurotisch symptoom. [Insincerity a neurotic symptom.] NTvG 1958, 102:933-937

51173 Prelude tot de psychiatrie. [Prelude to psychiatry.] Utrecht: Erven J Bijleveld 1956, 9-166

51174 Over stoornissen in de vorming en de functie van het geweten bij psychopathen. [About disturbances in formation and function of the super-ego in delinquency.] Maandblad voor de Geestelijke Volksgezondheid 1953, 8:1932-1941

51175 Symptomatologie. [Symptomatology.] In *Handboek der Psychiatrie*, Arnhem: V Loghum Slaterus 1958, 311-396

51176 Techniek en menselijkheid als probleem van caseworker en psychiater. [Technique and humanity as a problem for caseworker and psychiatrist.] In *Om de leefbaarheid van het bestaan*, 1958, 155-171

51177 An unusual case of juvenile delinquency. Folia Psychiat 1955, 58:77-90

51178 Over de verhouding van anthropologie en psychopathologie. [On the relation between anthropology and psychopathology.] Ned Tijdschr Psychol 1954, 9:273-288

51179 Verständliche Zusammenhänge bei der Entwicklung des sensitiven Charakters. [Some remarks about the development of the so-called sensitive character.] Arch Psychiat Nervenkr 1958, 196:591-610

51180 Over vrijheid en gebondenheid; enkele opmerkingen naar aanleiding van de daseinsanalytische methode van Binswanger. [Freedom and restraint; considerations on Binswanger's existential-analytic method.] Ned Tijdschr Psychol 1953, 8(5):414-438

See Boeke, P. E.; Dijk, W. K. Van

KULCER, SHLOMO

51181 [Drawing of mentally disturbed.] (Hebrew) Ofakim 1957, 11:7-15; 37
51182 [Freud and his generation.] (Hebrew) Ofakim 1956, 10:143-151

KUNKEL, FRITZ

51183 Growth through crises. In Doniger, S. *Religion and Human Behavior*, NY: Ass Pr 1954, 146-163

51184 What It Means to Grow Up. NY, London: Scribners 1936, 1955

KUNKEL, O.

51185 Enuresis und Enkopresis eines Dreizehnjährigen geheilt durch psychotherapeutische Behandlung der Mutter. [Enuresis and encropresis of a 13-year-old boy cured by psychotherapy of the mother.] Z Psychother med Psychol 1958, 8:236-239

KUNZ, HANS

51186 Zur Frage nach dem Wesen der Norm; mit Bemerkungen zur anthropologischen und daseinsanalytischen Perversionstheorie. [The problem of the nature of norm; with remarks on the theory of perversion, as developed in anthropology and existential analysis.] Psyche, Heidel 1954, 8:241-271; 321-366

51187 Die latente Anthropologie der Psychoanalyse. [The latent anthropology of psychoanalysis.] Schweiz Z Psychol 1956, 15:84-102

KUPFER, DAVID

51188 Hypnotherapy in a case of functional heart disorder. J clin exp Hyp 1954, 2:186-190

KUPPER, HERBERT I.

51189 (& Rollman-Branch, H. S.) Freud and Schnitzler—(Doppelgänger). J Am Psa Ass 1959, 7:109-126
Abs Rev Psicoanál 1959, 16:191. Shentoub RFPsa 1959, 23:520. TFr J 1960, 41:78-79. McLaughlin, J. T. Q 1960, 29:590

S-19290 Psychodynamics of the "intellectual."
Abs R 1953, 40:361-362

S-19271 Some aspects of the dream in psychosomatic disease.
Abs STa J 1948, 29:62

KUPPER, WILLIAM HOWARD

51190 (& Kelley, D. M.) Dictionary of Psychiatry and Psychology. Paterson, N.J.: Colt Press 1953, 194 p

KURAUCHI, HIROKAZU

51191 Discussion of Kosawa, H. "My own experience about didactic psycho-analysis." The Seishinbunseki Kenkyu 1956, 2(8):1-4

51192 Experimental studies on neuroses by the use of hypnosis. Report 1. On Freud's theory of lapsus linguae. Report 2. On the problem of dream symbolism. The Kyushu Neuro-Psychiatry 1954, 4(1-2):35-43; 44-49

51193 Some interesting phenomena observed during hypnoanalysis. The Seishinbunseki Kenkyu 1957, 4(1-2):24-26

51194 A trial discussion on hypnotic regression through the use of hypnosis. (Psychoanalysis and hypnosis, IV) The Seishinbunseki Kenkyu 1958, 5(4):1-8

See Shibaba

KURLAND, ALBERT ALEXANDER

51195 The drug placebo—its psychodynamic and conditional reflex action. Beh Sci 1957, 2:101-110

KURTH, GERTRUD M.
(See also Kieslinger, Gertrud M.)

51196 The image of the Fuehrer. A contribution to the role of imagery in hero worship. Unpubl master thesis, grad faculty of Pol & Soc Science, New School for Soc Res 1947

See Herma, Hans

REVIEWS OF:

51197   Kimble, G. A. Principles of General Psychology. Q 1957, 26:570-571
51198   Klopfer, B. et al: Developments in the Rorschach Technique. Q 1955, 24:595-597; 1958, 27:276-278
51199   Townsend, J. C. Introduction to Experimental Method. For Psychology and the Social Sciences. Q 1954, 23:289
51200   Zucker, L. J. Ego Structure in Paranoid Schizophrenia. Q 1959, 28:265-267

KURTH, W.

51201   Über eine seltene Sexopathie. [A rare sex deviation.] Psychotherapie 1957, 2:120-131

KUT, SARA

51202   The changing pattern of transference in the analysis of an eleven year old girl. Psa St C 1953, 8:355-378
Abs NRo An Surv Psa 1953, 4:293-296. RTh J 1955, 36:80. Rv Chaio, J. Rev Psicoanál 1958, 15:191

TRANSLATION OF:
Woolf, M. [62850]

KUTANIN, M.

51203   [Delirium and creativity.] (Russian) Klinicheskii arkhiv geneal'nosti i odarennosti 1929-30, 5:3-36

KUTNER, BERNARD

51204   Surgeons and their patients: a study in social perception. In Jaco, E. G. *Patients, Physicians and Illness*, Glencoe, Ill: Free Pr 1958, 384-397

See Harding, John

KWALWASSER, SIMON

51205   Adolescent pavilion—Hillside Hospital. In Denber, H. C. B. *Therapeutic Community*, Springfield, Ill: Thomas 1959

See Korin, Hyman; Miller, Joseph S. A.

L

LAB, J.

51205A Discussion of Perrotti, N. & Bouvet, M. de. "Aperçus théoriques de la dépersonnalisation." RFPsa 1960, 24:649-651

LA BARRE, WESTON

51206 Cynosures (points de mire) et structures sociales. [Cynosures (points for observation) and social structure.] Rev Psychol Peuples 1953, 8:362-377

S-19300 Family and symbol.
Abs GD An Surv Psa 1951, 2:496-497

51207 Freud and anthropology. Arch crim Psychodyn 1957, 2:450-453

51208 The Human Animal. Chicago: Univ of Chicago Pr 1954, 372 p
Abs J Am Psa Ass 1956, 4:189-190. Rv MG Q 1955, 24:597-598.
Axelrad, S. J Am Psa Ass 1960, 8:175-218

51209 The influence of Freud on anthropology. Am Im 1958, 15:275-328

51210 Obscenity: an anthropological appraisal. Law contemp Probl 1955, 20:533-543

51211 The patient and his families. In *Casework Papers*, Fam Serv Assoc of Amer 1958. Child-Fam Dig 1958, 18(1):9-18

51212 Religions, Rorschachs and tranquilizers. Ops 1959, 29:688-698

L'ABATE, LUCIANO

51213 Il linguaggio del fanciullo attraverso una tecnica proiettiva. [The language of the child through a projective technique.] Bollettino di psicologia e sociologia applicate 1956, 13-14:54-76

51214 Personality correlates of manifest anxiety in children. Am Psych 1959, 14:347

LABBÉ, P.

51215 Première conférence des psychanalystes de langues romanes; Paris, centre psychiatrique Sainte-Anne, 10-11 novembre 1952. Scalpel 1953, 106:101-103

REVIEWS OF:

51216 Azima, H. & Faure, H. Différents niveaux de dissolution psychique après hormono-thérapie hypophysosurrénale. RFPsa 1953, 17:354

51217 Macht, D. I. Médicaments, émotion et coagulation du sang. RFPsa 1953, 17:355

51218 Margolin, S. G. The behavior of the stomach during psychoanalysis.
       RFPsa 1953, 17:577
51219 Miller, M. L. Emotional conflicts in asthma. RFPsa 1953, 17:578
51220 Millet, J. A. P. et al: Raynaud's disease. RFPsa 1953, 17:354-355
51221 Rome, H. P. & Braceland, F. J. Psychological response to corticotropin,
       cortisone, and related steroid substances. RFPsa 1953, 17:355

LABHARDT
See Sapir, M.

LABRECQUE, J. P.

51222 De la personne de l'analyste, de son comportement dans le traitement
       psychanalytique. [On the personality of the analyst, from his behavior
       in psychoanalytic treatment.] Rev Can Psa 1954, 1:84-86
           Abs Stein, C. RFPsa 1955, 19:496
51223 De la psychanalyse. [About psychoanalysis.] Union méd du Canada
       1956, 85:691-695

LACAN, JACQUES M.

51224 La chose Freudienne ou sens du retour à Freud en psychanalyse. [The
       Freudian episode—a trend of return to Freudian psychoanalysis.]
       Evolut psychiat 1956, (1):225-252
51225 Commentaires sur des textes de Freud. Réponse au commentaire de
       Jean Hyppolite sur la "Verneinung" de Freud. [Commentaries to texts
       by Freud. Reply to Jean Hyppolite's commentary to "Verneinung" by
       Freud.] Psychanalyse 1953-55, 1:41-58
51226 Commentaires sur des textes de Freud. Séminaire de technique
       Freudienne du 10 février 1954. Introduction au commentaire de Jean
       Hyppolite sur la "Verneinung." [Commentaries to texts by Freud.
       Seminar of Feb. 10, 1954 on Freudian technique. Introduction to Jean
       Hyppolite's commentary to "Verneinung."] Psychanalyse 1953-55,
       1:17-28
51227 (& Levy, R.; Danon-Boileau, H.) Considérations psycho-somatiques
       sur l'hypertension artérielle. [Psychosomatic considerations in relation
       to arterial hypertension.] Evolut psychiat 1953, (3):397-409
51228 (& Granoff, W.) Fetishism: the symbolic, the imaginary and the real.
       In Lorand, S. Perversions: Psychodynamics and Therapy, NY: Random
       House 1956, 265-276
51229 Fonction et champ de la parole et du langage en psychanalyse. [Func-
       tion and range of the word and of language in psychoanalysis.] Psy-
       chanalyse 1953-55, 1:81-166
51230 L'instance de la lettre dans l'inconscient ou la raison depuis Freud.
       [The immediacy of the letter in the unconscious or the reason since
       Freud.] Psychanalyse 1957, 3:47-81
S-5407 (& Cénac, M.) Introduction théorique aux fonctions de la psychanalyse
       en criminologie.
           Abs JFr An Surv Psa 1951, 2:226. Edwards, F. H. J 1953, 34:69-74
51231 D'une question préliminaire à tout traitement possible de la psychose.
       [A question preceding all possible treatment of psychosis.] Psychana-
       lyse 1958, 4:1-50

51232 Le séminaire sur "La lettre volée." [Seminar on "The purloined letter."] Psychanalyse 1956, 2:1-44
51233 Some reflections on the ego. (Read at Brit Psa Soc, May 2, 1951) J 1953, 34:11-17
       Abs NRo An Surv Psa 1953, 4:114-115. HH-H Q 1954, 23:608
51234 (Ed) De l'usage de la parole et des structures de langage dans la conduite et dans le champ de la psychanalyse. [Use of the word and structures of speech during the course and in the field of psychoanalysis.] Psychanalyse 1953-55, 1, 291 p

       See Cénac, Michel

       TRANSLATION OF:
       Heidegger, M. [48586]

LACEY, JOHN I.

51235 Psychophysiological approaches to the evaluation of psychotherapeutic process and outcome. Res PT 160-208

LACHMAN, GEORGE S.
       See Wolff, Ernst

LACOMBE, PIERRE

51236 The problem of the identical twin as reflected in a masochistic compulsion to cheat. J 1959, 40:6-12
       Le problème du jumeau monozygote tel qu'il transparait dans une compulsion masochique de duper. RFPsa 1960, 24:169-186
       Abs Auth J 1954, 35:287. Tabak Rev Psicoanál 1959, 16:268-269. JBi Q 1960, 29:273
51237 Réactions inconscientes au conflit international du canal de Suez. [Unconscious reactions to the international conflict over the Suez canal.] RFPsa 1957, 21:827-837
51238 Du rôle de la peau dans l'attachement mère-enfant. [Role of the skin in mother-child attachment.] RFPsa 1959, 23:83-101
       Abs Puget Rev Psicoanál 1959, 16:141
51239 A special mechanism of pathological weeping. Q 1958, 27:246-251
       Abs JKl J 1960, 41:79

LACY, OSBORNE WILSON

51240 (& Lewinger, N.; Adamson, J. F.) Foreknowledge as a factor affecting perceptual defense and alertness. J exper Psychol 1953, 45:169-174

LAESSIG, URSULA

51241 Über den Heilungsvorgang in der Psychotherapie. [About the process of healing in psychotherapy.] In Bitter, W. Angst und Schuld, Stuttgart: Ernst Klett 1959
51242 Das Kind im Kraftfeld der Familie. Die unverheiratete Frau. [The child in the field of familial strife. The unmarried woman.] In Bitter, W. Psychotherapie und Seelsorge, Stuttgart 1954

51243 Triebe und Triebschicksale nach Freud. [Instincts and the fate of instincts according to Freud.] In Bitter, W. *Psychotherapie und Seelsorge*, Stuttgart 1954

51244 Das Vaterbild im Leben der Frau. [The father image in the life of woman.] In Bitter, W. *Das Vaterproblem in Psychotherapie, Religion und Gesellschaft*, Stuttgart: Hippokrates 1955

LAFFAL, JULIUS

51245 (& Sarason, I. G.; Ameen, L.; Stern, A.) Individuals in groups: a behaviour rating technique. Int J soc Psychiatry 1957, 2:254-262

51246 (& Sarason, I. G.) Limited goal group psychotherapy on a locked service. Dis nerv Syst 1957, 18:1-4

LAFITTE, VICTOR

51247 Psycho-somatique ou physio-pathologie cortico-viscérale? [Psychosomatics or cortico-visceral physiopathology?] Bull Gr Etud Psychol Univ Paris 1952, 6:376-380

LAFON, M. R.

See Blanc, M.

LAFON, O.

See Subes, J.

LAFORGE, ROLFE

See Hunt, John McV.

LAFORGUE, RENÉ

51248 Amour et structure de la personnalité individuelle et collective. [Love and the individual and collective structure of personality.] Psychologe 1959

Liebe und Struktur des individuellen und kollektiven Überichs. Psychologe, Bern 1959

51249 De l'aspect psychosomatique des névroses. [The psychosomatic aspect of neuroses.] Acta psychother psychosom orthopaedag 1953, 1:49-56. Maroc Méd 1953, 32

51250 Baudelaire et sa pensée. [Baudelaire and his thought.] Psyché, Paris 1955, 10:185-204

51251 Ein Bild von Freud. [A portrait of Freud.] Z Psychother med Psychol 1954, 4:209-217

51252 Crime et châtiment. [Crime and chastisement.] Revista espiritualidad, Madrid 1957

51253 Diagnose, Magie und Über-ich. [Diagnosis, magic and superego.] Z PSM 1955-56, 2:51-54

51254 L'enfant dans le monde moderne. [Children in the modern world.] Psyché, Paris 1956, 11:1-13

Das Kind in der modernen Welt. (Tr: Jaggi, J. W.) Prax Kinderpsychol 1957, 6:229-233

51255 La foi et l'équilibre psychique de l'homme. [Faith and the psychic equilibrium of man.] Psyché, Paris, 1953, 8:305-323

51256   Freud et son génie. [Freud; his genius.] Psyché, Paris 1955, 10:457-466. Acta psychother psychosom orthopaedag 1956, 4:265-274. Maroc méd 1956, 35:273-277

S-19389 Homosexualität. Psa Vkb 1957, 318-320

51257   De la médecine psychosomatique. [Psychosomatic medicine.] Acta psychother psychosom orthopaedag 1955, 3:289-304. Maroc méd 1955, 34:617-623

51258   Mystique et continence. [Mystic and continence.] In Les Etudes Carmélitaines: *Mystique et Continence,* Desclé & de Brouwer 1953

51259   Persönliche Erinnerungen an Freud. [Personal recollections of Freud.] In Speer, E. *Die Vorträge der 5. Lindauer Psychotherapiewoche 1954,* Stuttgart: Georg Thieme 1955, 42-56
       Mes souvenirs sur Freud. Action Pensée, Geneva 1956
       Recuerdos sobre Freud. Act luso-esp N P 1957, 16:255-267

51260   A propos du conditionnement dans les névroses. [Concerning the conditioning in neurosis.] Maroc méd 1959, 38:359-362

51261   A propos des règles du traitement psychanalytique. [Concerning the rules of psychoanalytic treatment.] (Read at French Soc Psa, March 1954) Act Pensée, Geneva 1955

51262   Psychanalyse et médecine psychosomatique. [Psychoanalysis and psychosomatic medicine.] Maroc méd 1958, 37

51263   Über Psyche und Konstitution in analytischer Sicht. [Analytic view on psyche and constitution.] Z PSM 1958-59, 5:230-238

51264   Die Rolle von Auge und Ohr in der Psychotherapie. [The role of eye and ear in psychotherapy.] Z PSM 1958-59, 5:167-171

51265   Scrupulosité névrotique et rédemption. [Neurotic scrupulosity and redemption.] Psyché, Paris 1955, 10:313-330
       Neurotische Hemmungen und Erlösung. Psychologe (Geneva) 1955, June

51266   De la souffrance sur le plan psychosomatique. [About suffering on a psychosomatic level.] Psyché, Paris 1955, 10:121-133. Maroc méd 1954, 33:688-692

51267   Die Sprache des Leidens. [The language of suffering.] Z PSM 1957-58, 4:125-128

51268   Structure et liberté. [Structure and freedom.] Extrait des Etudes Carmélitaines 1958

51269   Le super-ego individuel et collectif. [Superego; individual and collective.] Psyché, Paris 1954, 9:81-106
       Das individuelle und das kollektive Über-Ich. Z Psychother med Psychol 1955, 5:97-104; 141-152
       Abs GD An Surv Psa 1954, 5:427-428

51270   Les tendances modernes de la psychothérapie sous l'angle psychanalytique. [Present trends of psychotherapy in regard to psychoanalytic aspects.] Maroc méd 1958, 37:11-20. Acta psychother psychosom orthopaedag 1958, 6:220-238

S-19432 Du transfert.
       Abs NRo An Surv Psa 1952, 3:409-410

51271   La tuberculose du point de vue psychosomatique. [Tuberculosis seen from a psychosomatic point of view.] Maroc méd 1952, 31

LAGACHE, DANIEL

51272 Les artifices de la psychanalyse. [Artifices of psychoanalysis.] Les études philos 1956, 585-593

51273 Behavior and psychoanalytic experience. (Tr: Damman, V.) Dr Af Beh 120-125

51274 Conduit et communication en psychanalyse. [Behavior and communication in psychoanalysis.] Bull Psychol 1953

51275 La conscience en psychanalyse. [Consciousness in psychoanalysis.] Psychol Franc 1957, 2:49-50

S-19441 Définition et aspects de la psychanalyse.
Abs RdeS Q 1953, 22:312

51276 Deuil pathologique. [Pathologic mourning.] Psychanalyse 1956, 2:45-74

51277 Discussion of Lacan, J. "Fonction et champs de la parole et du langage en psychanalyse." Psychanalyse 1956, 1:211-220

51278 La doctrine Freudienne et la théorie du transfert. [Freudian doctrine and the theory of transference.] Acta psychother psychosom orthopaedag 1954, 2:228-249
Abs NRo An Surv Psa 1954, 5:338

51279 Eléments de psychologie médicale. [Elements of medical psychology.] Encycl Méd-Chirurg: Psychiatrie 1955, 37030 A-10, 2:1-11

51280 Fascination de la conscience par le moi. [Fascination of consciousness with the ego.] Psychanalyse 1957, 3:33-45; 325-329

S-19448 Un gangster.
The psychoanalysis of a gangster. (Tr: Damman, V.) Arch crim Psychodyn 1955, 1:832-865
Abs RdesS Q 1953, 22:313

S-19451 De l'homosexualité à la jalousie.
Abs R 1953, 40:355. Rv Pichon Rivière, E. Rev Psicoanál 1953, 10:121

51281 Introduction à la psychothérapie. [An introduction to psychotherapy.] Le Sud Médical et Chirurgical 1955, 88:4.044-4.056

51282 Sur le polyglottisme dans l'analyse. [Polyglottism in analysis.] Psychanalyse 1953-55, 1:167-178

S-19459 Le problème du transfert.
Spanish: (Tr: Baranger, M.) Rev Urug Psa 1956, 2(2)
Abs Koenig RFPsa 1958, 22:256-257

51283 La Psychanalyse. [Psychoanalysis.] Paris: PUF 1955, 126 p
Rv Garma, A. Rev Psicoanál 1955, 12:296-297

51284 La psychanalyse: évolution, tendances, et problèmes actuels. [Psychoanalysis: evolution, trends, and present problems.] Cahiers de l'Encyclop Franç 1955, 23-34

51285 Psychanalyse et psychologie. [Psychoanalysis and psychology.] Evolut psychiat 1956, (1):253-264

51286 De la psychanalyse à la sociologie. [From psychoanalysis to sociology.] (An answer to George Friedmann.) Bull Psychol 1956, 10:1-8

S-19461 La psycho-criminogenèse.
Abs CBr An Surv Psa 1951, 2:317-318. Edwards, F. H. J 1953, 34:74-75

51287 Quelques aspects de l'identification. Bull Int Sci Sociales, Unesco 1955, 7(1):37-46
  Some aspects of identification. Int soc Sci Bull 1955, 7:35-44
S-19466 Quelques aspects du transfert.
  Some aspects of transference. (Read at Brit Psa Soc, Apr 4, 1951) J 1953, 34:1-10
  Spanish: Rev Urug Psa 1956, 1:521-569
  Abs STa An Surv Psa 1951, 2:387-389. JLan An Surv Psa 1953, 4:427-428. Waldhorn, H. F. Q 1954, 23:607. Rev Psicoanál 1954, 11:392-393. Vega Q 1958, 27:621

51288 Réflexions sur De Greeff et le crime passionnel. [Reflections on De Greeff and the crime of passion.] In De Greeff, E. Autour de l'Oeuvre du Dr. E. De Greeff, Louvain, Belg: Edit Nauwelaerts 1956

51289 Résultats et critères de guérison de la psychanalyse. [Results and evaluation of psychoanalytic therapy.] Encycl Méd-Chirurg:Psychiatrie 1955, 37812 E-10, 2:1-5

51290 La rêverie imageante: conduite adaptive au test de Rorschach. [Imaginative reverie: adaptive response to the Rorschach.] Bull Group Franç Rorschach 1957, (9):3-11

51291 Socialisation et identification. [Socialization and identification.] Acta psychol 1955, 11:145-146

51292 Thérapie analytique en dispensaire. [Analytic therapy in an outpatients' service.] Psychanalyse 1956, 2:314-315

51293 Voisinage de la philosophie et de la psychanalyse. [Neighborliness between philosophy and psychoanalysis.] Encycl Franç: Philosophie 1957, 19.26.10-19.26.15

51294 Vues d'ensemble sur la psychanalyse. [General views concerning psychoanalysis.] Le Sud Méd et Chirurg 1956, 89:6592-6603

51295 Vues psychanalytiques sur les émotions. [Psychoanalytic views on the emotions.] Psychol Franç 1958, 3:66-75

TRANSLATION OF:
Balint, M. [41078]

REVIEWS OF:
51296 Balint, M. Primary Love and Psycho-Analytic Technique. J 1953, 34:328-329. RFPsa 1953, 17:359-361
51297 Sterba, R. F. Clinical and therapeutic aspects of character resistance. RFPsa 1953, 17:353

LA GUARDIA, ERIC

51298 Sire de Maletroit's door. Am Im 1958, 15:411-423

LAGUNA, FREDERICA DE

51299 Method and theory of ethnology. In author's American Anthropologist: Selected Papers, 1888-1920, Evanston, Ill: Row, Peterson 1960, 782-792

LAHA, S. C.

S-19480 Concept of time.
  Abs JAA An Surv Psa 1952, 3:86-88. Levinson, G. J 1953, 34:356

LAIBLIN, WILHELM

51300 Ein Krankenbericht, als tiefenpsychologischer Beitrag zum Problem einer geistig-politischen Neuorientierung. [A Case History, as a depth-psychological contribution to the problem of a psycho-political reorientation.] Heidelberg: L. Schneider 1949, 112 p

LAIDLAW, J. C.

See Rizzo, Nicholas Daniel

LAIDLAW, ROBERT W.

51301 Marriage counseling. In Liebman, S. *Understanding Your Patient*, Phila: Lippincott 1957, 131-146
51302 [Moderator: Discussion on] Psychiatric implications of surveys on sexual behavior. R 1956, 43:471-500
51303 Psychiatric uses of hypnosis. Tomorrow 1958, 6:15-29

See Saul, Leon J.

LAING, R. D.

51304 (& Esterson, A.) The collusion function of pairing in analytic groups. M 1958, 31:117-123
51305 An examination of Tillich's theory of anxiety and neurosis. M 1957, 30:88-91

LAING, W. A. R.

See-Wittkower, Eric D.

LAKIN, MARTIN

51306 Assessment of significant role attitudes in primiparous mothers by means of a modification of the TAT. PSM 1957, 19:50-60
51307 (& Lebovits, B.) Bias in psychotherapists of different orientations. An exploratory study. PT 1958, 12:79-86

See Lebovits, Binyamin Zeev

LAKOS, MARCILLE H.

See Ackerman, Nathan W.

LALOUM

See Lebovici, Serge

LAMANA, I. L. DE

51308 La asunción de rol sexual de una melliza univitelina. [The assuming of a sexual role in an identical twin.] Rev Psicoanál 1958, 15:98-102

REVIEWS OF:
51309 Klapman, J. W. Psychoanalytic or didactic group psychotherapy? Rev Psicoanál 1955, 12:429
51310 Munro, L. Steps in ego integration observed in a play analysis. Rev Psicoanál 1958, 15:140
51311 Riviere, J. On the genesis of psychical conflict in earliest infancy. Rev Psicoanál 1958, 15:130-131

LA MAR, NORVELLE C.

S-19512 (Reporter) Panel on current problems of psychoanalytic technique: failures and results.
      Abs STa An Surv Psa 1951, 2:420-429
S-19515 (Reporter) Panel: Schizophrenia in childhood.
      Abs NRo An Surv Psa 1952, 3:229-230; 234-240; 276-277

LAMB, GEORGE
TRANSLATION OF:
Nuttin, J. [24425]

LAMBERCIER, MARC
See Piaget, Jean

LAMBERT, ANNE
See Rose, John A.

LAMBLING, A.
See M'Uzan, M. De

LAMBRUSCHINI, CARLOS

51312 Analitica existencial de los sueños. [Existential analysis of dreams.] Act Np Arg 1959, 5:172
51313 La antropología filosófica y la psiquiatría actual. [Philosophical anthropology and modern psychiatry.] Act Np Arg 1958, 4:187-193
51314 Influencia del psicoanalisis en la psicoterapia actual. [The influence of psychoanalysis on the actual psychotherapy.] Rev Argent Neur Psiquiat 1939, 4:159
51315 Psicoanalisis y existencialismo. [Psychoanalysis and existentialism.] Rosario. Univ Nacional del Litoral, Instituto de Filosofia 1952, 40 p

LAMONT, JOHN H.

51316 Interpretation in therapy with children. Smith Coll Stud soc Wk 1958, 28:139-150

See Jessner, Lucie; Long, Robert T.

LAMPL, HANS

51316A On determinism. J 1955, 36:350-354
51317 The influence of biological and psychological factors upon the development of the latency period. (Tr: Maury, L. M.) Dr Af Beh 380-387

LAMPL-DE GROOT, JEANNE

51318 On adolescence. Psa St C 1960, 15:95-103
51319 On defense and development: normal and pathological. Psa St C 1957, 12:114-126.
      Abs Resta Riv Psa 1959, 5:195. RTh J 1959, 40:368-369
51320 Depression and aggression. Dr Af Beh 153-168
51321 Groepsbesprekingen met stiefmoeders. [Group discussion with stepmothers.] Maandbl Geest Volksgezondh 1954, 9:305-312

51322 Problems of psychoanalytic training. (Read at 18th Int Psa Cong, London, July 1953) J 1954, 35:184-187
Abs JFr An Surv Psa 1954, 5:403-404. Lebovici, S. RFPsa 1954, 18:467. JLan Q 1955, 24:605

51323 Psychoanalysis and its relation to certain other fields of natural science. J 1959, 40:169-179
Abs Weiss, J. Q 1960, 29:582-583

51324 Psychoanalytische Ich-Psychologie und ihre Bedeutung für die Fehlentwicklung bei Kindern. [Psychoanalytic ego psychology and its meaning in the faulty development of children.] Acta psychother psychosom orthopaedag 1956, 4:195-202

S-19533 Re-evaluation of the role of the Oedipus complex.
Abs JAA An Surv Psa 1952, 3:70-71. CBr Q 1954, 23:135

51325 The role of identification in psychoanalytic procedure. J 1956, 37:456-459
Abs JLan Q 1957, 26:581-582. Lebovici, S. RFPsa 1957, 21:617

51326 The theory of instinctual drives. (Read at 19th Int Psa Cong, Geneva, July 1955) J 1956, 37:354-359
Anmerkungen zur psychoanalytischen Triebtheorie. In Mitscherlich, A. Entfaltung der Psychoanalyse, Stuttgart: Klett 1956, 194-204. Psyche, Heidel 1956, 10:194-204
Abs JLan Q 1957, 26:577

LANDAUER, KARL

S-19545 Die Bewusstseinsstörungen. Psa Vkb 1957, 240-250
S-19549 Erkranken und Gesunden. Psa Vkb 1957, 215-222
S-19553 Die Gemütsbewegungen oder Affekte. Psa Vkb 1957, 172-190
S-19554 Gemütserkrankungen. Psa Vkb 1957, 289-294
S-19560 Die körperlichen Erkrankungen. Psa Vkb 1957, 223-225
S-19564 Paranoia. Psa Vkb 1957, 312-317
S-19571 Die Schizophrenie. Psa Vkb 1957, 295-304
S-19576 Die Triebe. Psa Vkb 1957, 191-202

LANDER, JOSEPH

51327 Psychoanalytic therapy. An Surv Psa 1953, 4:390-456
51328 When does an agency refer a child to a residential treatment center? Symposium 1954: The role of residential treatment for children. Ops 1955, 25:675-678
Abs Koenig RFPsa 1956, 20:583-584

ABSTRACTS OF:
51329 Abraham, H. C. A contribution to the problems of female sexuality. Q 1957, 26:577
51330 Abse, D. W. Early phases of ego structure adumbrated in the regressive ego states of schizophrenic psychosis, and elucidated in intensive psychotherapy. Q 1957, 26:139
51331 Adatto, C. P. Ego reintegration observed in analysis of late adolescents. Q 1959, 28:280
51332 Alexander, F. Current views on psychotherapy. An Surv Psa 1953, 4:415-417

51333   Alexander, V. K. A case of phobia of darkness. Q 1958, 27:289
51334   Alston, E. F. Psychoanalytic therapy conducted by correspondence. Q 1958, 27:127-128
51335   Arlow, J. A. On smugness. Q 1958, 27:127
51336   Ausubel, D. P. An evaluation of recent adolescent drug addiction. Q 1953, 22:138
51337   Bak, R. C. The schizophrenic defense against aggression. Q 1955, 24:602-603
51338   Balint, M. Analytic training and training analysis. Q 1955, 24:604
51339   Balint, M. Friendly expanses—horrid empty spaces. Q 1957, 26:278
51340   Balint, M. Notes on parapsychology and parapsychological healing. Q 1956, 25:442-443
51341   Baranger, W. The ego and the function of ideology. Q 1959, 28:280
51342   Barbara, D. A. The Demosthenes complex. Q 1958, 27:603
51343   Barbara, D. A. Neurosis in speaking. Q 1958, 27:288
51344   Bard, M. & Dyk, R. B. The psychodynamic significance of beliefs regarding the cause of serious illness. Q 1957, 26:583
51345   Bartemeier, L. H. A psychoanalytic study of pregnancy in an "as-if" personality. Q 1955, 24:606
51346   Baumeyer, F. The Schreber case. Q 1957, 26:434
51347   Bellak, L. An ego-psychological theory of hypnosis. Q 1957, 26:282
51348   Benedek, T. Dynamics of the counter-transference. An Surv Psa 1953, 4:432-435
51349   Bennitt, C. The psychological nature of sex. Q 1958, 27:289
51350   Berezin, M. A. Dynamic factors in pruritis ani: a case report. Q 1955, 24:467
51351   Bergler, E. Fear of heights. Q 1958, 27:603
51352   Bergler, E. Further contributions to the problem of blushing. Q 1958, 27:603
51353   Bergler, E. The "I'm damned if I do, and damned if I don't" technique. Q 1957, 26:438
51354   Bergler, E. On "negative" exhibitionism. Q 1958, 27:129-130
51355   Bergler, E. Salome, the turning point in the life of Oscar Wilde. Q 1957, 26:437
51356   Bergler, E. The second book and the second play. Q 1957, 26:141
51357   Bergler, E. Some atypical forms of impotence and frigidity. Q 1955, 24:312
51358   Bergler, E. Technical problems with couples simultaneously analyzed by the same analyst. An Surv Psa 1953, 4:449-450
51359   Bergler, E. Unconscious mechanisms in "writer's block." Q 1957, 26:138-139
51360   Bernard, V. Psychoanalysis and members of minority groups. An Surv Psa 1953, 4:455
51361   Beukenkamp, C. Clinical observations on the effect of analytically oriented group therapy and group supervision on the therapist. Q 1957, 26:436-437
51362   Bibring, G. L. The training analysis and its place in psychoanalytic training. Q 1955, 24:605
51363   Bienenfeld, F. R. Justice, aggression and Eros. Q 1958, 27:601
51364   Bion, W. R. On arrogance. Q 1959, 28:279

51365   Bion, W. R. Development of schizophrenic thought. Q 1957, 26:577
51366   Bion, W. R. Differentiation of the psychotic from the nonpsychotic personalities. Q 1958, 27:442-443
51367   Bion, W. R. Notes on the theory of schizophrenia. Q 1955, 24:602
51368   Bird, B. Feelings of unreality. Q 1958, 27:442
51369   Bird, B. Pathological sleep. Q 1955, 24:460-461
51370   Blau, A. A unitary hypothesis of anxiety and related displeasure emotions. Q 1954, 23:628-629
51371   Blauner, J. Existential analysis. Q 1958, 27:288
51372   Bonaparte, M. The fault of Orpheus in reverse. Q 1955, 24:602
51373   Bouvet, M. Technical variation and the concept of distance. Q 1959, 28:281
51374   Branfman, T. Modesty as a quasi-moral resistance. Q 1957, 26:141
51375   Brenner, C. et al: Discussion on the psi hypothesis. Q 1958, 27:128
51376   Bressler, B. Ulcerative colitis as an anniversary symptom. Q 1957, 26:587
51377   Breuer, J. & Freud, S. On the psychical mechanism of hysterical phenomena (1893). Q 1957, 26:432
51378   Brunswick, D. A revision of the classification of instincts or drives. Q 1955, 24:607
51379   Burlingham, D. Twins: A Study of Three Pairs of Identical Twins. An Surv Psa 1952, 3:579-581
51380   Bychowski, G. On the handling of some schizophrenic defense mechanisms and reaction patterns. Q 1955, 24:603-604
51381   Bychowski, G. The release of internal images. Q 1957, 26:576
51382   Bychowski, G. Struggle against the introjects. Q 1959, 28:280
51383   Caplan, G. Mental hygiene contributions to the resettlement of immigrants in Israel. Q 1953, 22:463-464
51384   Cath, S. H. et al: The role of the body image in psychotherapy with the physically handicapped. Q 1958, 27:288
51385   Cattell, J. P. The alternations of ego functioning after topectomy. Q 1955, 24:466
51386   Cattell, J. P. The holiday syndrome. Q 1956, 25:444
51387   Christoffel, H. Psychanalyse sous forme verbale et sous forme de jeu. An Surv Psa 1953, 4:435-436
51388   Colby, K. M. Gentlemen, the queen. Q 1954, 23:461
51389   Coleman, M. L. & Shor, J. Ego development through self-traumatization. Q 1954, 23:462
51390   Coleman, M. L. Externalization of the toxic introject. Q 1957, 26:585
51391   Dalmau, C. J. Post-Oedipal psychodynamics. Q 1958, 27:287
51392   Davidson, G. M. Concerning the biological aspects of the Oedipus complex. Q 1957, 26:140
51393   Desmonde, W. H. The ritual origin of Shakespeare's *Titus Andronicus*. Q 1956, 25:443-444
51394   Deutsch, F. Analytic synesthesiology. Analytic interpretation of intersensory perception. Q 1956, 25:113
51395   Devereux, G. The awarding of a penis as a compensation for rape. Q 1958, 27:600-601
51396   Devereux, G. Cultural factors in psychoanalytic therapy. An Surv Psa 1953, 4:455

51397 Dorn, R. M. The reintegration of a wish, a dream, and an error. Q 1956, 25:281

51398 Eidelberg, L. The concept of the unconscious. An Surv Psa 1953, 4:399-403

51399 Eisenbud, J. On the use of the psi hypothesis in psychoanalysis. Q 1957, 26:282

51400 Eisler, H. E. The development of the individual. Q 1957, 26:284

51401 Eissler, K. R. The effect of the structure of the ego on psychoanalytic technique. An Surv Psa 1953, 4:407-412

51402 Eissler, K. R. The experience and the mechanism of isolation. Q 1953, 22:123

51403 Eissler, K. R. Notes upon defects of ego structure in schizophrenia. Q 1955, 24:603

51404 Eissler, K. R. Notes upon the emotionality of a schizophrenic patient and its relation to problems of technique. An Surv Psa 1953, 4:453-454

51405 Eissler, K. R. Remarks on some variations in psychoanalytic technique. Q 1959, 28:281-282

51406 Ekstein, R. Structural aspects of psychotherapy. Q 1953, 22:302

51407 Ellis, A. An operational reformulation of some of the basic principles of psychoanalysis. Q 1957, 26:583

51408 Emch, M. The social context of supervision. Q 1957, 26:280

51409 English, O. S. (Reporter) Panel: The essentials of psychotherapy as viewed by the psychoanalyst. An Surv Psa 1953, 4:417-425

51410 Erikson, E. H. Freud's *The Origins of Psychoanalysis*. Q 1956, 25:442

51411 Evans, W. N. Evasive speech as a form of resistance. An Surv Psa 1953, 4:440-443

51412 Farrell, B. A. Psychological theory and the belief in God. Q 1956, 25:614

51413 Feldman, A. B. Shakespeare's early errors. Q 1956, 25:612

51414 Feldman, H. The illusions of work. Q 1957, 26:140

51415 Fingarette, H. Blame: its motive and meaning in everyday life. Q 1958, 27:443

51416 Fingert, H. H. Psychoanalytic study of the minor prophet, Jonah. Q 1955, 24:312-313

51417 Fleischl, M. F. Paroxysmal tachycardia. Q 1957, 26:141

51418 Flescher, J. On different types of countertransference. An Surv Psa 1953, 4:436-438

51419 Flescher, J. The "primary constellation" in the structure and treatment of psychoses. Q 1954, 23:461-462

51420 Fliess, R. The autopsic encumbrance. Q 1955, 24:459-460

51421 Fliess, R. Countertransference and counter-identification. An Surv Psa 1953, 4:428-431

51422 Fliess, R. The hypnotic evasion: a clinical observation. An Surv Psa 1953, 4:443-445

51423 Fliess, R. Phylogenetic vs. ontogenetic experience. Q 1957, 26:433-434

51424 Foulkes, S. H. Group analytic observations as indicator for psychoanalytic treatment. Q 1955, 24:609

51425 Fraiberg, L. Freud's writings on art. Q 1957, 26:434

51426 Freeman, T. Clinical and theoretical observations on male homosexuality. Q 1957, 26:281

51427 Freeman, T. Some notes on a forgotten religion. Q 1955, 24:311-312

51428 Freud, S. Memorandum on the electrical treatment of war neurotics (1920). Q 1957, 26:432-433

51429 (& Lester, M.) Freud, S. The Origins of Psychoanalysis. An Surv Psa 1954, 5:512-522

51430 Freud, S. Report on my studies in Paris and Berlin (1886). Q 1957, 26:432

51431 Freud, S. On the teaching of psychoanalysis in universities (1918). Q 1957, 26:432

51432 Fried, E. Self-induced failure. A mechanism of defense. Q 1956, 25:115

51433 Friedemann, M. Representative and typical dreams with emphasis on the masculinity-femininity problem. Q 1958, 27:601-602

51434 Friedenberg, F. S. A contribution to the problem of sadomasochism. Q 1957, 26:437

51435 Friedenberg, F. S. Thoughts on the latency period. Q 1958, 27:602

51436 Friedenberg, F. S. Two dreams. Q 1958, 27:130

51437 Fuller, R. G. A study of administration of state psychiatric services. Q 1955, 24:318

51438 Galdston, I. Prophylactic psychopathology: the rationality of the irrational in psychodynamics. Q 1954, 23:463

51439 Galdston, I. Psychiatry for everyman in his everyday life. Q 1953, 22:464

51440 Garma, A. The meaning and genesis of fetishism. Q 1957, 26:580

51441 Garma, A. Oral-digestive superego aggressions and actual conflicts in peptic ulcer patients. Q 1957, 27:437

51442 Garma, A. Peptic ulcer and pseudo-peptic ulcer. Q 1959, 28:277

51443 Gillespie, W. H. The general theory of sexual perversion. Q 1957, 26:579

51444 Gillspie, W. H. Neurotic ego distortion. Q 1959, 28:283

51445 Giovacchini, P. L. Defensive meaning of a specific anxiety syndrome. Q 1957, 26:586

51446 Gitelson, M. On ego distortion. Q 1958, 28:282-283

51447 Gitelson, M. Therapeutic problems in the analysis of the "normal" candidate. Q 1955, 24:605

51448 Glauber, I. P. The rebirth motif in homosexuality and its teleological significance. Q 1957, 26:580

51449 Glover, E. Ego distortion. Q 1959, 28:283

51450 Glover, E. Psychoanalysis and criminology: a political survey. Q 1957, 26:575

51451 Glover, E. Therapeutic criteria of psychoanalysis. Q 1955, 24:601

51452 Gloyne, H. F. Psychosomatic aspects of pain. Q 1955, 24:466-467

51453 Goldberger, E. The id and the ego. Q 1958, 27:444

51454 Goldfarb, A. I. Psychotherapy of the aged. Q 1957, 26:436

51455 Goldfarb, A. I. Psychotherapy of aged persons. Q 1957, 26:139

51456 Gombrich, E. H. Psychoanalysis and the history of art. Q 1956, 25:280

51457 Gordon, L. Incest as revenge against the preoedipal mother. Q 1957, 26:141

51458   Greenacre, P. Re-evaluation of the process of working through. Q 1957, 26:581

51459   Greenacre, P. Toward an understanding of the physical nucleus of some defense reactions. Q 1959, 28:276

51460   Greenacre, P. Woman as artist. Q 1960, 29:606-607

51461   Greenson, R. R. Variations in classic psychoanalytic technique: an introduction. Q 1959, 28:280-281

51462   Grinker, R. R. Growth inertia and shame: their therapeutic implications and dangers. Q 1957, 26:278

51463   Grinstein, A. Vacations: a psychoanalytic study. Q 1956, 25:614

51464   Grotjahn, M. Analytic psychotherapy with the elderly. Q 1957, 26:285

51465   Grotjahn, M. & Treusch, J. V. A new technique of psychosomatic consultations. Q 1958, 27:443

51466   Grotjahn, M. About the relation between psychoanalytic training and psychoanalytic therapy. Q 1955, 24:608-609

51467   Guy, W. & Finn, M. H. P. A review of autofellatio. A psychological study of two new cases. Q 1956, 25:115

51468   Haak, N. Comments on the analytic situation. Q 1958, 27:440

51469   Hambidge, G., Jr. On the ontogenesis of repression. Q 1957, 26:584

51470   Hart, H. H. Maternal narcissism and the Oedipus complex. Q 1959, 28:280

51471   Hartmann, H. The development of the ego concept in Freud's work. Q 1957, 26:580-581

51472   Hayman, M. Traumatic elements in the analysis of a borderline case. Q 1958, 27:127

51473   Heiman, M. (Ed) Psychoanalysis and Social Work. An Surv Psa 1953, 4:614-629

51474   Heimann, P. Dynamics of transference interpretations. Q 1957, 26:575

51475   Heimann, P. Problems of the training analysis. Q 1955, 24:604

51476   Hill, G. The dynamic you-and-I relationship with a borderline personality. Q 1957, 26:586

51477   Hitschmann, E. Some psychoanalytic aspects of biography. Q 1957, 26:573

51478   Hoch, P. H. Psychosomatic problems: methodology, research material and concepts. Q 1953, 22:301-302

51479   Hoffer, W. Defensive process and defensive organization: their place in psychoanalytic technique. Q 1955, 24:606

51480   Hoffer, W. Transference and transference neurosis. Q 1957, 26:578

51481   Hoffman, E. H. & Brody, M. W. The symptom, fear of death. Q 1958, 27:603

51482   Hora, T. The structural analysis of transvestitism. Q 1954, 23:462

51483   Hunter, D. Object-relation changes in the analysis of a fetishist. Q 1956, 25:113-114

51484   Isham, A. C. The ego, consciousness, motor processes, and thought. Q 1956, 25:444-445

51485   Isham, A. C. Emotion, instinct, and pain-pleasure. Q 1955, 24:466

51486   Isham, A. C. Imitation and identification. Q 1958, 27:128

51487   Jacobson, E. On psychotic identifications. Q 1955, 24:601

51488   Jones, E. The birth and death of Moses. Q 1959, 28:106

51489   Jones, E. Freud's early travels. Q 1955, 24:600

51490 Jones, E. The inception of *Totem and Taboo*. Q 1957, 26:433
51491 Jones, E. Pain. Q 1958, 27:442
51492 Kanzer, M. The communicative function of the dream. Q 1957, 26:279
51493 Kanzer, M. Past and present in the transference. An Surv Psa 1953, 4:425-426
51494 Kanzer, M. The reality testing of the scientist. Q 1957, 26:284
51495 Karpe, M. The origins of Peter Pan. Q 1957, 26:437
51496 Karson, M. The psychology of trade union membership. Q 1958, 27:299
51497 Katan, M. Contribution to the panel on ego distortion. Q 1959, 28:283
51498 Katan, M. The importance of the nonpsychotic part of the personality in schizophrenia. Q 1955, 24:602
51499 Kemper, W. The manifold possibilities of therapeutic evaluation of dreams. Q 1959, 28:278
51500 Klein, M. On the development of mental functioning. Q 1959, 28:276
51501 Kotkov, B. Common forms of resistance in group psychotherapy. Q 1958, 27:289
51502 Kowal, S. J. Emotions as a cause of cancer, eighteenth and nineteenth century contributions. Q 1957, 26:139
51503 Krapf, E. E. Cold and warmth in the transference experience. Q 1957, 26:579
51504 Kris, E. On some vicissitudes of insight in psychoanalysis. Q 1957, 26:581
51505 Lagache, D. Some aspects of transference. An Surv Psa 1953, 4:427-428
51506 Lampl-De Groot, J. Problems of psychoanalytic training. Q 1955, 24:605
51507 Lampl-De Groot, J. The role of identification in psychoanalytic procedure. Q 1957, 26:581-582
51508 Lampl-de Groot, J. The theory of instinctual drives. Q 1957, 26:577
51509 Langer, M. Sterility and envy. Q 1959, 28:278
51510 Lantos, B. On the motivation of human relationships. Q 1957, 26:279
51511 Lantos, B. The two genetic derivations of aggression with reference to sublimation and neutralization. Q 1959, 28:277
51512 Leavitt, H. C. A biographical and teleological study of "Irma's injection" dream. Q 1958, 27:129
51513 Leavitt, H. C. Generic relations between anxiety and fear. Q 1958, 27:288
51514 Leavitt, H. C. Interrelationships between unconscious fear patterns and function of repression. Q 1954, 23:462
51515 Leavitt, H. C. Organized qualities of the id structure. Q 1954, 23:463
51516 Leavitt, H. C. Relations between conditioned patterns and superego development. Q 1958, 27:288-289
51517 Leavitt, H. C. Relation between dream teleology and vigilance states. Q 1958, 27:129
51518 Leavitt, H. C. Teleological contributions of dreams to the waking ego. Q 1958, 27:443-444
51519 Leeuw, P. J. van der: On the preoedipal phase of the male. Q 1959, 28:277
51520 Lemkau, P. V. Toward mental health. Q 1953, 22:138

51521   Lemmertz, J. J. Valor clinico de las interpretaciones en terminos de identificaciones. An Surv Psa 1953, 4:445-446

51522   Lester, M. The analysis of an unconscious beating fantasy in a woman. Q 1958, 27:127

51523   Levin, A. J. Oedipus and Samson: the rejected hero-child. Q 1958, 27:438

51524   Levy, K. Silence in the analytic session. Q 1959, 28:107

51525   Lewinsky, H. The closed circle. Q 1957, 26:574-575

51526   Lewy, E. On micropsia, Q 1955, 24:460

51527   Lief, H. I. Should patients be presented in person? Q 1957, 26:436

51528   Linn, L. Some developmental aspects of the body image. Q 1956, 25:443

51529   Lipton, S. D. A note on the compatibility of psychic determinism and freedom of will. Q 1957, 26:281

51530   Little, M. On delusional transference (Transference psychosis). Q 1959, 28:278

51531   Little, M. "R"—the analyst's total response to his patient's needs. Q 1958, 27:442

51532   Lodge, A. Satan's symbolic syndrome. Q 1958, 27:128

51533   Loewenstein, R. M. Christians and Jews. An Surv Psa 1951, 2:653-662

51534   Loewenstein, R. M. Remarks on some variations in psychoanalytic technique. Q 1959, 28:281

51535   Loewenstein, R. M. Some remarks on defenses, autonomous ego and psychoanalytic technique. Q 1955, 24:606

51536   Loewenstein, R. M. Some remarks on the role of speech in psychoanalytic technique. Q 1957, 26:582

51537   Lomas, J. B. On maternal symbiotic depression. Q 1958, 27:129

51538   Lorand, S. Dream interpretation in the Talmud. Q 1958, 27:437

51539   Lorand, S. & Feldman, S. The symbolism of teeth in dreams. Q 1956, 25:612-613

51540   Lorand, S. & Console, W. A. Therapeutic results in psychoanalytic treatment without fee. Q 1959, 28:107

51541   Lowenhaupt, E. A consideration of psychic mechanisms in vasospastic disorders of the hand. Q 1953, 22:448

51542   Madison, P. Freud's repression concept. A survey and attempted classification. Q 1957, 26:434

51543   Mahler, M. S. Autism and symbiosis, two extreme disturbances of identity. Q 1959, 28:276

51544   Malamud, W. Developments in research on dementia praecox. Q 1953, 22:464

51545   Mann, T. Freud and the future. Q 1957, 26:435

51546   Mannheim, J. Notes on a case of drug addiction. Q 1956, 25:613

51547   Marcondes, D. The psychodynamism of the analytic process. Q 1957, 26:585

51548   Marty, P. The allergic object relationship. Q 1959, 28:277

51549   Masserman, J. H. The conceptual dynamics of person, religion and self. Q 1956, 25:115

51550   Mead, M. Changing patterns of parent-child relations in an urban culture. Q 1958, 27:599

51551 Meerloo, J. A. M. Freud, the creative scientist. Q 1958, 27:444
51552 Meerloo, J. A. M. Transference and resistance in geriatric psycho-
       therapy. Q 1956, 25:445
51553 Menaker, E. A note on some biologic parallels between certain innate
       animal behavior and moral masochism. Q 1957, 26:435-436
51554 Meng, H. & Stern, E. Organ-psychosis. Q 1957, 26:285
51555 Menninger, K. Regulatory devices of the ego under major stress. Q
       1956, 25:280
51556 Menninger, W. C. Men, machines, and mental health. Q 1953, 22:137
51557 Milner, M. The communication of primary sensual experience (the
       yell of joy). Q 1957, 26:574
51558 Mittelmann, B. Psychodynamics of motility. Q 1959, 28:280
51559 Modell, A. H. Some recent psychoanalytic theories of schizophrenia.
       Q 1957, 26:584
51560 Moloney, J. C. The precognitive cultural ingredients of schizophrenia.
       Q 1958, 27:598
51561 Moloney, J. C. Psychic self-abandon and extortion of confessions. Q
       1956, 25:443
51562 Money-Kyrle, R. E. Normal countertransference and some of its devia-
       tions. Q 1957, 26:578
51563 Money-Kyrle, R. E. On the process of psychoanalytical inference. Q
       1959, 28:278
51564 Murphy, W. F. Some clinical aspects of the body ego. Q 1958, 27:603-
       604
51565 Murphy, W. F. & Chasen, M. Spasmodic torticollis. Q 1957, 26:435
51566 Nacht, S. Causes and mechanisms of ego distortion. Q 1959, 28:284
51567 Nacht, S. Difficulté de la psychanalyse didactique par rapport à la
       psychanalyse thérapeutique. An Surv Psa 1953, 4:455. Q 1955, 24:608
51568 Nacht, S. et al: The ego in perverse relationships. Q 1957, 26:580
51569 Nacht, S. Technical remarks on the handling of the transference neu-
       rosis. Q 1958, 27:440-441
51570 Nacht, S. Variations in technique. Q 1959, 28:282
51571 Nielsen, N. The dynamics of training analysis. Q 1955, 24:608
51572 Nöllman, J. E. Consideraciones psicoanaliticas acerca de un enfermo
       esquizophrenico con mecanismos hipocondriaco-paranoides. An Surv
       Psa 1953, 4:454-455
51573 Novey, S. A re-evaluation of certain aspects of the theory of instinctual
       drives in the light of modern ego psychology. Q 1958, 27:438-439
51574 Novey, S. The role of the superego and ego-ideal in character forma-
       tion. Q 1957, 26:278
51575 Novey, S. Some philosophical speculations about the concept of the
       genital character. Q 1956, 25:611
51576 Novey, S. Utilization of social institutions as a defense technique in the
       neuroses. Q 1958, 27:437
51577 Nunberg, H. Character and neurosis. Q 1957, 26:433
51578 Nunberg, H. Evaluation of the results of psychoanalytic treatment. Q
       1955, 24:459
51579 Orbach, C. E. et al: Fears and defensive adaptations to the loss of anal
       sphincter control. Q 1958, 27:443

51580 Ostow, M. The death instincts—a contribution to the study of instincts. Q 1959, 28:106

51581 Ostow, M. Linkage fantasies and representations. Q 1957, 26:282

51582 Palm, R. A comparative study of symbol formation in the Rorschach Test and the dream. Q 1957, 26:585

51583 Parkin, A. Emergence of sleep during psychoanalysis. Q 1956, 25:613

51584 Pasche, F. & Renard, M. The reality of the object and economic point of view. Q 1957, 26:574

51585 Perestrello, D. Headache and primal scene. Q 1955, 24:606

51586 Peto, A. On so-called "depersonalization." Q 1957, 26:283

51587 Pichon-Rivière, A. A. de. Dentition, walking, and speech in relation to the depressive position. Q 1959, 28:279

51588 Pichon-Rivière, A. A. de. House construction play—its interpretation and diagnostic value. Q 1959, 28:107

51589 Podolsky, E. Hallucinosis. Q 1958, 27:130

51590 Polatin, P. & Douglas, D. B. Spontaneous orgasm in a case of schizophrenia. Q 1953, 22:609

51591 Pollaczek, P. P. & Homefield, H. D. The use of masks as an adjunct to role-playing. Q 1955, 24:318

51592 Pratt, J. S. Epilegomena to the study of Freudian instinct theory. Q 1959, 28:106

51593 Racker, H. A contribution to the problem of counter-transference. An Surv Psa 1953, 4:431-432

51594 Racker, H. Contribution to the problem of psychopathological stratification. Q 1958, 27:441-442

51595 Rado, C. Oedipus the King; an interpretation. Q 1957, 26:584

51596 Ramana, C. V. Preliminary notes on transference in borderline neurosis. Q 1957, 26:583

51597 Rangell, L. The psychology of poise. With a special elaboration of the psychic significance of the snout or perioral region. Q 1956, 25:114

51598 Rascovsky, A. Beyond the oral stage. Q 1957, 26:574

51599 Reich, A. A special variation of technique. Q 1959, 28:282

51600 Reider, N. Reconstruction and screen function. An Surv Psa 1953, 4:452-453

51601 Rein, D. M. Conrad Aiken and psychoanalysis. Q 1957, 26:284

51602 Repond, A. Invitation to action. Q 1953, 22:137

51603 Richardson, H. B. Love and the psychodynamics of adaptation. Q 1957, 26:586

51604 Richardson, H. B. The Pygmalion reaction. Q 1958, 27:130

51605 Richardson, H. B. Raynaud's phenomenon and scleroderma. A case report and psychodynamic formulation. Q 1956, 25:444

51606 Rodrigue, E. M. Notes on menstruation. Q 1957, 26:281

51607 Rodrigue, E. M. Notes on symbolism. Q 1957, 26:572

51608 Róheim, G. The basic dream. Q 1953, 22:469-470

51609 Rosen, S. R. & Appel, J. A speculation on the psychodynamics of certain psychosomatic disorders. Q 1953, 22:448

51610 Rosen, V. On mathematical "illumination" and the mathematical thought process. Q 1954, 23:163-164

51611 Rosenfeld, E. M. Dream and vision. Some remarks on Freud's Egyptian bird dream. Q 1957, 26:434

51612 Rosenfeld, H. Considerations regarding the psychoanalytic approach to acute and chronic schizophrenia. Q 1955, 24:603

51613 Rosenfeld, H. Discussion on ego distortion. Q 1959, 28:284

51614 Rosenfeld, H. Some observations on the psychopathology of hypochondriacal states. Q 1959, 28:278

51615 Rosenman, S. Black magic and superego formation. Q 1957, 26:585-586

51616 Rosow, H. M. The analysis of an adult nail biter. Q 1956, 25:114

51617 Rowley, J. L. Rehearsal and collusion. Q 1956, 25:281

51618 Rycroft, C. The nature and function of the analyst's communication to the patient. Q 1957, 26:582

51619 Rycroft, C. Symbolism and its relationship to the primary and secondary processes. Q 1957, 26:572

51620 Rycroft, C. Two notes on idealization, illusion and disillusion as normal and abnormal psychological processes. Q 1956, 25:611

51621 Sager, C. J. The psychotherapist's continuous evaluation of his work. Q 1958, 27:445

51622 Sandford, B. Some notes on a dying patient. Q 1958, 27:439

51623 Savage, C. Variations in ego feeling induced by D-lysergic acid Diethelamide (LSD-25). Q 1956, 25:444

51624 Schacht, M. The technique of employing doctor-patient transactions in psychoanalysis. An Surv Psa 1953, 4:450-452

51625 Schmideberg, M. Delinquent acts as perversions and fetishes. Q 1957, 26:580

51626 Schmideberg, M. Hypocrisy, detachment, and adaptation. Q 1958, 27:602

51627 Schmideberg, M. A note on transference. An Surv Psa 1953, 4:426-427

51628 Schmideberg, M. Some aspects of jealousy and of feeling hurt. Q 1953, 22:608-609

51629 Schmidl, F. The problem of scientific validation in psychoanalytic interpretation. Q 1956, 25:612

51630 Schneck, J. M. A hypnoanalytic exploration of the psychopathology of blushing and erythrophobia. Q 1957, 26:438

51631 Schneider, D. E. The image of the heart and the synergic principle in psychoanalysis (psychosynergy). Q 1957, 26:283

51632 Schnier, J. The Tibetan Lamaist ritual: chöd. Q 1958, 27:601

51633 Schur, M. Some modifications of Freud's theory of anxiety. Q 1953, 22:314-316

51634 Scott, W. C. M. A new hypothesis concerning the relationship of libidinal and aggressive instincts. Q 1955, 24:607

51635 Scott, W. C. M. Noise, speech, and technique. Q 1959, 28:277

51636 Scott, W. C. M. A note on blathering. Q 1957, 26:281

51637 Sechehaye, M. A. The transference in symbolic realization. Q 1957, 26:573-574

51638 Segal, H. Depression in the schizophrenic. Q 1957, 26:576-577

51639 Segal, H. Fear of death. Q 1959, 28:280

51640 Segal, H. Notes on symbol formation. Q 1958, 27:600

51641 Servadio, E. Magic and the castration complex. Q 1959, 28:279

51642 Servadio, E. A presumptively telepathic-precognitive dream during analysis. Q 1956, 25:442

51643 Servadio, E. Transference and thought transference. Q 1957, 26:579

51644 Seyler, C. A. Slips of the tongue in the Norse sagas. Q 1956, 25:612

51645 Siegman, A. J. Hybris—a reaction to positive transference. Q 1957, 26:139

51646 Silberer, H. The dream: introduction to the psychology of dreams. Q 1957, 26:283-284

51647 Silbermann, I. Two types of preoedipal character disorders. Q 1958, 27:598

51648 Sillman, L. The genesis of man. Q 1954, 23:158-160

51649 Silverberg, W. V. Childhood Experience and Personal Destiny. An Surv Psa 1952, 3:631-637

51650 Silverman, D. The analysis of an unconscious Pinocchio fantasy in an obsessional neurosis. Q 1956, 25:114-115

51651 Solomon, J. C. Nail biting and the integrative process. Q 1957, 26:283

51652 Sperling, M. Food allergies and the unconscious. Q 1953, 22:146-147

51653 Sperling, M. A psychoanalytic study of migraine and psychogenic headache. Q 1953, 22:124

51654 Sperling, M. The psychoanalytic treatment of ulcerative colitis. Q 1958, 27:598-599

51655 Sperling, M. Psychosis and psychosomatic illness. Q 1957, 26:280

51656 Sperling, S. J. On denial and the essential nature of defense. Q 1959, 28:106-107

51657 Spitz, R. A. A note on the extrapolation of ethnological findings. Q 1956, 25:613

51658 Spitz, R. A. Transference: the analytical setting and its prototype. Q 1957, 26:578-579

51659 Spotnitz, H. & Resnikoff, P. The myths of Narcissus. Q 1955, 24:467-468

51660 Stanley-Jones, D. The structure of emotion. Q 1958, 27:444-445

51661 Stanley-Jones, D. Training in cleanliness. Q 1958, 27:129

51662 Stein, M. H. Premonition as a defense. An Surv Psa 1953, 4:439-440

51663 Stengel, E. A re-evaluation of Freud's book On Aphasia. Q 1955, 24:600

51664 Sterba, R. & Sterba, E. The anxieties of Michelangelo Buonarroti. Q 1957, 26:576

51665 Sterba, R. F. Oral invasion and self-defense. Q 1958, 27:441

51666 Stern, M. M. The ego aspect of transference. Q 1958, 27:439

51667 Stern, M. M. Trauma, projective technique and analytic profile. An Surv Psa 1953, 4:446-449

51668 Stewart, D. A. Empathy, common ground of ethics and of personality theory. Q 1957, 26:138

51669 Stewart, K. Mental hygiene and world peace. Q 1955, 24:318-319

51670 Stokes, A. Psychoanalytic reflections on the development of ball games, particularly cricket. Q 1957, 26:573

51671 Stone, L. On the principal obscene word of the English language. Q 1955, 24:461

51672 Strauss, A. Unconscious mental processes and the psychosomatic concept. Q 1957, 26:280

51673 Sulzberger, C. F. An undiscovered source of heterosexual disturbance. Q 1957, 26:285

51674 Szasz, T. S. Entropy, organization and the problem of the economy of human relationships. Q 1957, 26:279

51675 Szasz, T. S. Psychoanalysis and the autonomic nervous system. Q 1953, 22:123

51676 Szasz, T. S. On the theory of psychoanalytic treatment. Q 1958, 27:440

51677 Székely, L. Biological remarks on fears originating in early childhood. Q 1955, 24:461

51678 Székely, L. On the origin of man and the latency period. Q 1958, 27:437-438

51679 Székely, L. A screen memory and myth formation in a case of apparent precognition. Q 1959, 28:279

51680 Thass-Thienemann, T. Left-handed writing. Q 1957, 26:140

51681 Thass-Thienemann, T. Oedipus and the sphinx. Q 1958, 27:287-288

51682 Thompson, C. Transference and character analysis. An Surv Psa 1953, 4:412-415

51683 Toman, W. Repetition and repetition compulsion. Q 1957, 26:577

51684 Veszy-Wagner, L. An Irish legend as proof of Freud's theory of joint parricide. Q 1958, 27:438

51685 Waals, H. G. Van der: Therapy of schizophrenia. Q 1955, 24:604

51686 Waelder, R. Introduction to the discussion on problems of transference. Q 1957, 26:578

51687 Waelder, R. Neurotic ego distortion. Q 1959, 28:282

51688 Waldhorn, H. F. Some technical and theoretical observations concerning assessment of analyzability. Q 1960, 29:605-606

51689 Walters, O. S. A methodological critique of Freud's Schreber analysis. Q 1957, 26:283

51690 Watters, T. A. Forms of the family romance. Q 1957, 26:584

51691 Wayne, G. J. Modified psychoanalytic therapy in senescence. Q 1954, 23:461

51692 Wayne, G. J. Some unconscious determinants in physicians motivating the use of particular treatment methods—with special reference to electroconvulsive treatment. Q 1956, 25:445

51693 Weigert, E. Countertransference and self-analysis of the psychoanalyst. Q 1955, 24:608

51694 Weiss, E. A comparative study of psychoanalytic ego concepts. Q 1958, 27:441

51695 Weyl, S. Retardation, acceleration, and psychoanalysis. Q 1955, 24:480-482

51696 Wheelis, A. The vocational hazards of psychoanalysis. Q 1957, 26:572-573

51697 Wilder, J. Dream analysis within dreams. Q 1957, 26:436

51698 Winnicott, D. W. Metapsychological and clinical aspects of regression within the psychoanalytic set-up. Q 1956, 25:442

51699 Winnicott, D. W. On transference. Q 1957, 26:579

51700 Winterstein, A. On the oral basis of a case of male homosexuality. Q 1957, 26:575

51701 Winterstein, A. A typical dream sensation and its meaning. Q 1955, 24:607

51702 Wittenberg, R. Lesbianism as a transitory solution of the ego. Q 1957, 26:596

51703 Wittenberg, R. On the superego in adolescence. Q 1957, 26:140
51704 Woolf, M. On castration anxiety. Q 1956, 25:611-612
51705 Woolf, M. Revolution and drive. Q 1958, 27:602-603
51706 Zetzel, E. R. Current concepts of transference. Q 1957, 26:578
51707 Zetzel, E. R. (Reporter) The traditional psychoanalytic technique and
       its variations. An Surv Psa 1953, 4:390-399
51708 Zilboorg, G. The contribution of psychoanalysis to forensic psychiatry.
       Q 1957, 26:576
51709 Zilboorg, G. Freud's fundamental psychiatric orientation. Q 1955,
       24:600

LANDES, R.

S-19651A (& Zborowski, M.) Hypotheses concerning the Eastern European
       Jewish family.
           Abs R 1954, 41:88-89

LANDFIELD, ALVIN W.

51710 A movement interpretation of threat. ASP 1954, 49:529-532

LANDIS, CARNEY

51711 El fenomeno psico-analitico. [The psycho-analytic phenomenon.] An
       Np 1958, 12(47):11-24
51712 Psicoanalisis y metodo cientifico. [Psychoanalysis and scientific
       method.] An Np 1958, 12(48):23-34
51713 Psicoterapie y religion. [Psychotherapy and religion.] An Np 1958,
       12(49):31-42

       See Lewis, Nolan D. C.

LANDMAN, LOUIS

51714 Group psychoanalysis. Psa 1955, 15:31-44

       See Weiss, Frederick A.

LANDQUIST, JOHN

TRANSLATIONS OF:
(& Landquist, S.; Andersson, O.) Freud, S. [10585]. (& Andersson, O.;
Schedin, G.) Freud, S. [10614]

LANDQUIST, SOLVEIG

See Landquist, John

LANDY, E.

See Waldfogel, Samuel

LANE, ELI W.

51715 The tuberculosis patient's private world. In Sparer, P. J. *Personality,
       Stress, and Tuberculosis,* NY: IUP 1956, 317-339

       See Beigler, Jerome S.

LANE, HOWARD
See Welsch, Exie E.

LANES, SAMUEL
ABSTRACT OF:
51716   Eidelberg, L. A second contribution to the theory of wit. Q 1960, 29:611-613

LANG, JEAN-L.
51717   L'abord psychanalytique des psychoses chez l'enfant. [Psychoanalytic view of psychoses in children.] Psychanalyse 1958, 4:51-82
51718   (& Fouquet, P.; Stern, A. L.) A propos d'une étude sur les conditions d'hospitalisation dans un service de pneumophtisiologie infantile. [Remarks on the hospitalization of children in a ward for childhood tuberculosis.] Compte-rendus des Journées Intern du Roc des Fiz, March 1959. L'Expansion Scientifique Franç
51719   Organisation des loisirs et prévention curative. [Organization of leisure and curative prevention.] R Np inf 1957, 5:600-604
51720   Les tics chez l'enfant. [Tics in children.] R Np inf 1955, 3:553-560

LANG, T.
51721   Die Homosexualität als genetisches Problem; in Verbindung mit einigen Fragen an die Psychologen. [Homosexuality as a genetic problem; including several questions to psychologists.] B Sexfschg 1957, (11):79-87

LANGE-EICHBAUM, WILHELM
S-19697 Genie, Irrsinn und Ruhm. Sec rev ed 1957

LANGER, DIETER
51722   Die wichtigsten Ergebnisse der Stress-Forschung (bis 1957) und deren Bedeutung für die Psychiatrie. [The most important results of stress-research (up to 1957) and their meaning for psychiatry.] Fortschr Neurol Psychiat 1958, 26(7):321-353

LANGER, MARIE
51723   Barrabás o la persecución por un ideal. [The novel Barrabas or the persecution by the ideal.] Rev Psicoanál 1956, 13:545-548
S-19706 Dos sueños de analistas.
        Abs NRo An Surv Psa 1952, 3:420. Vega Q 1954, 23:476
51724   (& Ochandorena, R. P.) El espasmo de las trompas como origen de esterilidad: sus causas, mecanismo y tratamiento. [Fallopian spasms causing sterility; cause, mechanism and treatment.] Rev Psicoanál 1953, 10:103-115
        Abs LCK An Surv Psa 1953, 4:499. Vega Q 1954, 23:623
51725   Fantasías Eternas a la Lux del Psicoanálisis. [Eternal Fantasies in the Light of Psycho-Analysis.] B. Aires: Edit Nova 1957, 220 p
        Rv Grinberg, L. Rev Psicoanál 1957, 14:335-336

51726 Freud y la sociología. [Freud and sociology.] Rev Psicoanál 1956, 13:212-219

51727 Die "Gestalt" einer Gruppe unfruchtbarer Frauen. [The "Gestalt" of a group of sterile women.] Z PSM 1958-59, 5:53-62

51727A Ideologia et idealización. [Ideology and idealization.] Rev Psicoanál 1959, 16:417-422

51728 La interpretación basada en la vivencia contra transferencial de conexión o desconexión con el analizado. [Interpretation based on the countertransference experience of connection with and separation from the analysand.] Rev Psicoanál 1957, 14:31-38

51729 Isabel I, Reina de Inglaterra. [Elizabeth I, Queen of England.] Rev Psicoanál 1955, 12:201-227

S-19708 Maternidad y Sexo.
Abs Auth An Surv Psa 1951, 2:645-653. Rv Brodsky, B. Q 1953, 22:261-264

51730 Mecanismo de cefalea en tres psicoanalistas. [Mechanism of headache in three psychoanalysts.] Rev Psicoanál 1954, 11:211-216
Abs JFr An Surv Psa 1954, 5:149-150. Vega Q 1956, 25:133-134

S-19714 Una sesión psicoanalítica.
Abs STa An Surv Psa 1951, 2:436

51731 Sterility and envy. (Read at 20th Int Psa Cong, Paris 1957) J 1958, 39:139-143
Abs J 1958, 39:292. JLan Q 1959, 28:278

See Grinberg, León

ABSTRACT OF:
51732 Schmideberg, M. A note on transference. Rev Psicoanál 1956, 13:78

REVIEWS OF:
51733 Bacon, L. C. et al: A psychosomatic survey of cancer of the breast. Rev Psicoanál 1953, 10:243-244

51734 Foulkes, S. H. Introduction to group-analytic psychotherapy. Rev Psicoanál, 1956, 13:321

51735 Freud, A. & Burlingham, D. Infants Without Families. Rev Psicoanál 1958, 15:115-116

51736 Gesell, A. & Amatruda, C. S. Development, diagnosis, normal and abnormal child development. Rev Psicoanál 1958, 15:114-115

51737 Krapf, E. E. Angustia, Tensión, Relajación. Rev Psicoanál 1953, 10:384

51738 Oliviero, W. I. de: El matricidio en la fantasia. Rev Psicoanál 1959, 16:84-85

51739 Pappenheim, E. & Sweenley, M. Separation anxiety in mother and child. Rev Psicoanál 1953, 10:244-245

51740 Powdermaker, F. B. & Frank, J. D. Group psychotherapy: studies on methodology of research and therapy. Rev Psicoanál 1955, 12:132-134

51741 Racker, H. Psicoanalisis del espiritu. Rev Psicoanál 1960, 17:120-121

51742 Sterba, E. & Sterba, R. Beethoven and His Nephew. Rev Psicoanál 1955, 12:130-132

51743 Zilboorg, G. Sigmund Freud: his exploration of the mind of man. Rev Psicoanál 1954, 11:527

LANGER, SUSANNE KATHERINA

51744 Philosophy in a New Key: a Study in the Symbolism of Reason, Rite, and Art. 3rd ed. Cambridge, Mass: Harvard Univ Pr 1957, 313 p

LANGER, WILLIAM L.

51745 The next assignment. Am Im 1958, 15:235-266

LANGEVELD, MARTIN J.

51746 Bevrijding door beeldcommunicatie. [Therapeutic cure through symbolic communication.] Ned Tijdschr Psychol 1955, 10(2):89-110

51747 Die "Projektion" im kindlichen Seelenleben. ["Projection" in children's psyche.] Psychol Rdsch 1957, 8:243-254

LANGFELDT, G.

51748 Psykoterapeutisk hjernevask. [Psychotherapeutic brain-washing.] Nord Psyk Medl 1957, 11:213-219

LANGFORD, WILLIAM S.

51749 Disturbance in mother-infant relationship leading to apathy, extranutritional sucking and hair ball. Emot Prob Early Child 57-76

See Freedman, Alfred M.

LANGHANS, SIEGFRIED

51750 Das Strukturmodell der menschlichen Psyche, ein wesentlicher Beitrag Freuds zur Psychologie. [The structural model of the human psyche, an important contribution of Freud to psychology.] In Riemann, F. *Lebendige Psychoanalyse,* Munich: C. H. Beck 1956, 114-123

LANGNER, HELEN P.

See Slavson, Samuel R.

LANGNER, THOMAS S.

51751 Environmental stress, degree of psychiatric impairment and type of mental disturbance. PPR 1960, 47(4):3-16

LANGSTROTH, LOVELL

51752 Structure of the Ego. An Anatomic and Physiologic Interpretation of the Psyche, Based on the Psychology of Otto Rank. Stanford, Calif: Stanford Univ Pr 1955, ix + 149 p
Abs J Am Psa Ass 1956, 4:189

LANGWORTHY, ORTHELLO R.

S-19727A Emotional issues related to certain cases of blepharospasm and facial tics.
Abs LRa Q 1953, 22:460-461

LANTER, R.

51753 La fonction onirique chez les malades mentaux. [The function of dreams in mental illness.] Evolut psychiat 1954, (4):685-720

LANTIS, MARGARET

S-19729 The symbol of a new religion.
Abs R 1954, 41:70-72

LANTOS, BARBARA

S-19731 Metapsychological considerations on the concept of work.
Abs JAA An Surv Psa 1952, 3:91-92. MGr Q 1954, 23:143-144
51754 On the motivation of human relationships. A preliminary study based on the concept of sublimation. J 1955, 36:267-288
Abs Morgan Rev Psicoanál 1956, 13:192. JLan Q 1957, 26:279
51755 Obituary: Julia Mannheim, 1895-1955. J 1956, 37:197-198
51756 The two genetic derivations of aggression with reference to sublimation and neutralization. (Read at 20th Int Psa Cong, Paris 1957) J 1958, 39:116-120
Die zwei genetischen Ursprünge der Aggression und ihre Beziehungen zu Sublimierung und Neutralisierung. Psyche, Heidel 1958, 12:161-169
Abs J 1958, 39:292. JLan Q 1959, 28:277

LA PIERE, RICHARD TRACY

51757 The Freudian Ethic. NY: Duell, Sloan & Pearce 1959, x + 299 p

LAPLANCHE, J.

See Lehmann, A.

TRANSLATION OF:
(& Lehmann, A.; Smirnoff, V. N.) Tausk, V. [33118]

LAPLANE, A.

See Duché, D.

LA PORTA, E. M.

51758 Generalidades e histórico da psicoterapia de grupo no Brasil. [Generalities and history of group psychotherapy in Brazil.] J Bras Psiquiat 1958, 7:293-303

LAPPLE

51759 [A case of sudden anxiety as a result of religious conflict.] (German) In Bitter, W. Angst und Schuld, Stuttg: Ernst Klett 1959

LAQUEUR, W.

51760 Psychoanalyse in sowjetischer Perspektive. [Psychoanalysis, as seen from the viewpoint of the Soviets.] Psyche, Heidel 1956, 10:588-596

LA RIVIÈRE, ANDRÉ

See Stern, Karl

LA ROCHE, JEAN
See Heyer, Gustav

LAROQUE, P.

51761 A propos de "De l'instinct à l'esprit" de Charles Baudouin. [Comments on "De l'instinct à l'esprit" by Baudouin.] Evolut Psychiat 1951, 3:497-516

LA RUE, LUCIEN

51762 Considérations générales sur la psychiatrie d'hier et d'aujourd'hui. [General observations on past and present psychiatry.] Canad Psychiat Ass J 1956, 1:169-172

LASHLEY, KARL S.

51763 An exchange of views on psychic energy and psychoanalysis. Beh Sci 1957, 2:231-240
51764 Introduction to Schiller, C. H. *Instinctive Behavior. The Development of a Modern Concept.*

LASKIN, DIANA
See Klein, George S.

LASSWELL, HAROLD DWIGHT

51765 Approaches to human personality: William James and Sigmund Freud. PPR 1960, 47(3):52-68
51766 Clarifying value judgment: principles of content and procedure. Inquiry 1958, 1:87-98
51767 Key symbols, signs, and icons. In Bryson, L. et al: *Conference on Science, Philosophy, and Religion in their Relation to the Democratic Way of Life.* 13th Symposium, NY: Harper Bros 1952, 1954; 199-204
51768 Political constitution and character. PPR 1959, 46(4):3-18
51769 (& Kaplan, A.) Power and Society. London: Routledge & Kegan Paul 1952, 295 p
	Rv Rowley, T. L. J 1953, 34:339
S-19746A Propaganda and mass insecurity.
	Abs R 1954, 41:78
S-19750 Psychopathology and Politics. New ed with afterthoughts by author. NY: Viking Pr 1960, 319 p
51770 The selective effect of personality on political participation. In Christie, R. & Jahoda, M. *Studies in the Scope and Method of "The Authoritarian Personality,"* Glencoe, Ill: Free Pr 1954, 197-225

REVIEWS OF:
51771 Biggs, J., Jr. The Guilty Mind: Psychiatry and the Law of Homicide. Q 1956, 25:426-429
51772 Levy, M. J. Jr. The Structure of Society. Q 1955, 24:458
51773 Neustatter, W. L. The Mind of the Murderer. Q 1958, 27:597
51774 Neustatter, W. L. Psychological Disorder and Crime. Q 1958, 27:597
51775 Tumin, M. Caste in a Peasant Society. Q 1954, 23:457-458
51776 Weihofen, H. The Urge to Punish. Q 1957, 26:560-561

LASZLO, CARL

51777 Zum Begriff der Paroxysmalität bei Szondi. [L. Szondi's concept of paroxysmality.] Psyche, Heidel 1953, 7:380-386
51778 Die Homosexualität des Mannes im Szondi-Test. Ein Beitrag zur Erforschung der Homosexualität und zur Kritik der Szondi-Methode. [The Szondi test of male homosexuality. A study of homosexuality and a critic of the Szondi method.] B Sexfschg 1956, (8):108 p
51779 Notes on various phenomena in male homosexuality. Int J Sexol 1955, 8:220-225
51780 Traumbilder eines zehnjährigen Knaben. [Dream images of a ten-year-old boy.] Heilpädag Werkbl 1954, 23:23-25

LASZLO, VIOLET STAUB DE

51781 Editor of Jung, C. G. *The Basic Writings of C. G. Jung.*
51782 Editor of Jung, C. G. *Psyche and Symbol.*

LA TENDRESSE, JOHN D.

See Azima, H.; Wittkower, Eric D.

LATHBURY, VINCENT T.

51783 An interesting screen memory. Bull Phila Ass Psa 1957, 7:81-84
51784 Obituary: Dr. William V. Fittipoldi. Bull Phila Ass Psa 1954, 4:21
51785 The possible psychogenesis of retracted nipples—a clinical observation. Bull Phila Ass Psa 1956, 6:121-122
51786 Relationship of reasoning in a child to neurotic symptom formation. A clinical observation. Bull Phila Ass Psa 1958, 8:22-24

See Strecker, Edward A.

LATIF, ISRAIL

51787 A case of localized amnesia. J Psa, Pakistan 1952, 1(1):51-54
51788 The central theme in the tragedy of Shakespeare's *Othello.* J Psa, Pakistan 1953, 1(4):47-57
51789 Our chaotic world as reviewed by a psychopathologist. J Psa, Pakistan 1953, 1(2):3-16
51790 Fear of insanity—a variant of castration complex. J Psa, Pakistan 1953, 1(3):2-12
51791 A psychoanalytic study of Adolf Hitler. J Psa, Pakistan 1953, 1(4):25-32
51792 The psychogenesis of epileptic seizures. J Psa, Pakistan 1952, 1(1):13-30
51793 Psychology at the Service of the State. (Monograph) Pakistan Philosophical Congress 1954, 16 p
51794 Puerperal insanity. J Psa, Pakistan 1953, 1(3):2-16
51795 The role of the father in the psychogenesis of male homosexuality. J Psa, Pakistan 1953, 1(2):29-44

REVIEW OF:
51796 Schoenfeld, C. God and Country. J 1957, 38:288-289

LATIL, J.

51797 Thérapeutique analytique et personne chrétienne. [Analytic therapy and the Christian personality.] Suppl Vie Spir 1953, (27):428-445

LATREYA, B.

51798 Freud ke Manovishleshana ke Siddhanta. [Principles of Freudian Psychoanalysis.] Freud Commemoration Vol of Balahita (Hindi), Udaipur

51799 Man as known to contemporary psychology. Contribution to Symposium "Mental life as pictured in contemporary psychology." Read at 31st Indian Sci Cong, Delhi; publ in Proc of Cong

51800 Principles and practice of psychotherapy. J Banaras Hindu Univ, Banaras

51801 [Psychoanalysis and Yogavasishtha.] (Hindi) Manovijnāna

51802 [Psychotherapy.] (Hindi) Kalpavriksha, Ujjain

51803 The Yoga of modern psychology. Yoga number of Kalyāna Kalpataru, Gorakhpur

LATTKE, HERBERT

51804 Psychoanalyse, soziale Arbeit und Erziehung. [Psychoanalysis, Social Work and Education.] Freiburg im Breisgau: Lambertus-Verlag 1951, 56 p

LAU, L. F.

See Seguin, Carlos Alberto

LAUBENTHAL, F.

51805 [Brain and Psyche. The Medical Problem of Body and Mind.] (German) Salzburg: O. Müller 1953

LAUBER, H. L.

51806 (& Lewin, B.) Über optische Halluzinationen bei Ausschaltung des Visus, klinisch und tiefenpsychologisch betrachtet. [Optic hallucinations accompanying impairment of vision, as analysed clinically and depth-psychologically.] Arch Psychiat Nervenkr 1958, 197:15-31

LAUFER, MAURICE W.

51806A (& Denhoff, E.; Solomons, G.) Hyperkinetic impulse disorder in children's behavior problems. PSM 1957, 19:38-49

LAUFFENBURGER

51807 La musique et l'inconscient collectif. [Music and the collective unconscious.] Polyphonie, Paris 1950, (7/8):10-23

LAUGHLIN, HENRY P.

51808 Anxiety, its nature and origins (an introductory essay to a series on the psychoneuroses.) Med Ann Distr Columbia 1953, 22:401-411, 444. Child-Fam Dig 1959, 18(4):52-69

51809 An approach to executive development; five years' experience with analytically oriented groups of executives. Dis nerv Syst 1954, 15:12-22

51810 King David's anger. Q 1954, 23:87-95
Abs JFr An Surv Psa 1954, 5:123-124. JKl J 1955, 36:422. Rev Psicoanál 1955, 12:307-308

51811 The Neuroses in Clinical Practice. Phila, London: W. B. Saunders 1956, xlii + 802 p
Rv Overholser, W. Q 1957, 26:128. ESt J 1957, 38:365

51812 The obsessive-compulsive neuroses. Med Ann Distr Columbia 1954, 23:322-331

51813 Seminars with executives on human relations in the United States Government. A group approach to management improvement. Int J grp PT 1954, 4:165-171

51814 Some dynamic and clinical features of depressive character defenses, psychoneurotic depression, and suicide. Med Ann Distr Columbia 1953, 22:653-671

LAUNAY, C.

51815 (& Bargues, R.) Carences paternelles et retard scolaire. [Lack of paternal care and scholastic retardation.] In Actes du Ier Congrès de Centres psycho-pédagogiques, Paris: 1954, July

51816 (& Doumic, A.; Bargues, R.) Les centres psychopédagogiques de l'enseignement du premier degré de la Seine. [The psychopedagogical training centers of the first grade in the province of Seine.] L'éducation nationale 1953, Jan 22

51817 Le rôle des parents dans la genèse des maladies mentales chez l'enfant. [The role of the parents in the genesis of mental illness in the child.] Hyg ment 1959, 48:233-253

51818 (& Bargues, R.) Les terreurs nocturnes chez l'enfant. [Nightmares in children.] Problèmes 1953, (1)

I AURENT, L.

51819 Réactions d'opposition et psychanalyse. [Reactions of opposition and psychoanalysis.] R Np inf 1958, 6:106-116

LAURIN, CAMILLE

51820 Essor de la psychiatrie française. 1. Le malade mental au XXᵉ siècle. [The scope of French psychiatry. 1. The mental patient in the 20th century.] Union Méd du Canada 1958, 87:1069-1071

51821 Essor de la psychiatrie française. 2. Psychologie médicale: bilan d'un demi-siècle. [The scope of French psychiatry. 2. Medical psychology: report on the last half-century.] Union Méd du Canada 1958, 87:1193-1197

51822 Essor de la psychiatrie française. 3. Courants doctrinaux contemporains. [The scope of French psychiatry. 3. Contemporary doctrinal ideas.] Union Méd Canada 1959, 88(Jan):53-57

51823 Essor de la psychiatrie française. 4. Présence de la psychanalyse. [The scope of French psychiatry. 4. The presence of psychoanalysis.] Union Méd Canada 1959, 88(Feb):3-7

51824 Essor de la psychiatrie française. 5. Humanisme et psychanalyse: Daniel Lagache. [The scope of French psychiatry. 5. Humanism and psychoanalysis: Daniel Lagache.] Union Méd Canada 1959, 88(Mar): 1-10

51825 Le médecin canadien en France. [The Canadian doctor in France.] Union Méd Canada 1956, Sept

51826 A propos des écrits techniques d'Edward Glover. [Edward Glover's writings on technique.] Psychanalyse 1956, 2:289-309

TRANSLATIONS OF:
Glover, E. [11909, 47343]

LAUS, O.

51827 Die Träume in Dostojewski's "Raskolnikoff." [Dreams in Dostoevski's "Raskolnikov."] Munich: 1923

LAUTER, PAUL

51828 Walt Whitman: lover and comrade. Am Im 1959, 16:407-435

LAUTERBACH, ALBERT

51829 Man, Motives and Money: Psychological Frontiers of Economics. London: Oxford Univ Pr; Cornell Univ Pr 1954, 366 p

See Wilder, Joseph

LAVELL, M.

See Tuckman, Jacob

LAVI, ZVI

51830 [How Marxists criticize presentday psychoanalysis.] (Hebrew) Ofakim 1956, 10:242-245

51831 [Situation of psychology to-day.] (Hebrew) Ofakim 1953, 7:2-5

51832 [Unconscious processes and consciousness.] (Hebrew) Ofakim 1953, 7:130-132, 142

LAW, S. G.

51833 Therapy through Interviews. NY: McGraw-Hill 1948

LAW, S. K.

51834 Girindrasekhar Bose. Samiksa 1955, Bose No, special issue:9-11

LAWRENCE, DAVID HERBERT

51835 Psychoanalysis and the Unconscious. (Introd: Rieff, P.) NY: Viking Pr 1960, 225 p

LAWRENCE, H. P.

See Collier, Rex M.

LAWRENCE, MARGARET MORGAN

51836 The application of psychiatric techniques to teaching. Nerv Child 1954, 10:378-386

51837   A comprehensive approach to the study of a case of familial dysau-
        tonomia. R 1956, 43:358-372
51838   How prejudice begins. Child Study 1955-56, 33:9-13

LAWRENCE, MARGARET SPERRY

See Chasdi, Eleanor Hollenberg

LAWTON, GEORGE

51839   Discussion of Bralove, R. S. & Milrod, D. "Clinical conference; a case
        of geriatric neurosis." J Hillside Hosp 1954, 3:247-249
51840   Straight to the Heart; A Personal Account of Thoughts and Feelings
        While Undergoing Heart Surgery. NY: IUP 1956, xxii + 347 p
          Rv Taylor, J. M. J 1959, 40:71

LAX, RUTH F.

51841   Infantile deprivation and arrested ego development. Q 1958, 27:501-
        517

REVIEW OF:
51842   Slavson, S. R. Child-Centered Group Guidance of Parents. Q 1959,
        28:412-413

LAYARD, JOHN

51843   Boar-sacrifice. J analyt Psychol 1956, 1:7-31
51844   Homo-eroticism in primitive society as a function of the self. J analyt
        Psychol 1959, 4:101-115

LAYMAN, EMMA

51845   Mental Health Through Physical Education and Recreation. Minnea-
        polis: Burgess Pub 1955, 520 p

See Lourie, Reginald S.

LAYNE, ERIC

51846   A comparison of supportive and analytically structured psychotherapy
        with ambulatory schizophrenic veterans. Diss Abstr 1954, 14:713

LAZARSFELD, SOFIE

51847   (& Kadis, A. L.) L' "âge critique" est-il un âge critique? [Is the
        "critical age" really a critical age?] Psyché, Paris 1954, 89:1-12
51848   (& Kadis, A. L.) Change of life—end of life? J ind Psychol 1958,
        14:167-170
51849   Pitfalls in psychotherapy. Int. J Indpsych 1953
51850   Sources of obstacles in the course of therapy. Am J Ind Psychol 1956,
        12:136-138

LAZARUS, RICHARD S.

See Shaffer, George Wilson

LAZEROWITZ, MORRIS

51851 The relevance of psychoanalysis to philosophy. Psa Sci Method Phil 133-156

LAZOWICK, LIONEL M.

51852 On the nature of identification. ASP 1955, 51:175-183

LEACH, BYRON E.

See Heath, Robert G.

LEACH, DAVID

51853 (Reporter) Technical aspects of transference. (Panel: Am Psa Ass, NY, Dec 1957) J Am Ass 1958, 6:560-566

REVIEW OF:
51854 Milner, M. On Not Being Able to Paint. Q 1959, 28:100-101

LEACH, JEAN M.

51855 Homemaker service as a way of strengthening families during illness. In *National Conference on Social Welfare. Casework Papers, 1958,* NY: Family Service Ass of Amer 1958, 132-143

LEAF, MUNRO

See Menninger, William C.

LEAKE, CHAUNCEY D.

51856 The prevention of the focusing of frustration in chronic illness. In Harrower, M. *Medical and Psychological Teamwork in the Care of the Chronically Ill,* Springfield, Ill: Thomas 1955, 60-64

LEARY, TIMOTHY

51857 (& Gill, M.) The dimensions and a measure of the process of psychotherapy: a system for the analysis of the content of clinical evaluations and patient-therapist verbalizations. Res PT 62-95
51858 Interpersonal Diagnosis of Personality: A Functional Theory and Methodology for Personality Evaluation. NY: Ronald Pr 1957, xix + 518 p
Rv Perr, H. M. Psa 1958, 18:201-204

LEAVITT, HARRY C.

51859 A biographical and teleological study of "Irma's injection" dream. R 1956, 43:440-447
Abs JLan Q 1958, 27:129
51860 Generic relations between anxiety and fear. R 1957, 44:65-72
Abs JLan Q 1958, 27:288
51861 Interrelationships between unconscious fear patterns and function of repression. R 1953, 40:218-224
Abs NRo An Surv Psa 1953, 4:117-118. JLan Q 1954, 23:462

51862 Organized qualities of the id structure. R 1953, 40:295-303
       Abs NRo An Surv Psa 1953, 4:63-65. JLan Q 1954, 23:463
51863 Relations between conditioned patterns and superego development. R
       1957, 44:73-80
       Abs JLan Q 1958, 27:288-289
51864 Relations between dream teleology and vigilance states. R 1956, 43:
       432-439
       Abs JLan Q 1958, 27:129
51865 Relationships between conditioned fear patterns and development of
       anxiety. R 1953, 40:27-35
       Abs NRo An Surv Psa 1953, 4:84-86
51866 Teleological contributions of dreams to the waking ego. R 1957, 44:
       212-219
       Abs JLan Q 1958, 27:443-444

LEAVITT, MAIMON

ABSTRACTS OF:
51867 Appel, K. et al: Prognosis in psychiatry. Q 1956, 25:122
51868 Battersby, W. S. et al: Figure-ground discrimination and the "abstract
       attitude" in patients with cerebral neoplasms. Q 1956, 25:123
51869 Bender, L. & Helme, W. H. A quantitative test of theory and diagnostic
       indicators of childhood schizophrenia. Q 1956, 25:121-122
51870 Brickner, R. M. Appetitive behavior and sign stimuli in human life.
       Q 1957, 26:146
51871 Brickner, R. M. A neural fractionating and combining system. Q 1957,
       26:145-146
51872 Cohen, B. D. et al: Effect of amytal and affect on conceptual thinking
       in schizophrenia, depression, and neurosis. Q 1956, 25:452
51873 Cohn, R. Role of "body image concept" in pattern of ipsilateral clinical
       extinction. Q 1956, 25:123
51874 Deutsch, C. P. Differences among epileptics and nonepileptics in terms
       of some memory and learning variables. Q 1956, 25:123
51875 Freeman, W. & Williams, J. Hallucinations in Braille. Q 1956, 25:123
51876 Grossman, C. Laminar cortical blocking and its relation to episodic
       aggressive outbursts. Q 1956, 25:620
51877 Hendrickson, W. J. et al: The initial interview. Q 1956, 25:451
51878 Hogger, A. Effect of atropine on blood pressure of patients with mental
       and emotional disease. Q 1956, 25:452
51879 Mahl, G. F. & Brody, E. B. Chronic anxiety symptomatology, experi-
       mental stress and HCI secretion. Q 1956, 25:452
51880 Manson, M. P. Some relationships of intelligence, mental efficiency,
       mental deterioration and disease. Q 1956, 25:123
51881 Reese, W. G. et al: Autonomic responses in differential diagnosis of
       organic and psychogenic psychoses. Q 1956, 25:123
51882 Rosenthal, M. J. Neurospychiatric aspects of infantile eczema. Q 1956,
       25:122
51883 Thigpen, F. B. et al: Use of electroconvulsive therapy in morphine,
       meperidine, and related alkaloid addictions. Q 1956, 25:122
51884 Weinstein, M. R. Histopathological changes in the brain in schizo-
       phrenia. Q 1956, 25:620

LEAVY, STANLEY A.

51885   Psychological understanding of religious experience. (Pamphlet) Nat Council of Episcopal Church, n.d.

51886   (& Freedman, L. Z.) Psychoneurosis and economic life. Social Problems 1956, 4:55-56

51887   A religious conversion in a four-year-old girl. A historical note. Bull Phila Ass Psa 1957, 7:85-90
  Japanese: (Tr: Ohtsuki, K.) Tokyo J Psa 1958, 16(6)

LEBENSOHN, ZIGMOND M.

51888   Contributions of Saint Elizabeths Hospital to a century of medico-legal progress. In Overholser, W. *Centennial Papers. Saint Elizabeths Hospital, 1855-1955*. Wash: Centennial Commission, Saint Elizabeths Hosp 1956, 37-65

LEBER, GABRIELE

51889   Über tiefenpsychologische Aspekte von Märchenmotiven. [Depth psychologic aspects of fairy tale themes.] Prax Kinderpsychol 1955, 4:274-285; 1956, 5:313-314

LEBO, DELL

51890   The development of play as a form of therapy: from Rousseau to Rogers. P 1955, 112:418-422

51891   The relationship of play to play therapy. J Educ Psychol, Baroda, India 1955, 13:114-121

51892   A theoretical framework for non-directive play therapy: concepts from psychoanalysis and learning theory. J consult Psychol 1958, 22:275-279

LEBOVICI, RUTH

51893   Le personnel des organismes de Sauvegarde de l'Enfance—l'Assistant de Psychothérapie. [The personnel of the organizations of Sauvegarde de l'Enfance—the Assistant in Psychotherapy.] Sauvegarde de l'Enfance (1/2/3):136-139

51894   Perversion sexuelle transitoire au cours d'un traitement psychanalytique. [Transitory sexual perversion in the course of a psychoanalytic treatment.] Bull Ass Psa Belg 1956, 25(March):1-15

LEBOVICI, SERGE

51895   L'action conjointe pédagogique et psychothérapique dans un internat spécialisé; modalités de collaboration entre psychiatres et pédagogues. [Teaching and psychotherapy combined in a specialized residential school; modalities of collaboration between psychiatrists and teachers.] R Np inf 1957, 5:408-415

51896   Approche psychodynamique et psychothérapique dans la schizophrénie infantile. [The psychodynamic and psychotherapeutic approach to infantile schizophrenia.] R Np inf 1956, 4:402-409

51897   Les aspects précoces de la relation objectale. La relation anaclitique. [Early aspects of object-relation. Anaclitic relation.] Bull Ass Psa Belg 1955, (25)

Die Aspekte der frühen Objekt-Beziehungen und die anaclitische Beziehung. Psyche, Heidel 1956, 10:82-92. In Mitscherlich, A. *Entfaltung der Psychoanalyse*, Stuttgart: Klett 1956, 82-92

51898 (& Diatkine, R.; Kestemberg, E.) Bilan de dix ans de thérapeutique par le psychodrame chez l'enfant et chez l'adolescent. [Ten years of treatment by psychodrama with children and adolescents.] In *Psychiatrie de l'Enfant*, Paris: PUF 1958, 1:63-177

51899 (& Diatkine, R.) Die Bilanz der Kinder-Psychoanalyse in Frankreich. [The state of child psychoanalysis in France.] Prax Kinderpsychol 1955, 4:178-187

51900 Buts et moyens de l'internat psychothérapique dans le domaine de l'enfance inadaptée. [Goals and ways of psychotherapeutic institutes for poorly adapted children.] Entretiens de Bichat, Paris 1958, 373-376

51901 (& McDougall, J.) Un Cas de Psychose Infantile. [A Case of Infantile Psychosis.] Paris: PUF 1960, 490 p

51902 (& Diatkine, R.) Le centenaire de la naissance de Sigmund Freud. [The centenary of Sigmund Freud's birth.] Evolut psychiat 1956, (4):959-962

51903 (& Buckle, D.) Les centres de guidance infantile. [Child Guidance Centers.] World Health Organization, Geneva 1958, 149 p

51904 Comment terminer le traitement psychanalytique. [How to terminate the psychoanalytic treatment.] Bull Ass Psa Belg 1954, (21). RFPsa 1955, 19:523-529

51905 Le Congrès international de psychiatrie infantile. [International Congress of infantile psychiatry.] R Np inf 1955, 3:80-81

51906 La connaissance de l'enfant par la psychanalyse. [Knowledge of the child through psychoanalysis.] Education Nationale 1956, 12(19)

51907 Considérations sur la relation d'objet psychotique. [Considerations on psychotic object relationship.] RFPsa 1959, 23:636-643
    Abs Puget Rev Psicoanál 1960, 17:269

51908 La contribution de la psychanalyse à la psychiatrie infantile. [The contribution of psychoanalysis to child psychiatry.] Acta neurol belg 1955, 55:539-550

51909 Contribution psychanalytique à la compréhension et au traitement de la mélancolie. [A psychoanalytic contribution to the understanding and treatment of melancholia.] Evolut psychiat 1955, (3):502-531
    Abs Garcia Reinoso, J. Rev Psicoanál 1956, 13:196

51910 Critères de la fin du traitement. [Criteria of the end of the psychoanalytic treatment.] Contribution to discussion. RFPsa 1954, 18:336, 344, 363

51911 (& Danon-Boileau, H.; Benhamou, F.; Barbier, M.) Débilité mentale évolutive, présentation de malades. [Evolutive mental deficiency; case presentation.] Ann méd-psychol 1954, 112:1(2):197-199

51912 (& Roumajon, Y.; Paumelle, P.; Simatos) Deux cas de paralysie générale infantile; présentation de malades. [Two cases of general paralysis in children; case presentation.] Ann méd-psychol 1954, 112:1(2): 188-191

51913 (& Roumajon, Y.; Morin; Bourreau) Deux cas de schizophrénie de l'adolescence, présentation de malades. [Two cases of schizophrenia in adolescents; case presentation.] Ann méd-psychol 1954, 112:1(2):195-197

51914 (& Paumelle, P.; Laloum; Kalmanson, D.) Deux cas de schizophrénie infantile; présentation de malades. [Two cases of schizophrenia in children; case presentation.] Ann méd-psychol 1954, 112:1(2):191-194

51915 Le développement récent du mouvement de la psychanalyse infantile en France. [Recent development of infantile psychoanalysis in France.] Pédiatrie 1956, (7):1-9

51916 Discussion of Luquet, C. J. "La place du mouvement masochique dans l'évolution de la femme." RFPsa 1959, 23:347-348

51917 (& Diatkine, R.) Discussion of Perrotti, N. "Aperçus théoriques de la dépersonnalisation." RFPsa 1960, 24:447-448

51918 L'entretien avec les parents comme aide diagnostique en psychiatrie infantile. [The interview with the parents, an aid to diagnosis in infantile psychiatry.] Entretiens de Bichat, Paris 1958, 369-372

51919 Essai sur la situation analytique et le processus de guérison. [About the analytic situation and the process of cure.] Discussion. RFPsa 1957, 21:434-437

51920 (& Diatkine, R.) Étude des fantasmes chez l'enfant. [Study of fantasies in children.] RFPsa 1954, 18:108-159
Abs NRo An Surv Psa 1954, 5:256-258. Pichon-Rivière, A. A. Rev Psicoanál 1955, 12:430

51921 Les facteurs psychologiques de la délinquance. [Psychological factors of delinquency.] Cahiers de l'Enfance 1956, 4(31)

51922 Group psychotherapy in France. Int J grp PT 1958, 8:471-472

51923 Indications et contre-indications de la psychanalyse chez l'enfant. [Indications and contra-indications of psychoanalysis with children.] R Np inf 1957, 5:608-614

51924 L'integrazione dei concetti psicoanalitici sullo sviluppo affettivo infantile nei dati neurobiologici e culturali. [Integration of psychoanalytic concepts of infantile affective development into neurobiological and cultural data.] Infanzia anormale 1958, 25(Jan-Feb)
Abs RFPsa 1959, 23:164

51925 Interprétation prégénitale. [Pre-genital interpretation.] Discussion of Grunberger's statement. RFPsa 1953, 17:488-491

S-19837 Introduction à la discussion sur les indications de la psychanalyse.
Abs NRo An Surv Psa 1952, 3:370-371

51926 Notes sur l'observation directe de l'enfant. [Notes on direct observations of the child.] RFPsa 1958, 22:213-218

51927 Notions psychodynamiques sur le groupe scolaire; applications thérapeutiques. [Psychodynamics of school groups; therapeutic applications.] R Np inf 1957, 5:146-150

51928 Une observation de cardiologie. Note du psychanalyste. [An observation of cardiology. Notes of the psychoanalyst.] RFPsa 1958, 22:234-241

51929 Une observation de psychose infantile: étude des mécanismes de défense. [An observation of an infantile psychosis: a study of defense mechanisms.] Evolut psychiat 1956, (4):843-859
Rv Masciangelo Riv Psa 1958, 4:59-60

51930   (& Diatkine, R.) Les obsessions chez l'enfant. [Obsessions in the child.]
        RFPsa 1957, 21:647-682
            Abs Roman, R. F. Q 1957, 21:149-150
51931   Der Platz der Psychoanalyse in der Psychotherapie des Kindes. [The
        role of psychoanalysis in psychotherapy with children.] (Tr: WHO)
        Prax Kinderpsychol 1957, 6:38-41
51932   Problèmes psychologiques et psychopathologiques posés par l'enfant
        à l'hôpital. [Psychological and psychopathological problems of the
        child at hospital.] Arch franç Pédiatrie 1955, 12(4)
S-19833 A propos du diagnostic de la névrose infantile.
            Abs RdeS Q 1953, 22:313
51933   A propos des facteurs de guérison non verbalisables. [About the non-
        verbal factors of cure.] RFPsa 1957, 21:211-212
51934   A propos des indications et des techniques psychanalytiques dans les
        états prépsychotiques de l'enfance. [Indications and psychoanalytic
        techniques in the prepsychotic states of children.] RFPsa 1956, 20:540-
        545
51935   (& Ajuriaguerra, J. De; Diatkine, R.) A propos de l'observation chez
        le jeune enfant. [About observation of the young child.] Psychiatrie de
        L'Enfant, Paris: PUF 1958, 2
51936   A propos de la psychanalyse de groupe. [Group psychoanalysis.] RFPsa
        1953, 17:266-278
            Abs LCK An Surv Psa 1953, 4:510
S-19846 A propos de la technique de marionettes en psychothérapie infantile.
            Abs RdeS Q 1953, 22:138
S-19842 (& Male, P.; Pasche, F.) Psychanalyse et criminologie: rapport
        clinique.
            Abs JFr An Surv Psa 1951, 2:224-226
51937   La psychanalyse chez l'enfant de 6 à 10 ans. [Child's psychoanalysis
        from 6 to 10 years.] A Criança Portuguesa, Lisbonne 1958, 17
51938   (& Diatkine, R.; Favreau, J.-A.; Luquet-Parat, P.) La psychanalyse des
        enfants. In Nacht, S. La Psychanalyse d'Aujourd'hui, Paris: PUF 1956,
        169-235
            Psychoanalysis of children. In Nacht, S. Psychoanalysis of Today,
        NY, London: Grune & Stratton 1959, 99-122
51939   Psychoanalytical applications of psychodrama. J soc Ther 1956, 2:280-
        291
51940   Psychoanalytical group psychotherapy. Group PT 1956, 9:282-289
51941   Die psychoanalytischen Auffassungen über die affektive Entwicklung
        des Kindes und ihre Integration in neurobiologische und kulturelle
        Gelegenheiten. [The psychoanalytic concepts of the emotional develop-
        ment of the child and their integration with neurobiologic and cultural
        conditions.] (Tr: WHO) Prax Kinderpsychol 1957, 6:33-38
51942   (& Diatkine, R.; Danon-Boileau, H.) Das Psychodrama und die Be-
        handlung von Psychosen. [Psychodrama and the therapy of psychoses.]
        Z PSM 1956-57, 3:220-231
            Psychodrame et traitement des psychotiques. Evolut psychiat 1958,
        (2):499-521
            Abs Auth RFPsa 1959, 23:429

51943 La psychogenèse du vol chez l'enfant. [The psychogenesis of theft in children.] R Np inf 1955, 3:426-433

51944 La psychothérapie analytique chez l'enfant. [Analytic psychotherapy with the child.] Semaine des Hopitaux, Ann Pédiatrie 1957, 33(4)

51945 Rapport sur les fantasmes. [Report about the fantasies.] (Presented at Cong of Psychoanalysts of Roman languages, Rome 1953.) Bull Ass Psa Belg (18)

51946 (& Diatkine, R.) Remarques méthodologiques à propos du diagnostic en neuro-psychiatrie infantile. [Methodological remarks about the diagnostic in infantile neuro-psychiatry.] Sauvegarde de l'Enfance 1954, 9(6)

51947 Les résultats de la reconnaissance d'une faute par l'analyste. [The results of the recognition of an error by the analyst.] Arch Sciences méd 1958, 14:542-549
    Abs Sakellaropoulos RFPsa 1959, 23:441-442

51948 Die Rolle der Prophylaxe für die seelisch-geistige Gesundheit des Kindes. [The role of prevention in the mental health of children.] (Tr: Bräuer, H. & Schwidder, W.) Prax Kinderpsychol 1959, 8:193-199; 241-246

51949 Social psychiatry in France. Prog PT 1959, 4:258-261

51950 Symposium on psychotic object relationships: I. A psychotic object relationship. (Read at 21st Int Psa Cong, Copenhagen, July 1959) J 1960, 41:540-543

51951 Le travail d'équipe en psychiatrie. [Teamwork in psychiatry.] Evolut psychiat 1959, 2:253-274
    Rv Puget Rev Psicoanál 1960, 17:123

51952 L'utilisation du psychodrame pour le diagnostic en psychiatrie infantile. Sauvegarde de l'Enfance 1954, 9(6). Z diagn Psychol 1957, 5:197-205
    Uses of psychodrama in psychiatric diagnosis. Int J Sociometry 1957, 1:175-180

51953 Le vol chez l'enfant. La psychogenèse du vol chez l'enfant. [Thieving in children. Psychogenesis of thieving in children.] Rv Np inf 1955, 3:426-433

See Diatkine, René; Heuyer, Georges; Lelong, M.; Nacht, Sacha; Schlumberger, Marc

ABSTRACTS OF:

51954 Balint, M. Friendly expanses, horrid empty spaces. RFPsa 1955, 19: 638-639

51955 Bartemeier, L. H. A psychoanalytic study of pregnancy in an "as-if" personality. RFPsa 1954, 18:470

51956 Baruk, H. Traité de psychiatrie. RFPsa 1959, 23:297

51957 Biehrer, J. The validity of psychiatric diagnoses. RFPsa 1955, 19:635

51958 Bonnard, A. The metapsychology of the Russian trials confessions. RFPsa 1954, 18:470

51959 Bromberg, W. Evolution of group psychotherapy. RFPsa 1958, 22:129

51960 Brunswick, D. A revision of the classification of instincts or drives. RFPsa 1954, 18:470

51961 Deutsch, F. Analytic synesthesiology. RFPsa 1955, 19:636

51962   Dracoulides, N. N. La complexualité de Platon. RFPsa 1957, 21:624
51963   Duchene, H. A propos d'un avortement provoqué pour causes psychi-
         atriques. RFPsa 1957, 21:299-300
51964   Emch, M. The social context of supervision. RFPsa 1955, 19:640
51965   Faure, H. L'investissement délirant de l'image de soi. RFPsa 1957,
         21:299
51966   Foulkes, S. H. Group analytic observation as indicator for psycho-
         analytic treatment. RFPsa 1954, 18:471
51967   Freeman, T. Clinical and theoretical observations on male homosexual-
         ity. RFPsa 1955, 19:641
51968   Fries, M. E. Some hypotheses on the role of the congenital activity type
         in personality development. RFPsa 1954, 18:469
51969   Greenacre, P. Re-evaluation of the process of working through. RFPsa
         1957, 21:616
51970   Grinker, R. R. Growth inertia and shame: their therapeutic implications
         and dangers. RFPsa 1955, 19:639-640
51971   Grotjahn, M. About the relation between psychoanalytic training and
         psychoanalytic therapy. RFPsa 1954, 18:469
51972   Hartmann, H. The development of the ego concept in Freud's work.
         RFPsa 1957, 21:615-616
51973   Held, R. Difficultés de l'analyse et certaines resistances intellectuelles.
         RFPsa 1957, 21:623
51974   Hoffer, W. Defensive process and defensive organization. RFPsa 1954,
         18:468-469
51975   Hunter, D. Object-relation changes in the analysis of a fetishist. RFPsa
         1955, 19:636
51976   Jacobs Van Merlen, T. De la psychothérapie des parents. RFPsa 1955,
         19:495
51977   Koupernik, C. Le développement du nourrison. RFPsa 1957, 21:299
51978   Kris, E. On some vicissitudes of insight in psychoanalysis. RFPsa 1957,
         21:616-617
51979   Lampl-de Groot, J. The role of identification in psychoanalytic pro-
         cedure. RFPsa 1957, 21:617
51980   Loewenstein, R. M. Some remarks on the role of speech in psycho-
         analytic technique. RFPsa 1957, 21:617-618
51981   Mannheim, J. Notes on a case of drug addiction. RFPsa 1955, 19:637
51982   Margat, P. Détails d'une psychothérapie de schizophrène. RFPsa 1957,
         21:299
51983   Menninger, K. The contribution of psychoanalysis to American psy-
         chiatry. RFPsa 1954, 18:456
51984   Mullan, H. Transference and countertransference: new horizons. RFPsa
         1955, 19:634
51985   Munro, L. Steps in ego-integration observed in a play-analysis. RFPsa
         1954, 18:469
51986   Nielsen, N. The dynamics of training analysis. RFPsa 1954, 18:471
51987   Paumelle, P. La conscience de l'état morbide chez les malades men-
         taux. RFPsa 1957, 21:874
51988   Perestrello, D. Céphalée et scène primaire. RFPsa 1954, 18:470
51989   Racamier, P. C. Introduction à une socio-pathologie des schizophrènes
         hospitalisés. RFPsa 1957, 21:874

51990 Rennie, T. A. C. Social psychiatry: a definition. RFPsa 1955, 19:635

51991 Rogers, C. R. Personality change in psychotherapy. RFPsa 1955, 19: 635-636

51992 Rosow, H. M. The analysis of an adult nail biter. RFPsa 1955, 19:636

51993 Roumajon, Y. Le problème de l'identité des psychoses à travers les facteurs ethniques. RFPsa 1957, 21:299

51994 Rycroft, C. The nature and function of the analyst's communication to the patient. RFPsa 1957, 21:618-619

51995 Saussure, R. de: Les mécanismes de défense et leur place dans la thérapeutique psychanalytique. RFPsa 1954, 18:469

51996 Schnadt, F. Techniques and goals in group therapy with schizophrenics. RFPsa 1955, 19:635

51997 Scott, W. C. M. A new hypothesis concerning the relationship of libidinal and aggressive instincts. RFPsa 1954, 18:470

51998 Segal, H. A note on schizoid mechanisms underlying phobia formation. RFPsa 1954, 18:470-471

51999 Servadio, E. Points de vue récents de la psychanalyse sur la genèse de l'homosexualité. RFPsa 1955, 19:495

52000 Siegman, A. J. La sentimentalité, une défense hysterique. RFPsa 1957, 21:624

52001 Sperling, M. Psychosis and psychosomatic illnesses. RFPsa 1955, 19: 640-641

52002 Teirich, H. R. Sociometry and group psychotherapy. RFPsa 1958, 22:129

52003 Victorius, K. Le Moise de Michel-Ange, de Sigmund Freud. RFPsa 1957, 21:623

52004 Voutsinas, D. Aperçu sur Freud. RFPsa 1957, 21:873-874

52005 Weigert, E. Countertransference and self-analysis of the psychoanalyst. RFPsa 1954, 18:471

52006 Winterstein, A. A typical dream sensation and its meaning. RFPsa 1954, 18:470

52007 Zilboorg, G. Aux frontières de la psychanalyse. RFPsa 1957, 21:623

REVIEWS OF:

52008 Allport, G. W. Becoming: Considerations for a Theory of Personality. RFPsa 1959, 23:297

52009 Bak, R. C. The schizophrenic defense against aggression. RFPsa 1954, 18:461-462

52010 Balint, M. Analytic training and training analysis. RFPsa 1954, 18:465

52011 Beigbeder: La symbolique. RFPsa 1957, 21:862

52012 Betlheim, S. Über die Bedeutung des Traumes in der Gruppentherapie. RFPsa 1959, 23:430

52013 Bibring, G. L. Training analysis and psychoanalytic training. RFPsa 1954, 18:466-467

52014 Bion, W. R. Notes on the theory of schizophrenia. RFPsa 1954, 18:460

52015 Bonaparte, M. Derrière les vitres closés; l'appel des sèves. RFPsa 1959, 23:296-297

52016 Bychowski, G. Some schizophrenic defense mechanisms. RFPsa 1954, 18:464

52017 Diatkine, R. & Stein, C. Les psychoses de l'enfance. RFPsa 1959, 23:428

52018 Eissler, K. R. Notes on defects of ego structure in schizophrenia. RFPsa 1954, 18:463

52019 Erwin, S. von: Wagner-Jauregg und die Psychotherapie. RFPsa 1959, 23:430

52020 Ey, H. Les problèmes cliniques des schizophrénies. RFPsa 1959, 23:427

52021 Follin, S. Sur la psychopathologie du processus schizophrénique. RFPsa 1959, 23:428

52022 Freud, M. Glory Reflected. RFPsa 1958, 22:251

52023 Freud, S. De la technique psychanalytique. RFPsa 1954, 18:450-454

52024 Gitelson, M. The analysis of the "normal" candidate. RFPsa 1954, 18:467

52025 Glover, E. Therapeutic criteria of psychoanalysis. RFPsa 1954, 18:458-459

52026 Heimann, P. Problems of the training analysis. RFPsa 1954, 18:465-466

52027 Jacobson, E. On psychotic identification. RFPsa 1954, 18:459-460

52028 Katan, M. The non-psychotic part of the personality in schizophrenia. RFPsa 1954, 18:461

52029 Lampl-de Groot, J. Problems of psychoanalytic training. RFPsa 1954, 18:467

52030 Leclaire, S. À la recherche des principes d'une psychothérapie des psychoses. RFPsa 1959, 23:429

52031 Loewenstein, R. M. On defenses, autonomous ego and technique. RFPsa 1954, 18:467-468

52032 Male, P. & Freen, A. Les préschizophrénies de l'adolescent. RFPsa 1959, 23:429

52033 Masserman, J. Principes de psychiatrie dynamique. RFPsa 1958, 22:740

52034 Pépin, J. Mythe et allégorie. RFPsa 1958, 22:739-740

52035 Perrier, F. Fondements théoriques d'une psychothérapie de la schizophrénie. RFPsa 1959, 23:429

52036 Racamier, P.-C. Connaissance et psychopathologie de la relation schizophrénique. RFPsa 1959, 23:429

52037 Rosenfeld, H. The psychoanalytic approach to acute and chronic schizophrenia. RFPsa 1954, 18:462-463

52038 Spitz, R. No and Yes. RFPsa 1958, 22:737-739

52039 Stengel, E. A re-evaluation of Freud's book "On Aphasia." RFPsa 1954, 18:457

52040 Van der Waals, G. Therapy of schizophrenia. RFPsa 1954, 18:464-465

52041 Volmat, R. Expression plastique de la folie. RFPsa 1957, 21:297-298

52042 Wall, W. D. Education et santé mentale. RFPsa 1957, 21:298

52043 Wittkower, E. D. Predictive psychophysiological studies. RFPsa 1959, 23:430

52044 Zilboorg, G. Freud's fundamental psychiatric orientation. RFPsa 1954, 18:458

LEBOVITS, BINYAMIN ZEEV

52045 (& Lakin, M.) Body image and paralytic poliomyelitis. An experimental approach. JNMD 1957, 125:518-523

See Lakin, Martin

LECHAT, FERNAND

52046 Sur l'acting-out [On acting-out.] Bull Ass Psa Belg 1953, (17), 8 p

52047 Considérations sur l'appartenance au groupe. [Some considerations on the belonging to a group.] Bull Ass Psa Belg 1955, (24), 17 p

52048 Hommage à S. Freud. [Homage to Freud.] RFPsa 1957, 21:325-330
Abs Roman, R. E. Q 1958, 27:148

52049 Importance de l'idéal du moi. [On the importance of the ego ideal.] Bull Ass Psa Belg 1949, (4), 13 p

52050 Sur l'instinct de mort. [On the death instinct.] Bull Ass Psa Belg 1953, (16), 9 p

52051 Jamais deux sans trois: considérations sur l'angoisse et sur les comportements névrotiques. [Trouble comes in threes: considerations on anxiety and neurotic behavior.] RFPsa 1953, 17:518-540. Bull Ass Psa Belg 1953, (18), 16 p
Abs JFr An Surv Psa 1953, 4:205-207. Marasse, H. F. Q 1956, 25:296-297

S-19856 Névrose et religiosité.
Abs RdeS Q 1953, 22:138

52052 Notes sur les premières relations objectales et sur leurs conséquences à l'âge adulte. [Notes on the first object relations and their consequences in adulthood.] RFPsa 1957, 21:715-750. Bull Ass Psa Belg 1956, 26, 33 p

52053 Autour du principe de plaisir. [About the pleasure principle.] RFPsa 1957, 21:769-789. Bull Ass Psa Belg 1957, (27), 12 p

52054 Du principe de sécurité. [On the principle of security.] RPFsa 1955, 19:11-101

52055 A propos du contre-transfert. [About counter-transference.] Bull Ass Psa Belg 1952, (13), 7 p

52056 Psychanalystes non médecins. [Non-medical psychoanalysts.] Bull Ass Psa Belg 1953, (17), 5 p

52057 Quelques réflexions sur l'amour et la haine. [Some considerations on love and hatred.] Bull Ass Psa Belg 1952, (14), 7 p

52058 Du surmoi. [On the superego.] Bull Ass Psa Belg 1951, (12), 9 p

See Nacht, Sacha

LECKY, PRESCOTT

52059 The personality. In author's *Self-Consistency*, (Ed: Thorne, F. C.) Island Pr Coop 1951. In Moustakas, C. E. *The Self. Explorations in Personal Growth*, NY: Harper & Bros 1956, 86-97

LECLAIRE, SERGE

52060 L'aspect psychanalytique de la sexualité infantile. [The psychoanalytic view of infantile sexuality.] R Np inf 1959, 7:1-7

52061 La fonction imaginaire du doute dans la névrose obsessionnelle. [The imaginary function of doubt in obsessional neurosis.] Entretiens Psychiat, Paris 1958, 4:193-216

52062 Les grands rythmes de la cure psychanalytique. [The important rhythmic features of psychoanalytic therapy.] In *Problèmes de Psychanalyse*, Paris: Fayard 1957, 44-55

52063 L'incurable psychanalyse. [Incurable psychoanalysis.] La Table Ronde 1956, Dec (108):36

52064 La mort dans la vie de l'obsédé. [Death in the life of obsessives.] Psychanalyse 1956, 2:111-144

52065 L'obsessionnel et son désir. [The obsessive and his desire.] Evolut psychiat 1959, (3):383-408

52066 A propos de "La cure-type en psychanalyse" de M. Bouvet. Essai critique. [Remarks on "La cure-type en psychanalyse" by M. Bouvet. A critical essay.] Evolut psychiat 1956, 2:515-540

52067 A propos de l'épisode psychotique que présenta "L'homme aux loups." [The psychotic episode that led to "The wolf man."] Psychanalyse 1958, 4:83-110

52068 A la recherche des principes d'une psychothérapie des psychoses. [In search of principles for a psychotherapy of psychoses.] Evolut psychiat 1958, (2):376-411
        Rv Lebovici RFPsa 1959, 23:429

52069 Réflexions sur l'étude clinique d'une manifestation de transfert. [Reflections on the clinical study of a transference manifestation.] Acta psychother psychosom orthopaedag 1955, 3(Suppl):201-210

LE COULTRE, RITSKE

52070 Elimination of guilt as a function of perversions. In Lorand, S. *Perversions: Psychodynamics and Therapy*, NY: Random House 1956, 42-54

52071 Enige bijzondere aspecten van het overdrachtsphenomeen. NTvG 1955, 99:3946-3949
        Some special aspects of the transference phenomenon. Acta psychotherap psychosom orthopaedag 1955, 3(Suppl):64-66

52072 Eine häufig vorkommende Lösung des Oedipuskonfliktes. [A frequent solution of the Oedipus conflict.] Acta psychother psychosom orthopaedag 1956, 4:289-296

LE CRON, L. M.

52073 A hypnotic technique for uncovering unconscious material. J clin exp Hyp 1954, 2:76-79

LEDER, H.

See Kaplan, Harold I.

LEDERER, HENRY D.

52074 How the sick view their world. J soc Issues 1952, 8:4-15. In Jaco, E. G. *Patients, Physicians and Illness*, Glencoe, Ill: Free Pr 1958, 247-256

See Blagg, David V.; Levine, Maurice

LEDERER, WOLFGANG

52075 Primitive psychotherapy. Ps 1959, 22:255-265
    Abs HRB Q 1960, 29:295

LEDERMANN, E. K.

52076 A review of the principles of Adlerian psychology. Int J soc Psychiat
    1956, 2:172-184

LEDERMANN, R. S.

52077 The significance of feeling in the therapeutic relationship. Brit J
    psychiat soc Work 1954, (9):12-17

LEE, A. RUSSELL

52078 (et al) Clinical symposium: Psychological and physiological aspects
    of marked obesity in a young adult female. J Hillside Hosp 1959,
    8:190-215
    Abs Gutstadt, J. P. Q 1960, 29:144-145

LEE, HARRY B.

REVIEW OF:
52079 Kris, E. Psychoanalytic Explorations in Art. Q 1953, 22:280-284

LEE, R. S.

52080 Psychology and Worship. London: S.C.M. Pr 1955, 110 p
    Rv EJ J 1955, 36:407-408

LEE, SIDNEY GILMORE

52081 Social influences in Zulu dreaming. Soc Psych 1958, 47:265-283

LEECH, CLIFFORD

52082 Studies in Hamlet, 1901-1955. Shakespeare Survey 1956, 9:1-15
52083 The year's contributions to Shakespearian study. Shakespeare Survey
    1955, 8:139-146

LEET, H. HALBERT

See Ross, W. Donald

LEEUW, P. J. VAN DER

52084 On the preoedipal phase of the male. (Read at 20th Psa Cong, Paris
    1957) J 1958, 29:112-115. Psa St C 1958, 13:352-374
    Zur präödipalen Phase des Mannes. Psyche, Heidel 1958, 12:81-87
    Abs J 1958, 39:292. Usandivaras & Tabak Rev Psicoanál 1959,
    16:88-89. RTh J 1960, 41:652-653
52085 Sigmund Freud: 6 Mei 1856—6 Mei 1956. [In commemoration of
    Freud's 100th birthday.] Het Parool 1956, May 6
52086 The techniques used in the Military Neurosis Hospital at Austerlitz.
    In *The Affective Contact*, Proc Int Cong for Psychotherapeutics,
    Leiden 1951, Sept 5-8

LEFEBRE, LUDWIG B.

S-19882A Eine Hypothese über den latenten Trauminhalt.
Abs JFr An Surv Psa 1952, 3:187
52087 Report on the 4th Intern. Congress of Psychotherapy. [On existential analysis.] PT 1958, 13(1)

LEFEBVRE, J.

52088 La personnalité de l'exhibitionniste. [The personality of the exhibitionist.] Acta Neurol Belg 1959, 59:253-267

LEFEBVRE, PAUL

See Gralnick, Alexander

LEFEVER, D. WELTY

See Bühler, Charlotte

LEFFORD, ARTHUR

See Barnett, Joseph

LEFKOVITS, AARON M.

See Mueller, Alfred D.

LEFORT, ROSINE

52089 L'enfant au loup. [The "wolf" child.] Psychanalyse 1956, 2:145-164

LE GALLAIS, PIERRE

52090 Arte e psicopatas. [Art and mental illness.] (Tr: Silveira, N. da; Souza Santos, J. de) Rev Bras Saúde ment 1955, 1(1):121-138
52091 A "concepção organo-dinâmica" da psiquiatria de Henri Ey. [The organ-dynamic conception of psychiatry of Henri Ey.] J brasil Psiquiat 1954, 3:61-69

LEGAULT, OSCAR

52092 Denial as a complex process in post lobotomy. Ps 1954, 17:153-161

LEGUE

See Soulairac, A.

LE GUILLANT, L.

52093 Introduction à une psycho-pathologie sociale. [Introduction to a social psychopathology.] Evolut psychiat 1954, (1):1-52

LEHFELDT, HANS

52094 Kinsey und der Frauenarzt. [Kinsey and the gynecologist.] Die Heilkunst 1955, 68:353-359

LEHMAN, IRVIN J.

52095 Responses of kindergarten children to the Children's Apperception Test. Clin Psych 1959, 15:60-63

LEHMANN, ANDRÉE

52096 Un cas de psychothérapie d'enfant. [A case of child psychotherapy.] Suppl Vie Spir 1958, 11:31-42

See Laplanche, J.

TRANSLATION OF:
(& Laplanche, J.) Matussek, P. [53529]

LEHMANN, HEINZ EDGAR

52097 A dynamic concept of the action of chlorpromazine at physiological and psychological levels. Enceph 1956, 4:1113-1118
52098 Selective inhibition of affective drive by pharmacological means. P 1954, 110:856-857
52099 Socio-psychiatric observations on displaced persons. Psychiat Q Suppl 1953, 27:245-256
52100 Stress dynamics in psychiatric perspective. Ps 1952, 15:387-393

LEHNER, GEORGE F. J.
See Katz, Barney

LEHNERT, BETTINA

52101 Participant in clinical conference: A problem of ego organization in a latency child. New Front Child Guid 173-209

LEHRMAN, NATHANIEL S.

52102 The analyst's sexual feelings. Their appropriateness and their value. PT 1960, 14:545-549
52103 The conflict within psychoanalysis. In Baran, P. A. et al: *Marxism and Psychoanalysis*, NY: Monthly Review Pr 1960, 26-32
52104 [Participant in] Discussion. Schiz Psa Off Pract 75
52105 Discussion of Toolan, J. M. "Changes in personality structure during adolescence." Sci Psa 1960, 3:200

LEHRMAN, PHILIP R.

52106 Introduction to Brill, A. A. *Freud's Principles of Psychoanalysis.*
S-19914A Obituary: Clarence Paul Oberndorf, 1882-1954. Q 1954, 23:424-428

REVIEWS OF:
S-19928A Oberndorf, C. P. A History of Psychoanalysis in America. Q 1954, 23:263-265
S-19929A Schilder, P. Medical Psychology. Q 1956, 25:105-106

LEHRMAN, SAMUEL R.

52107 A note on two characteristics of transference. Q 1959, 28:379-381
52108 Obituary: Frieda Fromm-Reichmann, 1890-1957. Q 1958, 27:104
52109 Obituary: Charles Otchin, 1900-1957. Q 1958, 27:105
52110 Psychoanalytic orientation in psychotherapy. AMA ANP 1958, 80:351-362

52111 Reactions to untimely death. Psychiat Q 1956, 30:564-578
52112 The role of the voluntary general hospital in the care of psychiatric patients. J Hillside Hosp 1959, 8:94-108

See Kaufman, M. Ralph

ABSTRACT OF:
52113 Stern, M. M. Trauma, dependency, and transference. Q 1957, 26:152-153

LEIBBRAND, WERNER

52114 Die biographische und geistesgeschichtliche Einordnung Sigmund Freuds. [The biographical and intellectual historical position of Freud.] Jb Psychol Psychother 1958, 5:82-89

LEICHTY, MARY M.

52115 The absence of the father during early childhood and its effect upon the Oedipal situation as reflected in young adults. Diss Abstr 1959, 19:1821

LEIDEN, IRVING

See Fineberg, Henry H.

LEIDER, ALLAN RICHARD

52116 (& Mangham, C. A.) A psychiatric study of the mothers of excessively crying infants. Psychiat Q 1957, 31:508-520

See Stewart, Ann H.; Weiland, Irvin H.

LEIDERMAN, GLORIA F.

52117 Effect of parental relationships and child-training practices on boys' interactions with peers. (Abs) Proc 15th Int Cong Psychol, Brussels 1957, Amsterdam: North-Holland Publ 1959, 469-470

LEIDERMAN, P. HERBERT

See Mendelson, Jack; Solomon, Philip; Wexler, Donald

LEIGH, DENIS

52118 Sudden death from asthma. PSM 1955, 17:232-239
       Abs EMW Q 1957, 26:145

See Lovett Doust, John W.

LEIGHTON, ALEXANDER H.

52119 (& Clausen, J. A.; Wilson, R. N.) (Eds) Explorations in Social Psychiatry. NY: Basic Books 1957, x + 452 p
52120 (& Clausen, J. A.; Wilson, R. N.) Orientation. In authors' *Explorations in Social Psychiatry*, 13-28

LEISER, RUDOLF

See Izner, Sanford M.

LEIST, FRITZ

52121 Die Grenzen zwischen Tiefenpsychologie und Seelsorge. [The boundaries between depth-psychology and pastoral care.] In Bitter, W.
Psychotherapie und Seelsorge, Stuttgart 1954

LEITE LOBO, F.

52122 Elementos para a avaliação do decurso do tratamento psicanalítico.
[Characteristic signs for the evaluation of progress during psychoanalytic therapy.] R Bras Saúde ment 1956, 2(2):25-36

52123 "Sociedade Psicanalítica do Rio de Janeiro": Sigmund Freud. ["The
Psychoanalytic Society of Rio de Janeiro": Sigmund Freud.] R Bras
Saúde ment 1956, 1(2):153-154

LEITER, L. H.

52124 A problem in analysis: Franz Kafka's "A Country Doctor." J Aesthet
1957, 16:337-347

LEITES, NATHAN

52125 Discussion of Bellak, L. "The unconscious." Ann NY Acad Sci 1959,
76:1092-1093

52126 Discussion of Pumpian-Mindlin, E. "Propositions concerning energetic-
economic aspects of libido theory: conceptual models of psychic energy
and structure in psychoanalysis." Ann NY Acad Sci 1959, 76:1058

52127 Panic and defenses against panic in the Bolshevik view of politics. Psa
Soc S 1955, 4:135-144

° ° °   "The Stranger." See [S-19947]

S-19947 Trends in affectlessness. Pers n s c 618-632. With title: "The Stranger."
Art Psa 247-267

See Wolfenstein, Martha

TRANSLATION OF:
Dolto, F. [44426]

LELONG, M.

52128 (& Lebovici, S.) Problèmes psychologiques et psychopathologiques
posés par l'enfant à l'hôpital. [Psychological and psychopathological
problems connected with the hospital stay of children.] Arch Franç
Pediat 1955, 12:349-367

LELORD, G.
See Heyer, Gustav R.

LEMAIRE, J. G.
See Delay, J.

LEMBKE, PERNILLA
See Charny, Israel W.

LEMKAU, PAUL V.

52129   Freud and prophylaxis. Bull NY Acad Med 1956, 32:887-893. In Gald-
        ston, I. *Freud and Contemporary Culture,* NY: IUP 1957, 42-52
S-19956A Toward mental health.
        Abs JLan Q 1953, 22:138

        See Kelman, Harold

LEMMERTZ, JOSÉ J.

52130   Valor clinico de las interpretaciones en términos de identificaciones.
        [Clinical value of interpretations in terms of identification.] Rev
        Psicoanál 1953, 10:90-102
        Abs JLan An Surv Psa 1953, 4:445-446. Vega Q 1954, 23:622.

LENIHAN, ELLENORA A.

See Prugh, Dane G.

LENKOSKI, DOUGLAS L.

See Pilot, Martin L.

LENNARD, HENRY L.
(See also Loeblowitz-Lennard, Henry)

52131   (& Jarvik, M. E.; Abramson, H. A.) Lysergic acid diethylamide (LSD
        25): III. A preliminary statement of its effects upon interpersonal
        communication. J Psychol 1956, 41:185-198
52132   (& Glock, C. Y.) Psychological factors in hypertension. J chronic
        Diseases 1957, 5:174-185
52133   (& Palmore, E.; Hendin, H.) Similarities of therapist and patient ver-
        bal behavior in psychotherapy. Sociometry 1959, March
52134   (& Calogeras, R.; Hendin, H.) Some relationships between verbal be-
        havior of therapist and patient in psychotherapy. J Psychol 1957,
        43:181-186

        See Palmore, Erdman

LENNARTZ, H.

52135   (& Spiegelberg, U.) [Psychopathological states in cases of myopathia.]
        (German) Nervenarzt 1956, 27:98

LENNEP, DAVID JACOB VAN

52136   Projection and personality. Pers Thy 259-277

LENOBLE, ROBERT

52137   Psychanalyse et science de l'homme. [Psychoanalysis and the science
        of man.] Rev Philosophique 1950, 1:36-71
        Rv Ostrov, L. Rev Psicoanál 1953, 10:249

LENZNER, ABRAHAM S.

52138 Countertransference and the resident on leaving his patient. J Hillside
Hosp 1955, 4:148-150

52139 (& Solovey, S.) Structure and process in limited-goal out-patient psychotherapy. J Hillside Hosp 1956, 5:449-459

LEON, H.

See Hallowitz, Emanuel

LEON, MAURICE J.

See Bowers, John E.

LEÓN MONTALBÁN, P.

52140 Algunas consideraciones sobre la psiquiatría norteamericana. [Com-
ments on North American psychiatry.] Rev Neuro-psiquiat 1956,
19:409-411

See Seguín, Carlos Alberto

LEONARD, MARJORIE R.

52141 Fear of walking in a two-and-a-half-year old girl. Q 1959, 28:29-39
Abs Rev Psicoanál 1959, 16:134-135

52142 Problems in identification and ego development in twins. (Read at
Los Angeles Institute for Psa, March 19, 1959)
Abs Tausend, H. Bull Phila Ass Psa 1959, 9:46

ABSTRACTS OF:
52143 Abraham, H. C. Twin relationship and womb fantasy in a case of
anxiety hysteria. Q 1955, 24:148-149

52144 Shields, J. Personality differences and neurotic traits in normal twin
school children: a study in psychiatric genetics. Q 1955, 24:474-475

REVIEWS OF:
52145 Burlingham, D. Twins: A Study of Three Pairs of Identical Twins.
Q 1953, 22:577-580

52146 Joseph, H. & Zern, G. The Emotional Problems of Children. Q 1955,
24:592-593

52147 Kallman, F. J. Heredity in Health and Mental Disorder. Q 1954,
23:436-441

LEONHARD, KARL

S-19983 Gesetze und Sinn des Träumens; zugleich eine Kritik der Traumdeutung und ein Einblick in das Wirken des Unterbewusstseins. 2nd
enlarged ed. Stuttgart: G. Thieme 1951, 146 p
Rv ESt J 1953, 34:171-172

52148 Über das Vorbeiträumen und seine Bedeutung in der Psychotherapie.
[Day dreams and their significance in psychotherapy.] Psychiat Neur
med Psychol, Leipzig 1956, 8:131-134

LEOPOLD, HAROLD

52149 Selection of patients for group psychotherapy. PT 1957, 11:634-637
Abs Usandivaras Rev Psicoanál 1957, 14:422

See Wolf, Alexander

LEOPOLD, ROBERT L.

52150 Contributing therapies. Am J Occupational Therapy 1955, 11:239-242
52151 (& Carroll, J. R.) The current influence of psychiatric concepts in
determining criminal responsibility in Pennsylvania. Temple Law
Quart 1958, 31:254-282
52152 Patient-therapist relationship: psychological consideration. Phys Therapy Rev 1954, 34(1):8-13
52153 The psychology of the interview. Personnel J 1958, 37:247-250

LEPINE, LOUIS T.

52154 (& Chodorkoff, B.) Goal setting behaviour, expressed feelings of adequacy, and the correspondence between the perceived and ideal self.
Clin Psych 1955, 11:395-397

LEPORE, M.

See Flood, C. A.

LEPP, IGNACE

52155 Clartés et ténèbres de l'âme; essai de psychosynthèse. [Brightnesses and
Shadows of the Soul; Attempt at Psychosynthesis.] Paris: Edit Mon-
taigne 1956, 295 p
52156 Psychanalyse de l'Amour. [Psychoanalysis of Love.] Paris: B. Grasset
1959, 283 p

LERNER, EUGENE

52157 Experiments in active play techniques. In Murphy, L. B. *Personality
in Young Children. Vol. I. Methods for the Study of Personality in
Young Children,* NY: Basic Books 1956, 267-333

LERNER, HARRY HERMAN

52158 (Ed) Group Methods in Psychotherapy, Social Work and Adult Education. J soc Issues 1952, 8(2). Wash: Div 9 Am Psychol Ass, 96 p
52159 (& Kelman, H. C.) Group therapy, group work and adult education:
the need for clarification. J soc Issues 1952, 8(2):3-10
52160 Methodological convergence and social action. J soc Issues 1952,
8(2):75-80

See Kelman, Herbert C.

LERNER, M.

52161 Enfoque actualizado de los conceptos de sugestión e hipnosis. [De-
velopment of the concepts of suggestion and hypnosis.] Act Np Arg
1958, 4:156-166

52162 Hipnoanálisis de un caso de anorexia y vómitos psicógenos. [Hypno-analysis of a case of psychogenic anorexia and vomiting.] Act Np Arg 1956, 2:308-312

52163 Relajación y neurosis con referencia al concepto de maduración del yo. [Relaxation and neurosis with reference to the concept of ego maturation.] Act Np Arg 1957, 3:155-158

52164 Valor de la relajación en medicina psicomatica y psicoterapia. [The value of relaxation in psychosomatic medicine and psychotherapy.] J ornada med 1955, 261:475

Abs Garcia Reinoso, D. Rev Psicoanál 1956, 13:327-328

LERNER, MAX

52165 Storm over Freud. NY Post 1956, May 2

LERNER, SAMUEL H.

52166 Effects of desertion on family life. Soc Casewk 1954, 35:3-8

52167 Some aggressive aspects of apathy. Bull Phila Ass Psa 1955, 5:91-106

LE ROY, D.

52168 Mythologie de l'Anxiété. [Mythology of Anxiety.] Paris: 1956, 170 p

LERSH, PHILIPP

52169 The levels of the mind. Pers Thy 212-217

LÉRTORA, A.

52170 El antirracionalismo existencialista frente a la psiquiatría. [Existential irrationalism confronting psychiatry.] Act Np Arg 1958, 4:307-321

LESCHNITZER, ADOLF F.

52171 Goethe und der Mythus von der Geburt des Helden. [Goethe and the myth of the birth of the hero.] Neue Schw Rundschau 1953, 9:549-557

LE SHAN, LAWRENCE L.

S-19989A Dynamics in accident-prone behavior. Encycl Aberr 4-10

Abs NRo An Surv Psa 1952, 3:293-294. Rosengarten, L. Q 1953, 22:613-614

52172 (& Worthington, R. E.) Loss of cathexes as a common psychodynamic characteristic of cancer patients; an attempt at statistical validation of a clinical hypothesis. Psychol Rep 1956, 2:183-193

52173 (& Worthington, R. E.) Personality as a factor in the pathogenesis of cancer: a review of the literature. M 1956, 29:49-55

52174 Psychological states as factors in the development of malignant disease: a critical review. J Nat Cancer Inst 1959, 22:1-18

52175 (& Gassmann, M. L.) Some observations on psychotherapy with patients with neoplastic disease. PT 1958, 12:723-734

52176 (& Worthington, R. E.) Some psychologic correlates of neoplastic disease: a preliminary report. J clin exp Psychopath 1955, 16:281-288

52177   (& Worthington, R. E.) Some recurrent life history patterns observed in patients with malignant disease. JNMD 1956, 124:460-465

S-19989B The safety prone.

Abs NRo An Surv Psa 1952, 3:294-295

LESSA, WILLIAM A.

52178   Oedipus-type tales in Oceania. J Am Folklore 1956, 69:63-73

LESSE, STANLEY

52179   Obituary: Emil A. Gutheil. Aufbau 1959, 25(31):7
52180   Psychodynamic relationships between the degree of anxiety and other clinical symptoms. JNMD 1958, 127:124-130

See Cattell, James P.; Malitz, Sidney

LESSER, GERALD S.

52181   Conflict analysis of fantasy aggression. J Pers 1958, 26:29-41
52182   The relationship between overt and fantasy aggression as a function of maternal response to aggression. ASP 1957, 55:218-221
52183   Religion and the defensive responses in children's fantasy. J proj Tech 1959, 23:64-68

LESSER, J.

REVIEW OF:

52183A Mann, T. Die Betrogene. Neue Schw Rundschau 1954, 21:686-687

LESSER, LEONA N.

See Halpern, Howard M.

LESSER, SIMON O.

52184   Arbitration and conciliation. Lit & Psych 1954, 4(2):25-27
52185   Fiction and the Unconscious. (Preface: Jones, E.) Boston: Beacon Pr 1957, xiii + 322 p
            Rv HRB Q 1958, 27:270-271
52186   Freud and *Hamlet* again. Am Im 1955, 12:207-220
52187   The functions of form in narrative art. Ps 1955, 18:51-63
            Abs Usandivaras Rev Psicoanál 1956, 13:324-325

S-19989B The image of the father. Art Psa 226-246

52188   Reply to review of author's *Fiction and the Unconscious* by Fiedler, L. J. in Lit & Psych 1958, 8(1):11-12. Lit & Psych 1958, 8(2):26-27
52189   Some unconscious elements in the responses to fiction. Lit & Psych 1953, 3(4):2-5
52190   Tragedy, comedy and the esthetic experience. Lit & Psych 1956, 6 (Freud Centenary issue):131-139

LESTER, MILTON

52191   The analysis of an unconscious beating fantasy in a woman. J 1957, 38:22-31. In Freeman, L. *Troubled Women*, Cleveland: World Publ 1959, 55-78
            Abs JLan Q 1958, 27:127

See Lander, Joseph

REVIEWS OF:

52192 Robertiello, R. C. Voyage from Lesbos. Q 1960, 29:579

52193 Schneider, D. E. The Image of the Heart and the Principle of Synergy in the Human Mind. Q 1957, 26:562-563

LETAYF, SONIA

52194 Psicanálise e arte. [Psychoanalysis and art.] Rev Psicol norm patol 1956, 2:519-533

LETHIN, ANTON N., JR.

See Barnes, George R.

LEUBA, CLARENCE

52195 The Sexual Nature of Man. NY: Doubleday 1954
Rv R 1955, 42:106

LEUBA, JOHN H.

S-20018 Women who fall.
Abs R 1953, 40:353

LEUNER, HANSCARL

52196 Genitalstörungen nach Vergewaltigung, ihre Manifestation und Psychotherapie. [Sex disorders after rape; their manifestation and psychotherapy.] Z PSM 1955-56, 2:28-34

52197 Kontrolle der Symbolinterpretation im experimentellen Verfahren. [Experimental control of symbol interpretations.] Z Psychother med Psychol 1954, 4:201-204

52198 Symbolkonfrontation. Ein nicht-interpretierendes Vorgehen in der Psychotherapie. Ergebnisse mit dem experimentellen katathymen Bilderleben. II. [Symbol confrontation. A non-interpreting procedure in psychotherapy. Results with the experimental catathymic experiences of images. II] Schweiz ANP 1955, 76:23-49

LEVBARG, J. J.

52199 Hypnosis as an aid in the practice of anesthesiology. Brit J med Hypnot 1956, 7(3):33-39

LEVENSON, E. A.

52200 Changing time concepts in psychoanalysis. PT 1958, 12:64-78

LEVI, FRITZ

52201 Zu C. G. Jung's Begriff der Synchronizität. [Concerning Jung's concept of synchronicity.] Neue Schw Rundschau 1955, 21:752-755

TRANSLATION OF:
Thompson, C. M. [33274]

LEVI, JOSEPH

52202 Hawthorne's *The Scarlet Letter:* a psychoanalytic interpretation. Am Im 1953, 10:291-306
Abs MK An Surv Psa 1953, 4:361-363

REVIEW OF:

52203   Jones, E. The Life and Work of Sigmund Freud, Vol. III. NPAP 1958,
6(1):74-77

LEVI, LEO H.

52204   Genital warts, a sex defense mechanism? Int J Sexol 1954, 7:122-124

LEVI-BIANCHINI, MARCO

52205   Alcuni rilievi clinici e psicoanalitici su denominazioni e diagnosi errate
nel campo delle psiconeurosi umane. [Some clinical and psychoanalytical data on erroneous terminology and diagnoses in the field of human
psychoneurosis.] Rass Studi Psichiat 1956, 45:647-657

52206   Commemorazione del centenario della nascita di Sigismondo Freud.
[Commemoration of the centenary of the birth of Sigmund Freud.]
Ann Np Psa 1956, 3:421-428

52207   Difesa della psicoanalisi di fronte alla neurosi cristiana antifreudiana.
[Defense of psychoanalysis against the Christian antifreudian neurosis.] Ann Np Psa 1955, 2:269-302

52208   L'epilessia paranoide. [Paranoid epilepsy.] Ann Np Psa 1955, 2:523-
528

52209   Le epilessie psicotraumatiche. [The psychotraumatic epilepsies.] Riv
Psipat Np Psa 1953, 21:203-210

52210   La fonte della vita o vero il bisogno di essere amati. [The source of
life or the need to be loved.] Ann Np Psa 1958, 5:49-99

52211   La neurosi anagapica infantile. [The anagapic neurosis in childhood.]
Ann Np Psa 1954, 1:159-166

52212   La neurosi anagapica e le sue forme cliniche. Psicoanalisi del "bisogno
di essere amati" e delle sue reaziono intrapsichiche de carenza (com-
plesso di anagapia). [The anagapic neurosis and its clinical forms.
Psychoanalysis of "the need to be loved" and of the intrapsychic reactions to lack of affection (complex of anagapia).] Riv Psipat Np Psa
1953, 21:11-105

52213   La neurosi antifallica nell'ambito della vita sociale ed in quella religiosa cattolica romana. [The antifallic neurosis in social life and in
Roman Catholic religious society.] Ann Np Psa 1956, 3:39-46

52214   Perizia neuropsichiatrica e medico-legale del Sig. A. A. [Neuropsy-
chiatric study and medico-legal testimony in the case of Mr. A. A.]
Ann Np Psa 1954, 1:531-538

52215   Perizia psichiatrica in persona di R. V. [Expert psychiatric testimony
in the case of the individual R. V.] Ann Np Psa 1958, 5:239-259

52216   Saggio psicoanalitico delle sconosciute neurosi anagapiche infantili di
Dostoiewski e di Baudelaire. [Psychoanalytic essay on the unfamiliar
anagapic childhood neuroses of Dostoevski and of Baudelaire.] Ann
Np Psa 1957, 4:5-12

LEVIN, A. J.

S-20098 The fiction of the death instinct.
Abs JAA An Surv Psa 1951, 2:37

52217   Oedipus and Samson: the rejected hero-child. J 1957, 38:105-116
Abs JLan Q 1958, 27:438

LEVIN, HARRY

52218   (& Sears, R. R.) Identification with parents as a determinant of doll play aggression. Child Developm 1956, 27:135-153
52219   (& Turgeon, V. F.) The influence of the mother's presence on children's doll play aggression. ASP 1957, 55:304-308
52220   Symbolism and Fiction. Charlottesville: Univ Virginia Pr 1956, 43 p

See Sears, Robert

LEVIN, I.

52221   Some psychoanalytic concepts in Richard Wagner's *The Ring of the Niblung.* Arch crim Psychodyn 1959, 3:260-316

LEVIN, MAX

52222   Aggression, guilt and cataplexy. AMA ANP 1953, 69:224-235. P 1959, 116:133-135
        Abs LRa Q 1954, 23:308-309. Loeb, L. Q 1960, 29:594
52223   Ego boundary in childhood and in schizophrenia. P 1953, 109:865
52224   The impact of Freud on psychiatry. Current Med Dig 1956, Aug:47-52. Child-Fam Dig 1956, 15(3):67-72

See Katcher, Allan

LEVIN, MEYER

52225   A new fear in writers. NPAP 1953, 2(1):34-38

LEVIN, SIDNEY

52226   Problems in the evaluation of patients for psychoanalysis. Bull Phila Ass Psa 1960, 10:86-95
52227   A study of fees for control analysis. Bull Phila Ass Psa 1958, 8:69-82

See Knapp, Peter H.

LEVINE, ABRAHAM

52228   A comparative evaluation of latent schizophrenic and overt schizophrenic patients with respect to certain personality variables. J Hillside Hosp 1958, 7:131-152
52229   (& Harris, J. B.; Caminsky, I.; Lurie, A.; Bachrach, M.; Miller, J. S. A.) An exploratory vocational counseling program in a mental hospital. J Hillside Hosp 1958, 7:153-161
52230   (& Abramson, H. A.; Kaufman, M. R.; Markham, S.) Lysergic acid diethylamide (LSD 25) XVI. The effect on intellectual functioning as measured by the Wechsler Bellevue intelligence scale. J Psychol 1955, 40:385-395
52231   (& Abramson, H. A.; Kaufman, M. R.; Markham, S.; Kornetsky, C.) LSD: XIV. Effect on personality as observed in psychological tests. J Psychol 1955, 40:351-366

See Abramson, Harold A.; Meyer, Bernard C.

LEVINE, DAVID

See Piotrowski, Zygmunt A.

LEVINE, JACOB

52232   (& Redlich, F. C.) Failure to understand humor. Q 1955, 24:560-572
        Abs JKl J 1956, 37:205-206
52233   (& Abelson, R.) Humor as a disturbing stimulus. J general Psychol
        1959, 60:191-200
52234   Inside story. In Redlich, F. C. & Bingham, J. *Psychiatry and Everyday
        Living*, NY: Alfred A. Knopf 1955

        See Redlich, Fredrick C.; Wolff, Peter

LÉVINE, JACQUES

52235   Représentation des étapes du développement et conscience de soi chez
        l'enfant. [Representation of developmental stages and the awareness
        of self by children.] Enfance 1958, (2):85-114

LEVINE, MAURICE I.

52236   Contribution to Alexander, F. *Psychoanalysis and Psychotherapy*, NY:
        W. W. Norton 1956, 236-243
52236A Contribution to Titchener, J. *Emotions and Surgery*, NY: Oxford Univ
        Pr 1959
52237   The education of the psychiatrist. Resident Physician J 1959
52238   Emotional maturity. From author's *Psychotherapy in Medical Practice*
        [20148]. In Linscott, R. N. & Stein, J. *Why You Do What You Do*,
        NY: Random House 1956, 261-274
52239   The evolution of psychiatry as an integral part of medical practice.
        J Michigan State méd Soc 1957, 56:218-222
52240   First International Congress of Psychiatry. P 1951, 107:555
52241   The impact of psychoanalysis on training in psychiatry. 20 Yrs Psa
        50-66
52242   Methods of teaching psychiatry. In *The Psychiatrist, His Training and
        Development*, Wash, D.C.: Am Psychiat Ass 1953, Appendix 4, p 175
52243   Oedipus, Cain and Abel, and the geographic full-time system. J med
        Educ 1960, 35:244-250
        Abs NR Q 1960, 29:443
S-20155 Pediatric observations on masturbation in children.
        Abs NRo An Surv Psa 1951, 2:82-83
52244   Preface to Balint, M. *The Doctor, His Patient and the Illness.*
52245   Preface to Ross, W. D. *Practical Psychiatry for Industrial Physicians*,
        Springfield, Ill: Thomas 1956
52246   Problem parents. From author's *Psychotherapy in Medical Practice*,
        [20148]. In Linscott, R. N. & Stein, J. *Why You Do What You Do*,
        NY: Random House 1956, 215-220
52247   (& Bell, A.) The psychological aspects of pediatric practice. II. Mas-
        turbation. Pediatrics 1956, 18:803-808

S-20148 Psychotherapy in Medical Practice.
Psicoterapia en la Práctica Médica. (Tr: Gonzalez, A.) B. Aires: Librería y Edit "El Ateneo" 1951, 302 p
Yugoslavia: 1959

52248 Summary discussion on psychiatric treatment. Proc Ass Res nerv Dis 1953, 31:35 p

52249 (& Lederer, H. D.) Teaching of psychiatry in medical schools. Am Hbk Psychiat 2:1923-1934

52250 The University Teaching Center and the mental hospital. In *Steps Forward in Mental Hospitals*, Am Psychiat Ass 1953, Sect 2, p 6

See Bell, Anita I.; Kubie, Lawrence S.; Titchener, James L.; Zwerling, Israel

LEVINE, S.

See Korchin, Sheldon J.

LEVINGER, LEAH

52251 Discussion. Symposium 1958: The teacher's role in creativity. Ops 1959, 29:291-297

52252 Interpretations of psychological tests to parents in a child guidance clinic. New Front Child Guid 5-45

52253 Participant in Clinical Conference: A problem of ego organization in a latency child. New Front Child Guid 173-209

LEVINSON, DANIEL J.

52254 Authoritarian personality and foreign policy. J Conflict Resolution 1957, 1:37-47

S-20155A Criminality from a sense of guilt: a case study and some research hypotheses.
Abs Holzman, P. S. Q 1953, 22:311

52255 The relevance of personality for political participation. Public Opinion Q 1958, 22:3-10

52256 Role, personality and social structure in the organizational setting. ASP 1959, 58:170-180

52257 (& Huffman, P. E.) Traditional family ideology and its relation to personality. J Pers 1955, 23:251-273. In Dulany, et al: *Contributions to Modern Psychology*, NY: Oxford 1958

See Adorno, T. W.; Frenkel-Brunswik, Else; Greenblatt, Milton; Hanfmann, Eugenia; Inkeles, Alex

LEVINSON, G.

ABSTRACTS OF:

52258 Agoston, T. & McCullough, M. W. Some observations on manic psychosis. J 1954, 35:447

52259 Bagchi, A. The Sanskritist's approach to the mental theory of Freud. J 1955, 36:435

52260 Barag, G. Clinical notes on kleptomania. J 1954, 35:448

52261 Bergler, E. Contributions to the psychology of homosexuals. J 1955, 36:434

52262 Bergler, E. Incognito exhibitionism. J 1953, 34:356-357

52263 Bergler, E. The infantile and adult forms of reducing to absurdity. J 1955, 36:434

52264 Bergler, E. The patient's suffering during analysis—a technical mistake on the part of the analyst. J 1953, 34:75

52265 Bergler, E. Technical problems with couples analysed simultaneously by the same analyst. J 1954, 35:448

52266 Bose, G. The mechanism of defiance. J 1953, 34:75

52267 Bose, G. & Ganguly, D. Psychological study of language. J 1953, 34:75

52268 Bose, G. Sex and anxiety. J 1953, 34:357

52269 Bose, N. K. Some facts of psychoanalytical interest in Ghandi's life. J 1953, 34:356

52270 Brody, M. W. A psycho-analytical interpretation of Rapunzel. J 1955, 36:434

52271 Crowley, R. M. Human reactions of analysts to patients. J 1953, 34:357

52272 Devereux, G. Belief, superstition and symptom. J 1955, 36:434

52273 Devereux, G. The Oedipal situation and its consequences in the epics of ancient India. J 1953, 34:75

52274 Dorsey, J. M. Some considerations of the psycho-analytical principle and religious living. J 1955, 36:434

52275 Eissler, K. R. On Hamlet. J 1954, 35:447-448

52276 Feldmann, S. S. A syndrome indicative of repressed oral aggression. J 1954, 35:447

52277 Ginsburg, S. W. The role of work. J 1955, 36:434

52278 Glover, E. Psychoanalysis and child psychiatry. J 1953, 34:356

52279 Hart, H. H. The meaning of circumstantiality. J 1954, 35:448

52280 Kamm, B. A. Reality: past and present. J 1954, 35:447

52281 Kris, E. The development of ego psychology. J 1953, 34:282

52282 Laha, S. C. Concept of time. J 1953, 34:356

52283 Masserman, J. H. Experimental approaches to psychoanalytic concepts. J 1953, 34:357

52284 Michel, A. Bibliography of psychoanalysis of music and musicians. J 1955, 36:435

52285 Racker, H. On the confusion between mania and health. J 1955, 36:434

52286 Ramana, C. V. Observations on the analysis of a musician. J 1953, 34:357

52287 Róheim, G. Wedding ceremonies in European folklore. J 1955, 36:434

52288 Roychoudhury, A. K. Sita myth of the Ramayana. J 1955, 36:435

52289 Safier, B. A psychological orientation to dance and pantomime. J 1954, 35:448

52290 Saul, L. J. Brief therapy of a case of torticollis. J 1954, 35:448

52291 Saul, L. J. Psycho-somatic aspects of peptic ulcer. J 1954, 35:448

52292 Schnier, J. Psycho-analysis of the artist. J 1955, 36:434

52293 Schwartz, L. A. Psychodynamic aspect of peptic ulcer. J 1953, 34:282-283

52294 Semrad, E. V. Psychotherapy of the psychoses. J 1955, 36:434

52295 Sinha, T. C. A case of aspermia. J 1955, 36:434

52296 Sinha, T. C. Formation of Garo clan. J 1953, 34:356

52297 Sinha, T. C. A psychological study of the colour preference of the Garos. J 1953, 34:75

52298 Tauber, E. S. Observations on countertransference phenomena. The supervisor-therapist relationship. J 1953, 34:357

52299 Thompson, C. Counter-transference. J 1953, 34:357

52300 Thompson, C. Transference and character analysis. J 1954, 35:448

LEVINSON, HARRY

52301 Emotional first aid on the job. Menn Q 1957, 11(3):6-15

52302 The illogical logic of accident prevention. Menn Q 1957, 11(1):19-25

52303 (& Menninger, W.) The machine that made pop; an industrial fable. Menn Q 1954, 8(3):20-26

52304 (Ed) Toward Understanding Men. Topeka, Kansas: Menninger Foundation 1956

See Menninger, Karl A.; Menninger, William C.

LEVINSON, MARIA HERTZ

See Adorno, T. W.

LEVITSKY, ABRAHAM

52305 A study of the defense mechanism of intellectualization. Diss Abstr 1955, 15:628

LEVITT, EUGENE E.

52306 (& Beiser, H. R.; Robertson, R. E.) A follow-up evaluation of cases treated at a community child guidance clinic. Ops 1959, 29:337-347 Abs Massoubre, J. RFPsa 1960, 24:212

52307 (& Lyle, W. H.) Punitiveness, authoritarianism, and parental discipline of grade school children. ASP 1955, 41:42-46

LEVITT, MORTON

52308 (& Rubenstein, B. O.) Acting out in adolescence: a study in communication. Ops 1959, 29:622-632

52309 (& Rubenstein, B. O.) The fate of advice: examples of distortion in parental counseling. MH, NY 1957, 41:213-216

52310 Freud and Dewey: a comparative study of their psychological systems. Diss Abstr 1956, 16:2386

52311 Freud and Dewey on the Nature of Man. NY: Philosophical Libr 1960, 180 p

52312 Freud's psychological system. Rd Psa Psychol 16-28

52313 Preface. Rd Psa Psychol ix-xii

52314 (& Sadler, H. H.) Psychological factors in clerkship grouping and their relationship to the learning process. J Med Educ 1958, 33:678

52315 (Ed) Readings in Psychoanalytic Psychology. NY: Appleton-Century-Crofts 1959, xiv + 413 p
Rv Niederland, W. G. Q 1960, 29:118-119

52316 Sigmund Freud: a biographical study. Rd Psa Psychol 1-15

See Falick, M. L.; Rubenstein, Ben O.

LEVY, DAVID M.

52317 Advice and reassurance. Am J publ Hlth 1954, 44:1113-1118
52318 Behavioral Analysis: Analysis of Clinical Observations of Behavior; as Applied to Mother-Newborn Relationships. Springfield, Ill: C. C Thomas 1958, 370 p
52319 Capacity and motivation. Ops 1957, 27:1-8
           Abs Jackel, M. M. Q 1958, 27:605
52320 Chairman's address. Chg Cpts Psa Med 1-3
52321 The Demonstration Clinic: for the Psychological Study and Treatment of Mother and Child in Medical Practices. Springfield, Ill: C. C Thomas 1959, 120 p
52322 The deprived and the indulged forms of psychopathic personality. In Karpman, B. *Symposia on Child and Juvenile Delinquency,* Wash: Psychodynamics Series 1959, 77-80
52323 Development and psychodynamic aspects of oppositional behavior. Chg Cpts Psa Med 114-134
S-20177 The hostile act. Under Hum Motiv 255-259
52324 Maternal feelings toward the newborn. In World Federation for Mental Health: *Mental Health in Home and School,* London: H. K. Lewis 1958
52325 A method of analyzing clinical observations of relational behavior. Curr App Psa 141-150
52326 Observational psychiatry: the early development of independent and oppositional behavior. In Grinker, R. R. *Mid-Century Psychiatry,* Springfield, Ill: C. C Thomas 1953, 113-121
52327 Oppositional syndromes and oppositional behavior. In Hoch, P. H. & Zubin, J. *Psychopathology of Childhood,* NY: Grune & Stratton 1955, 204-226
S-20192 Primary affect hunger. Under Hum Motiv 457-466
S-20203 Psychosomatic studies of some aspects of maternal behavior. Pers n s c 104-110
52328 The relation of animal psychology to psychiatry. In Galdston, I. *The New York Academy of Medicine. Medicine and Science.* NY: IUP 1954, 44-75

See Palmer, James O.

LEVY, E. Z.

52329 (& Ruff, G. E.; Thaler, V. H.) Studies in human isolation. JAMA 1959, 169:236-239

LEVY, ERWIN

52330 Some problems concerning ethics and the superego. PT 1956, 10:217-240

LEVY, JOHN

52331 (& Munroe, R.) Sexual satisfaction. In Linscott, R. N. & Stein, J. *Why You Do What You Do,* NY: Random House 1956, 139-148. From authors' *The Happy Family,* NY: Knopf 1938

LEVY, KATA

52332 Obituary: Dr. Endre Almásy. J 1956, 37:475
52333 Silence in the analytic session. J 1958, 39:50-58
    Abs JLan Q 1959, 28:107. Racamier RFPsa 1959, 23:153
52334 Simultaneous analysis of a mother and her adolescent daughter: the mother's contribution to the loosening of the infantile object tie. Psa St C 1960, 15:380-391

LEVY, LÁJOS

52335 Obituary: Istvan Hollos, 19 April 1872-2 February, 1957. J 1957, 38:280-281

REVIEW OF:
52336 Rehder, H. Konversion und Reversion klinischer Neurosen. J 1955, 36:399

LEVY, LEO B.

52337 Henry James' *Confidence* and the development of the idea of the unconscious. Amer Literature 1956, 28:347-358

LEVY, LEON H.

52338 Sexual symbolism: a validity study. J consult Psychol 1954, 18:43-46

LEVY, M.

See Sapir, M.

LEVY, NORMAN J.

52339 Anger, hate and jealousy. ACAAP pamphlet 1955
52340 El proceso neurotico. [The neurotic process.] Arch Neurol Psiquiat 1958, 8:54-62

LEVY, R.

See Lacan, Jacques M.

LEVY, RICHARD A.

See Levy, Sidney

LEVY, SIDNEY

52341 Case study of an adult: the case of Mr. P. In Hammer, E. F. *The Clinical Application of Projective Drawings*, Springfield, Ill: Thomas 1958, 135-161
52342 Projective figure drawing. In Hammer, E. F. *The Clinical Application of Projective Drawings*, Springfield, Ill: Thomas 1958, 83-112
52343 (& Levy, R. A.) Symbolism in animal drawings. In Hammer, E. F. *The Clinical Application of Projective Drawings*, Springfield, Ill: Thomas 1958, 311-343

See Sacks, Joseph

LÉVY-VALENSI, E. A.

52344 Aspects actuels, dans le champ de la psychopathologie, d'un vieux malentendu philosophique. [Practical aspects in the field of psychopathology of an old misunderstood philosophy.] Evolut psychiat 1957, (1):95-116

52345 L'échec du bon élève. [The honor student's failure.] Enfance 1954, 7:341-355

TRANSLATION OF:
Servadio, E. [59274]

LEWICKI, ANDRZEJ

52346 Zapominanie nazwisk; studium nad psychologicznymi podstawami uczenia sie i nauczania. [Forgetting of names; a study on the psychological foundations of learning and teaching.] Torun: Towarzystwo Naukowe 1950, 181 p

LEWIN, B.

See Lauber, H. L.

LEWIN, BERTRAM D.

52347 The analytic situation: topographic considerations. Q 1959, 28:455-469
52348 Ein Beitrag zum sensitiven Beziehungswahn bei Europäerinnen in Ägypten. [A contribution to "the sensitive delusion of reference" among European women in Egypt.] Z Psychother med Psychol 1956, 6:244-258
52349 Clinical hints from dream studies. BMC 1955, 19:73-85
Abs Racamier RFPsa 1956, 20:575. Rahman, L. Q 1956, 25:446
52350 Discussion of Kubie, L. S. "Some implications for psychoanalysis of modern concepts of the organization of the brain." Q 1953, 22:61-63
52351 Discussion of Loomie, L. S. et al: "Ernst Kris and the gifted adolescent project." Psa St C 1958, 13:58-60
52352 Dream psychology and the analytic situation. Q 1955, 24:169-199
Abs Dreyfus RFPsa 1956, 20:570. JKl J 1956, 37:202-203. Rv Weil, J. Rev Psicoanál 1957, 14:342-343
52353 Dreams and the Uses of Regression. NY: IUP 1958, 64 p
Abs J Am Psa Ass 1960, 8:220; 588. Rv Niederland, W. G. Q 1958, 27:574-575
52354 Education or the quest for omniscience. J Am Psa Ass 1958, 6:389-412
Abs TFr J 1959, 40:362-363. Shentoub RFPsa 1959, 23:435-438. TGS Q 1960, 29:430
52355 Edward Hitschmann—an appreciation. J Am Psa Ass 1955, 3:711-714
52356 Der Einfluss magischer und religiöser Vorstellungen auf die Pathoplastik reaktiver und endogener geistiger Störungen in Ägypten. [The influence of magic and religious concepts on symptom forms of reactive and endogenous mental disorders in Egypt.] Zschr Psychother 1956, 6:60-75
52357 The forgetting of dreams. Dr Af Beh 191-202
52358 Introduction to Ekstein, R. & Wallerstein, R. S. *The Teaching and Learning of Psychotherapy.*

52359 Introduction to Fenichel, O. *Collected Papers of Otto Fenichel.* NY: Norton 1953, vii-xii

S-20299 Phobic symptoms and dream interpretation. YBPsa 1953, 9:80-103
    Abs JFr An Surv Psa 1952, 3:113-117. CR J 1953, 34:354-355

52360 Problems of infantile neurosis. A discussion. Psa St C 1954, 9:44

S-20301 The Psychoanalysis of Elation.
    Psicoanálisis de la exaltación. (Tr: Remus Araico, J.) B. Aires: Edit Nova 1953, 189 p

52361 (& Ross, H.) Psychoanalytic Education in the United States. NY: Norton 1960, xviii + 478 p
    Rv Gitelson, M. Q 1960, 29:559-567

52362 Reconsideration of the dream screen. Q 1953, 22:174-199. YBPsa 1954, 10:193-213
    Abs Dreyfus RFPsa 1953, 17:532. JFr An Surv Psa 1953, 4:245-249. JKl J 1954, 35:440-441. Rev Psicoanál 1954, 11:388-389

52363 Sleep, narcissistic neuroses, and the analytic situation. Q 1954, 23:487-510
    Abs JFr An Surv Psa 1954, 5:90-92; 104; 215-216. NRo An Surv Psa 1954, 5:358-359. Dreyfus, L. RFPsa 1955, 19:507. JKl J 1955, 36:424-425

52364 Some psychoanalytic ideas applied to elation and depression. P 1959, 116:38-42
    Abs Loeb, L. Q 1960, 29:594

See Bunker, Henry Alden; Knight, Robert P.

TRANSLATION OF:
Anonymous [63271]

REVIEW OF:
52365 Roheim, G. The Gates of the Dream. Q 1954, 23:98-102

LEWIN, KARL KAY

52366 Psychosomatic research: problems in methodology. Ann intern Med 1959, 50:122-128

52367 Role of depression in the production of illness in pernicious anemia. PSM 1959, 21:23
    Abs Luchina, A. Rev Psicoanál 1959, 16:192-193

LEWINGER, N.

See Lacy, Osborne W.

LEWINSKY, HILDE

S-20352A The closed circle. An early image of sexual intercourse. (Read at NY Psa Soc, June 14, 1955; at 19th Int Psa Cong, Geneva, July 1955) J 1956, 37:290-297
    Abs Auth J 1956, 37:132. Moore, B. E. Q 1956, 25:302-304. JLan Q 1957, 26:574-575. Rv Morra Riv Psa 1957, 3:223-224

S-20353 Features from a case of homosexuality.
    Abs JFr An Surv Psa 1952, 3:178-180. Auth Rev Psicoanál 1953, 10:117. CR J 1953, 34:355

S-20357 Pathological generosity.
   Abs JFr An Surv Psa 1951, 2:210-211. MGr Q 1953, 22:296

LEWIS, A.

52368   La enfermedad obsesiva. [The obsessive illness.] Act Np Arg 1957,
        3:323-335

LEWIS, AUBREY

52369   Centenary tribute. Discovery 1956, 181-183
52370   Jung's early work. J anal Psych 1957, 2:119-136

LEWIS, CLAUDELINE P.

52371   The family-centered approach in a child development center. In
        National Conference on Social Welfare. Casework Papers, 1958, NY:
        Family Service Ass of Amer 1958, 114-131

LEWIS, CLIVE STAPLES

52372   Morality and psychoanalysis. In author's *Mere Christianity* (rev & enl
        ed), NY: Macmillan 1952, 69-73

LEWIS, HARVEY A.

52373   The effect of shedding the first deciduous tooth upon the passing of
        the Oedipus complex of the male. J Am Psa Ass 1958, 6:5-37
           Abs Shentoub RFPsa 1958, 23:141. TGS Q 1960, 29:424
52374   The unconscious castrative significance of tooth extraction. J Dent
        Child 1957, 3-16

LEWIS, HELEN BLOCK

52375   Organization of the self as reflected in manifest dreams. PPR 1959,
        46(2):21-35
52376   Over-differentiation and under-individuation of the self. PPR 1958,
        45(3):3-24

   See Witkin, Herman A.

LEWIS, HILDA

52377   Deprived Children, the Mersham Experiment, A Social and Clinical
        Study. London: Oxford Univ Pr 1954, 163 p

LEWIS, J. B. S.

52378   The psychiatrist, his patients, and the law. Med-leg J, Camb 1952,
        20:70-83

LEWIS, J. M.

52379   (& Osberg, J. W.) Observations on institutional treatment of character
        disorders. Workshop 1957: Treatment of the narcotic addict. Ops 1958,
        28:730-744
           Abs Koenig RFPsa 1959, 23:433

LEWIS, M. M.

S-20367 Infant Speech.
  Rv Mervis, S. J 1953, 34:168-170; Rev Psicoanál 1959, 15:160

LEWIS, MURRAY D.

52380 Experiences in teaching child psychiatry to fourth year medical students. J Med Educ 1956, 31:295-302

LEWIS, NOLAN D. C.

52381 American psychiatry from its beginnings to World War II. Am Hbk Psychiat 1:3-17

42382 (& Korkes, L.) Analysis of the relationship between psychological patterns and outcome in pulmonary tuberculosis. JNMD 1955, 122:524

52383 Chapter in Brings, L. D. *We Believe in the Value of Prayer*, Minneapolis: T. S. Dennison & Co. 1958

52384 (& Piotrowski, Z. A.) Clinical diagnosis of manic-depressive psychosis. In Hoch, P. H. & Zubin, J. *Depression*. NY: Grune & Stratton 1954, 25-38

52385 Comments on some aspects of the current (1953) research program of the New York State Psychiatric Institute. Psychiat Q 1953, 27:588-596

52386 Foreword to Barbara, D. A. *Your Speech Reveals Your Personality*.

52387 Foreword to Cassity, J. H. *Quality of Murder*, NY: Julian Pr 1958

52388 Foreword to Eisenstein, V. *Neurotic Interaction in Marriage*.

52389 Foreword to Kallmann, F. J. *Heredity in Health and Mental Disorder*, NY: W. W. Norton 1953

52390 Foreword to Meyer, A. *Psychobiology*, Springfield, Ill: Charles C Thomas 1957

52391 Foreword to Piotrowski, Z. *Percept-analysis*, NY: Macmillan 1957

52392 Foreword to Schneider, D. E. *Image of the Heart*

52393 Foreword to Yost, O. R. *What You Should Know about Mental Illness*.

52394 (& Landis, C.) Freud's library. R 1957, 44:327-354

52395 Historical roots of psychotherapy. P 1958, 114:795-799. Prog PT 1958, 3:20-26

52396 Impact of mentally ill children upon their families. J So Carolina Med Ass 1958, 54:322

S-20397 (& Pacella, B.) Modern Trends in Child Psychiatry.
  Rv Evelson, E. Rev Psicoanál 1958, 15:127-128

52397 Progress in psychiatry. J med Soc N Jersey 1956, 53:459-462

52398 Psychiatry. In Mackay, R. P. et al: *The Year Book of Neurology, Psychiatry, and Neurosurgery, 1952*. Chicago: Year Book Publ 1953, 205-405

52399 Psychiatry. In Mackay, R. P. et al: *The Year Book of Neurology, Psychiatry and Neurosurgery* (1953-1954 series). Chicago: Year Book Publ 1954, 211-381

52400 Psychiatry and the law. Chapter in *Proceedings of the Society of Medical Jurisprudence (1942-1950)*, 1954

52401 The reactions of adults in therapy. Workshop 1958: Indications and contraindications for adult therapy. Ops 1959, 29:69-74

52402   Review of the scientific contributions of Saint Elizabeths Hospital, 1855-1955. In Overholser, W. *Centennial Papers. Saint Elizabeth Hospital, 1855-1955,* Wash: Centennial Commission, Saint Elizabeth Hosp 1956, 25-35

52403   The role of self-image with respect to craving for alcohol. In Hoch, P. & Zubin, J. *Problems in Addiction and Habituation,* NY: Grune & Stratton 1958

52404   The scientific method in medicine. National Med J 1958

52405   (& Landis, C.; King, H. E.) (Eds) Studies in Topectomy. NY, London: Grune & Stratton 1956, viii + 248 p
        Rv ESt J 1958, 39:440

52406   (& Engle, B.) (Eds) Wartime Psychiatry; a Compendium of the International Literature. NY: Oxford Univ Pr 1954, vi + 952 p
        Rv MK Q 1955, 24:445-447

        See Gaudet, E. Louise; Hoch, Paul H.; Mackay, Roland P.; Piotrowski, Zygmunt A.

LEWIS, THEODORE N.

52407   Freud, the Jew and Judaism. Jewish Spectator, NY 1958, March: 11-14

LEWIS, THEOPHILUS

52408   Freud and the split-level drama. Catholic World 1958, 187:98-103

LEWIS, WILLIAM C.

52409   (& Lorenz, T. H.; Calden, G.) Irregular discharge from tuberculosis hospitals. PSM 1955, 17:270-290
        Abs Fain RFPsa 1956, 20:580-581

LEWY, E.

52410   On Micropsia. J 1954, 35:13-19
        Abs JFr An Surv Psa 1954, 5:129-130. JLan Q 1955, 24:460

LEYENDECKER, GERTRUDE T.

52411   Generic and specific factors in casework with the unmarried mother. In *Nat Conf on Soc Welfare, Casework Papers 1957,* NY: Fam Serv Ass of Amer 1957, 113-129

LEYS, DUNCAN

See Cameron, Kenneth

LHAMON, WILLIAM T.

See Appel, Kenneth E.; Loomis, Earl A., Jr.; Saul, Leon

LHERMITTE, JEAN

52412   Psychanalyse et médecine. Rapport au nom de la commission de la psychanalyse. [Psychoanalysis and medicine. Report from the Committee for Psychoanalysis.] Prog méd 1954, 82(23):483-484. Bull Acad Nat Med, Paris 1955, 139:65-66

LHOTSKY, J.

52413 Der Begriff "Prägung" in der vergleichend-analytischen Psychologie. [The concept of "imprinting" in comparative-analytic psychology.] B Sexfschg 1955, (6):57-67

52414 Gespräche mit dem Unbewussten; die Fortpflanzungstriebe und die Auslösermechanismen im Lichte der vergleichend-analytischen Psychologie. [Conversations with the unconscious; the procreative drive and its release mechanisms in the light of comparative-analytical psychology.] Nervenarzt 1953, 24:217-218

52415 Gespräche mit dem Unbewussten. Versuch einer Deutung im Sinne der vergleichend-analytischen Psychologie. [Conversations with the unconscious. An attempt at interpretation along the lines of comparative analytic psychology.] MMW 1952, 94:1857-1864

LIBERMAN, D.

52416 Acerca de la perceptión del tiempo. [Time perception.] Rev Psicoanál 1955, 12:370-375

52417 Actuación y realización en las relaciones humanas entre analistas. [Actuality and reality in the human relations between analysts.] Rev Psicoanál 1959, 16:423-431

52418 Autismo transferencial. Narcisismo: el mito de Eco y Narciso. [Transferential autism. Narcissism: the myth of Echo and Narcissus.] Rev Psicoanál 1958, 15:369-385
Abs Vega Q 1959, 28:436

52419 Cefaleas a raíz del fracaso por superar una fijación. [Headaches owing to failure in overcoming a fixation.] Rev Psicoanál 1954, 11:93-109
Abs JFr An Surv Psa 1954, 5:146. Vega Q 1956, 25:132

52420 Los efectos del conflicto matrimonial en el desarrollo del niño inferidos de la situación analítica. [The effects of matrimonial conflict upon the development of the child, as inferred from the analytic situation.] Rev Psicoanál 1958, 15:91-97
Abs Vega Q 1959, 28:435-436

52421 Fobia a la "Descompostura." ["Untidiness" phobia.] Rev Psicoanál 1956, 13:440

S-20614 Fragmento del análisis de una psicosis paranoide.
Abs JFr An Surv Psa 1952, 3:144-146. Vega Q 1954, 23:476-477

S-20615 Génesis de las elecciones de objeto en un homosexual.
Abs JFr An Surv Psa 1951, 2:214-217

52422 Humorismo en la transferencia e instinto de muerte, en un paciente obeso. [Humor in the transference and death instinct in an obese patient.] Rev Psicoanál 1957, 14:292-306
Abs Vega Q 1958, 27:453

52423 Identificación proyectiva y conflicto matrimonial. [Projective identification and matrimonial conflict.] Rev Psicoanál 1956, 13:1-20
Abs Vega Q 1957, 26:293-294

52424 Interpretación correlativa entre relato y repetición: su aplicación en una paciente con personalidad esquizoide. [Correlative interpretation between spoken material and repetition; its application to a patient with a schizoid personality.] Rev Psicoanál 1957, 14:55-62

52425 Reactivación del complejo de Edipo durante la evolución de un obeso. (Resumen). [Reactivation of the Oedipus complex during the change of an obese man. (Summary).] Rev Psicoanál 1955, 12:441

52426 Una sesión psicoanalitica de un paciente esquizofrénico. [A psychoanalytic session of a schizophrenic patient.] Rev Psicoanál 1953, 10:312

See Gioia, Gina; Zak, J.

REVIEWS OF:

52427 Brenner, C. et al: Psychological factors in the etiology and treatment of chronic headache. Rev Psicoanál 1954, 11:256

52428 Ferenzi, S. Sonntagsneurosen. Rev Psicoanál 1954, 11:246-247

52429 Grinker, R. R. & Gottschalk, L. Headaches and muscular pains. Rev Psicoanál 1954, 11:257-258

52430 Pichon-Rivière, E. Estudio psicoanalítico de la jaqueca. Rev Psicoanál 1954, 11:253

52431 Touraine, G. A. & Draper, G. The migrainous patient. Rev Psicoanál 1954, 11:235

52432 Wexler, M. The structural problem in schizophrenia. Rev Psicoanál 1953, 10:121-123

LICHTENBERG, JOSEPH D.

52433 Prognostic implications of the inability to tolerate failure in schizophrenic patients. Ps 1957, 20:365-371

LICHTENBERG, PHILIP

52434 Definition and analysis of depression. AMA ANP 1957, 77:519-527

52435 (& Kohrman, R.; MacGregor, H.) Motivation for Child Psychiatry Treatment. (Pref: Grinker, R. R.) NY: Russell & Russell 1960, 220 p

LICHTENSTEIN LUZ, C. S.

52436 A hipnose como auxiliar da psicoterapia. [Hypnosis as a tool in psychotherapy.] Rev Psicol norm patol 1958, 4:444-449

LIDDELL, D. W.

See Berrington, W. P.

LÌDDELL, HOWARD S.

52437 A biological basis for psychopathology. In Hoch, P. H. & Zubin, J. *Problems of Addiction and Habituation*, NY, London: Grune & Stratton 1958, 94-109

52438 The biology of wishes and worries. In Grinker, R. R. *Mid-Century Psychiatry*, Springfield, Ill: Thomas 1953, 104-112

52439 Emotional Hazards in Animals and Man. Springfield, Ill: Thomas 1956, xi + 97 p
       Rv Piotrowski, Z. A. R 1957, 44:229-230

52440 Obituary: Dr. Frieda Fromm-Reichmann. Curr App Psa xii

LIDZ, THEODORE

52441 Areas of interdoctrinal unacceptance. A psychodynamicist speaks. In Kruse, H. D. *Integrating the Approaches to Mental Disease*, NY: Hoeber-Harper 1957, 56-58

52442 Chronic situations evoking psychological stress and the common signs of the resulting strain. *Symposium on Stress.* Walter Reed Army Med Center 1953, 116-123

52443 Contributions in Calderone, M. S. *Abortion in the United States*, NY: Hoeber-Harper 1958, 125-128; 165-166

52444 Diabetes Mellitus. In Wittkower, E. D. & Cleghorn, R. A. *Recent Advances in Psychosomatic Medicine*, London: Sir Issac Pitman & Sons; NY: Lippincott 1954, 201-210

52445 (& Schafer, S.; Fleck, S.; Cornelison, A. R.; Terry, D.) Zur Differenzierung der Persönlichkeit und Symptome bei eineiigen Zwillingen. [Differentiation of personality and symptoms in identical twins.] Psyche, Heidel 1959, 13:345-364

52446 Discussion of Kubie, L. S. "Some unsolved problems of psychoanalytic psychotherapy." Prog PT 1956, 1:102-107

S-20625A (et al) Effects of CTH and cortisone on mood and mentation. Abs VC Q 1953, 22:616

52447 Emotional factors in the etiology of hyperthyroidism occurring in relation to pregnancy; summary of eleven cases. PSM 1955, 17:420-427
Abs Fain RFPsa 1956, 20:582. EFA Q 1957, 26:291

52448 Emotional factors in the etiology and therapy of hyperthyroidism. J Mt Sinai Hosp 1953, 20:27-40

52449 (& Rosen, H.) Emotional factors in the precipitation of recurrent diabetic acidosis. PSM 1949, 11:211-215

52450 Etiology of toxic diffuse goiter: emotional factors. In Werner, S. C. *The Thyroid Gland*, NY: Hoeber-Harper 1955

52451 Zur Familienumwelt des Schizophrenen. [The familial environment of the schizophrenic.] Psyche, Heidel 1959, 13:243-395

* * * (& Cornelison, A. R.; Fleck, S.; Terry, D.) The father in the intrafamilial environment of the schizophrenic patient. See [52455]

52452 General concepts of psychosomatic medicine. Am Hbk Psychiat 1:647-658

52453 Hypothyroidism: emotional factors in etiology of hypothyroid states. In Werner, S. C. *The Thyroid Gland*, NY: Hoeber-Harper 1955, 658

52454 Hyperthyroidism: emotions and mentation. In Werner, S. C. *The Thyroid Gland*, NY: Hoeber-Harper 1955, 572-575; 702-705

52455 (& Cornelison, A. R.; Fleck, S.; Terry, D.) The intrafamilial environment of the schizophrenic: I. The father. Ps 1957, 20:329-342. Adv Psychiat 180-206
Die intrafamiliäre Umwelt des Schizophrenen: Der Vater. Psyche, Heidel 1959, 13:268-286

52456 (& Cornelison, A. et al) The intrafamilial environment of the schizophrenic patient. II. Interaction between hospital staff and families. Ps 1957, 20:343-350

52457 (& Cornelison, A.; Fleck, S.; Terry, D.) The intrafamilial environment of schizophrenic patients. III. Marital schism and marital skew. P 1957, 114:241-248.

Spaltung und Strukturverschiebung in der Ehe. (Tr: Vogel, H.) Psyche 1959, 13:287-300

52458   (& Fleck, S.; Cornelison, A.; Terry, D.) The intrafamilial environment of the schizophrenic patient: IV. Parental personalities and family interaction. Ops 1958, 28:764-776

Elternpersönlichkeiten und Wechselbeziehungen in der Familie. Psyche, Heidel 1959, 13:301-314

Abs Dreyfus RFPsa 1959, 23:433-434

52459   (& Cornelison, A.; Terry, D.; Fleck, S.) Intrafamilial environment of the schizophrenic patient: VI. The transmission of irrationality. AMA ANP 1958, 79:305-316. (Abs) Cong Report of 2nd Int Cong Psychiat Zurich 1957, 4:37-39

Irrationalität als Familientradition. (Tr: Vogel, H.) Psyche, Heidel 1959, 13:315-329

S-20629 (& Whitehorn, J. C.) Life situations, emotions and Graves' disease. Res Publ Ass nerv ment Dis 1949, 29:445-450

52460   Nightmares and the combat neuroses. Ps 1946, 9:37-49

52461   The 1951 Ithaca Conference on psychiatry in medical education. J med Educ 1955, 30:689-697

52462   (& Carmichael, H. T.; Bandler, B.; Gregg, A.; Heath, R. G.; Jensen, R. A.; Luton, F.; Romano, J.; Rosenbaum, M.; Stokes, A. B.; Waggoner, R. W.) An outline of a curriculum for teaching psychiatry in medical schools. J med Educ 1956, 31:115-128

52463   Participant in symposium. In Kruse, H. D. *Integrating the Approaches to Mental Disease*, NY: Hoeber-Harper 1957, 160-383

52464   (& Greenblatt, M.; Hotchkiss, G.) Patient-family-hospital interrelations, some general considerations. In Greenblatt, M. & Hotchkiss, G. *The Hospital as a Social System*, Boston 1955

52465   Principles and techniques of therapy in psychosomatic disorders. Res Publ Ass nerv ment Dis 1953 (Proc 1951), 31:156-159

52466   (& Whitehorn, J. C.) Psychiatric problems in a thyroid clinic. JAMA 1949, 139:699-701

52467   (& Rubenstein, R.) Psychology of gastrointestinal disorders. Am Hbk Psychiat 1:678-689

52468   Reflections of a psychiatrist. In Rosen, H. *Therapeutic Abortion*, NY: Julian Pr 1954, 276-283

52469   (& Parker, B.; Cornelison, A.) The role of the father in the family environment of the schizophrenic patient. P 1956, 113:126-132

Abs DRub Q 1959, 28:124-125

52470   Schizophrenia and the family. Ps 1958, 21:21-27. (Abs) Report 2nd Int Cong Psychiatry, Zurich 1957, 4:196-197

Schizophrenie und Familie. Psyche, Heidel 1959, 13:257-267

Abs HRB Q 1959, 28:428

52471   (& Fleck, S.) Schizophrenia, human integration, and the role of the family. In Jackson, D. D. *The Etiology of Schizophrenia*, NY: Basic Books 1960, 323-345

52472   (& Greenblatt, M.) Some dimensions of the problem. In Greenblatt, M. & Hotchkiss, G. *The Hospital as a Social System*. Boston 1955

52473 The thyroid. In Wittkower, E. D. & Cleghorn, R. A. *Recent Advances in Psychosomatic Medicine,* London: Sir Isaac Pitman & Sons; NY: Lippincott 1954, 190-200

See Brosin, Henry; Fleck, Stephen; Rubenstein, R.; Sohler, Dorothy Terry

LIEBERMAN, MORTON A.

52474 (& Stock, D.: Whitman, R. M.) Self-perceptual patterns among ulcer patients. Arch gen Psychiat 1959, 1:267-276
Abs KRu Q 1960, 29:439-440

See Whitman, Roy M.

LIEBERMAN, SOLOMON S.

52474A The relationship of eye-hand dominance and fantasies in boys. Diss Abs 1954, 14:1620-1621

LIEBERMANN, LUCY P.

52475 (& Erdös, Z.) Les aspects psychologiques de la meningite tuberculeuse infantile traité par streptomycine. [The psychological aspects of tuberculous meningitis in children treated with streptomycin.] Rev Psychiatrie infantile 1959, 26:141-148
52476 Csoporttherápia a nevelési tanácsadásban. Gyermekgyogyászat 1956, (10):289-297
Joint interview technique: an experiment in group therapy. M 1957, 30:202-207
52477 (& Farago) Über Erscheinungsbild und Persönlichkeitsart von Suchtkranken. [Symptoms and personality of drug addicts.] Ann Np Psa 1957, 4:120-162
52478 (& Majláth) Fiatal anyagyilkos esete. [Case of a juvenile murderer.] Psychologiai Tanulmányok, vol 2, Hung Academy Sci 1959
52479 Gyermekkeri lepás esete. [A case of stealing.] Gyermekgyógyászat, Budapest 1953, (8):1-3
52480 Laterális dominantia. A balkezesség problémája. [Lateral dominance. The problem of left-handedness.] Gyermekgyogyászat 1954, (10):106-116
52481 Nevelési tanácsado esetek. [Child guidance cases.] Gyermekgyógyászat 1956, 4:105-107
52482 A nevelési tanácsadó tecznika problémii. [The problems of child guidance technique.] In *Psychologiai Tanulmányok kótete.* [Psychological Essays, Vol 1] Hung Academy of Sci 1958
52483 Pediatric concepts in child psychology. Acta Medica, Hung Academy of Sci 1959, 12
52484 A Rorschach-teszt grafikus ábrázolási médszere. [Graphic method of representation in the Rorschach test.] In Psychologiai Tanulmányok, Vol. II. Hung Academy of Sci 1959
52485 Three cases of attempted suicide in children. M 1953, 26:110-114
Abs R 1955, 42:209

LIEBMAN, SAMUEL

52486 (Ed) Emotional Problems of Childhood. Phila: Lippincott 1958,
viii + 176 p
52487 (Ed) Management of Emotional Problems in Medical Practice. Phila:
Lippincott 1956, vii + 152 p
52488 (Ed) Stress Situations. Phila: Lippincott 1955, 144 p
52489 (Ed) Understanding Your Patient. Phila: Lippincott 1957, 170 p

LIEF, HAROLD I.

52490 The effects of taraxein on a patient in analysis. AMA ANP 1957, 78:
624-627
52491 (& Browne, D. C.; Bargen, J. A.; Neefe, J. R.; McGlone, F. B.) On
functional disturbances of the gastrointestinal tract. Panel discussion.
Am J Gastroenterology 1959, 32:265-290
52492 The pediatrician's role in handling parental reactions to the sudden
death of a child. Bull Tulane Med Faculty 1952, 11:208-212
52493 Psychiatry and the law. Tulane Law Rev 1955, 29:819-822
52494 (& Stevenson, I. P.) Psychological aspects of prejudice with special
reference to desegregation. P 1958, 114:816-823
52495 Psychosomatic aspects of certain gastrointestinal diseases (special editor of symposium issue). J Digest Diseases 1958, 3(4)
52496 Sensory association in the selection of phobic objects. Ps 1955, 18:331-
338
52497 Should patients be presented in person? R 1956, 43:57-67
Abs JLan Q 1957, 26:436
52498 Some diagnostic errors in patients with a psychiatric label. Southern
Med J 1954, 47:756-761

See Millet, John A. P.; Rohrer, John H.

LIETAERT PEERBOLTE, MAARTEN

52499 The Orgastical Experience of Space and Metapsychologic Psychagogy;
An Outline of Practical Mental and Social Hygiene. Leiden: A. W.
Sijthoff 1955, 150 p
52500 Psychotherapeutic evaluations of birth-trauma analysis. A preliminary
contribution to Fodor's therapy. Psychiat Q 1951, 25:589-603
52501 Some problems connected with Fodor's birth-trauma therapy. Psychiat
Q 1952, 26:294-306

LIFSCHULTZ, JOSEPH EMANUEL

52502 Hysterical stigmatization. P 1957, 114:527-531

LIFTON, WALTER M.

52503 The implications of a study of empathy and aesthetic sensitivity for
art education. In 1959 Research Yearbook of the National Art Education Association
52504 The role of empathy and aesthetic sensitivity in counseling. J counsel
Psychol 1958, 5

52505 A study of amputee acceptance of prosthetic devices. J Physical and Mental Rehabil 1950, Feb-Mar, 17-19

52506 The teacher's role in mental hygiene, therapy, and social reconstruction. Progressive Educ 1955, May, 65-69

LIGHT, BERNARD H.

52507 The enigma of transference resistance in psychotherapy. Proc W Va Acad Sci 1954, 26:77-80

See Mowrer, O. Hobart

LIGNIERE, JEAN

52508 Françoise Sagan et le succès. [Françoise Sagan and success.] Paris: Edit du Scorpion 1957, 185 p

52509 Mademoiselle Narcisse. [Miss Narcisse.] Paris: Edit de la Table Ronde 1953, 315 p

LILIENFELD, ALFRED M.

See Pasamanick, Benjamin; Thomas, Alexander

LILLY, JOHN C.

52510 An anxiety dream of an 8-year-old boy and its resolution. Bull Phila Ass Psa 1955, 5:20-23

52511 Critical discussion of research project and results at conference in June 1952 by Dr. Robert G. Heath and Research group at Tulane University. In Heath, R. G. et al: *Studies in Schizophrenia: A Multidisciplinary Approach to Mind-Brain Relationships,* Cambridge, Mass: Harvard Univ Pr 1954, 528-532

52512 Discussion of Kubie, L. S. "Some implications for psychoanalysis of modern concepts of the organization of the brain." Q 1953, 22:63-64

52513 The psychophysiological basis for two kinds of instincts. Implications for psychoanalytic theory. J Am Psa Ass 1960, 8:659-670

52514 Rewarding and punishing systems in the brain. In *Central Nervous System and Behavior 1959.* First Conf, Josiah Macy Jr Found, Princeton, N J, 23-26 Feb 1958, 268-277

52515 Some considerations regarding basic mechanisms of positive and negative types of motivations. P 1958, 115:498-504

LIMENTANI, A.

REVIEW OF:
52516 Sullivan, H. S. Conceptions of Modern Psychiatry: the First William Alanson White Memorial Lectures. J 1957, 38:367

LIMENTANI, DAVIDE

52517 Symbiotic identification in schizophrenia. Ps 1956, 19:231-236

LINCKE, HAROLD

52518 Über Angstlust und infantile Sexualität. [Anxiety pleasure and infantile sexuality.] Psyche, Heidel 1954, 8:427-449
       Abs NRo An Surv Psa 1954, 5:50-52

52519   Bemerkungen zur Triebpsychologie der Ersatzbefriedigung und Sub-
         limierung. [Remarks on the drive psychology of substitute gratification
         and sublimation.] Psyche, Heidel 1953, 7:501-520
            Abs LRa An Surv Psa 1953, 4:32-34
52520   Einige Bemerkungen zur Triebentwicklung. [Some observations on the
         development of drives.] Psyche, Heidel 1957, 11:353-373
52521   Einige ergänzende Bemerkungen zu den Übersprungbewegungen des
         Menschen. [Some additional remarks concerning movements of shifting
         emphasis in humans.] Schweiz ANP 1955, 75:119-131

LINCOFF, HARVEY A.

52522   (& Ennis, J.) Differential diagnosis of hysteria and malingering in func-
         tional amblyopia: report of a case. Am J Ophthalmology 1956, 42:415-
         421

LINDBÄCK, ERLAND

52523   Gustaf Fröding. Temperamentsstudie och Diktanalys. [Gustaf Fröding.
         A Study of His Personality and a Poetic Analysis.] Stockholm: Svenska
         Bokförlaget—Norstedts 1957, 408 p
52524   Ida Bäckmann rehabiliterad. Pedagogisk-psykiatrisk kommentar till
         en bok om Fröding. [Ida Bäckmann rehabilitated. Pedagogic-psychi-
         atric comments to a treatise on Fröding. Germund Michanek, Fröding
         och Ida Bäckmann. Stockholm: 1955] Tidning för Sveriges läroverk
         1956, 56:80-81
52525   Krusentjerna-porträttet. Modern psykologi i akademisk tillämpning.
         Kommentar till en avhandling. [The Krusentjerna portrait. Modern psy-
         chology in academic application.] Tidning för sveriges läroverk 1952,
         52:150
52526   Sigmund Freud—profet och pedagog. Till minnet av hans födelse den
         6 maj 1856. [Sigmund Freud—a prophet and a pedagogue. In memory
         of his birth on the 6th of May 1856.] Tidning för sveriges läroverk
         1956, 56:364-365
52527   Studie över Frödings alkoholism. [A study of Fröding's alcohol addic-
         tion.] Pedagogisk tidskrift 1959, 95 (3/4)
52528   Thomas Manns budskap till ungdomen. Referat och kommentar.
         [Thomas Mann's appeal to the youth. Report and comments.] Tidning
         för sveriges läroverk 1955, 55:624-626
52529   Ungdomsvård i folkhemmet. Kommentar till Ungdomsvårdskommitténs
         slutbetänkande 1951. [Youth guidance in the Swedish welfare state.
         Comments on the result of the official research with suggestions of the
         Juvenile Care Committee 1951.] Tidning för sveriges läroverk 1952,
         52:548-552; 582-583

LINDEMANN, ELIZABETH

52530   (& Ross, A.) A follow-up study of a predictive test of social adaptation
         in preschool children. Emot Prob Early Child 79-93

LINDEMANN, ERICH

52531   Brief psychotherapy of a patient with headache and endometriosis. Am
         J Med 1956, 20:286-291

52532 Discussion of Ackerman, N. W. "Interlocking pathology in family relationships" and Marcus, I. M. "A family study unit." Chg Cpts Psa Med 162-164

52533 (& Mendelson, J.; Solomon, P.) Hallucinations of poliomyelitis patients during treatment in a tank type respirator. JNMD 1958, 126:421-428

52534 Interprofessional relationships. Ann NY Acad Sci 1955, 63:338-340

52535 The meaning of crisis in individual and family living. Teach Coll Rec 1956, 57:310-315

52536 The medical psychological dynamics of the gamut of normal experiences of the normal individual. In Galdston, I. *Ministry and Medicine in Human Relations,* NY: IUP 1955, 16-32

52537 The medical-psychological dynamics of the normal individual. Pastoral Psychol 1956, 7(62):47-56

52538 Mental Health—Fundamental to a Dynamic Epidemiology of Health. In *Epidemiology of Health,* NY: Health Education Council 1953, 109-124

S-20714 (& Clarke, L. D.) Modifications in ego structure and personality reactions under the influence of the effects of drugs.
Abs NRo An Surv Psa 1952, 3:292-293

52539 The nature of mental health work as a professional pursuit. In Strother, C. R. *Psychology and Mental Health,* Wash, DC: Am Psychological Ass 1957, 136-145

52540 Participant in symposium. In Kruse, H. D. *Integrating the Approaches to Mental Disease,* Hoeber-Harper 1957, 160-383

52541 (& Vaughan, W. T., Jr.; McGinnis, M.) Preventive intervention in a four-year-old child whose father committed suicide. Emot Prob Early Child 5-30

52542 Problems related to grandparents. In Liebman, S. *Understanding Your Patient,* Phila: Lippincott 1957, 147-158

52543 The psychosocial position on etiology. In Kruse, H. D. *Integrating the Approaches to Mental Disease,* NY: Hoeber-Harper 1957, 34-39

52544 (& Greer, I. M.) A study of grief: emotional responses to suicide. Pastoral Psychol 1953, Dec:9-13

S-20719 (& Dawes, L. G.) The use of psychoanalytic constructs in preventive psychiatry.
Abs NRo An Surv Psa 1952, 3:285-288. WH J 1953, 34:282

52545 The Wellesley Project for the study of certain problems in community mental health. In *Interrelations between the Social Environment and Psychiatric Disorders,* NY: Milbank Memorial Fund 1953, 167-186

LINDEN, MAURICE E.

52546 Geriatrics. Child-Fam Dig 1957, 16(3):46-61; (4):28-39. In Slavson, S. R. *Fields of Group Psychotherapy,* NY: IUP 1956, 129-152

52547 Group psychotherapy with institutionalized senile women: study in gerontologic human relations. Int J grp PT 1953, 3:150-170
Abs GPK Q 1955, 24:160

52548 The significance of dual leadership in gerontologic group psychotherapy: studies in gerontologic human relations III. Int J grp PT 1954, 4:262-273
Abs GPK Q 1955, 24:622

52549 Transference in gerontologic group psychotherapy: studies in ger-
       ontological human relations IV. Int J grp PT 1955, 5:61-79
           Abs GPK Q 1956, 25:453

       REVIEW OF:
52550 Colby, K. M. Energy and Structure in Psychoanalysis. Bull Phila Ass
       Psa 1957, 7:140-144

LINDGREN, HENRY CLAY

52551 The Art of Human Relations. NY: Hermitage House 1953, 287 p
52552 How to Understand Yourself and Other People. London: Rider & Co,
       Hutchinson House, Stratford Place 1954, 223 p
52553 Meaning: Antidote to Anxiety. NY: Thomas Nelson 1956, 271 p
52554 Psychology of Personal and Social Adjustment. NY: Amer Book Co
       1953, 481 p; 1959, 534 + ix p

LINDNER, HAROLD

52555 The Blacky Pictures test: a study of sexual and non-sexual offenders. J
       proj Tech 1953, 17:79-84
52556 Jack Rabbit: a study in character disturbance. Clin Stud Pers 290-306
52557 Perceptual sensitization to sexual phenomena in the chronic physically
       handicapped. Clin Psych 1953, 9:67-68
52558 Psychology of the adult criminal. In Dudycha, G. J. et al: *Psychology
       for Law Enforcement Officers*, Springfield, Ill: C. C Thomas; Oxford:
       Blackwell 1955, 272-294
52559 The work of court and prison psychologists. In Dudycha, G. J. et al:
       Psychology for Law Enforcement Officers, Springfield, Ill: C. C Thomas;
       Oxford: Blackwell 1955, 348-370

LINDNER, ROBERT MITCHELL

52560 Adolescents in mutiny. Pocket Book Mag 1955, Nov: No. 3
52561 Adultery—kinds and consequences as seen by a psychoanalyst. In
       Ellis, A. *Sex Life of the American Woman and the Kinsey Report*, NY:
       Greenberg 1954, 45-58
52562 Challenge for psychiatry. NY Gazette and Daily, York, Penna 1955,
       Apr 21
52563 The clinical uses of content analysis in Rorschach testing. NPAP 1955,
       3(3):12-17
52564 (Ed) Contemporary Criminal Hygiene. Baltimore: Oakridge Pr 1946
52565 Crime and criminals: a modern view. J Public Law 1955, Spring
52566 Crime and the child. Focus—National Probation & Parole Assn 1948,
       Sept
52567 Experimental studies in constitutional psychopathic inferiority. J crim
       Psychopathol 1942, 4(2); 1943, 4(3)
52568 (Ed) Explorations in Psychoanalysis; Essays in Honor of Theodor
       Reik, on the Occasion of His Sixty-fifth Birthday, May 12, 1953. NY:
       Julian Pr 1953, xiii + 308 p
52569 The Fifty-Minute Hour: A Collection of True Psychoanalytic Tales.
       (Introd: Lerner, M.) NY: Rinehart 1955; Toronto: Clarke, Irwin 1955,.

xvii + 293 p. With title: The Jet-Propelled Couch. London: Secker &
Warburg 1955
   Rv Schendler, D. NPAP 1955, 3(3):69
52570   Foreword and dedication. Expl Psa vii-viii
52571   (& Bently, M.) A functional and dynasomatic study of emoving. AJP
        1939, 52:186-209
* * *   The girl who couldn't stop eating. See [52591]
52572   Homeostasis as an explanatory principle in psychopathic personality.
        Proc 72nd Ann Cong of Correction of Amer Prison Assn. NY: Amer
        Prison Assn 1942
52573   Hypnoanalysis as a psychotherapeutic technique. Brit J med Hypnot
        1956, 7(3):2-12
* * *   The Jet-Propelled Couch. See [The Fifty-Minute Hour]
52574   The jet-propelled couch. Harper's 1954, Dec. From author's *The Fifty-
        Minute Hour*
52575   The jury system—good riddance. US Crime 1952, No 3, Feb
52576   Listen to a convict. Everybody's Digest 1946, August
52577   The meaning of punishment. J soc ment Ther 1955, 1:160-167
52578   Must You Conform? NY: Rinehart; Toronto: Clarke, Irwin 1956,
        xiii + 210 p
52579   Our mutinous young. Pocket Book Mag 1955, Oct: No 3
52580   Political creed and character. NPAP 1953, 2(2):10-33
52581   A postscript to *Stone Walls and Men.* The Prison World 1946, 8(1)
52582   Practical mental hygiene for the prisoner. Fed Probation 1946, 10(2)
52583   Predictions for 2001 A. D. Amazing 1956, Apr
52584   Prescription for Rebellion. NY: Rinehart; Toronto: Clarke, Irwin 1952
52585   The psychiatrist who caught his patient's craze. Liberty 1956, Dec
52586   Psychiatry challenges the law. U S Crime 1951, No 1, Dec
52587   Psychoanalysis in 2001 A. D. In *Psychoanalysis and the Future*, NY:
        Nat'l Psychol Ass for Psa 1957, 143-144
52588   The psychodynamics of gambling. Ann Amer Acad Polit Soc Sci 1950,
        May. Expl Psa 197-217
52589   Raise your child to be a rebel. McCall's Mag 1956, Feb
S-20731 Rebel Without a Cause. The Hypnoanalysis of a Criminal Psychopath.
        (Introd: Glueck, S. & Glueck, E. T.) NY: Grove Pr 1956, 296 p
52590   Sexual behavior in penal institutions. In Deutsch, A. *Sex Habits of
        American Men—A Symposium on the Kinsey Report*, NY: Prentice Hall
        1948
52591   Solitaire: Laura. From author's *The Fifty-Minute Hour*. In Freeman, L.
        Troubled Women, Cleveland: World Pub Co. 1959, 165-198. With
        title: The girl who couldn't stop eating. In Greenwald, H. *Great Cases
        in Psychoanalysis*, NY: Ballentine 1959, 107-151
52592   Stone Walls and Men. NY: Odyssey Pr 1946
S-20733 Who shall practice psychotherapy? PT 1950, 4(3):432-456
52593   Youth and conformity. Food for Thought 1955, 15(6)

LINDON, JOHN ARNOLD

52594   Castrophilia as a character neurosis. J 1958, 39:525-534
           Abs HW Q 1960, 29:131

LINDSAY, JOHN S. B.

52596   Abreaction and dreams. M 1953, 26:36-48
          Abs JFr An Surv Psa 1953, 4:254-256
52597   Nightmares. M 1954, 27:224-234
          Abs EMW Q 1956, 25:127

LINDSAY, S.

See Davidson, Audrey

LINDSAY, S. F.

REVIEWS OF:
52598   Baynes, H. G. Mythology of the Soul. J 1956, 37:495-496
52599   Huxley, A. Heaven and Hell. J 1956, 37:502-503
52600   Klein, M. & Riviere, J. Love, Hate and Reparation. J 1955, 36:138

LINDSTROM, CARL E.

52601   Dr. Kinsey and the press. Best Articles & Stories 1958, 2(2):27-29

LINDT, HENDRIK

52602   The nature of therapeutic interaction of patients in groups. Int J grp
          PT 1958, 8:55-69
          Abs GPK Q 1959, 28:431
52603   The "rescue fantasy" in group treatment of alcoholics. Int J grp PT
          1959, 9:43-52
S-20749 (& Sherman, M. A.) "Social incognito" in analytically oriented group
          psychotherapy.
          Abs GPK Q 1953, 22:308

LINDZEY, GARDNER

52604   (Ed) Assessment of Human Motives. NY: Rinehart 1958, 273 p
          Abs J Am Psa Ass 1960, 8:605. Rv Posinsky, S. H. Q 1959, 28:102-
          103
52605   The assessment of human motives. In author's *Assessment of Human
          Motives*, 3-32
52606   On the classification of projective techniques. Psychol Bull 1959, 56:
          158-168
52607   Hypothetical constructs, conventional constructs, and the use of
          physiological data in psychological theory. Ps 1953, 16:27-33
52608   (& Hall, C. S.) Psychoanalytic theory and its application in the social
          sciences. In author's *Handbook of Social Psychology*, Cambridge,
          Mass: Addison-Wesley 1954, 1:143-180
52609   (& Tejessy, C.) Thematic apperception test: indices of aggression in
          relation to measures of overt and covert behavior. Ops 1956, 26:567-
          576

          See Hall, Calvin S.

LINE, WILLIAM

S-20753A Anxiety and guilt in the modern community.
          Abs R 1953, 40:74-75

LINN, LOUIS

52610 The boundary line between psychiatry and religion. Judaism Psychiat 177-181

52611 Characteristics of the aged, ill and handicapped: mentally ill. Proc 2nd Hosp Recreat Inst, Nat Recreat Assn, Jan 1956, 17-28

52612 Color in dreams. J Am Psa Ass 1954, 2:462-465
Abs JFr An Surv Psa 1954, 5:218. TFr J 1955, 36:427. Shorr, J. Q 1957, 26:136

52613 The discriminating function of the ego. Q 1954, 23:38-47
Abs NRo An Surv Psa 1954, 5:41-43. JKl J 1955, 36:421-422. Rev Psicoanál 1955, 12:306

52614 Early recognition and management of psychiatric disorders in general practice. J Mt Sinai Hosp 1958, 25:Mar-Apr

52615 (& Strauss, H.; Ostow, M.) Electroencephalographic and neuropsychiatric observations in patients with senile cataract. Monthly Rev Psychiat Neurol 1955, 130:321-327

52616 (& Weinstein, E. A.; Kahn, R. L.) Encephalitis with a clinical picture of schizophrenia. J Mt Sinai Hosp 1955, 21:345

52617 A Handbook of Hospital Psychiatry. A Practical Guide to Therapy. NY: IUP 1955, 560 p
Abs J Am Psa Ass 1956, 4:184. Rv Overholser, W. Q 1956, 25:437. ESt J 1956, 37:496

52618 Hospital psychiatry. Am Hbk Psychiat 2:1829-1839

52619 The need to believe. Judaism Psychiat 129-134

52620 (& Kahn, R. L; Coles, R.; Cohen, J.; Marshall, D.; Weinstein, E. A.) Patterns of behavior disturbance following cataract extraction. P 1953, 110:281-289

52621 (& Kahn, R. L.; Weinstein, E. A.) Personality factors influencing the Rorschach response in organic brain disease. AMA ANP 1956, 76:226-227

52622 Psychiatric aspects of plastic surgery. In Bellak, L. *Psychology of Physical Illness,* NY: Grune & Stratton 1952

52623 (& Schwarz, L. W.) Psychiatry and Religious Experience. NY: Random House 1958, 307 p

52624 Psychoanalytic contributions to psychosomatic research. PSM 1958, 20:88-98
Abs Afterman, J. Q 1959, 28:130

52625 Psychological implication of the "activating system." P 1953, 110:61-65
Abs LCK An Surv Psa 1953, 4:481-483. NRo An Surv Psa 1953, 4:113. MK Q 1954, 23:303

52626 (& Weinstein, E. A.; Kahn, R. L.) Psychosis during electroshock therapy: its relation to the theory of shock therapy. P 1952, 109:22-26

52627 Psychosomatic aspects of backache. Conn State med J 1956, 20:288-290

52628 Psychosomatic medicine. *Collier's Yearbook for 1955,* 1956, 579-580

52629 "Pushing" in cattle: its relation to instinctive grasping in humans. J Animal Behav 1958, 6:(1/2)

52630 The renaissance of "neuropsychiatry." Psychiat Q 1955, 29:390-402

52631 The role of perception in the mechanism of denial. J Am Psa Ass 1953,
       1:690-705
           Abs NRo An Surv Psa 1953, 4:115-117. Vogel, B. F. Q 1953, 22:143-
       144. TFr J 1954, 35:447. Shentoub RFPsa 1954, 18:305. Rev Psico-
       anál 1954, 11:531. MGr Q 1955, 24:611-612
52632 Some comments on the origin of the influencing machine. J Am Psa
       Ass 1958, 6:305-308
           Abs TFr J 1959, 40:362. TGS Q 1960, 29:429
52633 Some developmental aspects of the body image. J 1955, 36:36-42
           Abs Rev Psicoanál 1955, 12:304. JLan Q 1956, 25:443
52634 The suggestion to dream about sickness. J Hillside Hosp 1954, 3:154-
       165
           Abs JFr An Surv Psa 1954, 5:212-214

       See Coles, Robert S.; Friedman, Paul; Schulman, D.

       ABSTRACTS OF:
52635 Heiman, M. On the role of animals. Q 1953, 22:147-149
52636 Margolin, S. On the psychological origin and function of symbols.
       Q 1954, 23:151-153

       REVIEWS OF:
52637 Janis, I. L. Psychological Stress. Psychoanalytic and Behavioral Studies
       of Surgical Patients. Q 1959, 28:271
52638 Malzberg, B. & Lee, E. S. Migration and Mental Disease. A Study of
       First Admissions to Hospitals for Mental Disease, New York, 1939-
       1941. Q 1957, 26:127

LINNEMANN, E. J.

52639 Indtryk under laereanalyse. [Impressions during the training analysis.]
       Nord psykiat Medlemsbl 1951, 5:142-144
52640 Studier i psykoterapi. [Studies in psychotherapy.] Nord psykiat Med-
       lemsbl 1954, 8:193-205

       See Juel-Nielsen, N.

LINSCOTT, ROBERT N.

52641 (& Stein, J.) (Ed) Why You Do What You Do. A Guide to Self-
       Understanding. NY: Random House 1956, iv + 305 p

LINTON, HARRIET

       See Gardner, Riley

LINTON, RALPH

52642 The Cultural Background of Personality. NY: Appleton-Century 1945
52643 Culture and Mental Disorders. (Ed: Devereux, G.) Springfield, Ill:
       Thomas 1956, 139 p
52644 The Tree of Culture. NY: Knopf 1955, xiv + 692 p
           Abs J Am Psa Ass 1956, 4:191. Rv Axelrad, S. J Am Psa Ass 1960,
       8:175-218

52645   What we know and what we don't. In Hsu, F. L. K. *Aspects of Culture and Personality,* NY: Abelard-Schuman 1954, 187-228

LIPIN, THEODORE

52646   Psychic functioning in patients with undiagnosed somatic symptoms; clinical evaluation. AMA ANP 1955, 73:329-337

LIPKOWITZ, HARRY

See Bender, Lauretta

LIPKOWITZ, MARVIN H.

See Green, Sidney L.

LIPPARD, VERNON W.

See Whitehorn, John C.

LIPPITT, RONALD

52647   (& Watson, J.; Westley, B.) The Dynamics of Planned Change. NY: Harcourt Brace 1958, 298 p
52648   (& Polansky, N.; Redl, F.; Rosen, S.) The dynamics of power, a field study of social influence in groups of children. In Swanson, G. E. et al: *Readings in Social Psychology,* NY: Henry Holt 1952, 623-636

See Redl, Fritz

LIPPMAN, HYMAN S.

52649   Antisocial acting out: symposium, 1954. Ops 1954, 24:667-696
52650   Difficulties in establishing the diagnosis of psychopathic personality in childhood. In Karpman, B. *Symposia on Child and Juvenile Delinquency,* Wash: Psychodynamics Series 1959, 118-124
52651   Emotional factors in family breakdown. Ops 1954, 24:445-453
52652   (& Reisman, S.) A neurotic adolescent struggling against a deep need for a criminal career. Case St Chd Dis 1953, 1:307-330
52653   (& Gerty, F.; Boyd, D. A., Jr.) Pastoral-psychiatric workshops: the St. John's Mental Health Institute. P 1958, 115:529-534. Prog PT 1959, 4:183-192
52654   The "psychopathic personality" in childhood. In Karpman, B. *Symposia on Child and Juvenile Delinquency,* Wash: Psychodynamics Series 1959, 4-8
52655   Psychopathic reactions in children. In Karpman, B. *Symposia on Child and Juvenile Delinquency,* Wash: Psychodynamics Series 1959, 53-56
52656   The relation between early childhood development and psychopathology. In Harris, D. *Concept of Childhood Development,* Minneapolis: Univ of Minn Pr 1957, 234-243
52657   Treatment of the Child in Emotional Conflict. NY: McGraw-Hill 1956, x + 298 p

See Palmer, James O.; Rose, John A.; Sontag, Lester W.

REVIEW OF:
52658 Heiman, M. (Ed) Psychoanalysis and Social Work. Q 1954, 23:116-118

LIPPMANN, HANNS LUDWIG

52659 Ludoterapia e orientação educacional. [Play therapy and child guidance.] Rio de Janeiro Faculdade de Filosofia, Ciências e Letras do Inst Santa Úrsula, Revista "Serviam" 1959, (9):11-38

LIPPMANN, WERNER O.

S-20786 Analyse eines Kriminellen.
Psychoanalytic study of a thief. (Ed: Karpman, B.) Arch crim Psychodyn 1957, 2:782-815

LIPSCHUTZ, LOUIS S.

52660 The written dream. J Am Psa Ass 1954, 2:473-478
Abs JFr An Surv Psa 1954, 5:234-235. TFr J 1955, 36:428. Shentoub RFPsa 1955, 19:499-500. Aldendorff, H. Q 1957, 26:136-137

LIPSCHUTZ, S.

52661 [Hypnoanalysis of Infantile Trauma in Hysteria.] (Russian) Moscow 1957, 79 p

LIPSHER, DAVID H.

See Bandura, Albert

LIPSHUTZ, DANIEL M.

52662 Combined group and individual psychotherapy. PT 1957, 11:336-344
Abs Viderman RFPsa 1958, 22:131-132
52663 Transference in borderline cases. R 1955, 42:195-200. Acta psychotherap psychosom orthopaedag 1955, 3(suppl):210-217

See Stein, Aaron

LIPSON, M. L.

See Plank, Emma N.

LIPTON, AARON

52664 (& Feiner, A. H.) Group therapy and remedial reading. J educ Psychol 1956, 47:330-334

LIPTON, EARLE L.

See Richmond, Julius B.

LIPTON, HERBERT

See Glasman, Rebecca

LIPTON, MORRIS A.

See Whitman, Roy M.

LIPTON, SAMUEL D.

52665 A clinical note on the occurrence of malingering in a case of paranoia. Bull Phila Ass Psa 1957, 7:91-95
 Abs de Saugy RFPsa 1959, 23:157

52666 A note on the compatibility of psychic determinism and freedom of will. J 1955, 36:355-356
 Abs Garcia Reinoso, D. Rev Psicoanál 1956, 13:80. JLan Q 1957, 26:281

52667 A note on the connection between preliminary communications and subsequently reported dreams. J Am Psa Ass 1958, 6:237-241
 Abs TFr J 1959, 40:361. Shentoub RFPsa 1959, 23:146-147. TGS Q 1960, 29:428

LISKA, EDWARD S.

See Berlin, Irving Norman; Szurek, Stanislaus A.

LISS, EDWARD

52668 (& Rosenthal, H.; Rivlin, H. N.; Harris, A. J.; Roswell, F. G.) Contemporary concepts of learning. Round table 1954. The genesis, evolution and dysfunction of learning and remedial measures. Ops 1954, 24:767-788

52669 The ego ideal role in learning. In Krugman, M. *Orthopsychiatry and the School*, NY: Am Ops Ass 1958, 102-104

52670 Motivations in learning. Psa St C 1955, 10:100-116
 Abs RTh J 1957, 38:294

52671 Preface to Elkisch, P. "Diagnostic and therapeutic value of projective techniques."

LISTWAN, I. A.

52672 Paranoid states: social and cultural aspects. Med J Australia 1956, 43:776-778

52673 Psychodrama. Med J Australia 1955, 42/I(15):524-527

LITIN, EDWARD M.

52674 (& Giffin, M. E.; Johnson, A. M.) Parental influence in unusual sexual behavior in children. (Read at Amer Psa Ass, NY, Dec 4, 1953) Q 1956, 25:37-55
 Abs Dreyfus RFPsa 1956, 20:573. JKl J 1957, 38:130

See Beckett, Peter G. S.; Giffin, Mary E.

LITMAN, ROBERT E.

52675 Some aspects of the treatment of the potentially suicidal patient. In Schneidman, E. S. & Farberow, N. L. *Clues to Suicide*, NY, Toronto, London: Blakiston Div, McGraw-Hill 1957, 111-118

LITTLE, JACK F.

52676 An experimental investigation of the libido theory. Doctoral Diss 1950, Library Univ of Southern Calif, Los Angeles

LITTLE, MARGARET

52677 On basic unity. (Read at 21st Int Psa Cong, Copenhagen, July 1959)
J 1960, 41:377-384; 637

S-20829 Counter-transference and the patient's response to it.
Abs STa An Surv Psa 1951, 2:389-393. Correal, J. Rev Psicoanál
1952, 9:367-369

52678 On delusional transference (transference psychosis). (Read at 20th
Int Psa Cong, Paris 1957) J 1958, 29:134-138
Über wahnhafte Übertragung (Übertragungspsychose). Psyche,
Heidel 1958, 12:258-269
Abs J 1958, 39:292-293. JLan Q 1959, 28:278. Usandivaras & Tabak
Rev Psicoanál 1959, 16:91. Zambonelli, F. Riv Psa 1959, 5:189-190

52679 Menopause: normal, or abnormal. Ment Hlth, Lond 1954, 14(1)

52680 "R"—the analyst's total response to his patient's needs. J 1957, 38:240-
254
Abs JLan Q 1958, 27:442

REVIEWS OF:

52681 Caprio, F. S. Female Homosexuality. A Psychodynamic Study of
Lesbianism. J 1955, 36:400-401

52682 Ferenczi, S. Final Contributions to the Problems and Methods of
Psycho-Analysis. J 1957, 38:121-123

52683 Harrower, M. (Ed) Medical and Psychological Teamwork in the Care
of the Chronically Ill. J 1956, 37:488-489

52684 Jones, E. Hamlet. J 1948, 29:64-65

LITTLE, S.

See Barnett, H. L.

LITTMAN, RICHARD A.

52685 Motives, history and causes. In Jones, M. R. *Nebraska Symposium
on Motivation: 1958.* Lincoln, Neb: Univ of Nebraska Pr 1958
114-168

52686 (& Moore, R. C. A.; Pierse-Jones, J.) Social class differences in
child rearing: a third community for comparison with Chicago and
Newton. Am Soc Rev 1957, 22:694-704

52687 (& Curry, J.: Pierse-Jones, J.) Where parents go for help. The
Coordinator 1957, 6:3-9

LITTNER, NER

52688 Discussion of Fradkin, H. & Krugman, D. "A program of adoptive
placement for infants under three months." Ops 1956, 26:590-593

52689 How to help the child welfare worker help herself. Child Welfare
1957, May

52690 The impact of the client's unconscious on the caseworker's reactions. Ego Psychol Dyn Casewk 73-82

52691 The institutional nursery—whence and whither. Child Welfare 1959,
Jan

52692 The natural parents. In Schapiro, M. *A Study of Adoption Practice,* Vol II, NY: Child Welfare League of Amer 1955, 21-33

52693 Some traumatic effects of separation and placement. Pamphlet F-17 Child Welfare League of Amer 1956

52694 The strains and stresses on the child welfare worker. Pamphlet AM-12. Child Welfare League of Amer 1957, May

52695 Traumatic effects of separation and placement. In *Nat Conf Soc Wk, Casework Papers, 1956,* NY: Fam Serv Ass of Amer 1956, 121-140

LITWINSKI, LEON

52696 Separation neuroses and infantile self-protection. Quart J Child Behavior 1952, 4(4)

Les névroses de séparation d'origine infantile et l'auto-protection. Enfance 1952, 5(3)

S-20829A Toward the restatement of the concept of the self.

Abs Holzman, P. S. Q 1953, 22:140-141

LIVERMORE, JEAN B.

52697 A schizophrenic child reviews her own treatment. Ops 1956, 26:365-375

See Eiduson, Bernice T.

LIVSON, FLORENCE

See Sampson, Harold

LLOPIS, BARTOLOMÉ

52698 The axial syndrome common to all psychoses. PPR 1959, 46(3):85-110; (4):92-96

LLORENTE, R. ALBERCA

52699 The basis of existential analysis. Rev Psiquiat Psicol Med 1953, 1:31-41

Abs Vega Q 1953, 22:618

LLUIS Y NAVAS-BRUSI, J.

52700 Un posible sentimiento de inseguridad en los reyes católicos proyectado en sus monedas. [A possible feeling of insecurity in the Catholic kings projected on their coins.] Rev Psiquiat Psicol 1955, 2:69-74

LOAR, L.

52701 An adventure in musical psychoanalysis. J Musicol 2(1):15-23

LOBO, F. L.

52702 Elementos para la avaluación del curso del tratamiento psicoanalítico. [Elements in evaluating the course of psychoanalytic therapy.] Rev Psicoanál 1956, 13:527-535

LOCH, WOLFGANG

52703   Begriff und Funktion der Angst in der Psychoanalyse. [Concept and function of anxiety in psychoanalysis.] Psyche, Heidel 1959, 13:801-816

LOCKE, NORMAN

52704   Bibliography on Group Psychotherapy. Vol II. NY: Amer Group Psychother Ass 1954

52705   Semantic psychotherapy: the misapplication of Korzybskian principles. ETC 1957, 15:31-36

52706   Trends in the literature on group psychotherapy. Int. J grp PT 1955, 5:181-184

52707   The use of dreams in group psychoanalysis. PT 1957, 11:98-110
      Abs Viderman RFPsa 1958, 22:129-130. Rv Teper, E. Rev Psicoanál 1957, 14:339-340

See Wolf, Alexander

LODGE, ANN

52708   Satan's symbolic syndrome. A psychological interpretation of Milton's Satan. R 1956, 43:411-422
      Abs JLan Q 1958, 27:128

LODGE, GEORGE TOWNSEND

52709   A method for the dynamic representation of personality data. J proj Techn 1953, 17:477-481

LOEB, LAURENCE

52710   Psychopathography and Toulouse-Lautrec. Am Im 1959, 16:213-224

ABSTRACTS OF:

52711   Carlson, H. B. Characteristics of an acute confusional state in college students. Q 1959, 28:424

52712   Eisenberg, L. School phobia: a study in the communication of anxiety. Q 1959, 28:424

52713   Gibson, R. W. et al: On the dynamics of the manic-depressive personality. Q 1960, 29:290

52714   Goldstein, N. P. & Giffin, M. E. Psychogenic hypersomnia. Q 1960, 29:290

52715   Horwitz, W. A. et al: A study of cases of schizophrenia treated by "direct analysis." Q 1959, 28:424

52716   Kolb, L. C. & Montgomery, J. An explanation for transference cure: its occurrence in psychoanalysis and psychotherapy. Q 1960, 29:289

52717   Levin, M. Aggression, guilt, and cataplexy. Q 1960, 29:594

52718   Lewin, B. D. Some psychoanalytic ideas applied to elation and depression. Q 1960, 29:594

52719   O'Neal, P. & Robins, L. N. The relation of childhood behavior problems to adult psychiatric status. Q 1959, 28:425

LOEBLOWITZ-LENNARD, HENRY

52720 The Jew as symbol: anti-Semitism and transference. Psychiat Q 1947, 21:253-260

LOEFFLER, FRANK J.

See Solomon, Adrian

LOEFFLER-DELACHAUX, MARGUERITE

52721 Le cercle, un symbole. [The Circle, a Symbol.] Geneva: Ed Mont-Blanc 1947, 207 p

LOEHRICH, ROLF RUDOLF

52722 Oneirics and Psychosomatics: An Introductory Treatise Concerning a New Theory of Psychoanalysis, Its Logic and Methodology. McHenry, Ill: Compass Pr 1953, xiv + 157 p

LOESER, LEWIS H.

52723 (& Bry, T.) The position of the group therapist in transference and countertransference: an experimental study. Int J grp PT 1953, 3:389-406
    Abs LCK An Surv Psa 1953, 4:519-521. GPK Q 1955, 24:163
52724 The role of group therapy in private practice. A clinical evaluation. J Hillside Hosp 1956, 5:460-467

LOEVINGER, JANE

52725 Diagnosis and measurement: a reply to Eysenck. Psychol Rep 1955, 1:277-278
52726 (& Ossorio, A.) Evaluation of therapy by self-report: a paradox. ASP 1959, 58:392-394
    Abs Applebaum, S. A. Q 1960, 29:442

LOEWALD, HANS W.

S-20831A Ego and reality.
    Abs JAA An Surv Psa 1951, 2:40; 132-135; NRo An Surv Psa 1951, 2:76-77
52727 Hypnoid state, repression, abreaction and recollection. J Am Psa Ass 1955, 3:201-210
    Abs TFr J 1956, 37:208. Young, B. Q 1959, 28:558-559
S-20831B The problem of defense and the neurotic interpretation of reality.
    Abs JAA An Surv Psa 1952, 3:88-89. Sloane, P. Q 1954, 23:144
S-20831c Psychoanalysis and modern views on human existence and religious experience. J pastoral Care 1953, 7:1-15
    Rv Casey, R. P. J 1954, 35:370-372
52728 (Reporter) Psychoanalytic curricula—principles and structure. (Panel: Am Psa Ass Atlantic City, May 1955) J Am Psa Ass 1956, 4:149-161
52729 On the therapeutic action of psychoanalysis. J 1960, 41:16-33
52730 Transference and the therapeutic action of psycho-analysis: metapsychological considerations. [Part 4 of author's "On the therapeutic action of psychoanalysis."]
    Abs J 1958, 39:293

LOEWALD, KATE S.

52731 Improvement and patients' perceptions of their therapists during initial stages of psychotherapy. Chicago: Library Dept of Photographic Reproduction, Univ of Chicago 1956, 83 p

LOEWENBERG, RICHARD D.

52732 Georg Christoph Lichtenberg: an eighteenth century pioneer of semantics. ETC 1943-44, 1(Winter):99-100
52733 From Immanuel Kant's Self-Analysis. Am Im 1953, 10:307-322. YBPsa 1954, 10:238-250
       Abs MK An Surv Psa 1953, 4:365-366

LOEWENSTEIN, RUDOLPH MAURICE

S-20852 Christians and Jews.
       Abs JLan An Surv Psa 1951, 2:653-662
52734 A contribution to the psychoanalytic theory of masochism. J Am Psa Ass 1957, 5:197-234
       Abs Shentoub RFPsa 1958, 22:125. HW Q 1960, 29:280. Rv de Chait Lia, B. Rev Psicoanál 1958, 15:302-303
52735 Discussion of Freud, A. "Problems of technique in adult analysis." Bull Phila Ass Psa 1954, 4:61-62
52736 Discussion of Ritvo, S. & Solnit, A. J. "Influences of early mother-child interaction on identification processes." Psa St C 1958, 13:86-87
52737 (Ed) Drives, Affects, Behavior. NY: IUP 1953, 399 p
       Abs Stein, A. An Surv Psa 1953, 4:629-657. Rv Bonaparte, M. RFPsa 1953, 17:556-567. Heilbrunn, G. Q 1954, 23:582. Sharoff, R. L. Psa 1954, 14:131-132. Gostynski, E. J 1955, 36:137-138
S-20840 Ego development and psychoanalytic technique.
       Abs STa An Surv Psa 1951, 2:417
52738 In memoriam: Ernst Kris, Ph. D., 1900-1957. J Am Psa Ass 1957, 5:741-743. RFPsa 1958, 22:136-140
S-20848 De la passivité phallique chez l'homme.
       Rv Oliveira, W. I. de. Rev Psicoanál 1948, 6:761-762
S-20850 The problem of interpretation.
       Abs STa An Surv Psa 1951, 2:415-416
52739 Problems of indications as viewed by a psychoanalyst. Dis nerv Syst 1959, 20:84-88
52740 Problems of infantile neurosis. A discussion. Psa St C 1954, 9:47-48
S-20856 Des pulsions vitales ou somatiques.
       Abs RdeS Q 1953, 22:139
52741 Réflexions sur le traitement d'un cas de névrose compulsionnelle. RFPsa 1956, 20:384-404
       Reflections on the treatment of a case of obsessional neurosis. (Tr: Damman, V.) In Freeman, L. Troubled Women, Cleveland: World Publ Co 1959, 295-316
52742 Remarks on some variations in psycho-analytic technique. (Read at 20th Int Psa Cong, Paris 1957) J 1958, 39:202-210; 240-242
       Abs Faergeman, P. M. Q 1958, 27:622-624. JLan Q 1959, 28:281

52743 Some reflections on the development of sadomasochistic fantasies. Bull
       Phila Ass Psa 1954, 4:20
52744 Some remarks on defenses, autonomous ego and psychoanalytic tech-
       nique. (Read at 18th Int Psa Cong, London, July 1953) J 1954,
       35:188-193
           Abs Auth J 1954, 35:287. Lebovici, S. RFPsa 1954, 18:467-468.
       NRo An Surv Psa 1954, 5:81; 323-324. JLan Q 1955, 24:606
52745 Some remarks on the role of speech in psychoanalytic technique. J
       1956, 37:460-467. Rd Psa Psychol 248-261.
           Abs Spiegel, L. A. Q 1953, 22:144-145. JLan Q 1957, 26:582.
       Lebovici, S. RFPsa 1957, 21:617-618
52746 Some thoughts on interpretation in the theory and practice of psycho-
       analysis. Psa St C 1957, 12:127-150
           Abs RTh J 1959, 40:369

       See Hartmann, Heinz; Knight, Robert P.

       REVIEW OF:
52747 Bonaparte, M. Female Sexuality. Q 1955, 24:119-120

LOGRE

52748 Psychanalyse et médecine. [Psychoanalysis and medicine.] Psyché,
       Paris 1954, 9:1-7

LOGRE, B. J.

52749 Freudisme et liberté. [Freudianism and liberty.] RFPsa 1955, 19:615-
       629

LOGRE, J.

52750 Le pré-inconscient et la psychologie amoureuse. [The pre-unconscious
       and affectional psychology.] RFPsa 1953, 17:541-547
           Abs NRo An Surv Psa 1953, 4:108-109
S-20879 À propos de Chronos, Eros et Thanatos.
           Abs JAA An Surv Psa 1952, 3:64-66

LOLIS, KATHLEEN

52751 New hope for deaf children. The Packer Alumni, Brooklyn, N.Y., 1957

LOLLI, GIORGIO

52752 The addictive drinker. Quart J Stud Alcohol 1949, 10. In Murphy, G.
       & Bachrach, A. J. *An Outline of Abnormal Psychology*, NY: Modern
       Library 1954, 295-310
52753 Alcoholism and homosexuality in Tennessee Williams' *Cat on a Hot
       Tin Roof*. Quart J Stud Alcohol 1956, 17:543-553

LOMAS, JACK B.

52754 Analysis of a case of migraine. Samiksa 1955, 9:232-254
52755 On maternal symbiotic depression. R 1956, 43:423-431
           Abs JLan Q 1958, 27:129

LOMAS, PETER ERIC SAMUEL

52756 The husband-wife relationship in cases of puerperal breakdown. M 1959, 32(2)

REVIEWS OF:

52757 Evelyn, J. The Theory of Gravitation in Mental Fields. J 1958, 39:430

52758 Galdston, I. (Ed) The Family in Contemporary Society. J 1959, 40:352

52759 Lafitte, P. The Person in Psychology: Reality or Abstraction? J 1959, 40:355

LOMAX, ALAN

52760 The cultural context of folk songs. In Goldschmidt, W. *Readings in the Ways of Mankind.* NY: Holt, Rinehart & Winston 1957; *Exploring the Ways of Mankind* 1960, 607-619

LOMBARD, CATHERINE

See Carter, Victor E.

LOMMEL, F.

52761 Ärzte als Patienten. [Physicians as patients.] Psychotherapie 1957, 2:181-192

LONDON, LOUIS SAMUEL

52762 Abnormal Sexual Behavior; Twenty-Three Detailed Case Studies. NY: Julian Pr 1957, viii + 427 p

S-20904 Ailurophobia and ornithophobia. (Cat phobia and bird phobia.) Abs JBi Q 1953, 22:449-450

52763 Dynamic Psychiatry. Vol. I. Basic Principles. NY: Corinthian Pr 1952; Vol. II. Transvestism—Desire for Crippled Women. NY: Corinthian Pr 1952; Vol. III. Frustrated Women. NY: Corinthian Pr 1953

52764 Hypnotherapy and narcotherapy of a bisexual struggle. Southern Med & Surg 1951, 113(2)

52765 The paraphiliac neuroses. Psychosexual infantilism. Psychogenesis and psychotherapy. Urol & Cutan Rev 1935, 39

52766 Psychoanalysis—a survey. Amer Med 1934, Jun

52767 Psychogenetic disturbances of hearing and vision. Delaware Med J 1945, Sept

52768 Psychosexual pathology of the sexual instinct. Urol & Cutan Rev 1932, 36(8)

52769 Psychosexual pathology of transvestism. Urol & Cutan Rev 1933, 37(9)

52770 Psychopathology of ereuthrophobia (blushing). Southern Med & Surg 1945, 107(9)

52771 Psychotherapeutic transfusions. Bol Assoc med P. Rico 1943, (11)

52772 Sexual Deviations in the Female. NY: Julian Pr 1957

LONERGAN, BERNARD J. F.

52773 Insight; A Study of Human Understanding. NY: Philos Lib; London: Longmans, Green 1957, 785 p

LONERGAN, W. G.

52774 Role playing in an industrial conflict. Group PT 1957, 10:105-110
Abs Lebovici, S. RFPsa 1958, 22:129

LONG, L. M. K.

52775 Alfred Adler and the problem of the unconscious. Am J Ind Psychol
1955, 11:163-166

LONG, ROBERT T.

52776 (& Lamont, J. H.; Whipple, B.; Bandler, L.; Blom, G. E.; Burgin, L.;
Jessner, L.) A psychosomatic study of allergic and emotional factors in
children with asthma. P 1958, 114:890-899

See Jessner, Lucie

LONGAKER, WILLIAM D.

See Cleveland, Eric J.

LÖNNERSTRAND, STURE

52777 Psykoanalys och erotik; tre artiklar. [Psychoanalysis and sex; three
essays.] Stockholm: Bokförlaget Indigo 1953, 39 p

LOO, P.

52778 (& Duflot, J. P.) L'anorexie mentale. [Mental anorexia.] Ann Med
Psychol 1958, 2:734-750

LOOMIE, LEO S.

52779 (& Rosen, V. H.; Stein, M. H.) Ernst Kris and the gifted adolescent
project. Psa St C 1958, 13:44-57
Abs RTh J 1960, 41:647-648

LOOMIS, EARL A., JR.

52780 (& Greenawalt, J. C.) A brief glossary of psychiatric terms for pastors.
Part I. Pastoral Psychol 1954, Jan
52781 (& Morrow, T., Jr.) A brief glossary of psychiatric terms for pastors.
Part II. Pastoral Psychol 1954, Jan
52782 The chaplain's emotional growth. Bull Amer Protestant Hosp Ass
1955, 19(3)
52783 Child psychiatry and religion. Group PT 1955, 8:291-297. Pastoral
Psychol 1956, 7(6):27-33
52784 The child's emotions and surgery. In Kiesewetter, W. B. *Pre- and
Postoperative Care in the Pediatric Surgical Patient,* Chicago: Yearbook Publ 1956
52785 A clinical curriculum in child development and care. Ops 1956,
26:643-645
52786 The concurrent presentation of a rare detail in the dreams of two
patients. J Am Psa Ass 1956, 4:53-55
Abs TFr J 1957, 38:134

52787 Discussion of Shugart, G. "Preventive and treatment methods of psychotic children." Prog PT 1956, 1:265-266

52788 The "foul disease" is no respecter of persons: a reply to Mr. Fitch. Christianity & Crisis 1958, 18(8)

52789 Group psychotherapy in a naval psychiatric service. Group PT 1953, 5:240-252

52790 Health, healing and forgiveness. The Witness: for Christ and His Church 1958, 45(38)

52791 Moody people. Pastoral Psychol 1954, Mar

52792 (& Meyer, L. R.) Observation and recording—a simultaneous process. Symposium 1958: Observational research with emotionally disturbed children: Session II. Ops 1959, 29:574-582

52793 (& Hilgeman, L. M.; Meyer, L. R.) Play patterns as nonverbal indices of ego functions: a preliminary report. Ops 1957, 27:691-700

52794 A psychiatrist reflects on his first year. *GAP Symposium No. 5, Some Considerations of Early Attempts in Cooperation between Religion and Psychiatry.* Group for the Advancement of Psychiatry 1958, Mar

52795 Psychiatry and the Christian ministry. Union Theol Sem Quart Rev 1957, 12:31-39. Prog PT 1958, 3:160-165

52796 (& Shugart, G.) Psychodrama with parents of hospitalized schizophrenic children. Group PT 1954, Oct

52797 Psychothérapie et formation pastorale. [Psychotherapy and pastoral structure.] Suppl vie Spir 1959, (49):217-221

52798 The symbolic meaning of the elbow. J Am Psa Ass 1955, 3:697-700
 Abs TFr J 1956, 37:511-512

52799 (& Lhamon, W. T.; Rashkis, H. A.) Tempo preference in hypnotically induced affective states. Brit J med Hypnot 1952-53, Winter

52800 The use of checkers in handling certain resistances in child therapy and child analysis. J Am Psa Ass 1957, 5:130-135
 Abs Shentoub RFPsa 1957, 21:613-614. HW Q 1960, 29:279-280

52801 What do children fear? Children's Religion 1958, 19:9-10

52802 [Discussant] When is grief healthy or morbid? and The pastor and suicide. In Section IV, Specific counseling problems, in *The Minister's Consultation Clinic: Pastoral Psychology in Action,* Great Neck, NY: Channel Pr 1955

See Maier, Henry W.; Morrow, Tarlton, Jr.

LOOSLEY, ELIZABETH W.

See Seeley, John R.

LOOSLI-USTERI, MARGUERITE

52803 Dr. Walter Morgenthaler zum 70. Geburtstag. [Dr. Walter Morgenthaler on his 70th birthday.] Rorschachiana 1952, 1:75-77

LOPAŠIĆ, P.

See Betlheim, Stjepan

LOPEZ, C.

52804 (& Benoit, G.; Abély, P.) Essai d'évaluation des mécanismes de défense, à l'aide des tests projectifs; à propos de 3 observations. [Attempt to evaluate defense mechanisms with the aid of projective tests; 3 case reports.] Ann méd psychol 1956, 2:868-875

LOPEZ, D.

52805 Discussant of Bouvet, M. de: "Dépersonnalisation et relations d'objet." RFPsa 1960, 24:619-620

LOPEZ IBOR, JUAN J.

52806 Analyse und Kommentar der ersten Krankengeschichte von Freud über Angst und Hysterie. [Analysis and commentary on Freud's first case history concerning anxiety and hysteria.] Jb Psychol Psychother 1953, 1:195-206

52807 Angoisse vécue et vocation religieuse. [Experience of anxiety and religious vocation.] (Tr: Fraenkel, E.) Psyché, Paris 1954, 9:433-446

52808 Bases biologicas de la histeria. [Biological bases of hysteria.] An Acad nac Med, Madrid 1952, 69:467-479

52809 Catharsis et transfert. [Catharsis and transference.] Psyché, Paris 1953, 8:248-261

52810 Die Dynamik der Angst. [The dynamics of anxiety.] Wien Z Nervenheilk 1955, 10:299-311

52811 Estructura de la neurosis y libertad. Homenaje al Prof. Kurt Schneider en su LXX aniversario. [The structure of neurosis and liberty. A tribute to Prof. Kurt Schneider on his 70th birthday.] Act luso-esp Neur 1956, 15:292-300

52812 Fundamentos de la psicoterapia. [Fundamentals of psychotherapy.] Act luso-esp Neur 1957, 16:11-27

52813 Obesidad y delgadez como formas de vida. [Obesity and leanness as patterns of life.] Act luso-esp Neur 1955, 14:279-287

52814 Percepción y humor delirante; análisis fenomenológico y existencial. [Perception and affective state in delirium; phenomenological and existential analysis.] Act luso-esp Neur 1953, 12:89-102

52815 Problems presented by asthma as a psychosomatic illness. J psychosom Res 1956, 1:115-119

52816 Psicopatologia de la angustia. [Psychopathology of anxiety.] Act luso-esp Neur 1955, 14:65-73

52817 Psychiatry and the existential crisis. In Braceland, F. J. *Faith, Reason and Modern Psychiatry,* NY: Kenedy 1955, 65-96

52818 Zwang, Phobie und Skrupel. [Compulsion, phobia and scruple.] Jb Psychol Psychother 1956, 4:92-101

LÓPEZ DE MESA, L.

52819 Algunas consideraciones acerca del hombre. [Various considerations about man.] An Np 1954, 8(33-34):5-43

LOPEZ RUEDA, JOSE

52820   Sigmund Freud heredero y donante. [Sigmund Freud, inheritor and giver.] In *Sigmund Freud, Homenaje,* Cuenca, Ecuador: Casa de la Cultura Ecuatoriana 1956, 153-182

LORAND, SANDOR

S-20942 Clinical Studies in Psychoanalysis.
          Estudios Clinicos de Psicoanalisis. (Tr: Evelson, E.) Buenos Aires: Biblioteca Psicoanal 1954
52821   Depressive reaction in women related to childbirth. J Hillside Hosp 1953, 2:131-142
52822   Dream interpretation in the Talmud. (Babylonion and Graeco-Roman period). J 1957, 38:92-97
          Abs JLan Q 1958, 27:437
52823   Introduction. In author's *Perversions: Psychodynamics and Therapy,* ix-x
52824   In Memoriam: Israel Strauss (1873-1955). J Hillside Hosp 1956, 5:127-128
52825   Obituary: Leonard Blumgart 1881-1959. J 1960, 41:640-641
52826   (& Balint, M.) (Eds) Perversions: Psychodynamics and Therapy. NY: Random House 1956, xii + 307 p
          Perversioni sessuali: Psicodinamica e Terapia. Milan: Parenti 1959
          Rv Williams, A. H. J 1957, 38:432
S-20972 (Ed) Psychoanalysis Today.
          Spanish: Buenos Aires: Ed Paidos 1953, 398 p
          Rv Garcia Reinoso, D. Rev Psicoanál 1953, 10:240-241
52827   Resistance. (Read at Psa Ass of NY, Oct 1957)
          Abs Hollander, E. E. Q 1958, 27:462-464
52828   (& Feldman, S.) The symbolism of teeth in dreams. J 1955, 36:145-161
          Abs JLan Q 1956, 25:612-613
52829   The teaching of psychotherapeutic technique to residents in psychiatry. Acta psychother psychosom orthopaedag 1955, 3 (suppl):218-224
52830   (& Console, W. A.) Therapeutic results in psycho-analytic treatment without fee. (Observations on therapeutic results). J 1958, 39:59-64
          Abs JLan Q 1959, 28:107. Racamier RFPsa 1959, 13:154-155
52831   The therapy of perversions. In author's *Perversions: Psychodynamics and Therapy* 290-307

REVIEW OF:
52832   Klein, M. et al (Eds) New Directions in Psycho-Analysis. J 1957, 38:283-285

LORAS, OLIVIER

52833   La psychanalyse extensive; origines et fondements de la psycho-thérapie. [Extensional psychoanalysis; origins and foundations of psychotherapy.] Paris: Payot 1957, 254 p
52834   L'Univers de Prométhée enchaîné. Le langage existentiel des hallucinations. [The universe of "Prometheus Bound." The existential language of hallucinations.] An Med Psychol 1958, 116:624-649

LORD, JOSEPH P.

See Prugh, Dane G.

LORD, RICHARD A.

52835 A note on stigmata. Am Im 1957, 14:299-302

LORENZ, EMIL

52836 Als Freud noch Einlasscheine ausgab. [When Freud still issued admission certificates.] Forum 1956, 3(29):177-179

LORENZ, KONRAD Z.

S-21018A King Solomon's Ring.
          Rv Spitz, R. A. Q 1953, 22:277-280
52837 The role of aggression in group formation. In Schaffner, B. *Group Processes*. NY: Josiah Macy Jr Found 1959

See Schiller, Claire H.

LORENZ, MARIA

52838 Expressive behavior and language patterns. Ps 1955, 18:353-366
52839 Language as expressive behavior. AMA ANP 1953, 70:277-285
          Abs LRa Q 1955, 24:617
S-21019 (& Cobb, S.) Language behavior in manic patients.
          Abs LRa Q 1953, 22:307
52840 Language behavior in manic patients. A qualitative study. AMA ANP 1953, 69:14-26
          Abs LRa Q 1954, 23:307-308
52841 (& Cobb, S.) Language behavior in psychoneurotic patients. AMA ANP 1953, 69:684-694
          Abs LRa Q 1955, 24:317

LORENZ, THOMAS H.

See Lewis, William C.

LORENZER, A.

52842 Ein Beitrag zur Paranoiafrage: II. Schuld und Gewissen in einer paranoischen Entwicklung. [A contribution to the problem of paranoia: II. Guilt and conscience in paranoid development.] Z Psychother med Psychol 1959, 9:97-108

LORR, MAURICE

52843 Discussion of Bordin, E. S. "Inside the therapeutic hour." Res PT 260-263
52844 Discussion of Snyder, W. U. "Some investigations of relationship in psychotherapy." Res PT 260-263

LORTON, WILLIAM L.

See Beckett, Peter G. S.

LOSSY, FRANK T.

ABSTRACTS OF:

52845 DiMascio, A. et al: Physiological correlates of tension and antagonism during psychotherapy: a study of "interpersonal physiology." Q 1958, 27:298

52846 Dixon, J. J. et al: Patterns of anxiety: the phobias. Q 1958, 27:147

52847 Freeman, T. et al: The state of the ego in chronic schizophrenia. Q 1958, 27:147

52848 Goy, R. W. & Young, W. C. Somatic basis of sexual behavior patterns in guinea pigs. Q 1958, 27:299

52849 Holstijn, A. J. W. The psychological development of Vincent Van Gogh. Q 1958, 27:147

52850 Malmo, R. B. et al: Physiological study of personal interaction. Q 1958, 27:298-299

52851 Meerloo, J. A. M. Human camouflage and identification with the environment: the contagious effect of archaic skin signs. Q 1958, 27:298

52852 Meyer, B. C. & Lyons, A. S. Rectal resection: psychiatric and medical management of its sequelae. Q 1958, 27:299

LOURIE, NORMAN V.

52853 The children's institution: one step in casework treatment. Soc Welfare Forum 1954

52854 Classification and grouping of juveniles adjudged delinquent. Survey by Univ of Penna Nov 1954

52855 Discipline: a consistent, non-punitive concept. Child Welfare 1951, Nov

52856 Juvenile delinquency. Social Work Yearbook 1957

52857 (& Schulman, R.) The role of the residential staff in resident treatment. Ops 1952, 22:798-808

LOURIE, REGINALD S.

52858 Basic problems involved in the use of the newer neuropharmacological drugs in childhood. In Fisher, S. *Child Research in Psychopharmacology,* Springfield, Ill: Thomas 1959, 48-55

52859 Basic science and the failure of orthopsychiatry. Ops 1958, 28:445-455
        Abs Koenig RFPsa 1959, 23:431

52860 Experience with therapy of psychosomatic problems in infants. In Hoch, P. & Zubin, J. *Psychopathology of Childhood,* NY: Grune & Stratton 1955, 254-266

52861 The pediatric-psychiatric viewpoint. In Karpman, B. *Symposia on Child and Juvenile Delinquency,* Wash: Psychodynamics Series 1959, 63-68

52862 The reversibility of psychopathic-like patterns in early childhood. In Karpman, B. *Symposia on Child and Juvenile Delinquency,* Wash: Psychodynamics Series 1959, 126-131

52863 Some basic elements in mental development. In Karpman, B. *Symposia on Child and Juvenile Delinquency,* Wash: Psychodynamics Series 1959, 8-10

52864 (& Layman, E. M.; Millican, F. K.; Sokoloff, B.; Takahashi, L. L.) A study of the etiology of pica in young children, an early pattern of addiction. In Hoch, P. H. & Zubin, J. *Problems of Addiction and Habituation,* NY, London: Grune & Stratton 1958, 74-86

See Bender, Lauretta; Hulse, Wilfred C.; Palmer, James O.; Sontag, Lester W.

LOVE, LEONORE R.

See Ingham, Harrington V.

LOVE, SIDNEY I.

52865 (& Mayer, H.) Going along with defenses in resistive families. Soc Casewk 1959, 40:69-74

52866 Participant in Clinical Conference: A problem of ego organization in a latency child. New Front Child Guid 173-209

LOVETT DOUST, JOHN W.

52867 (& Leigh, D.) Studies on the physiology of awareness; the interrelationship of emotions, life situations, and anoxemia in patients with bronchial asthma. PSM 15:292-311

LOW, BARBARA

S-21040A Bibliography. J 1956, 37:474

REVIEW OF:

S-21072A Friedmann, M. V. Olive Schreiner. A Study in Latent Meanings. J 1955, 36:408-409

LOW-BEER, M.

52868 Considerazioni psicoanalitiche a proposito di un case di neurodermite. [Psychoanalytic comments on a case of neurodermatitis.] Riv Psa 1959, 5:235-244

52869 Discussant of Perrotti, N. "Aperçus théoriques de la dépersonnalisation." RFPsa 1960, 24:420-428

LOWE, WARNER L.

52870 Value systems in the psychotherapeutic process. In Wolff, W. *Psychiatry and Religion,* NY: MD Publications 1955, 40-43

LOWELL, F. C.

See Knapp, Peter H.

LOWEN, ALEXANDER

52871 Physical Dynamics of Character Structure: Bodily Form and Movement in Analytic Therapy. NY, London: Grune & Stratton 1958, x + 358 p

LOWENFELD, HENRY

S-21096 Psychic trauma and productive experience in the artist. Art Psa 292-305

52872 Sigmund Freud. J Am Psa Ass 1956, 4:682-691

REVIEWS OF:
52873 Erikson, E. H. Young Man Luther. Q 1960, 29:108-111
52874 Fromm, E. The Forgotten Language: An Introduction to the Understanding of Dreams, Fairy Tales and Myths. Q 1953, 22:108-110
52875 May, R. et al: Existence. Q 1959, 28:256-261
52876 Reik, T. The Search Within. Q 1958, 27:111-113

LOWENFELD, MARGARET

52877 The structure of transference. Acta psychotherap psychosom orthopaedag 1955, 3(suppl):224-229

LOWENFELD, YELA

REVIEWS OF:
52878 Binswanger, L. Erinnerungen an Sigmund Freud. Q 1957, 26:416-419; 1959, 28:265
52879 Fromm, E. Sigmund Freud's Mission. Q 1960, 29:252-254
52880 Jahoda, M. Current Concepts of Positive Mental Health. Q 1960, 29:122-124

LOWENHAUPT, ELIZABETH

S-21147 A consideration of psychic mechanisms in vasospastic disorders of the hand.
Abs JAA An Surv Psa 1952, 3:341-342. JLan Q 1953, 22:448
52881 Two cases of chicken phobia. J Hillside Hosp 1955, 4:211-217

LOWINGER, LOUIS

See Hulse, Wilfred C.

LOWINGER, PAUL

52882 (& Huston, P. E.) Transference and the physical presence of the physician. JNMD 1955, 121:250-256

LÖWNAU, H. W.

52883 Differentialdiagnostische Erwägungen zur Frage der Neurose im Kindesalter. [Differential diagnostic considerations on the problem of neurosis in childhood.] Prax Kinderpsychol 1958, 7:241-251
52884 Über Exhibitionismus bei einem Jugendlichen. [On exhibitionism in an adolescent boy.] Prax Kinderpsychol 1955, 4:168-174

LOWREY, LAWSON G.

52885 Adolescent frustrations and evasions. In Hoch, P. & Zubin, J. *Psychopathology of Childhood*, NY: Grune & Stratton 1955, 267-284

52886 The development of psychopathic reactions. In Karpman, B. *Symposia on Child and Juvenile Delinquency*, Wash: Psychodynamics Series 1959, 68-74

52887 Introduction. Symposium, 1954: Therapeutic play techniques. Ops 1955, 25:574-575
    Abs Koenig, J. RFPsa 1956, 20:584-585

See Palmer, James O.; Welsch, Exie E.

LOWTZKY, FANNY

52888 L'angoisse de la mort et l'idée du bien chez L. N. Tolstoi. [Fear of death and the idea of the good in L. N. Tolstoi.] RFPsa 1959, 23:495-525

S-21169 Mahatma Gandhi. A contribution to the psychoanalytic understanding of the causes of war and the means of preventing wars.
    Abs STa An Surv Psa 1952, 3:471-473. Grinberg, L. Rev Psicoanál 1953, 10:245-246. MGr Q 1954, 23:147-148

52889 Das Problem des Masochismus und des Strafbedürfnisses im Lichte klinischer Erfahrung. [The problem of masochism and the desire for punishment in the light of clinical experience.] Psyche, Heidel 1956, 10:331-347

LOWY, SAMUEL

52890 (& Gutheil, E. A.) Active analytic psychotherapy (Stekel). Prog PT 1956, 1:136-143

52891 A psychoanalytic view of psychosis. PPR 1960, 47(1):34-50

52892 Transference in modified analytical therapies; supplementary communication. Acta psychotherap psychosom orthopaedag 1955, 3(suppl):230-237

LUBIN, ALBERT J.

52893 A boy's view of Jesus. Psa St C 1959, 14:155-168

52894 A feminine Moses. J 1958, 39:535-546
    Abs HW Q 1960, 29:131

52895 Psychoanalytically oriented landscaping. Space '58, Dept. Landscape Architecture, Univ Calif. 1958, 9

LUBORSKY, LESTER B.

52896 (& Shevrin, H.) Dreams and day-residues: a study of the Poetzl observation. BMC 1956, 20:135-137
    Abs Weiss, J. Q 1959, 27:292

52897 (& Shevrin, H. S.) An experimental study of visual sources of dreams and waking images. Am Psych 1958, 13:354

52898 Intraindividual repetitive measurements (P technique) in understanding psychotherapeutic change. In Mowrer, O. H. et al: *Psychotherapy: Theory and Research*, NY: Ronald Pr 1953, 389-413

52899 (& Siegal, R.; Gross, G. A.) Neurotic depression and masochism. Clin Stud Pers 191-212

52900 A note on Eysenck's article: "The effects of psychotherapy: an evaluation." BJP 1954, 45:129-131

52901   The personality of the psychotherapist. Menninger Quart 1952, 6:1-6
52902   The personality requisites for work in psychiatry as revealed in the
        TAT. Am Psychol 1949, 4:258
52903   Psychotherapy. Ann Rev Psychol 1959, 10:317-344
52904   Research on the outcome of psychotherapy. Proc Kansas Univ Psychol
        Inst on Res in Psychother, 1955, Lawrence, Kans: Kansas Univ 1957
52905   Selecting psychiatric residents: survey of the Topeka research. BMC
        1954, 18:252-259
            Abs Rahman, L. Q 1956, 25:117-118
52906   (& Holt, R. R.) The selection of candidates for psychoanalytic training.
        J clin exp Psychopathol 1957, 18:166-176
52907   Self-interpretation of the TAT as a clinical technique. J proj Tech
        1953, 17:217-223
52908   (& Fabian, M.; Hall, B. H.; Ticho, E.; Ticho, G.) Treatment variables.
        BMC 1958, 22:126-147
52909   (& Cattell, R. B.) The validation of personality factors in humor. J
        Personality 1947, 15:283-291

        See Cattell, Raymond B.; Holt, Robert R.; Shevrin, Howard; Waller-
        stein, Robert S.

LUCAS, S. H.
REVIEW OF:
52910   Ralli, E. P. Adrenal Cortex. J 1955, 36:141; 403

LUCHINA
ABSTRACTS OF:
52911   Beech, H. R. An experimental investigation of sexual symbolism in
        anorexia nervosa employing a subliminal stimulation technique. Rev
        Psicoanál 1959, 16:139
52912   Friedman, M. et al: Changes in the blood cholesterol and in the coagu-
        lation among men under stress cyclic due to their work. Rev Psicoanál
        1959, 16:139-140
52913   Kaplan, S. M. & Gottschalk, L. A. Modifications of the oropharyngeal
        bacteria with changes in the psychodynamic state. Rev Psicoanál
        1958, 15:426
52914   Perrin, G. & Pierce, I. Psychosomatic aspects of cancer—a review. Rev
        Psicoanál 1959, 16:141
52915   Seitz, P. F. D. Infantile experience and adult behavior in animal sub-
        jects. Rev Psicoanál 1959, 16:140

REVIEWS OF:
52916   Groethuysen, U. C. et al: Depth electrographic recording of a seizure
        during a structural intervention. Rev Psicoanál 1956, 14:427
52917   Stuntz, E. C. The beard as an expression of body feelings in a schizo-
        phrenic. Rev Psicoanál 1959, 16:191-192

LUCHINA, A.
ABSTRACTS OF:
52918   Lewin, K. K. Role of depression in the production of illness in per-
        nicious anemia. Rev Psicoanál 1959, 16:192-193

52919 Orgel, S. Z. Effect of psychoanalysis on the course of peptic ulcer. Rev Psicoanál 1958, 15:426

REVIEW OF:
52920 Luby, E. D. et al: Stress and the precipitation of acute intermittent porphyria. Rev Psicoanál 1959, 16:193

LUCHINA, ISAAC LÉON

ABSTRACT OF:
52921 Berner, A. S. & Simer, P. J. Effect of hypnosis on intraocular pressure in normal and glaucomatous subjects. Rev Psicoanál 1958, 15:427

REVIEW OF:
52922 Renneker, R. E. Countertransference reactions to cancer. Rev Psicoanál 1957, 14:427-428

LUCHINS, ABRAHAM S.

52923 Patients view the therapist: a training and research device. J consult Psychol 1951, 15:24-31
52924 (& Luchins, E. H.) Rigidity of Behavior; A Variational Approach to the Effect of *Einstellung*. Eugene, Ore: Univ of Oregon Pr 1959, xxv + 623 p
52925 A social experimental approach to group psychotherapy. Soc Psych 1955, 42:121-127
52926 On the theories and problems of adolescence. J genet Psychol 1954, 86:47-63
52927 Toward an experimental clinical psychology. J Personality 1952, 20:440-456

LUCHINS, EDITH HIRSCH

See Luchins, Abraham S.

LUCOTTE, D.

52928 Névrose familiale. [Familial neurosis.] Psyché, Paris 1956, 11:213-235

LUCOTTE, H.

52929 L'attitude psycho-somatique en médecine. [The psychosomatic attitude in medicine.] Maroc méd 1958, 37(392):32-42
52930 Obsession et milieu familial. [Obsession and family environment.] Maroc méd 1958, 37(392):56-60
52931 Ulcères et traumatismes; chirurgie et psychanalyse. [Ulcers and traumatisms; surgery and psychoanalysis.] Maroc méd 1955, 34:624-629

LÜDERS, WOLFRAM

52932 Die Bedeutung der ersten Objektsbeziehungen des Kleinkindes für die Entwicklung der Persönlichkeit nach R. Spitz. [The role of early object relations in infancy in personality development according to R. Spitz.] Prax Kinderpsychol 1959, 8:280-284

LUDWIG, ALFRED O.

52933 [Discussant] Is the term "mysterious leap" warranted? Mind-Body 19-20

52934 Emotional factors in rheumatoid arthritis: their bearing on the care and rehabilitation of the patient. The Physical Therapy Rev 1949, 29 (Aug)

52935 Malingering in combat soldiers, "combat psychiatry." Bull US Army Med Dept 1949, Nov 9:26-32

52936 The practical importance of modern concepts of psychosomatic relations. New England J Med 1958, 238:(Feb 5)175-178

52937 Psychiatric considerations in rheumatoid arthritis. Med Clin N Amer 1955, 39:447-458

52938 Psychiatric studies of patients with rheumatoid arthritis. In *Rheumatic Diseases*, W. B. Saunders 1952

52939 (Reporter) Psychoanalysis and psychotherapy: dynamic criteria for treatment choice. Panel report. J Am Psa Ass 1954, 2:346-350
       Abs NRo An Surv Psa 1954, 5:389-392

52940 Psychogenic factors in rheumatoid arthritis. Bull Rheumatic Dis 1952, 2:April

52941 Rheumatoid arthritis. In Wittkower, E. D. & Cleghorn, R. A. *Recent Developments in Psychosomatic Medicine,* London: Pitman & Sons 1954

52942 The role of identification in the conversion process. Mind-Body 98-110

52943 Some psycho-social factors in cases of severe medical disease. Applied Anthropology: Problems of Human Organization 1948, 7(1)

LUDOWYK GYOMROI, EDITH

52944 Pubertätsriten der Mädchen in einer in Umwandlung begriffenen Gesellschaft. [Puberty rites of girls in a changing society.] In Pfister-Ammende, M. *Geistige Hygiene, Forschung und Praxis,* Basel: Benno Schabe 1955, 237-251

LUFT, JOSEPH

52945 Interaction and projection. J proj Tech 1953, 17:489-492

LUJÁN, N.

52946 Influencia de Freud en la concepción psicológica de los personajes de la novela moderna. [Freud's influence on the psychologic concept of personages of the modern novel.] Rev Psiquiat Psicol 1956, 2:783-794

LUKAS, K. H.

52947 Primäre Dysmenorrhoe und Neurose; ein Beitrag zur Psychotherapie in der Frauenheilkunde. [Primary dysmenorrhoea and neurosis; a contribution to psychotherapy in gynecology.] Z Geburtsh Gynäk 1956, 147:339-370

LULOFF, HARRY

52948 Participant in Clinical conference: A problem of ego organization in a
latency child. New Front Child Guid 173-209

LULOW, WILLIAM V.

See Hulse, Wilfred C.; Stein, Aaron

LUMERMANN, S.

REVIEW OF:
52949 Saul, L. J. Bases of Human Behavior. Rev Psicoanál 1960, 17:256

LUMINET, DANIEL

52950 Les céphalalgies du point de vue psychosomatique. [Headaches from
the psychosomatic point of view.] Bruxelles-Médical 39(5):159-175
52951 Examen critique des modèles théoriques en recherche psychosomatique.
[Critical examination of theoretical models in psychosomatic research.]
Acta neurol psychiat Belg 1959, 59:471-489
52952 Psychothérapie brêve de l'asthme bronchique. [Short psychotherapy
with bronchial asthma.] Acta neurol Belg 1957, 57:582-587

LUN, WENZEL VAN

See Ringel, Erwin

LUND, FREDERICK H.

52953 Biodynamics vs. Freudian psychodynamics. Education 1957, 78:41-54
52954 (& Glosser, H. J.) The nature of mental illness: diversity of psychiatric
opinion. Education 1957, 78:154-166

LUNDY, R. L.

See Gordon, Jesse E.

LUNSKY, L. L.

52955 Murderous "acting out" as a primitive defense to master anxiety. PT
1955, 9:262-268
Abs Racamier RFPsa 1956, 20:575

REVIEW OF:
52956 Miller, H. & Baruch, D. Practice of Psychosomatic Medicine as Illustrated in Allergy. R 1957, 44:230-231

LUQUET, C. J.

See LUQUET-PARAT, C. J.

LUQUET, PIERRE

52957 Les critères de la fin du traitement psychanalytique. [The criteria of
the termination of psychoanalytic therapy.] Symposium. RFPsa 1954,
18:345
52958 Discussion of Berge, A. "L'équation personnelle ou de l'art psychanalytique." RFPsa 1959, 23:469-476

52959 Discussion of Grunberger, B. "Essai sur la situation analytique et le processus du guérison." RFPsa 1957, 21:446-448

52960 Discussion of Grunberger, B. "Étude sur la relation objectale anale." RFPsa 1960, 24:160-163

52961 Discussion of Marty, P. "Importance du rôle de la motricité dans la relation d'objet." RFPsa 1955, 19:313-317

52962 Fugue et homosexualité. [Fugue and homosexuality.] Rv Np inf 1955, 3:547-552

52963 Interprétation prégénitale. [Pregenital interpretation.] RFPsa 1953, 17:465-467

52964 Observation d'un cas de frigidité. Observation du psychanalyste. [Observation on a case of frigidity—the psychoanalyst's observation.] RFPsa 1957, 21:809-826

52965 À propos des facteurs de guérison non verbalisables de la cure analytique. [Nonverbal factors in analytic cure.] RFPsa 1957, 21:182-224
    Abs Roman, R. E. Q 1958, 27:148. Rv Garcia Reinoso, J. P. Rev Psicoanál 1957, 14:340-341

52966 (& Diatkine, R.; Luquet-Parat, C. J.) Psychothérapie chez l'enfant. Indications. Contre-indications. Résultats. [Child psychotherapy. Indications. Contra-indications. Results.] Encycl médico-chir—Psychothérapie 1955, 37818 A 10—37818 C 10—37818 E 10, 18 p

52967 (& Luquet-Parat, C. J.) Troubles des conduites excrémentielles. [Difficulties in elimination behavior.] Encycl médico-chir—Psychiatrie 1955, 37105 D 10, 6 p

52968 L'utilisation du matériel onirique en thérapeutique psychanalytique chez l'adulte. Colloque. [The use of dream material in adult psychoanalytic therapy. Symposium.] RFPsa 1959, 23:62-64

See Fain, Michel; Lebovici, Serge; Michel-Wolfromm, Helene; Schlumberger, Marc

LUQUET-PARAT, C. J.

52969 La place du mouvement masochique dans l'évolution de la femme. [The place of masochism in the development of the female.] RFPsa 1959, 23:305-336; 349-352

See Luquet, Pierre

REVIEW OF:
52970 Caprio, F. S. Female Homosexuality. RFPsa 1959, 23:776

LURIA, ALEXANDER ROM

52971 [On the problem of genetic analysis of psychological functions in relation to their development.] (Russian) [*Problems in Neurological Physiology and Behavior*.] Tiflis: 1936, 361-367

LURIA, ZELLA
See Mowrer, O. Hobart

LURIE, ABRAHAM
See Bellak, Leopold

LURIE, LOUIS A.

52972 Psychopathic behavior of little known or idiopathic origin. In Karpman, B. *Symposia on Child and Juvenile Delinquency*, Wash: Psychodynamics Series 1959, 49-51

52973 Psychopathic delinquent behavior of possible idiopathic origin. In Karpman, B. *Symposia on Child and Juvenile Delinquency*, Wash: Psychodynamics Series 1959, 1-4

52974 The role of endocrine factors in delinquency. Ops 1953, 23:21-30. In Karpman, B. *Symposia on Child and Juvenile Delinquency*, Wash: Psychodynamics Series 1959, 166-175

See Karpman, Ben; Palmer, James O.

LUSSHEIMER, PAUL

52975 On daydreams. Psa 1954, 14:83-92
52976 Psychoanalysis and religion. Psa 1953, 13:88
52977 (& Kelman, H.: Kilpatrick, E.; Gersham, H.; Gutheil, E. A.; Oberndorf, C.) Tributes (to Karen Horney). Psa 1954, 14:8-13

See Kelman, Harold

LUSSIER, ANDRÉ

52978 The analysis of a boy with a congenital deformity. Psa St C 1960, 15:430-453

See Burlingham, Dorothy

ABSTRACT OF
52979 Mailloux, N. Psychic determinism, freedom, and personality development. J 1955, 36:435

LUSTIG, G.

52980 Migración y regresión. [Migration and regression.] 2nd Cong Lat-Am de Higiene y Salud mental, Buenos Aires, Oct 1956
       Abs Rev Psicoanál 1958, 15:197

LUSTIG, S.

52981 (& Tomas, J.) Aspectos prenatales en la literatura de cienca-ficción; análisis del *Hombre Illustrado*, de R. Bradbury. [Prenatal aspects of science fiction; analysis of Ray Bradbury's *Illustrated Man*.] Rev Psicoanál 1956, 13:548-551

See Rascovsky, Arnaldo

REVIEWS OF:
52982 Affemann, R. Beiträge zur Psychologie und Anthropologie der Depression. Rev Psicoanál 1958, 15:304
52983 Hoff, H. & Ringel, E. Zur psychosomatischer Erkrankungen. Rev Psicoanál 1958, 15:303-304

LUSTMAN, SEYMOUR L.

52984 Psychic energy and mechanisms of defense. Psa St C 1957, 12:151-165
    Abs RTh J 1959, 40:369
52985 Rudiments of the ego. Psa St C 1956, 11:89-98
    Abs RTh J 1959, 40:73-74

See Richmond, Julius B.

LUTHY, HERBERT

52986 Democracy and its discontents: France. Encounter 1954, 2(5):23-31

LUTON, F.

See Lidz, Theodore

LUTZ, JAKOB

52987 Entwicklungen in der Kinderpsychiatrie. [Developments in child psychiatry.] Schweiz med Wschr 1954, 84:1355-1359
52988 Psychic damage in early childhood and its consequences from the point of view of the child psychiatrist. J med Liban 1957, 10:212-221

LYKETSOS, GEORGE C.

52989 On the formation of mother-daughter symbiotic relationship patterns in schizophrenia. P 1959, 22:161-166
    Abs HRB Q 1960, 29:293

REVIEW OF:
52990 Kouretas, D. [Abnormal Characters in the Ancient Drama.] Q 1953, 22:110-112

LYKKEN, DAVID THORSON

52991 A study of anxiety in the sociopathic personality. Diss Abst 1956, 16:795

LYLE, J. G.

52992 (& Gilchrist, A. A.) Problems of TAT interpretation and the diagnosis of delinquent trends. M 1958, 31:51-59
    Abs Johnston, M. Q 1959, 28:134

LYLE, WILLIAM HENRY

See Levitt, Eugene E.

LYNCH, H.

See Fineberg, Henry H.

LYND, HELEN M.

52993 Identifications and the growth of personal identity. Merrill-Palmer Q 1956, 3:2-12

52994 On Shame and the Search for Identity. London: Routledge & Kegan
Paul 1958, 318 p
Abs J Am Psa Ass 1960, 8:220-221; 593. Rv Fountain, G. Q 1960,
29:119-121. CR J 1960, 41:85-86

LYON, PETER

See Fox, Ruth

LYONS, ALBERT S.

See Meyer, Bernard C.

LYONS, H.

See Chodoff, Paul

LYONS, JOHN W.

52995 (& Saul, L. J.) Motivation and respiratory disorders. In Wittkower,
E. D. & Cleghorn, R. A. *Recent Developments in Psychosomatic Medicine,* Phila, Montreal: Lippincott 1954, 267-281

See Weiss, Edward

LYONS, JOSEPH

52996 An annotated bibliography of phenomenology and existentialism. Psychol Rep 1959, 5:613-631

See Mendel, Werner M.; Wallerstein, Robert S.

LYRA CHEBABI, WILSON DE

52997 A evolução do conceito de neurose. [The evolution of the concept of
neurosis.] J Bras Psiquiat 1957, 6:197-212

M

M., R

52998 Zur hundertsten Wiederkehr des Geburtstages von Sigmund Freud, 6. Mai 1856. [On the one hundredth anniversary of the birthday of Sigmund Freud, May 6, 1856.] Schweiz Z Psychol 1956, 15:81-83

MABILLE

See Parrot, P.

MACALPINE, IDA

S-30166 (& Hunter, R. A.) Daniel Paul Schreber, Memoirs of My Illness. (Ed, tr, with notes and discussion) Cambridge, Mass: Robert Bentley 1955, 146 p
　　　Abs J Am Psa Ass 1955, 3:544-545. Rv ESt J 1955, 36:399-400. Kohut, H. J Am Psa Ass 1960, 8:567-586

52999 (& Hunter, R. A.) The importance of the concept of transference for present-day theories of mental diseases. Acta psychother psychosom orthopaedagog 1955, 3(suppl):237-243

53000 "Meet it is I write it down . . ." R 1953, 40:158-159
　　　Abs LRa An Surv Psa 1953, 4:26

53001 (& Hunter, R. A.) Observations on the psychoanalytic theory of psychosis: Freud's "A Neurosis of Demoniacal Possession in the Seventeenth Century." M 1954, 27:175-192
　　　Abs LRa An Surv Psa 1954, 5:26-27. EMW Q 1956, 25:125-126

53002 Present status of psychosomatic medicine: reviewed on the basis of a recent publication. PT 1954, 8:454-465

53003 Pruritis ani: a psychiatric study. PSM 1953, 15:498-508

53004 Psychiatric observations on facial dermatoses. Brit J Derm 1953, 65:177-182

S-21418A Psychosomatic symptom formation.
　　　Abs JAA An Surv Psa 1952, 3:330-331

S-21419 (& Hunter, R. A.) Rossini: piano pieces for the primal scene. Morceaux de piano et scène primitive. RFPsa 1952, 16:319-324
　　　Abs MK An Surv Psa 1952, 3:526-527

53005 (& Hunter, R. A.) Schizophrenia 1677. A Psychiatric Study of an Illustrated Autobiographical Record of Demoniacal Possession. Psychiat Monogr Series No. 2. London: W. Dawson 1956, ix + 197 p
　　　Rv Niederland, W. G. Q 1958, 27:107-111

53006   (& Hunter, R. A.) The Schreber case. A contribution to schizophrenia, hypochondria, and psychosomatic symptom-formation. Q 1953, 22:328-371
        Abs LRa An Surv Psa 1953, 4:42-45. Rev Psicoanál 1954, 11:390. JKl J 1955, 36:218. Rv Dreyfus RFPsa 1953, 17:582
53007   Tribute to Freud. J Hist Med 1956, 11:247-260

        See Greenberg, Phillip; Hunter, Richard A.

        REVIEW OF:
53008   Devereux, G. (Ed): Psychoanalysis and the Occult. Q 1954, 23:268-270

MacBRAYER, CAROLINE TAYLOR

53009   Symbolism validity and learning without awareness. J consult Psychol 1959, 23:357-360

MACCOBY, ELEANOR E.

53010   Effects upon children of their mothers' outside employment. In *Work in the Lives of Married Women*, NY: Columbia Univ Pr 1958, 150-172

        See Sears, Robert

MacDONALD, JOHN M.

53011   (& Galvin, J. A. V.) Experimental psychotic states. P 1956, 112:970-976
        Abs DRu Q 1959, 28:121
53012   Pathological firesetting. J forens Med 1959, 6:53-61
53013   Psychiatry and the Criminal. A Guide to Psychiatric Examination for the Criminal Courts. Springfield, Ill: Thomas 1957, 227 p; Oxford: Blackwell Scientific Publ 1958, xvi + 228 p
        Rv MG Q 1958, 27:435. Williams, H. J 1959, 40:350

MACE, CECIL ALEC

53014   (& Vernon, P. E.) (Eds) Current Trends in British Psychology. London: Methuen; NY: British Book Centre 1953, viii + 262 p
        Abs DRu Q 1959, 28:121

MacFARLANE, JEAN W.

53015   (& Allen, L.; Honzik, M.) A developmental study of the behavior problems of normal children between twenty-one months and fourteen years. Univ of Calif Publications in Child Development, vol 2. Univ Calif Pr 1954, 221 p

MacGREGOR, HELEN

        See Lichtenberg, Philip

MACHADO GOMES, E.

53016   O exame psíquico na prática psiquiátrica. Introdução ao estudo de uma psiquiatria filosófica. [The psychologic examination in psychiatric practice. Introduction to the study of a philosophic psychiatry.] Rev Psicol norm patol 1958, 4:283-291

MACHOVER, KAREN

53017   A destructive juvenile delinquent. Clin Stud Pers 582-599

See Machover, Solomon

MACHOVER, SOLOMON

53018   (& Puzzo, F. S.) Clinical and objective studies of personality variables in alcoholism. I. Clinical investigation of the "alcoholic personality." II. Clinical study of personality correlates of remission from active, chronic alcoholism. Quart J Stud Alcoh 1959, 20:505-519; 520-527

53019   (& Puzzo, F. S.; Machover, K.; Plumeau, F. E.) Clinical and objective studies of personality variables in alcoholism. III. An objective study of homosexuality in alcoholism. Quart J Stud Alcoh 1959, 20:528-542

53020   A compulsive personality with psychosomatic reactions. Clin Stud Pers 21-48

MACHT, DAVID I.

53021   Influence of some drugs and of emotions on blood coagulation. JAMA 1952, 148:265-270
    Rv Labbé, P. RFPsa 1953, 17:355

MacINTYRE, A. C.

53022   The Unconscious. A Conceptual Analysis. London: Routledge & Kegan Paul 1958, 100 p
    Rv ESt J 1959, 40:348

MacIVER, JOHN

53023   (& Redlich, F. C.) Patterns of psychiatric practice. P 1959, 115:692-697

MacIVER, R. M.

53024   Signs and symbols. J Relig Thought 1952-53, 10:101

MacKEITH, RONALD

53025   Children in hospital. Lancet 1953, Oct:843. Child-Fam Dig 1954, 10(3):44-52

53026   Foreword to Robertson, J. *Young Children in Hospital*

53027   The psychosomatic approach in paediatrics. Mod Tr PSM 60-72

MACKENZIE, J.

See Gifford, Sanford

MACKENZIE, JEAN N.

See Stein, Morris I.

MACKENZIE, MARION

See Bowlby, John

MacKINNON, DONALD W.

53028 A topological analysis of anxiety. Char Pers 1944, 12:163-177. Stud Pers 136-147

MacKINNON, HARRY L.

53029 (& Allen, A.) Special techniques in brief psychotherapy. Dis nerv Syst 1955, 16:277-283

MACKWOOD, JOHN C.

53030 Remedial and educational psychotherapy during penal detention. In East, W. N. *The Roots of Crime,* London: Butterworth 1954, 90-119

MACLAY, DAVID THOMSON

53031 The Approach to Mental Health. London: Thorsons Publ 1956, 144 p

MacLEAN, MALCOLM S.

See Hahn, Milton Edwin

MacLEAN, PAUL D.

53032 Discussion of Kubie, L. S. "Some implications for psychoanalysis of modern concepts of the organization of the brain." Q 1953, 22:52-54

REVIEW OF:
53033 Cannon, W. B. Bodily Changes in Pain, Hunger, Fear and Rage. Q 1954, 23:282-283

MacLENNAN, BERYCE

See Slavson, Samuel Richard

MacLEOD, ALISTAIR W.

53034 (& Wittkower, E. D.; Margolin, S. G.) Basic concepts of psychosomatic medicine. In Wittkower, E. D. & Cleghorn, R. A. *Recent Developments in Psychosomatic Medicine,* Phila: Lippincott 1954, 2-38

REVIEW OF:
53035 Balint, M. Thrills and Regressions. J 1959, 40:342-343

MacLEOD, JOHN A

See Gottschalk, Louis A.

MacNAUGHTON, DOROTHY

53036 Discussion of Dunbar, F. "Symbiosis of parent and child." Ops 1952, 22:823-824
53037 The inner world of the pre-school child. Child Study Quart 1950, 6-8, 38-40

MADDALONI, ARNOLD

53038 Psychologic evolution in character formation. Am Im 1956, 13:241-257

MADDEN, EDWARD H.

53039 Psychoanalysis and moral judgeability. Phil phenomenol Res 1957, 18:68-79

MADIA, A.

53040 (& Spadaro, P.) Il parricidio. Osservazioni sulla dinamica psicologica criminale. [Parricide. Observations on the psychodynamics of criminality.] Pisani 1959, 73:561-580

MADISON, PETER

53041 Freud's repression concept. A survey and attempted clarification. J 1956, 37:75-81
       Abs JLan Q 1957, 26:434

MAEDA, SHIGEHARU

53042 My experience of didactic analysis. Jap J Psa 1958, 5(3):24-28
53043 My experience of didactic analysis. (I) On free association. In *Susume* of psychoanalysis. Yokohama: Hiyoshi Hosp 1958, (1):21-38
53044 My experience of didactic analysis. (II) Spider-phobia and primal scene. In *Susume* of Psychoanalysis, Yokohama: Hiyoshi Hosp 1958, (2):1-19
53045 Our problems of learning psychoanalysis. Jap J Psa 1958, 5(6):25-29
53046 A psychoanalytic case report on anthropophobia. Jap J Psa 1956, 3(7):7-10
53047 A psychoanalytic case report on leprophobia. Jap J Psa 1955, 2(7):2-5
53048 Some considerations on the dream of neurotics. Jap J Clin & Exper Med 1956, 33(12):50-55

MAEDER, ALPHONSE

53049 Die Bedeutung der Person des Erziehers für seine Aufgabe. [The importance of the educator's personality for his task.] Acta psychother psychosom orthopaedagog 1953, 1(2):120-135
53050 Kontakt und Übertragung. Die zwischenmenschliche Beziehung Arzt-Patient. [Contact and transference. The doctor-patient interpersonal relationship.] In Stern, E. *Handbuch der klinischen Psychologie*. Vol. II: *Die Psychotherapie in der Gegenwart*, Zürich: Rascher Verlag 1958, 335-349
53051 A new concept of the psychotherapist's role. J Psychother relig Proc 1955, 2:38-46
53052 Persönliche Erinnerungen an Freud und retrospektive Besinnung. [Personal recollections about Freud and retrospective consideration.] Schweiz Z Psychol 1956, 15:114-122
53053 Psychosynthese—Psychagogik. [Psychosynthesis—Psychagogy.] Hndb N P 1959, 3:392-412
53054 Der Psychotherapeut als Partner; eine appelative Psychotherapie. [The psychotherapist as partner; an appelative psychotherapy.] Zürich: Rascher 1957, 140 p

53055 Sendung und Aufgabe des Arztes; Ausblick eines Psychotherapeuten. [Mission and Task of the Physician; Outlook of a Psychotherapist.] Zürich: Rascher 1952, 281 p

53056 Übertragung und Beziehung; eine zentrale Frage der Psychotherapie. [Transference and doctor-patient relationship; a fundamental problem of psychotherapy.] MPN 1953, 125:605-614

53057 Ways to Psychic Health. NY: Charles Scribner's Sons 1953, x + 200 p

53058 Wesen und Wirken der Deutung. [What is interpretation and how does it work?] Psyche Heidel 1958, 12:538-549

53059 Über die zwischenmenschliche Beziehung in der Psychotherapie. [The interpersonal relationship in psychotherapy.] Acta psychother psychosom orthopaedagog 1955, 3(1):50-58

MAENCHEN, ANNA

53060 Notes on early ego disturbances. Psa St C 1953, 8:262-270
Abs NRo An Surv Psa 1953, 4:279-281. RTh J 1955, 36:78-79

MAGEIRA, ESTELLE A.

See Watters, Thomas A.

MAGNUSSEN, F.

See Bressler, Bernard

MAGNUSSEN, MAX G.

53061 (& Kidorf, I. W.) Bibliography on repression. Psychol Newsltr, NYU 1959, 10:92-95

53062 Body size and body-cathexis replicated. Psychol Newsltr, NYU 1958, 10:33-34

MAGONET, A. PHILIP

53063 Hypnosis in Asthma. London: Heinemann Med Books 1955, 95 p
Rv ESt J 1956, 37:501

MAGRUDER, BETTY ALLEN

ABSTRACT OF:

53064 Fessler, L. The "exceptional performance" as a biological concept. Q 1958, 27:303-304

REVIEWS OF:

53065 De Kok, W. You and Your Child. Q 1956, 25:433-434

53066 Valentine, C. W. Parents and Children. Q 1956, 25:434-435

MAHL, GEORGE F.

53067 (& Brody, E. B.) Chronic anxiety symptomatology, experimental stress, and HCl secretion. AMA ANP 1954, 71:314-325
Abs Leavitt, M. Q 1956, 25:452

53068   Disturbances and silences in the patient's speech in psychotherapy. ASP 1956, 53:1-15
53069   (& Karpe, R.) Emotions and hydrochloric acid secretion during psychoanalytic hours. PSM 1953, 15:312-327
        Abs LCK An Surv Psa 1953, 4:489-491. VC Q 1954, 23:471. Rev Psicoanál 1954, 11:545
53070   (& Dollard, J.; Redlich, F. C.) Facilities for the sound recording of interviews. Science 1954, 120(3111):235-239

        REVIEW OF:
53071   Skinner, B. F. Verbal Behavior. Q 1958, 27:595-597

MAHLER, MARGARET S.

53072   Autism and symbiosis, two extreme disturbances of identity. J 1958, 29:77-83
        Abs J 1958, 29:293. JLan Q 1959, 28:276. Usandivaras & Tabak Rev Psicoanál 1959, 16:86
S-21538 On child psychosis and schizophrenia: autistic and symbiotic infantile psychosis.
        Abs NRo An Surv Psa 1952, 3:230-234. RTh J 1953, 34:281. Rv Bensoussan, P. RFPsa 1954, 18:301-302
53073   Discussion of Freud, A. "Problems of technique in adult analysis." Bull Phila Ass Psa 1954, 4:53
53074   Discussion of Loomie, L. S. et al: "Ernst Kris and the Gifted Adolescent Project." Psa St C 1958, 13:61-63
S-21542 Discussion of Sperling, M. "The neurotic child and his mother." Rv Goldfarb RFPsa 1955, 19:493-495
53075   (& Rabinovitch, R.) The effects of marital conflict on child development. In Eisenstein, V. W. Neurotic Interaction in Marriage, NY: Basic Books 1956, 44-56
        Rv Fiasche, D. N. de Rev Psicoanál 1959, 15:146
53076   Obituary: Prof. August Aichhorn. Quart J Child Beh 1950, 2(3):35-51
53077   (& Furer, M.) Observations on research regarding the "symbiotic syndrome" of infantile psychosis. Q 1960, 29:317-327
53078   Problems of infantile neurosis. A discussion. Psa St C 1954, 9:65-66
53079   On psychological problems of adolescence. NY State Comm on Mental Hygiene Pamphlet 1944
53080   (& Silberpfennig, I.) Der Rorschach'sche Formdeutversuch als Hilfsmittel zum Verständnis der Psychologie Hirnkranker. [The Rorschach test as an auxiliary psychological method for understanding the organic brain-damaged patient.] Schweiz ANP 1938, 40:302-327
53081   (& Furer, M.; Settlage, C. F.) Severe emotional disturbances in childhood: psychosis. Am Hbk Psychiat 1:816-839
53082   (& Elkisch, P.) Some observations on disturbances of the ego in a case of infantile psychosis. Psa St C 1953, 8:252-261
        Abs NRo An Surv Psa 1953, 4:281-284. RTh J 1955, 36:78
53083   (& Gosliner, B. J.) On symbiotic child psychosis. Genetic, dynamic and restitutive aspects. Psa St C 1955, 10:195-212
        Abs RTh J 1957, 38:295-296

53084 Symposium on psychotic object relationships: III. Perceptual dedifferentiation and psychotic "object relationship." (Read at 21st Int Psa Cong, Copenhagen, July 1959) J 1960, 41:548-553

See Elkisch, Paula; Gardner, George E.; Herskovitz, Herbert H.

MAHLER, VERA

53085 [Educational conclusions of depth psychology for the teacher's and educator's work.] (Hebrew) Hahinukh 1957-58, 30:254-273

MAHONY, FRANK

See Fischer, J. L.

MAIDER, A.

See Boss, Medard

MAIER, HENRY WILLIAM

53086 (& Loomis, E. A., Jr.) Effecting impulse control in children through group therapy. Int J grp PT 1954, 4:312-320

53087 (& Campbell, S. G.) Routines: a pilot study of three selected routines and their impact upon the child in residential treatment. Ops 1957, 27:701-709

53088 (& Hilgeman, L. M.; Shugart, G.; Loomis, E. A., Jr.) Supervision of child care workers in a residential treatment service. Symposium 1954: The role of residential treatment for children. Ops 1955, 25:699-704
    Abs Koenig RFPsa 1956, 20:583-584

53089 Three current child development theories applied to child rearing tasks: a study of three child development theories as postulated by Jean Piaget, Erik H. Erikson and Robert R. Sears for the purpose of applying principles derived from these theories to child caring tasks in children's institutions. Diss Abstr 1959, 20:1432-1433

MAIER, JOSEPH

53090 The sociologic definition of religion. In Wolff, W. *Psychiatry and Religion*, NY; MD Publications 1955, 28-31

MAILLOUX, NOËL

53091 Aspects cliniques de la tentation morale. [Clinical aspects of moral temptation.] In *Conducta religiosa y salud mental*, 7th Int Cong of Psychotherapy & Clin Psychol, Madrid 1959, 201-206

53092 The contribution of clinical research to personality theory. Canad J Psychol 1955, 9:133-143

53093 Déterminisme psychique, liberté et développement de la personnalité. Suppl Vie Spir 1952, (22):257-276
    Psychic determinism, freedom, and personality development. Canad J Psychol 1953, 7:1-11
    Determinismo psichico, libertà e sviluppo della personalità. Arch Psicol Neur Psich 1956, 17:853-865
    Abs Lussier, A. J 1955, 36:435

53094　(& Ancona, L.) La dinamica del conflitto psicologico. [The dynamics of psychological conflict.] Arch Psicol Neur Psich 1957, 18:395-400. Contributi del Laboratorio di Psicologia, Milano 1957, 21:112-116

53095　Foi et psychopathologie. [Faith and psychopathology.] Suppl Vie Spir 1948, (7):284-292

53096　Modern psychology and moral values. (Read at Am Psa Ass, May 17, 1948) In *Christianity in an Age of Science,* Toronto: Canad Broadcasting Corp Publ Branch 1952, 50-57. Pastoral Psychol 1954, 5(47):11-16

53097　Obstacles to the realisation of the ascetic ideal. In *Christian Asceticism and Modern Man,* NY: Philos Library 1955, 237-252

53098　La pastorale et les scrupuleux. Suppl Vie Spir 1956, (39):425-439
　　　　The problem of scrupulosity in pastoral work. *Proc Inst for Clergy on Problems in Pastoral Psychology,* NY: Fordham Univ 1956, 53-65

53099　Psychology and spiritual direction. In Braceland, F. J. *Faith, Reason and Modern Psychiatry,* NY: Kenedy 1955, 247-263
　　　　Psychologie pastorale et problèmes de la direction de conscience. Contributions à l'Étude des Sciences de l'Homme 1959, 4:66-130

53100　Quelques observations sur les attitudes psychologiques de la mère célibataire. [Some observations on the psychological attitudes of the unmarried mother.] Suppl Vie Spir 1957, (43):399-412

53101　Religious and moral issues in psychotherapy and counseling. Ann NY Acad Sci 1955, 63:427-428

53102　Sanctity and the problem of neurosis. Pastoral Psychol 1959, 10:37-43

53103　(& Ancona, L.) Uno studio clinico degli atteggiamenti religiosi e un nuovo punto di vista nella psicopatologia. Contributi del Laboratorio di Psicologia, Milano 1957, 21:102-111

MAIN, TOM F.

53104　Notes on an adult head-banger. (Read at Chicago Psa Soc Oct 20, 1959)
　　　　Abs Seitz, P. F. D. Bull Phila Ass Psa 1959, 9:107-109

53105　Perception and ego function. M 1958, 31:1-8
　　　　Abs Johnston, M. Q 1959, 28:132

MAINZER, F.

53106　[Concerning the influence of anxiety on the electrocardiogram.] (German) Med Klin 1953, 1651

MAIRE, FERDINAND

See Piaget, Jean

MAISKII, I.

53107　[Freudism and religion.] (Russian) In [*The Atheist.*] (Russian). Moscow: 1930, 78 p

MAISNER, EDNA A.

53108　Contributions of play-therapy techniques to total rehabilitative design in an institution for high-grade mentally deficient and borderline children. Am J Ment Defic 1950, 55:235-250. Couns PT Ment Retard 241-255

MAITI, H. P.

53109 Unconscious parental resistance to child's improvement in therapy. (Read at 19th Int Psa Cong, Geneva 1955)
Abs Auth J 1956, 37:132

MAJLÁTH

See Liebermann, Lucy P.

MAJLUF, E.

53110 Naturaleza y razón. Ensayo sobre la significación de la teoría en el conocimiento psiquiátrico. [Nature and reason. An essay on the significance of theory in psychiatric knowledge.] Rev psiquiát Peru 1957, 1:141-146

53111 Sobre una sencilla clasificación de las alteraciones de la noción de tiempo. [A simple classification of the changes in the time sense.] Rev Neuro-psiquiat 1954, 17:484-487

MAJORE, I.

53112 Psicoanalisi in Italia: discussioni e controversie. [Psychoanalysis in Italy: discussions and controversies.] Note Psichiat, Pesaro 1957, 50:147-158

TRANSLATION OF:
Moloney, J. C. [54410]

MAJUMDER, KANAK

53113 Adure meye. [Pet daughter.] Chitta 1959, 1(3)
53114 Amil keno. [Why conjugal quarrel?] Ujjwal Bharat 1956, 9(9):536-540
53115 Ghurni. [Mental conflict.] Ujjwal Bharat 1958, 11(9):550-552
53116 Heenata bodh. [Inferiority feeling.] Ujjwal Bharat 1959, 12(9):523-527
53117 Kanna. [Crying.] Ujjwal Bharat 1957, 10(9):550-553
53118 Maner ashukh lukoyee keno. [Why do we conceal mental disease?] Ujjwal Bharat 1955, 8(9):604-608
53119 [Mental treatment in school.] (Bengali) Ujjwal Bharat 1953, 6(9)

MAKKAY, ELISABETH S.

See Kaufman, Irving

MALAMUD, DANIEL

53120 A workshop in self-understanding designed to prepare patients for psychotherapy. PT 1958, 12:771-786

MALAMUD, WILLIAM

53121 Current trends in basic psychiatric research. J Hillside Hosp 1956, 5:171-184
53122 Developments in research on dementia praecox. MH 1953, 37:14-21
Abs JLan Q 1953, 22:464

53123   (& Overholser, W.) Multidisciplinary research in schizophrenia. P 1958, 114:865-872

See Whitehorn, John C.

MALAN, DAVID H.

53124   On assessing the results of psychotherapy. M 1959, 32:86
53125   (& Phillipson, H.) The psychodynamics of diagnostic procedures. A case study reporting the effects on the patient of psychiatric interview and Rorschach investigation. M 1957, 30:92-98

MALCOLM, NORAN ADRIAN

53126   Dreaming. London: Routledge & Kegan Paul; NY: Humanities Pr 1959, 128 p
    Rv Young, N. Q 1960, 29:264-266

MÂLE, P.

53127   Etude psychanalytique de l'adolescence. [Psychoanalytic study of adolescence.] In Nacht, S. *La psychanalyse d'aujourd'hui*, Paris: PUF 1956, 237-286
53128   (& Freen, A.) Les préschizophrénies de l'adolescent. [Pre-schizophrenias in the adolescent.] Evolut psychiat 1958, 2:323-374

See Favreau, Jean; Lebovici, Serge

MALEV, MILTON

53129   The value of ritual. Judaism Psychiat 135-142

ABSTRACT OF:
53130   Rapaport, D. On psychoanalytic metapsychology. Q 1959, 28:297-298

MALINOWSKI, BRONISLAW

S-21621 Sex and Repression in Savage Society. NY: Meridian Books 1955, 251 p

MALITZ, SIDNEY

53131   [Participant in] Conference on d-lysergic acid diethylamide (LSD-25). In Abramson, H. A. *The Use of LSD in Psychotherapy: Transactions,* NY: Josiah Macy Jr Found 1960, 7-240
53132   Psychoanalytic psychotherapy with LSD. In Abramson, H. A. *The Use of LSD in Psychotherapy; Transactions.* NY: Josiah Macy Jr Found 1960, 7-24
53133   (& Hoch, P. H.; Lesse, S.) A two-year evaluation of chlorpromazine in clinical research and practice. P 1956, 113:540-545

See Cattell, James P.; Weinstein, Edwin A.

MALL, GERHARD

53134   Metodi e fondamenti della psicoterapia. [Methods and foundations of psychotherapy.] Clin nuova 1951, 12(1546):558-563

MALLESON, JOAN

53135 Deviations: their cause and effect. In Linscott, R. N. & Stein, J. *Why You Do What You Do,* NY: Random House 1956, 178-186. From author's *Any Wife or Any Husband,* NY: Random House 1951.

MALLESON, NICHOLAS

53136 (Ed) The Matrix of Medicine: Some Social Aspects of Medical Practice. London: Pitman 1958
Rv Bonnard, A. J 1959, 40:357

MALLET, C. H.

53137 Analyse des Grimm'schen Märchens "Der starke Hans." [Analysis of Grimm's fairy tale "Strong John."] Prax Kinderpsychol 1953, 2:53-62; 321

MALLET, JEAN

53138 Contribution à l'étude des phobies. [Contribution to the study of phobias.] RFPsa 1956, 20:237-282
53139 La dépression névrotique. [Neurotic depression.] Évolut psychiat 1955, (3):483-501
53140 L'évolution de W. Reich ou l'analyste et l'instinct de mort. [The development of Wilhelm Reich or the analyst and the death instinct.] RFPsa 1953, 17:279-298
Abs LRa An Surv Psa 1953, 4:48-49. NRo An Surv Psa 1953, 4:79
53141 Hystérie de conversion [Conversion hysteria.] In *Psychiatrie Encyclopédie Médico-Chirurgicale,* Paris 1955, 37340-A 10, 15 p
53142 Névroses phobiques. [Phobic neuroses.] In *Psychiatrie Encyclopédie Médico-Chirurgicale,* Paris 1955, 37360-A 10, 5 p
53143 Les troubles névrotiques de la sexualité (Etude centrée sur la point de vue économique). [Neurotic sexual disturbances. A study focused on the economic point of view.] In Nacht, S. *La psychanalyse d'aujourd'hui,* Paris: PUF 1956, 1:346-359

MALMO, ROBERT B.

53144 Hysterical deafness in a young girl. Clin Stud Pers 213-230
53145 Research: experimental and theoretical aspects. In Wittkower, E. D. & Cleghorn, R. A. *Recent Developments in Psychosomatic Medicine,* Phila: Lippincott 1954, 84-100

See Shagass, Charles

MALONE, THOMAS P.

53146 Countertransference. In Whitaker, C. A. *Psychotherapy of Chronic Schizophrenic Patients,* Boston: Little, Brown 1958, 144-183

See Whitaker, Carl A.

MALTZMAN, IRVING

53147 (& Morrisett, L., Jr.; Fox, J.) Some effects of manifest anxiety on mental set. J exp Psychol 1953, 46:50-54

MANDEL, HENRY

53148 A Q-methodology investigation of the oral and anal character as described by psychoanalytic theory. Diss Abstr 1959, 19:2148

MANDELBAUM, ARTHUR

See Ekstein, Rudolf; Hirschberg, J. Cotter

MANDELBROTE, B. M.

53149 (& Wittkower, E. D.) Emotional factors in Graves' disease. PSM 1955, 17:109-123
       Abs Fain, M. RFPsa 1955, 19:632. EMW Q 1957, 26:144. R 1957, 44:481

See Wittkower, Eric D.

MANDOLINI, H.

53150 El problema de la creación artistica. [The problem of artistic creativity.] Rev Criminol Psiquiat Med leg 1931, 18:434-443

MANDOLINI, M.

53151 Die geschlechtlichen Konflikte bei künstlerischen Genies. [Sexual conflicts in artistic genius.] Rev Criminol Psiquiat Med leg 1927, 17 (82)

MANDY, ARTHUR J.

See Mandy, T. E.

MANDY, T. E.

53152 (& Scher, E.; Farkas, R.; Mandy, A. J.) The psychic aspects of sterility and abortion. Southern med J 1951, 44:1054-1059

MANFREDINI, J.

53153 A bio-afetividade. [Bio-affectivity.] J Bras Psiquiat 1954, 3:40-60
53154 Fundamentos de um programa de psicopatologia. [Outline of a course in psychopathology.] J Bras Psiquiat 1956, 5:316-326

MANGANARO, D.

See Imberciadori, E.

MANGHAM, CHARLES A.

See Leider, Allan R!; Stewart, Ann H.; Weiland, Irvin H.

REVIEW OF:
53155 Slavson, S. R. Child Psychotherapy. Q 1954, 23:134

MANHÃES, M. P.

53156 Assistência psiquiátrica infantil. [Child psychiatry services.] Rev Bras Saúde ment 1957, 3(1):5-27
53157 Influência das tensões familiares no estudo das convulsões infantis. [The influence of family tensions on convulsions of children.] Rev Bras Saúde ment 1957, 3(1):55-71

MANHEIM, ELEANOR B.

53158 Pandora's Box. Persistent fantasies as themes in the plays of Jean Anouilh. Lit & Psych 1958, 8(1):6-10

MANHEIM, LEONARD FALK

53159 The law as "father." An aspect of the Dickens pattern. Am Im 1955, 12:17-23

S-21639A The personal history of David Copperfield.
　　　　Abs MK An Surv Psa 1952, 3:522-524

53160 A *Tale of Two Cities* (1859): a study in psychoanalytic criticism. English Rev 1959, Spring: 13-28

53161 Thanatos: the death instinct in Dickens' later novels. PPR 1960, 47(4):17-31

MANIORI, E.

See Missaglia, A.

MANN, HAROLD

See Sperry, Bessie M.

MANN, JAMES

53162 Childhood schizophrenia. Acta med Orient, Jerusalem 1956, 15:33-48

53163 The contributions of Freud to the understanding of psychosis. Acta med Orient, Jerusalem 1956, 15:177-182
　　　　Hebrew: In Halpern, L. et al: [*Freud's Festival*], Jerusalem: Magnes Pr, Hebrew Univ 1957, 36-42

53164 (& Semrad, E. V.) Conversion as process and conversion as symptom in psychosis. Mind-Body 131-154

53165 Dynamics of hostility in schizophrenia. JNMD 1953, 117(Mar)

53166 Group therapy with adults—general observations. Ops 1953, 23:332-337

53167 (& Robinson, A.) Praise, blame and gossip. Nursing Outlook 1954, Dec

S-21641 (& Menzer, D.; Standish, C.) Psychotherapy of psychoses
　　　　Abs R 1954, 41:67-68

53168 Psychotherapy of schizophrenia in an outpatient setting. P 1953, 110:448-453

53169 Some theoretic concepts of the group process. Int J grp PT 1955, 5:235-241
　　　　Abs GPK Q 1956, 25:622-623

See Semrad, Elvin V.; Standish, Christopher T.

MANN, JOHN WILLIAM

53170 The folktale as a reflection of individual and social structure. A depth-psychological study of seven tales from the brothers Grimm. Diss Abstr 1959, 19:1514-1515

MANN, LESTER

53171 Child-physician; patient-therapist: role and transference problems. NPAP 1955-56, 4(2):67-70

53172 Persuasive doll play: a technique of directive psychotherapy for use with children. Clin Psych 1957, 13:14-19

MANN, THOMAS

S-21644 Freud and the future. J 1956, 37:106-115. Daedalus (Proc Am Acad Arts & Sci) 1959, 88:374-378. Art Psa 369-389. From author's *Freud, Goethe, Wagner.*
> Abs JLan Q 1957, 26:435
53173 Freuds Humanismus. [Freud's humanism.] Psa Vkb 1957, 46-52
S-21647 Die Stellung Freuds in der modernen Geistesgeschichte.
> Freud's position in the history of modern culture. (Tr: Willard, C. & Jelliffe, S. E.) Arch crim Psychodyn 1957, 2:495-506
53174 About "Totem and Tabu." In [S. Freud-centenary of his birth.] (Hebrew) Urim 1955-56, 13:618

MANNES, MARYA

53175 Riggs: where psychiatrists learn. Reporter, 1954, Nov 4:35-39. In Daniel, R. S. *Contemporary Readings in General Psychology,* Boston: Houghton Mifflin 1959, 378-382

MANNHEIM, JULIA

53176 Notes on a case of drug addiction. J 1955, 36:166-173
> Abs Lebovici RFPsa 1955, 19:637. JLan Q 1956, 25:613

MANNHEIM, KARL

53177 Essays on Sociology and Social Psychology. (Ed: Kecskemeti, P.) London: Routledge & Kegan Paul; NY: Oxford Univ Pr 1953, 310 p
> Rv Schmidl, F. Q 1955, 24:306-307. Turquet, P. M. J 1955, 36:360-361. MG Q 1957, 26:132-133. Williams, A. H. J 1957, 38:127-128
53178 Systematic Sociology. An Introduction to the Study of Society. (Ed: Erös, J. S. & Stewart, W. A. C.) NY: Philos Libr 1958, 169 p
> Rv Posinsky, S. H. Q 1958, 27:428

MANNONI VAN DER SPOEL, MAUD
(See also Spoel, Maud Van Der)

53179 Problèmes posés par la psychothérapie des débiles. [Problems in the psychotherapy of feeble-minded children.] La Psychanalyse 1959, (5)
53180 Réactions de la famille à la débilité. [Family reactions to feeble-mindedness.] Rev belge de Psychanalyse (22)
S-21658 Regression in infantile psychotherapy.
> Abs RdeS Q 1953, 22:312

MANNONI, O.

53181 Poésie et psychanalyse. [Poetry and psychoanalysis.] Psychanalyse 1957, 3:139-163
53182 Le théatre du point de vue de l'imaginaire. [Theater from the point of view of fantasy.] Psychanalyse 1959, 5
53183 Le tour de vis. [The turn of the screw.] (An analytical study of James' novel). Les temps modernes 1951, (73)

MANOR, A.

53184 [On the paths of psychology.] (Hebrew) Urim 1953-54, 11:481-484

MANOR, RAHEL

53185 [On transference in education.] (Hebrew) Ofakim 1958, 12:155-160

MANRIQUE, M.

53186 Comentario psicoanalitico sobre los milagros. [Psychoanalytic comments on miracles.] Arch Neurol Psiquiat 1958, 8:129-133

53187 (& Kubie, L. S.) El proceso psicodinámico del descubrimiento de la realidad. [Psychodynamic process of the discovery of reality.] Rev Psicoanál 1956, 13:372-378

MANSON, MORSE P.

See Bühler, Charlotte

MANTHEY, H. G.

53188 (& Droste, R.) Thyreotoxikosen in psychosomatischer Betrachtung. [Psychosomatic considerations in thyrotoxicoses.] Z PSM 1957, 3:95-109

53189 (& Droste, R.) Thyreotoxikosen und psychischer Stress. [Thyrotoxicoses and mental stress.] Dtsche med Wschr 1957, 82:1227-1230

MANZANILLA, LUIS M.

See Mendoza-Hoyos, H.; Quijada, Hernán

MAQUET, JEAN

53190 Le docteur Freud, grand détective des rêves. [Doctor Freud, great dream detective.] Paris Match 1956, Dec 1 (399):50

MARABINI, ENRICO

53191 Sogno paragnosico; contributo casistico. [Paragnostic dream; case report.] Minerva med 1956, 47:1928-1938

MARASSE, HENRY F.

53192 (Reporter) Isolation. (Panel: Am Psa Ass, San Francisco, May 1958) J Am Psa Ass 1959, 7:163-172

ABSTRACTS OF:
53193 Dracoulides, N. N. The "displaced" Oedipus complex. Q 1956, 25:295
53194 Lechat, F. Things always come in threes. Q 1956, 25:296-297
53195 Nacht, S. Difficulties of didactic as compared to therapeutic analysis. Q 1956, 25:296
53196 Racamier, P. C. Clinical studies of infantile frustration. Q 1956, 25:296
53197 Rosen, V. H. Reconstruction of a traumatic childhood event in a case of derealization. Q 1955, 24:324-325
53198 Roumajon, Y. Anxiety state following combat wound. Q 1956, 25:297
53199 Savitt, R. A. Phobic and counterphobic attitudes in a research scientist. Q 1957, 26:150-152

MARBURG, RUDOLF

See Bing, James F.

MARCH, HANS

53200 Zur Frage der Neurosen-Begutachtung. Ein kasuistischer Beitrag. [Contribution to the appraisal of neuroses. A case report.] Die Medizinische 1959 (10)

53201 Lebensschicksale in psychiatrischen Gutachten. Schuld und Verantwortung. [Life Biographies in Psychiatric Investigations. Guilt Feelings and Responsibility.] Stuttgart: Enke 1959, 353 p

53202 Menschenschicksale in Gutachten. [Human destinies in expert testimony.] Psyche, Heidel 1953, 7:301-317

53203 Menschenschicksale in Gutachten. III. (4) Ein Krankenhauswanderer. [Human destinies and expert testimony. III (4). A hospital vagrant.] Psyche, Heidel 1954, 7:711-720

53204 Der Psychotherapeut. [The psychotherapist.] Stimmen der Zeit 1954, Oct (1)

MARCHAND, H.

53205 [Concerning vegetative function-tests on hypnotized experimental patients.] (German) Medizinische 1956, 1:382

MARCHESI, C.

53206 An evaluation of hypnosis as a conscious state. Brit J med Hypnot 1957, 8(4):2-15

MARCONDES, DURVAL

53207 The concept of interpretation in psychoanalysis. JNMD 1958, 127:443-447

53208 Formação psicossomática do médico. [The psychosomatic training of the physician.] Rev Assoc médica brasileira, São Paulo 1957, 3:167-171

S-21733A A Medicina e a Psicologia. [Medicine and Psychology.]
Rv Kairys, D. Q 1953, 22:442-443

53209 Nuevos aspectos de la entrevista médica: dificultades contra-transferenciales. [New aspects of the medical interview: countertransferential aspects.] Actas médico-psicol, Buenos Aires, 1959, 2

53210 Psicologia médica. [Medical psychology.] In Klineberg, O. *Psicologia Moderna*, Rio de Janeiro: Livraria Agir Editora 1953, 181-203

53211 A psicoterapia na clínica general. [Psychotherapy in general medical practice.] Rev brasileira de Med, Rio de Janeiro 1954, 11:800-802

53212 The psychodynamism of the analytic process. R 1956, 43:261-271
Abs JLan Q 1957, 26:585

MARCOVITZ, ELI

53213 Discussion of Freud, A. "Problems of technique in adult analysis." Bull Phila Ass Psa 1954, 4:62-63

53214 Discussion of Kolansky, H. "Treatment of a three-year-old girl's severe infantile neurosis." Bull Phila Ass Psa 1960, 10:134-135

53215 Discussion of Sloane, P. "Resistance as a narcissistic defense." Bull Phila Ass Psa 1957, 7:21-23

S-21744 The meaning of *déjà vu*. YBPsa 1953, 9:250-256
Abs JFr An Surv Psa 1952, 3:133-135. CR J 1954, 35:437

53216 Obituary: Edward Weiss, 1895-1960. Bull Phila Ass Psa 1960, 10:100-101

MARCUS, BERNARD

53217 Status of the psychological factor in criminal research. Brit J Delinq 1954, 4:283-288

MARCUS, IRWIN M.

53218 Clinical aspects of childhood schizophrenia, viewed from integrative levels. New Orleans med surg J 1952, 104:541-548

53219 Diagnostic problems with adolescents. Bull Tulane Univ med Faculty 1954, 14(1). Child-Fam Dig 1956, 14(5):3-13

53220 A family study unit. Chg Cpts Psa Med 151-161

53221 An interdisciplinary approach to accident patterns in children. Lafayette, Ind: Child Development Publ, Purdue Univ 1959, 86 p

53222 The problem of evaluation. In *The Adolescent Exceptional Child* (Proc 1954 Spring Conf, Child Res Clin of Woods Schools), Langhorne, Pa: Woods Schools 1954, 10-18

53223 Psychoanalytic group therapy with fathers of emotionally disturbed preschool children. Int J grp PT 1956, 6:61-76
Abs GPK Q 1958, 27:144

See Newton, Niles

MARCUSE, HERBERT

53224 Editor of Neuman, F. L. *The Democratic and Authoritarian State*

53225 Eros and Civilization. A Philosophical Inquiry into Freud. Boston: Beacon Pr; London: Routledge & Kegan Paul, 1955; xii + 277 p
Eros und Kultur. Ein philosophischer Beitrag zu Sigmund Freud. (Tr: Eckardt, M. von) Stuttgart: Ernst Klett 1957, 264 p
Rv MG Q 1956, 25:429-431. Jones, R. M. Am Im 1958, 15:175-180. William, A. H. J 1959, 40:359-360. Axelrad, S. J Am Psa Ass 1960, 8:175-218

53226 Die Idee des Fortschritts im Lichte der Psychoanalyse. [The idea of progress in the light of psychoanalysis.] In Alexander, F. et al: *Freud in der Gegenwart*, Frankfurt: Europäische Verlagsanstalt 1957, 425-441

53227 The ideology of death. In Feifel, H. *The Meaning of Death*, NY, Toronto, London: McGraw-Hill 1959, 64-76

53228 The indictment of western philosophy in Freud's theory. J Philos 1957, 54:154-155

53229 Kritik des Neo-Freudianischen Revisionismus. [Critique of neo-Freudian revisionism.] Psyche, Heidel 1957, 11:801-820

53230 Revisioni Freudiane. [Freudian revisions.] In Zolla, E. *La Psicoanalisi*, Milan: Garzanti 1960, 38-67

53231   Trieblehre und Freiheit. [Theory of instincts and freedom.] In Alexander, F. et al: *Freud in der Gegenwart,* Frankfurt: Europäische Verlagsanstalt 1957, 401-424

MARCUSE, LUDWIG

53232   Der Fall C. G. Jung. [The case of C. G. Jung.] Aufbau 1955, 21(52):13-15
53233   Freuds Aesthetik. Modern Language Ass Publ 1957, 72:446-463
        Freud's aesthetic. J Aesthet 1958, 17:1-21
53234   "Heine und Freud": Vortrag von Ludwig Marcuse. [Report of a lecture on Heine and Freud by Ludwig Marcuse.] Aufbau 1955, 21(51):11
53235   Ein vorläufiges Schlusswort. [Finis, for the present, to the Jung controversy.] Aufbau 1956, 22(17):20
53236   Zwischen Rechts und Links. [Pro and con psychoanalysis.] Aufbau 1956, 22(21):19-20

MARCUSSEN, ROBERT

53237   (& Wolff, H. G.) A formulation of the dynamics of the migraine attack.
        Abs Rev Psicoanál 1954, 11:258-259

MARGAT, P.

53238   Détail d'une psychothérapie de schizophrène. [Detail from the psychotherapy of a schizophrenic.] Evolut psychiat 1956, (3):717-749
        Abs Lebovici, S. RFPsa 1957, 21:299

See Schweich, M.

MARGETTS, EDWARD L.

53239   The concept of the unconscious in the history of medical psychology. Psychiat Q 1953, 27:115-138
        Abs JBi Q 1953, 22:610-611. SG An Surv Psa 1953, 4:20-21. NRo An Surv Psa 1953, 4:52
53240   Historical notes on psychosomatic medicine. In Wittkower, E. D. & Cleghorn, R. A. *Recent Developments in Psychosomatic Medicine,* Phila: Lippincott 1954, 41-68

MARGOLIN, SYDNEY G.

S-21818 The behavior of the stomach during psychoanalysis.
        Abs STa An Surv Psa 1951, 2:355-358. CR J 1953, 34:68. Rv Labbé, P. RFPsa 1953, 17:577
53241   Discussion of Kubie, L. S. "Some implications for psychoanalysis of modern concepts of the organization of the brain." Q 1953, 22:54-57
53242   (& Gunther, H.) Editors of Hitschmann, E. *Great Men: Psychoanalytic Studies*
53243   Genetic and dynamic psychophysiological determinants of pathophysiological processes. Psm Cpt Psa 3-36

53244 On the psychological origin and function of symbols. (Read at NY Psa Soc, Feb 24, 1953)
    Abs Linn, L. Q 1954, 23:151-153
53245 Psychophysiological basis of medical practice. P 1953, 110:204-207
    Abs MG J 1954, 35:450
53246 Psychophysiological properties of the adrenal cortex; recent, unpublished advances. Introductory remarks. PSM 1953, 151:563-564
53247 Psychotherapeutic principles in psychosomatic practice. In Wittkower, E. D. & Cleghorn, R. A. *Recent Development in Psychosomatic Medicine*, Phila: Lippincott 1954, 134-153
53248 La signification du terme psychogenèse dans les symptomes organiques. [The meaning of the term psychogenesis in organic symptoms.] Évolut psychiat 1953 (3):371-386
53249 On some principles of therapy. P 1958, 114:1087-1096

    See Macleod, Alistair W.

MARGOLIS, JOSEPH

53250 On alleged contributions of religion to ethics. Rev Religion 1954, 18:163-167

MARGOLIS, NORMAN M.

53251 A theory on the psychology of jazz. Am Im 1954, 11:263-291
    Abs MK An Surv Psa 1954, 5:468

MARGOLIS, VERA S.

53252 Ego-centered treatment of an adolescent girl. In *Nat Conf Soc Wk, Casework Papers, 1956.* NY: Fam Serv Ass of Amer 1956, 91-106

MARIA, G.

53253 La narcoanalisi nella diagnostica differenziale dell'epilessia. [Narco-analysis in the differential diagnosis of epilepsy.] Cervello 1956, 32:477-486

MARIANO, JOHN HORACE

53254 The Case Study Method in Psychoanalytic Legal Aid. NY: Council on Marriage Relations 1958, 21 p
53255 The Use of Psychotherapy in Divorce and Separation Cases. NY: American Pr 1958, 179 p

MARIAS, JULIAN

53256 En el centenario de Freud. La generación de 1856. [In connection with the Freud centennial; the generation of 1856.] Rev Psicol gen apl, Madrid 1957, 12:155-161

MARITAIN, JACQUES

53257 Freudianism and psychoanalysis: a thomist view. Freud 20th Cent 230-258

MARJA, FERN

53258 Freud's bouncing Boswell at 77. NY Post 1956, May 6

MARK, JOSEPH C.

53259 The attitudes of the mothers of male schizophrenics toward child behavior. ASP 1953, 48:185-189

MARKHAM, SYLVIA

53260 The dynamics of post-partum pathological reactions as revealed in psychological tests. J Hillside Hosp 1958, 7:178-189

See Levine, Abraham

MARKILLIE, RONALD E. D.

53261 Group psychotherapy in psychosomatic disorders. Mod Tr PSM 317-332

REVIEWS OF:
53262 Balint, M. The Doctor, His Patient and the Illness. J 1958, 39:427-428
53263 Braatøy, T. Fundamentals of Psychoanalytic Technique. J 1955, 36:411-412
53264 Roback, A. A. The Psychology of Character, with a Survey of Personality in General. J 1953, 34:343
53265 Schaffner, B. (Ed) Group Processes. Transactions of the Second Conference, 1955. J 1958, 39:439-440
53266 Simmons, L. W. & Wolff, H. G. Social Science in Medicine. J 1956, 37:494

MARKOWITZ, IRVING

53267 Psychotherapy of narcolepsy in an adolescent boy: case presentation. Psychiat Q 1957, 31:41-56

MARKOWITZ, JOEL

53268 The nature of the child's initial resistances to psychotherapy. Soc Wk 1959, 4:46-51

MARKUS, RUDI

53269 Aggressivitet hos boern. [Children's aggressivity.] Paedagogisk-psykologisk Tidsskr 1952
53270 Nogle betragninger om den saakaldte normale trodsperiode. [Commenting on the so-called normal "Trotz"-period.] Paedagogisk- psykologisk Tidsskr 1951

MARKUSZEWICZ, R.

53271 Des nouveaux courants en psycho-pathologie. [Recent trends in psychopathology.] Schweiz ANP 1955, 75:132-147

MARLOWE, BARBARA

See Eisenberg, Leon

MARMOR, JUDD

53272 Case Studies in Seward, G. *Psychotherapy and Culture Conflict*
53273 Discussion of Maskin, M. "Adaptations of psychoanalytic technique to specific disorders." Sci Psa 1960, 3:357-359
53274 [Contribution to panel discussion on] The family in psychotherapy. Sci Psa 1959, 2:198-199
53275 The feeling of superiority: an occupational hazard in the practice of psychotherapy. P 1953, 110:370-376
53276 Indications for psychiatric therapy or social casework. Soc Casewk 1955, 36:60-63
53277 (& Ashley, M.; Storkan, M.; Tabachnick, M.; McDonald, F.) The mother-child relationship in the genesis of neurodermatitis. AMA Arch Dermat 1956, 74:599-605
53278 Orality in the hysterical personality. J Am Psa Ass 1953, 1:656-671
         Abs JFr An Surv Psa 1953, 4:179-181. TFr J 1954, 35:446. MGr Q 1955, 24:611. Rv Shentoub RFPsa 1954, 18:306
53279 (& Kert, M. J.) Paroxysmal ventricular tachycardia: a case study. California M 1958, 88:325-329
53280 Psychiatric aspects of chronic disease and rehabilitation. California M 1958, 88:350-353
53281 The psychodynamics of realistic worry. Psa Soc S 1958, 5:155-163
53282 Self acceptance and self esteem. Recall 1959, 1(1)
53283 Some comments on ego psychology. J Hillside Hosp 1958, 7:26-31
53284 Some considerations concerning orgasm in the female. PSM 1954, 16:240-245
         Abs VC Q 1956, 25:120-121
53285 Some observations on superstition in contemporary life. Ops 1956, 26:119-130
         Abs DRu Q 1959, 28:113
53286 (under pseud: Stone, Judson T.) Theory and practice of psychoanalysis. Sci & Soc 1946, 10:54-79
53287 A therapeutic approach to the narcotics problem. Proc 6th Ann Training Inst for Probation, Parole & Institutional Staff, Univ of Calif Aug 1954
53288 (Reporter) Validation of psychoanalytic techniques. (Panel: Am Psa Ass, NY, Dec 1954) J Am Psa Ass 1955, 3:496-505
53289 What shall we tell the cancer patient? Bull L. A. County Med Ass 1954, Nov 18

See Martin, Alexander Reid

MAROGER
TRANSLATION OF:
Horney, K. [15229]

MARONE, SILVIO

53290 Homosexuality and art. Int J Sexol 1954, 7:175-190

MAROUN, J.
See Piaget, Jean

MARS, L.

S-6813 (& Devereux, G.) Haitian voodoo and the ritualization of the nightmare.
    Abs JAA An Surv Psa 1951, 2:120;544-546. GD An Surv Psa 1951, 2:530
53291 La higiene mental y la etnopsicologia. [Mental hygiene and ethnopsychology.] Arch Neurol Psiquiat 1958, 8:64-70

MARSCHAK, MILDRED
See Fromm, Erika

MARSH, JAMES T.

53292 (& Worden, F. G.) Perceptual approaches to personality. Psychiat Res Rep 1956, (6):171-176

See Rasmussen, A. F., Jr.

MARSHALL, DOROTHY
See Linn, Louis

MARSHALL, MARY LOUISE
See Doe, Janet

MARSMAN, W.

53293 Anthropologische psychiatrie en psychotherapie. [Anthropological psychiatry and psychotherapy.] Ned Tijdschr Psychol 1958, 13:345-358
53294 Fenomenologia y psicoanalisis. [Phenomenology and psychoanalysis.] Rev Psiquiat Psicol 1959, 4:313-318

See Janse de Jonge, A. L.

MARTENSEN-LARSEN, OLUF

53295 Group psychotherapy with alcoholics in private practice. Int J grp PT 1956, 6:28-37
    Abs GPK Q 1958, 27:144

MARTET, P.
TRANSLATION OF:
Freud, S. [10582)

MARTI-IBÁÑEZ, FÉLIX

53296 On Christmas and neuroses: an editorial introduction. In Wolff, W. *Psychiatry and Religion,* NY: MD Publications 1955, 57-62
53297 The historical and philosophic background of psychobiology. J clin exp Psychopath 1956, 17:360-369
53298 (& Sackler, R. R.; Sackler, A. M.; Sackler, M. D.) The philosophy of organicism in psychiatry. J clin exp Psychopath 1954, 15:179-190
53299 On the psychology of symbolism in oriental rugs. Int Rec Med 1956, 169:651-662
53300 (& Sackler, A. M.; Sackler, M. D.; Sackler, R. R.) The quest for Freud. J clin exp Psychopath 1956, 17:117-127

See Sackler, Arthur M.

MARTÍ-TUSQUETS, J. L.

53301 Influencia de Freud en el psicodrama. [Freud's influence on psychodrama.] Rev Psiquiat Psicol 1956, 2:767-780

53302 I Congreso iberoamericano de intercambio médico psicológico (Barcelona, 3-6 de agosto de 1955). [First Ibero-American congress of medical psychologic interchange (Barcelona, August 3-6, 1955).] Rev Psiquiat Psicol 1955, 2:389-395

53303 Psicodrama. [Psychodrama.] Rev Psiquiat Psicol 1958, 3:600-602

53304 (& Turó, P.; González Monclús, E.) El psicodrama en el diagnóstico y tratamiento de los enfermos mentales. [Psychodrama in the diagnosis and treatment of mental patients.] Rev Psiquiat Psicol 1955, 2:326-336

53305 Reunión de la sociedad española de psicoterapie y medicina psicosomática. El Escorial, Diciembre de 1955. [Meeting of the Spanish society of psychotherapy and psychosomatic medicine. El Escorial, December 1955.] Rev Psiquiat Psicol 1956, 2:494-498

53306 II Congreso internacional de psicoterapia de grupo. Zurich, 28 al 31 de agosto 1957. [Second International congress of group psychotherapy. Zurich, August 28-31, 1957.] Rev Psiquiat Psicol 1957, 3:270-273

MARTIN, ALEXANDER REID

53307 (& Van Bark, B.; Marmor, J.; Weigert, E.; Anderson, C. M.; Kelman, H.; Whitaker, C. A.) The doctor-patient relationship in therapy: a symposium. Psa 1955, 15:3-21

53308 The dynamics of insight. Psa 1952, 12:24-38

53309 Nostalgia. Psa 1954, 14:93-104

53310 The whole patient in therapy. Prog PT 1956, 1:170-179

See Kelman, Norman

MARTIN, B. C.

See Gordon, Jesse E.

MARTIN, D. V.

53311 Problems in developing a community approach to mental hospital treatments. Brit J psychiat soc Wk 1959, 5:56-63

MARTIN, IAN H.

53312 Cortical neurology and the body-image. Med J Australia 1951, Sept 15; 1952, Feb 16

MARTIN, JACQUES YVES

53313 Psychanalyse et psychologie. [Psychoanalysis and psychology . . . Chronicle of human science.] Concourse méd 1955, 77:4717-4722

MARTIN, PETER A.

53314 Afraid of life? Mental Hlth Bull 1952, 10(1)

53315 (& Bird, H. W.) An approach to the psychotherapy of marriage partners. Ps 1953, 16:123-127. In Vincent, C. E. Readings in Marriage Counseling, NY: Crowell 1957, 323-330

53316 Clinical manifestations of anxiety. J Mich State med Soc 1957, 56:1252-1254

53317 The cockroach as an identification; with reference to Kafka's *Metamorphosis*. Am Im 1959, 16:65-71

53318 Convulsive therapies: review of 511 cases at Pontiac State Hospital. JNMD 1949, 109(2)

53319 Emotional preparation for atomic bombing. In *Tentative Reports Prepared by the Sub-Committee on Uniform Medical Treatment*, Detroit: Civil Defense and Disaster Committee, Wayne County Medical Society, 1951, October 9

53320 The Haven; A home for the disturbed child in the community. World Hlth Org: Preparatory Commiss Rep on Planning for Ment Hlth, Organization, Training, Propaganda, 1948

53321 Hostility and mental health in the home. Ment Hyg Bull 8(1). Child-Fam Dig 1955, 12(2):3-12

53322 The kaleidoscopic nature of psyche and soma. J Mich State med Soc 1957, 56:1249-1251

53323 (& Bird, H. W.) A marriage pattern: the "lovesick" wife and the "cold, sick" husband. Ps 1959, 22:245-249
        Abs HRB Q 1960, 29:294

53324 Mental illness is treatable. Ment Hlth Bull 1954, 11(1). Child-Fam Dig 1955, 12(4):25-31

53325 Note on inhibition of scientific productivity. Q 1956, 25:415-417
        Japanese: Tokyo J Psychoanal 1957, 15(9):1-3
        Abs JKl J 1957, 38:133. Rev Psicoanál 1957, 14:424

53326 One type of earliest memory. Q 1959, 28:73-77
        Abs Sapochnik Rev Psicoanál 1959, 16:137

53327 A psychiatric viewpoint on civil defense, J Mich State med Soc 1952, 51:304-309. Child-Fam Dig 1955, 12(3):40-50

53328 A psychotic episode following a dream. Q 1958, 27:563-567

53329 The Rochester Plan, a community mental health program. Ment Hyg Bull 1948, 6(4)

53330 On scierneuropsia: a previously unnamed psychogenic visual disturbance. J Am Psa Ass 1960, 8:71-81

See Bird, H. Waldo

MARTIN, WILLIAM E.

53331 (& Stendler, C. B.) Child Development: The Process of Growing Up in Society. NY: Harcourt, Brace 1953, xxii + 519 p

53332 Learning theory and identification. III. The development of values in children. J. genet Psychol 1954, 84(2):211-217

53333 (& Stendler, C. B.) (Eds) Readings in Child Development. NY: Harcourt, Brace 1954 xi + 512 p

MARTÍN-SANTOS, L.

53334 Jaspers y Freud. [Jaspers and Freud.] Rev Psiquiat Psicol 1956, 2:694-699

MARTINEZ, H.

TRANSLATION OF:
Brenner, C. [42766]

MARTINEZ ARANGO, C.

53335 Psicoterapia, utilizando el T.A.T. como via de acceso al inconsciente. [Psychotherapy, utilizing the T.A.T. to gain access to the unconscious.] Arch Neurol Psiquiat 1958, 8:146-156

MARTINS, CYRO

53336 Aspectos clínicos de la modificación superyoica en la situación de grupo. [Clinical aspects of superego modification in the group situation.] Primer Congreso latinoamericano de Psicoterapia de grupo, Buenos Aires 19--, 131

53337 Aspectos de la elaboración del complejo de Edipo en un grupo terapéutico. [Elaboration of the Oedipus complex in a therapeutic group.] Rev Psicoanál 1956, 13:540-544

53338 Avidez y repetición. [Avidity and repetition.] Rev Psicoanál 1956, 13:136-151

53339 Freud e o sonho. [Freud and the dream.] "Correio do Povo," Porto Alegre, Brazil 1959, Supl Literário, May 12

53340 Do mito à verdade científica. (Sintese histórica da psicoterapia). [From myth to scientific truth. (Historical synthesis of psychotherapy).] Rev Ass méd Rio Grande do Sul 1957, 1:51-57
Síntesis histórica de la psicoterapia. (Del mito a la verdad científica). Psique en la Universidad, Buenos Aires 1958, 1(1):31

53341 Psicoterapia del grupo. [Group psychotherapy.] Rev Psicoanál 1959, 16:184

MARTINS, M.

53342 Contribución al estudio psicoanalitico de la epilepsia. [Contribution to the psychoanalytic study of epilepsy.] Rev Psicoanál 1955, 12:245-271

53343 Mecanismos de defensa en la epilepsia. [Defense mechanisms in epilepsy.] Rev Psicoanál 1955, 12:389-403

MARTINY, MARCEL

53344 Different planes of the unconscious. In *Proceedings of Four Conferences of Parapsychological Studies.* NY: Parapsychology Found 1957, 170-172

MARTIRE, JOHN G.

53345 Identification in the counseling process. J counsel Psychol 1955, 2:91-95

MARTY, PIERRE

53346 Les céphalalgies. [Headaches.] Encyclop Méd-Chirur, Psychiatrie 2, Paris 1955

53347 Discussion of Fain, M. "Sur un cas d'hypertension artérielle." RFPsa 1957, 21:483-484

53348 Discussion of Grunberger, B. "Essai sur la situation analytique et le processus de guérison." RFPsa 1957, 21:448-452

53349 Discussion of Grunberger, B. "Interprétation prégénitale." RFPsa 1953, 17:491-495

53350 Discussion of Racker, H. "À propos de musique." RFPsa 1955, 19:402-405

53351 (& Fain, M.) Importance du rôle de la motricité dans la relation d'objet. [Importance of the role of motility in the object relation.] RFPsa 1955, 19:205-322

53352 Maurice Bouvet familier. [The man Maurice Bouvet.] RFPsa 1960, 24:709-710

53353 (& Fain, M.; Kervran, R.; Duprès, P.) Notes sur certains aspects psychosomatiques de la tuberculose pulmonaire. [Notes on certain psychosomatic aspects of pulmonary tuberculosis.] RFPsa 1954, 18:244-275

      Abs JFr An Surv Psa 1954, 5:158-160

53354 (& Volmat, R.) Point de vue psychanalytique sur l'ulcère d'estomac. [Psychoanalytical point of view on stomach ulcers.] Rev méd, Nancy 1956, 81:568-583

53355 (& Fain, M.) Psychanalyse et médecine psychosomatique. Le mouvement psychosomatique dans la médecine. [Psychoanalysis and psychosomatic medicine. The psychosomatic trend in medicine.] In Nacht, S. La Psychanalyse d'Aujourd'hui, Paris: PUF 1956, 499-531

53356 (& Gosset, J.; Fain, M.) Les rachialgies fonctionelles, leur mécanisme et leur traitement. [Functional backaches, their mechanism and their treatment.] Semaine des Hôpitaux, Ann de Chir 1953, (2)

53357 La relation objectale allergique. RFPsa 1958, 22:5-35

      The allergic object relationship. (Read at 20th Int Psa Cong, Paris 1957) J 1958, 29:98-103

      Abs J 1958, 29:293. Fiasche, D. N. de. Rev Psicoanál 1958, 15:423. JLan Q 1959, 28: 277. Roman, R. E. Q 1959, 28:296. Usandivaras & Tabak Rev Psicoanál 1959, 16:88

53358 Le rôle des facteurs affectifs dans les difficultés de réhabilitation fonctionnelle des opérés et des traumatisés. [The role of emotional factors in the difficulties of functional rehabilitation among operated and traumatized people.] Vie médicale 1957, (37)

      See Bouvet, Maurice; Fain, Michel; Schlumberger, Marc

MARUI, KIYOYASU

53359 Psychoanalytical investigation of hysteroepilepsy. Folia psychiat neur jap 1953, 6:231-235

53360 The role of the parents in the education of children. Folia psychiat neur jap 1952, 6: 221-230

MARULLI, G.

53361 Il contenuto psicodinamico instintivo e affettivo del bacio nell'ambito della storia, dell'arte e della letteratura. [The psychodynamic instinctual and affective meaning of the kiss in history, art and literature.] Riv Psipat Np Psa 1953, 21:157-174

MARX, MELVIN

53362   Comments on Beach, F. A. "Characteristics of masculine 'sex drive'."
In Jones, M. R. *Nebraska Symposium on Motivation: 1956*, Lincoln,
Neb: Univ of Nebraska Pr 1956, 39-41

MARZUOLI, UGO

53363   Contributo alla psicoterapia dinamica delle nevrosi. [Contribution to
the dynamic psychotherapy of the neuroses.] Arch Psicol Neur Psich
1956, 17:19-32

MÁS DE AYALA, I.

53364   Algunas ideas de Freud a la luz de la neurofisiología. Psicopatología de
lapsus y omisiones. [Some of Freud's ideas in the light of neurophysiology. Psychopathology of lapses and omissions.] Rev Psiquiat Psicol
1957, 3:208-212

53365   Las neurosis a la luz de la actual neurofisiología. [The neuroses in the
light of modern neurophysiology.] Rev Psiquiat Psicol 1958, 3:504-510

MASCHIO, G.

53366   Medicina e psicanalisi. [Medicine and psychoanalysis.] Minerva med
1956, 47:Varia, 692-700

MASCIANGELO, PIER M.

53367   Applicazione del reattivo mentale di Zülliger (Z-test) all'età evolutiva.
[Application of Zülliger mental reaction (Z-test) in developmental
stage.] Riv sper freniat 1955, 79:825-836

53368   Un caso di negazione delirante di morte. [Delusional negation of death;
case report.] Riv Psa 1957, 3:209-220

53369   Considerazioni sui rapporti fra angoscia e rimozione. [Considerations
on the relations between anxiety and separation.] Riv Psa 1956, 2:141-
148

53370   Una "gang" minorile. [A juvenile "gang."] Riv Psa 1958, 4:17-24

REVIEWS OF:

53371   Lebovici, S. Une observation de psychose infantile. Riv Psa 1958,
4:59-60

53372   Nacht, S. et al: La Psychanalyse d'aujourd'hui. Riv Psa 1958, 4:73-75

53373   Racamier, P. C. & Blanchard, M. De l'angoisse à la manie. Riv Psa
1958, 4:58-59

MASCIO, ALBERTO DI

See DiMASCIO, ALBERTO

MASIH, Y.

53374   Metapsychology of James and Freud. J Bihar Univ 1956, 1:61-69

MASKIN, MEYER

53375   Adaptations of psychoanalytic technique to specific disorders. Sci Psa
1960, 3:321-352

MASLING, J. M.
See Stern, G. G.

MASLOW, ABRAHAM H.

53376 A comparative approach to the problem of destructiveness. Ps 1942, 5:517-522

53377 Conflict, frustration and threat. ASP 1943, 38:81-86. In Tomkins, S. *Contemporary Psychopathology: A Sourcebook,* Cambridge: Harvard Univ Pr 1943

53378 Creativity in self-actualizing people. Electro-Mechanical Design 1958. In Anderson, H. H. *Michigan Creativity Symposium,* NY: Harpers 1959

53379 Defense and growth. Merrill-Palmer Quart 1956, 3:36-47

53380 Deficiency motivation and growth motivation. In Jones, M. R. *Nebraska Symposium on Motivation: 1955,* Lincoln, Neb: Univ of Nebraska Pr 1955, 1-30

53381 Deprivation, threat, and frustration. Psychol Rev 1941, 48:364-366. Under Hum Motiv 259-261

53382 A dynamic theory of human motivation. Psychol Rev 1943, 50:370-396. In Harriman, P. *Twentieth Century Psychology: Recent Developments in Psychology,* NY: Philos Libr 1946. In Remmer, H. et al: *Growth, Teaching and Learning,* NY: Harpers 1957

53383 (& Mintz, N.) Effects of esthetic surroundings: I. Initial effects of three esthetic conditions upon perceiving "energy" and "well-being" in faces. J Psychol 1956, 41:247-254

53384 Emotional blocks to creativity. J ind Psychol 1958, 14:51-56. Electro-Mechanical Design 1958, 2:66-72. Humanist 1958, 18:325-332

53385 The expressive component of behavior. Psychol Rev 1949, 56:261-272. Stud Pers 363-376

53386 The instinctoid nature of basic needs. J. Personality 1954, 22:326-347

53387 Love in healthy people. In Montagu, M. F. A. *The Meaning of Love,* NY: Julian Pr 1953, 57-93

53388 Motivation and Personality. NY: Harper 1954, 411 p
      Rv JAA Q 1955, 24:447-448

53389 (Ed) New Knowledge of Human Values. NY: Harper 1958

53390 Normality, health and values. Main Currents 1954, 10:75-81

53391 Personality problems and personality growth. In Moustakas, C. E. *The Self: Explorations in Personal Growth,* NY: Harper 1956, 232-246

53392 A philosophy of psychology. Main Currents 1956, 13:27-32. ETC 1957, 14:10-22. In Fairchild, J. *Personal Problems and Psychological Frontiers,* Sheridan Pr 1957. Manas 1958, 11(17-18)

53393 Power relationships and patterns of personal development. In Kornhauser, A. *Problems of Power in American Democracy,* Detroit: Wayne Univ Pr 1957

53394 A preface to motivation theory. PSM 1943, 5:85-92

S-21947 (& Mittelmann, B.) Principles of Abnormal Psychology: The Dynamics of Psychic Illness
      Rv Scott, W. C. M. J 1953, 34:171

53395 (& Mittelmann, B.) Psychoanalytic therapy. Out Psa 1955, 565-592. From authors' *Principles of Abnormal Psychology*

53396 Psychological data and human values. In author's *New Knowledge of Human Values*, NY: Harper 1958

53397 Resistance to being rubricized. In Kaplan, B. & Wapner, S. *Perspectives in Psychological Theory*, NY: IUP 1960, 173-178

53398 (& Kessler-Szilagyi, I.) Security and breastfeeding. ASP 1946, 41:83-85

53399 (& Bossom, J.) Security of judges as a factor in impressions of warmth in others. ASP 1957, 55:147-148

53400 Self-actualizing people: a study of psychological health. In Wolff, W. *Symposium No. 1, 1950, Values in Personality Research*, NY: Grune & Stratton 1950. In Moustakas, C. E. *The Self: Explorations in Personal Growth*, NY: Harper 1956, 160-194

53401 Self-esteem (dominance-feeling) and sexuality in women. See Psych 1942, 16:259-294

53402 Some theoretical consequences of basic need-gratification. J Personality 1947, 16:402-416

53403 A theory of human motivation. Psychol Rev 1943, 50:370-396. In Gorlow, L. & Katkovsky, W. *Readings in the Psychology of Adjustment*, NY: McGraw-Hill 1959, 202-222

53404 Two kinds of cognition and their integration. Gen Semantics Bull 1957, (20-21)

53405 (& Mittelmann, B.) Unconscious psychological processes: conflict. Under Hum Motiv 369-371. From authors' *Principles of Abnormal Psychology*

MASON, D. G.

53406 Psychoanalysis and music. Art & Decorations 1920, Jan, 13:106

MASON, E. M.

53407 The centenary of Freud: understanding and misunderstanding. Brit J psychiat soc Wk 1956, 3(4):12-14

MASON, PERCY

53408 Suicide in adolescents. R 1954, 41:48-54

MASON, RUSSELL E.

53409 Three studies relating internal sensory experiences and feeling reactions. J gen Psychol 1959, 60:211-228

MASSERMAN, JULES HOMAN

53410 (& Gross, Z.; Pechtel, C.) Abnormalities of behavior. Ann Rev Psychol 1954, 5:263-280

53411 Alcohol and other drugs as preventives of experimental trauma. Quart J Stud Alcohol 1959, 20:464-466

S-21952 (& Yum, K. S.) An analysis of the influence of alcohol on experimental neuroses in cats.
Abs STa J 1946, 27:65

53412 The biodynamic approaches. Am Hbk Psychiat 2:1680-1696

53413 A biodynamic summary. Sci Psa 1959, 2:73-84

53414 Biodynamic therapy in the aging. Imprensa med 1957, 21:275

53415 Biodynamic therapy in the aging—an integration. Prog PT 1957, 2:121-131

53416 (Ed) Biological Psychiatry. NY: Grune & Stratton 1959, 354 p

53417 Can anthropology be weaned from its formulae: problems of invariance. Discussion. In Hsu, F. L. K. *Aspects of Culture and Personality*, NY: Abelard-Schuman 1954, 161-168

53418 Comparative research in ethology, biodynamics and psychoanalysis. (Read in part at Acad of Psa, NY, Dec 1958) Sci Psa 1960, 3:20-80

53419 The conceptual dynamics of person, religion, and self. R 1954, 41:303-329

       Abs JLan Q 1956, 25:115

53420 (& Pechtel, C.) Conflict-engendered neurotic and psychotic behavior in monkeys. JNMD 1953, 118:408-411

53421 Una contribución experimental al problema de la neurosis. [An experimental contribution to the problems of neurosis.] Rev argent Neurol Psiquiat 1946, 11:3

53422 (& Pechtel, C.; Cain, J.) Création de névroses expérimentales chez le chat par un traumatisme psychologique. [Production of experimental neuroses in the cat by psychological trauma.] Compt rend Soc Biol 1954, 148:2041

53423 (& Pechtel, C.) Differential effects of cerebral lesions on susceptibility of animals to induction and relief of experimental neuroses. Army Med Serv Res Prog Rep, 1st Quarter, 1954, 433

53424 Discussant. In Gerty, F. Round Table Discussion. Psych Res Rep 1956, 114-129

53425 Discussion of Moreno, J. L. "Interpersonal therapy, group psychotherapy and the function of the unconscious." Group Psychother 1955, 8:62

53426 Discussion of Moreno, J. L. "Transference, countertransference and tele: their relation to group research and group psychotherapy." Group Psychother 1954, 7:309

53427 Discussion of symposium on "Psychoanalysis and Values." Sci Psa 1960, 3:138-139

53428 Emotional reactions to death and suicide. Am Pract Dig Treatment 1954, 5:41. In Liebman, S. *Stress Situations*, Phila: Lippincott 1955, 117-134

53429 Evolution vs. "revolution" in psychotherapy: a biodynamic integration. Beh Sci 1957, 2:89-100. Prog PT 1957, 2:231-253

       Evolución y "revolución" en psicoterapia. Actas medico-psicologicas 1958, 1:267

53430 Experimental and historical perspectives in psychopharmacology. Trans First Res Conf on Chemotherapy in Psychiat, Wash, D. C.: Veterans Admin 1957, 20

S-21966 Experimental approaches to psychoanalytic concepts.

       Abs STa An Surv Psa 1952, 3:26-29. Levinson, G. J 1953, 34:357

53431 Experimental approaches to psychodynamic problems. J. Mt. Sinai Hosp 1953, 19:639-652. In Murphy, G. & Bachrach, A. J. *An Outline of Abnormal Psychology*, NY: Modern Library 1954, 435-462

       Experimente über psychodynamische Probleme. Psyche, Heidel 1952, 5:102-120

53432 (& Pechtel, C.) An experimental investigation of factors influencing drug action. Psychiat Res Rep 1956, 4:95-113

53433 Experimental neuroses. *Scientific American Reader,* NY: Simon & Schuster 1953, 441

53434 Experimental psychopharmacology and behavioral relativity. In Hoch, P. & Zubin, J. *Problems of Addiction and Habituation,* NY: Grune & Stratton 1958, 110-148

53435 Faith and delusion in psychotherapy (the ur-defenses of man). P 1953, 110:324-333

53436 Fundamentals of psychotherapy, with special reference to respiratory diseases. In Sparer, P. J. *Personality, Stress, and Tuberculosis,* NY: IUP 1956, 235-247

53437 An historical-biodynamic integration of psychotherapy. Prog PT 1956, 1:188-198

53438 (& Pechtel, C.) How brain lesions affect normal and neurotic behavior. P 1956, 112:865-872
　　　Abs DRu Q 1959, 28:119

53439 Humanitarian psychiatry. Public Welfare Dept Publ, Springfield, Ill: 1957

53440 Hypnotic treatment of acute hysterical depression: the dynamics of hypnosis and brief psychotherapy. AMA ANP 1941, 48:488

53441 Hysteria. In *American Peoples Encyclopedia,* Chicago: Spencer Pr 1958
* * * (Ed) Individual and Family Dynamics. See [Science and Psychoanalysis, Vol. II]

53442 An integration of group therapeutic techniques. Dept Med & Surg Infor Bull, Veterans Admin 1954, 4

53443 [Contribution to panel discussion on] Masochism: psychogenesis and therapeutic principles. Sci Psa 1959, 2:53

53444 Memorial to Dr. Frieda Fromm-Reichmann. Sci Psa 1958, 1:iv

53445 Mental disorders. In *American Peoples Encyclopedia,* Chicago: Spencer Pr 1948, 13:423

53446 Mental hygiene. In *American Peoples Encyclopedia,* Chicago: Spencer Pr 1959

53447 Motion picture films. Psychological Cinema Register Catalogue. State College, Pa: 1954, 69

53448 Music as a tool of delightful delusion. Music Therapy 1953

53449 Music and the child in society. PT 1954, 8:63-67

53450 National Foundation for Psychiatric Research: what it is, how it concerns you. Chicago: Northwestern Univ 1958

53451 Neurasthenia. In *American Peoples Encyclopedia,* Chicago: Spencer Pr 1948

53452 (& Pechtel, C.) Neurophysiologic and pharmacologic influences on experimental neuroses. P 1956, 113:510-514

53453 (et al) The neuroses. Prog Neurol Psychiat 1948, 3:507

53454 (& Murrin, F. H.; et al) The neuroses. Prog Neurol Psychiat 1950, 5, chap 26

53455 (& Tourlentes, T.; et al) The neuroses. Prog Neurol Psychiat 1951, 6: chap 25

53456 (& Dushkin, M. A.) The neuroses. Prog Neurol Psychiat 1953, 8:475-485

53457   (& Berkwits, G.; Pauncz, A.) The neuroses. Prog Neurol Psychiat 1954, 9:507-524

53458   (& Pauncz, A.) The neuroses. Prog Neurol Psychiat 1955, 10:496-509

53459   (& Pauncz, A.; Nathan, R.) The neuroses. Prog Neurol Psychiat 1956, 11:327-337

53460   (& Alan, B.; Klotz, M.) The neuroses. Prog Neurol Psychiat 1957, 12:515-530

53461   (& Pauncz, A.; Scher, J.; Norton, A.) The neuroses. Prog Neurol Psychiat 1958, 13:331-346

53462   (& Pechtel, C.) Neuroses in monkeys: a preliminary report of experimental observations. Ann NY Acad Sci 1953, 56:253-265

53463   (& Pechtel, C.) Normal and neurotic olfactory behavior in monkeys: a motion picture. JNMD 1956, 124:518-519. Trans Soc Biol Soc 1956, 11:30

53464   (& Pechtel, C. T.) The osmotic responses of normal and neurotic monkeys. Ann NY Acad Sci 1954, 58:256-260

53465   The Practice of Dynamic Psychiatry. Phila: W. B. Saunders 1955, xxx + 790 p
           Principes de Psychiatrie dynamique. Paris: PUF 1957
           Rv ESt J 1956, 37:497. Lebovici RFPsa 1958, 22:740. Scolni, F. Rev Psicoanál 1958, 15:301

53466   (& Moreno, J. L.) Preface. Prog PT 1957, 2:v; 1959, 4:vii-viii

53467   (& Moreno, J. L.) Preface in memoriam [of Dr. Frieda Fromm-Reichmann]. Prog PT 1958, 3:vii

53468   President's message. Newsletter, Acad Psychoanal 1957, 1:Spring, Nov; 1958, 2

53469   Principles of biodynamics. Trans NY Acad Sci 1944, 61-71

53470   Proceedings of the annual banquet. Music Therapy 1954, 5

53471   (& Moreno, J. L.) (Ed) Progress in Psychotherapy. Vol II, Anxiety and Therapy. NY: Grune & Stratton 1957, 264 p
           Abs J Am Psa Ass 1960, 8:594-595. Rv Kaplan, D PPR 1958, 45(1-2):147-150

53472   (& Moreno, J. L.) (Ed) Progress in Psychotherapy Vol. III, Techniques of Psychotherapy. NY: Grune & Stratton 1958, 324 p

53473   (& Moreno, J. L.) (Ed) Progress in Psychotherapy. Vol. IV, Social Psychotherapy. NY: Grune & Stratton 1959, 361 p

53474   Psiquiatria humanista. [Humanistic psychiatry.] Rev Psiquiat Psicol 1959, 4:65-69

53475   Psychiatry. In American Peoples Encyclopedia, Chicago: Spencer Pr 1948, 16:229; 1952, 9:37; 1953, 803; 1954, 811; 1955, 881; 1956, 906; 1958, 895

53476   Psychiatry in Latin America. Quart Bull Northwest Univ med School 1956, 30:270-277; 1957, 31:78

53477   Psychiatry in Rio: the Institute of Psychologic Medicine. Imprensa med 1957, 21:254

53478   Psycho-analysis and biodynamics—an integration. J 1953, 34(Suppl): 13-42
           Psychanalyse et biodynamique; une intégration. Enceph 1954, 43:1-39; 121-148

53479   The psychodynamics of aging. Geriatrics 1957, 12:115-122

53480 Psychosomatic medicine. In *American Peoples Encyclopedia,* Chicago: Spencer Pr 1948, 16:250

53481 Psychotherapeutic progress in Latin America. Prog PT 1958, 3:282-310

53482 Psychotherapy. In *American Peoples Encyclopedia,* Chicago: Spencer Pr 1948, 16:255

53483 Psychotherapy: an outline and an integration. Impr Med, Lisboa 1957, 21:231-241

53484 Psychotherapy—a review and an integration. BMC 1954, 18:162-170
    Abs Rahman, L. Q 1956, 25:116-117

53485 (& Carmichael, H. T.) Results of treatment in a psychiatric outpatient department—a follow-up study of 166 cases. JAMA 1939, 113:2292

53486 Review of experimental catatonia. Science 1946, 103:28

53487 (& Pechtel, C.; Schreiner, L.) The role of olfaction in normal and neurotic behavior in animals. PSM 1953, 15:396-404
    Abs Rev Psicoanál 1954, 11:548-549

53488 Say Id isn't so—with music. Sci Psa 1958, 1:176-187

53489 (Ed) Science and Psychoanalysis. Vol I, Integrative Studies. NY, London: Grune & Stratton 1958, vi + 201 p. Vol II, Individual and Familial Dynamics. NY: Grune & Stratton 1959, vi + 218 p. Vol III, Psychoanalysis and Human Values. NY, London: Grune & Stratton 1960, xiv + 377 p
    Abs J Am Psa Ass 1960, 8:597. Rv JBi Q 1959, 28:533-536; 1960, 29:402-404

53490 Science, psychiatry and religion. Prog PT 1959, 4:324-350

53491 Sociologic and psychologic correlates of music therapy. Music Therapy 1956, 15-16

S-22002 Some current concepts of sexual behavior.
    Abs JAA An Surv Psa 1951, 2:29-30

53492 Some practical aspects of a Veterans Administration Residency Training Program. Northwestern Univ Quart Bull 1949, 23:487

53493 Therapeutic efficacy of electrocoma. Mod Med 1952, April

53494 The truth about nervous breakdowns. This Week Magazine 1958, Sept 27:18-19

53495 (& Balken, E. R.) Use of Phantasy tests in differential psychiatric diagnosis. AMA ANP 1940, 42:1249

See Alexander, Franz; Schreiner, Leon

MASSION-VERNIORY, L.

53496 La kleptomanie. [Kleptomania.] Acta Neurol Psychiat Belg 1957, 57(11):869-889

53497 (& Dumont, E.) À propos de quatre cas d'ondinisme. [Four cases of urolagnia.] Acta neurol Belg 1958, 58:446-459

MASSOUBRE, J.

ABSTRACTS OF:

53498 Chess, S. et al: Characteristics of the individual child's behavioral responses to the environment. RFPsa 1960, 24:218; 340

53499 Esman, A. Parents of schizophrenic children. RFPsa 1960, 24:214-215

53500 Goldsmith, J. et al: Changing delinquents' concept of school. RFPsa 1960, 24:211-212

53501 Lapouse, R. & Monk, M. A. Fears and worries in a representative sample of children. RFPsa 1960, 24:218; 341

53502 Levitt, E. et al: A follow-up evaluation of cases treated at a community child guidance clinic. RFPsa 1960, 24:212

53503 Pfeiffer, F. A modified nursery school program in a mental hospital. RFPsa 1960, 24:217-218; 340

53504 Polsky, H. & Kohn, M. Participant observation in a delinquent subculture. RFPsa 1960, 24:217; 340

53505 Prall, R. C. Observational research with emotionally disturbed children. RFPsa 1960, 24:210-211; 215

53506 Redl, F. The concept of a therapeutic milieu. RFPsa 1960, 24:217; 339-340

53507 Saksida, S. Motivation mechanisms and frustration stereotypes. RFPsa 1960, 24:215-216

53508 Verley, B. K. "Reaching out" therapy with schizophrenic patients. RFPsa 1960, 24:129-132

53509 Zier, A. Meprobamate (Miltown) as an aid to psychotherapy in an outpatient child guidance clinic. RFPsa 1960, 24:212

MASTER, REGINA

See Saul, Leon

MASTERSON, JAMES FRANCIS, JR.

53510 Psychotherapy of the adolescent: a comparison with psychotherapy of the adult. JNMD 1958, 127:511-517

MATALON, B.

See Gressot, Michel

MATARAZZO, JOSEPH D.

See Saslow, George

MATHENEY, RUTH V.

53511 (& Topalis, M.) Psychiatric Nursing. St. Louis: C V Mosby 1953, 247 p

MATHEWS, ARTHUR GUY

53512 Start Living Today, A Guide to Positive Living; A Thesis and Modern Interpretation of Mental, Nervous, Emotional, and Psychosomatic Disorders, Comprehensively Written in Non-Medical Language Especially for the Layman. Daytona Beach, Fla: College Pub Co 1956, 271 p

MATHEWS, W. MASON

53513 (& Wineman, D.) Problems of supervision and training in clinical psychology. Round Table, 1952. 3. The supervision of clinical diagnostic work. Ops 1953, 23:301-306

MATSON, FLOYD W.

53514 History as art: the psychological-romantic view. J Hist Ideas 1957, 18:270-279

53515 Political implications of psychoanalytic theory. J Politics 1954, 16:704-725

MATTE-BLANCO, IGNACIO

53516 The constitutional approach to the study of human personality. Psychiat Res Rep 1955, 2:132-154

53517 La enseñanza de psiquiatría dinámica a los estudiantes de medicina: nuestra experiencia, sus resultados y sugerencias. [The teaching of dynamic psychiatry to medical students: our experience, its results and suggestions.] Actas medico-psicologicas 1958, 1(2):164-176

53518 Estudios de Psicología dinámica. [Studies in Dynamic Psychology.] Santiago (Chile): Edit Universitaria 1955, 329 p
   Rv Garma, A. Rev Psicoanál 1955, 12:534-535

53519 Expression in symbolic logic of the characteristics of the system Ucs or the logic of the system Ucs. J 1959, 40:1-5
   Abs JBi Q 1960, 29:273. Rv Tabak Rev Psicoanál 1959, 16:268

53520 La Psíquico y la Naturaleza humana; hacia un Planteamiento experimental. [The Psychical and Human Nature; Towards an Experimental Formulation.] Santiago (Chile): Edit Universitaria 1954, 263 p

53521 [The role of constitutional diagnosis in clinical practice.] (German) In Tribute to Ernst Kretschmer on his 70th birthday, Stuttgart: Georg Thieme 1958

See Ganzaraín, Ramón

MATTHEWS, ROBERT A.

See Watkins, Charles

MATUSSEK, PAUL

53522 Die allgemeine Bedeutung Freuds für die Psychiatrie. [The general significance of Freud for psychiatry.] In Riemann, F. *Lebendige Psychoanalyse*, Munich: Verlag C H Beck 1956, 124-135. Jb Psychol Psychother 1958, 5:90-97

53523 Freud und die gegenwärtige Psychiatrie. Zum 100. Geburtstag Sigmund Freuds am 6. Mai 1956. [Freud and modern psychiatry. On the occasion of the centenary of Sigmund Freud's birth on May 6, 1956.] Fortschr Neurol 1956, 24:531-561

53524 [Functional sexual disturbances.] (German) In Giese, F. [*Human Sexuality.*] Stuttgart: Enke 1955

53525 Funktion und Erleben bei Potenzstörungen mit besonderer Berücksichtigung der impotentia satisfactionis. [Function and emotion in potency disorders and particularly in impotentia satisfactionis.] Z PSM 1955-56, 2:12-19

53526 Liebesleben: Störungen des Sexuallebens. [The love life: disturbances of sexual life.] Hndb N P 1959, 2:580-598

53527 Psychotherapie bei Schizophrenen. [Psychotherapy with schizophrenics.] Hndb N P 1959, 4:385-417

53528 Zur Psychotherapie des Glücksspielers. [On the psychotherapy of the
       gambler.] Vorträge 3. Lindauer Psychotherapie-Woche 1952, 135-146
53529 La psychothérapie des schizophrènes. [Psychotherapy of schizophren-
       ics.] (Tr: Lehmann, A. & Laplanche, J.) Psychanalyse 1958, 4:320-333
53530 Süchtige Fehlhaltungen. [Failures due to addiction] Hndb N P 1959,
       2:188-212

MAUCO, GEORGES

53531 Le caractère de votre enfant. [The character of your child.] Paris:
       Sudel 1959
53532 Conférence à l'école des parents et des éducateurs de 1945 à 1959.
       [Lecture at the school of parents and educators from 1945 to 1959.]
       Paris: Editions de l'École des Parents
53533 Deux mois à l'hôpital. [Two months in the hospital.] Psyché, Paris
       1954, 9:640-651. L'Express (Paris) 1956, Oct 5
53534 L'Education de la Sensibilité chez l'Enfant. Essai sur l'Évolution de
       la Sensibilité. [Training of Sensitivity in the Child. Essay on the Devel-
       opment of Sensitivity.] (2nd ed) Paris: Éditions familiales 1950
53535 L'Inadaptation Scolaire et Sociale et Ses Remèdes. [School and Social
       Maladjustment and Its Remedies.] Paris: Bourrelier 1959, 192 p
          Rv Shentoub RFPsa 1960, 24:125-126

MAUDE, ANGUS

53536 Why is gambling? Encounter 1957, 8(4):25-30

MAUDE, JOHN

53537 Foreword to Neustatter, W. L. *Psychological Disorder and Crime*

MAUERHOFER, H.

53538 Sicología de la experiencia cinematográfica. [Psychology of the cine-
       matographic experience.] (Tr: Carrión Estella, F.) Arch Crimin Neu-
       ropsiq 2. ep. 1958, 6:432-436

MAUGHS, SYDNEY B.

53539 Criminal psychopathology. Prog Neurol Psychiat 1957, 12:494-500
53540 Psychopathic personality. Review of the literature 1947-54. Arch Crim
       Psychodyn 1955, 1:291-325

MAULTSBY, MAXIE

See Badal, Daniel W.

MAURON, CHARLES

53541 Notes sur la structure de l'inconscient chez Vincent van Gogh. [The
       structure of Vincent van Gogh's unconscious.] Psyché, Paris 1953,
       8:24-31; 124-143; 203-209

MAURY, LOTTIE M.

TRANSLATION OF:
Lampl, H. [51317]

MAVES, PAUL B.

53542   (Ed) The Church and Mental Health. NY: Scribner 1953, 303 p

MAXWELL, GROVER
See Feigl, Herbert

MAY, ROLLO
53543   Anxiety and values. Prog PT 1957, 2:82-90
53544   Anxiety in chronic illness. In Harrower, M. *Medical and Psychological
Teamwork in the Care of the Chronically Ill*, Springfield, Ill: Thomas
1955, 55-57
53545   Contributions of existential psychotherapy. In author's *Existence*, 37-91
53546   (& Angel, E.; Ellenberger, H. F.) (Ed) Existence. A New Dimension
in Psychiatry and Psychology. NY: Basic Books 1958, x + 445 p
Rv Lowenfeld, H. Q 1959, 28:256-261. Blauner, J. PPR 1960,
47(2):114-118
53547   The existential approach. Am Hbk Psychiat 2:1338-1361
53548   Fear and anxiety: a psychologist's view. Judaism Psychiat 35-44
53549   Foreword to Guntrip, H. *Psychotherapy and Religion*, 7-10
53550   Freud's evolving theories of anxiety. Out Psa 1955, 97-112. From
author's *The Meaning of Anxiety*
53551   The historical meaning of psychology as a science and profession. Trans
NY Acad Sci 1955, 17:312-314
53552   Historical and philosophical presuppositions for understanding therapy.
In Mowrer, O. H. *Psychotherapy*, NY: Ronald Pr 1953, 9-43
53553   Man's Search for Himself. NY: W W Norton 1953, 281 p
Rv Nydes, J. NPAP 1953, 1(3):68-72. Gendel, E. Psa 1955, 15:86
53554   The origins and significance of the existential movement in psychology.
In author's *Existence*, 3-36
53555   A psychologist looks at mental health in today's world. MH 1954,
38:1-11
53556   Religious psychotherapy and achievement of selfhood. Pastoral Psychol
1951, 2(18):15-20; 1952, 2(20):26-35
53557   The significance of symbols. In author's *Symbolism in Religion and
Literature*. NY: G Braziller 1960, 11-49
53558   Toward an understanding of anxiety. Pastoral Psychol 1950, 1(2):25-31

MAYER, A.
53559   [Concerning psychically-determined disturbances of menstruation.]
(German) Wien med Wschr 1950, 443
53560   Moderne Psychosomatik. [Modern psychosomatics.] Die Heilkunst
1953, 66:119-123
53561   [Psychic roots of gynaecological complaints.] (German) Dtsch med
Wschr 1949, 252

MAYER, FELIX
53562   Dynamische Tiefenpsychologie. [Dynamic Depth Psychology.] Bern:
P Haupt 1953, 343 p

MAYER, HERTA

See Love, Sidney I.

MAYER, M,

TRANSLATION OF:
Freud, S. [10554]

MAYER, MORRIS F.

53563   Introduction. Symposium, 1954: The role of residential treatment for children. Ops 1955, 25:667-668
Abs Koenig RFPsa 1956, 20:583-584

MAYER, WILLIAM

53564   Emil Kraepelin (1856-1926). PT 1956, 10:273-274

MAYER-GALLIN, EMILIA

53565   Lebenswege und Lebensentscheidungen; eine Auseinandersetzung mit der Psychoanalyse. [Ways of Life and Crises of Life; Coming to Terms with Psychoanalysis.] Vienna: W Braumüller 1952-57

MAYER-GROSS, WILLIAM

53566   (& Slater, E.; Roth, M.) Clinical Psychiatry. London: Cassell 1954, 652 p
Rv ESt J 1955, 36:414

MAYMAN, MARTIN

53567   Ego strength and the potential for recovery from mental illness. In Peatman, J. G. & Hartley, E. L. *Festschrift for Gardner Murphy,* NY: Harper 1960, 344-357
53568   (& Schlesinger, H. J.) The Menninger Foundation. In Rubinstein, E. A. & Lorr, M. *Survey of Clinical Practice in Psychology,* NY: IUP 1954, 57-68
53569   A narcissistic character. Clin Stud Pers 307-321

See Ekstein, Rudolf; Menninger, Karl; Sargent, Helen D.

MAYNARD, FREDELLE BRUSER

53570   Your child can train himself. My Baby 1957, Jan. Child-Fam Dig 1957, 16(2):47-49

MAYS, W.

53571   Introduction to Piaget, J. *Logic and Psychology*

MAYZNER, MARK S.

53572   Bibliography on cognitive processes: I. Consciousness, II. Creativity-Invention, III. Dreams, IV. Concepts, V. Intuition, VI. Symbols, VII. Set-Rigidity, VIII. Imaginal Processes—Fantasy, IX. Emotions, X. Thinking—Thought, XI. Judgment, XII. Problem-solving, XIV. Anxiety and stress. Psychol Newsletr, NYU 1956, 7:92-102; 121-132; 8:12-18; 33-36; 1957, 8:77-82; 149-158

MAZAR, B.

53573 (& Winnik, H. Z.; Halpern, L.) [Foreword.] (Hebrew) In Halpern, L. et al: [Freud's Festival.], Jerusalem: Magnes Pr, Hebrew Univ 1957, 7

MAZÉ, D.

TRANSLATIONS OF:
Brun, D. [4644]. Caprio, F. S. [43417]

MAZER, JUNE

See Goodrich, D. Wells

MAZER, MILTON

See Thompson, Clara; Witenberg, Earl G.

MAZZANTI, VINCENT E.

53574 (& Bessell, H.) Communication through the latent language. PT 1956, 10:250-260
Rv Goldberg, L. Rev Psicoanál 1957, 14:343

McALLISTER, JOSEPH B.

53575 Psychoanalysis and morality. New Scholast 1956, 30:310-329

See Garner, Harry H.

McALLISTER, WINSTON K.

53576 The pleasure-pain principle in Bentham and Freud: some relations between factual hedonism, normative hedonism, and criminality. Arch crim Psychodyn 1957, 2:458-476

McARTHUR, CHARLES C.

See Sanford, Nevitt

McCALL, LILLIAN BLUMBERG

53577 (& Meyerhoff, H.) Freud and scientific truth. An exchange. Commentary 1958, 25:343-349
53578 The hidden springs of Sigmund Freud. Does the oedipus complex unlock his personality? Commentary 1954, 18:102-110

McCANDLESS, BOYD R.

53579 Problems of childhood and adolescence. Intro Clin Psych 2, 223-243

McCARTER, ROBERT H.

See Knapp, Peter H.

McCARTNEY, JAMES LINCOLN

53580 The application of electroshock to expedite transference. Acta psychotherap psychosom orthopaedagog 1955, 3(Suppl):243-246

53581 Hypnosis: a rational form of psychotherapy in the treatment of the psychoneuroses. Brit J med Hypnot 1957, 8(4):32-41; 9(1):32-40

53582 Integration of the disintegrated personality. Dis nerv Syst 1953, 14:305-307

53583 Psychotherapy, with special reference to the use of hypnosis. Brit J med Hypnot 1957, 8(3):10-26

53584 Understanding Human Behavior. NY: Vantage Pr 1956, 258 p

McCARY, JAMES L.

53585 Introduction. In author's *Psychology of Personality*, xi-xvi

53586 Introduction. In author's *Six Approaches to Psychotherapy*, 1-7

53587 (Ed) Psychology of Personality; Six Modern Approaches. NY: Logos Pr 1956, xvi + 383 p
    Abs J Am Psa Ass 1958, 6:180. Rv ESt J 1958, 39:441. Hill, G. Q 1959, 28:407-408

53588 (& Sheer, D. E.) (Eds) Six Approaches to Psychotherapy. NY: Dryden Pr 1955, vi + 402 p
    Rv Rosen, V. H. J Am Psa Ass 1958, 6:154-167

McCLARY, ALLAN R.

53589 (& Edgerton, M. D.) Augmentation mammaplasty: psychiatric implications and surgical indications. J Plastic Reconstructive Surg 1958, 21(4)

53590 Depression and chronic illness. Paper and panel discussion. (Abs) Proc Amer Acad PSM 1958

53591 (& Meyer, E.; Weitzman, E. L.) Observations of the role of the mechanism of depression in some patients with disseminated lupus erythematosus. PSM 1955, 17:311-321
    Abs Fain RFPsa 1956, 20:581. EFA Q 1957, 26:290-291. R 1957, 44:482

53592 Separation anxiety in bronchial asthma. (Abs) Proc Med Soc, St. Elizabeth's Hosp, Wash, D.C. 1952

McCLELLAND, DAVID CLARENCE

53593 Comments on Maslow, A. "Deficiency motivation and growth motivation." In Jones, M. R. *Nebraska Symposium on Motivation: 1955*. Lincoln, Neb: Univ of Nebraska Pr 1955, 31-37

53594 Freud and Hull: Pioneers in scientific psychology. Amer Sci 1957, 45:101-113
    Freud y Hull, precursores de la psicologia cientifica. Rev Psicol gen apl, Madrid 1957, 12:111-128

53595 The importance of early learning in the formation of motives. In Atkinson, J. W. *Motives in Fantasy, Actions, and Society*, NY: Van Nostrand 1958, 437-452. From author's *Personality*, NY: Sloane Pr 1951

53596 Methods of measuring human motivation. In Atkinson, J. W. *Motives in Fantasy, Action, and Society*, NY: Van Nostrand 1958, 7-42

53597 Notes for a revised theory of motivation. In author's *Personality*, NY: Sloane 1951, 466-475. In author's *Studies in Motivation*, 226-234

53598 Personality. Ann Rev Psychol 1956, 7:39-62
53599 Personality: an integrative view. In McCary, J. L. *Psychology of Personality*, NY: Logos Pr 1956, 322-365
53600 Psychoanalysis and Religious Mysticism. Wallingford, Pa: Pendle Hill 1959, 32 p
53601 (Ed) Studies in Motivation. NY: Appleton-Century-Crofts 1955, xi + 552 p
53602 Toward a science of personality psychology. Pers Thy 355-382

McCLINTOCK, CHARLES

See Sarnoff, Irving

McCORD, H.

53603 Hypnotherapy and stuttering. J clin exp Hyp 1955, 3:210-214

McCORD, JOAN

See McCord, William

McCORD, WILLIAM

53604 (& McCord, J.) Two approaches to the cure of delinquents. J crim Law Criminol 1944, 44:442-467. In Glueck, S. *The Problem of Delinquency*, Boston: Houghton Mifflin 1959, 721-737

McCORKLE, L. W.

53605 The present status of group therapy in United States correctional institutions. Int J grp PT 1953, 3:79-87

McCORMICK, CHARLES G.

53606 Group dynamics: homeopathic treatment. Int J grp PT 1957, 7:103-112
53607 Objective evaluation of the process and effects of analytic group psychotherapy with adolescent girls. Int J grp PT 1953, 3:181-190

McCRAVEN, VIVIAN

See Singer, Jerome L.

McCULLOCH, WARREN STURGIS

53608 The past of a delusion. Chicago: Chicago Literary Club 1953, 37 p

McCULLOUGH, GWEN

See Berlin, Irving Norman; Szurek, Stanislaus A.

McCULLOUGH, MILTON W.

See Agoston, Tibor; Bateman, J. F.

McCULLY, ROBERT S.

53609 A projective study of a true hermaphrodite during a period of radical surgical procedures. Psychiat Q Suppl 1958, 32:1-35

McCURDY, HAROLD GRIER

53610 The history of dream theory. Drms Pers Dyn 44-54
53611 The Personality of Shakespeare. A Venture in Psychological Method.
       New Haven: Yale Univ Pr; London: Geoffrey Cumberlege, Oxford
       Univ Pr 1953, xi + 243 p
S-21298 A study of the novels of Charlotte and Emily Brontë as an expression
       of their personalities.
           Abs Schafer, R. Q 1953, 22:134

McDANALD, EUGENE C., JR.

53612 Anxiety, chronic disease and the psychologist. In Harrower, M. *Medical
       and Psychological Teamwork in the Care of the Chronically Ill*, Spring-
       field, Ill: Thomas 1955, 52-55
53613 Deliberate lying and unwitting distortion of fact as a mode of resistance
       in psychotherapy. Dis nerv Syst 1956, 17:84-87

McDEVITT, J. B.

ABSTRACT OF:
53614 Thorner, H. A. Examination anxiety without examination. Q 1953,
       22:602

McDONALD, FRANKLIN R.

53615 Psychological flight from "black identity." Clin Stud Cult Confl 63-89

See Marmor, Judd

McDONALD, M.

See Hoffman, Julius

McDONNELL, KILIAN

53616 Psychiatry and pastoral psychology: the experience of an "Institute for
       Mental Health." Lumen Vitae 1957, 12:253-259

McDOUGALL, JOYCE

See Lebovici, Serge

TRANSLATIONS OF:
Nacht, S. et al: [54890]. Pasche, F. & Renard, M. [55511]

McDOWALL, R. J. S.

53617 A biological approach to psychology. Practitioner 1953, 170(1021):
       59-65

McDOWELL, MEHL

53618 An abrupt cessation of the major neurotic symptoms following an hyp-
       notically induced conflict. BMC 1948, 12:168-178
53619 Hypnosis in dermatology. In Schneck, J. *Hypnosis in Modern Medicine*,
       Springfield, Ill: Thomas 1953, 1959, 101-115

McELROY, W. A.

53620 A sex difference in preferences for shapes. BJP 1954, 45:209-216

McFARLAND, MARGARET B.

53621 A discussion of "An experiment in group upbringing," by Anna Freud in collaboration with Sophia Dann; a report on the development of children deprived of both parents. Bull Nat Ass for Nursery Educ 1955, 10(3). Child-Fam Dig 1955, 13(3):3-10

53622 Research concerning the curiosity of children. Child-Fam Dig 1955, 13(4):64-68

McGHIE, ANDREW

See Cameron, J. L.; Chapman, James; Freeman, Thomas

McGINNIS, MANON

See Lindemann, Erich; Winch, Robert F.

McGINNIS, ROBERT

See Winch, Robert F.

McGLASHAN, ALAN

53623 Daily Paper Pantheon, a new fantasia of the unconscious. The Lancet 1953, 1:238-239. The Listener 1953, 50:65-66

53624 Remembering and forgetting. The Lancet 1955, 2:1332-1333

McGLONE, FRANK B.

See Lief, Harold I.

McGOLDRICK, JAMES B.

See Cavanagh, John R.

McGRANAHAN, DONALD V.

S-21367 Critical and experimental study of repression. Under Hum Motiv 371-382

McGUIRE, IVÁN A.

S-21370 The role of the serpent in mental development.
Rv Garma Rev Psicoanál 1953, 10:123

McKAY, B. M.

See Powers, D.

McKELLAR, PETER

53625 Imagination and Thinking: A Psychological Analysis. NY: Basic Books 1957, xi + 219 p

53626 Scientific theory of psychosis: the "model psychosis" experiment and its significance. Int J soc Psychiat 1957, 3:170-182

53627 (& Simpson, L.) Between wakefulness and sleep: hypnagogic imagery. BJP 1954, 45:266-276

McKINNEY, BETSY MARVIN

53628 The sexual aspects of breast feeding. Child-Fam Dig 1955, 13(4):45-57

McKINNON, KATHERN M.

53629 A clinical evaluation of the method of direct analysis in the treatment of psychosis. Clin Psych 1959, 15:80-96

ABSTRACT OF:
53630 Rosen, J. M. Direct Analysis: Selected Papers. An Surv Psa 1953, 4:686-693

McLAUGHLIN, FRANCIS

53631 (Reporter) Problems of reanalysis. (Panel: Am Psa Ass, NY, Dec 1958) J Am Psa Ass 1959, 7:537-547

See Bing, James F.

McLAUGHLIN, JAMES T.

53632 (& Zabarenko, R. N.; Diana, P. B.; Quinn, B.) Emotional reactions of rheumatoid arthritis to ACTH. PSM 1953, 15:187-199
53633 (& Shoemaker, R. J.; Guy, W. B.) Personality factors in adult atopic eczema. AMA Arch Dermatol & Syphil 1953, 68:506-615. Pennsylvania med J 1954, 57:133-137

See Guy, William B.; Shoemaker, Robert J.

ABSTRACTS OF:
53634 Bandler, B. et al: Seizures and the menstrual cycle. Q 1959, 28:287-288
53635 Blumstein, A. Masochism and fantasies of preparing to be incorporated. Q 1960, 29:592-593
53636 Bowman, K. M. & Engle, B. Medicolegal aspects of transvestism. Q 1959, 28:287
53637 Brenner, C. The masochistic character: genesis and treatment. Q 1960, 29:590-591
53638 Brodsky, B. The self-representation, anality, and the fear of dying. Q 1960, 29:589-590
53639 Bromberg, N. Stimulus-response cycles and ego development: with special reference to the masochistic ego. Q 1960, 29:591
53640 Bychowski, G. Some aspects of masochistic involvement. Q 1960, 29:591-592
53641 Eidelberg, L. Humiliation in masochism. Q 1960, 29:592
53642 Fisher, C. & Paul, I. H. The effect of subliminal visual stimulation on images and dreams: a validation study. Q 1960, 29:588-589
53643 Izner, S. M. On the appearance of primal scene content in dreams. Q 1960, 29:593-594
53644 Klein, G. S. Consciousness in psychoanalytic theory: some implications for current research in perception. Q 1960, 29:588
53645 Kucera, O. On teething. Q 1960, 29:592
53646 Kupper, H. I. & Rollman-Branch, H. A. Freud and Schnitzler—(Doppelgänger). Q 1960, 29:590

53647 Miller, J. G. Mental health implications of a general behavior theory. Q 1959, 28:289

53648 Pumpian-Mindlin, E. Changing concepts of therapy in a Veterans Administration mental hygiene clinic. Q 1959, 28:289-290

53649 Rochlin, G. The loss complex: a contribution to the etiology of depression. Q 1960, 29:593

53650 Socarides, C. W. Meaning and content of a pedophilic perversion. Q 1960, 29:589

53651 Thorne, F. C. Epidemiological studies of chronic frustration-hostility-aggression states. Q 1959, 28:288

53652 Weyl, S. Retardation, acceleration, and psychoanalysis. Q 1960, 29:594

McLEAN, HELEN VINCENT

S-21385 Corrective emotional experience through rapport.
Expérience émotionnelle grâce aux relations. (Tr: Comandré, M.) In Alexander, F. & French, T. M. *Psychothérapie analytique*, Paris: PUF 1959, 254-274

53653 Looking ahead in the fields of orthopsychiatric research; a symposium. Ops 1950, 20:73-114

53654 Psychoanalysis as concerned with the problem of values. (Read at Acad of Psa, NY, Dec 1958) Sci Psa 1960, 3:104-109

McLEAN, PRESTON G.

53655 Psychiatry and philosophy. Am Hbk Psychiat 2:1760-1776

McMURRIN, STERLING W.

See Branch, C. H. Hardin

McMURRY, ROBERT N.

53656 The executive neurosis. Harvard Business Rev 1952, 30(6)

53657 Mental illness in industry. Harvard Business Rev 1959, 37(2)

53658 The problem employee. Iron Age 1959, Aug 6:13, 20

McNAUGHTON, F. L.

See Ross, William Donald

McNEILL, HARRY V.

53659 Freudians and Catholics. The Commonweal 1947, 46:350-353

McNEMAR, QUINN

See Farnsworth, Paul R.

McPEEK, JAMES A. S.

53660 Richard and his shadow world. Am Im 1958, 15:195-212

McQUITTY, LOUIS L.

53661 Developing pattern-analytic methods to isolate fruitful psychological concepts. Canad J Psychol 1958, 12:109-114

MEAD, MARGARET

53662   Adolescence in primitive and in modern society. In Calverton, V. F. & Schmalhausen, S. D. *The New Generation*, NY: Macaulay 1930. Read Soc Psychol 341-349

53663   Anthropological data on the problem of instinct. PSM 1942, 4:396-397. Pers n s c 115-118

53664   Changing patterns of parent-child relations in an urban culture. (In somewhat altered form, the Ernest Jones Lecture 1957) J 1957, 38: 369-378
Abs J 1957, 38:301

53665   (& Wolfenstein, M.) (Ed) Childhood in Contemporary Cultures. Chicago: Univ Chicago Pr 1955, xi + 473 p
Rv Axelrad, S. J Am Psa Ass 1960, 8:175-218

53666   Children and ritual in Bali. Childhood Contemp Cult 40-51

53667   The concept of culture and the psychosomatic approach. Ps 1947, 10:57-76. In Weider, A. *Contributions toward Medical Psychology*, Vol I, NY: Ronald Pr 1953, 368-397

53668   The cross-cultural approach to the study of personality. In McCary, J. L. *Psychology of Personality*, NY: Logos Pr 1956, 202-252

53669   Cultural contexts of puberty and adolescence. Bull Phila Ass Psa 1959, 9:59-79

53670   Cultural determinants of behavior. In Roe, A. & Simpson, G. G. *Behavior and Evolution*, New Haven: Yale Univ Pr 1958, 480-503

53671   Cultural discontinuities and personality transformation. J soc Issues, Suppl Series No 8, 1954 (Kurt Lewin Memorial Award Issue)

53672   Effects of anthropological field work models in interdisciplinary communication in the study of national character. J soc Issues 1955, 11(2): 3-11

53673   Illness as a psychological defense. In Fairchild, J. A. *Personal Problems and Psychological Frontiers*, NY: Sheridan House 1957, 60-79

53674   Implications of insight—II. Childhood Contemp Cult 449-461

53675   Introduction to Krich, A. M. *Men*, 9-25

53676   Introduction to Krich, A. M. *Women*, 9-24

53677   Mental health in world perspective. In Opler, M. K. *Culture and Mental Health*, NY: Macmillan 1959, 501-516

53678   (& Wolfenstein, M.) "Monkey": a Chinese children's classic. Childhood Contemp Cult 246-252

53679   National character. In Kroeber, A. L. *Anthropology Today*, Chicago: Univ of Chicago Pr 1953, 642-667

53680   Participant in symposium. In Tanner, J. M. & Inhelder, B. *Discussions on Child Development*, Vol III, NY: IUP 1958, 223 p

53681   (& Calas, N.) (Ed) Primitive Heritage. An Anthropological Anthology. NY: Random House 1953, 592 p
Rv Muensterberger, W. Q 1954, 23:288-289

53682   Research on primitive children. In Carmichael, L. *Manual of Child Psychology*, 2nd ed, NY: John Wiley & Sons 1954, 735-780

53683   Sex and censorship in contemporary society. In *New World Writing*, Third Mentor Selection, NY: New Am Library of World Lit 1953, 7-24

53684 Sharing child development insights around the globe. Understanding the Child 1952, 21(4):98-103. Child-Fam Dig 1953, Feb

53685 Some theoretical considerations on the problem of mother-child separation. Ops 1954, 24:471-483

53686 (& Métraux, R.) (Ed) The Study of Culture at a Distance. Chicago: Univ Chicago Pr; London: Cambridge Univ Pr 1954, x + 480 p
     Rv Jaques, E. J 1955, 36:416-417

53687 The study of national character. In Lerner, D. & Lasswell, H. *The Policy Sciences: Recent Development in the Scope and Methods,* Hoover Institute Studies, Stanford: Stanford Univ Pr 1951, 70-85

53688 The swaddling hypothesis: its reception. Am Anthropologist 1954, 56:395-409

53689 Theoretical setting—1954. Childhood Contemp Cult 3-20

53690 The unique value of the family. In Gruenberg, S. M. *The Encyclopedia of Child Care and Guidance,* NY: Doubleday 1954. In Linscott, R. N. & Stein, J. *Why You Do What You Do,* NY: Random House 1956, 187-190

REVIEW OF:
53691 Abramson, H. A. The Patient Speaks. PPR 1959, 46(2):126-127

MEADOW, A.

53692 (& Vetter, H. J.) Freudian theory and the Judaic value system. Int J soc Psychiat 1959, 5:197-207

MEARES, AINSLIE

53693 The Door of Serenity; A Study in the Therapeutic Use of Symbolic Painting. Springfield, Ill: Thomas; London: Faber & Faber 1958, 119 p

53694 A dynamic technique for the induction of hypnosis. Brit J med Hypnot 1958, 9:22-28

53695 Hypnography, A Study in the Therapeutic Use of Hypnotic Painting. Springfield, Ill: Thomas 1957, 271 p

53696 Hypnography—a technique in hypnoanalysis. JMS 1954, 100:965-974
     Abs EMW Q 1956, 25:295

53697 A note on hypnosis and the mono-symptomatic psychoneurotic. Brit J med Hypnot 1956, 8(2):26-28

53698 A note on the motivation for hypnosis. J clin exp Hyp 1955, 3:222-228

53699 Recent work in hypnosis and its relation to general psychiatry. Med J Australia 1956, 43:1-5

MECHLER, A.

53700 Der Tod als Thema der neueren medizinischen Literatur. [The theme of death in recent medical writing.] Jb Psychol Psychother 1955, 3:371-382

MEDALIA, N. Z.

53701 Authoritarianism, leader acceptance, and group cohesion. ASP 1955, 51:207-213

MEDEIROS, M. DE

53702 Centenário de Freud. [Centennial of Freud.] Rev Bras Saúde ment 1956, 2(2):5-9

MEDNICK, SARNOFF A.

53703 (& Garner, A. M.; Stone, H. K.) A test of some behavioral hypotheses drawn from Alexander's specificity theory. Ops 1959, 29:592-598

MEDUNA, LADISLAS J.

See Grinker, Roy R.

MEEHL, PAUL E.

53704 Psychotherapy. Ann Rev Psychol 1955, 6:357-378

See Sanford, Nevitt

MEER, BERNARD

See Stein, Morris I.

MEER, SAMUEL J.

53705 Authoritarian attitudes and dreams. ASP 1955, 51:74-78

MEERLOO, JOOST A. M.

53706 Abstention, rebound, and readjustment; addiction abstention, acute deprivation, starvation, shock, withdrawal of chronic medication; a study in experimental adaptation. JNMS 1954, 120:46-55
53707 On ambivalence. NPAP 1953, 2(1):16-22
53708 Archaic behavior and the communicative act; the meaning of stretching, yawning, rocking and other fetal behavior in therapy. Psychiat Q 1955, 29:60-73
S-22170A Artificial ecstasy. Encycl Aberr 195-206
        Abs NRo An Surv Psa 1952, 3:297-302
53709 Brainwashing and menticide. Some implications of conscious thought control. PPR 1958, 45(1-2):83-99
53710 Children's language. Child-Fam Dig 1956, 14(3):34-46. From author's *Conversation and Communication* [22171A]
S-22171 (& Klauber, L. D.) Clinical significance of starvation and oral deprivation.
        Abs R 1954, 41:289
53711 Contribution of the psychiatrist to the management of crisis situations. P 1952, 109:352-355
53712 Contribution of psychoanalysis to the problems of the aged. Psa Soc Wk 321-337
S-22171A Conversation and Communication: A Psychological Inquiry.
        Rv JKl J 1953, 34:161-163. R 1954, 41:295
53713 Danger, panic and first aid. Milit Rev Ft Leavenworth 1953, 33(2): 40-45
53714 The delusion of the flying saucer. Am Practit 1958, 9:1631-1636

53715 Discussant, Conference on "Morale and communication." In Galdston, I. *Panic and Morale*, NY: IUP 1958, 46-48

53716 Discussant, Conference on "Morale: its nature and meaning." In Galdston, I. *Panic and Morale*, NY: IUP 1958, 82-83

53717 Discussant, Conference on "The sociology of morale." In Galdston, I. *Panic and Morale*, NY: IUP 1958, 137-141

53718 Emergency methods in psychotherapy. PT 1956, 10:117-140

53719 Emergency psychotherapy and mental first aid, JNMD 1956, 124:535-545

53720 The fate of one's face. Psychiat Q 1956, 30:31-43
     Abs JBi Q 1957, 26:287-288

53721 The father cuts the cord. The role of the father as an initial transference figure. PT 1956, 10:471-480. Child-Fam Dig 1956, 15(3):56-66
     Abs Viderman RFPsa 1957, 21:624

53722 First aid in acute panic states. PT 1951, 5:367-371

S-22176 Free association, silence and the multiple function of speech.
     Abs JAA An Surv Psa 1952, 3:90-91. NRo An Surv Psa 1952, 3:375-376

53723 Freud: the creative scientist. Reflections upon some pictures of Sigmund Freud. R 1957, 44:225-227
     Abs JLan Q 1958, 27:444

53724 Human camouflage and identification with the environment: the contagious effect of archaic skin signs. PSM 1957, 19:89-98
     Abs Lossy, F. T. Q 1958, 27:298

53725 Justice as a psychological problem. Arch crim Psychodyn 1959, 3:7-51

53726 Koprolalia—the child's urge to use indecent words. Child-Fam Dig 1958, 17(5):19-20

53727 Kos against Knidos. Ambivalence as the psychiatric outlook on man. J Hillside Hosp 1957, 6:67-86
     Abs Afterman, J. Q 1958, 27:146

53728 Living by proxy: a frequent form of transference and mental symbiosis. PT 1953, 7:241-253
     Abs Rev Psicoanál 1955, 12:141

53729 Man's wish for eternity. Tomorrow 1954, 2:67-71

53730 Medication into submission; the danger of therapeutic coercion. JNMD 1955, 122:353-360

53731 Mental contagion. PT 1959, 13:66-82

53732 Mental contagion—fear—and the flu pandemic. Child-Fam Dig 1958, 17(4):21-24

53733 Mental danger, stress and fear. I. A semantic and clinical inquiry. JNMD 1956, 123:513-530

53734 Mental danger, stress and fear. II. Man and his morale. JNMD 1957, 125:357-379

53735 Mental first aid. Child-Fam Dig 1958, 17(1):20-24

53736 Mental hygiene in medical practice. Amer Practit Dig Treatment 1959, 10(4). Child-Fam Dig 1959, 18(4):21-25

53737 The monument as a delusional token. Am Im 1954, 11:363-374
     Abs MK An Surv Psa 1954, 5:466-467

53738 Morale. Milit Rev, Ft Leavenworth 1954, 33(11):44-50

53739 Obituary: Clinton P. McCord 1881-1953. Q 1953, 22:421

S-22180 Patterns of Panic.
    Rv Piotrowski, Z. A. R 1953, 40:290
53740 Pavlovian strategy as a weapon for menticide. P 1954, 110:809-813.
    Child-Fam Dig 1954, 11(1):3-11
53741 People's reaction to danger. In Galdston, I. *Panic and Morale*, NY:
    IUP 1958, 174-178
53742 Pep pills and the emotional challenge of sports. Child-Fam Dig 1958,
    17(2):8-10
53743 Psychiatric ecology. JNMD 1959, 129:385-390
53744 Psychoanalysis as an experiment in communication. PPR 1959, 46(1):
    75-89
54745 Psychological implications of malignant growth. (A survey of hypoth-
    eses.) M 1954, 27:210-215
53746 The psychology of treason and loyalty. PT 1954, 8:648-666
    Abs Rev Psicoanál 1955, 12:148
53747 Psychotherapy with elderly people. Geriatrics 1955, 10:583-587
53748 The Rape of the Mind. Cleveland: World Publ Co 1956, 320 p
53749 Rock 'n Roll: a modern aspect of St. Vitus Dance. Implications for the
    theory of mental contagion. Amer Practit Dig Treatment 1959, 10:
    1029-1032. Child-Fam Dig 1959, 18(6):15-21
53750 Sea- and air-sickness and man's hidden fears. Child-Fam Dig 1958,
    17(3):3-5
53751 Some psychological problems of the aged patient. NYSJM 1958, 58:
    3810-3814. Child-Fam Dig 1959, 18(2):3-12
53752 Suicide, menticide, and psychic homicide. AMA ANP 1959, 81:360-362
53753 Television addiction and reactive apathy. JNMD 1954, 120:290-291.
    Child-Fam Dig 1955, 12(4):3-6
53754 Thought control and confession compulsion. Expl Psa 28-37
53755 The thousand delights of yoghurt. Child-Fam Dig 1959, 18(1):81-82
53756 Three artists. An essay on creative urge and artistic perturbation. Am
    Im 1953, 10:247-263
    Abs MK An Surv Psa 1953, 4:368-369
53757 Transference and resistance in geriatric psychotherapy. R 1955, 42:72-
    82
    Abs JLan Q 1956, 25:445
S-6023 (& Coleman, M. L.) The transference function: a study of normal and
    pathological transference.
    Abs JAA An Surv Psa 1951, 2:161. STa An Surv Psa 1951, 2:386-387
53758 The Two Faces of Man; Two Studies on the Sense of Time and on
    Ambivalence. NY: IUP 1954, x + 237 p
    Abs J Am Psa Ass 1955, 3:551-552
53759 Who are these: I, me, my ego and myself? A survey of ego aspects.
    PPR 1960, 47(2):83-96
53760 Why do they yield. The psychodynamics of false confession. Child-
    Fam Dig 1956, 15(1):44-57. From author's *The Rape of the Mind*

See Meerloo, Lucy; Weiss, Frederick A.

REVIEWS OF:
53761 Emde-Boas, C. Van: Shakespeare's Sonnetten en Hun Verband Met de
    Travesti-Double Spelen. Q 1953, 22:593-594

53762 Van Den Berg, J. H. The Phenomenological Approach to Psychiatry. Q 1956, 25:436

MEERLOO, LUCY

53763 (& Meerloo, J. A. M.) Some psychological problems in cerebral palsy children. Quart J Child Behav 1950, 2(4). Child-Fam Dig 1955, 12(1):12-20

MEEROVICH, R.

53764 [Psychological analysis of the ascending tendency in progressive paralysis.] (Russian) Nevropat psichiatriya i psikhologiya 1936, 5:793-813

MEERWEIN, F.

53765 Die Bedeutung der Anstalt für die Gegenübertragung der Therapeuten. [Significance of the institution for the therapist's countertransference.] Acta psychother psychosom orthopaedag 1957, 5:248-253

MEHTA, HOSHANG P.

S-22192 The ego and its object.
Abs JAA An Surv Psa 1952, 3:48-49

MEHTA, PERIN H.

53766 A comparative evaluation of client-centered therapy and psychoanalysis. Educ & Psychol, Delhi 1955, 2(1):1-10

MEIER, CARL ALFRED

53767 Jung and Analytical Psychology. Newton Centre, Mass: Dept of Psychol, Andover Newton Theolog School 1959, 80 p
53768 Projektion, Übertragung, und Subjekt-objektrelation. Dialectica 1954, 8:4

Projection, transference, and the subject-object relation. J analyt Psychol 1959, 4:21-34. In *Proceedings of Four Conferences of Parapsychological Studies*, NY: Parapsychology Foundation 1957, 155-157

MEIER, LOTTE

See Meng, Heinrich

MEIERS, JOSEPH

53769 Discussion of Rosen, J. N. "The treatment of schizophrenic psychosis by direct analytic therapy." Psychiat Q 1947, 21. Direct Anal 87-90

MEIGNANT, P.

53770 Médecine et psychologie. Réponse à M. Pierre Salzy. [Medicine and psychology. Answer to Mr. Pierre Salzy.] Psyché, Paris 1954, 9:298-309

MEIGNIEZ, ROBERT

53771 Réflexions pour une sociologie psychanalytique. [Considerations on a psychoanalytical sociology.] Psyché, Paris 1954, 9:246-254

53772 Le thème de la mort-mère dans les cas graves de tuberculose pulmonaire. [Theme of the dead mother in severe cases of pulmonary tuberculosis.] Psyché, Paris 1956, 11:73-84

MEIJERING, W. L.
(See also Meyering, W. L.)

53773 Group psychotherapy and the "frame of reference." Int J grp PT 1955, 5:242-248

53774 The use of multiple transferences in community psychotherapy. Acta psychotherap psychosom orthopaedag 1955, 3(Suppl):246-252

MEILI, RICHARD

53775 Anfänge der Charakterentwicklung. [Beginnings of character development.] Pro Juventute 1957, 37:435-439

53776 Angstentstehung bei Kleinkindern. [The development of anxiety in infancy.] Schweiz Z Psychol 1955, 14:195-212

53777 Les débuts de la psychanalyse en Suisse romande. [The beginnings of psychoanalysis in French-speaking Switzerland.] Schweiz Z Psychol 1956, 15:139-141

53778 Zur hundertjährigen Wiederkehr des Geburtstages von Sigmund Freud: 6. Mai 1856. [On the hundredth anniversary of Sigmund Freud's birthday: May 6, 1856.] Schweiz Z Psychol 1956, 15:81-83

53779 A longitudinal study of personality development. Dynam Psychopath Child 106-123

MEILI-DWORETZKI, GERTRUD

TRANSLATIONS OF:
Duss, L. [7329]. Spitz, R. A. [60082]

MEINERTZ, F.

53780 Über das Werk von Werner Wagner; Daseinsanalyse und Psychiatrie. [The work of Werner Wagner; existential analysis and psychiatry.] MMW 1956, 98:1439-1441

MEINERTZ, JOSEF

53781 Bemerkungen zum Begriff der Entwicklung in der Tiefenpsychologie. [Remarks on the concept of development in depth psychology.] Psyche, Heidel 1956, 10:401-403

53782 Kant und die Tiefenpsychologie. [Kant and depth-psychology.] Psyche, Heidel 1949, 3:241-282

53783 Psychologie, Existenz, Anthropologie. [Psychology, existence, anthropology.] Psyche, Heidel 1953, 6:577-583

53784 [The specific mode of comprehending deep-psychological processes.] (German) Stud gen 1950, 3:284

53785 Die Tiefenpsychologie in ihren Bezügen zu wesentlichen Strömungen der gegenwärtigen geistigen Atmosphäre. [The relations of depth psychology to basic trends of the contemporary intellectual atmosphere.] Psyche, Heidel 1957, 11:473-504

MEISS, MARGARET L.

S-22247 The Oedipal problem of a fatherless child.
Abs NRo An Surv Psa 1952, 3:262-264; 268. WH J 1953, 34:280

MEISSNER, W. W.

53786 Affective response to psychoanalytic death symbols. ASP 1958, 56:295-299

MEISTRA Y FALABELLA

TRANSLATION OF:
Berge, A. [41691, 41696]

MELAMED, L.

See Halevy, Meyer

MELLETT, THOMAS PAUL

53787 Recall of tasks and expressed self-acceptance among patient groups. Diss Abstr 1954, 14:2402

MELLEY, A.

REVIEW OF:
53788 Dracoulides, N. N. Psychanalyse de l'Artiste et de son Oeuvre. RFPsa 1953, 17:361-362

MELLO, A. DA S.

S-22250 Ilusões da terapêutica psicanalítica. Rev bras Med 1953, 10(1):14-20; 10(2):101-108

MELTZER, DONALD

53789 Toward a structural concept of anxiety. Ps 1955, 18:41-50

MELTZER, E.

53790 [Experimental psychological researches on pulmonary tuberculosis patients with the aid of the Rorschach test.] (German) Psychol Rdsch 1950, 1:103
53791 [Psychodiagnostic investigations into pulmonary patients with the aid of the Rorschach test.] (German) Beitr Klin Tuberk 1950, 103:303

MENAKER, ESTHER

53792 A contribution to the study of the neurotic stealing symptom. Ops 1939, 9:368-377
53793 Hypermotility and transitory tic in a child of seven. Nerv Child 1945, 4:335-341
53794 Masochism—a defense reaction of the ego. Q 1953, 22:205-220
Abs JFr An Surv Psa 1953, 4:209-211. JKl J 1954, 35:441-442. Rv Dreyfus RFPsa 1953, 17:351-352

53795   A note on some biologic parallels between certain innate animal be-
        havior and moral masochism. R 1956, 43:31-41
            Abs JLan Q 1957, 26:435-436
53796   The self-image as defense and resistance. Q 1960, 29:72-81

MENDEL, WERNER M.

TRANSLATION OF:
(& Lyons, J.) Binswanger, L. [2827]

MENDELL, DAVID

53797   [Participant in] Discussion. Schiz Psa Off Pract 74
53798   (& Fisher, S.) A multi-generation approach to treatment of psycho-
        pathology. JNMD 1958, 126:523-529
            Abs Smolensky Rev Psicoanál 1959, 16:92

See Fisher, Seymour

MENDELL, RALPH WALDO

53799   Contemporary histories of psychology. Pres-Day Psychol 487-506

MENDELSOHN, B.

53800   La victimologie. [Victimology.] RFPsa 1958, 22:95-119
            Rv Fiasche, D. N. de. Rev Psicoanál 1958, 15:425-426

MENDELSOHN, ROBERT S.

See Falstein, Eugene I.; Judas, Ilse

MENDELSON, JACK P.

53801   (& Wexler, D.; Leiderman, P. H.; Solomon, P.) A study of addiction
        to nonethyl alcohols and other poisonous compounds. Quart J Stud
        Alcohol 1957, 18:561-580

See Lindemann, Erich; Solomon, Philip; Wexler, Donald

MENDELSON, MYER

53802   (& Hirsch, S.; Webber, C. S.) A critical examination of some recent
        theoretical models in psychosomatic medicine. PSM 1956, 18:363-373
            Abs Powelson, D. H. Q 1958, 27:136
53803   Psychiatric views of depression: a critical and historical review. Bull
        Marit psychol Assoc 1954 (spring), 21-32
53804   Psychoanalytic Concepts of Depression. Springfield, Ill: Thomas 1960,
        xii + 170 p

MENDEZ, SUSANA A. DE

53805   (& Rascovsky, A.) La percepción interna como fenómeno visual. [Inner
        perception as a visual phenomenon.] Rev Psicoanál 1956, 13:379-382
            Abs Rev Psicoanál 1958, 15:199

MENDONÇA, DARCY

53806 Alguns aspectos da psicanálise da esquizofrenia. [Some aspects of the psychoanalysis of schizophrenia.] J bras Psiquiat 1953, 2

53807 Alguns aspectos da teoria kleiniana das psicoses. [Some aspects of the Klein theory of psychoses.] Neurobiol 1955, 18(1)

53808 Arte e psicose. [Art and psychosis.] Foldha de Manhã, São Paulo 1954, Jan 31

53809 A conversão e a fobia como "defesa" na histeria. [The conversion and the phobia as "defense" in hysteria.] J bras Psiquiat 1954, 4

53810 Importância dos instintos sexuais em psicopatologia. [The importance of the sexual instincts in psychopathology.] Arquivos Neuro-Psiquiat, São Paulo 1959, 17(4)

53811 Sobre o problema da transferencia. [About the problem of transference.] Neurobiol 1952, 15(3-4)

53812 Sobre o problema do "contato social" do analista com o paciente. [About the problem of the "social relations" between the psychoanalyst and the patient.] Neurobiol (Recife) 1952, 15(3-4)

53813 Psicanálise e medicina psicossomática. [Psychoanalysis and psychosomatic medicine.] Neurobiol 1953, 16(3)

53814 Psicodinâmica da despersonalização. [Psychodynamics of depersonalization.] Arquivos Neuro-Psiquiat, São Paulo 1959, 17(3)

53815 A psicologia da angústia. [The psychology of anxiety.] Neurobiol 1955, 18(4)

53816 Sôbre a psicopatologia da despersonalização. [On the psychopathology of depersonalization.] Thesis, Univ of Brazil, São Paulo 1958, 258 p Empresa Gráfica da Revista dos Tribunais, ed.

MENDOZA-HOYOS, H.

53817 (& Manzanilla, L.; Torres, M.) Psicopatias tirotocicas. [Psychopathic thyrotoxicosis.] Rev Soc endocrin Columbia (Bogotà) 1956, 1:107-115

MENG, HEINRICH

53818 Die Akzentverschiebung in der Psychohygiene. [The shift of emphasis in mental hygiene.] Schweiz Z Psychol 1955, 14:81-87. Prak Psychiat 1955, 34:205-211

53819 Andragogik. [Andragogics.] Berner Schulblatt 1957, (1-2) Arbeitsgem. Basel

53820 August Aichhorns Weg, Vergangenes, Gegenwärtiges, Zukünftiges. [The path of August Aichhorn, past, present, and future.] In Aichhorn: Erziehungsberatung, Erziehungshilfe, Bern; Stuttgart: Huber 1959

53821 Die Bedeutung der prämorbiden Persönlichkeit für den seelischen Gesundheitsschutz. [Role of the premorbid personality in mental hygiene.] Z Präventivmedizin 1956, 1(10). Agnes Karll-Schwester 1957, 11(10). Prak Psychiat 1957, 36:87-92

53822 Discussion of Graber, G. Psychologie des Mannes. Hippokrates 1958, 29(23)

53823 Discussion of Lauterburg, "Wozu leben wir?" Landarzt 1958, 34(17)

53824 Discussion of Petri, H., "Psychohygiene und die Entwicklung der Menschlichkeit." Hippokrates 1958, 29(24)

53825 Einwände und Widerstände gegen die Psychohygiene. [Objections and resistances to mental hygiene.] Medizinische 1956, (2)

53826 Über Entwurzelung. [On uprooting.] Hippokrates 1958, 29(9). Basler Psychol Arbeitsgemeinschaft 1958

53827 Erforscher der Menschenseele. [Explorers of the human psyche.] Frankfurter Rundschau 1958, June 27

53828 Erinnerungen (an S. Freud). [Reminiscences of Sigmund Freud.] Aufbau 1956, 22(21):20

53829 Le facteur psychique dans la médecine dentaire. [The psychologic factor in dentistry.] Psyché, Paris 1953, 8:350-361

53830 Foreword to second ed of *Praxis der seelischen Hygiene*. Basel; Stuttgart: Schwabe 1959

53831 Zur Frage des "Climacterium virile." Acta psychother psychosom orthopaedagog 1953, 1:97-101. Med Klinik 1958, 53(24)
The male climacteric. (Tr: Elkan, E.) Int J Sexol 1954, 7:246-248

53832 Freud und der Bildhauer. [Freud and the sculptor.] Schweiz Z Psychol 1956, 15:149-151

53833 Gedenken—Sigmund Freud. [In memoriam—Sigmund Freud.] Hippokrates 1956, 27(9)

53834 Geistige Hygiene. [Mental hygiene.] Nationalzeitg, special issue May 6, 1956, No 206

53835 Geistige Hygiene—Forschung und Praxis. [Mental hygiene—research and practice.] Realität und Utopie 1956, 12

53836 Über den Heilerfolg begünstigende Faktoren in der psychoanalytischen Therapie. [Factors favoring the success of psychoanalytic therapy.] Schweiz med Wschr 1955, 85:1096-1099

53837 Der Heilweg der Psychoanalyse S. Freuds. [The healing method of Freud's psychoanalysis.] In *Heilwege der Tiefenpsychologie*, Bern; Stuttgart: Huber 1957

53838 Implications of the "miracles of Lourdes." In *Proceedings of Four Conferences of Parapsychological Studies*, NY: Parapsychology Foundation 1957, 82-84

53839 Lehrer und Schüler. [Teachers and pupils.] Med Klinik 1958, (15)

53840 Über eine Magersuchtsform als Äquivalent der Organpsychose. [A certain kind of dieting fad as an equivalent to organ psychosis.] Ars Medici 1957, 47(8)

53841 Nachwort. [Epilogue.] In Hoff, H. *Lehrbuch der Psychiatrie*. Basel: Benno Schwab 1956

53842 Über Neurosenfragen, Psychosenpsychologie, Endokrinium. [On the problems of neuroses, psychology of psychoses, endocrine system.] Psyche, Heidel 1959, 13:499-523

53843 Obituary: Dr. Leo Kaplan, 1876-1956. Schweiz Z Psychol 1955, **14**:316. J 1957, 38:277

53844 Preface to *Aichhorn: Erziehungsberatung und Erziehungshilfe*. Bern; Stuttgart: Huber, "Bücher des Werdenden," zweite Reihe, 1959

53845 (& Stern, E.) Zum Problem der Organpsychose. Z PSM 1954-55, 1:286-294.
Organ-psychosis. R 1955, 42:428-434
Abs JLan Q 1957, 26:285

53846 Zum Problem der Wunderheilungen. [On the problem of miraculous cures.] Heilkunst, Munich 1956, (4)

S-22319 (Ed) Die Prophylaxe des Verbrechens.
Rv Salomon, F. RFPsa 1957, 21:863-864

53847 Prophylaxe des Verbrechens. [Prevention of crime.] Schule und Nation 1957, 4(1). Pro Juventute 1957, 38(1-2). Der öffentliche Dienst 1957, June 7. Stimme der Arbeit, Bern 1957, 25(4). From author's *Prophylaxe des Verbrechens* [22319]
La prophylaxie du crime. Psyché, Paris 1954, 9:164-168

53848 Psyche, Hormon und menschliche Konflikte. [Mind, hormone and human conflicts.] Int J für prophylaktische Med und Sozialhygiene 1959, 3(5)

53849 Psyche und Hormon. [Psyche and hormone.] In *Therapie des Monats,* Mannheim: Boehringer 1959

53850 Die Psychoanalyse und die dynamische Betrachtungsweise des Psychischen. [Psychoanalysis and the dynamic way of looking at the psyche.] Praxis, Schweiz Rundschau f Med 1958, 47(22)

53851 Psychoanalysis, ethics and worldly care of the soul. Tr: Dunner, A.) Am Im 1956, 13:335-346

53852 Psychoanalytische Voraussetzungen einer aktiven Psychohygiene. [Psychoanalytic conditions for an active mental hygiene.] Prak Psychiat 1954, 33:227-231

53853 Psychohygiene 1 and 2. [Mental hygiene, pts 1 and 2.] In Hoff, H. *Lehrbuch der Psychiatrie,* Basel: Schwabe 1956

53854 Über Psychohygiene als akademisches Unterrichtsfach. [On mental hygiene as an academic subject.] Psyche, Heidel 719-720

53855 Psychohygiene gestern und heute. [Mental hygiene past and present.] Prak Psychiat 1958, 37:88-92

53856 (& Meier, L.) Psychohygiene gestern und heute. [Mental hygiene past and present.] Pro Juventute 1958, 39:94-96

53857 Psychohygiene heute (Idee und Wirklichkeit). [Mental hygiene today. Idea and reality.] In *Aktuelle Psychotherapie,* Munich: Lehmann 1958

53858 Zur Psychohygiene mitmenschlicher Beziehungen. [Contribution to mental hygiene of interpersonal relations.] *Handbuch der Neurosenlehre,* 1959

53859 Psychohygienische Vorlesungen. [Lectures in Mental Hygiene.] Basel; Stuttgart: Schwabe 1958
Rv Barande, I. RFPsa 1959, 23:291

53860 Psychologie in der zahnärztlichen Praxis. [Psychology in Dental Practice.] Bern, Stuttgart: Hans Huber 1952
Rv Salomon, F. RFPsa 1953, 17:567-568

53861 Psychosomatik, Krankheit und Suggestibilität. [Psychosomatics, disease and suggestibility.] Die Heilkunst 1957, 70:409-412

53862 Psychotherapie heute. [Psychotherapy today.] Zürichsee-Zeitung 1957, April 6, (82)

53863 Psychotherapie und Strukturwandel. [Psychotherapy and structural change.] Psychologe 1957, 9(11)

53864 Rainer Maria Rilke als Problem der Tiefenpsychologie. [Rainer Maria Rilke as a problem of depth psychology.] Psychotherapie 1956, 1:66-68

53865 Schulkind, Eltern und Zahnarzt. [School-age child, parents, and dentist.] Pro Juventute 1956, 37(2-3). Schweiz Erziehungsrundschau 1957, 30(8)

53866 Zum 6. Mai 1936 (80. Geburtstag von Freud). [On the occasion of the 80th birthday of Freud on May 6, 1936.] Psa Vkb 1957, 73-74

53867 6. Mai 1956 (100. Geburtstag Freuds). [On the occasion of the 100th birthday of Freud on May 6, 1956.] Psa Vkb 1957, 75

53868 Seelische Entwicklung und Asthmabereitschaft. [Psychic development and predisposition for asthma.] Landarzt, Stuttgart 1957, 33(32)

53869 Seelischer Gesundheitsschutz—eine individuelle und gesellschaftliche Aufgabe. [The protection of mental health—an individual as well as social task.] In *Seelische Gesundheit,* Bern; Stuttgart: Huber 1959

53870 Shortcuts to mental health. Tomorrow 1958, 6:36-42

53871 Zum 70. Geburtstag von H. Christoffel. [On the occasion of the 70th birthday of H. Christoffel.] Psychologe 1958, 10(6)

53872 Sigmund Freud. Hippokrates, Stuttg 1956, 27:292-295

53873 Sigmund Freud. Psychologe (special issue) 1956, 8(5-6)

53874 Sigmund Freud. Psa Vkb 1957, 11-19

53875 Sigmund Freud in Brief, Gespräch, Begegnung und Werk. [Sigmund Freud in letters, conversations, interviews and work.] Psyche, Heidel 1956, 10:517-529. Prak Psychiat 1957, 36:165-167; 182-189

53876 Sigmund Freud, the one hundredth anniversary. J Am Med Women's Ass, Nashville, Tenn 1957, 12(6)

53877 Sigmund Freud und die Soziologie. Sociologica. Frankfurter Beiträge zur Soziologie 1955, 1:67-76

53878 Sigmund Freud zum 100. Geburtstag. [On the 100th birthday of Sigmund Freud.] Frankfurter Rundschau 1956, May 5, (105)
       Sigmund Freud—pour commémorer le 100ᵉ anniversaire de sa naissance. Ciba Symposium 1956, 4(1)

53879 Zu Sigmund Freuds 100. Geburtstag am 6. Mai. [On Sigmund Freud's 100th birthday, May 6th.] Landarzt 1956, 32(13)

53880 Die Therapie der Neurosen. [Therapy of neuroses.] In Hoff, H. *Lehrbuch der Psychiatrie,* Basel: Benno Schwab 1956

53881 Tie'enpsychologische Therapie der Neurosen. [Depth-psychological therapy of neuroses.] In Hoff, H. *Lehrbuch der Psychiatrie,* Basel: Benno Schwab 1956

S-22386 Wir lesen Freud. Psa Vkb 1957, 117-122

53882 Worte des Freundes. (Ernst Schneider). [Words of a friend. (Ernst Schneider).] Psychologe 1957, Feb 20. Berner Schulblatt 1957, 90(1-2)

53883 Zeitfragen in einer sich wandelnden Welt. [Timely questions in a changing world.] Prak Psychiat 1953, 32:102-104. Psychologe 1953, 5:125-128. From author's *Zwang und Freiheit in der Erziehung* [22390]

S-22390 Zwang und Freiheit in der Erziehung. (2nd ed) Bern: Hans Huber 1953, xi + 227 p

53884 Zwang und Freiheit in der Erziehung. [Coercion and freedom in education.] Schweiz Lehrerzeitung 1957, (21)

53885 Die Zwangsneurose und ihr verwandte Störungen. [Obsessional neurosis and related disturbances.] Psa Vkb 1957, 263-271

See Bettschart, W.; Federn, Paul; Grote, L. R.

MENNINGER FOUNDATION

53886 Children at the edge of schizophrenia. Menn Q 1955, 9(3):19-20
53887 Far more than a monument. Menn Q 1954 8(3):1-8
53888 1953 The Menninger Foundation. Topeka, Kans: Menninger Found 1953, 48 p
53889 Report of Progress for the Year from July 1, 1954, to June 30, 1955. Topeka, Kans: Menninger Found 1955, 104 p
53890 Report of Progress for the Year from July 1, 1955, to June 30, 1956. Topeka, Kans: Menninger Found 1956, 100 p
53891 Report of Progress for the Year from July 1, 1956, to June 30, 1957. Topeka, Kans: Menninger Found 1957, 116 p
53892 Report of Progress. Topeka, Kans: Menninger Found 1958, 106 p
53893 Review: industrial mental health. Menn Q 1957, 11(2):17-21
53894 The training of a psychiatrist. Menn Q 1955, 9(3):14-18

MENNINGER, CATHERINE F.

See Ackerman, Nathan W.

MENNINGER, KARL AUGUSTUS

S-22459 The abuse of rest in psychiatry. Psychiat World 370-377
53895 The academic lecture: Hope. P 1959, 116:481-491
53896 Acceptance address for the 1954 CIO-CSC Philip Murray award. NY: Nat CIO Community Services Committee 1955
53897 Address before Assembly of California Legislature. Assembly Daily J 1957, Jan 15:387-394
53898 Address before 80th General Assembly of State of Tennessee. Nashville, Tenn: Dept Mental Hlth 1957, Feb 20
53899 Address before Joint Assembly of Vermont Legislature. J of Joint Assembly 1957, Apr 9:84-94
53900 Address before Joint Convention of Iowa Legislature. Iowa State House J 1957, Feb 1:156-166
53901 Address before Joint Session of Texas Legislature. Texas Soc Mental Hlth 1957, Feb 12
53902 Alcohol addiction. In Linscott, R. N. & Stein, J. *Why You Do What You Do,* NY: Random House 1956, 125-138. From author's *Man Against Himself* [22520]
53903 All About You. Life Adjustment Booklet. Chicago: Science Res Assoc 1955, 40 p
S-22462 The amelioration of mental disease by influenza. Psychiat World 156-166
53904 Angels unaware: How are you emotionally? Crippled Child 1955, April, 32:4-7, 27
S-22466 The approach to the psychiatric patient. Psychiat World 378-390
S-22467 Are policemen supermen? Psychiat World 749-753
53905 Are you really grown-up? This Week Mag 1955, Sept 4:7. Hum Relat 1955, Nov 20, (45):2-3
53906 The banker and his mental health. Chicago: Financial Public Relations Assn 1957, 14 p
53907 The best in your life. Home in Review 1957, Jan 14-25:17-19

53908 Bibliography 1919-1959. Psychiat World 891-907
53909 The billion dollar hangover. In *Annual Meeting of the National Council on Alcoholism*, NY: Nat Council on Alcoholism 1957, 51-59
S-22470 Bleeding Kansas. Psychiat World 16-22
53910 Blueprint for Teen-age Living. NY: Sterling 1958
53911 Boom! In Gilliland, E. G. *Music Therapy 1952*, Lawrence, Kans: Nat Assn Music Therapists 1953
53912 Brill memorial address: the homeostatic regulatory function of the ego. (Read at NY Psa Soc, Mar 24, 1953)
    Abs Rosen, V. H. Q 1954, 23:156-157
S-22471 Changing concepts of disease. Psychiat World 670-679
53913 The character of the therapist. Pastoral Psychol 1958, 9:14-18. From author's *Theory of Psychoanalytic Technique*
S-22474 The Cinderella of medicine. Psychiat World 646-653
53914 Citizens and schools. Menn Q 1952, 6:7-10. Better Schools 1957, May, 3:6. Psychiat World 770-773
53915 Communication and mental health. Mississippi Valley Med J 1959, 81:18-20
53916 Constructive and destructive motivation trends. In Levinson, H. *Toward Understanding Men*, Topeka, Kans: Menninger Found 1956
53917 The contribution of psychoanalysis to American psychiatry. BMC 1954, 18:85-91. Psychiat World 834-843. With title: "Psychiatry and psychoanalysis" in *Encyclopédie Médico-Chirurgicale* 1955
    Abs SG An Surv Psa 1954, 5:11-12. Lebovici, S. RFPsa 1954, 18:456. Rahman, L. Q 1955, 24:471
S-22479 Contributions of A. A. Brill to psychiatry. Psychiat World 830-833
53918 Contributor to discussion on varieties of homosexual manifestations. Homosex 181-183
53919 Criticism of "Speak Truth to Power," Progressive Mag 1955, Oct, 19:12-13
53920 Defense mechanisms. (N-P-T Quiz program). Nat Parent-Teacher 1955, Jan, 49:15
53921 The dilemma of psychiatry and the law. Menn Q 1953, 8(2):16-19. From Iowa Law Rev
S-22488 The dirt beneath our feet; why do we despise it? Psychiat World 27-37
53922 Discussion of Rado, S. "Dynamics and classification of disordered behavior." P 1953, 110:417-421
S-22490 The doctor as leader. Psychiat World 680-689
53923 Editorial. Bull Northern Colorado Psychiat Services 1957, Spring, 1
S-22630 Elmer Ernest Southard. 1876-1920. Psychiat World 813-815
53924 Emotional maturity. Mental Hlth Progress 1956, Feb. Bull Northern Colorado Psychiatric Services 1957, spring, 2-14
53925 (& Mayman, M.) Episodic dyscontrol: a third order of stress adaptation. BMC 1956, 20:153-165
    Abs Racamier RFPsa 1957, 21:123
53926 Executive problems. In Levinson, H. *Toward Understanding Men*, Topeka, Kans: Menninger Found 1956, 155-165; 1957 ed, 213-223
53927 Faith healing. Monday Morning 1955, Nov 21, 20:7-8

53928 The first years of marriage are crucial years. McCalls 1955, 82(Apr):53, 90, 91

53929 Footprints. Psychiat World 856-875

53930 Foreword to Eaton, J. W. & Weil, R. J. *Culture and Mental Disorders. A Comparative Study of the Hutterites and Other Populations.* Glencoe, Ill: Free Pr 1955

53931 Foreword to Fletcher, J. *Morals and Medicine.* Princeton: Princeton Univ 1954

53932 Foreword to Schneidman, E. S. & Farberow, N. L. *Clues to Suicide,* v

53933 Freedom. BMC 1955, 19:240-243. Menn Q 1956, 10(1):14-18. Psychiat World 803-808

53934 Freedom from dependence for crippled. Bull Nat Soc Crippled Children 1954, Nov-Dec, 17:7-8

53955 Freud and American psychiatry. J Am Psa Ass 1956, 4:614-625. Psychiat World 844-855
        Abs TFr 1957, 38:433. Shentoub RFPsa 1957, 21:613

S-22501 The genius of the Jew in psychiatry. Psychiat World 415-424

53936 The goals of psychiatric education. Introduction to the 1959 Catalogue of the Menninger School of Psychiatry. Psychiat World 717-725

53937 Growing up emotionally. Chicago: Science Res Assoc 1957, 48 p

53938 A Guide to Psychiatric Books, with Some Suggested Reading Lists. NY, London: Grune & Stratton 1956, xvi + 157 p
        Rv ESt J 1956, 37:501

S-22504 Havelock Ellis. 1859-1939. Psychiat World 816-818

53939 Healthier than healthy. Psychiat World 635-645

53940 At the heart of scouting. Scouting 1954, 42(Nov):8-9

53941 How To Be a Successful Teen-ager. NY: Sterling Publ 1954, 256 p

53942 How to keep friends. This Week Mag 1953, Dec 13

53943 How to Understand the Opposite Sex. NY: Sterling 1956, 192 p

S-22507 The Human Mind.
        Ningen no Kokoro. (Tr: Kosawa, H. & Kusano, E.) Tokyo: Nihon Kyobunsha 1950, Vol 1, 482 p; 1951, Vol 2, 436 p
        Korean transl: 1957

53944 Human needs in urban society. Menn Q 1959, 13(3):1-8

53945 (& Levinson, H.) Human Understanding in Industry. Chicago: Science Res Assoc 1957, 102 p

53946 The hydrogen-cobalt bomb. Pulpit Dig 1954, 34 (June):38-41

53947 If you go to the psychiatrist. Bull Milwaukee Co Soc Ment Hlth 1953, 5(3)

S-22510 Impotence and frigidity. In Krich, A. M. *Men,* NY: Dell 1954, 99-114

S-22511 Impotence and frigidity from the standpoint of psychoanalysis. Psychiat World 237-257

53948 Improving Productivity Through Human Relations. Los Angeles Police Academy 1954, Jan 15, 9 p

53949 Improving understanding and productivity through human relations. Vital Speeches 1953, 20:122-126

53950 (& Levinson, H.) Industrial mental health. Industrial Med & Surg 1955, 24:89-93. Mental Hlth Bull, Michigan 1955, 11:1-5

53951 Introduction to issue commemorating centennial of Freud's birth. BMC 1956, 20:101-102. Menn Q 1956, 10:4-5

53952   Introductory remarks [To 3rd Regional Research Conference]. BMC
        1954, 18:126-129
S-22517 The isolation type of personality. Psychiat World 192-206
53953   Is there hate in your house? This Week Mag 1958, Oct 5:14-15
53954   The job ahead. Austin, Tex: Hogg Found for Ment Hyg 1956, 11 p
53955   Let's Be Friends. J. Life Adjustment Booklet. Chicago: Science Res
        Assoc 1953, 40 p
53956   Let's take wives to conventions. This Week Mag 1959, Jan 11:11, 13
53957   A letter to men in prison. In *The Inside Story*, Tennessee State Peni-
        tentiary 1953, fall, 13-15. Menn Q 1955, 9(4):8-9. Psychiat World
        754-756
53958   Like leader, like girl. Campfire Girl 1954, 34 (Oct):3
53959   The limits of counseling with neurotics. In Doniger, S. *The Minister's
        Consultation Clinic*, Great Neck, NY: Channel Pr 1955, 55-57
53960   Listen! In Thayer Gaston, E. *Music Therapy 1956*, Lawrence, Kans:
        Nat Assn Music Therapy 1957. Psychiat World 9-15
53961   Looking backward. The Land 1953, 11(Jan):251-254. Psychiat World
        58-66
S-22519 Love Against Hate.
        Rakkaus vai Viha. (Tr: Havu, T. & Mikkola, S.) Helsinki: Kustan-
        nusosakuyhtio Otava 1953
        Korean transl: 1955
53962   (& Levinson, H.) The machine that made pop. Menn Q 1954, summer.
        8:20-26. Personnel Panorama 1955, 8:6-7
53963   The meaning of the hospital. Menn Q 1954, 8(3):9-12. Psychiat World
        54-57
S-22525 Men, women, and hate. Psychiat World 608-625
53964   Mental attitudes and safety. Menn Q 1959, 13(2):1-7
S-22528 Mental health. Scouting 1954, 42 (April):2-3, 22
53965   Mental Health and the Mass Media. NY: Thomas Alva Edison Fd
        1956
53966   Mental Health of the Executive. NY: Am Assn Advertising Agencies
        1957, 10 p
53967   Mental health problem acute. Town Hall 1954, June 29, 16(26)
53968   Mental patients can be cured. Reader's Dig 1956, 69 (Aug):13-16
53969   [Participant in] Mental responsibility panel. *Army Judge Advocates'
        Conference*. Charlottesville, Va: US Army 1956, Sept 24-27: 44-59
53970   To my father on his ninetieth birthday, July 11, 1952. Psychiat World
        38-42
53971   My favorite tree. Amer Forests 1950, 56(June):4, 39. Psychiat World
        7-8
53972   My town. Menn Q 1954, 8(1):21-30. Look Mag 1958, 22(Sept 30):89-
        92. Psychiat World 43-53
53973   Myth of incurable mental illness laid to understaffed hospitals. Pastoral
        Psychol 1955, 6(May):57-58
S-22538 Observations of a psychiatrist in a dermatology clinic. Psychiat World
        319-327
S-22541 The origins and masques of fear. Psychiat World 560-571
S-22542 Orpheus and Psyche. Psychiat World 23-26
S-22543 Paranoid psychoses. Psychiat World 185-191

53974 Personally yours. Menn Q 1954, 8(winter):30-32; (spring):32; (summer):32; (fall):31-32

53975 Perspectives in psychiatric research. P 1955, 112:289

53976 A picture of mental health. Nat Parent-Teacher 1953, 68(Oct):10-12

53977 A plea for understanding. Nat Parent-Teacher 1953, 68(Dec):27-28

53978 Poor little good child. Household Mag 1932, Aug. Psychiat World 556-559

53979 Prescription for the executive. Variety 1958, 101 (Nov 4):52, 354

S-22552 Present trends in psychoanalytic theory and practice. Psychiat World 461-465

53980 The president plans the future with his family. YPO Enterprise 1958, 8(June):15-18

S-22553 Presidential address to the American Psychoanalytic Association. Psychiat World 447-460

S-22554 Pseudoanalysis. Psychiat World 536-546

53981 The psychiatric aide. In Hall, B. et al: *Psychiatric Aide Education,* NY: Grune & Stratton 1952. Psychiat World 712-716

S-22555 Psychiatric aspects of contraception. Pastoral Psychol 1954, 5(49):28-33. In Rosen, H. *Therapeutic Abortion,* NY: Julian Pr 1954, 247-253

53982 Psychiatric aspects of physical disability. In *Selected Readings on Rehabilitation.* Ill Public Aid Commission 1955, 101-107

S-22557 A psychiatric fable. Psychiat World 709-711

53983 [Participant in discussion on] Psychiatric implications of surveys on sexual behavior. (Round table at Am Psychiatric Ass, St. Louis, Mo., May 1954) R 1956, 43:471-500

53984 Psychiatric responsibilities in nursing home care. BMC 1955, 19:16-18. Psychiat World 391-394
    Abs Racamier, P. C. RFPsa 1955, 19:630

53985 The psychiatric view. Police Chief 1956, 23(Oct):37

53986 A psychiatric view of the police. Police Chief 1956, 23(Dec):41-45

S-22561 The psychiatrist in relation to crime. Psychiat World 729-736

53987 A Psychiatrist's World; Selected Papers. (Ed & Intro: Hall, B. H.; Foreword: Kenworthy, M. E.) NY: Viking Pr 1959, 931 p
    Rv Murphy, W. F. Q 1960, 29:113-116

S-22562 Psychiatry. Psychiat World 572-607

53988 Psychiatry: facts for trust officers. Trusts & Estates 1954, 93(Aug):695-696

53989 Psychiatry looks at religion. Psychiat World 793-802

S-22563 Psychiatry and medicine. J Student Am Med Assn 1953, 2:28. Psychiat World 660-669

S-22566 Psychiatry and psychology. Psychiat World 690-695

53990 Psychiatry and social problems. In Lee, E. B. *Social Problems in America,* NY: Henry Holt 1955, 459-461

53991 Psychoanalysis and the ministry. Pastoral Psychol 1958, 9(Nov):59

53992 Psychoanalysts are indeed serving in a sense as priests. New Republic 1955, May 16:132

53993 The psychoanalytic approach to alcoholism. Blue Book 1955, 7:30-50

S-22570 Psychoanalytic aspects of suicide. Psychiat World 330-346

53994 Psychoanalytic psychiatry. In Engle, L. *New Worlds of Modern*

Science, NY: Dell 1956, 307-322. From Menninger, W. C. *Psychiatry: Its Evolution and Present Status* [22732]

S-22573 Psychoanalytic psychiatry: theory and practice. Psychiat World 428-446

S-22574 Psychoanalytic study of a case of organic epilepsy. Psychiat World 215-228

S-22576 Psychogenic influences on the appearance of the menstrual period. Psychiat World 298-303

53995 Psychological aspects of the organism under stress. Part 1. The homeostatic regulatory function of the ego. Part 2. Regulatory devices of the ego under stress. J Am Psa Ass 1954, 2:67-106; 280-310. In Bertalanffy, L. v. & Rapoport, A. *General Systems: Yearbook of the Society for General Systems Research*, Ann Arbor, Mich: Univ of Mich 1957, vol 2
   Abs JFr An Surv Psa 1954, 5:85-88. Rev Psicoanál 1954, 11:533-534. TFr J 1955, 36:221; 224. Shentoub RFPsa 1955, 19:472. Aldendorf, H. Q 1956, 25:282-283

53996 The psychological examination in the psychiatric case study. BMC 1959, 23:131-143. Psychiat World 395-411. From author's *A Manual for Psychiatric Case Study*, Rev Ed, 1952

S-22577 The psychological factor in disease. Psychiat World 654-659

53997 Psychological factors in the choice of medicine as a profession. Quart Phi Beta Pi 1956, 53:12-23. BMC 1957, 21:51-58; 99-106. Psychiat World 477-496
   Abs Weiss, J. Q 1958, 27:447-448

53998 Psychological factors in obstetrics. Child-Fam Dig 1957, 16(3):26-27. From author's "Psychological factors in the choice of medicine as a profession."

S-22578 Psychological factors in urological disease. Psychiat World 258-281

S-22579 Psychology of a certain type of malingering. Psychiat World 357-368

53999 Psychoses associated with influenza. JAMA 1919, 72:235-241. Psychiat World 110-125

54000 Reading notes. Psychiat World 68-103

S-22585 Recognizing and renaming "psychopathic personalities." Psychiat World 207-212

S-22586 Recording the findings of the psychological examination ("mental status").
   Abs MK Q 1953, 22:124

54001 Regulatory devices of the ego under major stress. (Read at 18th Int Psa Cong, London, July 1953) J 1954, 35:412-420. Psychiat World 497-515. From author's "Psychological aspects of the organism under stress."
   Abs Auth J 1954, 35:287. Rev Psicoanál 1955, 12:302. JLan Q 1956, 25:280

S-22590 Religio Psychiatri. In Doniger, S. *Religion and Human Behavior*, NY: Association Pr 1954, 1-19. Psychiat World 774-784

54002 Religious psychiatry: there is a basic parallelism in psychiatric-religious practice. Pastoral Psychol 1951, 2(16):10-16

S-22593 Research in psychiatry. Psychiat World 696-708

54003 Reverence for life. Psychiat World 67

S-22594 Reversible schizophrenia. Psychiat World 126-133

S-22596 The schizophrenic syndrome as a product of acute infectious disease. Psychiat World 134-155

54004 Sigmund Freud, 1856-1939. The Nation 1939, 149(Oct):373-374. Psychiat World 819-822

54005 Sigmund Freud, 1856-1939. BMC 1949 (Sept). Psychiat World 822-824

54006 Sigmund Freud. Menn Q 1956, 10(3):4-5. Psychiat World 824-825

S-22598 Smith Ely Jelliffe, 1866-1945, and Peter Bassoe, 1874-1945. Psychiat World 826-829

S-22599 Somatic correlations with the unconscious repudiation of femininity in women. Psychiat World 282-297

S-22600 Some clinical examples of indirect suicide. Psychiat World 347-356

S-22601 Some observations on the psychological factors in urination and genitourinary afflictions. Psychiat World 304-318

S-22603 Some unconscious psychological factors associated with the common cold. Psychiat World 229-236

54007 Staying mentally healthy. NY: Nat Fed B&PW Clubs 1954, 8 p

S-22608 Take your choice. Psychiat World 5-6

54008 Taking the psychiatric history. In State of Mind, Summit, N. J.: CIBA 1956

54009 Teaching emotional first aid. Family Service Highlights 1956, 17(June): 93-94

54010 Theory of Psychoanalytic Technique. NY: Basic Books 1958, 206 p; London: Imago Publ Co 1958
    Abs J Am Psa Ass 1960, 8:218-219; 601. Rv Coleman, M. L. PPR 1958, 45(3):118-121. EG Q 1958, 27:569-574. Viderman, S. RFPsa 1959, 23:421-425. Racker Rev Psicoanál 1960, 17:117-120

54011 There is something you can do about mental health. NY: Nat Assn Ment Hlth 1959, 3 p

54012 Things I never would have learned at home. Reader's Digest 1954, 65:129-132. The Army Reservist 1955, 1(Jan):3

54013 This is prejudice. In Wallace, W. The Baltimore Sun Panel. One of 22 interviews in The Sun from Oct 11 through Nov 1, 1954

S-22612 Totemic aspects of contemporary attitudes toward animals.
    Abs GD An Surv Psa 1951, 2:520-524

54014 Toughest problem—human relations. Industrial News Rev 1954, 84:22-30

54015 Toward a unitary concept of mental illness. Psychiat World 516-528

54016 Understanding ourselves. Bull Nat Assn Secondary School Principals 1954, 38:413-414

54017 (& Ellenberger, H.; Pruyser, P.; Mayman, M.) The unitary concept of mental illness. BMC 1958, 22:1-12
    Abs Weiss, J. Q 1959, 28:284

54018 Unprofitable investments in love. Ladies Home Journal, 1931, May. Psychiat World 547-555

54019 Verdict guilty—now what? Harper's Magazine 1959, Aug. Psychiat World 757-769

S-22619 The Washburn college course in mental hygiene. Psychiat World 531-535

54020 "We hardly know we are alive." BMC 1954, 18:17-18

54021 We're not so lonesome. Kansas Teacher 1953, 62(Sept):20-22
S-22620 What Are the Goals of Psychiatric Education?
       Abs RRG Q 1953, 22:450
S-22621 What is economy in mental illness? Psychiat World 626-634
S-22622 What is wrong with our prisons? Psychiat World 737-748
54022 What Makes an Effective Man? A Psychiatrist Looks at Industry To-
       day. NY: Am Management Assn 1953, 8 p. Condensed: News and
       Views on Industrial Relations Bull 1953, Aug, No 56
54023 What's happening in health? Nat Cong PTA Convention Dig 1953,
       May: 28-31
54024 What you can do about mental health. Scouting 1958, 46(Apr):20-21,
       28
54025 Why men fail. This Week Mag 1955, Mar 27:7, 26. Virginia Re-
       habilitator 1955, May, 11:7-9. Traffic Topics 1955, July, 29:19, 48-
       49. Manage 1955, Oct, 8:34-36
       Japanese: Thai Airways 1955, 9(Apr):16-17
54026 Why you need a vacation. This Week 1957, May 12:17-18, This Week
       1959, March 24
       Japanese: Pan American 1957, 18(June 23):14-16
54027 Worry while you work. Manage 1955, 7(March):17, 27
54028 You and your friends. Am Jr Red Cross J 1954, March:4-7
54029 You as a person. Childcraft 1954, 12:24-31

       See Chidester, Leona

       REVIEWS OF:
54030 Freud, S. Moses and Monotheism. Psychiat World 785-792
54031 Horney, K. New Ways in Psychoanalysis. Psychiat World 425-427
54032 Kinsey, A. C. et al: Sexual Behavior in the Human Male. Psychiat
       World 466-476
S-22632 White, W. A. Forty Years of Psychiatry. Psychiat World 811-812

MENNINGER, R.
See Semrad, Elvin V.

MENNINGER, WILLIAM CLAIRE
54033 Alcoholism: a national emergency. Menn Q 1957, 1(2):7-10. On
       Center 1957, 3:1-3. Pastoral Psychol 1958, 9:7-8
54034 Attributes of mental health. Nat Parent-Teacher 1953, 48:10-12
54035 "Brains before bricks." Menn Q 1955, 9(3):1-13
54036 Effective human relations. Menn Q 1954, 8(2):1-8
54037 Facing up to the stress and strain of modern life. Menn Q 1959,
       13(1):12-19. Child-Fam Dig 1959, 18(4):71-74
54038 (et al) How You Grow Up. NY: Sterling 1957, 187 p
54039 Medicine and society: the role of psychiatry. J Mount Sinai Hosp
       1953, 19:790-811
S-22688 Men, machines, and mental health.
       Abs JLan Q 1953, 22:137
54040 (& Levinson, H.) The Menninger Foundation survey of industrial
       mental health. Observations and perspectives. Menn Q 1954, 8(4):1-13.
       Industr Med Surg 1955, 24:89-93

54041 (& Leaf, M.) Mental mechanism. In Linscott, R. N. & Stein, J. *Why You Do What You Do*, NY: Random House 1956, 16-32. From authors' *You and Psychiatry* [22785A]

54042 (& Leaf, M.) The oedipus complex. In Linscott, R. N. & Stein, J. *Why You Do What You Do*, NY: Random House 1956, 197-201. From authors' *You and Psychiatry* [22785A]

54043 Prescription for the executive. Menn Q 1958, 12(2):22-26

54044 Principles of psychiatry applicable to industry. In Levinson, H. *Toward Understanding Men,* Topeka, Kansas: Menninger Found 1956, 2-10; 1957, 3-11

54045 Psychiatric principles applicable to industry. Menn Q 1956, 10(3):9-14

54046 (& Levinson, H.) Psychiatry in industry: some trends and perspectives. Personnel 1955, 32:90-99

54047 Psychiatry; An Orientation to Life's Problems. Los Angeles: College Pr 1949, 26 p

54048 Psychiatry and the practice of medicine. BMC 1953, 17:170-179. Philadelphia Med 1955, 50:1359-1363. Mississippi Valley med J 1956, 78:93-97
       Abs RRG Q 1954, 23:469

54049 The psychological key to success. Menn Q 1955, 9(2):19-21

S-22767 Self Understanding, A First Step in Understanding Children.
       Rv Cremieux RFPsa 1957, 21:297

54050 (& Levinson, H.) Seminars for executives and industrial physicians. P 1956, 113:451-454

54051 Social Change and Scientific Progress. Cambridge, Mass: 1951, 42 p

54052 Ten points. Menn Q 1956, 10(2):19-20

54053 Tensions in family life. Pastoral Psychol 1953, 4(33):11-18

54054 The therapy of friendship. Fed Probation 1957, 21:41-46. Reprint: Dept. Hlth, Educ, Welfare 1957. Int Assn Pupil Personnel Workers J 1957, Sept:19-27

54055 (& Pratt, J. F.) The therapy of gardening. Menn Q 1958, 12(2):27-28

S-22778 Understanding Yourself
       Arabic: (Ed: Koussy, Abdel Aziz) (Tr: Barrakat, M.) Cairo: Renaissance 1954

S-22785A (& Leaf, M.) You and Psychiatry.
       Psychotherapie für Jedermann. Munich: Reinhart 1954, 190 p
       Rv Salomon RFPsa 1958, 22:122

       See Levinson, Harry

MENNINGER-LERCHENTHAL, E.

54056 Periodische Träume. [Periodic dreams.] Wien Z Nervenheilk 1954, 10:121-126

MENSH, IVAN NORMAN

54057 Neurodermatitis: a psychosomatic disease. Clin Stud Pers 341-361

54058 Research in counseling and psychotherapeutic processes. Prog Clin Psych 1956, 2:340-360

MENZER, DORIS
(Menzer-Benaron, Doris)

54059   The importance of the psychologic factor in gynecology. New England J Med 1953, 249:519-522

54060   (& Morris, T.; Gates, P.; Sabbath, J.; Robey, H.; Plaut, T.; Sturgis, S. H.) Patterns of emotional recovery after hysterectomy: first in a series of reports. PSM 1957, 19:379-388

      Abs Johnston, McC. Q 1958, 27:606-607

54061   Psychobiological study of the conversion process in women. Mind-Body 155-181

54062   (& Sturgis, S. H.) Relationship between emotional and somatic factors in gynecologic disease. In *Progress in Gynecology, Vol 3*, NY: Grune & Stratton

  See Mann, James; Semrad, Elvin V.; Standish, Christopher T.

MENZIES, ISABEL E. P.
REVIEWS OF:

54063   Jaques, E. Measurement of Responsibility. J 1957, 38:287-288

54064   Newcomb, T. M. Social Psychology. J 1953, 34:338

MERENCIANO, M.

54065   Neurosis. [Neurosis.] Act luso-esp Neur 1953, 12:22-23

MERIN, JOSEPH H.

54066   Family role in ambulatory treatment. Schiz Psa Off Pract 92-94

MERLEAU-PONTY, MAURICE

54067   Preface to Hesnard, A. L. M. *L'Oeuvre de Freud et son Importance pour le Monde moderne.*

MERLEN, T. J. VAN

54068   Obituary: Fernand Lechat 1895-1959. J 1960, 41:641

MERRILL, BRUCE R.

S-22807 Childhood attitudes toward flatulence and their possible relation to adult character.

      Abs JAA An Surv Psa 1951, 2:161-162. NRo An Surv Psa 1951, 2:80. CR J 1953, 34:271

54069   Some psychosomatic aspects of pulmonary tuberculosis. A review of the English language literature. JNMD 1953, 117:9-28

MERRILL, G. G.

54070   Sexual complications of hypnosis. J clin exp Hyp 1957, 5:138-146

MERRY, J.

54071   The relative roles of individual psychotherapy and group psychotherapy in the industrial neurosis unit. JMS 1953, 99(415):301-307

MERTENS, GERARD M.

54072 Hemingway's *Old Man and the Sea* and Mann's *The Black Swan.* Lit
& Psych 1956, 6(3):96-99

MERTENS DI WILMARS, CHARLES

54073 Studio critico del concetto di "motivazione." [Critical study of the
concept of "motivation."] Boll Psicol Sociol appl 1956, (13-16):9-19

MERTZ, PHILIP

54074 Therapeutic considerations in masturbation. PT 1955, 9:630-639

MERVIS, SADIE

REVIEW OF:
54075 Lewis, M. M. Infant Speech. J 1953, 34:168-170. Rev Psicoanál 1958,
15:160

MESSINGER, EMANUEL

54076 Psychiatric chronology; a systematic technique for promoting insight
in psychotherapy. Dis nerv Syst 1955, 16:270-274

METH, JOHANNES M.

See Arieti, Silvano

METMAN, PHILIP

54077 The ego in schizophrenia. Part I. The accessibility of schizophrenics
to analytic approaches. J anal Psychol 1956, 1:161-176
54078 The trickster figure in schizophrenia. J anal Psychol 1958, 3:5-20

METRAUX, RHODA

See Mead, Margaret

METTE, ALEXANDER

54079 Emil Kraepelin und Sigmund Freud. Zur 100. Wiederkehr ihrer
Geburtstage. [Emil Kraepelin and Sigmund Freud, to their 100th
anniversaries.] Psychiat Neurol med Psychol, Leipzig 1956, 8:99-100
54080 Freud und Pawlow. [Freud and Pavlov.] Psychiat Neurol med Psychol,
Leipzig 1957, 9:217-225
54081 [Remarks on Freud's conception of regression.] (Russian) Z Nevropat
Psikhiat 1958, 58:67-71
54082 Sigmund Freud. Berlin: Verlag Volk und Gesundheit 1956, 79 p. 3rd
enl ed with an Appendix: Von Freud zu Pawlow [From Freud to
Pavlov.] Berlin: Verlag Volk und Gesundheit 1958, 111 p
54083 Sind Kinder grausam? [Are children cruel?] Psychiat Neurol med
Psychol, Leipzig 1953, 5:328-334
54084 Spekulation und exakte Wissenschaft in der Typenlehre. [Speculation
and exact science in type theory.] Psychiat Neurol med Psychol,
Leipzig 1956, 8:225-234

METZGER, EMY A.

54085 Karen Horney on psychoanalytic technique: understanding the patient as the basis of all technique. Psa 1956, 16:26-31

See Sheiner, Sara B.

METZGER, WOLFGANG

54086 Frühkindlicher Trotz. [Early defiance in infants and children.] Psychol Prax, Basel 1956, (18):1-70

METZINGER, J.

54087 Critique d'art et psychanalyse. [Art criticism and psychoanalysis.] Psyché, Paris 1953, 8:64-66

MEYER, A.

See Slater, Eliot

MEYER, ADOLF

54088 Preface to Kanner, L. *Child Psychiatry.*
54089 Psychobiology; A Science of Man. (Comp & ed: Winters, E. E. & Bowers, A. M.) (Foreword: Lewis, N. D. C.) Springfield, Ill: Thomas 1957, 257 p
　　　　Rv Meyer, E. Q 1958, 27:273-275

MEYER, BERNARD C.

54090 Alcuni aspetti psichiatrici dell'artrite reumatoide. [Some psychiatric aspects of rheumatoid arthritis.] Med psicosom 1956, 1:13-22
54091 Aspects de la psychothérapie en médecine psychosomatique. [Aspects of psychotherapy in psychosomatic medicine.] RFPsa 1955, 19:357-380
S-22876 Betty M and the seven dwarfs.
　　　　Abs R 1954, 41:373
54092 (& Blacher, R. S.) The creative impulse—biologic and artistic aspects: report of a case. (Read at NY Psa Soc, Oct 15, 1957) Psa St Soc 1960, 1:251-271
　　　　Abs Q 1958, 27:624-626
54093 (& Brown, F.; Levine, A.) Observations on the house-tree-person drawing test before and after surgery. PSM 1955, 17:428-454
　　　　Abs EFA Q 1957, 26:291
54094 (& Weinroth, L. A.) Observations on psychological aspects of anorexia nervosa: report of a case. PSM 1957, 19:389-398
　　　　Abs Johnston, McC. Q 1958, 27:607
54095 On the plight of the not-so-sick ward patient. NYSJM 1957, 57:2665
54096 Psychiatric aspects of ulcerative colitis. Proc Rud Virchow Soc 1953, 12
　　　　Alcuni aspetti psichiatrici della collite ulcerosa cronica. Med psicosom 1956, 1:116
54097 Psychosomatic medicine and plastic surgery. Psychiatric discussion. In *Psychosomatic Aspects of Surgery*, NY: Grune & Stratton 1956

54098   (& Lyons, A. S.) Rectal resection: psychiatric and medical management of its sequelae: report of a case. PSM 1957, 19:152-157
        Abs Lossy, F. T. Q 1958, 27:299. Rv de M'Uzan RFPsa 1958, 22:389-390
54099   Should the patient know the truth. J Mount Sinai Hosp 1954, 20:344
54100   Some gynecological implications of the castration complex. J Mount Sinai Hosp 1953, 20:267
54101   Some psychiatric aspects of surgical practice. PSM 1958, 20:203-214
        Abs Simon, J. Q 1959, 28:291

MEYER, EUGENE

54102   Acute psychologic disturbances in the course of hospitalization of patients with chronic illness. J chronic Diseases 1956, 3:111-121
54103   .The psychosomatic concept, use and abuse. J chronic Diseases 1959, 9:298-314

        See McClary, Allan R.

        REVIEWS OF:
54104   Meyer, A. Psychobiology. Q 1958, 27:273-275
54105   Steinfeld, J. I. Therapeutic Studies on Psychotics. Q 1953, 22:112-113

MEYER, H.-H.

54106   Die Therapie der endogenen Psychosen. [The treatment of endogenous psychoses.] Dtsch med Wschr 1957, 82:76-80

MEYER, ILSE

54107   Bemerkungen zu dem Aufsatz von Nelly Wolffheim, London, "Überlegungen zur Frage der Privatkindergärten." [Remarks on the article by Nelly Wolffheim of London, "The question of private preschools."] Prax Kinderpsychol 1955, 4:72-73, 267

        TRANSLATION OF:
        Barag, G. [1464]

MEYER, J.-E.

54108   Studien zur Depersonalisation. II. Depersonalisation und Zwang als polare Störungen der Ich-Aussenwelt-Beziehung. [Studies on depersonalization. II. Depersonalization and obsession as polar disturbances of the relation between the ego and the outer world.] Psychiat Neurol, Basel 1957, 133:63-79

MEYER, LUCILLE R.

        See Loomis, Earl A., Jr.

MEYER, LUISE

54109   Neurotische Erziehungsschwierigkeiten nach ungünstigen frühkindlichen Umwelteinflüssen. [Neurotic upbringing difficulties after unfavorable early childhood environmental influences.] Prax Kinderpsychol 1953, 2:262-266

MEYER, MORTIMER M.

See Tolman, R. S.

MEYER, P. S.

54110 Psychologie und Psychotherapie in der Dermatologie. [Psychology and psychotherapy in dermatology.] Z Haut-und Geschlechts-Krankh 1953, 14(2):45-55

MEYER, R.

54111 (& Sussman, I.) [Group psychotherapy with psychotic patients.] (Hebrew) English and French summaries. Harefuah 1956, 51:197-199

MEYERHOFF, HANS

54112 Freud and the ambiguity of culture. Partisan Rev 1957, 24:117-130
54113 Freud the philosopher. Commentary 1958, 25:62-67
54114 By love redeemed. A fantasy on "God and Freud." Commentary 1959, 28:202-206

See McCall, Lillian Blumberg

MEYERING, W. L.
(See also Meijering, W. L.)

54115 (& Wielen, G. H. van de) Groepstherapie binnen het kader van een kliniek. [Group therapy within the clinic.] Maandbl Geest Volksgezondh 1954, 9:326-330

MEYERS, F. S.

54116 Enkele beschouwingen omtrent de leer van Sigmund Freud. [Some considerations about the doctrine of Sigmund Freud.] Ned Tijdschr Psychol 1953, 8:201-243

MEYERS, HAROLD L.

54117 The therapeutic function of the evaluation process. BMC 1956, 20:9-19
Abs Racamier RFPsa 1956, 20:576

MEYERS, THOMAS J.

54118 Countertransference. J Amer osteop Ass 1953, 53(3):195-197

MEYERSBURG, HERMAN A.

See Eldred, Stanley H.

MEZER, ROBERT R.

54119 Dynamic Psychiatry in Simple Terms. NY: Springer 1956, xi + 174 p

MICHAEL, CARMEN MILLER

54120 (& Morris, D. P.; Soroker, E.) Follow-up studies of shy, withdrawn children. II. Relative incidence of schizophrenia. Ops 1957, 27:331-337
Abs KHG Q 1959, 28:566

MICHAEL, ROBERT

54121 Was kränkt macht krank; eine Gesundheitsphilosophie. [What injures makes ill; a philosophy of health.] Munich: Kindler 1959, 259 p

MICHAEL, STANLEY T.

See Volkart, Edmund H.

MICHAELS, JOSEPH J.

54122 Character disorder and acting upon impulse. Rd Psa Psychol 181-196

54123 Character structure and character disorders. Am Hbk Psychiat 1:353-377

54124 Considerations regarding the loyalty oath as a manifestation of current social tension and anxiety. (With Comm on Soc Issues of GAP) Group for the Advancement of Psychiatry Symposium, 1954, Oct, No. 1

54124A Contributor to Report of the Survey Steering Committee (American Psychoanalytic Association) to Board on Professional Standards (Problems and Methods of Evaluation) Dec. 1, 1955. J Am Psa Ass 1956, 4:351

54125 Delinquency and control. Ops 1954, 24:258-265
Abs NRo An Surv Psa 1954, 5:289-290. MK Q 1955, 24:315

54126 Discussion. Psm Cpt Psa 144-149

54127 Disorders of Character: Persistent Enuresis, Juvenile Delinquency and Psychopathic Personality. Springfield, Ill: Thomas 1955, x + 148 p
Abs J Am Psa Ass 1955, 3:545. Rv Harris, H. I. Q 1956, 25:106. ESt J 1956, 37:499; Rev Psicoanál 1959, 15:162

54128 Disorders of character: persistent enuresis, juvenile delinquency and psychopathic personality. JNMD 1954, 120:408-410. AMA ANP 1954, 72:641-643

54129 The management of the juvenile delinquent: a point of view. In Liebman, S. *Emotional Problems of Childhood*, Phila: Lippincott 1958, 107-123

54130 Obituary: Dr. Ruth Burr. J 1954, 35:434

54131 Psychiatric aspects of school desegregation. (With Comm on Soc Issues of the Group for the Advancement of Psychiatry). Report No. 37, May 1957

54132 (& Adler, M. H.) Statistical analysis of 1,994 veteran patients. JNMD 1952, 116:138

See Bibring, Grete; Valenstein, Arthur F.

MICHAL-SMITH, HAROLD

54133 (& Gottsegen, M.; Gottsegen, C.) A group technique for mental retardates. Int J grp 1955, 5:84-90. Couns PT Ment Retard 201-207
Abs GPK Q 1956, 25:454

54134 (& Hammer, E.; Spitz, H.) Use of the Blacky Pictures with a child whose oedipal desires are close to consciousness. Clin Psych 1951, 7:280-282

See Hulse, Wilfred C.

MICHAUX, L.

54135 Etude cliniques de la névrose obsessionnelle de l'enfant. [Clinical study of obsessional neuroses in children.] R Np inf 1957, 5:467-493

54136 (& Duché, D. J.) Les impulsions de l'enfant. [Impulses of children.] R Np inf 1958, 6:225-236

54137 (& Gallot, H. M.; Benoit, P.) De la réduction alimentaire déliberée à l'anorexie intentionnelle. Première communication à propos d'une observation gemellaire. [From deliberate food reduction to intentional anorexia. First communication with reference to a study in a pair of twins.] R Np inf 1956, 4:205-212

See Duché, D.

MICHAUX, WILLIAM W.

54138 Traumatic implications of psychiatric disability discharge from the Armed Services. Military med 1959, 124:273-283

MICHEL, ANDRÉ

54139 Bibliography of psychoanalysis of music and musicians. Samiksa 1954, 8:222-234; 1955, 9:169

S-22977 Psychanalyse de la Musique.
         Abs Auth & Kohut, H. An Surv Psa 1951, 2:662-675

See Kohut, Heinz

MICHEL, ERNST

54140 Das Vaterproblem heute in soziologischer Sicht: seine Bedeutung für die Tiefenpsychologie. [The modern father problem from a sociological viewpoint; its significance for depth psychology.] Psyche, Heidel 1954, 8(3):161-190. In Bitter, W. *Das Vaterproblem in Psychotherapie, Religion und Gesellschaft,* Stuttgart: Hippokrates 1955

MICHEL, H.

54141 Versuch einer vergleichenden Darstellung der Neurose bei Freud und Jung am Beispiel einer leib-seelischen Erkrankung. IV. [Essay in comparative portrayal of neurosis according to Freud and Jung with reference to a clinical case of psychosomatic disorder. IV] Schweiz ANP 1955, 76:91-109

MICHELOUD, PIERRETTE

54142 Dictionnaire psychanalytique des Rêves. [Psychoanalytic Dictionary of Dreams.] Paris: Nouvelles Editions Debresse 1957, 155 p

MICHELSON, A. L.

See Knapp, Peter H.

MICHEL-WOLFROMM, HÉLÈNE

54143 (& Luquet, P.) Observation d'un cas de frigidité. [Observations on a case of frigidity.] RFPsa 1957, 21:809-826

MICK, ROGER MARCUS

54144 A study of resistance during psychotherapy. Diss Abstr 1956, 16:1174

MIDDENDORP-MOOR, V.

54145 Katamnestische Untersuchungen nach poliklinisch durchgeführter Kurz-psychotherapie. [Follow-up studies after brief psychotherapy in an out-patient clinic.] Psyche, Heidel 1957, 10:662-675

MIDDLEMORE, MERELL P.

54146 The mother's emotional attitude. Child-Fam Dig 1953, 8(1):27-32

MIDELFORT, CHRISTIAN FREDRIK

54147 The Family in Psychotherapy. NY, London: McGraw-Hill, Blakiston Div 1957, 203 p

MIELKE, F.

See Benedetti, Gaetano; Mitscherlich, Alexander

MIERKE, KARL

54148 Entwicklungsanomalien als Folgeerscheinungen seelischer Überforde-rung. [Developmental anomalies resulting from mental strain.] Prax Kinderpsychol 1953, 2:33-38

MIGEON, CLAUDE J.

See Bliss, Eugene L.

MIK, G.

See Kuiper, P. C.

MIKKOLA, SIRPPA

See Havu, Toini

MIKSZTAL, W. M.

See Piotrowski, Zygmunt A.

MILAM, JAMES R.

54149 Examiner influences on Thematic Apperception Test stories. J proj Tech 1954, 18:221-226

MILBERG, IRVING L.

54150 Group psychotherapy in the treatment of some neurodermatoses. Int J grp PT 1956, 6:53-60
Abs GPK Q 1958, 27:144

See Wolf, Alexander

MILECK, JOSEPH

54151 A comparative study of "Die Betrogene" (The Deceived Woman) and "Der Tod in Venedig" (Death in Venice). Modern Language Forum 1957, 42:124-129

MILES, DWIGHT W.

54152 The importance for clinical psychology of the use of tests derived from theories about infantile sexuality and adult character. Genet Psychol Monogr 1954, 50:227-288

MILES, HENRY H. W.

S-23007 (& Barrabee, E. L.; Finesinger, J. E.) Evaluation of psychotherapy. Abs R 1953, 40:165-166

54153 (& Waldfogel, S.; Barrabee, E. L.; Cobb, S.) Psychosomatic study of forty-six young men with coronary artery disease. PSM 1954, 16:455-477

Abs Fain RFPsa 1955, 19:507. EMW Q 1956, 25:450

See Cobb, Stanley

MILHOLLAND, W.

See Janis, Irving L.

MILL, CYRIL R.

54154 The effect of thorazine on fantasy. Virginia M Month 1958, 85:446-447

MILLÁN, ALFONSO

54155 Discussion of symposium. Psychiat Res Rep 1955, (2):24-29
54156 The use of reports on movie stories as a means of studying personalities during psychoanalytic treatment. Psychiat Res Rep 1955, (2):15-23

MILLAR, E. C. P.

See Wolstenholme, G. E. W.

MILLAR, MARGARET W.

54157 Casework services for the unmarried mother. In Nat Conf Soc Wk, Casework Papers, 1955. NY: Fam Serv Assoc of Amer 1955, 91-100

MILLER, ARTHUR A.

54158 An interpretation of the symbolism of Medusa. Am Im 1958, 15:389-399

See Biegler, Jerome S.

MILLER, BENJAMIN

See Pinner, Max

MILLER, DANIEL R.

54159 (& Swanson, G. E.) The Changing American Parent. A Study in the Detroit Area. NY: Wiley; London: Chapman & Hall 1958, 302 + xiv p

S-23011 (& Stine, M. E.) The prediction of social acceptance by means of psychoanalytic concepts. J Personality 1951-52, 20:162-174

Abs Holzman, P. S. Q 1953, 22:309-310

54160   (& Swanson, G. E.) The study of conflict. In Jones, M. R. *Nebraska Symposium on Motivation: 1956.* Lincoln, Neb: Univ of Nebraska Pr 1956, 137-174

See Blom, Gaston E.

MILLER, EMANUEL

54161   The challenge of psycho-analysis. The Listener 1956, June 7:762
54162   Facts and fictions in the study of child psychiatry. JMS 1956, 102(426):96-104
54163   Freud and after: the rooted sorrow. 20th Century 1956, May:443-452

MILLER, G.

See Greene, William A., Jr.

MILLER, GEORGE A.

54164   Langage et communication. [Language and Communication.] Paris: PUF 1956
Rv Benassy, M. RFPsa 1957, 21:857-861

MILLER, H. MILTON

54165   The compensation neurosis. J Forens Sciences 1959, 4:59-166

MILLER, HERBERT C.

See Davis, Herbert V.

MILLER, HYMAN

54166   (& Baruch, D. W.) Practice of Psychosomatic Medicine as Illustrated in Allergy. NY: McGraw-Hill 1956, 196 p
Rv Lunsky R 1957, 44:230-231
54167   (& Baruch, D. W.) Psychotherapy in acute attacks of bronchial asthma. Ann Allergy 1953, 11:438-444

See Baruch, Dorothy W.; Sapir, M.

MILLER, JACOB J.

54168   Symposium on atropine toxicity therapy: repression and atropine toxicity therapy. JNMD 1956, 124:269-275

MILLER, JAMES G.

54169   Closing comments. Sci Psa 1958, 1:173-174
54170   Criteria and measurement of change during psychiatric treatment. BMC 1954, 18:130-137
Abs Rahman, L. Q 1956, 25:116
54171   Mental health implications of a general behavior theory. P 1957, 113:776-782
Abs McLaughlin, J. T. Q 1959, 28:289
54172   Psychoanalysis and systems theory. Sci Psa 1958, 1:109-125
54173   Psychology. Encyclop Britannica 1953, 18:682-690

54174   Special problems of psychotherapy. Prog PT 1957, 2:188-196

54175   Toward a general theory for the behavioral sciences. Am Psych 1955, 10:513-531

54176   Unconscious. Encyclop Britannica 1951, 22:680-681

54177   Unconscious processes and perception. In Blake, R. & Ramsey, G. V. *Perception: an Approach to Personality*, NY: Ronald Pr 1951, 258-282

MILLER, JASON

54178   Psychoanalytic observations on self-frustration. Auxil Pamphlet, Am Inst Psa, NY 1956, Nov

54179   Socio-cultural aspects of homosexuality. Bull Cand Assn, Am Inst Psa, NY 1958, 11(6):6-8

54180   Some psychoanalytic observations on luck. Bull Cand Assn, Am Inst Psa 1958, 11(5):7-9

MILLER, JOSEPH S. A.

54181   (& Kwalwasser, S.; Stein, A.) Observations concerning the use of group psychotherapy in a voluntary mental hospital. Effects of group psychotherapy on the training residents. Int J grp PT 1954, 4:86-94
     Abs GPK Q 1955, 24:620

See Bellak, Leopold; Graubert, David N.; Levine, Abraham

MILLER, LEE H.

See Ross, William Donald

MILLER, LOVICK

See Young, Robert A.

MILLER, M. D.

54182   Jazz and aggression. Psychiat Comm 1958, 1:7-10

MILLER, MICHAEL M.

54183   Certain factors pertaining to the value of narcoanalysis in securing testimony. J Nat Med Ass 1954, 46:238-241

54184   Combined use of ethyl alcohol and amobarbital (amytal) sodium for ambulatory narcoanalysis. AMA ANP 1952, 67:620-624
     Abs LRa Q 1953, 22:307

54185   A group therapeutic approach to a case of bed wetting and fire setting with the aid of hypnoanalysis. Group Psychother 1957, 10:181-190

54186   The use of psychodrama in the treatment of psychoneurotic patients. J Nat Med Ass 1955, 47:30-34

MILLER, MILTON L.

S-23038 Emotional conflicts in asthma.
     Rv Labbé, P. RFPsa 1953, 17:578

54187   Nostalgia: A Psychoanalytic Study of Marcel Proust. Boston: Houghton Mifflin 1956, xii + 306 p
     Rv Beres, D. Q 1957, 26:539-541

54188   The relation between submission and aggression in male homosexuality. In Lorand, S. *Perversions: Psychodynamics and Therapy*, NY: Random House 1956, 160-179

54189   On street fear. J 1953, 34:232-240
    Abs Auth Q 1955, 24:150. JFr An Surv Psa 1953, 4:168-170

S-23046 The traumatic effect of surgical operations in childhood on the integrative function of the ego.
    Abs JFr An Surv Psa 1951, 2:220-221. CR Rev Psicoanál 1959, 15:159

MILLER, NEAL E.

54190   (& Kraeling, D.; Murray, E. J.) Displacement. J exp Psychol 1952, 43:217-231

54191   (& Kraeling, D.) Displacement: greater generalization of approach than avoidance in a generalized approach-avoidance conflict. J exp Psychol 1952, 43:217-226. With title: "An experimental approach to the psychoanalytic concept of displacement," In McGuigan, F. J. & Calvin, A. D. *Current Studies in Psychology*, NY: Appleton-Century-Crofts 1958, 139-142

S-23057 (& Sears, R. R.; Mowrer, O. H.; Doob, L. W.; Dollard, J.) Frustration-aggression hypothesis. Under Hum Motiv 251-255

54192   Theory and experiment relating psychoanalytic displacement to stimulus-response generalization. ASP 1948, 43:155-178. Stud Pers 459-485

See Dollard, John; Murray, Edward J.

MILLER, PAULA E.
See Bandura, Albert

MILLER, ROBERT E.
See Mirsky, I. Arthur

MILLER, SAUL
See Burgum, Mildred

MILLER, STUART C.

54193   Metapsychology. (Read at Los Angeles Psa Soc Oct 20, 21, 22, 1959)
    Abs Tausend, H. Bull Phila Ass Psa 1960, 10:25-29

See Polansky, Norman A.

MILLER, WAYNE
See Spock, Benjamin

MILLET, JOHN A. P.

54194   Body, mind, and spirit. Pastoral Psychol 1950, 1(5):9-16. In Doniger, S. *Healing: Human and Divine*, NY: Association Pr 1957, 23-40

54195   Considerazioni psicodinamiche sulle malattie vascolari periferiche con particolare riferimento alla tromboflebite migrante ed al morbo di Raynaud. [Psychodynamic considerations regarding peripheral vascular diseases with special reference to thrombophrebitis migrans and to Raynaud's disease.] Gazz int med chir 1954, 59:62-68

54196 Dedication. Sandor Rado, Samuel W. Hamilton Memorial Lecturer, 1956. Psychopathol Communic ix-xii

54197 Erich Fromm's art of dream interpretation. Pastoral Psychol 1952, 2(23):46-48

54198 [Contribution to panel review on] Masochism: a biodynamic summary. Sci Psa 1959, 2:85-86

54199 Masochism: psychogenesis and therapeutic principles. Sci Psa 1959, 2:44-52

54200 Motivations, positive and negative, in the rehabilitation of the disabled. Bull Am Rehabil Com 1953, 2(2):1-5

54201 A psychoanalyst's viewpoint on sexual problems. Pastoral Psychol 1953, 4(31):38-41; 44-46

54202 Psychoanalytic psychotherapy in Raynaud's disease. PSM 1956, 18:492-505
        Abs Fain RFPsa 1957, 21:621. Powelson, D. H. Q 1958, 27:136-137

54203 (& Dyde, J. F.) Psychoanalytical observations in two cases of thrombophlebitis migrans. PSM 1957, 19:275-286
        Abs Powelson, D. H. Q 1958, 27:451

54204 Psychosomatic aspects of breast surgery. Proc Acad of PSM Meeting 1954, Oct. NY: Grune & Stratton 1956

54205 (& Lief, H.; Mittelmann, B.) Raynaud's disease. Psychogenic factors and psychotherapy. PSM 1953, 15:61-65
        Abs VC Q 1954, 23:307. Rv Labbé, P. RFPsa 1953, 17:354-355

54206 Response to Presidential Address. (Read at Acad of Psa, Phila, April 1959) Sci Psa 1960, 3:xiii-xiv

54207 Shock therapies, old and new. Pastoral Psychol 1959, 10(97):44-50

54208 Sigmund Freud and pastoral psychology. Pastoral Psychol 1956, 7(68):7

54209 Understanding the emotional aspects of disability. Soc Wk 1957, 2:16-21

MILLICAN, FRANCIS K.

See Lourie, Reginald S.

MILLS, C. WRIGHT

See Gerth, Hans H.

MILNER, MARION
(See also Field, Joanna)

S-23083A Aspects of symbolism in comprehension of the not self. Shortened, with titles: The role of illusion in symbol formation. New Dir Psa 82-108
        Abs JAA An Surv Psa 1952, 3:53-54. MK An Surv Psa 1952, 3:515-516

54210 The communication of primary sensual experience (the yell of joy). (Read at 19th Int Psa Cong, Geneva, July 1955) J 1956, 37:278-281
        Abs Auth J 1956, 37:132. JLan Q 1957, 26:574

S-9423 A Life of One's Own
    Spanish: Mexico: Edit Novaro 1959
54211 On Not Being Able to Paint (Foreword: Freud, A.) NY: IUP 1957, xxii + 184 p
    Rv Leach, D. Q 1959, 28:100-101
S-23085 A note on the ending of an analysis. R 1953, 40:368-369
54212 Obituary: Karin Stephen 1889-1953. J 1954, 35:432-433
54213 Psycho-analysis and art. In Sutherland, J. M. *Psycho-Analysis and Contemporary Thought,* London: HPI 1958, 77-101
° ° ° The role of illusion in symbol formation. See [S-23083A]
54214 The sense in non-sense. (Freud and Blake's "Job"). New Era, London 1956, 7:29-41.
    Der Sinn im Sinnlosen: Freud und der "Hiob" von Blake. Psyche, Heidel 1957, 10:688-713

MILROD, DAVID

54215 Some prognostic factors in schizophrenia related to childbirth with a report of two cases. J Hillside Hosp 1954, 3:107-125

MINER, HORACE
See De Vos, George

MINKOWICH, ABRAM

54216 Correlates of superego functions. Diss Abstr 1959, 19:3356-3357

MINKOWSKI, EUGENE

54217 Findings in a case of schizophrenic depression. J Psychol norm et path 1923, 20:543-558. In *Le Temps Vécu,* Paris: J. L. L. d'Artrey 1933, 169-181. (Tr: Bliss, B.) Existence 127-138
54218 Hommage de Françoise Minkowska à Hermann Rorschach. [Tribute from Françoise Minkowska to Hermann Rorschach.) Z diag Psychol 1955, 3:280-288
54219 Les modes d'existence en fonction de certaines activités psychomotrices; introduction à l'analyse existentielle. [Modes of existence as a function of certain psychomotor activities; introduction to existential analysis.] Evolut psychiat 1955, (3):413-427
54220 Preface to Gayral, L. *La Psychiatrie Contemporaine: Principes, Méthodes, Applications*
54221 Psychopathologie, science humaine. [Psychopathology, a human science.] Note Psichiat, Pesaro 1956, 49:25-47
54222 Psikhopatologia u filosofia. [Psychopathology and philosophy.] Iyun 1956, 7:193-209

    See Fusswerk Fursay, Joseph

MINKOWSKI, M.

54223 Gedenkfeier zum 70. Geburtstag von Hermann Rorschach im psychiatrisch-neurologischen Verein Zürich am 8. Nov. 1954. [Memorial celebration of Hermann Rorschach's 70th birthday at the Zürich Psychiatric-Neurologic Society on November 8, 1954.] Z diag Psychol 1955, 3:271-279

MINNEHAN, ROBERT W.
See Hofling, Charles K.

MINOR, JOHN B.
See Scheidlinger, Saul

MINSKI, LOUIS

54224 (& Desai, M. M.) Aspects of personality in peptic ulcer patients.
M 1955, 28:113-134
Abs EMW Q 1956, 25:624

MINTZ, ELIZABETH E.

54225 An example of assimilative projection. ASP 1956, 52(2)
54226 Personal problems and diagnostic errors of clinical psychologists. J
proj Tech 1957, 21:123-128
54227 (& Schmeidler, G. R.; Bristol, M.) Rorschach changes during psychoanalysis. J proj Tech 1956, 20:414-417

MINTZ, N.
See Maslow, Abraham H.

MINTZ, YA.

54228 [Aleksandr Blok. Pathographic outline.] (Russian). Klinicheskii arkhiv
geneal'nosti i odarennosti 1928, 4(3):45-54
54229 [Jesus Christ as a type of mental illness.] (Russian). Klinicheskii arkhiv
geneal'nosti i odarennosti 1957, 3(3):243-252
54230 [On the pathography of Pushkin.] (Russian). Klinicheskii arkhiv geneal'nosti i odarennosti 1925, 1(2):29-46

MIOTTO, ANTONIO

54231 Las Psicanalisi. [Psychoanalyses.] Milan: Garzanti 1954, 101 p

MIRA y LÓPEZ, EMILIO

54232 Características generales de las actividades psíquicas. [General characteristics of mental activities.] Act Np Arg 1957, 3:217-222
54233 Personalidad y psicoterapia. [Personality and psychotherapy.] Arch
Neurol Psiquiat 1958, 8:43-46

MIRACLE, LUIZ

54234 Editor of Nacht, S. La psychanalyse d'aujourd'hui (Spanish edition)

MIRSKY, I. ARTHUR

54235 (& Miller, R. E.; Murphy, J. V.) The communication of affect in
rhesus monkeys. I. An experimental method. J Am Psa Ass 1956, 6:433-
441
Abs TFr J 1959, 40:363. Shentoub RFPsa 1959, 23:436. TGS Q
1960, 29:430-431

54236 Discussion of Ostow, M. "The structural model: ego, id, and super-ego." Ann NY Acad Sci 1959, 76:1133-1134

54237 Discussion of Stanton, A. H. "Propositions concerning object choices." Ann NY Acad Sci 1959, 76:1035

54238 Discussion of Szasz, T. S. "A critical analysis of some aspects of the libido theory: the concepts of libidinal zones, aims, and modes of gratification." Ann NY Acad Sci 1959, 76:998

54239 Physiologic, psychologic, and social determinants in the etiology of duodenal ulcer. Amer J dig Dis 1958, 3:285-314

54240 Psychoanalysis and the biological sciences. 20 Yrs Psa 155-176

54241 Psychologic and endocrinologic interrelations. Int Rec Med 1953, 166:204-210

54242 The psychosomatic approach to the etiology of clinical disorders. PSM 1957, 19:424-430

54243 (& Miller, R.; Stein, M.) Relation of adrenocortical and adaptive behavior. PSM 1953, 15:574-588

54244 (& Thaler, M.; Weiner, H.; Reiser, M.) Studies on the physiological, psychological and social determinants in the etiology of duodenal ulcer. PSM 1956, 18:514

See Persky, Harold; Wiener, Herbert

MISCHEL, ELLIS

See Stein, Aaron

MISES, R.

REVIEW OF:

54245 Spitz, R. A. La Première Année de la Vie de l'Enfant, RFPsa 1959, 23:283-284

MISPELBLOM BEYER, F.

54246 Over bet begrip "autoritaire personlijkheid." [The concept of "authoritarian personality."] Ned Tijdschr Psychol 1957, 12:367-391

MISSAGLIA, A.

54247 (& Maniori, E.) Algolagnia sessuale passiva in una schizofrenica. [Passive sexual algolagnia in a schizophrenic woman.] Ann Np Psa 1955, 2:407-425

54248 Osservazioni sull'indagine dell'inconscio mediante il test di Rorschach. [Observations in the investigation of the unconscious by means of the Rorschach test.] Ann Np Psa 1955, 2:223-231

MITCHELL, HOWARD E.

54249 (& Preston, M. G.; Mudd, E. H.) Anticipated development of the case from the content of the first interview. Marriage Fam Living 1953, 15:226-231

54250 (& Mudd, E. H.) Anxieties associated with the conduct of research in a clinical setting. Ops 1957, 27:310-330
Abs Koenig RFPsa 1958, 22:258

54251 "Color conflict" as a defense. Clin Stud Cult Confl 91-118

54252   (& Preston, M. G.; Mudd, E. H.) Counselors' attitudes toward technical aids to the counseling process. Soc Casewk 1955, 36:165-174

54253   (& Mudd, E. H.) The development of a research methodology for achieving the cooperation of alcoholics and their nonalcoholic wives. Quart J Stud Alcohol 1957, 18:647-657

54254   (& Mudd, E. H.) Interpersonal perception theory applied to conflicted marriages in which alcoholism is and is not a problem. Ops. 1959, 29:547-559

54255   Upward social mobility in a new American. Clin Stud Cult Confl 561-584

MITCHELL, JOHN D.

54256   André Gide, rebel and conformist. Am Im 1959, 16:147-153

54257   Applied psychoanalysis in the director-actor relationship. Am Im 1956, 13:223-239

54258   Applied psychoanalysis in the drama. Am Im 1957, 14:263-280

54259   The Sanskrit drama "Shakuntala": a psychologic sounding board for Hindu culture. Am Im 1959, 16:329-348

MITRA, SUHRIT CHANDRA

54260   Causes of crime. Science and Culture 1946

54261   Children's education through rhythm. Rhyme and Rhythm 1954

54262   The concept of instinct. IJP 1928, 3

54263   Contributions of abnormal psychology to normal psychology. IJP 1938, special No.

54264   Education of the criminal. Calcutta Police J 1953

54265   Gestalt psychology. Calcutta Rev 1935

54266   On Indian juvenile delinquency. Calcutta Police J 1953

54267   Laws in psychology. IJP 1936, 11

54268   Life of W. Wundt. IJP 1932, 7

54269   Need for a psychology to replace psychologies. IJP 1943, 18

54270   Professor Girindrasekhar Bose. An appreciation. Science and Culture 1953, 19(3). Samiksa 1955, Bose No., special issue: 57-61

54271   Dr. Girindrasekhar Bose (Obituary). Educ & Psychol, Delhi 1954, 1(1):63-64

54272   Politics and psychology. IJP 1928, 3

54273   Psychological studies of crime. Calcutta Police J 1953

54274   Psychology and life. IJP 1935, 10

54275   The right approach to psychology. Science and Culture 1946

54276   The spirit of nation in peace and war. IJP 1927, 2

54277   Studies in aesthetic perception. IJP 1936, 11; 1942, 17

MITSCHERLICH, ALEXANDER

54278   Aggression und Anpassung. Psyche, Heidel 1956, 10:177-193; 1958, 12:523-537. In author's *Entfaltung der Psychoanalyse*, Stuttgart: Klett 1956, 177-193

54279   Ansprache im Namen der Medizinischen Fakultät der Universität Heidelberg. [Address on behalf of the Medical Faculty of Heidelberg University.] In Alexander, F. et al: *Freud in der Gegenwart*, Frankfurt: Europäische Verlagsanstalt 1957, 36-42

54280 Ansprache im Namen der Medizinschen Fakultät. [Address in the name of the medical faculty.] In *Reden gehalten in der Universität zu Frankfurt a/M anlässlich der Wiederkehr des Geburtstages von Sigmund Freud,* Frankfurt: Klostermann 1956, 43-47

54281 Anweisungen zu einer neuen Menschenkunde. Zum Tode Viktor von Weizsäckers. [Instructions for a new anthropology. On the death of Viktor von Weizsäcker.] Die Zeit 1957, 12(3):4

54282 Über die Bedeutung der Enuresis. [The meaning of enuresis.] Med Klin 1947, 42

54283 Bemerkungen zum klinisch-ärztlichen Allergieproblem. [Remarks on clinical and therapeutic problems of allergy.] Hippokrates, Stuttgart 1950

54284 Bemerkungen zur gesellschaftlichen Funktion psychologischen Wissens. [Comments on the social function of psychological knowledge.] Psyche, Heidel 1954, 7:641-647

54285 Die Bewertung des "Schöpferischen" in der psychosomatischen Medizin. [The evaluation of the "creative faculties" in psychosomatic medicine.] Trans Ier Cong mondial de Psychiat, 1950, Paris: 1952

54286 [Concerning the Origin of Disease. A Pathogenetic Investigation of Diabetes Insipidus.] (German) Stuttgart: Klett 1947

54287 Contribution à la théorie psychanalytique des maladies psychosomatiques. [Psychoanalytic theory of psychosomatic diseases.] Évolut psychiat 1953, 3:529-546

54288 Doctors of Infamy. The Story of the Nazi Medical Crimes. NY: Henry Schuman 1949

54289 Über den Einbau der Tiefenpsychologie in das Medizinstudium. [On the insertion of psychoanalysis into the medical curriculum.] Ärztl Mitteilungen 1957, 42:384-387

54290 Der Einzelne in seiner Angst. Ein Wort zu den Massenreaktionen unserer Zeit. [The individual in anxiety. A word on the mass reactions of our time.] Deutsche Zeitung u Wirtschaftszeitung 1956, 11(80):4

54291 Das Ende einer Simplifizierung. [The end of a simplification.] Materia med Nordmark 1958, 10:265-267

54292 Endlose Diktatur? [Unending dictatorship?] Zurich: Artemis-Verlag 1947

54293 (Ed) Entfaltung der Psychoanalyse; das Wirken Sigmund Freuds in die Gegenwart. [The Unfolding of Psychoanalysis; The Effect of Sigmund Freud on the Present.] Stuttgart: Ernst Klett 1956, 276 p
    Rv ESt J 1958, 39:441. Stern, M. M. Q 1958, 27:428-430

54294 Geleitwort. [Introductory Remarks.] In Alexander, F. et al: *Freud und die Gegenwart,* Frankfurt: Europäische Verlagsanstalt 1957, xiii-xvi

54295 Geschichtsschreibung und Psychoanalyse. [Historiography and psychoanalysis.] Schweiz Ann 1947

54296 Der geteilte Vater. Generationskonflikte in der modernen Welt. [The divided father. Generation conflicts in the modern world.] Deutsch Kommentare 1955, 7:5

54297 Gewinn und Grenzen der Psychoanalyse. Zur Diskussion einer päpstlichen Ansprache. [Gain and limits of psychoanalysis. Discussion of a papal speech.] Merkur 1953, 7:901-918

54298   Gibt es politische Neurosen? [Are there political neuroses?] Der Monat
         1953-54, 6:479-482
54299   Groszstadt und Neurose. [Big cities and neurosis.] Merkur 1955,
         9:201-219. Studium generale 1955, 8:135-150
54300   Hindernisse in der sozialen Anwendung der Psychotherapie. [Obstacles
         in the social application of psychotherapy.] Psyche, Heidel 1954,
         8:284-305. In Geistige Hygiene, Basel 1955, 213-235
54301   Jugend in der technischen Welt. [Youth in the technical world.] Neue
         deutsche Hefte 1957-58, 4:396-405
54302   Jugend ohne Bilder. [Youth in trouble for lack of identificational
         prototypes.] "Du," Zurich 1947
54303   Die Krankheiten der Gesellschaft und die psychosomatische Medizin.
         [Diseases of human societies and psychosomatic medicine.] In Krank-
         heit im Wandel der Welt, Forschungen des Landes Hessen. 3. Sitzg.
         Wiesbaden 1957. Bad Homburg o. J. 37-54
S-23258 Kritische Anmerkungen zur Problementfaltung in der Tiefenpsycholo-
         gie.
            Abs JAA An Surv Psa 1951, 2:23-25
54304   Leib und Seele. [Body and mind.] In Das Weltbild unserer Zeit,
         Nürnberg 1954, 35-64
S-23259 Lust- und Realitätsprinzip in ihrer Beziehung zur Phantasie.
            Abs JAA An Surv Psa 1952, 3:85-86
54305   Massenpsychologie ohne Ressentiment. [Mass psychology without
         resentments.] Die neue Rundschau 1953, 64:36-79
54306   Meditationen zu einer Lebenslehre der modernen Massen. [Reflections
         on the living conditions of modern masses.] Merkur 1957, 11:201-213;
         335-350
54307   Die Metapsychologie des Komfort [Metapsychology of easy living.]
         Baukunst und Werkform 1954, 7:190-193
54308   Neuere pathogenetische Fragestellungen in der psychosomatischen
         Klinik. [New approaches in pathogenesis as derived from psychoso-
         matic clinical observations.] Med Klin 1958, 53:165-171
54309   Neurosen und Psychosen als soziale Phänomene. [Neuroses and psy-
         choses as sociological phenomena.] In Viktor von Weizsäcker, Arzt im
         Irrsal der Zeit, Göttingen 1956, 157-168
54310   Oedipus und Kaspar Hauser. Der Monat 1950, Oct 25
54311   Person und Kollektiv aus psychologischer Sicht. [Individual and col-
         lective from the psychologist's viewpoint.] In Synthetische Anthropo-
         logie, Bonn: 1950
54312   Das Phantomglied—seine Deutung und Bedeutung. [Phantom limb—
         its interpretation and significance.] Schweiz med Wochenschr 1947,
         77:423
54313   Preface to Freud, S. Zur Psychopathologie des Alltagslebens
54314   Zur psychoanalytischen Auffassung psychosomatischer Krankheitsent-
         stehung. [Contribution to the psychoanalytic theory of psychosomatic
         disorders.] Psyche, Heidel 1954, 7:561-578
54315   Der psychologische Zugang zur Krankheit. [A psychological approach
         to illness.] Medizinische 1958, 766-769
54316   Die Psychosomatik in der Allergie. [The psychosomatic approach to

allergy.] Verhandlungsberichte des I. International Allergy Congress, Basel, New York, 1951

54317 Psychosomatik vom Standpunkt der Psychoanalyse. [Psychosomatics, as seen from the standpoint of psychoanalysis.] Med Klin 1954, 49:1789-1793

54318 Psychosomatische Aspekte der Allergie. [Psychosomatic aspects of allergy.] Int Arch Allergy & Appl Immunol (Basel), 1950

54319 Pubertät und Tradition. [Adolescence and traditionalism.] Verh Dt Soziologentag 13, Bad Meinberg. Köln 1957, 65-86

54320 Pubertät und Tradition heute. [Adolescence and tradition today.] Neue deutsche Hefte 1957-58, 4:498-508

54321 Rationale Therapie und Psychotherapie. [Rational therapy and psychotherapy.] Psyche, Heidel 1958, 12:721-731

54322 Scheinfütterung. Kollektive Ersatzbefriedigung in der heutigen Kultur. [Sham feeding. Collective substitutes for gratifications in modern civilization.] Deutsche Studentenzeitung 1955, 5:10

54323 (& Ruffler, G.) Der Schmerz als Symbol. [Pain as a symbol.] Med Klin 1956, 51:909-913

54324 Sigmund Freuds Beitrag zur modernen Psychologie. [Sigmund Freud's contribution to modern psychology.] In Festschrift für Alfred Weber, Heidelberg: Lambert Schneider, 1948

54325 Soziologisches Denken in der Medizin. [Sociological thinking in medicine.] Dt Arzt 1958, 8:459-475

54326 Spezifische Voraussetzungen moderner Massenreaktionen. [Some specific preconditions of modern mass reactions.] In Polizei und ihre Aufgaben, Essen 1957, 111-128

54327 Die störenden Illusionen. [Disturbing illusions.] Frankfurter Allg Zeitung 1956, May 5 (105)

54328 Zum Streit um die Psychoanalyse. [Controversy about psychoanalysis.] Der Monat 1956, 8:56-60

54329 Der Strukturwandel der Persönlichkeit in tiefenpsychologischer und entwicklungspsychologischer Sicht. [Structural changes in personality from the psychoanalytic and genetic viewpoints.] Ber Kongress d Deut Ges f Psych 1956, 20:80-88

54330 Auf der Suche nach der Identität von Leib und Seele. [The search for identity of body and mind.] Die Zeit 1956, 11(16):6

54331 Die Symptomwahl in den Neurosen. [Choice of symptoms in neurosis.] Dtsche med Wschr 1946, 71:147

54332 Tiefenpsychologie und soziale Krankenversicherung. [Psychoanalysis and social health insurance.] Soz Fortschritt 1953, 2:265-269

54333 Die unsichtbare Gestalt des Vaters. Ein Phänomen der modernen Zivilisation. [The invisible father. A phenomenon of modern civilization.] Die Zeit 1955, 10(39):4

54334 Der unsichtbare Vater; ein Problem für Psychoanalyse und Soziologie. [The invisible father; a psychoanalytical and sociological problem.] Kölner Z Soziol 1955, 7:188-201

54335 Über die Vielschichtigkeit sozialer Einflüsse auf Entstehung und Behandlung von Psychosen und Neurosen. [On the various social influences on pathogenesis and treatment of psychoses and neuroses.] Med Klin 1957, 52:125-129; 161-164

54336 Die Wandlung des Leib-Seele-Problems in der modernen Medizin. [The transformation of the body-mind problem in modern medicine.] Die Neue Weltschau, Stuttgart 1951

54337 Was von der Psychoanalyse geblieben ist? [What of psychoanalysis has survived?] Dtsche Z u Wirtschaftszeitung 1954, 9(3):5

54338 Die wechselseitige Beeinflussung des Freiheits-und Krankheits-begriffes in einer anthropologischen Heilkunde. [Interaction of the concepts of freedom and illness in an anthropologically oriented therapy.] Dialectica (Zurich) 1951

54339 Widerstand und Einsicht—Sigmund Freuds Anliegen in der Psychoanalyse. [Resistance and insight—Sigmund Freud's contribution to psychoanalysis.] Studium Generale 1950, 3:7

54340 (& Mielke, F.) Wissenschaft ohne Menschlichkeit. [Science without Humane Responsibility.] Heidelberg: Lambert Schneider 1949

See Oehme, C.; Thomae, Hans

MITTELMANN, BELA

54341 Analysis of reciprocal neurotic patterns in family relationships. In Eisenstein, V. W. *Neurotic Interaction in Marriage*, NY: Basic Books 1956, 81-100

S-23281 The concurrent analysis of married couples. In Vincent, C. E. *Readings in Marriage Counseling*, NY: Crowell 1957, 330-342

54342 Intrauterine and early infantile motility. Psa St C 1960, 15:104-127

54343 Motility in infants, children, and adults: patterning and psychodynamics. Psa St C 1954, 9:142-177
    Abs NRo An Surv Psa 1954, 5:252-254. RTh J 1956, 37:213-214

54344 Motility in the therapy of children and adults. Psa St C 1957, 12:284-319
    Abs RTh J 1959, 40:372

54345 Motor patterns and genital behavior: fetishism. Psa St C 1955, 10:241-263
    Abs Kloth, E. Q 1956, 25:306-307, RTh J 1957, 38:296

54346 Problems of infantile neurosis. A discussion. Psa St C 1954, 9:63-64

54347 Psychodynamics of motility. (Read at 20th Int Psa Cong, Paris 1957) J 1958, 39:196-199
    Abs J 1958, 39:293-294. JLan Q 1959, 28:280. Rv Tabak Rev Psicoanál 1959, 16:267

54348 Psychosomatic medicine and the older patient. In Kaplan, O. J. *Mental Disorders in Later Life*, Stanford: Stanford Univ Pr; London: Geoffrey Cumberlege, Oxford Univ Pr 1945, 349-372; 2nd Ed 1956, 398-422

S-23301 The simultaneous treatment of both parents and their child.
    Abs NRo An Surv Psa 1952, 3:433-435

54349 Symposium on disturbances of the digestive tract; V. Psychosomatic disorders, psychosis, and therapeutic accessibility. (Read at 21st Int Psa Cong, Copenhagen, July 1959) J 1960, 41:465-466

See Bellak, Leopold; Maslow, Abraham H.; Millet, John A. P.; Weider, Arthur

MITTELMANN, M.

54350 L'homme et son univers [Man and his universe.] Psyché, Paris 1954, 9:319-338

MIURA, TAIEI

54351 Psychoanalysis and religion. Jap J Psa 1955, 2(11):5-10

REVIEW OF:
54352 Ey, H. Psychiatrie et Psychanalyse. Jap J Psa 1958, 5(6):59-64

MIYAGI, O.

See Griffith, Richard Marion

MIYATE, BOSI

54353 Über den Nihilismus des Dichters Basio. [On the nihilism of the poet Basio.] Tokio Z Psa 1938, 6

MODE, DORIS

54354 A psychoanalytic view of miracles. J Psychother 1956, 3:47-52

MODEIROS, M. DE

54355 As personalidades psicopáticas no casamento. [Psychopathic personalities in marriage.] J Bras Psiquiat 1955, 4:135-155

MODEL, A.

54356 (& Shepheard, E.) The child who refuses to go to school. Med Offr 1958, 100:39-41

MODELL, ARNOLD H.

54357 Some recent psychoanalytic theories of schizophrenia. R 1956, 43:181-194
Abs JLan Q 1957, 26:584
54358 The theoretical implications of hallucinatory experiences in schizophrenia. J Am Psa Ass 1958, 6:442-480
Abs TFr J 1959, 40:363. Shentoub, RFPsa 1959, 23:436-437. TGS Q 1960, 29:431

MODLIN, HERBERT C.

54359 An evaluation of the learning process in a psychiatric residency program. BMC 1955, 19:139-159
Abs Rahman, L. Q 1956, 25:618
54360 (& Faris, M.) Follow-up study of psychiatric team functioning. BMC 1954, 18:242-251
54361 (& Faris, M.) Group adaptation and integration in psychiatric team practice. Ps 1956, 19:97-103
54362 (& Gardner, R.; Faris, M.) Implications of a therapeutic process in evaluations by psychiatric teams. Ops 1958, 28:647-655
54363 The M. M. P. I. in clinical practice. In Welch, G. S. & Dahlstrom, W. G. *Basic Readings on the M.M.P.I.* Minneapolis: Univ of Minn Pr 1956

54364   (& Hall, B. H.) The patient bridges the gap between the hospital and
        the community. In *Better Social Service for Mentally Ill Patients*, NY:
        Amer Assn Psychiat Soc Workers 1954
54365   Personality mechanisms. In Levinson, H. *Toward Understanding Men*,
        Topeka, Kans: Menninger Foundation 1956
54366   The position of the psychiatrist in the administration of the criminal
        law. Kans Law Rev 1956, 4:350-355
54367   Psychiatry and criminal law. Menn Q 1956, 10(2):1-6
54368   Schizophrenia. Menn Q 1954, 8(2):25-31
            Jap: J Tokyo Inst Psa 1956, 4:7-11
54369   (& Sargent, H.; Faris, M.; Voth, H. M.) Situational variables. BMC
        1958, 22:148-166
54370   Training of the modern psychiatrist. J Phi Rho Sigma 1954, 49:1-3
54371   Traumatic neurosis. J Bar Assn State of Kans 1956, 24:341-352

        See Wallerstein, Robert S.

MODONESI, C.

54372   Sulle alterazioni del carattere in rapporto a squilibri affettivi in neuro-
        psichiatria infantile. [Character disorder in relation to emotional imbal-
        ance in child neuropsychiatry.] Neuropsichiatria 1954, 10:45-68

MOFFITT, J. WELDON

        See Stagner, Ross

MÖGLICH, H.-J.

54373   Kasuistischer Beitrag zur Frage fehlgeleiteter kindlicher Gewissens-
        reaktionen. [Contribution of a case study on the problem of misdirected
        infantile conscience reactions.] Prax Kinderpsychol 1958, 7:64-68

MOHR, GEORGE J.

54374   Discussion of Murphy, G. "Psychoanalysis as a unified theory of be-
        havior." Sci Psa 1960, 3:179-180
54375   Discussion of Rabin, A. I. "Infants and children under conditions of
        'intermittent' mothering in the Kibbutz." Ops 1958, 28:584-586
            Abs Koenig RFPsa 1959, 23:431-432
54376   (& Richmond, J. B.; Garner, A. M.; Eddy, E. J.) A program for the
        study of children with psychosomatic disorders. Emot Prob Early Child
        251-268
54377   Psychoanalysis: some present-day assessments. (Read at Acad of Psa,
        NY, Dec 1958) Sci Psa 1960, 3:1019
54378   Psychoanalytic training. 20 Yrs Psa 235-241
54379   Psychological factors in marital adjustment. In Fishbein, M. & Reeves
        Kennedy, R. J. *Modern Marriage and Family Living*, NY: Oxford Univ
        Pr 1957, 248
54380   (& Despres, M. A.) The Stormy Decade: Adolescence. NY: Random
        House 1958, 272 p
54381   (& Josselyn, I. M.; Spurlock, J.; Barron, S. H.) Studies in ulcerative
        colitis. P 1958, 114:1067-1076

        See Rabin, Albert I.

REVIEWS OF:

54382 Alexander, F. & Staub, H. The Criminal, the Judge, and the Public. Q 1959, 28:263-265

54383 Erikson, E. H. Identity and the Life Cycle. Q 1960, 29:105-108

54384 Overholser, W. The Psychiatrist and the Law. Q 1954, 23:126-128

MOLHUYSEN-VAN DER WALLE, S. M.

See Musaph, H.

MOLINA, JERONIMO

54385 Freud en el Tiempo. [Freud and his times.] Rev Psicol gen apl, Madrid 1957, 12:203-206

MOLINA NÚÑEZ, J.

54386 Complejo de Edipo. [Oedipus complex.] Act luso-esp Neur 1957, 16:296-304

54387 Eros y libido. [Eros and libido.] Act luso-esp Neur 1959, 18:34-38

MOLINARI, EGON

54388 Considerazioni sulle situazioni conflittuali in alcuni casi di impotenza psicogena. [Considerations on the conflicting situations in several cases of psychogenic impotence.] Riv Psa 1955, 1(2):57-65

54389 Meccanismi di difesa e paralogismi. [Mechanisms of defense and paralogisms.] Riv Psa 1958, 4:25-52

54390 Sentimento di inferiorità e sentimento di colpa. [Feeling of inferiority and guilt feeling.] Riv Psa 1955, 1(3):37-42

54391 Il silenzio in analisi. [The silence in analysis.] Riv Psa 1957, 3:19-34

TRANSLATION OF:
Freud, S. [10609]

MOLISH, HERMAN B.

54392 (& Beck, S. J.) Further explorations of the "6 schizophrenias": type S-3. Ops 1958, 28:483-505
Abs Koenig RFPsa 1959, 23:431

54393 (& Beck, S. J.) Mechanisms of defense in schizophrenic reaction types as evaluated by the Rorschach test. Workshop 1956: Psychoanalytic concepts and principles discernible in projective personality tests. Ops 1958, 28:47-60

See Beck, Samuel J.; Thetford, William H.

MOLL, ALBERT E.

54394 Suicide (psychopathology). Canad Med Ass J 1956, 74:104-112

MOLLEGEN, A. T.

54395 Utilization of religious attitudes in clinical psychiatry. Bull Isaac Ray med Libr 1954, 2:116-135

MOLLER, A.

54396 Ut patet ex quotidiana experientia. [As shown by daily experience.]
Ugeskrift for Laeger 1953, 115(17):649

MOLONEY, JAMES CLARK

54397 Anthropological clues to mental conflicts. Child-Fam Dig 1954, 10(3):
69-70. From author's *The Battle for Mental Health* [23408]
54398 The cultural source of power drives. Child-Fam Dig 1959, 18(1):3-7
54399 Does rooming-in cost more? Child-Fam Dig 1954, 10(6):35-36
54400 Etiology of mental health. Med Bull Henry Ford Hosp (Detroit) 1955,
3(1). Child-Fam Dig 1955, 12(5):3-14
54401 Fear: Contagion and Conquest. NY: Philos Library 1957, xii + 140 p
Rv Williams, A. H. J 1959, 40:356
54402 Fear is the most dangerous contagion in the world. Child-Fam Dig
1958, 17(2):3-7. From author's *Fear: Contagion and Conquest*
54403 A fragment of the core. A new slant on the pleasure-pain principle.
Child-Fam Dig 1957, 16(5):21-23
54404 Interpersonalism and someikonics. Pres-Day Psychol 733-769
54405 Japanese conformity and insanity. Child-Fam Dig 1954, 11(2):3-12.
From author's *Understanding the Japanese Mind*
S-23418 The Magic Cloak
Rv Christensen, E. O. R 1953, 40:61-72
54406 Maternocentric child rearing. Child-Fam Dig 1956, 15(3):17-32. Merrill-Palmer Q 1957, 3:54-66
54407 A memorandum on emotional disorganization in this culture. In Trans
2nd Conf on Prob of Early Infancy, March 2, 1948, NY. NY: Josiah
Macy Jr Found, 82-88. Child-Fam Dig 1956, 14(3):20-26
54408 Mother, God and superego. J Am Psa Ass 1954, 2:120-151
Abs RJA An Surv Psa 1954, 5:438-439. TFr J 1955, 36:222. Shentoub RFPsa 1955, 19:472. MGr Q 1956, 25:283-284
54409 The origin of the rejected and crippled hero myths. Am Im 1959,
16:271-328
S-23423 Planned infancy and the paranoid block to human progress.
Abs R 1954, 41:370
54410 The precognitive cultural ingredients of schizophrenia. J 1957, 38:325-
340
Componenti culturali prelogiche nella schizofrenia. (Tr: I. Majore)
Riv Psa 1959, 5:3-30
Abs Racamier RFPsa 1959, 23:152-153
54411 Psychic self-abandon and extortion of confessions. J 1955, 36:53-60
Abs Rev Psicoanál 1955, 12:304-305. JLan Q 1956, 25:443
54412 The relation between infant care and adult neurosis among the Oki-
nawans. Child-Fam Dig 1954, 10(1):43-49
54413 The shuttlecock. Child-Fam Dig 1959, 18(3):11-14
54414 A string of fish. The Humanist 1956, 16:163-166
54415 Understanding the Japanese Mind. NY: Philos Library 1954, 252 p
Rv Williams, A. H. J 1955, 36:407. R 1956, 43:389
54416 Understanding the paradox of Japanese psychoanalysis. J 1953, 34:291-
303
Abs Auth Q 1955, 24:308-309. GD An Surv Psa 1953, 4:336-337

MOLONEY, ROBERT

54417 Freud and moral theory. Month, London 1957, Sept:169-174

MOM, JORGE M.

54418 Algunas consideraciones sobre el concepto de distancia en las fobias. [Various findings on the concept of distance in phobias.] Rev Psicoanál 1956, 13:430-435

54419 Algunas consideraciones sobre interpretación en las fobias. [Various findings on the interpretation of phobias.] Rev Psicoanál 1957, 14:63-71

54420 Aspectos teoricas y tecnicos en las fobias y en las modalidades fobicas. [Theoretical and technical aspects of phobias and of phobic modalities.] Rev Psicoanál 1960, 17:190-218

MOM, M. T.

ABSTRACT OF:

54421 Pichon-Rivière, A. A. de. Como repercute en los niños la conducta de los padres con sus animales preferidos. Rev Psicoanál 1958, 15:189

MONARD, HÉLÈNE PERRENOUD

54422 Actualités pédagogiques et psychologiques: les enfants nerveux. [Present pedagogic and psychologic realities: nervous children.] Neuchatel, Paris: Delachaux & Niestle 1946, 20 p

MONASHKIN, IRWIN

See Zuckerman, Marvin

MONCHAUX, CECILY DE

54423 The contribution of psycho-analysis to the psychology of thinking. Advanc Sci 1956, 12:558-562

54424 The contributions of psychoanalysis to the understanding of child development. In Symposium on the contribution of current theories to an understanding of child development. M 1957, 30:230-269
    Abs EMW Q 1958, 27:620-621

54425 (& Schachter, S. et al) Cross-cultural experiments on threat and rejection. Human Relat 1954, 7:403-439

54426 Obituary: Dr. John Carl Flugel, 1884-1955. Bull Brit psychol Soc 1955, 27:2

54427 (& Dixon, J. J.; Sandler, J.) Patterns of anxiety: the phobias. M 1957, 30:34-40

54428 Pooling of case material: a methodological project. Proc RSM 1958, 51(11):8-9

54429 Psychological aspects of world affairs. Year Book of World Affairs 1958, 12:381-391; 1959, 13:338-400

54430 (& Shimmin, S.) Some problems of method in experimental group psychology. Hum Relat 1955, 8:53-60

54431 The theories of Freud: a revaluation. The Listener 1954, 52(1335):517-518

See Dixon, James J.; Nuttin, Joseph; Sandler, Joseph J.

REVIEWS OF:
54432 Stone, C. P. & Taylor, D. W. Annual Review of Psychology. J 1954, 35:367
54433 Whiting, J. M. & Child, I. L. Child Training and Personality. J 1954, 35:365-367

MONCHY, RENE DE

S-23443 Masochism as a pathological and as a normal phenomenon in the human mind.
    Abs R 1953, 40:362
S-23446 Oral components of the castration complex.
    Abs JAA An Surv Psa 1952, 3:74-76. Hunt, S. P. Q 1954, 23:144-145
54434 Psykoanalysen och läkaren. [Psychoanalysts and physicians.] Med Förēn Tidskr 1956, 34:237-249

MONCHY, S. J. R. DE

54435 Beschouwingen naar aanleiding van Zilboorg's: The psychology of the criminal act and punishment. [Reflections on Zilboorg's The psychology of the criminal act and punishment.] Maandbl voor de geest volksgezondheid 1956, 11:342-352
54436 Psychotherapeutische mogelykheden by delinquenten. [Psychotherapeutic possibilities with delinquents.] Maandbl voor berechtigung en reclasseering 1956, 35(4):77-91

MONEY, JOHN

54437 An examination of the concept of psychodynamics. Ps 1954, 17:325-330
54438 (& Hampson, J. G.) Idiopathic sexual precocity in the male: management; report of a case. PSM 1955, 17:1-15
    Abs EMW Q 1957, 26:142-143
54439 Linguistic resources and psychodynamic theory. M 1955, 28:264-266
S-23449 Observations concerning the clinical method of research, ego theory and psychopathology.
    Abs JAA An Surv Psa 1951, 2:114-116. NRo An Surv Psa 1951, 2:49-50
54440 The Psychologic Study of Man. Springfield, Ill: C C Thomas 1957, xi + 216 p

See Hampson, Joan G.

MONEY-KYRLE, ROGER E.

54441 The anthropological and the psychoanalytic concept of the norm. Psa Soc S 1955, 4:51-60
54442 An inconclusive contribution to the theory of the death instinct. New Dir Psa 499-509
54443 Introduction. New Dir Psa ix-xiii
54444 Normal countertransference and some of its deviations. (Read at 19th Int Psa Cong, Geneva, July 1955) J 1956, 37:360-366
    Contra-transferência normal e alguns dos seus desvios. (Tr: Cabernite, L.) Rev Bras Saúde ment 1956, 2(2):105-110
    Abs Auth J 1956, 37:132-133. JLan Q 1957, 26:578

54445 On the process of psychoanalytical inference. (Read at 20th Int Psa
       Cong, Paris 1957) J 1958, 29:129-133
              Abs J 1958, 29:294. JLan Q 1959, 28:278. Usandivaras & Tabak
              Rev Psicoanál 1959, 16:90
S-23457 Psychoanalysis and ethics. New Dir Psa 421-439
              Abs STa An Surv Psa 1952, 3:467-469. VC Q 1953, 22:606-607.
              Rv Weil Rev Psicoanál 1953, 10:117-118
54446 Psycho-analysis and philosophy. In Sutherland, J. M. *Psycho-Analysis
       and Contemporary Thought,* London: HPI 1958, 102-124
S-23458 Psychoanalysis and Politics.
              Abs Stein, A. An Surv Psa 1951, 2:675-684
S-23470 Some aspects of state and character in Germany.
              Abs GD An Surv Psa 1951, 2:510-511
54447 Towards a rational attitude to crime. J Howard League for Penal
       Reform 1953
54448 The world of the unconscious and the world of commonsense. Brit J
       Philos Sci 1956, 7:86-96

       See Klein, Melanie

       REVIEW OF:
54449 Fortes, M. Oedipus and Job—in West African Religion. J 1960, 41:645

                              MONK, MARY
       See Bernstein, Lotte

                            MONOD, MIREILLE
54450 Problèmes du transfert dans les psychothérapies d'enfants soignés en
       sanatorium. [Transference problems in psychotherapy of children cared
       for in a sanitarium.] Schweiz Z Psychol 1955, 14:88-105

                            MONROE, JACK J.
       See Cutler, Robert P.

                          MONROE, RUSSELL R.
54451 Discussion of Maskin, M. "Adaptations of psychoanalytic techniques to
       specific disorders." Sci Psa 1960, 3:352-357
54452 (& Weiss, V. W.) A framework for understanding family dynamics. Soc
       Casewk 1959, 40:3-9, 80-87

       See Kelley, Kenneth

                           MONSALLUT, A. J.
S-23535A Réflexions sur "La médecine psychosomatique" d'Alexander.
              Abs JAA An Surv Psa 1952, 3:327-329

                         MONSERRAT VALLE, L.
54453 Autoanálisis de Freud. [Freud's selfanalysis.] Rev Psiquiat Psicol 1956,
       2:650-661
54454 Psicoterapia de grupo. [Group psychotherapy.] Rev Psiquiat Psicol
       1953, 1:204-220

MONSOUR, KAREM J.

54455 Asthma and the fear of death. Q 1960, 29:56-71
54456 Migraine: dynamics and choice of symptoms. Q 1957, 28:476-493
       Abs Auth J 1958, 39:452. Dreyfus RFPsa 1958, 22:742-743

MONTAGU, M. F. ASHLEY

54457 Man—and human nature. P 1955, 112:401-410
54458 (Ed) The Meaning of Love. NY: Julian Pr 1953, viii + 248 p
54459 The origin and meaning of love. In author's *The Meaning of Love*, 3-24

MONTANARI, C.

54460 Sulla patogenesi dell'isterismo. [On the pathogenesis of hysteria.] Note
       Psichiat, Pesaro 1953, 79:239-260

MONTESANO, G.

54461 L'isterismo al lumi de la psicologia biologica. [Hysteria in the light of
       psychobiology.] Riv Psipat Np Psa 1953, 21:5-10
54462 Marco Levi Bianchini. Ann Np Psa 1956, 3:178-180

MONTESSORI, MARIA M.

54463 Das Kind in der Familie und andere Vorträge. [The Child in the
       Family and Other Lectures.] Stuttgart: Ernst Klett 1954, 93 p
54464 Obituary: Dr. Hans Lampl, 1889-1958. J 1960, 41:163-164

MONTGOMERY, JOHN

See Kolb, Lawrence C.

MONTSERRAT, SANTIAGO

54465 En Torno de Freud y su Tiempo. [Concerning Freud and his time.]
       Rev Psicol gen apl, Madrid 1957, 12:197-202

MONTSERRAT ESTEVE, S.

54466 Cibernética y psicología médica. [Cybernetics and medical psychol-
       ogy.] An Med, Barcelona 1956, 42(4):spec no:449-453

MOODY, ROBERT L.

54467 On the function of counter-transference. J anal Psych 1955, 1:49-58
54468 On Jung's concept of the symbol. M 1956, 29:9-14
       Abs EFA Q 1957, 26:292-293
54469 The relation of personal and transpersonal elements in the transference.
       Acta psychotherap psychosom orthopaedagog 1955, 3(Suppl):253-259

MOON, SHEILA

54470 Some aspects of redemption in the Navajo creation myth. J Psychother
       1956, 3:53-72

MOORE, A. ULRIC

See Hersher, Leonard

MOORE, ANN LESLIE

54471 (& Moore, M.) Notes on re-reading Dr. Hanns Sachs' last book. (P.S.P. —a re-view). Am Im 1954, 11:3-9

MOORE, BURNESS E.

54472 Congenital versus environmental: an unconscious meaning. J Am Psa Ass 1960, 8:312-316

54473 (& Atkinson, M.) Psychogenic vertigo: the importance of its recognition. AMA Arch Otolaryngol 1958, 67:347-353

See Redlich, Fredrick C.

ABSTRACT OF:
54474 Lewinsky, H. The closed circle. Q 1956, 25:302-304

MOORE, CLIFFORD D.

See Bonime, Walter

MOORE, H. C.

See Dittman, Allen T.

MOORE, MERRILL

54475 Case Record from a Sonnetorium. NY: Twayne Pub 1952
Rv Oberndorf, C. P. J 1953, 34:173

54476 Concerning the creative process in literature. In Hoch, P. & Zubin, J. *Experimental Psychopathology*, NY: Grune & Stratton 1957, 120-128

54477 Note on a limerick. Am Im 1956, 13:147-148

54478 Papers, 1903-1958. Lib Cong, Manuscript Div

54479 Psychiatry in modern life. New England J Med 1955, 253:1114-1116

See Moore, Ann Leslie

MOORE, ROBERT C. A.

See Littman, Richard A.

MOORE, ROBERT F.

See Semrad, Elvin V.

MOORE, WILLIAM T.

54480 Concern about a bee-sting in the analysis of an eleven-year-old boy. Bull Phila Ass Psa 1958, 8:9-15
Abs EFA Q 1959, 28:108. Saugy, de RFPsa 1959, 23:160

MOOS, RUDOLPH

54481 (& Mussen, P.) Sexual symbolism, personality integration, and intellectual functioning. J consult Psychol 1959, 23:521-523

MORA, GEORGE

54482 Concezione psicodinamica delle lesioni cerebrali croniche infantili. [Psychodynamic concept of brain-damaged children.] Minerva pediatrica 1954, 6:36-54

54483 Considérations sur les problèmes psychologiques de l'amygdalectomie chez les enfants. [Psychologic problems of tonsillectomy in children.] R Np inf 1955, 3:191-218

54484 Einige Aspekte der Übertragung bei der Behandlung skrupuloser Kranker. [On some aspects of transference in the treatment of scrupulous patients.] Anima 1956, 11:50-65

Notes sur quelques aspects du transfert dans le traitement des malades scrupuleux. Suppl Vie Spir 1956, (36):81-98

54485 L'enuresi come problema psichiatrico: eziopatogenesi e sintomatologia. [Enuresis as a psychiatric problem: pathogenesis and symptomatology.] Minerva pediatrica 1952, 4:322-342

54486 Le psicosi infantili: quadri clinici, concezione dinamica, tentativi terapeutici. [Childhood psychoses: clinical pictures, dynamic concepts, therapeutic attempts.] Minerva pediatrica 1955, 7:165-187

54487 The psychotherapeutic treatment of scrupulous patients. Cross Currents 1957, 7:29-40

54488 Recent American psychiatric developments (since 1939). Am Hbk Psychiat 1:18-57

54489 Valore dell'umanesimo in psichiatria. [Value of humanism in psychiatry.] Arch di psicologia, psichiatria e neurologia 1954, 17:485-502

MORAES PASSOS, A. C. DE

54490 Teorias da hipnóse. [Theories of hypnosis.] Rev Psicol norm patol 1957, 3:667-682

MORAGAS, JERONI DE

54491 Conséquences psychiques chez l'enfant repoussé. [Psychic sequelae in the rejected child.] Z Kinderpsychiat 1958, 25:49-52

MORALES, FRANCISCO PÉREZ

54492 Aspectos del análisis de una prostituta. [Aspects of the analysis of a prostitute.] Rev Psicoanál 1960, 17:66-81

54493 Un caso de neurosis de examen. [A case of examination neurosis.] Rev Psicoanál 1958, 15:278-292

MORALES BELDA, F. J.

TRANSLATION OF:
Binswanger, L. [42131]

MORAN, MARION LOUISE

54494 Some emotional responses of patients' husbands to the psychotherapeutic course as indicated in interviews with the psychiatric caseworker. Ops 1954, 24:317-325

MOREIRA, A.

54495 Sexo e moralidade. Experiência sociológica e conflito de psiquiatria. [Sex and morality. Sociologic experience and conflict with psychiatry.] Rev Psicol norm patol 1957, 3:581-588

MORENO, J. L.

54496 (& Fromm-Reichmann, F.; Alexander, F.; Grotjahn, M. et al) Comments on Moreno's "Transference, countertransference and tele." Group PT 1954, 7:307-333
54497 The current climate of social psychotherapy. Prog PT 1959, 4:1-31
54498 Die epochale Bedeutung der Gruppenpsychotherapie. [The epochal importance of group psychotherapy.] Z diag Psychol 1957, 5:139-150
54499 Freud's hundredth birthday. Group PT 1956, 9:251
54500 Fundamental rules and techniques of psychodrama. Prog PT 1958, 3:86-131
54501 Global psychotherapy and prospects of a therapeutic world order. Prog PT 1957, 2:1-31
54502 Group psychotherapy, psychodrama and the warming up process to the sexual act. Int J Sexol 1954, 8:12-15
54503 Interpersonal therapy, group psychotherapy and the function of the unconscious. Group PT 1954, 7:191-204
54504 (& Enneis, J. M.) Ipnodrama e psicodrama. [Hypnodrama and psychodrama.] In Zolla, E. *La Psicoanalisi*, Milan: Garzanti 1960, 108-114
54505 Philosophy of the third psychiatric revolution, with special emphasis on group psychotherapy and psychodrama. Prog PT 1956, 1:24-53
54506 (& Yablonsky, L.) Progress in psychodrama. Prog Clin Psych 1956, 2:216-222
54507 Psychodrama of a dream. Prog PT 1959, 4:193-211
54508 Psychodrama and sociatry. Pres-Day Psychol 679-686
54509 Psychotherapy, present and future. Prog PT 1956, 1:324-342
54510 The significance of the therapeutic format and the place of acting out in psychotherapy. Group PT 1955, 8:7-19
54511 Some comments to the trichotomy, tele-transference-empathy. Group PT 1952, 5:87-90
54512 Transference, countertransference and tele: their relation to group research and group psychotherapy. Group PT 1954, 7:107-117

See Fromm-Reichmann, Frieda; Masserman, Jules H.

MORERA, MARÍA ESTHER

54513 Algunos aspectos del análisis de un niño. [Some aspects of the analysis of a child.] Rev Psicoanál 1959, 16:242-257
54514 Fantasías hétero y homosexuales subyacentes a un síntoma histérico. [Hetero- and homosexual phantasies underlying a hysterical symptom.] Rev Psicoanál 1958, 15:36-40

REVIEWS OF:
54515 Brenner, C. The masochistic character. Rev Psicoanál 1959, 16:271
54516 Fisher, C. The effect of subliminal visual stimulation on images and dreams. Rev Psicoanál 1959, 16:189-190

54517   Isaacs, S. Fatherless children. Rev Psicoanál 1954, 11:410; 1958, 15:118
54518   Isaacs, S. Intellectual growth in young children. Rev Psicoanál 1958, 15:107-108
54519   Isaacs, S. The mental hygiene of the preschool child. Rev Psicoanál 1958, 15:116
54520   Isaacs, S. Property and possessiveness. Rev Psicoanál 1953, 10:524
54521   Isaacs, S. Recent advances in the psychology of young children. Rev Psicoanál 1958, 15:117-118
54522   Isaacs, S. Social development in young children. Rev Psicoanál 1958, 15:108
54523   Isaacs, S. A special mechanism in a schizoid boy. Rev Psicoanál 1953, 10:523-524
54524   Izner, S. M. Primal scene content in dreams. Rev Psicoanál 1959, 16:270-271
54525   Klein, G. S. Consciousness in psychoanalytic theory; some implications for current research in perception. Rev Psicoanál 1959, 16:189
54526   Kucera, O. On teething. Rev Psicoanál 1959, 16:271-272
54527   Piers, G. & Singer, M. B. Shame and Guilt. Rev Psicoanál 1953, 10:506-508
54528   Rochlin, G. The loss complex, a contribution to the etiology of depression. Rev Psicoanál 1959, 16:127-128
54529   Socarides, C. W. Meaning and content of a pedophiliac perversion. Rev Psicoanál 1959, 16:190
54530   Wolffheim, N. Psychoanalyse und Kindergarten. Rev Psicoanál 1953, 10:504-506; 1958, 15:145

MORF, ALBERT

See Gressot, Michel; Piaget, Jean

MORGAN

ABSTRACTS OF:
54531   Emch, M. The social context of supervision. Rev Psicoanál 1956, 13:193
54532   Lantos, B. On the motivation of human relations. Rev Psicoanál 1956, 13:192
54533   Szasz, T. Entropy, organization and the problem of the economy of human relations. Rev Psicoanál 1956, 13:192-193

MORGAN, CLIFFORD THOMAS

54534   (et al) Introduction to Psychology. NY, London: McGraw-Hill 1956, 676 p

MORGAN, DOUGLAS N.

54535   Psychology and art today: a summary and critique. J Aesthetics Art Crit 1950, 10:81-96. In Vivas, E. & Krieger, M. *The Problems of Aesthetics,* NY: Holt, Rinehart & Winston 1960, 30-47

MORGAN, EDITH E.

REVIEW OF:
54536   Muller, T. G. The Nature and Direction of Psychiatric Nursing. R 1954, 41:93-94

MORGAN, J. J. B.
See Watson, John B.

MORGAN, PATRICIA K.

54537 (& Gaier, E. L.) The direction of aggression in the mother-child punishment situation. Child Developm 1956, 27:447-457

54538 (& Gaier, E. L.) Types of reaction in punishment situations in the mother-child relationship. Child Developm 1957, 28:161-166

MORGAN, W.
See Kluckhohn, C.

MORGENSTERN, H. S.
See Shaskan, Donald A.

MORGENSTERN, SOPHIE

S-23620 Psychoanalyse Infantile.
Rv Pichon-Rivière, A. A. de. Rev Psicoanál 1958, 15:108-109

MORGENTHALER, FRITZ
See Parin, Paul

MORGENTHALER, WALTER

54539 (et al) Begegnungen von Schweizern mit Freud und seinem Werk. [Meetings of Swiss with Freud and his work.] Schweiz Z Psychol 1956, 15:103-151

54540 Deutung eines erfundenen Traumes. [Interpretation of a fabricated dream.] MPN 1953, 125:622-627

54541 Erinnerungen an Freud. [Reminiscences about Freud.] Schweiz Z Psychol 1956, 15:103-104

54542 Erinnerungen an Hermann Rorschach. Die Waldauzeit. [Recollections about Hermann Rorschach. At Waldau.] Schweiz Z Psychol 1958, Suppl 35, Rorschachiana VI:5-11

54543 Heinrich Meng zum 70. Geburtstag 9. Juli 1957. [Heinrich Meng on his 70th birthday July 9, 1957.] Schweiz Z Psychol 1957, 16:131-132

54544 Hermann Rorschach zum 70. Geburtstag. [The 70th anniversary of Hermann Rorschach's birthday.] Schweiz Z Psychol 1954, 13:315

54545 Der Kampf um das Erscheinen der Psychodiagnostik. Hermann Rorschach zum 70. Geburtstag (8. November 1954). Z diagn Psychol 1954, 2:255-262

The battle for the publication of the "Psychodiagnostics." For Hermann Rorschach's 70th birthday (November 8, 1954). (Tr: Bash, K. W.) Z diagn Psychol 1954, 2:355-362

La bataille pour la publication du Psychodiagnostic. Pour le 70e anniversaire de Hermann Rorschach (8 novembre 1954). (Tr: Mme Reymond-Rivier) Z diagn Psychol 1954, 2:263-270

La lotta intorna all'apparire della "Psicodiagnostica." Nel 70° anniversario della nascita di Ermanno Rorschach (8. XI. 1954). (Tr: Rizzo, C.) Z diagn Psychol 1954, 2:363-370

54546 Obituary: Dr. Henri Bersot. Schweiz Z Psychol 1955, 14:316-317

MORIN, JACQUES

54547 (& Ravaud, G.) Passion morbide, imagination et anomalies des conduites. [Morbid passion, imagination and anomalies of behavior.] Ann méd-psychol 1957, 1(5):837-864

See Lebovici, Serge

MORLAN, GEORGE K.

54548 A note on the frustration-aggression theories of Dollard and his associates. Psychol Rev 1949, 56:1-8. Under Hum Motiv 283-292

MOROCUTTI, C.

See Tolentino, Isidor; Vizioli

MOROZOV, V. M.

54549 [Depth psychology and psychiatry.] (Russian) Zh Nevropat Psikhiat 1958, 58(11):1399-1406

54550 [The philosophy of voluntarism and Freud's psychoanalysis.] (Russian) Zh Nevropat Psikhiat 1959, 59:609-620

MORRA, MAURO

REVIEWS OF:

54551 Jones, E. De la nature du génie. Riv Psa 1957, 3:224-225

54552 Lewinsky, H. The closed circle: an early image of sexual intercourse. Riv Psa 1957, 3:223-224

54553 Reding, Les états de dépendance en clinique psychanalytique. Riv Psa 1957, 3:226-228

54554 Payne, S. Notes sur quelques types de défense du moi qui ont leur origine dans les phases prégénitales du développement libidinal. Riv Psa 1957, 3:225-226

MORRICE, J. K. W.

54555 The psychiatric treatment of habitual criminals. Brit J Delinq 1959, 10:14-21

MORRIS, BEN

54556 Personality study: its aims and implications for students of education. Sociol Rev Monogr 1958, (1):75-86

MORRIS, DON P.

See Michael, Carmen Miller

MORRIS, GARY O.

See Weinstein, Edwin A.

MORRIS, HAROLD H., JR.

54557 (& Escoll, P. J.; Wexler, R.) Aggressive behavior disorders of childhood: a follow-up study. P 1956, 112:991-997
      Abs DRu Q 1959, 28:122

See Appel, Kenneth E.

MORRIS, P.

54558 The psychiatric social worker as a research interviewer. Brit J psychiat soc Wk 1959, 5:64-69

MORRIS, T.

See Sturgis, Somers H.

MORRISETT, LLOYD, JR.

See Maltzman, Irving

MORROW, TARLTON, JR.

54559 (& Loomis, E. A., Jr.) Symbiotic aspects of a seven-year-old psychotic. Emot Prob Early Child 337-361

See Loomis, Earl A., Jr.

MORROW, WILLIAM R.

See Adorno, T. W.; Holt, Robert R.

MORSE, NANCY CARTER

54560 (& Allport, F. H.) The causation of anti-semitism; an investigation of seven hypotheses. J Psychol 1952, 34:197-233

MORSE, PHILIP W.

54561 (& Gessay, L. H.; Karpe, R.) The effect of group psychotherapy in reducing resistance to individual psychotherapy: a case study. Int J grp PT 1955, 5:261-269
Abs GPK Q 1956, 25:623
54562 Psychotherapy with the non-reflective aggressive patient. Ops 1958, 28:352-361

MORSE, ROBERT T.

54563 The neuroses. *The Book of Health*. Elsevier Pr 1953
54564 (Cm & Ch Ed) A Psychiatric Glossary; the Meaning of Words Most Frequently Used in Psychiatry. Wash: Am Psychiat Ass 1957, 66 p
54565 A serious and little-recognized deficit in post-war psychiatric residency training. P 1958-59, 115:899-904

MORSE, WILLIAM C.

54566 (& Wineman, D.) Group interviewing in a camp for disturbed boys. J soc Issues 1957, 13(1):23-31
54567 (& Small, E. R.) Group life space interviewing in a therapeutic camp. Workshop 1957: The life space interview. Ops 1959, 29:27-44
54568 (& Wineman, D.) The therapeutic use of social isolation in a camp for ego-disturbed boys. J soc Issues 1957, 13(1):32-39

MORSELLI, G. E.

54569 Arte e schizofrenia nel pensiero di Karl Jaspers. [Art and schizophrenia according to the ideas of Karl Jaspers.] Arch Psicol Neur Psich 1954, 15:177-187

54570 Experience mescalinique et vécu schizophrénique. [Mescalinic experience and schizophrenic functioning.] Évolut Psychiat 1959
Rv Puget Rev Psicoanál 1960, 17:123-124

MORSIER, G. DE

54571 Jean Martin Charcot. In Kolle, K. *Grosse Nervenärzte*, Stuttgart: Thieme 1956, 1:39-55

MOSAK, HAROLD H.

54572 Early recollection as a projective technique. J proj Tech 1958, 22:302-311

54573 Language and the interpretation of "sexual" symbolism. J consult Psychol 1955, 19:108

MOSBACHER, ERIC

TRANSLATIONS OF:
Bonaparte, M. [3468, 4252]. (& Strachey, J.) Freud, S. [10393].
Richard, G. [57035]

MOSCHINI, G. A.

See Barison, F.

MOSER, ULRICH

54574 Die Bestimmung der psychosexuellen Triebproportion im Szondi-Test. [Determination of psychosexual drive proportions on the Szondi test.] Beih Schweiz Z Psychol 1954, (25):130-147

54575 Diskussion über die Heilwege in der Tiefenpsychologie. [Discussion and comparison of psychotherapeutic methods.] In Szondi, L. *Heilwege der Tiefenpsychologie*, Bern: Hans Huber 1956, 155-180

54576 Die experimentelle Triebdiagnostik (Szondi-Test). [Experimental Diagnostics of Drives.] In Stern, E. *Handbuch der klinischen Psychologie. Vol. I: Die Tests in der klinischen Psychologie, Part 1*, Zürich: Rascher Verlag 1954, 350-382

54577 Ichkrisen der Nachpubertät, Probleme der Berufs- und Partnerwahl. [Ego-crisis in adolescence, problems of choice in love and vocation.] Schweiz Z Psychol 1958, 17:81-97

54578 Psychologie der Arbeitswahl und der Arbeitsstörungen. [Psychology of occupational choice and maladjustment.] Bern: Hans Huber 1953, 183 p
Rv Salomon, F. RFPsa 1953, 17:568-570. Dale, M. J 1955, 36:412

54579 Psychologie der Partnerwahl. [Psychology of Partner Choice.] Stuttgart: Hans Huber 1957, 228 p

See Gressot, Michel; Szondi, Leopold

MOSES, LEON

54580 [Contribution to panel discussion on] Masochism: psychogenesis and therapeutic principles. Sci Psa 1959, 2:60-66

54581 (& Daniels, G. E.; Nickerson, J. L.) Psychogenic factors in essential hypertension. PSM 1956, 18:471
  Abs Fain RFPsa 1957, 21:621

See Rubin, Sidney

MOSES, PAUL J.

54582 The Voice of Neurosis. NY: Grune & Stratton 1954, 131 p
  Rv Glauber, I. P. Q 1955, 24:587-590. Rowley, J. L. J 1956, 37:498

MOSES, R.

See Rubenstein, R.

MOSHER, MARGARET M.

See Silverman, Jerome S.

MOSONYI, D.

54583 [Psychology of music by new methods.] (Hungarian) Budapest: 1934

MOSS, CLAUDE SCOTT

54584 Dream symbols and disguises. ETC 1957, 14:267-273
54585 A forced hypnoprojective fantasy used in the resolution of pseudo-epileptic seizures. J clin exp Hyp 1957, 5:59-66
54586 A quantitative semantic analysis of the dream in psychotherapy. Diss Abstr 1953, 13:1261

MOSS, H. A.

54587 (& Kagan, J.) Maternal influences on early IQ scores. Psychol Reports 1958, 4:656-661

MOSS, LEONARD M.

54588 (& Hamilton, D. M.) Psychotherapy of the suicidal patient. P 1956, 112:814-820. In Schneidman, E. S. & Farberow, N. L. Clues to Suicide, NY, London, Toronto: Blakiston Div, McGraw-Hill 1957, 99-110
  Abs DRu Q 1958, 27:617-618

MOSSA, G.

54589 (& Coda, G.) Psicopatologia della automutilazione. [The psycho-pathology of self-mutilation.] Rass Studi Psichiat 1955, 44:311-332

MOSSE, ERIC P.

54590 The Conquest of Loneliness. NY: Random House 1957, 241 p
54591 The handling of relatives in the psychoanalytic situation. R 1954, 41:258-262
  Abs JLan Q 1955, 24:614
54592 Nine psychiatric commandments. Med Rec 1947

S-23688 Psychological mechanisms in art production.
    Abs JAA An Surv Psa 1951, 2:152-153. MK An Surv Psa 1951,
    2:442-443
54593 Psychotherapy in action. Proc Rudolf Virchow Med Soc 1947, 6:117-
    124
54594 On psychotic episodes. Proc Rudolf Virchow Med Soc 1940, 9:75-81

MOSSE, HILDA L.

54595 The Duess Test. PT 1954, 8:251-264
    Abs Rev Psicoanál 1955, 12:145
54596 Is there an Ishmael complex? PT 1953, 7:72-79

MOTTO, ROCCO L.

54597 Emotional factors in physically handicapped children. California Med
    1956, 84:106-109

MOULTON, RUTH

54598 Dental and facial pain: a symposium. J Am Dent Ass 1955, 51:393-419
54599 (& Ewen, S.; Thiemann, W.) Emotional factors in periodontal disease.
    Oral Surg 1952, 5:833-860
    Abs Rahman, L. Q 1954, 23:309-310
54600 Oral and dental manifestations of anxiety. Ps 1955, 18:261-273
54601 Psychiatric considerations in maxillofacial pain. J Am Dent Ass 1955,
    51:408-414
54602 Psychological considerations in the treatment of occlusion. J Prosthetic
    Dentistry 1957, 7:148-157
54603 The role of stress in dentistry. NYJ Dentistry 1958, 28(3):93-96

MOUNIER, EMMANUAL

54604 The Character of Man (Tr: Rowland, C.) London: Rockliffe 1956,
    341 p
    Rv ESt J 1958, 39:441

MOURA, A.

54605 Psicanálise e psicoterapia; sobre a necessidade da validação objectiva
    dos resultados conseguidos com estes métodos de tratamento. [Psycho-
    analysis and psychotherapy; necessity for objective evaluation of the
    results obtained by these methods of treatment.] Jornal do Médico
    1954, 25(614):369-374

MOURAD, YOUSSEF

54606 [From introspection to psychoanalysis.] (Arabic) Egypt J Psychol
    1952, 7:301-310
54607 [New trends in the field of psychoanalysis.] (Arabic) Egypt J Ment
    Hlth 1958, 1(3):29-44
54608 [The psychoanalytical method and its integrative nature.] (Arabic)
    Egypt J Psychol 1952, 8:15-32
54609 [Sexuality biologically and integratively viewed.] (Arabic) Egypt
    Yearb Psychol 1954, 1:9-28

MOUSTAKAS, CLARK E.

54610 (& Schalock, H. D.) An analysis of therapist-child interaction in play therapy. Child Develpm 1955, 26:143-157

54611 True experience and the self. In author's *The Self. Explorations in Personal Growth*, NY: Harper 1956, 3-14

MOWRER, O. HOBART

54612 Changes in verbal behavior during psychotherapy. In author's *Psychotherapy; Theory and Research*, 463-545

54613 Changing concepts of the unconscious. JNMD 1959, 129:222-234

54614 Comments on Trude Weiss-Rosmarin's "Adler's psychology and the Jewish tradition." J indiv Psychol 1959, 15:128-129

54615 Ego psychology, cybernetics, and learning theory. In Kentucky Symposium, *Learning Theory, Personality Theory, and Clinical Research*, NY: Wiley 1954, 81-90

54616 Emerging conceptions of neurosis and normality. In Hsu, F. L. K. *Aspects of Culture and Personality*, NY: Abelard-Schuman 1954, 119-131

S-23716 (& Viek, P.) An experimental analogue of fear from a sense of helplessness. In McClelland, D. C. *Studies in Motivation*, NY: Appleton-Century-Crofts 1955, 190-199

54617 Hearing and speaking: an analysis of language learning. J Speech Dis 1958, 23:143-152

54618 (& Keehn, J. D.) How are intertrial "avoidance" responses reinforced? Psychol Rev 1958, 65:209-221

54619 Learning theory: historical review and reinterpretation. Harvard educ Rev 1954, 25:37-58

54620 Learning theory and identification. 1. Introduction. J genet Psychol 1954, 84:197-199

54621 Motivation and neurosis. In *Current Theory and Research in Motivation, A Symposium*, Lincoln, Neb: Univ Neb Pr 1953, 162-184

54622 Neo-analytic theory. J counsel Psychol 1956, 3:108-111

54623 Neurosis: a disorder of conditioning or problem solving. Ann NY Acad Sci 1953, 56:273-288. In Gorlow, L. & Katkovsky, W. *Readings in the Psychology of Adjustment*, NY: McGraw-Hill 1959, 293-311

54624 Neurosis and psychotherapy as interpersonal processes: a synopsis. In author's *Psychotherapy; Theory and Research*, 69-94

54625 Neurosis, psychotherapy, and two-factor learning theory. In author's *Psychotherapy; Theory and Research*, 140-149

54626 The psychologist looks at language. Am Psych 1954, 9:660-694

54627 (Ed) Psychotherapy; Theory and Research. NY Ronald Pr 1953, 700 p
    Abs J Am Psa Ass 1955, 3:162-163

54628 Some philosophical problems in mental disorder and its treatment. Harvard educ Rev 1953, 23:117-127

54629 Some philosophical problems in psychological counseling. J counsel Psychol 1957, 4:103-111

54630 Summary of "Family impact upon personality." In Hulett, J. E., Jr. & Stagner, R. *Problems in Social Psychology*, Champaign, Ill: Univ Ill Pr 1952, 61-66

54631 Symposium on relationships between religion and mental health: Discussion. Am Psych 1958, 13:577-579

54632 (& Light, B. H.; Luria, Z.; Zeleny, M. P.) Tension changes during psychotherapy, with special reference to resistance. In author's *Psychotherapy; Theory and Research*, 546-640

54633 The therapeutic process. III. Learning theory and the neurotic fallacy. Ops 1952, 22:679-689

54634 Two-factor learning theory reconsidered, with special reference to secondary reinforcement and the concept of habit. Psychol Rev 1956, 63:114-128

54635 The unconscious re-examined in a religious context. Read Psychol Relig 244-250

54636 What is normal behavior? In Pennington, L. A. & Berg, I. A. *An Introduction to Clinical Psychology*, NY: Ronald Pr 1948, 17-46. In Weider, A. *Contributions toward Medical Psychology, Vol. I*, NY: Ronald Pr 1953, 136-170. Intro Clin Psych 2, 58-88

54637 The whole human enterprise. In Beck, S. J. & Molish, H. B. *Reflexes to Intelligence*, Glencoe, Ill: Free Pr 1959, 557-566. From author's "Neurosis: a disorder of conditioning or problem solving."

See Dollard, John; Frank, Lawrence K.; Miller, Neal E.

MUCKLER, FREDERICK A.

See O'Kelly, Lawrence I.

MUDD, EMILY HARTSHORNE

54638 Knowns and unknowns in marriage counseling research. Marriage Fam Living 1957, 19:75-81

54639 (& Krich, A.) (Ed) Man and Wife. A Source Book of Family Attitudes, Sexual Behavior and Marriage Counseling. NY: Norton 1957, xxvi + 291 p
    Rv Sherman, M. H. PPR 1958, 45(1-2):146

54640 (& Goodwin, H. M.) Marriage counseling. Prog PT 1958, 3:171-175

54641 Marriage Counseling: A Case Book. NY: Association Pr 1958, 479 p

54642 Premarital counseling. In Liebman, S. *Understanding Your Patient*, Phila: Lippincott 1957, 109-130

54643 Psychiatry and marital problems. Proc 14 Japan Med Cong, Kyoto, Japan, April 1-5, 1955, 1:367-372. Eugenics Quart 1955, 2(2)

54644 Women's conflicting values in relation to marriage adjustment. In Fishbein, M. *Modern Marriage and Family Living*, Oxford Univ Pr 1957

See Appel, Kenneth E.; Bullock, Samuel C.; Mitchell, Howard E.; Preston, M. G.; Saul, Leon J.

MUELLER, ALFRED D.

54645 (& Lefkovits, A. M.) Personality structure and dynamics of patients with rheumatoid arthritis. Clin Psych 1956, 12:143-147

MUELLER, E. E.

54646 A psychiatric social worker's experience in group psychotherapy with discharged patients. PT 1954, 8:276-292

MUELLER, WILLIAM R.

54647 Psychoanalysis and poet: a note. NPAP 1957, 5(2):55-66

MUENSTERBERGER, WARNER

54648 On the biopsychical determinants of social life. In memoriam, Geza Róheim 1891-1953. Psa Soc S 1955, 4:7-25
54649 Editor of Róheim, G. *The Individual, the Group, and Mankind.*
54650 Über einige Beziehungen zwischen Individuum und Umwelt, unter besonderer Berücksichtigung der Pomo-Indianer. [On some special interrelationships between individual and milieu, with special reference to the Pomo Indians.] In Sociologus, Berlin, 1951, 1:127-137
54651 Über einige psychologische Fundamente der menschlichen Gesell-schaftsbildung. [Certain psychological fundamentals of the formation and growth of human society.] Psyche, Heidel 1953, 6:683-698
　　　Abs GD An Surv Psa 1953, 4:311-315
54652 Ethnologie und Ichforschung. [Anthropology and ego analysis.] In Federn, P. & Meng, H. *Die Psychohygiene,* Bern: Huber 1949, 145-153
54653 Foreword to Róheim, G. *Hungarian and Vogul Mythology*
54654 Observations on the collapse of leadership. Psa Soc S 1955, 4:158-165
S-23738 Orality and dependence: characteristics of Southern Chinese.
　　　Abs GD An Surv Psa 191, 2:499-500. NRo An Surv Psa 1951, 2:80
54655 Perversion, cultural norm and normality. In Lorand, S. *Perversions: Psychodynamics and Therapy,* NY: Random House 1956, 55-67
54656 (& Axelrad, S.) (Eds) The Psychoanalytic Study of Society, Vol. I. NY: IUP 1960, 384 p
S-23739 Roots of primitive art.
　　　Abs GD An Surv Psa 1951, 2:499-500. NRo An Surv Psa 1951, 2:80
54657 Sculpture of Primitive Man. NY: Harry N. Abrams 1955; London: Thames & Hudson 1955
　　　Amsterdam: Uitgeverij Contact 1955
　　　Paris: Flammarion 1955
　　　Munich: Wilh. Goldmann 1956
54658 The use of psychoanalytic concepts in anthropology. Int J grp PT 1951, 1:200-207
54659 Vincent van Gogh. NY: Beechhurst Pr 1947
　　　Holland: Krooner, Bussum 1947
　　　Paris: Noble 1947

REVIEWS OF:
54660 Bettelheim, B. Symbolic Wounds. Q 1955, 24:593-595
54661 Kroeber, A. L. et al: Culture: A Critical Review of Concepts and Definitions. Q 1954, 23:604
54662 Mead, M. & Calas, N. (Eds): Primitive Heritage. An Anthropological Anthology. Q 1954, 23:288-289

54663 Parsons, T. & Shils, E. A. (Eds): Toward a General Theory of Action. Q 1953, 22:120-122

54664 Potter, D. M. People of Plenty. Economic Abundance and the American Character. Q 1955, 24:456-457

MUENZINGER, KARL F.

See Bruner, Jerome S.

MUFTIC, M. K.

54665 The psychosomatic aspect of the etiology of chronic sinusitis. Brit J med Hypnot 1957, 8(3):2-8

See Atia, I. M.

MUHLEN, NORBERT

54666 Democracy and its discontents: Germany. Encounter 1954, 2(4):27-31

MUKERJEE, RADHAKAMAL

54667 The Dynamics of Morals. London: Macmillan 1952, 530 p
        Rv Rowley, T. L. J 1953, 34:338-339

54668 The Social Function of Art. NY: Philos Library 1954, xxii + 280 p

54669 The Symbolic Life of Man. Bombay: Hind Kitabs 1959, xii + 294 p

MUKHERJEE, M. B.

54670 Michael Madhusudan Dutt in the eyes of a psychoanalyst. Calcutta med J 1953, 50:229-232

MULLAHY, PATRICK

54671 Interpersonal psychiatry versus the philosophy of I-Thou and I-It. Ps 1956, 19:401-408

S-23799 A philosophy of personality.
        Abs R 1954, 41:86-87

54672 Some aspects of Sullivan's theory of interpersonal relations. In Gorlow, L. & Katkovsky, W. Readings in the Psychology of Adjustment, NY: McGraw-Hill 1959, 167-181. From author's Oedipus, Myths, and Complex 280-301

S-23780 (Ed) A Study of Interpersonal Relations: Contributions to Psychiatry. NY: Grove Pr 1957, 507 p
        Rv Zinkin, J. R 1953, 40:94-95

S-23784 Will, choice, and ends.
        Abs R 1953, 40:88

See Thompson, Clara

MULLAN, HUGH

54673 Conflict avoidance in group psychotherapy. Int J grp PT 1953, 3:243-253

54674 Counter-transference in groups. PT 1953, 7:680-688
        Abs Rev Psicoanál 1955, 12:143

54675 (& Sangiuliano, I. A.) The existential matrix of psychotherapy. PPR 1960, 47(4):87-99
54676 Fathers and children. ACAAP 1952 (pamphlet)
54677 The group analyst's creative function. PT 1955, 9:319-334
54678 The group patient as therapist. Psychiat Q 1957, 31:91-101
54679 The group psychotherapeutic experience. PT 1957, 11:830-838
54680 Group psychotherapy in private practice: practical considerations. J Hillside Hosp 1957, 6(1)
54681 (& Sangiuliano, I. A.) Interpretation as existence in analysis. PPR 1958, 45(1-2):52-64
54682 The nonteleological in dreams in group psychotherapy. J Hillside Hosp 1956, 5:480-487
54683 Status denial in group psychoanalysis. JNMD 1955, 122:345-352
54684 The training of group psychotherapists. PT 1958, 12:495-500
54685 Transference and countertransference. New horizons. Int J grp PT 1955, 5:169-180
       Abs Lebovici, S. RFPsa 1955, 19:634. GPK Q 1956, 25:454
54686 Trends in group psychotherapy in the United States. Int J soc Psychiat 1957, 3:224-230

       See Bowers, Margaretta K.; Wolf, Alexander

MULLER, A. D.

54687 Die antropologiese psigologie van Hans Trüb. Grondbeginsels van 'n nuwe psigoterapeutiese metode. [The anthropological psychology of Hans Trüb. The origins of a new psychotherapeutic method.] Amsterdam: Swets & Zeitlinger 1958, 123 p

MULLER, ARMAND

54688 L'art et la psychanalyse. [Art and psychoanalysis.] RFPsa 1953, 17:297-319
54689 Petite incursion dans la mythologie grecque. [Brief excursion into Greek mythology.] Acta psychother psychosom orthopaedag 1957, 5:74-87
S-23789 À propos du transfert.
       Abs NRo An Surv Psa 1952, 3:408-409

MÜLLER, CHRISTIAN

54690 Anstaltsfragen in der modernen Psychiatrie. [Mental hospital questions in modern psychiatry.] Prak Psychiat 1959, 38:182-187; 202-209
54691 Die Bewährung neurose-verdächtiger Anwärter in der Pilotenschule. [Follow-up studies of suspect neurotics among candidates for pilot's training.] Vjschr Schweiz San Offiziere 1953, 30:39-49
54692 Die Enuresis als Selektionsproblem in der Flugwaffe. [Problem of enuresis in selection of air force personnel.] Vjschr Schweiz San Offiziere 1954, 31:210-213
54693 Die Freudsche Auffassung der psychotherapeutischen Kommunikation und ihr Einfluss auf die Beziehung des Psychiaters zum Kranken. [The Freudian concept of psychotherapeutic communication and its

influence on the relationship between psychiatrist and patient.] Schweiz ANP 1957, 79:413-414

54694 (& Burner, M.; Villa, J. L.) Hystérie ou schizophrénie? Contribution au diagnostic différentiel. [Hysteria or schizophrenia? A contribution to differential diagnosis.] Enceph 1956, 45:256-266

54695 Zur Katamnese der Enuresis nocturna. [Catamnesis in enuresis nocturna.] Schweiz ANP 1955, 75:172-180

54696 Mikropsie und Makropsie; eine klinisch-psychopathologische Studie. [Micropsia and macropsia; a clinico-psychopathological study.] Bibl psychiat neur, Basel 1956, (98):1-60

54697 Paul Dubois. In Kolle, K. *Grosse Nervenärzte,* Stuttgart: Thieme 1959, 2:217-223

54698 Die Pioniere der psychoanalytischen Behandlung Schizophrener. [Pioneers of the psychoanalytical treatment of schizophrenics.] Nervenarzt 1958, 29:456-462

54699 Über Psychotherapie bei einem chronischen Schizophrenen. [Psychotherapy in a chronic schizophrenic patient.] Psyche, Heidel 1955, 9:350-369

54700 Psychotherapie der Psychosen. [Psychotherapy of the psychoses.] In Stern, E. *Handbuch der klinischen Psychologie. Vol. II: Die Psychotherapie in der Gegenwart,* Zurich: Rascher Verlag 1958, 350-367

54701 Rorschachbefunde bei Zwangsneurotikern. [Rorschach findings in obsessional neurosis.] Schweiz ANP 1953, 72:226-231

54702 Schizophrénie et psychothérapie. [Schizophrenia and psychotherapy.] Rev med Suisse rom 1955, 85:752-759

54703 Symposium international sur la psychothérapie de la schizophrénie. [International symposium on psychotherapy of schizophrenia.] Basel: Karger-Verlag 1957, 264 p

54704 Les thérapeutiques analytiques des psychoses. [Analytic therapeutics in psychoses.] RFPsa 1958, 22:575-647
Abs RFPsa 1958, 22:4-5. J 1959, 40:250. Stewart, S. Q 1960, 29:145

54705 Der Übergang von Zwangsneurose in Schizophrenie im Lichte der Katamnese. [The transition from obsessional neurosis to schizophrenia as revealed in catamnestic studies.] Schweiz ANP 1953, 72:218-225

See Benedetti, Gaetano

MÜLLER, M.

54706 Besuch bei Freud. [A visit with Freud.] Schweiz Z Psychol 1956, 15:147-148

MÜLLER, R.

54707 Zur Differentialdiagnose regressiver Reaktionen bei Schulkindern. [Differential diagnosis of regressive reactions in school children.] Prax Kinderpsychol 1959, 8:277-280

MULLER, THERESA GRACE

54708 The Nature and Direction of Psychiatric Nursing: The Dynamics of Human Relationships in Nursing. Phila: Lippincott 1950, 379 p
Rv Morgan, E. E. R 1954, 41:93-94

MÜLLER-BEK, H.

54709 Das Berufsmilieu des Volksschullehrers. [The occupational environment of public school teachers.] Psyche, Heidel 1958, 12:50-62

MÜLLER-BRAUNSCHWEIG, CARL

54710 Die erste Objektsbesetzung des Mädchens in ihrer Bedeutung für Penisneid und Weiblichkeit. [The girl's first object cathexis in relation to penis envy and femininity.] Psyche, Heidel 1959, 13:1-24

54711 Zur menschlichen Grundhaltung, Psychologie und Technik der psychoanalytischen Therapie. [Basic human attitudes, psychology, and technique of psychoanalytic therapy.] Psychol Beitr 1955, 2:56-69
        Abs Aufreiter, J. J 1956, 37:512

54712 Zur Methodik und Technik in der Praxis der Psychoanalyse. [Contribution to the method and technique of psychoanalytic practice.] Psyche, Heidel 1954, 7:676-688

54713 Obituary: Margarete Steinbach. J 1955, 36:73

MÜLLER-ECKHARD, HANS

54714 Analyse eines jugendlichen Voyeurs. [Analysis of an adolescent voyeur.] Prax Kinderpsychol 1955, 4:285-289

54715 Conjunctivitis als Angst-Abwehrsymptom. Beitrag zur Psychologie der Weltbewältigung. [Conjunctivitis as defense symptom against anxiety. Contribution to the psychology of conquering the world.] Acta psychother psychosom orthopaedag 1958, 6:29-42

54716 [The Disease of Not Being Able to be Ill.] (German) Stuttgart: Klett 1954

54717 Zur Phäno-analyse des Zwangs. [Contribution to the pheno-analysis of the obsessive-compulsive neurosis.] Psyche, Heidel 1954, 8:143-160

54718 Teufelshalluzinationen eines Elfjährigen im Beichtstuhl. [Hallucinations of the devil by an 11-year-old boy in confession.] Prax Kinderpsychol 1954, 3:208-211

54719 Das unverstandene Kind. [The misunderstood child.] Stuttgart: Ernst Klett 1953, 269 p

MÜLLER-ERZBACH, I.

54720 Märchenmotive im Stupor—Stupormotive im Märchen. [Fairy tale motives in stupor and stupor motives in fairy tales.] MPN 1953, 126:403-408

MÜLLER-HEGEMANN, D.

54721 Neue Wege der psychiatrisch-neurologischen Forschung auf Grund der Arbeiten der Pawlowschen Schule. [New directions of neuropsychiatric research on the basis of the work by the Pavlov School.] Psychiat Neurol med Psychol, Leipzig 1955, 7:193-203

MUMFORD, LEWIS

54722 The rise of Caliban. Virginia Q Rev 1954, 30:321-341

MUMFORD, ROBERT S.

54723 [Contribution to panel discussion on] Masochism: psychogenesis and therapeutic principles. Sci Psa 1959, 2:62-63

54724 Discussion of Spiegel, H. "Hypnosis and transference: a theoretical formulation." Sci Psa 1960, 3:242-243

MUNCIE, WENDELL

54725 A principle of Meyerian psychobiologic treatment as illustrated by a crucial episode in the treatment of a severe phobic neurotic. Ann Psychother, Monogr 1959, (1):44-50

54726 The private practice of psychiatry and the community. Prog PT 1959, 4:85-91

MUNDEN, KENNETH J.

54727 A contribution to the psychological understanding of the origin of the cowboy and his myth. Am Im 1958, 15:103-148

MUNHOZ DA ROCHA, G.

54728 O testemunho de um professor. [A professor's testimony.] Rev Psicol norm patol 1955, 1:147-159

MUNIZ, RAMON DE LA FUENTE

See FUENTE-MUNIZ, RAMON DE LA

MUNRO, CLARE

See Kepecs, Joseph G.

MUNRO, LOIS

S-23941A Clinical notes on internalization and identification.
Abs JFr An Surv Psa 1952, 3:108-110. RRG Q 1953, 22:600

54729 Steps in ego-integration observed in a play-analysis. (Read at 18th Int Psa Cong, London, July 1953) J 1954, 35:202-205. New Dir Psa 109-139
Abs Auth J 1954, 35:287-288. Lebovici, S. RFPsa 1954, 18:469. NRo An Surv Psa 1954, 5:290-292. Lamana, I. L. Rev Psicoanál 1958, 15:140. Resta Riv Psa 1958, 4:67

MUNRO, THOMAS

54730 Suggestion and symbolism in the arts. J Aesthet 1956, 15:152-180

MUNROE, RUTH LEARNED

54731 Intellectualizing techniques in psychotherapy. Case St Couns PT 382-404

54732 Other psychoanalytic approaches (Adler, Jung, Rank). Am Hbk Psychiat 2:1453-1465

54733 Schools of Psychoanalytic Thought; An Exposition, Critique, and Attempt at Integration. NY: Dryden Pr 1955, xvi + 670 p
Abs J Am Psa Ass 1956, 4:188-189. Rv MBr J 1957, 38:123-125

See Levy, John

MUNSTERBERG, ELIZABETH

54734 (& Mussen, P. H.) The personality structures of art students. J Pers 1953, 21:457-466

MUNZER, JEAN

54735 (& Greenwald, H.) Interaction process analysis of a therapy group. Int J grp PT 1957, 7:175-190

MURAKAMI, MASASHI

See Ogino, Koichi

MURAKAMI, TOSHIO

54736 A case report of psychoanalysis in adult enuresis. Psychiat et Neurol Jap 1955, 59(11):578

54737 Studies on psychotherapy of hysteria. Psychiat et Neurol Jap 1953, 55(4):567

MURAMATSU, T.

54738 Koichi Miyake 1876-1954. Folio psychiat neur jap 1955, 9:1-2

MURATORI, ANNA MARIA

See Bartoleschi, B.

MURAWSKI, BENJAMIN J.

See Fox, Henry M.; Hill, S. R.

MURPHY, GARDNER

54739 Affect and perceptual learning. Psychol Rev 1956, 63:1-15

54740 Creativeness. Menn Q 1957, 11(2):1-6

54741 The current impact of Freud upon psychology. Am Psych 1956, 11:663-672. Freud 20th Cent 102-122

54742 Discussion. In Feifel, H. *The Meaning of Death*, NY, Toronto, London: McGraw-Hill 1959, 317-340

54743 Discussion of Whiting, J. W. M. "Totem and taboo—a re-evaluation." Sci Psa 1960, 3:177-178

54744 The Dreamer. Drms Pers Dyn 3-29

54745 The hospital as a therapeutic community. Planning for the future. Neuropsychiatry 1956, 4:10-26

54746 Human Potentialities. NY: Basic Books 1958, 340 p
Rv GPK Q 1959, 28:537-539. Bradley, N. J 1960, 41:642-643

54747 Introduction. In author's *An Outline of Abnormal Psychology*, xi-xxxiii

54748 (& Solley, C. M.) Learning to perceive as we wish to perceive. BMC 1957, 21:225-237

54749 In the Minds of Men: The Study of Human Behavior and Social Tensions in India. Based on UNESCO studies by social scientists conducted at the request of the Government of India. NY: Basic Books 1953, 366 p
Rv Eisenbud, J. Q 1954, 23:284-285. Sanai, M. J 1954, 35:367-368

54750 New knowledge about family dynamics. Menn Q 1959, 13(3):12-18

54751   (& Bachrach, A. J.) (Eds) An Outline of Abnormal Psychology. Rev
        ed. NY: Modern Library 1954, xxxiii + 597 p
54752   The patient's psychological resources in fighting diseases. Neuropsy-
        chiatry 1952-53, 2:121-140
54753   (& Wallerstein, R.) Perspectives of the Research Department of the
        Menninger Foundation. BMC 1954, 18:223-231
54754   Plans for research. In *Proceedings of Four Conferences of Parapsycho-
        logical Studies,* NY: Parapsychology Foundation 1957, 95-96
54755   Psychoanalysis as a unified theory of behavior. (Read at Acad of Psa,
        NY, Dec 1958) Sci Psa 1960, 3:140-149
54756   Psychoanalysis as a unified theory of human behavior. Ps 1960, 23:341-
        346
54757   Research at the Menninger Foundation. The situation today and pros-
        pects for the future. Menn Q 1953, 7(1-2):16-19
54758   Social motivation. In Lindzey, G. *Handbook of Social Psychology,* Cam-
        bridge, Mass: Addison-Wesley 1954, 2:601-633
54759   Social Psychology. Am Hbk Psychiat 2:1733-1742
54760   Some needed research in personality structure. In Overholser, W.
        Centennial Papers. Saint Elizabeths Hospital, 1855-1955, Wash: Cen-
        tennial Commission, Saint Elizabeths Hospital 1956, 177-192
54761   Toward a dynamic trace-theory. BMC 1956, 20:124-134
            Abs Weiss, J. Q 1958, 27:291-292
54762   What constitutes a well-integrated personality? Menn Q 1956, 10(1):
        1-9

MURPHY, H. B. M.

54763   (Ed) Flight and Resettlement. Paris: UNESCO; NY: Columbia Univ
        Pr 1955, 231 p

MURPHY, JOHN J.

See Davis, William S.; Hulse, Wilfred C.

MURPHY, JOHN V.

See Mirsky, I. Arthur

MURPHY, LOIS BARCLAY

54764   (et al) Personality in Young Children. Vol. I. Methods for the Study of
        Personality in Young Children. Vol. II. Colin—A Normal Child. NY:
        Basic Books 1956, xx + 424 p; xii + 267 p
            Abs J Am Psa Ass 1958, 6:178. Rv Anthony, J. J 1959, 40:348-349.
        Bernstein, I. Q 1960, 29:271-272
54765   Psychoanalysis and child development. BMC 1957, 21:177-188; 248-
        258
            Abs Koenig RFPsa 1958, 22:127. Weiss, J. Q 1959, 28:109

MURPHY, ROBERT C., JR.

54766   The defense mechanisms of a six-year-old. Ops 1954, 24:185-199.
        Case St Chd Dis 1956, 2:43-57
54767   Man without a conscience. Northwest Med 1953, 52:27-28. Child-Fam
        Dig 1954, 10(6):4-8

MURPHY, WILLIAM F.

54768 Character, trauma, and sensory perception. J 1958, 39:555-568
    Abs HW Q 1960, 29:131

54769 A comparison of psychoanalysis with the dynamic psychotherapies.
JNMD 1958, 126:441-450

54770 [Contributor to] Discussion. Psm Cpt Psa 168-174

54771 Ego integration, trauma, and insight. Q 1959, 28:514-532

54772 [Discussant] Is the term "mysterious leap" warranted? Mind-Body 20-23

54773 A note on the significance of names. (Read at Boston Psa Soc, Oct 26,
1955) Q 1957, 26:91-106
    Abs Dreyfus RFPsa 1958, 22:128

54774 Psychosomatic disorders in the service. USAF med J 1953, 4:1003-1010

54775 Some clinical aspects of the body ego. (With some especial reference
to phantom limb phenomena.) R 1957, 44:462-477

54776 (& Chasen, M.) Spasmodic torticollis: a case presentation and discussion. R 1956, 43:18-30
    Abs JLan Q 1957, 26:435

See Deutsch, Felix

ABSTRACTS OF:

54777 Desmonde, W. H. Psychoanalysis and legal origins. Q 1954, 23:610-611

54778 Garma, A. The internalized mother as harmful food in peptic ulcer
patients. Q 1954, 23:612-613

54779 Scott, W. C. M. Patients who sleep or look at the psychoanalyst during
treatment—technical considerations. Q 1954, 23:146-147

REVIEWS OF:

54780 Berglund, H. J. & Nichols, H. L., Jr. It's Not All In Your Mind. Q 1954,
23:459-460

54781 Cranston, R. The Miracle of Lourdes. Q 1956, 25:602-607

54782 Firth, R. The Fate of the Soul. Q 1956, 25:602-607

54783 Frankel, V. E. The Doctor and the Soul: An Introduction to Logotherapy. Q 1956, 25:602-607

54784 Frosch, J. (Ed): The Annual Survey of Psychoanalysis, Vol. 2, 1951.
Q 1955, 24:440-441

54785 Goldbrunner, J. Holiness Is Wholeness. Q 1956, 25:602-607

54786 Helweg, H. Soul Sorrow. Q 1956, 25:602-607

54787 Kardiner, A. Sex and Morality. Q 1955, 24:581-584

54788 Menninger, K. A. A Psychiatrist's World. Q 1960, 29:113-116

54789 Sullivan, H. S. The Interpersonal Theory of Psychiatry. Q 1954, 23:
446-450

54790 Thompson, C. et al (Eds): An Outline of Psychoanalysis. Q 1956,
25:266-270

54791 Vander Veldt, J. H. & Odenwald, R. P. Psychiatry and Catholicism.
Q 1953, 22:580-586

MURRAY, EDWARD J.

54792 A case study in a behavioral analysis of psychotherapy. ASP 1954,
49:305-310

54793 Conflict and repression during sleep deprivation. ASP 1959, 59:95-101

54794 A content-analysis method for studying psychotherapy. Psychol Monogr 1956, 70(13), (No. 420), 32 p
54795 (& Miller, N. E.) Displacement and conflict: learnable drive as a basis for the steeper gradient of avoidance than of approach. J exper Psychol 1952, 43:227-231
54796 (& Berkun, M. M.) Displacement as a function of conflict. ASP 1955, 51:47-56
54797 (& Miller, N. E.) Displacement: steeper gradient of generalization of avoidance than of approach with age of habit controlled. J exper Psychol 1952, 43:222-226
54798 (& Cohen, M.) Mental illness, milieu therapy and social organization in ward groups. ASP 1959, 58:48-54

See Auld, Frank, Jr.; Miller, Neal E.

MURRAY, HENRY A.

54799 American Icarus. Clin Stud Pers 615-641
54800 Notes on the Icarus syndrome. Folia Psychiat Neerl 1958, 61:140-144
54801 (& Kluckhohn, C.) Outline of a conception of personality. Pers n s c 3-49
54802 Toward a classification of interactions. In Parsons, T. & Shils, E. A. *Toward a General Theory of Action,* Cambridge: Harvard Univ Pr 1952, 434-464
54803 Types of human needs. In author's *Explorations in Personality.* Oxford Univ Pr 1938, 80-85; 109-115. In McClelland, D. C. *Studies in Motivation,* NY: Appleton-Century-Crofts 1955, 63-70

See Kluckhohn, Clyde

MURRIN, F. H.

See Masserman, Jules H.

MURSTEIN, BERNARD I.

54804 The projection of hostility on the Rorschach and as a result of ego threat. J proj Tech 1956, 20:418-428
54805 Studies in projection: a critique. J proj Tech 1957, 21:129-136

See Wheeler, John I., Jr.

MUSAPH, H.

54806 (& Molhuysen-van der Walle, S. M.; Barendregt, J. T.) Bullosis psychogenica and epidermolysis bullosa. PSM 1957, 19:30
54807 (& Molhuysen-van der Walle, S. M.; Barendregt, J. T.) Een geval van bullosis psychogenica. [A case of psychogenic bullosis.] Ned Tijdschr Geneesk 1954, 98:497-504
54808 Over huwelijksvoorlichting. [On pre-marriage guidance.] Maandbl geest Volksgezondh 1956, 11:367
54809 (& Prakken, J. R.) Pruritis anogenitalis. Ned Tijdschr Geneesk 1953, 97:290

54810 Psychiatrisch onderzoek van patienten met chronische urticaria. [Psychiatric research on patients suffering from urticaria chronica.] Ned Tijdschr Geneesk 1956, 100:3169

54811 Psychologische achtergronden van sexuele moelijkheden bij volwassenen. [Psychological backgrounds of sexual difficulties in adults.] Maandbl geest Volksgezondh 1954, 9:271-281

54812 (& Prakken, J. R.) Psychosomatische beschouwingen over het constitutionele eczeem. [Psychosomatic observations on atopic dermatitis.] In Kroese, S. *Psyche en Allergische Ziekten,* Leiden, Holland 1953, 120-140

54813 Sigmund Freud herdenking. [Sigmund Freud in commemoration.] Tijdschr Maatschappelijk Werk 1956, 10:162

54814 De toekomst der sexuele hervorming. [The future of sexual reform.] Inzichten 1957, 1(2):45

54815 De wenselijkheid van social casework aan een consultatiebureau voor geslachtskunde. [On the desirability of social casework in a clinic for sexual disorders.] Maandbl geest Volksgezondh 1959, 14(3):89

MUSATTI, CESARE LUIGI

54816 A cento anni dalla nascita di Freud. [A hundred years after the birth of Freud.] Riv Psa 1956, 2:223-255

54817 Una fantasia isterica alla base di una vicenda giudiziaria. [A hysterical fantasy causing a judicial mix-up.] Riv Psa 1957, 3:47-58

54818 I fondamenti della psicoanalisi nella critica di F. V. Bassin. [The bases of psychoanalysis in the critic of F. V. Bassin.] Riv Psa 1959, 5:125-141

54819 Freud, Breuer e Janet. [Freud, Breuer and Janet.] Riv Psa 1956, 2:149-152

54820 Freud e le origine della psicoanalisi. [Freud and the origins of psychoanalysis.] Riv Psa 1956, 2:223-234

54821 L'opera di Freud e la situazione attuale della psicologia. [The work of Freud and the current state of psychology.] Riv Psa 1956, 2:234-245

54822 Per una classificazione psicologica delle condotte criminose contro la vita e la integrità personale ai fini di un'opera sociale di prevenzione. [A psychologic classification, particularly in regard to preventive social work, of criminal behavior against life and personal integrity.] Riv Psa 1956, 2:17-23

54823 Problemi tecnico-psicologici della democrazia. [Technical-psychological problems of democracy.] Riv Psa 1958, 4:139-149

54824 Psicoanalisi e Vita Contemporanea. [Psychoanalysis and contemporary life.] Torino: Boringhieri 1960, 375 p

54825 La psicoanalisi nella cultura moderna. [Psychoanalysis in contemporary culture.] Riv Psa 1956, 2:245-255

54826 Psicologia clinica e clinica psicologica. [Clinical psychology and psychological clinic.] Arch Psicol Neurol Psichiat 1953, 14:140-153

54827 Psicoterapia analitica delle schizofrenie e tecnica della realizzazione simbolica. A proposito del "Diario di una schizofrenica" di M. A. Sechehaye. [Analytic psychotherapy of schizophrenia and technique of symbolic realization. Comments on "Diary of a schizophrenic" by M. A. Sechehaye.] Riv Psa 1957, 3:87-106

54828 La suggestione. [Suggestion.] Riv Psa 1955, 1(3):23-36
S-24019 Trattato di Psicoanalisi.
       Rv Abadi, M. Rev Psicoanál 1957, 14:417-418

TRANSLATION OF:
Freud, S. [10647, 10648]

MUSHATT, CECIL

54829 [Discussant] Is the term "mysterious leap" warranted? Mind-Body 24
54830 Loss of sensory perception determining choice of symptom. Mind-Body
       201-234
54831 Psychological aspects of non-specific ulcerative colitis. In Wittkower,
       E. D. & Cleghorn, R. A. *Recent Developments in Psychosomatic Medi-
       cine,* Phila: Lippincott 1954, 345-363

MUSSEN, PAUL HENRY

54832 (& Conger, J. J.) Child Development and Personality. NY: Harper
       1956, xii + 569 p
54833 (& Scodel, A.) The effects of sexual stimulation under varying condi-
       tions on TAT sexual responsiveness. J consult Psychol 1955, 19:90
54834 (& Kagan, J.) Group conformity and perceptions of parents. Child
       Developm 1958, 29:57-60
54835 (& Distler, L.) Masculinity, identification, and father-son relationships.
       ASP 1959, 59:350-356

See Moos, Rudolph; Munsterberg, Elizabeth; Payne, Donald E.; Sewell,
W. H.

MUSTA, WALTER

54836 A technical problem of acting out. Bull Phila Ass Psa 1956, 6:110-118

MUTTER, ARTHUR Z.

See Silverman, Samuel

MUUSS, ROLF E.

54837 Existentialism and psychology. Educ Theory 1956, 6:135-153

M'UZAN, MICHEL DE

54838 Discussant of Bouvet, M. de: "Dépersonnalisation et relations d'objet."
       RFPsa 1960, 24:630-634
54839 Discussant of Perrotti, N. & Bouvet, M. de: "On depersonalization."
       RFPsa 1960, 24:659-660
54840 (& Bonfils, S.; Lambling, A.) Étude psychosomatique de 18 cas de
       recto-colite hémorragique. [A psychosomatic study of 18 cases of
       hemorrhagic rectocolitis.] Sem Hop Paris 1958, 34:922-928
54841 Quelques remarques sur les écrits de M. Bouvet. [Some remarks on
       M. Bouvet's writings.] RFPsa 1960, 24:719-720
54842 (& David, C.) Préliminaires critiques à la recherche psychosomatique.
       [Preliminary critique of psychosomatic research.] RFPsa 1960, 24:19-39

See Ajuriaguerra, Julien de; Bonfils, S.

ABSTRACTS OF:

54843 Thaler, M. et al: Exploration of the doctor-patient relationship through projective techniques. RFPsa 1958, 22:390

54844 Weiner, H. et al: Etiology of the duodenal ulcer. RFPsa 1958, 22:745

REVIEWS OF:

54845 Meyer, B. C. Rectal resection: psychiatric and medical management of its sequelae. RFPsa 1958, 22:389-390

54846 Nacht, S. (Ed) Psychanalyse d'aujourd'hui. RFPsa 1957, 21:465-468

54847 Pierlott, R. Problèmes généraux de psycho-somatique clinique. RFPsa 1958, 22:121

MYDEN, WALTER D.

54848 An interpretation and evaluation of certain personality characteristics involved in creative production: an investigation and evaluation of personality structure and characteristics of creative individuals in the context of psychoanalytic theory and ego psychology. Diss Abstr 1957, 17:897-898

MYERS, BARBARA

See Wittenborn, John Richard

MYERS, CHAUNCIE KILMER

54849 Light the Dark Streets. Greenwich, Conn: Seabury Pr 1957, 156 p

MYERS, J. MARTIN, JR.

54850 The role of the administrative psychiatrist in intensive psychotherapy in a mental hospital. P 1956, 113:71-74

See Appel, Kenneth E.

MYERS, JEROME KEELEY

54851 (& Roberts, B. H.) Family and Class Dynamics in Mental Illness. NY: John Wiley & Sons 1959, 295 p
Rv GPK Q 1960, 29:267-270

See Redlich, Fredrick C.; Robinson, H. A.; Schaffer, Leslie

MYERSON, DAVID J.

54852 Clinical observations on a group of alcoholic prisoners with special reference to women. Quart J Stud Alcohol 1959, 20:555-572

ABSTRACT OF:

54853 Silverman, S. Ego function and body language. Bull Phila Ass Psa 1960, 10:102-103

MYERSON, PAUL G.

54854 Awareness and stress: post-psycho-analytic utilization of insight. J 1960, 41:147-156
Abs Weisman, A. D. Bull Phila Ass Psa 1959, 9:35

N

NACHT, SACHA

54855 De la agresividad como fuente de las contradicciones humanas. [About aggressivity as a source of human contradictions.] Arch Med Mex 1956, A-XIV, n 1938; Vida Universitaria, Univ de Nuevo Léon, Monterrey NL, Mexico # 285, Sept 5, 1956

54856 Allocution. [Remarks on Freud at the Salpêtrière.] In *1856-1956: Centenaire de la Naissance de Sigmund Freud*, Paris: PUF 1957, 18-21

54857 Allocution. [Address (in honor of Maurice Bouvet.)] RFPsa 1960, 24:675-676

54858 Allocution prononcée à l'occasion de l'inauguration de l'institut de psychanalyse. [Address for the opening of the Institute of Psycho-analysis, Paris.] RFPsa 1954, 19:166-170

54859 Avant-propos. [Foreword.] In *1856-1956: Centenaire de la Naissance de Sigmund Freud*, Paris: PUF 1957, 1-6

54860 Causes et mécanismes des déformations névrotiques du moi. (Read at 20th Int Psa Cong, Paris 1957) RFPsa 1958, 22:197-203
   Causes and mechanisms of ego-distortion. J 1958, 29:271-274
   Abs JLan Q 1959, 28:284

54861 Ce que le malade attend du médecin. [What the patient expects from the physician.] RFPsa 1959, 23:479-486

54862 Colloque sur l'utilisation du matériel onirique en thérapeutique psy-chanalytique chez l'adulte. [Discussion of the use of dream material in psychoanalytic treatment of adults.] RFPsa 1959, 23:49-52

54863 (& Lebovici, S.; Shentoub, S. A.; Held, R.; Bouvet, M.) Comment terminer le traitement psychanalytique? [How terminate psychoanalytic treatment?] RFPsa 1955, 19:509-568. Bull Ass Psa Belg 1955, 23

54864 Contribution à la discussion du symposium sur les variantes techniques. 20e Cong intern de Psychanalyse 1958, 22:191-195
   Variations in technique. (Read at 20th Int Psa Cong, Paris 1957) J 1958, 29:235-237
   Abs JLan Q 1959, 28:282

54865 (& Bouvet, M.; Bénassy, M.; Lechat, F.) Les critères de la fin du traitement psychanalytique. [Criteria for terminating psychoanalytic treatment.] RFPsa 1954, 18:328-365
   Abs NRo An Surv Psa 1954, 5:331-335

54866 Difficulté de la psychanalyse didactique par rapport à la psychanalyse thérapeutique. (Read at 18th Int Psa Cong, London, July 1953) RFPsa 1953, 17:320-327

The difficulties of didactic psychoanalysis in relation to therapeutic psychoanalysis. J 1954, 35:250-253

Abs Auth J 1954, 35:288. JFr An Surv Psa 1953, 4:462-463. JLan An Surv Psa 1953, 4:455. JFr An Surv Psa 1954, 5:409-410. JLan Q 1955, 24:608. Marasse, H. F. Q 1956, 25:296

54867 Discussion of Bénassy, M. "Théorie des instincts." RFPsa 1953, 17:99-102; 109-110

54868 Discussion of Berge, A. "L'équation personnelle ou de l'art psychanalytique." RFPsa 1959, 23:467-468

54869 Discussion of Bouvet, M. "Le moi dans la névrose obsessionnelle." RFPsa 1953, 17:206

54870 Discussion of Grunberger, B. "Essai sur la situation analytique et le processus de guérison." RFPsa 1957, 21:437-440

54871 Discussion of Grunberger, B. "Interprétation prégénitale." RFPsa 1953, 17:452-457

54872 Discussion of Lebovici, S. & Diatkine, R. "L'étude des fantasmes chez l'enfant." RFPsa 1954, 18:155-156

54873 Discussion of Lechat, F. "Du principe de sécurité." RFPsa 1955, 19:102-104

54874 Discussion of Luquet, P. "À propos des facteurs de guérison non verbalisables de la cure analytique." RFPsa 1957, 21:210-211

54875 Discussion of Marty, P. "Importance du rôle de la motricité dans la relation d'objet." RFPsa 1955, 19:286-289

54876 Discussion of Pasche, F. "L'angoisse et la théorie freudienne des instincts." RFPsa 1954, 18:104-105

54877 Discussion of Pasche, F. "Le génie de Freud." RFPsa 1957, 21:364-365

54878 Discussion of Renard, M. "La conception freudienne de névrose narcissique." RFPsa 1955, 19:432

54879 Discussion of Schlumberger, M. "Introduction à l'étude du transfert en clinique psychanalytique." RFPsa 1952, 16:163-166

54880 (& Lebovici, S.; Diatkine, R.) L'enseignement de la psychanalyse. [The teaching of psychoanalysis.] RFPsa 1960, 24:225-240

S-24101 Essai sur la peur.

Abs JAA An Surv Psa 1952, 3:83-85

54881 (& Racamier, P. C.) Les états dépressifs: étude psychanalytique. [A psychoanalytic study of depressive states.] RFPsa 1959, 23:567-605

Abs Puget Rev Psicoanál 1960, 17:267-268

54882 La France a-t-elle fait une maladie de jeunesse ou de vieillesse? [Has France made an illness of youth or of old age?] Réalités, Femina-Illustration Paris 1958, (155):74-75, 149

54883 The French as seen by themselves and as others see them. Réalités, NY 1959, (100):34-36

54884 Homosexualité. Étude psychanalytique. [Homosexuality. A psychoanalytic survey.] Encycl Medico-Chirur, Psychiatrie 1955, 37-105, I-20

54885 De l'importance du masochisme primaire organique comme condition traumatisante pré-Oedipienne. Intervention à propos de "Le rôle des conflits préoedipiens" par E. Servadio. [Importance of primary organic masochism as a preoedipal traumatising condition. Discussion of "The role of preoedipal conflicts" by E. Servadio.] RFPsa 1954, 18:46-51, 75

54886 (& Lebovici, S.) Indications et contre-indications de la psychanalyse.

[Indications and contraindications for psychoanalysis.] RFPsa 1955, 19:135-188; 201-202. Encycl Medico-Chir, Psychiatrie 1955, 37810, I-10

54887 (& Lebovici, S.) Indications et contre-indications de la psychanalyse chez l'adulte. In author's *La Psychanalyse d'aujourd'hui* 1-39
Indications and contraindications for psychoanalysis of adults. In author's *Psychoanalysis of Today* 1-18

54888 Instinct de mort ou instinct de vie? [Death instinct or life instinct?] RFPsa 1956, 20:405-416. Bull Assoc Psa Belg 1957, 26. Arch Sciences méd d'Athènes 1958, July

54889 Lecciones de tecnica psicoanalítica. [Lessons on psychoanalytic technique.] Arch Med Mex 1955, A-XIII, N 131

54890 (& Diatkine, R.; Favreau, J.) Le moi dans la relation perverse. (Read at 19th Int Psa Cong, Geneva, July 1955) RFPsa 1956, 20:457-478
The ego in perverse relationships. (Tr: McDougall, J.) J 1956, 37:404-413
Abs Auth J 1956, 37:132-133. JLan Q 1957, 26:580

54891 (& Viderman, S.) Du monde préobjetal dans la relation transférentielle. (Read at 21st Int Psa Cong, Copenhagen, July 1959) RFPsa 1959, 23:555-562
The pre-object universe in the transference situation. J 1960, 41:385-388
Abs Puget Rev Psicoanál 1960, 17:267

S-24106 The mutual influences in the development of ego and id: discussion.
Abs JAA An Surv Psa 1952, 3:42-46. WH J 1953, 34:278

54892 La névrose de transfert et son maniement technique. RFPsa 1958, 22:675-691. Bull Assoc Psa Belg 1958, (29-30)
Technical remarks on the handling of the transference neurosis. J 1957, 38:196-203
Abs JLan Q 1958, 27:440-441. Recamier RFPsa 1959, 23:150. Stewart, S. Q 1960, 29:145. Rv Fiasche, de Rev Psicoanál 1959, 16:278-279

S-24107 Les nouvelles théories psychanalytiques sur le moi et leurs répercussions sur l'orientation methodologique.
Abs JAA An Surv Psa 1951, 2:104-105

S-24111A Presidential address.
Abs Edwards, F. H. J 1953, 34:69

54893 (Ed) La psychanalyse d'aujourd'hui. 2 vols. Paris: PUF 1956, viii + 867 p; 1 vol. 436 p
Psychoanalysis of Today. (Adapt: Roman, R. E.) NY, London: Grune & Stratton 1959, 228 p
El psicoanalisis, hoy. (Ed: Miracle, L.) 2 vols. Barcelona 1959
Abs J Am Psa Ass 1958, 6:177. Rv M'Uzan, de RFPsa 1957, 21:465-468. Masciangelo Riv Psa 1958, 4:73-75. JAA Q 1960, 29:401-402

54894 La psychanalyse des enfants. In author's *La psychanalyse d'aujourd'hui*

54895 (& Diatkine, R.; Racamier, P. C.) Psychanalyse et sociologie. RFPsa 1957, 21:244-282
Psychoanalysis and sociology. In author's *Psychoanalysis of Today*, 203-228
Abs Roman, R. E. Q 1958, 27:148

54896 Psychanalyse freudienne. Historique. [Freudian psychoanalysis. An historical survey.] Encycl Med-Chir, Psychiatrie 1955, 37810 I-10-2, 7 p
54897 (& Racamier, P. C.) Symposium on "Depressive Illness": II. Depressive states. (Read at 21st Int Psa Cong, Copenhagen, July 1959) J 1960, 41:481-496
54898 Sur la technique du début de la cure psychanalytique. [On the technique for beginning a psychoanalytic treatment.] RFPsa 1960, 24:5-18
54899 (& Racamier, P. C.) La théorie psychanalytique du délire. [The psychoanalytic theory of delirium.] RFPsa 1958, 22:417-574
        Abs J 1959, 20:249-250. Stewart, S. Q 1960, 29:145
54900 La thérapeutique psychanalytique. In author's *La Psychanalyse d'aujourd'hui* 123-168
        Psychoanalytic therapy. In author's *Psychoanalysis of Today,* 78-98

        See Schlumberger, Marc

NAESGAARD, SIGURD

54901 Vore neuroser. [Our Neuroses.] Odense, Denmark: Psykoanalytisk forlag 1952, 237 p

NAFTALIN, MOSES

54902 Correspondence with Max M. Stern, October 31, 1958, November 18, 1958, and November 28, 1958. Q 1958, 27:630-631
54903 Footnote to the genesis of Moses. Q 1958, 27:402-405
        Abs JKl J 1960, 41:166
54904 Reply to letters of Ernst L. Freud. Q 1959, 28:147

NAGEL, ERNEST

54905 Methodological issues in psychoanalytic theory. Psa Sci Method Phil 38-56

NAGELBERG, LEO

54906 (& Spotnitz, H.; Feldman, Y.) The attempt at healthy insulation in the withdrawn child. New Front Child Guid 141-156
S-24186A (& Spotnitz, H.) Initial steps in analytic therapy of schizophrenia.
        Abs NRo An Surv Psa 1952, 3:281-282
54907 The meaning of help in psychotherapy. PPR 1959, 46(4):50-63

        See Feldman, Yonata; Rosenthal, Leslie; Spotnitz, Hyman; Sternbach, Oscar

NAGLER, SIMON H.

54908 Discussion of Chrzanowski, G. "Treatment of asocial attitudes in ambulatory schizophrenic patients." Schiz Psa Off Pract 119-122
54909 Fetishism: a review and a case study. Psychiat Q 1957, 31:713-741
        Abs JBi Q 1959, 28:117-118

NAGY, MARIA H.

54910 The child's view of death. In Feifel, H. *The Meaning of Death,* NY, Toronto, London: McGraw-Hill 1959, 79-98
54911 Children's birth theories. J genet Psychol 1953, 83:217-226

54912   Children's conceptions of some bodily functions. J genet Psychol 1953, 83:199-216

54913   The representation of "germs" by children. J genet Psychol 1953, 83: 227-240

NAIMAN, JAMES

See Shagass, Charles

NÁJERA PEREZ, H.

54914   Psicoterapia de la esquizofrenia; revisión y comentariós de las teorías y técnica del análisis directo del doctor Rosen. [Psychotherapy of schizophrenia: review and comments on Dr. Rosen's theories and technics of direct analysis.] Arch med Cuba 1954, 5:451-458

NAMNUM, ALFREDO

54915   The relationship of intellectual achievement to the processes of identification. In Wedge, B. M. *Psychosocial Problems of College Men*, New Haven: Yale Univ Pr 1958, 242-259

NANDI, DHIRENDRA NATH

54916   Importance of exciting factors in the aetiology of psychoses. Samiksa 1956, 10:85-98

54917   Psychopathology of megalomania. Samiksa 1953, 7:133-138
      Abs JFr An Surv Psa 1953, 4:163-164

54918   The self-analysis of Arjuna—as recorded in Bhagwat-Gita. Samiksa 1958, 12:166-212

NARDO, RAMON DI

See DiNARDO, RAMON

NASH, HARVEY

54919   Assignment of gender to body regions. J genet Psychol 1958, 92:113-115

54920   The behavioral world. J Psychol 1959, 47:277-288

54921   Incomplete sentences tests in personality research. Educ Psychol Measmt 1958, 18:569-581

54922   Metaphor in personality theory. Amer Psychol 1959, 14:697-698

NATANSON, MAURICE

54923   Death and situation. Am Im 1959, 16:447-457

NATENBERG, MAURICE

54924   The Case History of Sigmund Freud; a Psycho-Biography. Chicago: Regent House 1955, vii + 245 p

54925   Freudian Psycho-Antics; Facts and Fraud in Psychoanalysis. Chicago: Regent House 1953, 101 p

NATHAN, EDWARD

See Kaplan, Maurice

NATHAN, M.
See Bonaparte, Marie

NATHAN, R.
See Masserman, Jules H.

NATHAN, W.
REVIEW OF:
54926 Balint, M. The Doctor, His Patient and the Illness. Q 1957, 26:553-555

NATHANSON, JEROME
See Kelman, Norman

NATHANSON, MORTON
S-24202A (& Bergman, P. S.; Gordon, G. G.) Denial of illness.
Abs LRa Q 1953, 22:459

NAUMBURG, GEORGE W., JR.
See Buchenholz, Bruce

NAUMBURG, MARGARET
54927 Art as symbolic speech. J Aesthet 1955, 13:435-450. In Anshen, R. N.
Language: An Enquiry into Its Meaning and Function, NY: Harper
1957
54928 Art therapy with 17-year-old schizophrenic girl. In Hammer, E. F.
The Clinical Application of Projective Drawings, Springfield, Ill:
Charles C Thomas 1958, 518-561
54929 Children's art expression and war. Nerv Child 1943, 2:360
54930 The psychodynamics of the art expression of a boy with tic syndrome.
Nerv Child 1945, 4(4)
54931 Psychoneurotic Art: Its Function in Psychotherapy. (Pref: Appel, K.
E.; Correlation of tests: Woltmann, A. G.; Comments on Rorschach:
Piotrowski, Z. A.) NY: Grune & Stratton 1953, 148 p
Rv Spitz, R. A. Q 1954, 23:279-282
54932 Religious symbols in the unconscious of man. Int Med Rec 1958, Dec
S-24205 Schizophrenic Art: Its Meaning in Psychotherapy.
Rv Khan, M. M. R. J 1953, 34:164. Kris, E. Q 1953, 22:98-101
54933 Spontaneous art in therapy and diagnosis. Prog Cl P 1952, 1
54934 A study of the art expression of a behavior problem boy as an aid in
diagnosis and therapy. Nerv Child 1944, 3
54935 La terapia por el arte—su alcance y función. Act Np Arg 1957, 3:10-14
Art therapy: its scope and function. In Hammer, E. F. *The Clinical
Application of Projective Drawings*, Springfield, Ill: Charles C Thomas
1958, 511-517
54936 The use of spontaneous art in analytically oriented group therapy of
obese women. Proc Int grp Ther Assoc 1959

REVIEWS OF:
54937 Dracoulidès, N. N. Psychanalyse de l'Artiste et de son Oeuvre. Q 1955,
24:296-298

54938 Kraus, G. The Relationship between Theo and Vincent Van Gogh. Q 1956, 25:275-278
54939 Reitman, F. Insanity, Art, and Culture. Q 1957, 26:563-564

NAVARRO, SOEIRO

54940 Personalidade psicopática e personalidade neurótica. [Psychopathic personality and neurotic personality.] An Portug P 1953, 5:82-101

NAVEILLAN FERNÁNDEZ, P.

See Beca, M. F.

NAVRATIL, LEO

54941 (& Strotzka, H.) Die Kind-Mutter-Relation bei epileptischen Kindern. [The child-mother-relation of epileptic children.] Wien Arch Psychol Psychiat Neurol 1954, 4(1)
54942 Zur Psychodynamik der Colitis ulcerosa. [On the psychodynamics of ulcerative colitis.] WMW 1954, 104:156-159
54943 Die Rolle der Ehefrau in der Pathogenese der Trunksucht. [The role of the wife in the pathogenesis of male alcohol addiction.] Wien Z f Nervenheilk 1957, 14:90-97

NAYEL, K. A.

54944 [Aggression.] (Arabic) EJP 1952, 7:357-381

NEAVLES, JACK S.

54945 (& Winokur, G.) The hot rod driver. BMC 1957, 22:28-35
    Abs Weiss, J. Q 1958, 27:447

NEEDLES, WILLIAM

54946 Gesticulation and speech. J 1959, 40:291-294
    Abs Weiss, J. Q 1960, 29:586
54947 A note on orgastic loss of consciousness. Q 1953, 22:512-518
    Abs JFr An Surv Psa 1953, 4:195. JKl J 1955, 36:219

REVIEWS OF:
54948 Bond, D. D. The Love and Fear of Flying. Q 1953, 22:113-114
54949 Frosch, J. (Ed) The Annual Survey of Psychoanalysis, Vol. III. Q 1957, 26:116-117
54950 Lorand, S. (Ed) The Yearbook of Psychoanalysis, Vol. VI. Q 1952, 21:107

NEEFE, JOHN R.

See Lief, Harold I.

NEEL, ANN MARIE (FILINGER)

54951 The nature of defensive behavior as studied by perceptual distortion. Diss Abstr 1954, 14:713-714

NEHNEVAJSA, JIRI

54952 Psychoanalyse und Psychodrama. [Psychoanalysis and psychodrama.] Die Heilkunst 1956, 69:162-164

54953 Sociocultural models in psychiatry. Group Psychother 1956, 9:268-273

NEILSON, FRANCIS

54954 The Freudians and the Oedipus Complex. Lancaster, Pa: Business Pr 1957, 83 p

NEISWANGER, D.

54955 The Menninger Foundation, past, present, and future. Menn Q 1958, 12(4):1-6

NELKEN, SAM

See Gwartney, R. H.

NELSON, BENJAMIN N.

54956 On Dr. Walker's "Five Theories." NPAP 1957, 5(3):26-27

54957 Editor of Freud, S. *On Creativity and the Unconscious.*

54958 Foreword to *Psychoanalysis and the Future.* NY: Nat'l Psychol Ass for Psa 1957, v-x

54959 (Ed) Freud and the 20th Century. NY: Meridian Books; London: Ruskin House 1957, 314 p
   Abs J Am Psa Ass 1958, 6:170. Rv Kaplan, D. PPR 1959, 46(1):122-124. Stewart, W. A. Q 1959, 28:99-100

54960 The future of illusions. NPAP 1954, 2(4):16-37

54961 The great divide. PPR 1959, 46(2):66-68

54962 Preface. Freud 20th Cent 7-10

54963 (Ed) Psychoanalysis and the Future: A Centenary Commemoration of the Birth of Sigmund Freud. NY: Nat'l Psychol Ass for Psa 1957, 160 p
   Abs J Am Psa Ass 1958, 6:171-172. Rv GPK Q 1958, 27:271-272

54964 Psychological systems and philosophical paradoxes. PPR 1960, 47(3): 43-51

54965 Questions on existential psychotherapy. PPR 1958, 45(4):77-78

54966 Social science, utopian myths, and the oedipus complex. PPR 1958, 45(1-2):120-126

See Coleman, Marie L.

NELSON, J. G.

See Saul, Leon J.

NELSON, MARIE COLEMAN
(See also Coleman, Marie L.)

54967 (& Schendler, D.) Changing patterns of transference and fetishism: a cultural inquiry. PPR 1960, 47(3):13-31

54968 Comment on Mullan, H. & Sangiuliano, I. A. "The existential matrix of psychotherapy." PPR 1960, 47(4):102-104

NELSON, SHERMAN EUGENE

54969 Psychosexual conflicts and defenses in visual perception. ASP 1955,
51:427-433. Diss Abstr 1955, 15:629-630

NELSON, VIRGINIA F.

See Kagan, Jerome

NEME, M.

54970 La neurofisiologia y la ampliación del concepto de "accidentes de tra-
bajo." [Neurophysiology and enlargement of the concept of industrial
accidents.] Arch Crimin Neuropsiq 2. ep. 1957, 5:346-375

NEMETZ, MIRIAM GROSSMAN

54971 Child psychoanalysis of Melanie Klein and of Anna Freud: a comparative study of their theories and methods. Diss Abstr 1954, 14:634-
635

NEMETZ, S. JOSEPH

See Knapp, Peter Hobart

NEMIAH, JOHN C.

54972 Contribution of psychiatry to research in physical medicine and rehabilitation. Arch phys med Rehabilit 1956, 37:341-344
54973 (Reporter) The loss complex. (Meeting Boston Psa Soc Sept 24,
1958). Bull Phila Ass Psa 1959, 9:19-20

NEMON, OSCAR

54974 Comment j'ai fait le buste de Freud. [How I made the bust of Freud.]
Psyché, Paris 1955, 10:483

NEUBAUER, PETER B.

54975 Basic considerations in the application of therapy and education to
parent groups. Int J grp PT 1953, 3:315-319
54976 (& Fishman, R. P.; Steinert, J.) Consultation services in nursery
schools. Child Welfare 1951, 30(2)
54977 (& Beller, E. K.) Differential contributions of the educator and
clinician in diagnosis. In Krugman, M. Orthopsychiatry and the
School, NY: Am Orthopsychiat Ass 1958, 36-45
54978 Group living: new patterns in family life. Child Study 1950, Fall
54979 Inner sources of responsibility: the child's growth toward maturity.
Child Study 1956, Summer
54980 (& Alpert, A.; Bank, B.) The nursery group experience as part of a
diagnostic study of a preschool child. New Front Child Guid 124-138
54981 The one-parent child and his Oedipal development. Psa St C 1960,
15:286-309
54982 The place of education and psychotherapy in mental health. Ops 1953,
23:280-283
54983 The psychoanalyst's contribution to the family agency. Psa Soc Wk
109-123

54984 (& Steinert, J.) Schizophrenia in adolescence. Nerv Child 1953, 10(1)
54985 We need not wait. In Baran, P. A. et al: *Marxism and Psychoanalysis,*
       NY: Monthly Review Pr 1960, 33-36

       See Alpert, Augusta; Wolf, Katherine M.

NEUMAN, GERARD G.

54986 (& Salvatore, J. C.) The Blacky Test and psychoanalytic theory: a
       factor-analytic approach to validity. J proj Tech 1958, 22:427-431

NEUMANN, ERICH

54987 Amor and Psyche: the Psychic Development of the Feminine, a Com-
       mentary on the Tale by Apuleius. NY: Pantheon Books 1956, 181 p
54988 The Great Mother: An Analysis of the Archetype. NY: Pantheon
       Books 1955, xliii + 352 p
54989 In honour of the centenary of Freud's birth. J anal Psych 1956, 1:195-
       201
54990 The Origins and History of Consciousness. (Foreword: Jung, C. G.)
       (Tr: Hull, R. F. C.) London: Routledge & Kegan Paul 1954, xxiv +
       493 p
         Rv MBr J 1956, 37:499

NEUMANN, FRANZ L.

54991 Angst und Politik. Tübingen: Mohr 1954, 44 p
         Anxiety and politics. (Tr: Gay, P.) In author's *The Democratic and
       Authoritarian State* (Ed: Marcuse, Herbert) Chicago: Free Pr 1957,
       270-303

NEUMANN, HEINZ

TRANSLATION OF:
Horney, K. [15209]

NEUMANN, JOHANNES

54992 Die Entstehung des Selbst aus der Angst. [The development of the
       ego out of anxiety.] In Bitter, W. *Angst und Schuld in theologischer
       und psychotherapeutischer Sicht,* Stuttgart: Ernst Klett 1959
54993 Der nervöse Charakter und seine Heilung. [The Neurotic Character
       and Its Treatment.] Stuttgart: Hippokrates Verlag 1954, 294 p

NEUSS, K. A.

54994 Zur Kasuistik aktiv-klinischer Psychotherapie. [Case material for active
       clinical psychotherapy.] Psychotherapie 1957, 2:174-176

NEUSTATTER, W. LINDESAY

54995 Homosexuality: the medical aspect. Practitioner 1954, 172(1030):364-
       373
54996 The Mind of the Murderer. NY: Philos Libr 1957, 232 p
         Rv Lasswell, H. D. Q 1958, 27:597

54997 Psychological Disorder and Crime. London: Christopher Johnson 1953; NY: Philos Libr 1957, 248 p
       Rv Overholser, W. Q 1954, 23:128-129. Lasswell, H. D. Q 1958, 27:297. Williams, A. H. J 1959, 40:356-357

NEWBOLD, GEORGE

See Ambrose, Gordon

NEWCOMB, MARGARET L.

54998 (& Gay, E.; Young, R. L.; Smith, S. R.; Weinberger, J. L.) The function of a psychiatric social worker in a mental hygiene clinic. MH 1952, 36:257
54999 Progress in psychiatric social work treatment. Prog PT 1959, 4:153-158

NEWCOMB, THEODORE M.

55000 Comments on papers by Professors Nowlis & Mowrer. In *Current Theory and Research in Motivation, a Symposium,* Lincoln, Neb: Univ Nebraska Pr 1953, 185-189
55001 Motivation in social behavior. In *Current Theory and Research in Motivation, a Symposium,* Lincoln, Neb: Univ Nebraska Pr 1953, 139-161
55002 Social Psychology, London: Tavistock Pub, 690 p
       Rv Menzies, I. E. P. J 1953, 34:338

NEWELL, H. WHITMAN

55003 (& Schultz, K. L.) Brief therapy for acute anxiety in a five-year-old girl. Ops 1953, 23:186-203. Case St Chd Dis 1953, 1:247-264
55004 Childhood intuition. Bull Phila Ass Psa 1955, 5:54
55005 Hippocratic use of psychotherapy. Bull Phila Ass Psa 1953, 3:75-78
55006 An interpretation of the Hindu worship of Siva Linga. Bull Phila Ass Psa 1954, 4:82-86

NEWMAN, M. F.

See Hilgard, Josephine R.

NEWMAN, R. E.

55007 The application of the Rorschach technique to a primitive group. Z diag Psychol 1955, 3:187-222
55008 Personality development in a primitive "adolescent" group as revealed by the Rorschach technique. Z diag Psychol 1958, 6:241-253

NEWMAN, RICHARD

See Gill, Merton M.; Redlich, Fredrick C.

NEWTON, MILES

55009 (& Marcus, I. M.) The Family Book of Child Care. NY: Harper 1957, 477 p
55010 Maternal Emotions. NY: Paul B. Hoeber 1955

55011   Maternal emotions. I. Introduction. II. Women's feelings about menstruation. III. Women's feelings about pregnancy. IV. Women's feelings about childbirth. V. Women's feelings about breast feeding. VI. Women's feelings about care of their babies. VII. Women's envy of men. VIII. Sexual intercourse: its relation to the rest of women's sexual role. IX. Biological femininity *versus* cultural femininity. Child-Fam Dig 1957, 16(5):67-72; 16(6):70-77; 1958, 17(1):25-29; 17(2):40-50; 17(3):47-60; 17(4):7-19; 17(5):55-63; 17(6):37-44; 1959, 18(1):37-44. From author's *Maternal Emotions*

NGUYEN, ANH

55012   Le rire et la dérision. [Laughter and derision.] Evolut psychiat 1955, (1):67-118

NICE, RICHARD W.

55013   (Ed) Crime and Insanity. NY: Philos Libr 1958, 280 p
          Rv Schmidl, F. Q 1959, 28:104
55014   (& Podolsky, E.) A Handbook of Abnormal Psychology. NY: Philos Libr 1959, 245 p

NICEFORO, A.

55015   Alcuni aspetti della struttura e della condotta dell' "Io." [Some aspects regarding the structure and behavior of the ego.] Scientia 1955, 90(513):29-36; 90(514):74-82

NICHOLLS, GRACE

55016   Treatment of a disturbed mother-child relationship: a case presentation. Smith Coll Stud Soc Wk 1956, 26(3). Ego Psychol Dyn Casewk 117-125

See Blom, Gaston E.

NICHOLS, C. R.

55017   (& Busse, E. W.) Some aspects of mental health and illness in the aged. N C med J 1958, 19:352-354

See Busse, Ewald William

NICHOLS, F.

See Peltz, William L.

NICHOLS, ROBERT C.

55018   A study of psychoanalytic symbolism in relation to stimulus generalization. (Abs) Am Psych 1955, 10:351

NICHTENHAUSER, ADOLF

55019   (& Coleman, M. L.; Ruhe, D. S.) Films in Psychiatry, Psychology and Mental Health. NY: Health Education Council 1953, 269 p
          Rv Gustav, A. NPAP 1954, 2(4):68-71

NICHTERN, SOL
See Bender, Lauretta

NICKERSON, J. L.
See Moses, Leon

NICOLAOU, GEORGE T.

55020 Evaluation of ward occupational therapy with regressed patients. Psychiat Q Suppl 1951, 25:202-205
55021 Reserpine in the treatment of disturbed adolescents. Psychiat Res Rep 1955, July:122-132
55022 The selection of psychiatric patients for research. P 1953, 110:179-185
55023 State hospital adolescent treatment unit. Psychiat Q 1956, 30:450-457

NIEBAUER, EVA L.

55024 Logotherapie und Existenzanalyse. [Logotherapy and existential analysis.] Die Heilkunst 1958, 71:279-283

See Kocourek, Kurt

NIEBUHR, REINHOLD

55025 Human creativity and self-concern in Freud's thought. Freud 20th Cent 259-276
55026 The Self and the Dramas of History. NY: Scribner 1955, ix + 246 p; London: Faber 1956, 264 p

NIEBUHR, URSULA M.

55027 "Sex in Christianity and Psychoanalysis." Religion in Life 1956, 25:613-618

NIEDERER, W.

55028 Die Beziehung zwischen Seelsorge und Analyse. [The relation between psychoanalysis and pastoral counseling.] Pro Juventute 1958, 39:85-86

NIEDERLAND, WILLIAM G.

55029 Clinical observations on the "Little Man" phenomenon. Psa St C 1956, 11:381-395
          Abs RTh J 1959, 40:77
55030 Discussion of Teirich, H. R. "Ein Fall von Zoophilie." Z diagn 1955, 3:72-73
55031 The earliest dreams of a young child. Psa St C 1957, 12:190-208
          Abs RTh J 1959, 40:370
55032 Early auditory experiences, beating fantasies, and primal scene. Psa St C 1958, 13:471-504
          Abs RTh J 1960, 41:654-655
55033 The first application of psychoanalysis to a literary work. Q 1960, 29:228-235
55034 (& Shatzky, J.) Four unpublished letters of Freud. Q 1956, 25:147-154

55035 Freuds Lebenswerk. [Freud's life work.] Aufbau 1956, 22(21):17-18
55036 Further remarks on river symbolism. J Hillside Hosp 1959, 8:109-114
        Abs Osher, S. Q 1959, 28:569
55037 Jacob's dream: with some remarks on ladder and river symbolism.
        J Hillside Hosp 1954, 3:73-97
        Abs RJA An Surv Psa 1954, 5:444-447. JFr An Surv Psa 1954,
        5:234. Friedman, P. Q 1955, 24:473-474
55038 Linguistic observation on beating fantasies. J Hillside Hosp 1958,
        7:202-207
        Abs Powelson, D. H. Q 1959, 28:567-568
55039 The "miracled-up" world of Schreber's childhood. Psa St C 1959,
        14:383-413
        Abs Donadeo, J. Q 1960, 29:301-304
55040 The psychoanalysis of a severe obsessive-compulsive neurosis. Bull
        Phila Ass Psa 1958, 8:83-93
        Analisi di una grave nevrosi ossessiva. (Tr: Auth & Zambonelli, F.)
        Riv Psa 1959, 5:31-37
        Abs EFA Q 1959, 28:419
55041 River symbolism. Q 1956, 25:469-504; 1957, 26:50-75
        Abs JK J 1957, 38:434. Zambonelli Riv Psa 1959, 5:85-86
55042 Schreber: father and son. Q 1959, 28:151-169
        Abs Sapochnik Rev Psicoanál 1959, 16:138-139. Dreyfus RFPsa
        1960, 24:207
55043 Schreber's father. J Am Psa Ass 1960, 8:492-499
55044 Some technical aspects concerning the analysis of obsessive-compulsive
        patients. (Read at NY Psa Soc, Feb 16, 1959) Bull Phila Ass Psa 1960,
        10:148-153
        Abs Drooz, R. B. Q 1959, 28:450
55045 The symbolic river-sister equation in poetry and folklore. J Hillside
        Hosp 1957, 6:91-99
        Abs Afterman, J. Q 1958, 27:146
S-24327 Three notes on the Schreber case.
        Abs JFr An Surv Psa 1951, 2:188-190. CR J 1953, 34:272

REVIEWS OF:
55046 Bychowski, G. Psychotherapy of Psychosis. Q 1954, 23:596-597
55047 Freeman, T. et al: Chronic Schizophrenia. Q 1959, 28:86-87
55048 Freud, S. & Oppenheim, D. E. Dreams in Folklore. Q 1958, 27:576-578
55049 Jones, E. Sigmund Freud: Four Centenary Addresses. Q 1957, 26:118-119
55050 Levitt, M. Readings in Psychoanalytic Psychology. Q 1960, 29:118-119
55051 Lewin, B. D. Dreams and the Uses of Regression. Q 1958, 27:574-575
55052 Macalpine, I. & Hunter, R. A. Schizophrenia 1677. Q 1958, 27:107-111
55053 Rifkin, A. H. (Ed) Schizophrenia in Psychoanalytic Office Practice.
        Q 1958, 27:420
55054 Schreber, D. P. Memoirs of My Nervous Illness. Q 1956, 25:93-94

NIEL, ANDRÉ

55055 Le moi et l'amour. [The ego and love.] Critique 1958, 14:976-987

NIEL, HENRI

55056 Destin biologique et psychologie de la femme. [Biological destiny and the psychology of woman.] Critique 1955, 11:848-866
55057 Etudes de psychologie génétique. [Studies in genetic psychology.] Critique 1955, 11:237-249; 339-351
55058 Psychanalyse et philosophie. [Psychoanalysis and philosophy.] Critique 1953, 9:973-980
55059 Psychanalyse et religion d'après C. G. Jung. [Psychoanalysis and religion according to C. G. Jung.] Critique 1954, 10:1056-1066
55060 La psychanalyse existentiale de Ludwig Binswanger. [The existential psychoanalysis of Ludwig Binswanger.] Critique 1957, 13:877-888

NIELSEN, NILS

55061 The dynamics of training analysis. (Read at 18th Int Psa Cong, London, July 1953) J 1954, 35:247-249
       Abs Auth J 1954, 35:288. JFr An Surv Psa 1954, 5:418. Lebovici RFPsa 1954, 18:471. JLan Q 1955, 24:608
55062 Några synpunkter på psykoanalytisk utbildning. [Some viewpoints on psychoanalytical training.] Nord psykiat Medlemsbl 1951, 5:135-142
55063 Specialistutbildningen i psykiatri. [Postgraduate training of psychiatric specialists.] Svenska Läkartidningen 1957, 54:1112-1116
55064 Value judgements in psychoanalysis. (Read at 21st Int Psa Cong, Copenhagen, July 1959) J 1960, 41:425-429
55065 Vem är psykoterapeut? [Who is a psychotherapist?] Svenska Läkartidningen 1956, 53:777-780
55066 What is homosexuality? Int J Sexol 1953, 6:188

NIMKOFF, MEYER F.

See Allee, W. C.

NININGER, ENGEL SCOTT

55067 The high and the low. Am Im 1957, 14:333-341

NININGER, EUGENE V.

ABSTRACTS OF:
55068 Arlow, J. A. & Brenner, A. The concept of regression and the structural theory. Q 1960, 29:603-605
55069 Frosch, J. Transference derivatives of the family romance. Q 1959, 28:143-145
55070 Schur, M. The ego and the id in anxiety. Q 1959, 28:141-143
55071 Stern, M. M. Remarks about an oral character disorder with blank hallucinations. Q 1960, 29:452-454

NISHIZONO, MASAHISA

55072 Clinical study on neuroses. Kuyshu Neuro-Psychiatry 1958, 7(1):1-51
55073 On conversion-mechanism of hysterical symptom. Kyushu Neuro-Psychiatry 1958, 6(3-4):39-44
55074 Hypnotic therapy of neuroses. Jap J Clin & Exper Med 1956, 33(8):109-113

55075 Mother-fixation on female. Its influence on superego formation. Jap J Psa 1957, 4(7-8):10-12

55076 On an obsessive-compulsive case. Jap J Psa 1955, 2(7):11-16

55077 Oral regression observed in the course of psychoanalytic therapy. Jap J Psa 1958, 5(2):1-3

55078 A psychoanalytic case report on erythrophobia. Kyushu Neuro-Psychiatry 1956, 1:169-173. Jap J Psa 1956, 3(7-8):11-14

See Okonogi, Keigo

NISSEN, G.

55079 Psychogener Tic und Altersdisposition bei Kindern. [Psychogenic tic and age disposition in children.] Z Kinderpsychiat 1956, 23:97-107

NISSEN, HENRY W.

55080 Comments on Klein, G. S. "Needs and regulation." In Jones, M. R. *Nebraska Symposium on Motivation: 1954*, Lincoln, Neb: Univ Nebraska Pr 1954, 277-280

See Allee, W. C.

NIXO, NORMAN

55081 A child guidance clinic explores ways to prevention. Children 1957, 4:9-14

NIXON, W. C. W.

55082 Foreword to Hegeler, S. *Peter and Caroline. A Child Asks about Childbirth and Sex*

NOBLE, DOUGLAS

S-24350 Hysterical manifestations in schizophrenic illness.
        Abs JFr An Surv Psa 1951, 2:192-193

55083 (& Price, D. B.; Gilder, R., Jr.) Psychiatric disturbances following amputation. P 1954, 110:609-613
        Abs MK Q 1954, 23:464

S-24354 Psychodynamics of alcoholism in a woman.
        Abs R 1953, 40:89

S-24356 A study of dreams in schizophrenic and allied states.
        Abs JFr An Surv Psa 1951, 2:257-259

NODET, CHARLES-HENRI

55084 Considérations psychanalytiques à propos des attraits névrotiques pour la vie religieuse. [Psychoanalytic considerations regarding neurotic attractions to the religious life.] Suppl Vie Spir 1950, (14):279-306

55085 Note sur l'aspect psychologique de l'angoisse. [A note on the psychological aspect of anxiety.] Suppl Vie Spir 1954, (28):53-63

55086 À propos du livre du Docteur Daim: Transvaluation de la psychanalyse. [A discussion of the book of Dr. Daim: The transvaluation of psychoanalysis.] Suppl Vie Spir 1957, (40):94-107

55087   Psychanalyse et sens du péché. [Psychoanalysis and guilt feelings.]
        RFPsa 1957, 21:791-805
             Abs Roman, R. E. Q 1958, 27:618
55088   Le psychanalyste. [The psychoanalyst.] Evolut psychiat 1957, (4):677-
        692. In *Problèmes de Psychanalyse*, Paris: Fayard 1957, 28-43
55089   Quelques réflexions sur les valeurs engagées dans la cure analytique.
        [Thoughts on the values implicit in analytic treatment.] RFPsa 1958,
        22:343-374
             Rv Zmud, F. & Fiasche, D. N. Rev Psicoanál 1959, 16:195-196
55090   Troubles nerveux et vocation. [Nervous troubles and vocation.] Suppl
        Vie Spir 1957, (40):17-23
55091   Vie affective infantile et vie morale adulte: notions "analogues." [The
        affective life of the child and the moral life of the adult: analogous
        concepts.] Suppl Vie Spir 1948, (4):390-410

NOGALES, C. DE

55092   (& Folch Mateu, P.; Abella Gibert, D.) Anorexia mental. [Anorexia
        nervosa.] Rev Psiquiat Psicol 1957, 3:265-270

NOGUEIRA, H.

55093   Freud e a renovação da psicologia. [Freud and the revival of psy-
        chology.] Rev Bras Saúde ment 1956, 2(2):53-57

NOLAN, WILLIAM

See Carlson, Helen B.

NOLLMANN, JORGE ENRIQUE

55094   Consideraciones psicoanalíticas acerca de un enfermo esquizofrénico
        con mecanismos hipocondriaco-paranoideos. [Psychoanalytic study of a
        case of schizophrenia with hypochondriacal-paranoid mechanisms.]
        Rev Psicoanál 1953, 10:37-74
             Abs JLan An Surv Psa 1953, 4:454-455. Vega Q 1954, 23:622

REVIEW OF:
55095   Geleerd, E. R. A contribution to the problem of psychosis in child-
        hood. Rev Psicoanál 1958, 15:125-126

NORD, CHARLES L.

55096   Handling stress through identification. J soc Therapy 1956, 2(4)

NØRGAARD, K.

55097   (& Zahle, V.) Forsøg med gruppeterapi på et sindssygehospital. [Group
        therapy trial in a mental hospital.] Nord Psyk Medl 1953, 7:26-70

NORMAN, ELIZABETH

55098   Reality relationships of schizophrenic children. M 1954, 27:126-142
             Abs Weiss, J. Q 1956, 25:124-125

NORMAN, HASKELL F.

ABSTRACTS OF:

55099 Foulkes, S. F. Some similarities and differences between psychoanalytic principles and group-analytic principles. Q 1954, 23:618-619

55100 Freud, A. Problems of technique in adult analysis. Q 1956, 25:284-285

55101 Glover, E. The indications for psychoanalysis. Q 1955, 24:623-624

55102 Hunter, R. A. & Macalpine, I. Follow-up study of a case treated in 1910 by "The Freud Psychoanalytic Method." Q 1954, 23:619

55103 Jones, E. The early history of psychoanalysis. Q 1955, 24:319-320

55104 Pëto, A. The interrelations of delinquency and neurosis: the analysis of two cases. Q 1955, 24:320-321

55105 Tarachow, S. et al: Studies in ambivalence. Q 1959, 28:131-132

55106 Winnicott, D. W. Psychoses and child care. Q 1954, 23:619-620

55107 Wisdom, J. O. A general hypothesis of psychosomatic disorder. Q 1954, 23:618

55108 Zilboorg, G. Scientific psychopathology and religious issues. Q 1955, 24:624

NORMAN, RALPH D.

55109 The interrelationships among acceptance-rejection, self-other identity, insight into self, and realistic perceptions of others. Soc Psych 1953, 37:205-235

55110 (& Ainsworth, P. A.) The relationships among projection, empathy, reality, and adjustment, operationally defined. J consult Psychol 1954, 18:53-58

NORTHRUP, GORDON

55111 Transsexualism: report of a case. AMA Arch gen psychiat 1959, 1:332-337

NORTON, ALAN

55112 (& Hall-Smith, P.) A psychiatric view of skin disorder. Mod Tr PSM 126-145

NORTON, ARTHUR

See Masserman, Jules H.

NORTON, JOSEPH L.

55113 Some doubts about current use of defense mechanisms. Am Psych 1957, 12:421

NORTON, NEA

See Coleman, Jules V.; Fleck, Stephen

NOSHPITZ, JOSEPH D.

55114 Opening phase in the psychotherapy of adolescents with character disorders. BMC 1957, 21:153-164

NOTCUTT, BERNARD

55115 The Psychology of Personality. NY: Philos Libr 1953, 259 p
Rv Evans, W. N. Q 1955, 24:143-144. Knapp, B. W. R 1955, 42:308

NOTT, KATHLEEN

55116 My life and hard cash. Encounter 1957, 9(2):28-37

NOVECK, SIMON

55117 (Ed) Judaism and Psychiatry. Two Approaches to the Personal Problems and Needs of Modern Man. NY: Basic Books 1956, xiii + 197 p
Rv BB Q 1957, 26:263. NRo J Am Psa Ass 1958, 6:519-539

NOVELL-SMITH, PATRICK

55118 Psycho-analysis and moral language. Rationalist Annu 1954, 36-45

NOVEY, SAMUEL

55119 A clinical view of affect theory in psychoanalysis. J 1959, 40:94-104
Abs JBi Q 1960, 29:276-277
55120 The meaning of the concept of mental representation of objects. Q
1958, 27:57-79
Abs Dreyfus RFPsa 1958, 22:744. Sapochnik, L. Rev Psicoanál
1958, 15:305. JKl J 1959, 40:366
55121 The outpatient treatment of borderline paranoid states. Ps 1960,
23:357-364
55122 A re-evaluation of certain aspects of the theory of instinctual drives
in the light of modern ego psychology. J 1957, 38:137-145
Abs JLan Q 1958, 27:438-439
55123 The role of the superego and ego-ideal in character formation. J 1955,
36:254-259. Rd Psa Psychol 114-123
Abs Garcia Reinoso, D. Rev Psicoanál 1956, 13:78-79. JLan Q 1957,
26:278
55124 Some philosophical speculations about the concept of the genital
character. J 1955, 36:88-94
Abs JLan Q 1956, 25:611
55125 The technique of supportive therapy in psychiatry and psychoanalysis.
Ps 1959, 22:179-187
Rv Euredjian Rev Psicoanál 1959, 16:275
55126 Utilization of social institutions as a defence technique in the neuroses.
J 1957, 38:82-91
Abs JLan Q 1958, 27:437

NOWLIS, VINCENT

55127 Comments on papers by Professors Newcomb and Mowrer. In *Current
Theory and Research in Motivation, a Symposium,* Lincoln, Neb:
Univ Nebraska Pr 1953, 190-194

See Sears, Robert R.

NOWOTNY, J.

55128 Der derzeitige Stand der Individualpsychologie. [Present status of
individual psychology.] Wien Arch Psychol Psychiat Neurol 1952,
2:83-95

NOYES, ARTHUR PERCY

55129 The administrator's place in psychiatry. In Overholser, W. *Centennial Papers. Saint Elizabeths Hospital, 1855-1955,* Wash: Centennial Commission, Saint Elizabeths Hospital 1956, 127-140

55130 Modern Clinical Psychiatry. 4th ed. Phila: Saunders 1953, 609 p

55131 (& Kolb, L. C.) Modern Clinical Psychiatry. 5th ed. Phila: Saunders 1958, 694 p

55132 Presidential address. P 1955, 112:1-7

NUNBERG, HERMAN

S-24392 Allgemeine Neurosenlehre auf psychoanalytischer Grundlage. (2nd ed) Bern: Hans Huber 1959, 435 p
      Principles of Psychoanalysis. Their Application to the Neuroses. (Foreword: SF) (Tr: Kahr, M. & Kahr, S.) NY: IUP 1956, 382 p
      Abs J Am Psa Ass 1957, 5:185. Rv EG Q 1956, 25:586-589. Foulkes, S. R. J 1957, 38:121

55133 Character and neurosis. J 1956, 37:36-45. From author's *Principles of Psychoanalysis—Their Application to the Neuroses* [24392]
      Abs JLan Q 1957, 26:433

S-24399 Discussion of M. Katan's paper on Schreber's hallucinations.
      Abs JFr Surv Psa 1952, 3:150-152. MGr Q 1954, 23:145-146

55134 Evaluation of the results of psychoanalytic treatment. J 1954, 35:2-7. Rd Psa Psychol 311-320
      Abs NRo An Surv Psa 1954, 5:327-329. JLan Q 1955, 24:459

55135 Über körperliche Begleiterscheinungen assoziativer Vorgänge. In Jung, C. G. *Diagnostische Assoziationsstudien, Vol II,* Leipzig: Barth 1910
      On the physical accompaniments of association processes. In Jung, C. G. *Studies in Word-Association; Experiments in the Diagnosis of Psychopathological Conditions carried out at the Psychiatric Clinic of the University of Zürich under the direction of C. G. Jung,* NY: Moffat, Yard & Co 1919

S-24415 Transference and reality.
      Abs STa An Surv Psa 1951, 2:383-386. R 1955, 42:202

S-24416 Über den Traum. Psa Vkb 1957, 146-157

NUNES DA COSTA

55136 Personalidade e despersonalização. [Personality and depersonalization.] An Portug P 1953, 5:102-117

NÚÑEZ, MOLINA

55137 Eros y libido. [Eros and libido.] Act luso-esp N P 1959, 18:34-38

NÚÑEZ SANCHEZ, E.

55138 Las categorias basicas de lo real en los planos de la existencia humana; introducción a una ontología de la existencia vital. [Basic categories of the real in the theories of human existence; introduction to an ontology of vital existence.] Act luso-esp N P 1955, 14:27-34

NUTTIN, JOSEPH

55139 Consciousness, behavior, and personality. Psychol Rev 1955, 62:349-355

55140 (& Curle, A. C. T. W.; Monchaux, C. de) Contribution of psychoanalysis to the understanding of human behaviour. Advancement of Sci 1956, 12(44):548-562

55141 Human motivation and Freud's theory of energy discharge. Canad J Psychol 1956, 10:167-178
La motivación humana y la teoría de Freud de la descarga de la energía. Rev Psicol gen apl, Madrid 1957, 12:93-110

55142 Personality. Ann Rev Psychol 1955, 6:161-186

55143 Personality dynamics. Pers Thy 183-196

S-24425 Psychoanalyse en spiritualistische opvatting van de mens.
Psychoanalysis and Personality. A Dynamic Theory of Normal Personality. (Tr: Lamb, G.) NY: Sheed & Ward 1953, 310 p
Psychanalyse et Conception spiritualiste de l'homme. (2 rev enl ed.) Louvain: Pub univ Louvain 1955, 367 p
Abs Auth An Surv Psa 1953, 4:657-661. Rv MG Q 1954, 23:450

NYDES, JULE

55144 Comment on Mullan, H. & Sangiuliano, I. A. "The existential matrix of psychotherapy." PPR 1960, 47(4):100-102

S-24427 Interpersonal relations: personal and depersonalized.
Abs STa An Surv Psa 1952, 3:8-9

55145 The magical experience of the masturbation fantasy. PT 1950, 4:303-310

55146 Within the pleasure principle. Expl Psa 3-15

REVIEW OF:
55147 May, R. Man's Search for Himself. NPAP 1953, 1(3):68-72

NYHUS, PER

See Bressler, Bernard

NYMAN, LAWRENCE

See Esman, Aaron H.

NYPELSEER, JEAN-LOUIS VAN

55148 (& Robaye, F.) Essai de validation des indices du test de Rorschach, particulièrement des F Clob, des G et du type d'économie intime, au regard du niveau d'aspiration et d'expectation. [Attempt to validate the Rorschach indices, especially F Ch, W and experience balance, in face of level of aspiration and level of expectation.] Bull du CERP, Paris 1955, Jan

55149 Notes sur la psychologie de l'imprudence. [Notes on the psychology of imprudence.] Rev Droit Pénol et Criminol, Brussels 1958, Nov

NYSWANDER, MARIE

55150 The Drug Addict as a Patient. NY: Grune & Stratton 1955
55151 Drug Addiction. In Wohl, *Long Term Illness,* Phila: Saunders 1958
55152 Drug addictions. Am Hbk Psychiat 1:614-622
55153 Narcotic addiction. Interview. Modern Med 1957, Oct
55154 The treatment of drug addiction. Med Clin N Amer 1958, May
55155 (& Winick, C.; Bernstein, A.; Brill, L.; Kaufer, G.) The treatment of drug addicts as voluntary outpatients: a progress report. Workshop 1957: Treatment of the narcotic addict. Ops 1958, 28:714-727
      Abs Koenig RFPsa 1959, 23:433
55156 Withdrawal treatment of drug addiction. New England J Med 1950, 242:128-130

See Brown, Bernard Sydney

O

OAKESHOTT, EDNA M.

55157 Means by which students of education may learn about personality development. Sociol Rev Monogr #1, 1958:51-60

OATES, WAYNE EDWARD

55158 Anxiety in Christian Experience. Phila: Westminster Pr 1955, 156 p
55159 The cult of reassurance. Religion in Life 1954-55, 24:72-82
55160 Introduction to Ikin, A. G. *New Concepts of Healing*
55161 Pastoral psychology and faith healing. In Doniger, S. *Healing: Human and Divine,* NY: Association Pr 1957, 229-254
55162 The Religious Dimensions of Personality. NY: Association Pr 1957; London: Mayflower Publ Co 1958, 320 p
55163 Religious Factors in Mental Health. NY: Association Pr 1955; London: Allen & Unwin 1957, xv + 239 p
　　Rv NRo J Am Psa Ass 1958, 6:519-539. Zeitlyn, B. B. J 1958, 39:435
55164 The role of religion in the psychoses. In Doniger, S. *Religion and Human Behavior,* NY: Association Pr 1954, 88-106
55165 What Psychology Says about Religion. NY: Association Pr 1958, 128 p

OBERHOLZER, EMIL

See DuBois, Cora Alice

OBERMAYER, MAXIMILIAN ERNEST

55166 Neurodermatitis diseminada. La enfermedad problema. [Neurodermatitis disseminata. The problem disease.] Dermatologia, Mexico 1957, 1:228-236
55167 Psychocutaneous Medicine. Springfield, Ill: Thomas; Oxford: Blackwell 1955, 487 p

OBERNDORF, CLARENCE PAUL

S-24456 (Ed, Tr) Autobiography of Josef Breuer (1842-1925). J 1953, 34:64-67
　　Abs SG An Surv Psa 1953, 4:10-11
S-24461 Child-parent relationship. In Linscott, R. N. & Stein, J. *Why You Do What You Do,* NY: Random House 1956, 190-197

55168 Diagnostic and etiological concepts in the neuroses. In Hoch, P. H. & Zubin, J. *Current Problems in Psychiatric Diagnosis*, NY: Grune & Stratton 1953, 80-88

S-24489 Function in psychiatry. P 1953, 110:13-18
   Abs MK Q 1954, 23:303

S-24493 A History of Psychoanalysis in America. NY: Grune & Stratton 1953, vii + 280 p
   Abs SG An Surv Psa 1953, 4:662-673. Rv Lehrman, P. R. Q 1954, 23:263-265. Staff, C. NPAP 1954, 3(1):77-79. Zinkin, J. R 1954, 41:403-404. Scott, W. C. M. J 1955, 36:415-416

S-24507A Obituary: Henry Alden Bunker 1889-1953. J Am Psa Ass 1953, 1:757-758

55169 Psychoanalytic concepts of criminality. Encycl Aberr 158-163

S-24536 Psychopathology at work.
   Abs JAA An Surv Psa 1951, 2:163-165

S-24546 Results to be effected with psychoanalysis. AMA ANP 1953, 69:655

S-24548 The role of anxiety in depersonalization.
   Abs R 1953, 40:352.

S-24551 Selectivity and option for psychiatry. P 1954, 110:754-758

  See Lussheimer, Paul; Spiegel, Leo A.

OBERS, SAMUEL J.

  See Wolf, Alexander

OBIOLS VIÉ, J.

55170 Técnicas psicoterápicas usadas en la infancia; estado actual de la psicoterapia infantil en España. [Psychotherapeutic technics used in childhood; present state of child psychotherapy in Spain.] Rev Psiquiat Psicol 1956, 2:439-457

OBLER, PAUL C.

55171 Psychology and literary criticism: a summary and critique. Lit & Psych 1958, 8(4):50-59

OCHANDORENA, RAÚL PARKS

  See Langer, Marie

ØDEGÅRD, Ø.

55172 Emil Kraepelin og Sigmund Freud—100 år. (Emil Kraepelin and Sigmund Freud—100 years.] Nord Psyk Medl 1956, 10:388-390

ODENWALD, ROBERT P.

S-24609A Advisability of undertaking psychotherapy against the will of the patient.
   Abs MK Q 1953, 22:125

55173 Cleanliness is next to neurosis: the case of the unwashed child. Jubilee 1954, 1(2):32-37

55174   (& Shea, J. A.) Emotional problems of maladjustment in children with reading difficulties. P 1951, 107:890-893
55175   Psychiatry and psychoanalysis. The Sign, Nat Catholic Mag 1950, March
55176   Psychotherapy against the will of the patient. PT 1952, 6:274-279
55177   Your Child's World: From Infancy Through Adolescence. NY: Random House 1958, viii + 211 p

See Vander Veldt, James H.

ODIER, CHARLES

S-24610 L'Angoisse et la Pensée magique.
        Anxiety and Magic Thinking. (Tr: Schoelly, M.-L. & Sherfey, M. J.) NY: IUP 1956, xii + 302 p
        Abs J Am Psa Ass 1958, 6:175-176. Rv Ziferstein, I. Q 1957, 26:546-548. Williams, A. H. J 1958, 39:432-433
S-24611A Bibliography. J 1955, 36:216-217
55178   Comment faul-il écouter la musique? [How should one listen to music?] La Sem litt 1919, Feb 22, 15
55179   Essai sur la sublimation. Schweiz Z Psychol 1954, 13:97-113
        Essay on sublimation. (Tr: Damman, V.) Dr Af Beh 104-119
55180   Le problème musical et le point de vue de l'origin. [The musical problem and the point of view of origin.] La Sem litt 1924, Jan 12, 19, 26; Feb 2

O'DONOVAN

TRANSLATION OF:
(& Rosenthal) Freud, S. [10494A)

OEHME, C.

55181   [On the question of a psychosomatic medicine.] (German) Forsch Fortschr 1950, 26:162
55182   (& Mitscherlich, A.) [Remarks on the clinical problem of allergy.] (German) Hippokrates 1950, 21:429

OELZE, M.

See Cremerius, Johannes

OFFENKRANTZ, WILLIAM

55183   (& Church, E.; Elliott, R.) Psychiatric management of suicide problems in military service. P 1957, 114:33-41
55184   (& Allen, E.; Clow, H.; Tibbitts, C.) Panel discussion on "Some psychologic and psychiatric problems of old age." J Am Geriatrics Soc 1956, 4:1956
55185   A rapid interdisciplinary method for neuropsychiatric evaluation of family groups. JNMD 1957, 125:570-573

See Vitanza, Angelo

OGINO, KOICHI

55186 [Delusion] (Japanese) Tokyo: Misuzu-Shobo 1954, 76 p
55187 (& Murakami, M.) On Pierre Janet. Tokyo: Misuzu-Shobo 1958
55188 The psychological mechanism of ideas of reference seen in the sensitive character. Psychiat et Neurol jap 1953, 54:627-634; Engl abstr 41
55189 The psychological structure and the psychodynamism of influence-syndrome. Academia 1953, 4
55190 The psychological structure and the psychodynamism of the delusion of jealousy. Academia 1957, 19:43-73
55191 The psychopathological considerations on the sensitive ideas of reference. Psychiat et Neurol jap 1953, 55:33-41; Engl abstr 4
55192 The starting point of existential analysis. Psychol Rev 1958, 2(2):184-198

OHM, G.

55193 Konversionsneurosen und deren Behandlung bei einfach strukturierten Menschen. [Conversion neuroses and their treatment in patients of simple structure.] MMW 1954, 96:611-614

OHRBACH, C.

55194 (& Bieber, I.) Depressive and paranoid reactions. AMA ANP 1957, 78:301-311

OHTSUKI, KENJI

55195 [The Disease and the Personality.] (Japanese) Tokyo: Ikeda Publ 1954, 245 p
55196 [How to Find and Develop Your Natural Talent.] (Japanese) Tokyo: Ikeda Publ 1957, 269 p
55197 [How to Get Self-Confidence.] (Japanese) Tokyo: Ikeda Publ 1956, 227 p
55198 [Illustratory Introduction to Psychoanalysis.] (Japanese) Tokyo: Ikubunsha 1956, 222 p
55199 [The Masculine and the Feminine.] (Japanese) Tokyo: Ikeda Publ 1956, 240 p
55200 [Personality Can Be Changed.] (Japanese) Tokyo: Ikeda Publ 1956, 255 p
55201 [Psychology of Love and Sex.] (Japanese) Tokyo: Ikubunsha 1952, Vol. 1, 393 p; 1955, Vol. 2, 230 p; Vol. 3, 302 p
55202 [Psychology of Marriage.] (Japanese) Tokyo: Ikubunsha 1952, 291 p
55203 Report of the discussion with Dr. Harold Kelman. Tokyo J Psa 1958, 16(9):1-3
          Japanese: Tokyo J Psa 1958, 16(9):10-17
55204 [Sexual Education Is Needless.] (Japanese) Nagoya: Reimei Publ 1957, 232 p
55205 [Study on the Good and the Bad.] (Japanese) Tokyo: Tokyo Inst for Psa 1947, 128 p

See Karpe, Richard

TRANSLATIONS OF:
Kelman, H. [50198, 50202, 50224]. Leavy, S. A. [51887]

O'KELLEY, ELIZABETH

55206 Some observations on relationships between delinquent girls and their parents. M 1955, 28:59-66
Abs EMW Q 1956, 25:458

O'KELLY, LAWRENCE I.

55207 (& Muckler, F. A.) Introduction to Psychopathology. 2nd ed. Englewood Cliffs, NJ: Prentice-Hall 1955, 704 p

OKEN, DONALD
See Basowitz, Harold

OKONOGI, KEIGO

55208 Dr. Paul Federn's ego psychology and his psychotherapy of psychoses. Jap J Psa 1956, 3(2)-3(8)
55209 The meaning of the primary operational reaction—on the operational-structural aspect. Jap J Psa 1957, 4(3-4):1-16
55210 Our problems of learning psycho-analysis. Jap J Psa 1958, 5(6):32-40
55211 Psychoanalytic concept of sex and psychosomatic medicine. In Lectures on Psychosomatic Medicine, Nippon Kyobunshya 1957, 4:207-260
55212 Psychoanalytic studies on Rorschach-Test. II. Obsessive and compulsive defensive operations. Jap J Psa 1959, 6(2)
55213 Psychoanalytic therapy. In Clinical Psychology, Seishin-Shobo 1958, 279-302
55214 Report on my experience of control-analysis received from the supervisor (Dr. H. Kosawa). Jap J Psa 1954-55, 1(8)-2(6)
55215 (& Takahashi, S.; Takeda, M.; Suzuki, K.; Nishizono, M.) Studies on free association and analytic situation. I. A study on the primary operational reaction. Jap J Psa 1957, 4(3-4):17-36, 36-40
55216 Studies on free association and analytic situation. V. A study on the secondary operational reaction. Jap J Psa 1958, 5(2):10-51
55217 Studies on the patients' reactions to the psychoanalytical rules of fee and time-appointment. Jap J Psa 1957, 4(7-8):13-25
55218 Technique of free association—on problems of the introductory phase of psycho-analytic therapy. Jap J Psa 1955, 2(9):1-21

See Kosawa, H.; Takahashi, Susumo

TRANSLATIONS OF:
Freud, S. [10405, 10471, 10580]. Reich, W. [26812]

REVIEWS OF:
55219 Jones, E. Young Freud. Jap J Psa 1956, 2(9-10)
55220 Solomon, J. C. Synthesis of Human Behavior. Jap J Psa 1957, 4(3-4): 40-48

OLDEN, CHRISTINE

55221 On adult empathy with children. Psa St C 1953, 8:111-126
Abs NRo An Surv Psa 1953, 4:296-298. RTh J 1955, 36:76-77

S-24679 Notes on child rearing in America.
　　　Abs NRo An Surv Psa 1952, 3:206. STa An Surv Psa 1952, 3:484-
　　　485. RTh J 1953, 34:281
55222　Notes on the development of empathy. Psa St C 1958, 13:505-518
　　　Abs RTh J 1960, 41:655

OLDHAM, A. J.

See Stengel, E.

OLDS, JAMES

55223　Comments on Maslow, A. "Deficiency motivation and growth motiva-
　　　tion." In Jones, M. R. *Nebraska Symposium on Motivation: 1955,*
　　　Lincoln, Neb: Univ Nebraska Pr 1955, 37-39

See Parsons, Talcott

OLINGER, LEONARD B.

55224　(& Sommers, V. S.) The divided path: "Psychocultural" neurosis in a
　　　Nisei man. Clin Stud Cult Confl 359-408

OLINICK, STANLEY L.

55225　Questioning and pain, truth and negation. J Am Psa Ass 1957, 5:302-
　　　324
　　　Abs Shentoub RFPsa 1958, 22:126. HW Q 1960, 29:281-282
55226　Some considerations of the use of questioning as a psychoanalytic
　　　technique. J Am Psa Ass 1954, 2:57-66
　　　Abs NRo An Surv Psa 1954, 5:366-369. TFr J 1955, 36:221. Shen-
　　　toub RFPsa 1955, 19:471. Aldendorf, H. Q 1956, 25:282

OLIVEIRA, WALDEREDO ISMAEL DE

55227　"Acting-out" y la situación analítica. ["Acting out" and the analytic
　　　situation.] Rev Psicoanál 1955, 12:500-510
　　　Abs Vega Q 1956, 25:626
55228　O alcoolismo em Pernambuco. [Alcoholism in Pernambuco.] Arch
　　　Neuropsiq 1945, 3(1):15-33
55229　Um caso de Sindrome de Déjerine-Reussy. [A case of Déjerine-Reussy's
　　　Syndrome.] Neurobiol, Recife 1940, 3:383-395
55230　Experiência com narcoanalise nas psicoses funcionais. [Experience with
　　　narcoanalysis in functional psychoses.] Neurobiol, Recife 1949, 12:99-
　　　126
55231　The legend of Orestes: a psychoanalytical approach to the study of
　　　matricide. (Read at 19th Int Psa Cong, Geneva, 1955)
　　　Greek: Arch Med Sci, Athens 1959, 15:35-46; 196-207
　　　Abs Auth J 1956, 37:133
55232　El Matricidio en la Fantasía. [Matricide in Fantasy.] Buenos Aires:
　　　Edit Nova 1957, 204 p
　　　Rv Langer, M. Rev Psicoanál 1959, 16:84-85
55233　Notas psicanalíticas sôbre o choque hipoglicêmico de Sakel. [Psycho-
　　　analytic comments on the hypoglycemic shock of Sakel.] Rev Bras
　　　Saúde ment 1957, 3(1):37-53

55234 Observações psicologicas em esquizofrenicos tratados pelo método de Sakel. [Psychological remarks on schizophrenics treated by Sakel's method.] Neurobiol, Recife 1939, 2:303-315

55235 Psicanálise e antropologia. A personalidade e a cultura. [Psychoanalysis and anthropology. Personality and culture.] Rev Bras Saúde ment 1957, 3(2):75-103

55236 Psicanálise e educação. [Psychoanalysis and education.] J bras Psiquiat 1959, 8(1)

55237 Psicoanálisis de una fobia a la desfloración. [Psychoanalysis of a defloration phobia.] Rev Psicoanál 1953, 10:3-36
        Abs JFr An Surv Psa 1953, 4:171-172. Vega Q 1954, 23:621

55238 O Psicodiagnostico de Rorschach em Epilepticos. [Rorschach's Psychodiagnostic in Epileptics.] Rio de Janeiro: Companhia Editora Ameriana 1945, 95 p

55239 Sôbre psicoterapia analítica de grupo. [Analytic group psychotherapy.] J bras Psiquiat 1958, 7:287-292

S-24685 El simbolismo de la Torre de Babel; la confusión de lenguas y la disociación esquizofrenica.
        Abs STa An Surv Psa 1951, 2:564-566

REVIEWS OF:
55240 Loewenstein, R. De la passivité phallique chex l'homme. Rev Psicoanál 1948, 6:761-762

55241 Sharpe, E. The psycho-analyst. Rev Psicoanál 1948, 6:244-248

OLIVEN, JOHN F.

55242 Sexual Hygiene and Pathology; A Manual for the Physician. Phila: Lippincott 1955, xiii + 481 p

OLSEN, CLARENCE

S-24686A The relationship between psychoses and visceral crises.
        Abs LRa Q 1953, 22:130-131

OLSON, ROBERT G.

55243 Ignorance, false belief and unconscious desire. J Philos 1957, 54:466-474

OMBREDANE, ANDRÉ

55244 Distinction et mise en place des aspects de la projection. [The aspects of projection and their distinction.] Rorschachiana 1953, 1:287-306

O'NEAL, PATRICIA

55245 (& Robins, L. N.) The relation of childhood behavior problems to adult psychiatric status: a 30-year follow-up study of 150 subjects. P 1958, 114:961-969
        Abs Loeb, L. Q 1959, 28:425

O'NEILL, WILLIAM M.

55246 The relation of clinical and experimental methods in psychology. M 1953, 26:158-162
        Abs LRa An Surv Psa 1953, 4:23-24

O'NEILL, DESMOND

55247 Doctor, patient and student. Mod Tr PSM 49-59

55248 (Ed) Modern Trends in Psychosomatic Medicine. London: Butterworth 1955, xi + 375 p

55249 Psychological aspects of gynecology and obstetrics. In Wittkower, E. D. & Cleghorn, R. A. *Recent Developments in Psychosomatic Medicine,* Phila: Lippincott 1954, 212-231

55250 Uterine bleeding in tension states. J Obstet Gynaec Brit Emp 1952, 59:234-239

ONQUÉ, GLORIA COCHRANE

See Stone, Alan A.

OOSTERBAAN, W. M.

See Havermans, Franciscus M.

OPLER, MARVIN KAUFMANN

55251 Anthropological aspects of psychiatry. Prog PT 1959, 4:125-130

55252 Cultural anthropology and social psychiatry. P 1956, 113:302-311
Abs DRu Q 1959, 28:125-126

55253 The cultural backgrounds of mental health. In author's *Culture and Mental Health,* 1-17

55254 Cultural differences in mental disorders: an Italian and Irish contrast in the schizophrenias. In author's *Culture and Mental Health,* 425-442. Psychiat Q 1959, July

55255 Cultural dilemma of a Kibei youth. Clin Stud Cult Confl 297-316

55256 (Ed) Culture and Mental Health. Cross-Cultural Studies. NY: Macmillan 1959, xxi + 533 p
Abs J Am Psa Ass 1960, 8:603

55257 Culture, Psychiatry, and Human Values; The Methods and Values of a Social Psychiatry. (Foreword: Rennie, T. A. C.) Springfield, Ill: Thomas 1956, 242 p

55258 Dilemmas of two Puerto Rican men. Clin Stud Cult Confl 223-244

55259 Dream analysis in Ute Indian therapy. In author's *Culture and Mental Health,* 97-117

55260 Entities and organization in individual and group behavior: a conceptual framework. Group PT 1956, 9:290-300

55261 Epidemiological studies of mental illness. Methods and scope of the midtown study in New York. In *Symposium on Preventive and Social Psychiatry,* April 15-17, 1957, Wash: Govt Printing Off 1958, 111-145

See Singer, Jerome L.

OPLER, MORRIS EDWARD

55262 Considerations in the cross-cultural study of mental disorders. Int J soc Psychiat 1959, 5:191-196

OPPENHEIM, A. LEO

55263 The Interpretation of Dreams in the Ancient Near East, with a Trans-
lation of an Assyrian Dream Book. Trans Am Philos Soc, vol 46. Phila:
American Philosophical Soc 1956, 371 p
Rv Fisher, C. Q 1959, 28:88-89

OPPENHEIM, D. E.

See Freud, Sigmund

OPPENHEIM, SADI

See Abel, Theodora M.

ORAISON, MARC

55264 Le médecin psychanalyste et le confesseur. [The medical psychoanalyst and the confessor.] In *Problèmes de Psychanalyse*, Paris: Fayard
1957, 153-172

ORANGE, ARTHUR J.

55265 A note on brief group psychotherapy with psychotic patients. Int J grp
PT 1955, 5:80-83
Abs GPK Q 1956, 25:453-454

ORBACH, C. E.

55266 (& Bard, M.; Sutherland, A. M.) Fears and defensive adaptations to
the loss of anal sphincter control. R 1957, 44:121-175
Abs JLan Q 1958, 27:443

ORBACH, CHANNING H.

55267 (& Saxe, C. H.) Role confusion in a Negro-Indian woman. Clin Stud
Cult Confl 125-150

ORCHINIK, CARLTON W.

55268 On tickling and stuttering. PPR 1958, 45(3):25-39

ORENS, MARTIN H.

55269 The genesis of environment. J Hillside Hosp 1958, 7:162-177
55270 Setting a termination date—an impetus to analysis. J Am Psa Ass 1955,
3:651-665
Abs TFr J 1956, 37:511. Shentoub RFPsa 1956, 20:568. Young, B.
Q 1959, 28:564
55271 The shift of object in regression. Bull Phila Ass Psa 1957, 7:56-61
Abs EFA Q 1958, 27:446

ABSTRACTS OF:
55272 Taylor, F. K. The scapegoat motif in society and its manifestations in a
therapeutic group. Q 1955, 24:152
55273 Weiss, E. Paul Federn's scientific contributions: in commemoration.
Q 1953, 22: 298-299

ORGEL, SAMUEL ZACHARY

55274   (et al) Clinical symposium on group psychotherapy: a problem of oral aggression experienced in group psychotherapy. J Hillside Hosp 1955, 4:32-58

55275   Discussion of Sperling, O. E. "Some observations on failure of leadership." Psa Soc S 1955, 4:101-103

55276   Effect of psychoanalysis on the course of peptic ulcer. PSM 1958, 20:117-123
            Abs Luchina, I. Rev Psicoanál 1958, 15:426. Afterman, J. Q 1959, 28:130

55277   The part of the disease that is fear. In Standard, S. & Nathan, H. "Should the Patient Know the Truth?" A Response, NY: Springer 1955, 59-65

55278   The problem of bisexuality as reflected in circumcision. J Hillside Hosp 1956, 5:375-383
            Abs Afterman, J. Q 1958, 27:610-611

55279   Symposium on disturbances of the digestive tract: III. Oral regression during psychoanalysis of peptic ulcer patients. (Read at 21st Int Psa Cong, Copenhagen, July 1959) J 1960, 41:456-461

ORIGLIA, D.

55280   Aspetti della personalità del ragazzo difficile. [Personality aspects of the difficult child.] Minerva Med 1955, 46(II):635-640

55281   Possibilità di una psicoterapia su basi non-freudiane in sede neuropsichiatrica. [The possibility of a psychotherapy on non-Freudian basis in neuropsychiatry.] Arch Psicol Neurol Psichiat 1953, 14:306-309

ORLINSKY, NANCY

55282   Patients' and therapists' conceptions of the therapist's role in relation to outcome of therapy. Chicago: Dept of Photoduplication, Univ Chicago Lib 1959

ORMAECHAEA, JOSE LUIS DE

55283   Psicoterapía Kretschmeriana: sugestión, psicoanalisis y entrenamiento. [Kretschmerian psychotherapy: suggestion, psychoanalysis and training.] Rev Psicol gen apl, Madrid 1952, 7:261-270

ORMIAN, H.

55284   Child psychology and "controversy of schools." Acta Psychol, Amsterdam 1953, 9:16-52

ORMONT, LOUIS R.

55285   The preparation of patients for group psychoanalysis. PT 1957, 11:841-848

ORMBEY, R.

See Saul, Leon J.

ORNE, MARTIN T.

55286 The nature of hypnosis: artifact and essence. ASP 1959, 58:277-299
       Abs Applebaum, S. A. Q 1960, 29:441

ORR, DOUGLAS W.

55287 Transference and countertransference: a historical survey. J Am Psa
       Ass 1954, 2:621-670
       Abs NRo An Surv Psa 1954, 5:335-337; 346. TFr J 1955, 36:430.
       Shentoub RFPsa 1955, 19:503. Asch, S. Q 1958, 27:282

REVIEW OF:
55288 Alexander, F. Our Age of Unreason. Q 1953, 22:93-95

ORROK, DOUGLAS HALL

55289 Lenormand's Don Juan. Lit & Psych 1956, 6(3):87-89

ORTEGA, MAGNO J.

55290 Delusions of jealousy. PPR 1959, 46(4):102-103

OSBERG, JAMES W.

See Lewis, J. M.

OSGOOD, CHARLES E.

See Bruner, Jerome S.

OSHER, STANLEY

ABSTRACTS OF:
55291 Balint, M. Opening moves in psychotherapy. Q 1959, 28:568
55292 Bertalanffy, L. von: Some biological considerations on the problem of
       mental illness. Q 1960, 29:138-139
55293 Feldman, S. S. Notes on some religious rites and ceremonies. Q 1959,
       28:568
55294 Frank, J. Treatment approach to acting-out character disorders. Q 1959,
       28:568
55295 Glauber, I. P. Notes on the early stages in the development of stutter-
       ing. Q 1959, 28:568
55296 Kanzer, M. The recollection of the forgotten dream. Q 1959, 28:569
55297 Niederland, W. G. Further remarks on river symbolism. Q 1959, 28:569
55298 Rubin, S. A study of the daydream illustrating some aspects of ego
       functioning. Q 1959, 28:569
55299 Sperling, M. Equivalents of depression in children. Q 1959, 28:569
55300 Sperling, O. E. Thought control and creativity. Q 1959, 28:570
55301 Stern, M. M. Hysterical spells. Q 1959, 28:570

OSMOND, HUMPHREY

55302 (& Smythies, J. R.) The present state of psychological medicine. Hib-
       bert J 1952-53, 51:133-142

OSSIPOW, N.

55303 [The analysis of sexual experiences.] Czechosl psa annual 1947
55304 ["The Double. Petersburg Poem" of Dostoevskii.] (Russian) Collection *On Dostoevskii*. Prague: 1929, 39-63
55305 [Interpretation of dreams. (Chapters on Freudian psychology).] Czechosl psa annual 1948
55306 [The neurosis of fear.] (Russian) Report of Lecture to Moscow Society of Neuropathology and Psychiatry. Psikhoterapiya 1910, 98-101
55307 [Psychology of complexes and experiment with association according to the work of the Zürich clinic.] (Russian) Zhurnal nevropat i psikhiat im Korsakova 1908, 4
55308 [Recent works of the Freudian School.] (Russian) Moscow: 1909, 61 p

OSSORIO, ABEL

See Loevinger, Jane

ØSTERGAARD, LISE

55309 On psychogenic obesity in childhood. Acta paediatr, Stockh 1954, 43:507-521

See Bruch, Hilde

OSTOW, MORTIMER

55310 Behavior correlates of neural function. Amer Scientist 1955, 43:127-133
55311 Biologic basis of religious symbolism. Int Rec Med 1958, 171:709-717
55312 Clinical estimation of ego energy content. (Read at Phila Ass Psa, Oct 16, 1959)
　　　Abs Ecker, P. G. Bull Phila Ass Psa 1960, 10:64-66
55313 The control of human behavior. J 1959, 40:273-286
　　　Abs Weiss, J. Q 1960, 29:585
55314 The death instincts—a contribution to the study of instincts. J 1958, 39:5-16
　　　Abs JLan Q 1959, 28:106. Racamier RFPsa 1959, 23:153-154
55315 Depression: a psychiatric view. Judaism Psychiat 61-72
55316 Discussion of Bellak, L. "The unconscious." Ann NY Acad Sci 1959, 76:1091-1092
55317 Discussion of Kubie, L. S. "Some implications for psychoanalysis of modern concepts of the organization of the brain." Q 1953, 22:57-61
55318 Discussion of Pumpian-Mindlin, E. "Propositions concerning energetic-economic aspects of libido theory: conceptual models of psychic energy and structure in psychoanalysis." Ann NY Acad Sci 1959, 76:1057-1058
55319 Discussion of Stanton, A. H. "Propositions concerning object choices." Ann NY Acad Sci 1959, 76:1032-1033; 1036-1037
55320 Discussion of Szasz, T. S. "A critical analysis of some aspects of the libido theory: the concepts of libidinal zones, aims, and modes of gratification." Ann NY Acad Sci 1959, 76:996-997; 1003-1004; 1006-1007

55321   The erotic instincts—a contribution to the study of instincts. J 1957,
         38:305-324
            Abs Auth Q 1958, 27:598. Golden, M. M. Q 1956, 25:627-629.
         Racamier RFPsa 1959, 23:152
55322   Fluctuations of temporal lobe electroencephalographic abnormality
         during psychic function. P 1953, 110:55-60
55323   The illusory reduplication of body parts in cerebral disease. Q 1958,
         27:98-103
            Abs JKl J 1959, 40:366-367
55324   The limitations of reason. PPR 1959, 46(1):3-27
55325   Linkage fantasies and representations. J 1955, 36:387-392
            Abs JLan Q 1957, 26:282
55326   The metapsychology of autoscopic phenomena. (Read at Am Psa Ass,
         Apr 1959) J 1960, 41:619-625
55327   The nature of religious controls. Am Psych 1958, 13:571-574
55328   (& Scharfstein, B. A.) The Need to Believe. The Psychology of Re-
         ligion. NY: IUP 1954, 162 p
            Rv MBr J 1955, 36:408. GZ Q 1955, 24:291-293. NRo J Am Psa
         Ass 1958, 6:519-539
55329   (& Scharfstein, B. A.) The need to believe. Read Psychol Relig 190-
         193. From authors' The Need to Believe
55330   The need to believe; persistent religious behavior in non-believers. Int
         Rec Med 1955, 168:798-802
55331   A primal horde dream. Q 1959, 28:470-480
55332   Psychic contents and processes of the brain. I. The brain as a com-
         puting machine. PSM 1955, 17:396-406
55333   (& Kline, N. S.) The psychic effects of chlorpromazine and reserpine.
         In Kline, N. S. Psychopharmacology Frontiers, Boston: Little, Brown
         1959
55334   Psychic effects of the newer drugs. In The Dynamics of Psychiatric
         Drug Therapy, Springfield, Ill: Thomas; England: Blackwell 1959
55335   The psychic function of depression: a study in energetics. (Read at NY
         Psa Soc, June 9, 1959) Q 1960, 29:355-394
            Abs Donadeo, J. Q 1959, 28:580-581
55336   Psychic function of temporal lobe as inferred from seizure phenomena.
         AMA ANP 1957, .77:79-85
55337   (Reporter) Psychoanalysis and ethology. (Panel: Amer Psa Ass, NY,
         Dec 1959) J Am Psa Ass 1960, 8:526-534
55338   Psychoanalysis and the brain. Acta med orient, Jerusalem 1956, 15:167-
         176
55339   A psychoanalytic contribution to the study of brain function. I. The
         frontal lobes. Q 1954, 23:317-338
            Abs Auth J 1955, 36:423. NRo An Surv Psa 1954, 5:37-41. Schloss-
         man, H. Q 1954, 23:157-158. Dreyfus RFPsa 1955, 19:505. Rev
         Psicoanál 1955, 12:308-309
55340   A psychoanalytic contribution to the study of brain function. II. The
         temporal lobes; III. Synthesis. Q 1955, 24:383-423
            Abs Schlossman, H. Q 1954, 23:311-312. Dreyfus RFPsa 1956,
         20:570. JKl J 1956, 37:204

55341 Psychodynamic disturbances in patients with temporal lobe disorder. J Mt Sinai Hosp 1954, 20(5):293-308

55342 Psychodynamics of depression. JNMD 1955, 121:181. AMA ANP 1955, 73:462-463

55343 The psychology of depression and its management. Bull NY Acad Med 1955, 31:757-773

55344 Religion and psychoanalysis: the area of common concern. Pastoral Psychol 1959, 10(94):33-38

55345 The structural model: ego, id, and superego. In *Conceptual and Methodological Problems in Psychoanalysis.* Ann NY Acad Sci 1959, 76:1098-1125

55346 (Reporter) Theory of aggression. (Panel at Am Psa Ass, Dec 1956) J Am Psa Ass 1957, 5:556-563

55347 Toilet symbols and fantasies. J Am Psa Ass 1955, 3:682-696
Abs TFr J 1956, 37:511

55348 Use of drugs to overcome technical difficulties in psychiatry. In *The Dynamics of Psychiatric Drug Therapy,* Springfield, Ill: Thomas 1959

55349 Virtue and necessity. Am Im 1957, 14:243-261

See Appel, Kenneth E.; Linn, Louis; Scharfstein, Ben-Ami

REVIEWS OF:

55350 Foerster, H. von, et al (eds): Cybernetics. Circular Causal and Feed-Back Mechanisms in Biological and Social Systems. Q 1953, 22:272-277; 1954, 23:591-594

55351 Jeffress, L. A. (Ed) Cerebral Mechanisms in Behavior. The Hixon Symposium. Q 1953, 22:105-108

55352 Stern, K. The Third Revolution. Q 1955, 24:448-450

OSTROV, LEÓN

55353 Sobre algunos aspectos especificos de las relaciones entre analistas. [Certain specific aspects of the relations between analysts.] Rev Psicoanál 1959, 16:432-437

REVIEWS OF:

55354 Bergler, E. Conflict in Marriage. Rev Psicoanál 1953, 10:239-240

55355 Blajan-Marcus, E. Erreurs, tâtonnements et tentations des apprentis analystes. Rev Psicoanál 1953, 10:514-515

55356 Lenoble, R. Psychanalyse et Science de l'Homme. Rev Psicoanál 1953, 10:249

OSTROVSKY, EVERETT S.

55357 Father to the Child; Case Studies of the Experiences of a Male Teacher with Young Children. NY: Putnam 1959, 173 p

OSTROW, ELLEN K.

See Kazan, Avraam T.

OSTWALD, E.

55358 [Clinical investigations into the influence of personality on blood pressure and peripheral hemorrhage.] (German) Med Klin 1949, 861

OSTWALD, PETER FREDERIC

55359 (& Regan, P. F., III) Psychiatric disorders associated with childbirth. JNMD 1957, 125:153-165

OTAOLA, J. R. DE

55360 El Análisis de los Suenos. [The Analysis of Dreams.] Barcelona: Argos 1954
  Rv Garcia Badaracco, J. RFPsa 1954, 18:303-304. Garma, A. Rev Psicoanál 1955, 12:297-298

55361 XVIII Congreso psicoanalítico internacional. [18th International Psychoanalytic Congress.] Rev Psiquiat Psicol 1953, 1:311-313

55362 Nuevas aportaciones a la interpretación biográfica de Freud. [New contributions to a biographic interpretation of Freud.] Rev Psiquiat Psicol 1956, 2:637-649

OTTENBERG, PERRY

See Stein, Marvin

OTTENHEIMER, LILLY

55363 On the nature and early development of the ego ideal. PT 1955, 9:612-623

OUTLER, ALBERT COOK

55364 Psychotherapy and the Christian Message. NY: Harper 1954, 286 p

OVERHOLSER, WINFRED

55365 (Ed) Centennial Papers. Saint Elizabeths Hospital, 1855-1955. Wash: Centennial Commission, Saint Elizabeths Hospital 1956, ix + 251 p

55366 (& Werkman, S. L.) Etiology, pathogenesis, and pathology. Schiz Rev Syn 82-106

55367 Forensic psychiatry. Prog Neurol Psychiat 1957, 12:490-493

55368 Foreword to Bromberg, W. *Man Above Humanity: A History of Psychotherapy*

55369 An historical sketch of Saint Elizabeths Hospital. In author's *Centennial Papers. Saint Elizabeths Hospital, 1855-1955*, 1-24

See Malamud, William; Mettler, Fred A.

REVIEWS OF:

55370 Arieti, S. (Ed) American Handbook of Psychiatry. Q 1960, 29:266-267

55371 Bennett, A. E. et al (Eds) The Practice of Psychiatry in General Hospitals. Q 1957, 26:128-129

55372 Evaluation in Mental Health. Report of a Subcommittee on Evaluation of Mental Health Activities. Q 1956, 25:108

55373 Goldhammer, H. & Marshall, A. W. Psychosis and Civilization: Two Studies in the Frequency of Mental Disease. Q 1954, 23:129-130

55374 Greenblatt, M. et al (Eds) The Patient and the Mental Hospital. Q 1958, 27:430-432

55375 Guttmacher, M. S. & Weihofen, H. Psychiatry and the Law. Q 1953, 22:586-587
55376 Hoch, P. & Zubin, J. (Eds) Psychiatry and the Law. Q 1956, 25:594-596
55377 Interrelations between the Social Environment and Psychiatric Disorders. Q 1954, 23:597-599
55378 Laughlin, H. P. The Neuroses in Clinical Practice. Q 1957, 26:128
55379 Linn, L. A Handbook of Hospital Psychiatry. Q 1956, 25:437
55380 Neustatter, W. L. Psychological Disorder and Crime. Q 1954, 23:128-129
55381 Stanton, A. H. & Schwartz, M. S. The Mental Hospital. Q 1955, 24:591-592

OVESEY, LIONEL

55382 (& Jameson, J.) The adaptational technique of psychoanalytic therapy. Chg Cpts Psa Med 165-179
55383 The homosexual conflict: an adaptational analysis. Ps 1954, 17:243-250 Abs JFr An Surv Psa 1954, 5:194-195
55384 Masculine aspirations in women; an adaptational analysis. Ps 1956, 19:341-351
55385 The pseudohomosexual anxiety. Ps 1955, 18:17-26
55386 Pseudohomosexuality, the paranoid mechanism, and paranoia. Ps 1955, 18:163-173. In Crow, L. D. & Crow, A. *Readings in Abnormal Psychology,* Ames, Iowa: Littlefield, Adams 1958, 348-364. Psychopathol 380-403
55387 The theoretical approaches: round table discussion. Curr App Psa 47-54

See Kardiner, Abram

OWEN, JOSEPH H.

55388 Obituary: William H. Dunn, M.D. 1898-1955. J Am Psa Ass 1955, 3:357-358

OWEN, JOSEPH W.

REVIEWS OF:
55389 Association for Research in Nervous and Mental Disease: The Neurologic and Psychiatric Aspects of the Disorders of Aging. Q 1958, 27:424-426
55390 Strachey, A. The Unconscious Motives of War. Q 1958, 27:121-122

OWEN, M.

55391 Over-identification in the schizophrenic child and its relationship to treatment. JNMD 1955, 121:223-229

OWENS, CHARLOTTE

See Caplan, Gerald

OWENS, GWINN

55392 The coming choice for psychiatry. Johns Hopkins Mag 1957, 8(8):4-7, 21-23

ŌYAMA, JUNDO

55393 Comparative study on the psychoanalysis and Buddhism-theory. Sendai J Psychoanal 1953, 4-5

55394 Consideration of mental conflict and Ādāna-Vījñāna. Sendai J Psychoanal 1953, 18-20

55395 Psycho-analysis of religious exaltation. Jap J Psa 1957, 4:1-9

55396 The theories of personality in psychoanalysis and the concept of the Three Consciousnesses (Vījñāna) in Buddhism. I. On Es and mano-vījñāna. Jap J Psa 1958, 5:9-14

55397 On the unconsciousness-theory in Buddhism in view of the psycho-analysis. Sendai J Psychoanal 1953, 13-14

OYARZÚN, F.

55398 Identificación y problemas psicológicos en la adolescencia. [Identification and psychological problems in adolescence.] Rev psiquiat, Santiago 1956-57, 21-22:96-103

See Ganzaraín, Ramón

P

PACELLA, BERNARD L.

55399 The delinquent. J S Carolina Med Assn 1959, 55:41-49
55400 (& Impastato, D. J.) Focal stimulation therapy. P 1954, 110:576-578
55401 (& Doltolo, J. J.; Fleischer, M. S.) Narcophotic stimulation of psychiatric patients. AMA ANP 1953, 69:772-773
55402 "Nonshock" therapies in clinical practice. P 1955, 111:845-850
55403 Photic stimulation of psychiatric patients. Conf neurol 1953, 13:309-312
55404 (& Doltolo, J.; Cerulli, R. R.) Sub-convulsive metrazol therapy. JNMD 1953, 117:50-54

See Impastato, David J.; Lewis, Nolan D. C.

PACHECO E SILVA, A. C.

55405 Apreciações da psicanálise. [Evaluation of psychoanalysis.] Gaz méd Portug 1953, 6(2):311-314

PACI, ENZO

55406 Sulla concezione psicanalitica dell'angoscia. [About the psychoanalytic concept of anxiety.] Arch Filos 1952, 71-79

PAGE, HORACE A.

55407 Studies in fantasy—daydreaming frequency and Rorschach scoring categories. J consult Psychol 1957, 21:111-114

PAILLERETS

See Duché, D.

PAIVA, L. M. DE

55408 Estudo psicossomático e psicanalítico das dispepsias gástricas. [The psychosomatic and psychoanalytic study of gastrointestinal disorders.] Med cir farm, Rio 1956, (244):430-439
55409 Pseudo-frigidez; etiologia e tratamento (hormonal e psicanalítico). [Pseudo-frigidity; etiology and treatment (with hormones and with psychoanalysis).] Rev paul med 1956, 48:449-466

PALEÓLOGO, C.

55410 Psicanálise e criação literária. [Psychoanalysis and literary creation.] Rev Bras Saúde ment 1956, 2(2):69-74

PALEOLOGOS, M.

55411   Psychoneurosis in childhood. Ann Np Psa 1959, 6:61-86

PALEY, AARON

S-24916A Hypnotherapy in the treatment of alcoholism.
Abs RRG Q 1953, 22:127

PALM, ROSE

55412   A comparative study of symbol formation in the Rorschach Test and
the dream. R 1956, 43:246-251
Abs JLan Q 1957, 26:585
55413   Contribution of Rorschach research in Fowler, E. & Zeckel, A. *Psychophysiological Factors in Menière's Disease.* PSM 1953, 15(2)
55414   Identification and magical thinking. PPR 1960, 47(4):32-36
55415   A note in the bisexual origin of man. NPAP 1957, 5(3):77-80
55416   The psychodynamics of enuresis. A psychoanalytical study in Rorschach
symbolism. Am Im 1953, 10:167-180
55417   [Contributor to] Research Project for the Study and Treatment of
Persons Convicted of Crimes involving Sexual Aberrations. NY State
Dept of Mental Hygiene 1956
55418   (& Abrahamsen, D.) A Rorschach study of the wives of sex offenders.
JNMD 1954, 119:167-172
55419   On the symbolic significance of the Star of David. Am Im 1958, 15:
227-231

REVIEW OF:
55420   Schafer, R. Psychoanalytic Interpretations in Rorschach Testing. NPAP
1955, 3(4):73-75

PALMER, DWIGHT M.

55421   Mental reactions following injuries in which there is no evidence of
damage to nervous tissues. J Forens Med 1954, 1:222-230

PALMER, F. CLAUDE

55422   The death instinct and Western man. Hibbert J 1952-53, 51:329-337

See Buck, Alice E.

PALMER, HAROLD ANSTRUTHER

55423   Psychopathic Personalities. NY: Philos Libr 1957, 179 p

PALMER, JAMES N.

ABSTRACT OF:
55424   Eidelberg, L. An Outline of a Comparative Pathology of the Neuroses.
An Surv Psa 1954, 5:496-503

PALMER, JAMES O.

55425   (& Cutter, A. W.; Zuger, B.; Rabinovitch, R. D.; Lowrey, L. G.;
Lippman, H. S.; Levy, D. M.; Lourie, R. S.; Lurie, L. A.; Karpman, B.)

Discussion. Round Table 2; Psychopathic behavior. In Karpman, B. *Symposia on Child and Juvenile Delinquency*, Wash: Psychodynamics Series, 1959, 91-101

PALMIERI, V. M.

55426   Relazione di perizia medico-legale sullo stato di mente di Otello. [Report of medico-legal assessment of the state of mind of Othello.] Ann Np Psa 1955, 2:81-92

PALMORE, ERDMAN

55427   (& Lennard, H. L.; Hendin, H.) Similarities of therapist and patient verbal behavior in psychotherapy. Sociometry 1959, 22:12-22

See Lennard, Henry L.

PANETH, LUDWIG

55428   Zahlensymbolik im Unbewusstsein. [The Symbolism of Numbers in the Unconscious.] Zurich: Rascher 1952, xii + 235 p

PANKOW, GISELA

55429   Darstellung der Übertragung in der analytischen Behandlung einer paranoischen Patientin. [Representation of transmission in the treatment of a female paranoical patient.] Int Cong Psychotherapy, Zurich 1954. Proc of Cong, Basel 1955, 537 (Suppl 259)
55430   Das doppelte Spiegelbild. [The double mirror image.] Z Psychother med Psychol 1958, 8(2):45-50
55431   Dynamic structurization and Goldstein's concept of the organism. Psa 1959, 19:157-160
55432   Dynamic structurization in schizophrenia. In *The Psychotherapy of the Psychoses*, NY: Basic Books 1959
55433   Dynamische Strukturierung in der Psychose. [Psychodynamic Organization in Schizophrenia.] (Pref: Favez-Boutonier, J.) Bern: Hans Huber 1957, 171 p
55434   La estructuración dinamica de la imagen del cuerpo en los enfermos mentales. [Dynamic structuration of the body image in mental patients.] Rev Psiquiat Psicol 1959, 4:335-340
55435   Das Gesetz und die Stimmen. Ein Beitrag zur analytischen Psychotherapie der Psychosen. [The law and the voices—A contribution to the analytical psychotherapy of psychosis.] Der Psychologe 1956, 8:262-269
55436   L'image du corps dans la psychose. [The body image in psychosis.] Cahiers Montagien, Nouvelle série, Paris 1959, 4:1-11
55437   Das Körperbild bei einer Asthma-Kranken. [The body image of a female asthmatic patient.] Z PSM 1958-59, 5:191-204
55438   La méthode de la structuration dynamique appliquée à un cas d'état hallucinatoire chronique. [The method of dynamic structurization applied in a case of a chronic hallucinatory state.] Psychanalyse 1958, 4:111-133

55439 Der Ring am Fuss der Zigeunerin. Ein Zugang zur psychotischen Welt eines Philosophen. [The ring on the foot of a gypsy.—An approach to the psychotic world of a philosopher.] Der Psychologe 1959, 11:145-150

55440 Die Schauspielerin und die Schallplatte. Ein Beitrag zur Psychopathologie des Alltagslebens. [The actress and the record. A contribution to the psychopathology of everyday life.] Der Psychologe 1957, 9:344-346

55441 Das Spiel der Hand. Ein Beitrag zur Psychotherapie des Stehlens. [The game of the hand. A contribution to the psychotherapy of stealing.] Der Psychologe 1955, 7:240-246

55442 Structuration dynamique dans la schizophrénie. Contribution à une psychothérapie analytique de l'expérience psychotique du monde. [Dynamic structure in schizophrenia; a contribution to psychoanalytic therapy in a psychotic experience of the world.] Schweiz Z Psychol 1956, Suppl 27:1-80

55443 Über eine visuelle Primitivreaktion bei einer paranoischen Patientin. [A visual "primitive reaction" of a paranoid female patent.] Z Psychother méd Psychol 1955, 5:19-29

55444 Die wiedergefundene Sprache. [The recovered speech.] In *Mehrdimensionale Diagnostik und Therapie*. Publication on the occasion of 70th anniv of Prof Dr. Ernst Kretschmer, Stuttgart

See Kelman, Harold

TRANSLATION OF:
Decourt, J. [44167]

PANSE, F.

55445 [Anxiety and Terror from the Point of View of Clinical Psychology and Social Medicine.] (German) Stuttgart: Thieme 1952

PAP, ARTHUR

55446 On the empirical interpretation of psychoanalytic concepts. Psa Sci Method Phil 283-297

PAPANEK, E.

55447 Das Kinderheim, seine Theorie und Praxis im Lichte der Individualpsychologie. [The children's home, its theory and practice as seen in the light of individual psychology.] Acta psychother psychosom orthopaedag 1956, 4:53-72

PAPANEK, H.

55448 Combined group and individual therapy in private practice. PT 1954, 8:679

55449 Ethical values in psychotherapy. J ind Psychol 1958, 14:160-166

PAPATHOMOPOULOS, EVANGELOS

See Seidenberg, Robert

PAPERTE, FRANCES
See Taylor, Irving A.

PAPPENHEIM, ELSE
S-24937 (& Sweeney, M.) Separation anxiety in mother and child.
Abs NRo An Surv Psa 1952, 3:288-289. RTh J 1953, 34:279. Rv
Langer, M. Rev Psicoanál 1953, 10:244-245

REVIEW OF:
55450 Wyss, D. Der Surrealismus. Eine Einführung und Deutung surrealistischer Literatur und Malerei. Q 1953, 22:101-105

PARAD, HOWARD J.
55451 (Ed) Ego Psychology and Dynamic Casework. Papers from Smith
College School for Soc Work. NY: Family Serv Assoc of Amer 1958,
282 p
Rv Woolf, P. J. Q 1959, 28:104-105

PARCELLS, FRANK H.
55452 (& Segel, N. P). Oedipus and the prodigal son. Q 1959, 28:213-227
Abs Sapochnik Rev Psicoanál 1960, 17:265

PARCHEMINEY, GEORGES
S-24947A La conception psychanalytique de l'angoisse. Vie méd 1953, 33(5):
26-31
S-24949A Exposé d'un cas d'hystérie. Encéph 1954, 43:40-54
S-24962A Psychanalyse et psychologie clinique. Arch Psicol Neur Psich 1953,
14(1-2):85-95

PARDEL, TOMÁŠ
55453 Niektoré kritické poznámky na okraj buržoáznej psychologie. [Critical
remarks about bourgeois psychology.] Psychol Časopis 1953, 1:29-54

PARIN, PAUL
55454 (& Morgenthaler, F.) Charakteranalytischer Deutungsversuch am Verhalten "primitiver" Afrikaner. [Character-analytical interpretation of
the behavior of "primitive" Africans.] Psyche, Heidel 1956, 10:311-330
55455 Einige Charakterzüge "primitiver" Afrikaner. [Some traits of character
found among the West African Negroes.] Psyche, Heidel 1958, 11:692-
706
55456 Die Indikation zur Analyse. [The indication for psychoanalysis.] Psyche,
Heidel 1958, 12:367-387
55457 Das "sinnlose" Fragen der Patienten. ["Silly questions" by patients.]
Schweiz med Wschr 1952, 82:568-572

PARK, EDWARDS A.
55458 Preface to Kanner, L. Child Psychiatry.

PARK, PAUL D.
See Goldfarb, Walter

PARKER, BEULAH
See Lidz, Theodore

PARKER, JAMES W.
See Klopfer, Bruno

PARKER, SEYMOUR
55459 Role theory and the treatment of the antisocial acting-out disorders. Brit J Delinq 1956-57, 7:285-300
    Abs Roumajon RFPsa 1958, 22:260-261

PARKES, ERNEST
See Bellak, Leopold

PARKIN, ALAN
55460 Emergence of sleep during psychoanalysis. A clinical note. J 1955, 36:174-176
    Abs JLan Q 1956, 25:613

See Foulkes, S. H.

PARKS OCHANDORENA, RAÚL
See OCHANDORENA, RAUL PARKS

PARLAND, OSKAR
55461 On the psychogenic background of several female epileptics. Acta psychiat, Kbh 1953, Suppl 80:222-232
55462 Some views on sexual factors in the pathogenesis of schizophrenia. Acta psychiat, Kbh 1953, Suppl 80:60-66

PARLOFF, MORRIS B.
55463 (& Kelman, H. C.; Frank, J. D.) Comfort, effectiveness and self-awareness as criteria of improvement in psychotherapy. P 1954, 111:345-351
55464 (& Rubinstein, E. A.) Research problems in psychotherapy. Res PT 276-293
55465 Some factors affecting the quality of therapeutic relationships. ASP 1956, 52:5-10

See Kelman, Herbert; Rubinstein, Eli A.; Stone, Anthony R.

PARNES, HERBERT S.
55466 Mobility and the process of labor allocation. In author's *Research on Labor Mobility*, Soc Science Research Council Bull 1954, (65):144-190

PARRAL, J. J.

55467 Tres instantáneas psicoanalíticas. [Three cases of psychoanalysis.] Rev Publ nav, B. Aires 1953, 6(3-4):183-191

PARRES, RAMON

See Ramirez, Santiago

PARROT, P.

55468 (& Gueneau, M.) L'angoisse de dévalorisation chez l'adolescent délinquant. [Self-devaluation and anxiety in delinquent adolescents.] Ann méd-psychol 1957, 2(2):241-255

55469 (& Gueneau, M.) Un cas de bouc-émissaire dans un foyer de sémi-liberté (filles). [A scapegoat in a semi-free home (for girls).] Rv Np inf 1957, 5:25-28

55470 (& Gueneau, M.) Une formule de rééducation: la semi-liberté. [A formula for re-education: semi-freedom.] Ann méd-psychol 1957, 1(5): 801-827

55471 (& Romain, R. P.; Mabille; Courtelare, A.) Une maison médico-psychologique réservée à des prêtres. [A medical-psychological house reserved for priests.] Suppl Vie Spir 1958, (46):355-368

55472 (& Romain, R. P.) Maturité affective et vocation sacerdotale. [Affective maturity and the vocation of priesthood.] Suppl Vie Spir 1958, (46): 307-322

PARSONS, TALCOTT

55473 Boundary relations between sociocultural and personality systems. Unif Theory Behav 325-339

55474 (& Shils, E. A.) Categories of the orientation and organization of action. In authors' *Toward a General Theory of Action*, 53-109

55475 (& Shils, E. A.) Conclusions. In authors' *Toward a General Theory of Action*, 234-243

55476 The definitions of health and illness in the light of American values and social structure. In Jaco, E. G. *Patients, Physicians and Illness*, Glencoe, Ill: Free Pr 1958

55477 (& Bales, R. F.) The dimensions of action space. In author's *Working Papers in the Theory of Action*.

55478 Essays in Sociological Theory. Rev ed. Glencoe, Ill: Free Pr 1954, 459 p
         Rv Schmidl, F. Q 1955, 24:306-307

55479 (& Bales, R. F.; Olds, J.; Slater, P.; Zelditch, M., Jr.) Family, Socialization, and Interaction Process. Glencoe, Ill: Free Pr 1955, 422 p
         Rv HRB Q 1957, 26:125-127

55480 Father symbol: an appraisal in the light of psychoanalytic and sociological theory. In Bryson, L. et al: *Conference on Science, Philosophy, and Religion in Their Relation to the Democratic Way of Life; 13th Symposium: Symbols and Values. NY: 1952.* NY: Harper Bros 1954, 523-544

55481 (& Shils, E. A.) A general statement. In authors' *Toward a General Theory of Action*, 3-29

55482 Illness and the role of the physician: a sociological perspective. Ops 1951, 21:452-460. Pers n s c 609-617

55483 (& Fox, R.) Illness, therapy and the modern urban American family. J soc Issues 1952, 8(4):2-3; 31-44. In Jaco, E. G. *Patients, Physicians and Illness*, Glencoe, Ill: Free Pr 1958, 234-245

55484 The incest taboo in relation to social structure and the socialization of the child. Brit J Sociol 1954, 5:101-117

55485 (& Shils, E. A.) Introduction. In authors' *Toward a General Theory of Action*, 47-52

55486 (& Shils, E. A.) Personality as a system of action. In authors' *Toward a General Theory of Action*, 110-158

55487 (& Bales, R. F.; Shils, E. A.) Phase movement in relation to motivation, symbol formation, and role structure. In authors' *Working Papers in the Theory of Action*,

55488 Psychoanalysis and social science. 20 Yrs Psa 186-215

55489 Psychology and sociology. In Gillin, J. *For a Science of Social Man*, NY: Macmillan 1954, 67-101

55490 The relation between the small group and the larger social system. Unif Theory Behav 190-200

55491 Social structure and the development of personality: Freud's contribution to the integration of psychology and sociology. Ps 1958, 21:321-340
　　　Abs HRB Q 1959, 28:571-572

55492 The social system: a general theory of action. Unif Theory Behav 55-69

55493 Some comments on the state of the general theory of action. Amer sociol Rev 1953, 18:618-631

55494 Suggestions for a sociological approach to the theory of organizations. I. Adm sci Quart 1956, 1:63-85; 225-239

S-24999 The superego and the theory of social systems. In author's *Working Papers in the Theory of Action*, 13-28.
　　　Abs STa An Surv Psa 1952, 3:456-459

55495 (& Shils, E. A.) (Ed) Toward a General Theory of Action. Cambridge: Harvard Univ Pr 1951, 506 p
　　　Rv Muensterberger, W. Q 1953, 22:120-122

55496 (& Bales, R. F.; Shils, E. A.) Working Papers in the Theory of Action. Glencoe, Ill: The Free Pr 1953

PARTRIDGE, MAURICE

See Curran, Desmond

PAS, J. H. VAN DER

55497 Übertragung und Existenz. [Transference and existence.] Acta psychotherap psychosom orthopaedag 1955, 3(Suppl):260-265

PASAMANICK, BENJAMIN

55498 (Chm) Group discussion on therapist-patient relationship. Res PT 264-275

55499 (& Rogers, M. E.; Lilienfeld, A. M.) Pregnancy experience and the development of behavior disorders in children. P 1956, 112:613-618

55500 (& Knobloch, H.; Lilienfeld, A. M.) Socioeconomic status and some precursors of neuropsychiatric disorders. Ops 1956, 26:594-601

PASCAL, GERALD R.

55501 (& Sipprelle, C. N.) Development of a neurotic fear of contamination. Clin Stud Pers 322-340

55502 The psychoneuroses. Intro Clin Psych 2:276-395

PASCHE, FRANCIS

55503 L'angoisse et la théorie freudienne des instincts. [Anxiety and the Freudian theory of instincts.] RFPsa 1954, 18:76-104
       Abs NRo An Surv Psa 1954, 5:48-50

55504 La Génie de Freud. [Freud's Genius.] Paris: PUF 1956, 30 p. RFPsa 1957, 21:333-372. In *1856-1956: Centenaire de la Naissance de Sigmund Freud.* Paris: PUF 1957, 23-52

55505 Intervention sur un rapport du Dr. Benassy. [Comments on a lecture by Dr. Benassy.] RFPsa 1953, 17(1-2), 10 p

55506 Notes sur les perversions. [Notes on perversions.] RFPsa 1955, 19:381-384

55507 (& Renard, M.) Pregenital anxiety, pregenital phantasies and economic point of view. (Read at 19th Int Psa Cong, Geneva, July 1955)
       Abs Auth J 1956, 37:133-134

55508 (& Renard, M.) Psychanalyse et troubles de la sexualité: des problèmes essentiels de la perversion. [Psychoanalysis and sexual disorders: about the main problems of perversion.] In Nacht, S. *La Psychanalyse d'Aujourd'hui,* Paris: PUF 1956, 1:319-345

55509 Autour de quelques propositions freudiennes contestées. [On certain controversial Freudian propositions.] RFPsa 1956, 20:417-431

55510 Réactions pathologiques à la réalité. [Pathologic reactions to reality.] RFPsa 1958, 22:705-717
       Abs De Fiasche Rev Psicoanál 1959, 16:280. Zambonelli Riv Psa 1959, 5:191-192. Stewart, S. Q 1960, 29:146

55511 (& Renard, M.) Réalité de l'objet et point de vue économique. (Read at 19th Int Psa Cong, Geneva, July 1955) RFPsa 1956, 20:517-523
       The reality of the object and economic point of view. (Tr: McDougall, J.) J 1956, 37:282-285
       Abs JLan Q 1957, 26:574

55512 (& Racamier, P. C.) Le terrain psychique es tuberculeux pulmonaires. [The psychic predisposition to pulmonary tuberculosis.] CR First Int Cong Psychiatry, Paris 1950, Paris: Hermann 1951, 5:416-422

See Lebovici, Serge; Schlumberger, Marc

PASCHE, M.

See Glatzel, Hans

PASETTI, ANGELO

55513 Fobia del parto: contributo clinico. [Fear of childbirth: clinical contribution.] Riv Psa 1955, 1(1):78-86

55514 Fughe impulsive [Compulsive fugues.] Riv Studi Psichiat 1955, 44(4)

PASQUARELLI, BLAISE

55515   Psychoanalysis and religion—a postulated autonomy in function. Bull
Phila Ass Psa 1960, 10:10-17

See Bellak, Leopold

PASSONI, JOHN A.

55516   Constructive and obstructive forces in prognosis. Psa 1952, 12:74-77

PASTO, TARMO A.

55517   (& Kivisto, P.) Art and the clinical psychologist. J Aesthet 1953, 12:
76-82

PASTRANA-BORRERO, H. Y.

55518   (& Rascovsky, A.) Vivencias de nacimiento en la situación analítica.
[Birth experiences in the analytic situation.] Rev Psicoanál 1958,
15:86-90

See Rascovsky, Arnaldo; Wencelblat, Simon

PATEL, RAMANLAL M.

55519   Fear of death and the ideas to kill. Samiksa 1959, 12:11-28
55520   Freud, the father of psychoanalysis. Time of India 1956, May 6
55521   The Indian dowry system: a clinical study. Psa 1959, 19:216-219
55522   The phenomena of "identity of perception" and the problem of neurosis. Samiksa 1953, 7:216-223

PATHMAN, JULIAN H.

55523   (& Clark, V.) Psychoanalytically oriented therapy. Intro Clin Psych
2:557-585

See Carlson, Helen B.

PATRICK, CATHERINE

55524   What is Creative Thinking? NY: Philos Lib 1955, xix + 205 p
Rv R 1955, 42:443-444

PATTERSON, CHARLES HENRY

55525   The place of values in counseling and psychotherapy. J counsel Psychol 1958, 5:216-223

PATTERSON, GERALD

55526   (& Schwartz, R.; Van der Wart, E.) The integration of group and
individual therapy. Ops 1956, 26:618-629. In Glueck, S. The Problem
of Delinquency, Boston: Houghton Mifflin 1959, 899-907

PATTERSON, VIRGINIA

See Jackson, Don D.

PATTIE, FRANK A.

55527 Theories of hypnosis. In Dorcus, R. M. *Hypnosis and Its Therapeutic Applications*, NY: McGraw-Hill 1956, 1:1-30

S-25035A (& Cornett, S.) Unpleasantness of early memories and maladjustment of children.
Abs Holzman, P. S. Q 1953, 22:311

PATTON, JOHN D.

See Hill, Lewis B.

PAUL, BENJAMIN D.

55528 Sibling rivalry in San Pedro. Amer Anthropologist 1950, 52:205-218.
Pers n s c 321-334

PAUL, HELMUT

55529 [The psychic life of the dystrophic on the basis of personal experience.] (German) Z Psychother 1955, 5:168

55530 Psychologie und Grenzgebiete der ärztlichen Psychotherapie. [Psychology and the limitations of medical psychotherapy.] Die Heilkunst 1953, 66:242-245

PAUL, IRVING H.

55531 Studies in Remembering. The reproduction of connected and extended verbal material. Psych Issues 1959, 1(2):1-152
Rv Gardner, R. W. Q 1960, 29:410-413

55532 (& Fischer, C.) Subliminal visual stimulation: a study of its influence on subsequent images and dreams. JNMD 1959, 129:315-340

See Fisher, Charles

PAUL, LOUIS

55533 Beyond laughter (letter). Contemp Psychol 1958, 3:80

55534 Implications of general semantics for psychosomatic medicine. PSM 1945, 7:246-248. ETC 1945, 3:58-62

55535 The Mental Health Book Review Index (letter), an answer to Dr. Kahn's query. P 1958, 114:756

55536 A note on the private aspect and professional aspect of the psychoanalyst. Bull Phila Ass Psa 1959, 9:96-101

55537 (& Burdon, A. P.) Obesity: a review of the literature, stressing the psychosomatic approach. Psychiat Q 1951, 25:568-580

55538 Psychoanalytic reduction of an affect block. AMA ANP 1959, 81:100-113

55539 Psychosomatic aspects of low back pain: a review of recent articles. PSM 1950, 12:116-124

55540 Some remarks on psychosomatic issues. ETC 1947, 4:268-274

55541 A treat, not a treatment. (Letter) ETC 1950, 8:68-69

55542 When psychiatrist and patient talk together. MH 1953, 37:425-429.
Wisdom 1957, 2:75-76

PAUL, NORMAN L.

55543   (& Greenblatt, M.) Psychosurgery and schizophrenia. Schiz Rev Syn
         501-530

PAULEEN, MORRIS M.

55544   Some relationships between personality and behavior in hospitalized
         tuberculosis patients. Am Rev Tuber 1957, 76:232-246

PAULI, W.

See Jung, C. G.

PAULSEN, ALMA D.

55545   (Chm) School phobias. Workshop 1955. Ops 1957, 27:286-309
         Abs Koenig RFPsa 1958, 22:258

PAULSEN, LOLA

55546   Transference and projection. J analyt Psychol 1956, 1:203-206

PAUMELLE, P.

55547   La conscience de l'état morbide chez les malades mentaux. [Awareness
         of the state of illness in mental patients.] Évolut psychiat 1957, (1):
         25-45
         Abs Lebovici, S. RFPsa 1957, 21:874

See Lebovici, Serge

PAUNCZ, ARPAD

S-25047 The concept of adult libido and the Lear complex.
         Abs NRo An Surv Psa 1951, 2:93-94
55548   The Lear complex in world literature. Am Im 1954, 11:51-83
         Abs MK An Surv Psa 1954, 5:461-462
S-25047A Psychopathology of Shakespeare's *King Lear:* exemplification of the
         Lear complex (a new interpretation).
         Abs MK An Surv Psa 1952, 3:531-532

See Masserman, Jules H.

PAVENSTEDT, ELEANOR

55549   (& Anderson, I. N.) Complementary treatment of mother and child
         with atypical development. Case St Chd Dis 1953, 1:201-235
55550   The effect of extreme passivity imposed on a boy in early childhood.
         Psa St C 1956, 11:396-409
         Abs RTh J 1959, 40:77
55551   History of a child with an atypical development, and some vicissitudes
         of his treatment. Emot Prob Early Child 379-405
55552   (& Gordon, E.; Roblin, M.; Gilbert, R. R.) Is trying enough? A report
         of treatment during the latency period of a girl with atypical develop-
         ment. Workshop 1954. Ops 1955, 25:398-427. Case St Chd Dis 1956,
         2:231-260
         Abs DRu Q 1956, 25:448

55553 Psychological development of the child. In *Pediatric Dentistry*, St. Louis: C. V. Mosby 1957, Chapt 4

See Jessner, Lucie

PAVLOV, I.

55554 Experimental Psychology and Other Essays. NY: Philos Libr 1957, 653 p
Rv ESt J 1959, 40:358-359

PAYCHERE, E.

See Courchet, J. L.

PAYNE, D. H.

55555 Transference in psychotherapy. J Amer osteop Ass 1953, 53(3):192-195

PAYNE, DONALD E.

55556 (& Mussen, P. H.) Parent-child relations and father identification among adolescent boys. ASP 1956, 52:358-362

PAYNE, L. M.

See Hunter, Richard A.

PAYNE, SYLVIA M.

55557 Concerning defence originating in pregenital phases of libidinal development. (Read at 18th Int Psa Cong, London, July 1953)
Notes sur quelques types de défense du moi. [Several types of ego defense.] RFPsa 1957, 21:83-92
Abs Auth J 1954, 35:288. Rv Morra Riv Psa 1957, 3:225-226
55558 Introduction to Rickman, J. *Selected Contributions to Psychoanalysis.*
55559 Introduction to Sutherland, J. M. *Psycho-Analysis and Contemporary Thought.* London: HPI 1958, 11-14

OBITUARIES:
55560 Iseult Grant Duff. J 1958, 39:619
55561 Dr. Ethilda Budgett-Meakin Herford. J 1957, 38:276
55562 Dr. Ernest Jones. J 1958, 39:307-308
55563 Sir Arthur George Tansley, F.R.S. 1871-1955. J 1956, 37:197
S-25150 Short communication on criteria for terminating analysis.
Abs R 1953, 40:370

PEABODY, GEORGE A.

55564 (& Rowe, A. T.; Wall, J. H.) Fetishism and transvestism. JNMD 1953, 118:339-349

PEAK, HELEN

55565 Attitude and motivation. In Jones, M. R. *Nebraska Symposium on Motivation: 1955*, Lincoln, Neb: Univ of Nebraska Pr 1955, 149-189

55566 Comments on Rotter, J. B. "The role of the psychological situation in determining the direction of human behavior." In Jones, M. R. *Nebraska Symposium on Motivation: 1955*, Lincoln, Neb: Univ Nebraska Pr 1955, 269-270

PEAK, HORACE M.

55567 Search for identity by a young Mexican-American. Clin Stud Cult Confl 201-222

See Bühler, Charlotte

PEALE, NORMAN VINCENT

55568 (& Blanton, S.) How to have a successful marriage. In authors' *The Art of Real Happiness*, NY: Prentice-Hall 1950. Child-Fam Dig 1953, 9(1):59-78

PEAR, TOM H.

55569 Dr. John Carl Flugel. (Obit and portrait) BJP 1956, 47:1-4

PEARCE, ARTHUR J.
See Beard, John H.

PEARLMAN, JACK

S-25192A Psychodynamics in a case of severe hypochondriasis. Abs JFr An Surv Psa 1952, 3:128-129. RRG Q 1953, 22:303

PEARSON, GERALD H. J.

55570 Adolescence and the Conflict of Generations: An Introduction to Some of the Psychoanalytic Contributions to the Understanding of Adolescence. NY: Norton 1958, 186 p
       Abs J Am Psa Ass 1960, 8:221; 587. Rv Belmont, H. S. Bull Phila Ass Psa 1960, 10:154-155
55571 A brief survey of psychosis in children. Bull Phila Ass Psa 1955, 5:15-19
       Abs Herman, M. Q 1958, 27:289-290
55572 The fear of going beserk. Bull Phila Ass Psa 1955, 5:43-44
       Abs Herman, M. Q 1958, 27:290
55573 The most effective help a psychiatrist can give to the teacher. In Krugman, M. *Orthopsychiatry and the School*, NY: Am Ops Ass 1958, 3-22
55574 A note on the connection between urethral erotism and ambition. Bull Phila Ass Psa 1956, 6:29-30
55575 A note on identification and melancholia. Bull Phila Ass Psa 1953, 3:39
55576 A note on oral incorporation. Bull Phila Ass Psa 1955, 5:55
55577 (Reporter) A note on primal repression. (Meeting of Regional Committee on Psychoanalysis of Children and Adolescents, Philadelphia, April 6, 1953) Bull Phila Ass Psa 1953, 3:42
55578 Obituary: Sydney Geoffrey Biddle, M.D. 1889-1954. J Am Psa Ass 1955, 3:355-356
55579 Obituary: H. Whitman Newell (1898-1955). Bull Phila Ass Psa 1955, 5:57-58

55580   Psychoanalysis and the Education of the Child. NY: W. W. Norton
        1954, 357 p
            Rv Spranger, O. NPAP 1954, 3(1):80. Zinkin, J. R 1955, 42:311-312.
        Fountain, G. Q 1956, 25:91-92
55581   The psychoanalytic contributions to the theory and practice of educa-
        tion. Rd Psa Psychol 338-354
55582   The psychopathology of mental defect. Nerv Child 1942, 2:9-20.
        Couns PT Ment Retard 130-141
55583   Some developmental problems in children. Bull Phila Ass Psa 1955,
        5:9-14
55584   Some notes on masochism. Bull Phila Ass Psa 1956, 6:1-20
            Abs EFA Q 1957, 26:285
55585   (Reporter) Some observations on infant behavior. (Meeting of Re-
        gional Committee on Psychoanalysis of Children and Adolescents, May
        18, 1953) Bull Phila Ass Psa 1953, 3:60-61
S-25217 A survey of learning difficulties in children.
            Abs NRo An Surv Psa 1952, 3:244-251. WH J 1953, 34:281
55586   Training program in the Institute of the Philadelphia Association for
        Psychoanalysis. III. The curriculum of the professional school. Bull
        Phila Ass Psa 1953, 3:18-24
55587   What is ego weakness? Bull Phila Ass Psa 1956, 6:43-48
            Abs EFA Q 1957, 26:286
55588   The wise vultures. Bull Phila Ass Psa 1955, 5:115-116

        See English, O. Spurgeon

PEARSON, MANUEL

See Appel, Kenneth E.

PEBERDY, G. R.

55589   The psychiatry of infertility. Med Pr 1958, 240:702-704

PECHEY, B. M.

55590   The direct analysis of the mother-child relationship in the treatment
        of maladjusted children. M 1955, 28:101-112

PÉCHOUX, RAYMOND J. A.

55591   (& Defayolle, M.) Rorschach et libido. [Rorschach and libido.] Ror-
        schachiana 1952, 1:221-238

PECHTEL, C.

See Masserman, Jules H.; Schreiner, L.

PECK, ALICE L.

See Coolidge, John C.; Hahn, Pauline B.; Kaufman, Irving

PECK, HARRIS B.

55592   (Chm) Our young citizens: promise and problem. Symposium 1955.
        Ops 1956, 26:471-496

55593 Psychodynamics of child delinquency. Further contributions. Round Table, 1953. Ops 1955, 25:266-273
55594 Theoretical concepts of delinquency. In Karpman, B. *Symposia on Child and Juvenile Delinquency,* Wash: Psychodynamics Series 1959, 245-252

See Karpman, Ben; Rose, John A.; Slavson, Samuel R.

PECK, ROBERT F.

55595 The child patterns himself after his favorite models. In *Fostering Mental Health in Our Schools,* 1950 Yearbook A.S.C.D., NEA, Wash 1950, 146-157
55596 Family patterns correlated with adolescent personality structure. ASP 1958, 57:347-350
55597 Individuality develops. In *Fostering Mental Health in Our Schools,* 1950 Yearbook of A.S.C.D., NEA, Wash 1950, 64-76

PEDERSEN, STEFI

55598 Autoritär moral. [Authoritarian morals.] Tiden 1952, 5:290-295
55599 Den bortglömde faderen. [The forgotten father.] Barn, Stockholm 1949, 4:2-23
55600 Eidetics, obsessions and modern art. Am Im 1954, 11:341-362
55601 Om evnen til toleranse. [On the ability of being tolerant.] Samtiden 1938
55602 Fall 13. Legal abort. [Case 13. Legal abortion. Case history of a survivor of the Ghetto of Warsaw.] All Världens Berättare, Stockholm 1951, 10:788-798
55603 Flukt og virkelighet. [Flight and reality.] Samtiden 1945, 188-194
55604 Har neurosene ökat? [Have the neuroses increased?] Tiden, Stockholm 1957, (10):598-608
55605 Kjarlighet og arbeid. [Love and Work.] Oslo: Fritt Ord 1938
55606 Korsfareren uten kors. [Crusader without a cross.] Tiden, Stockholm 1955, (9):550-554
55607 Kroppsfölelse og gymnastikk. [Body image and gymnastics.] Norsk Pedagogisk Tidskrift 1939, (4)
55608 Lengselen efter trygghet. Tilpasningsproblem hos flyktningsbarn. [Longing for security. Adaptational difficulties of refugee children.] Norsk Peragogisk Tidskrift 1948, 7
55609 Mennesket mellem norm og drift. [Man between norm and drive.] Samtiden, Oslo 1957, (2):98-108
55610 Moral som behov. [The need for morals.] Tiden 1951, 6:377-378
55611 Den oändliga psykoanalysen. [Psychoanalysis infinite.] Tiden, Stockholm 1956, (5):295-301
55612 Opdragelsesfeil som ikke kan gjöres godt igjen. [Educational errors that cannot be repaired.] Norsk Pedagogisk Tidskrift 1941, 9
55613 Phallic fantasies, fear of death, and ecstasy. Am Im 1960, 17:21-46
55614 Reaching safety. In Murphy, H. B. M. *Flight and Resettlement,* UNESCO 1955, 33-43
55615 Sigmund Freud 100 år. Hans personlighet og dens inflytelse på utformningen av den psykoanalytiske teori. [Sigmund Freud 100 years. His

personality and its influence upon the formation of psychoanalytical theory.] Nordisk Psykologi 1956, 187-194

55616 Tilbakeblik på Sigmund Freuds hundrearsjubileum. [On the occasion of the Freud centenary.] Samtiden 1957, 66:98-108

55617 Trygve Braatøy og Arthur Köstler. [Trygve Braatøy and Arthur Köstler.] Vinduet, Oslo 1950, 5:379-386

S-25257 Unconscious motives in pro-Semitic attitudes.
Abs GD An Surv Psa 1951, 2:515. JFr An Surv Psa 1951, 2:213-214

55618 Att vara ensam. [About loneliness.] In Samuelsson, *Hemmets Samlingsverk*, Malmö: Bernces Forlag 1953, 384-390

PEDERSON-KRAG, GERALDINE

S-25259 The genesis of a sonnet.
Abs MK An Surv Psa 1951, 2:449-451

S-25260 The Pederson-Krag findings. Discussion of Ellis, A. "Telepathy and psychoanalysis: a critique of recent findings." In Devereux, G. *Psychoanalysis and the Occult*, NY: IUP 1953, 326-330

55619 Personality Factors in Work and Employment. NY: Funk & Wagnalls 1955, 269 p
Abs J Am Psa Ass 1955, 3:547. Rv Herma, J. L. NPAP 1955, 4(1):78-79. Hendricks, R. C. Q 1956, 25:601-602

S-25261 "Oh poetry! For thee I hold my pen."
Abs MK An Surv Psa 1951, 2:451-452

S-25262 A psychoanalytic approach to mass production.
Abs GD An Surv Psa 1951, 2:524-525. CR J 1953, 34:69

55620 Similarities in the dynamic functioning of industrial and therapeutic groups. Int J grp PT 1956, 6:280-285

S-25264 Telepathy and repression. In Devereux, G. *Psychoanalysis and the Occult*, NY: IUP 1953, 277-282

55621 The use of metaphor in analytic thinking. Q 1956, 25:66-71
Abs JKl J 1957, 38:131

See Eisenbud, Jule; Glatzer, Henriette T.

ABSTRACTS OF:

55622 Ackerman, N. W. Group psychotherapy with a mixed group of adolescents. Q 1956, 25:623

55623 Ackerman, N. W. Some structural problems in the relations of psychoanalysis and group psychotherapy. Q 1955, 24:621

55624 Adler, J. Therapeutic group work with tuberculous displaced persons. Q 1955, 24:161

55625 Amster, F. Application of group psychotherapy principles to nonstructured groups. Q 1955, 24:622

55626 Beard, J. H. et al: The effectiveness of activity group therapy with chronically regressed adult schizophrenics. Q 1959, 28:431-432

55627 Bion, W. R. Psychoanalysis and ethics. Q 1953, 22:608

55628 Bowers, M. et al: Therapeutic implications of analytic group psychotherapy of religious personnel. Q 1959, 28:432

55629 Braunthal, H. A casework training course as a group therapeutic experience. Q 1953, 22:309

55630 Brody, M. W. & Harrison, S. I. Group psychotherapy with male stutterers. Q 1955, 24:621
55631 Bross, R. B. The "deserter" in group psychotherapy. Q 1958, 27:145-146
55632 Bry, T. Acting out in group psychotherapy. Q 1955, 24:159
55633 Carmichael, D. M. Potential of group practices in mental hospitals. Q 1955, 24:161-162
55634 Clapham, H. I. & Sclare, A. B. Group psychotherapy with asthmatic patients. Q 1959, 28:430-431
55635 Davids, M. Integration of activity group therapy for a ten-year-old boy with casework services to the family. Q 1956, 25:453
55636 Fabian, A. A. Group treatment of chronic patients in a child guidance clinic. Q 1955, 24:621
55637 Flescher, J. On different types of countertransference. Q 1955, 24:162
55638 Fort, J. P. The psychodynamics of drug addiction and group psychotherapy. Q 1956, 25:454
55639 Fortin, J. N. & Abse, D. W. Group psychotherapy with peptic ulcer. Q 1958, 27:145
55640 Freedman, M. B. & Sweet, B. S. Some specific features of group psychotherapy and their implications for selection of patients. Q 1955, 24:622-623
55641 Fried, E. Combined group and individual therapy with passive-narcissistic patients. Q 1956, 25:455
55642 Fried, E. The effect of combined therapy on the productivity of patients. Q 1955, 24:620
55643 Fried, E. Ego emancipation of adolescents through group psychotherapy. Q 1958, 27:145
55644 Friedlander, K. Varieties of group therapy patterns in a child guidance service. Q 1955, 24:159-160
55645 Gabriel, B. & Halpert, A. The effect of group therapy for mothers on their children. Q 1953, 22:134
55646 Glatzer, H. T. Analysis of masochism in group therapy. Q 1960, 29:598
55647 Gliedman, L. H. Concurrent and combined group therapy of chronic alcoholics and their wives. Q 1959, 28:295
55648 Graham, F. W. Observations on analytic group psychotherapy. Q 1960, 29:597-598
55649 Greenbaum, H. Group psychotherapy with alcoholics in conjunction with antabuse treatment. Q 1955, 24:620
55650 Grotjahn, M. Special aspects of countertransference in analytic group psychotherapy. Q 1955, 24:163
55651 Hadden, S. B. Countertransference in the group psychotherapist. Q 1955, 24:164
55652 Hill, L. B. On being rather than doing in group psychotherapy. Q 1959, 28:431
55653 Hinckley, W. W. The Chestnut Lodge kiosk: observations on a psychiatric hospital's work project. Q 1959, 28:296
55654 Hulse, W. C. Transference, catharsis, insight and reality testing during concomitant individual and group psychotherapy. Q 1956, 25:453
55655 Jackson, J. & Grotjahn, M. The efficacy of group therapy in a case of marriage neurosis. Q 1960, 29:598

55656 Kaldeck, R. Group psychotherapy with mentally defective adolescents and adults. Q 1959, 28:432

55657 Kassoff, A. I. Advantages of multiple therapists in a group of severely acting-out adolescent boys. Q 1959, 28:431

55658 Klein-Lipschutz, E. Comparison of dreams in individual and group psychotherapy. Q 1955, 24:160

55659 Klemes, M. A. & Kallejian, V. J. The group psychotherapist in industry: a preventive approach. Q 1956, 25:454

55660 Kubie, L. S. Some theoretical concepts underlying the relationship between individual and group psychotherapies. Q 1959, 28:430

55661 Linden, M. E. Group psychotherapy with institutionalized senile women: study in gerontologic human relations. Q 1955, 24:160

55662 Linden, M. E. The significance of dual leadership in gerontologic group psychotherapy: studies in gerontologic human relations. Q 1955, 24:622

55663 Linden, M. E. Transference in gerontologic group psychotherapy: studies in gerontologic human relations. Q 1956, 25:453

55664 Lindt, H. The nature of therapeutic interaction of patients in groups. Q 1959, 28:431

55665 Lindt, H. The "rescue fantasy" in group treatment of alcoholics. Q 1960, 29:597

55666 Lindt, H. & Sherman, M. A. "Social incognito" in analytically oriented group psychotherapy. Q 1953, 22:308

55667 Loeser, L. H. & Bry, T. The position of the group therapist in transference and countertransference: an experimental study. Q 1955, 24:163

55668 Mann, J. Some theoretic concepts of the group process. Q 1956, 25:622-623

55669 Marcus, I. M. Psychoanalytic group therapy with fathers of emotionally disturbed preschool children. Q 1958, 27:144

55670 Martensen-Larsen, O. Group psychotherapy with alcoholics in private practice. Q 1958, 27:144

55671 Michal-Smith, H. et al: A group technique for mental retardates. Q 1956, 25:454

55672 Milberg, I. L. Group psychotherapy in the treatment of some neurodermatoses. Q 1958, 27:144

55673 Miller, J. S. A. et al: Observations concerning the use of group psychotherapy in a voluntary mental hospital: effects of group psychotherapy on training of residents. Q 1955, 24:620

55674 Morse, P. W. et al: The effect of group psychotherapy in reducing resistance to individual psychotherapy: a case study. Q 1956, 25:623

55675 Mullan, H. Transference and countertransference: new horizons. Q 1956, 25:454

55676 Orange, A. J. A note on brief group psychotherapy with psychotic patients. Q 1956, 25:453

55677 Perl, W. R. Benefits from including one psychopath in a group of mildly delinquent patients. Q 1958, 27:144-145

55678 Perry, E. The treatment of aggressive juvenile delinquents in "family group therapy." Q 1956, 25:454

55679 Potts, L. R. The use of art in group psychotherapy. Q 1958, 27:145

55680 Rice, K. K. The importance of including fathers. Q 1953, 22:309
55681 Rosenthal, L. & Nagelberg, L. Limitations of activity group therapy: a case presentation. Q 1958, 27:145
55682 Schindler, W. Countertransference in "family-pattern group psychotherapy." Q 1955, 24:164
55683 Schnadt, F. Techniques and goals in group psychotherapy with schizophrenics. Q 1956, 25:454-455
55684 Sears, R. Leadership among patients in group therapy. Q 1955, 24:161
55685 Shea, J. E. Differentials in resistance reactions in individual and group psychotherapy. Q 1955, 24:621-622
55686 Shellow, R. et al: Group therapy and the institutionalized delinquent. Q 1959, 28:432-433
55687 Slavson, S. R. Common sources of error and confusion. Q 1955, 24:159
55688 Slavson, S. R. A contribution to a systematic theory of group psychotherapy. Q 1955, 24:619-620
55689 Slavson, S. R. Criteria for selection and rejection of patients for various types of group psychotherapy. Q 1956, 25:452
55690 Slavson, S. R. et al: Report to the World Federation for Mental Health. Q 1953, 22:132-133
55691 Slavson, S. R. Some problems in group psychotherapy as seen by private practitioners. Q 1953, 22:132
55692 Slavson, S. R. Sources of countertransference and group induced anxiety.. Q 1955, 24:162-163
55693 Solomon, A. et al: An analysis of co-therapist interaction in group psychotherapy. Q 1955, 24:160
55694 Sommers, V. S. An experiment in group psychotherapy with members of mixed minority groups. Q 1955, 24:161
55695 Spanjaard, J. Transference neurosis and psychoanalytic group psychotherapy. Q 1960, 29:597
55696 Stein, A. et al: Experimental and specific types of group psychotherapy in a general hospital. Q 1953, 22:132
55697 Stone, A. R. et al: The use of "diagnostic" groups in a group therapy program. Q 1955, 24:622
55698 Stranahan, M. et al: Activity group therapy with emotionally disturbed and delinquent adolescents. Q 1959, 28:295
55699 Thorpe, J. J. & Smith, B. Operational sequence in group therapy with young offenders. Q 1953, 22:132
55700 Thorpe, J. J. & Smith, B. Phases in group development in the treatment of drug addicts. Q 1955, 24:160
55701 Votos, A. S. & Glenn, J. Group techniques in overcoming medical students' resistance to learning psychiatry. Q 1955, 24:161
55702 Winder, A. E. & Hersko, M. A thematic analysis of an outpatient psychotherapy group. Q 1959, 28:433
55703 Wolf, A. et al: The psychoanalysis of groups: the analyst's objections. Q 1953, 22:308-309

REVIEWS OF:
55704 Fodor, N. On the Trail of the Poltergeist. PPR 1959, 46(3):125-126
55705 Grotjahn, M. Beyond Laughter. Q 1957, 26:541-542
55706 Havemann, E. The Age of Psychology. Q 1958, 27:275-276

55707 Murphy, G. Human Potentialities. Q 1959, 28:537-539
55708 Myers, J. K. & Roberts, B. H. Family and Class Dynamics in Mental Illness. Q. 1960, 29:267-270
55709 Nelson, B. (Ed) Psychoanalysis and the Future. Q 1958, 27:271-272
55710 Raven, J. C. Controlled Projection for Children. Q 1953, 22:589-590
55711 Ruesch, J. & Bateson, G. Communication. The Social Matrix of Psychiatry. Q 1954, 23:594-596
55712 Saul, L. J. The Hostile Mind. Q 1957, 26:543
55713 Smith, H. C. Psychology of Industrial Behavior. Q 1956, 25:438-439
55714 Weisskopf, W. A. The Psychology of Economics. Q 1957, 26:129-131
55715 Wheelis, A. The Quest for Identity. Q 1958, 27:588-589

PEDROSA, M.

55716 Arte e psicanálise. [Art and psychoanalysis.] Rev Bras Saúde ment 1956, 2(2):37-47

PEEK, JOSEPHINE E.

See Kerdman, Louis

PEERBOLTE, MAARTEN LIETAERT

See LIETAERT PEERBOLTE, MAARTEN

PELLER, LILI

55717 The concept of play and ego development. (Read at 18th Int Psa Cong, London, July 1953)
      Abs Auth J 1954, 35:288
55718 The daydream behind the story. Child Study 1957, 34(2):8-12
55719 Daydreams and children's favorite books. Psychoanalytic comments. Psa St C 1959, 14:414-433
55720 Discussion of Kolansky, H. "Treatment of a three-year-old girl's severe infantile neurosis." Bull Phila Ass Psa 1960, 10:133-134
S-25293 Incentives to development and means of early education. In *Studying Psychology and Teaching*, Scott, Foresman 1957, 77-83
55721 Language and symbols: their use in childhood. (Read at Phila Ass Psa, April 15, 1960)
      Abs Kaplan, E. Bull Phila Ass Psa 1960, 10:108-110
55722 Libidinal development as reflected in play. NPAP 1955, 3(3):3-11
55723 Libidinal phases, ego development and play. (Read at NY Psa Soc, June 22, 1954) Psa St C 1954, 9:178-198
      Abs NRo An Surv Psa 1954, 5:258-260. Rosen, V. H. Q 1955, 24:325-326. RTh J 1956, 37:214
55724 Models of children's play. MH 1952, 36:66-83
55725 Reading and daydreams in latency, boy-girl differences. J Am Psa Ass 1958, 6:57-70
      Abs Shentoub RFPsa 1959, 23:142-143. TGS Q 1960, 29:425
55726 The school's role in promoting sublimation. Psa St C 1956, 11:437-449
      Abs RTh J 1959, 40:78

55727   Significant symptoms in the behavior of young children: a check list for teachers. In *Growth, Teaching and Learning*. NY: Harper & Bros 1957, 336-343

REVIEWS OF:
55728   Coveney, P. Poor Monkey. The Child in Literature. Q 1959, 28:271-272
55729   Gerard, M. W. The Emotionally Disturbed Child. Q 1957, 26:268-271
55730   Kornberg, L. A Class for Disturbed Children. Q 1957, 26:123-125
55731   Kramer, E. Art Therapy in a Children's Community. Q 1960, 29:125-126
55732   Redl, F. & Wineman, D. Children Who Hate. Q 1953, 22:289-291
55733   Wolfenstein, M. Children's Humor. A Psychological Analysis. Q 1956, 25:106-108

PELTZ, WILLIAM L.

55734   Adolescence in the age of longing. In *Religion in the Schools*, Council for Religion in Indep Schools, NY 1956, 3-7. Modified version: Friends J (Quaker weekly) 1956, 2:748-750
55735   (& Goldberg, M.) A dynamic factor in group work with post-adolescents and its effects on the role of the leader. MH, NY 1959, 43:71-72
55736   (& Steel, E.; Wright, S.) Group experiences with medical students as a method of teaching psychiatry. Ops 1957, 27:145-166
        Abs Koenig RFPsa 1957, 21:873
55737   (& Steel, E. H.; Hadden, S. B.; Schwab, M. L.; Nichols, F.) A group method of teaching psychiatry to medical students. Int J grp PT 1955, 5:270-279
55738   Practical aspects of marriage counseling. In Mudd, E. H. & Krich, A. *Man and Wife, a Source Book of Family Attitudes, Sexual Behavior and Marriage Counseling*, NY: W. W. Norton 1957, 242-257
55739   (& Rickels, K.) Die psychiatrische Ausbildung in den Vereinigten Staaten. [Psychiatric training in the United States.] Fortsch Neur Psychiat 1958, 26:311-315
55740   Psychotherapy of adolescents at private practice plus school practice level. In Balser, B. H. *Psychotherapy of the Adolescent*, NY: IUP 1957, 39-66
55741   Sexual adjustment before marriage. In Mudd, E. H. & Krich, A. *Man and Wife, A Source Book of Family Attitudes, Sexual Behavior and Marriage Counseling*, NY: W. W. Norton 1957, 165-174
55742   Transference in psychoanalytic case supervision. Bull Phila Ass Psa 1956, 6:49-52
        Abs EFA Q 1957, 26:286

See Preston, Malcolm G.

PELZMAN, O.
See Conigliaro, V.

PÈNE, F.
See Piaget, Jean

PENNES, HARRY H.

See Cattell, James P.; Hoch, Paul H.

PENNINGTON, LEON ALFRED

55743 (& Berg, I. A.) (Eds) An Introduction to Clinical Psychology. 2nd ed. NY: Ronald Pr 1954, vii + 709 p
55744 Psychopathic and criminal behavior. Intro Clin Psych 2:421-447
55745 Rehabilitative approaches. Intro Clin Psych 2:632-657

PENROSE, L. S.

55746 Genetics and the criminal. Brit J Delinq 1955, 6:15-25
55747 Psycho-analysis and experimental science. (Read at Brit Psa Soc, Jan 1947) J 1953, 34(Suppl):74-82

PENTTI, IKONEN

55748 Mitä on psykoanalyysi. [What is psychoanalysis.] Koulusanomat 1957, 2(10):12-13, (11):12-13, (14):14-16
55749 Psykoanalyysi. [Psychoanalysis.] Mitä—Missä—Milloin 1957, 7:282-283
55750 Psykoanalyysi. [Psychoanalysis.] Iso Tietosanakirja Täydennysosa 1958, 2:522-523

PEPIN, J.

55751 Mythe et allégorie. [Myth and Allegory.] Paris: Aubier 1958, 522 p
Rv Lebovici RFPsa 1958, 22:739-740

PEPINSKY, HAROLD B.

55752 (& Pepinsky, P. N.) Counseling Theory and Practice. NY: Ronald Pr 1954, viii + 307 p

PEPINSKY, PAULINE NICHOLS

See Pepinsky, Harold B.

PEREIRA ANAVITARTE, JUAN

55753 Acerca de la interpretación del silencio. [Interpretation of silence.] Rev Urug Psa 1958, 2:298-318
Abs Vega Q 1959, 28:134-135
55754 Notas sobre la actividad lúdicra del adulto: el ajedrez. [Notes on the game-playing activity of adults: chess.] Rev Urug Psa 1956, 1:183-196
Abs Koenig RFPsa 1958, 22:256
55755 Omnipotencia, enfermedad y síntoma. [Omnipotence, illness and symptom.] Rev Urug Psa 1956, 1:503-520
55756 Psicoanálisis de la esquizofrenia. Breve reseña histórica. [Psychoanalysis of schizophrenia. Brief historical survey.] Rev Urug Psa 1957, 2:150-177
55757 Significados del juego de ajedrez en un caso de autismo. [The meaning of chess in a case of autism.] Rev Psicoanál 1956, 13:473-478

PEREPEL', I.

55758 [Analysis of a Jealousy Murder.] (Russian) Leningrad: 1927, 36 p
55759 [Experiment on the Application of Psychoanalysis to the Study of Childhood Defects.] (Russian) Leningrad: 1925, 26 p
55760 [Psychoanalysis and the Physiological School.] (Russian) Leningrad: 1926, 28 p
55761 [Soviet Neurology and Psychoanalysis.] (Russian) Leningrad: 1927, 60 p

PÉRES, H.

55762 Psicanálise e psiquiatria. [Psychoanalysis and psychiatry.] Rev Bras Saúde ment 1956, 2(2):93-102

PERESTRELLO, DANILO

55763 Sôbre um caso de Pitiríase Rósea—contribuição psicanalítica. [About a case of Pityriasis Rosea—psychoanalytic contribution.] Neurobiologia 1956, 19:108-113
55764 Headache and primal scene. (Read at 18th Int Cong, London, July 1953) J 1954, 35:219-223
　　Abs Auth J 1954, 35:288-289. JFr An Surv Psa 1954, 5:141-142. Lebovici RFPsa 1954, 18:470. Rev Psicoanál 1954, 11:263. JLan Q 1955, 24:606-607
55765 Medicina Psicossomática. [Psychosomatic Medicine.] Rio de Janeiro: Borsói 1958, 217 p

PERESTRELLO, MARIALZIRA

55766 A finalidade didática como dificuldade na tratamento analítico. [Termination of training as difficulty in analytic treatment.] J Bras Psiquiat 1956, 5:253-261
　　Abs Rev Psicoanál 1959, 16:97
55767 Manifestações de uma estrutura oral. [Manifestations of an oral structure.] Neurobiologia 1956, 19:141-147
55768 O psicanalista e o psicótico. [The psychoanalyst and the psychotic.] Neurobiologia 1955, 18:9-23

ABSTRACTS OF:
55769 Hermann, I. The giant mother, the phallic mother, obscenity. Rev Psicoanál 1956, 13:83
55770 Kepecs, J. G. A waking screen, analogous to the dream screen. Rev Psicoanál 1956, 13:80-81

REVIEWS OF:
55771 Balint, A. La vida intima del niño. Rev Psicoanál 1958, 15:113
55772 Dolto, F. Cure psychanalytique à l'aide de la poupée-fleur. Rev Psicoanál 1958, 15:186-187
55773 Schweich, M. Principes d'action thérapeutique de la psychothérapie des schizophrènes hospitalisés. Rev Psicoanál 1959, 16:97-98

PÉREZ, SANZ B.

55774 La transferencia. [Transference.] Arch méd Cuba 1955, 6:124-129

PÉREZ MORALES, FRANCISCO

55775 Un caso de neurosis de examen. [A case of examination neurosis.] Rev Psicoanál 1958, 15:278
Abs Kestenberg, J. RFPsa 1959, 23:442-443
55776 Psicoanálisis y dietilamida del ácido lisérgico. [Psychoanalysis and LSD 25.] Act Np Arg 1958, 4:28
55777 Psicoterapia de grupo y dietilamida del ácido lisérgico. [Group psychotherapy and LSD 25.] Act Np Arg 1958, 4:258

See Alvarez de Toledo, Luisa G. de

PERKINS, GEORGE L.

55778 The consultant's view. Workshop 1957: Psychiatric consultation in residential treatment. Ops 1958, 28:266-275
Abs Koenig RFPsa 1959, 23:173
⇥ 55779 The emotional conflicts of the school-age child. In Liebman, S. *Understanding Your Patient*, Phila: Lippincott 1957, 65-76

PERKINS, ROLLIN M.

55780 (& Holstrom, J. D.; Haines, W. H.; Regan, L. J.; Zilboorg, G.) Section on legal aspects of psychiatry: summary of symposium on privileged communications. P 1954, 111:13-21

PERL, WILLIAM R.

55781 Benefits from including one psychopath in a group of mildly delinquent patients. Int J grp PT 1956, 6:77-79
Abs GPK Q 1958, 27:144-145

PERLMAN, A.

55782 [Some Material From the Psychoanalytic Study of the Personality of Paul Cézanne.] (Russian) Moscow: 1917, 10 p

PERLMAN, HELEN HARRIS

55783 The basic structure of the casework process. Soc S R 1953, 27:308-315
55784 Classroom teaching of psychiatric social work. Ops 1949, 19:306-315
55785 The client's treatability. Soc Wk 1956, 1(4):32-40
55786 Freud's contribution to social welfare. Soc S R 1957, 31:192-202

PERLMAN, MELVIN

55787 An investigation of anxiety as related to guilt and shame. AMA ANP 1958, 80:752-759

PERLS, FREDERICK S.

55788 Morality, ego boundary and aggression. Complex 1953-54, 9:42-52

PERLS, LAURA POSNER

55789 Notes on the psychology of give and take. Complex 1953-54, 9:24-30

PERMAN, JOSHUA M.

55790   (& Rapoport, J.) Psychotherapy of a hospitalized orthopedic patient.
PSM 1953, 15:252-255
Abs Rev Psicoanál 1954, 11:544

ABSTRACTS OF:
55791   Bell, A. I. The psychological consequences of physical illness in the
first three years of life. Q 1959, 28:576-577
55792   Brenner, C. The masochistic character: genesis and treatment. Q 1959,
26:447-449
55793   Brodsky, B. Self-representation, anality, and the fear of dying. Q 1959,
28:137-139
55794   Greenacre, P. Toward an understanding of the physical nucleus of
some defense reactions. Q 1959, 28:139-141
55795   Pfeffer, A. Z. The follow-up study of a satisfactory analysis. Q 1960,
29:450-452

PERR, HERBERT MILTON

55796   Criteria distinguishing parents of schizophrenic and normal children.
AMA ANP 1958, 79:217-224

REVIEW OF:
55797   Leary, T. Interpersonal Diagnosis of Personality: A Functional Theory
and Methodology for Personality Evaluation. Psa 1958, 18:201-204

PERRIER, FRANÇOIS

55798   Fondements théoriques d'une psychothérapie de la schizophrénie. [The
psychotherapy of schizophrenia. Contribution to the theory of the
cure.] Evolut psychiat 1958, 2:421-444
Rv Lebovici RFPsa 1959, 23:429
55799   Phobies et hystérie d'angoisse. [Phobias and anxiety hysteria.] Psychanalyse 1956, 2:165-195
55800   Psychanalyse de l'hypocondriaque. [Psychoanalysis of the hypochond-
riac.] Évolut psychiat 1959, (3):413-433
55801   Sens du transfert dans les psychothérapies de schizophrènes. [The
meaning of transference in the psychotherapy of schizophrenics.] Acta
psychotherap psychosom orthopaedag 1955, 3(Suppl):266-272

PERRIN, GEORGE M.

55802   (& Pierce, I. R.) Psychosomatic aspects of cancer: a review. PSM
1959, 21:397-421
Abs Luchina Rev Psicoanál 1959, 16:141. Towne, R. D. Q 1960,
29:435

PERROTTI, NICOLA

S-25344 L'aggressione umana.
Abs JAA An Surv Psa 1951, 2:35-37. NRo An Surv Psa 1951, 2:84
55803   Aperçus théoriques de la dépersonnalisation. [Theoretical considerations on depersonalization.] RFPsa 1960, 24:365-412; 663-667

55804 Considérations psychanalytiques sur la musique. [Psychoanalytic considerations on music.] (Report of 13th Int Cong Psa, Lucerne, Aug 26-31, 1934) RFPsa 1935, 8:346

55805 Contributo della psicoanalisi alla psícologia sociale. [Contribution of psychoanalysis to social psychology.] Riv psicol soc 1954, 2(Apr-Jun): 9-11

55806 (& Tolentino, I. I.) Contributo allo studio dell' ansia per mezzo della psicoanalisi. [Contribution to study of anxiety through psychoanalysis.] Cong Soc Ital Psichiat, Genova 1959. Neuropsichiat 1959, 15(Suppl 1)

55807 Premesse psicoanalitiche alla dottrina del Casework. [Psychoanalytic principles applied in the field of case work.] Riv Psa 1957, 3:189-207

55808 La profilassi delle nevrosi. [Prevention of neuroses.] Riv Psa 1955, 1(1):23-45

55809 La psicoanalisi e la medicina psicosomatica. [Psychoanalysis and psychosomatic medicine.] Med psicosom 1956, 1:209-216

PERRUSI, LEONARDO C.

55810 El Factor Emocional en la Etiopatogenia de la Enfermedad de Basedow. El Mecanismo Causal Analizado en 24 Casos: Conclusiones Patogenicas, Terapeuticas, Pronosticas y Profilacticas. [The Emotional Factor in the Etiopathogenesis of Basedow's Disease. The Casual Mechanism Analyzed in 24 Cases: Pathogenic, Therapeutic, Prognostic and Prophylactic Conclusions.] B. Aires: El Ateneo 1939, 190 p

PERRY, ETHEL

55811 The treatment of aggressive juvenile delinquents in "family group therapy." Int J grp PT 1955, 5:131-149
Abs GPK Q 1956, 25:454

PERRY, HELEN SWICK

55812 (& Gawel, M. L.) Editors of Sullivan, H. S. *Clinical Studies in Psychiatry*

55813 (& Gawel, M. L.) Editors of Sullivan, H. S. *The Interpersonal Theory of Psychiatry*

PERRY, JOHN WEIR

55814 A Jungian formulation of schizophrenia. PT 1956, 10:54-65

55815 The Self in Psychotic Process: Its Symbolization in Schizophrenia. (Foreword: CGJ) Berkeley, L. Angeles, Cal: Univ Calif Pr 1953, xvii + 184 p
Rv R 1954, 41:295. Jackson, D. D. Q 1955, 24:138-140

PERRY, STEWART E.

55816 Observations on social processes in psychiatric research; definitions of knowledge, method, and science in psychiatry. Beh Sci 1956, 1:290-302

See Bloch, Donald A.; Silber, Earle; Stanton, Alfred H.

PERRY, SYLVIA

55817   Casework with the neurotic client. Smith Coll Stud soc Wk 1957, 27:193-202. With title: The conscious use of a relationship with the neurotic client. Ego Psychol Dyn Casewk 164-173

° ° °   The conscious use of a relationship with the neurotic client. See under: Casework with the neurotic client [55817]

PERRY, WILLIAM, G., JR.

55818   (& Estes, S. G.) The collaboration of client and counselor. In Mowrer, O. H. *Psychotherapy: Theory and Research,* NY: Ronald Pr 1954, 95-119

55819   On the relation of psychotherapy and counseling: the findings of the Commission in Counseling and Guidance. Annals NY Acad Sci 1955, 63:396-407

PERSKY, HAROLD

55820   (& Grinker, R. R.; Gamm, S. R.) Correlations between fluctuation of free anxiety and quantity of hippuric acid excretion. PSM 1952, 14:34-40

55821   (& Korchin, S. J.; Basowitz, H.; Board, F. A.; Sabshin, M.; Hamburg, D. A.; Grinker, R. R.) Effect of two psychological stresses on adreno-cortical function. Studies on anxious and normal subjects. AMA ANP 1959, 81:219-226

55822   (& Grinker, R. R.; Mirsky, I. A.; Gamm, S. R.) Life situations, emotions, and the excretion of hippuric acid in anxiety states. In *Life Stress and Bodily Disease,* Proc Ass Res Nerv & Ment Dis 1950, 29:297-306

55823   (& Hamburg, D. A.; Basowitz, H.; Grinker, R. R.; Sabshin, M.; Korchin, S. J.; Herz, M.; Board, F. A.; Heath, H. A.) Relation of emotional responses and changes in plasma hydrocortisone level after stressful interview. AMA ANP 1958, 79:434-447

See Basowitz, Harold; Board, Francis A.; Grinker, Roy R.; Hamburg, David A.; Korchin, Sheldon J.; Sabshin, M.

PESCH, EDGAR

55824   La Psychologie Affective. [Affective Psychology.] Paris: Bordas 1947, 476 p

PESCHKES, ERICH

See Carlson, Helen B.

PESSAC, P.

55825   Le roman d'amour de Freud et de Martha Bernays d'après les lettres présentées par Ernest Jones. [The love story of Freud and Martha Bernays according to the letters presented by Ernest Jones.] Psyché, Paris 1955, 10:495-500

PETER, PRINCE OF GREECE AND DENMARK

55826 Melgarsh: the study of a Toda polyandrous family. Dr Af Beh 327-369
55827 The polyandry of Ceylon and South India. The polyandry of Tibet.
Actes 4ème Cong Int des Sci Anthrop et Ethnolog, Vienna. Ethnologica
1952, 2:88
   Polyandri i Tibet of Indien. [Polyandry of Tibet and India.] Men-
neskets Mangfoldighed, Kopenhagen: E. Wangel 1957, 16

PETERS, C. M.

See Harris, Herbert I.

PETERS, GEORGE A.

55828 (& Phelan, J. G.) Relieving personality conflicts by a kind of group
therapy. Personnel J 1957, 36:61-64

PETERS, JOSEPH J.

See Hayward, Malcolm M.

PETERS, MILDRED

See Falick, M. L.

PETERS, R. S.

55829 The Concept of Motivation. NY: Humanities Pr 1958, 166 p
55830 Freud's theory. Brit J Phil Sci 1956, 7:4-12
55831 Psychology becomes self-conscious. In author's *Brett's History of Psychology,* London: Allen & Unwin 1953, 507-583
55832 (Ed) Twentieth century trends. In author's *Brett's History of Psychology,* London: Allen & Unwin, 1953, 658-725

REVIEW OF:
55833 Wisdom, J. O. Foundations of Inference in Natural Science. J 1953,
34:334